The Sanctuary House Case

AN ARBITRATION WORKBOOK

The Sanctuary House Case

AN ARBITRATION WORKBOOK

BY

D. Mark Cato
MSc, FRICS, FCIArb

VOLUME 2

LONDON   NEW YORK   HONG KONG
1996

LLP Limited
Legal & Business Publishing Division
27 Swinton Street
London WC1X 9NW
Great Britain

USA AND CANADA
LLP Inc.
Suite 308, 611 Broadway
New York, NY 10012, USA

SOUTH-EAST ASIA
LLP Asia Limited
Room 1101, Hollywood Centre,
233 Hollywood Road
Hong Kong

First published 1996

British Library Cataloguing in Publication Data
A catalogue record for this book
is available from the
British Library

ISBN 1-85044-853-1

Text set in 10/12pt Bembo and Helvetica by
Mendip Communications Ltd., Frome, Somerset
Printed in Great Britain by
Hartnolls Ltd., Bodmin, Cornwall

Contents – Volume 2

[Chapter numbers relate to the Chapter numbers in Volume 1]
[References in brackets thus (7.2 Arb) relate to documents referred to in Volume 1]

CONTENTS

CONTENTS

Extracts of Relevant Correspondence

07.01.91 Invitation to Tender, PC/1   PC/1

You are invited to tender for the refurbishment and extension of Sanctuary House, Woodbridge, Suffolk.

Tenders are due back in this office not later than 12 o'clock on Thursday 31 January 1991, accompanied by your priced Bill of Quantities.

Our client is not obliged to accept the lowest, or any tender.

The following are enclosed on which your tender should be based.

    1 Specification of Works—dated November 1990—including Preambles and Preliminaries.

    2 Drawing Nos:
        TAP/1A, 2, 3B, 4C, 5, 6, 7A, 8 & 9
        MECH/ENG 1029/1, 2 & 3
        ELEC 78/1 & 2
        Site Level Drawing S1.70
        Drainage—Schematic D1 & 2

    3 Schedules: Ironmongery, Finishes, Bathroom Fittings, Joinery, Doors & Windows

    4 Tender Budget—November 1990

    Draft Bill of Quantities—For Guidance Only. Sanctuary House Limited are not liable for any inaccuracies in quantities or dimensions.

The successful tenderer will be bound by the appropriate conditions of the standard JCT Intermediate Form of Building Contract (IFC '84) 1990 Edition.

31.01.91 Reliable Builders Limited Tender to TAP, PC/2   PC/2

Further to your invitation to tender for the above works we have pleasure in quoting a figure of £617,148.24 ex VAT as per the attached summary sheet.

If you require any additional information please contact the undersigned.

20.03.91 TAP/RBL, PC/3   PC/3

Further to our recent telephone conversation, we write to confirm that it is our client's intention to enter into a Contract with your Company, in accordance with the Tender that you submitted on 31 January last, but in the agreed Revised Sum of £550,000.00 ex VAT.

As specified, the Contract is the JCT Intermediate Form—IFC '84—and my assistant, Miss Hutch, will prepare a document for your signature and forward it to you shortly. This is, of course, a Fixed Price Lump Sum Contract, not subject to remeasurement.

In the meantime, we are pleased to confirm that you should proceed with the works commencing on Monday 2 April, and that you will be reimbursed all reasonable costs incurred in the unlikely event that a contract is not entered into.

PC/4   28.03.91 RBL/TAP, PC/4

Thank you for your letter 20 March . . .

. . . We note that you consider our quotation as a lump sum at the fixed price of £550,000.00 ex VAT. We would point out that our tender was compiled on the basis of the quantities which you sent to us with your invitation to tender. We did not have time to prepare our own Bill, nor the opportunity to check yours, so we cannot see how the contract can be fixed price.

With regard to the main superstructure items in your Bill, we have no reason to beleive [*sic*] that these are not correct and we will check them and do not intend to argue over minor percentages either way. Our concern is more for the earthworks and the effect of soft spots, deeper topsoil and the effect it would have on the muck away and the imported sub-base filling. We will of course have your interest at heart as well as our own and will try to keep all costs to a minimum, but we hope that your site agent will agree the formation levels as they are agreed and accepted by the engineer. To this end the earthworks and infilling quantities can be agreed and will be paid for accordingly.

PC/5   07.04.91 Diary Note Max D'Iffy, PC/5

Spoke Hocking RBL re their letter 28/3. Suggested best resolved tomorrow's site meeting.

PC/6   10.04.91 RBL/TAP, PC/6

Having commenced demolition of the internal 'non-load-bearing walls' shown on your original drawings, undue movement in the floor and roof structure would indicate that the walls are in fact load-bearing. As a result, demolition work has now ceased and will only be recommenced once we have received the necessary revised drawings.

Accordingly we are entitled to an appropriate extension of time in accordance with clause 2.3 of the Contract.

PC/7   15.04.91 TAP/RBL, PC/7

Further to our meeting 8 April we confirm that the IFC '84 Terms and Conditions will apply except that remeasurement will take place, limited to items agreed at that meeting and listed on the attached sheet.

Please confirm, in writing, your agreement to this list so that it can be incorporated into the contract documents.

PC/8   22.04.91 RBL/TAP, PC/8

We acknowledge your letter 15 April and confirm our acceptance of the items listed which are to be remeasured.

We must, however, reserve the right to ask for a remeasure of any item which we find are substantially more than your Bill of Quantities. We will only ask for this to be done if we feel that the financial effect is a significant increase in the value of a particular Bill item.

PC/9   15.10.91 RBL/TAP, PC/9

As you are aware, the works at Sanctuary House are already well behind schedule. We were therefore somewhat surprised when the direct contractors you have employed to install the kitchen and laundry equipment arrived on-site yesterday seeking storage space—apparently with your authority—for all their equipment. This equipment is unlikely to be needed by your contractors before the end of November. In the meantime we have been forced to allocate two large rooms for storage purposes, but will doubtless have to move this equipment from room to room to complete our own works which can only lead to further delay and disruption.

25.10.91 RBL/TAP, PC/10   PC/10

Alert Alarms & Co, the contractor you have instructed to install the nurse call alarm system is currently delaying the commencement of the plastering and screed operations to the new extension. This is because the wiring, which we understand is to be run through conduits beneath the plaster, has not been installed, nor, despite our repeated requests has Alert Alarms been able to give any indication of the route the wiring is likely to take.

At the very least we require a wiring diagram in the very near future to enable plastering to commence. However, it is now inevitable that our workmen will have to work alongside those of Alert Alarms which will cause interference with our work and lead to further delay and disruption. Please treat this letter as our application for an extension of time and notification of disruption in accordance with the contract.

We believe that, as you are fully aware of the circumstances, these are all the particulars you need to agree to this request.

01.01.92 RBL/TAP, PC/11   PC/11

As you are aware from our previous correspondence in which we have claimed extensions of time, the works programme is now some 14 weeks behind schedule. So as to minimise any further delay we would be grateful to receive the colour schedules for the decorating works to enable us to order the necessary materials. We would estimate being in a position to commence decorating in two to three weeks time.

15.03.92 RBL/TAP, PC/12   PC/12

Our attempt to complete the floor finishing operation is currently being disrupted by Wonder Units Limited, the contractor you have employed to install the kitchen units. To date only two of nine wall mounted units have been fitted and no base units. It seems likely that the floor finishing task will not now be completed within the revised programme. This is because we are unable to commence this operation in the kitchen until the base units have been fitted.

Kindly treat this letter as our application for an extension of time and notification that we will be making a disruption claim pursuant to the contract.

15.04.92 TAP/RBL, PC/13   PC/13

Yesterday the basement of Sanctuary House flooded and the laundry machines shorted out the entire home.

It took some time to restore the electrical system which I need hardly tell you is a very serious problem in a home where so many elderly and sick people reside.

Please attend the site immediately and remedy the defect which is causing the flooding.

02.11.92 TAP/RBL, PC/14   PC/14

We are in receipt of your remeasure and we would refer you to our letter 15 April 1991.

We are currently analysing your figures and will advise you of our findings in due course.

PC/15   **09.11.92 RBL/TAP, PC/15**

We note your reference to your letter 15 April 1991 but, in turn, would refer you to our reply dated 22 April 1991 and also our concern, mentioned on numerous occasions, both to your Mr D'Iffy and to Miss Hutch, over the original quantities compared to the revised design layout and the scheme as being built.

PC/16   **18.11.92 RBL/TAP, PC/16**

Further to our letter 9 November and our subsequent discussion on site between our quantity surveyors and Miss Hutch, we are still very concerned by your interpretation of the agreed tender discount and its application to the rates for additional work.

We would therefore appreciate a further site meeting, if possible, for Monday 23 November to resolve this matter . . . .

PC/17   **20.11.92 TAP/RBL, PC/17**

We refer to your two letters 9 and 18 November.

The original intention was that this, is a lump sum contract based on your tender figure—as adjusted—and subsequently reduce, by agreement, by 12%.

At our meeting together on 8 April 1991, we agreed to a limited remeasurement based on your tender rates, less 12%. The list of items which we agreed would be remeasured was sent to you with our letter 15 April 1991.

PC/18   **25.11.92 RBL/TAP, PC/18**

We note that you believe that the original tender documents should form a lump sum without variations despite our telling you, at the time, that this was not acceptable to us.

As we pointed out, quantities could change for reasons beyond our control.

We were led to believe that the design and layout of the works was final and that the quantities set out in your Tender Budget, which accompanied your invitation to tender, were accurate within minor amounts either way. We refer to our reservations stated in our letter 28 March 1991 and 22 April 1991.

Since then . . . all elements have been revised . . . to incorporate various changes which have resulted in major increases in each element.

For many months you have refused to accept these changes . . . we cannot allow this matter to drift on.

On the question of discount we cannot accept that the percentage reduction applies to the rates for all additional work. We were led to believe that in agreeing to a reduction of £72,171.95 to get the job, the overall contract value would not materially change. It was your surveyor, not ours, who decided to convert this reduction into a percentage.

Of course, we stand by the reduction in the tender figure but we require the full rates for our tender to be applied to all additional work.

PC/19   **27.11.92 TAP/RBL, PC/19**

We only agree to remeasure those items listed following the 8 April meeting and rates for this remeasure are subject to the 12% adjustment.

The quants sent to you, at tender stage, were indicative only—it was for you to assess the quantities of work to be done. We do not agree that the design has radically altered since tender stage.

10.12.92 RBL/TAP, PC/20

PC/20

Both Mr D'Iffy and Miss Hutch have constantly assured us that we would be treated fairly over our final account but that does not seem to be the case . . .

. . . We must reiterate our previous position; we cannot accept that your quantities were only indicative. At the tender stage you requested us to accept these as the basis for a lump sum agreement but we said that this was not acceptable due to the lack of detail and the shortness of time before we had to start on-site. You led us to believe that your quantities were reasonably accurate within minor percentages and your letter 27 November is the first time we have heard it suggested that these quantities were indicative only.

11.12.92 TAP/RBL, PC/21

PC/21

We refer to your letter 10.12.92. We have clearly stated our position on a number of occasions and cannot usefully add to what we have already said.

24.12.92 SHL/RBL—Collapse of Ceiling, PC/22

PC/22

Early this morning almost the entire Gibbs ceiling in the lounge collapsed. Fortunately it occurred before any residents were up. However, the room has had to be closed and the Health Authority has been here today and demanded that we evacuate the entire floor above the lounge. The consequences of such evacuation are not only immensely inconvenient, but very distressing for elderly residents, particularly on Christmas Eve.

I know that you close down, from today, for two weeks for the Christmas break, but I urge you to attend the site immediately to see what can be done as quickly as possible to ameliorate this highly distressing occurrence.

19.01.93 RBL/TAP, PC/23

PC/23

Little progress has been made over the past two months or so in connection with our differences over the remeasure items. Indeed, we feel that we are further apart than ever and the overall position is little changed.

We have no option but to give notice of dispute and unless you can agree our choice of arbitrator as listed below we will have no choice but to apply to the RICS for a nomination.

03.03.93 Arbitrator to Parties, re Attendance of Pupil, PC/24

PC/24

Would both parties kindly confirm that they have no objection to my pupil Thomasina Tyro sitting in on the forthcoming Preliminary Meeting and, indeed, attending any other interlocutory meetings in this reference and the Hearing itself, should a Hearing eventually take place?

Of course, this pupil is aware of the private nature of arbitration and understands the confidential nature of the proceedings and the outcome of the dispute.

29.03.93 Jayrich Associates to the Arbitrator, re Joinder, PC/25

PC/25

Having considered further the question of possible joinder and specifically joining in the Georgian Restoration Group, who carried out the repair to the Gibbs ceiling, we have decided not to proceed with this course of action.

PC/26   **05.07.93 Jayrich Associates to the Arbitrator, PC/26**

Due to my absence on holiday recently I find that I am unlikely to meet the date of 8 July, as directed by you, for service of my Client's Statement of Case.

I have spoken to Mr Catchpole, for the Respondent, and he has agreed to my having an extension until Monday 12 July.

PC/27   **05.07.93 Arbitrator to Parties, re Extension of Time to serve Statement of Case, PC/27**

I acknowledge receipt of Jayrich Associates' letter received by fax today.

I note that the Claimant will not be able to meet the date for the service of his Statement of Case, as directed by me in item 5.02 of my Order for Directions No 2. Accordingly, the Claimant has informed me that the Respondent has agreed to extend the date of service to Monday 12 July.

As this is the first application of this nature in this reference I refer both parties to Rule 6.7.1 for the procedure to be followed in the event of either being unable to meet any dates which I have directed. Having refreshed their memories they will recall that the discretion as to whether to grant an extension of time for service of any Statement, is entirely mine, having taken into account comments from either party. I will take the Claimant's letter to be a Request and

ACCORDINGLY I HEREBY DIRECT

that the date for the service of the Statement of Case, as directed by me in item 5.02 of my Order for Directions, shall now be 12 July.

PC/28   **16.07.93 Jeremy Catchpole to the Arbitrator, re F. & B.P.'s, PC/28**

I have now received and had an opportunity to review the Claimant's Statement of Case. I consider it to be vague in certain respects, to a degree such that it is not possible for my client to ascertain the full extent of the case against him or to be able to draft a meaningful Defence. I do not wish to make a formal application for Further and Better Particulars at this stage, but rather to request that Jayrich Associates provide voluntary further particulars. The areas about which I am most concerned which I consider to be under particularised are as follows:

(1) Paragraph 7.2.3 is contradictory. Is it the Claimaint's case that it was necessary to erect scaffolding in order to fit replacement windows or, as stated lower down in the same paragraph, that it was necessary to remove scaffolding in order to fit replacement windows?

(2) In paragraphs 11 and 12, it is not clear whether the rates used to calculate Variations and the Remeasurable items are correctly discounted. Without prejudice to my client's case, that the Contract was a Lump Sum Contract with limited remeasure, the rates in the tender budget should be discounted in accordance with the Interim Declaratory Award.

(3) In Appendix D paragraph 2 the calculation of uneconomic working is wholly unclear. For example, what do the figures 16.8, 45 and 7 represent in the calculation at paragraph 2.1 and how have they been calculated?

(4) In Appendix E, how has the overhead profit percentage been calculated and what is the formula used to calculate overheads and profit?

(5) In paragraph 10.4, interest and bank charges have been claimed, however, only interest would seem to have been particularised. Do bank charges include interest?

I have not yet had an opportunity to review the Appendices in any detail and I therefore reserve the right to make further requests for particulars.

19.07.93 Arbitrator to Parties, re F. & B.P.'s & Interest, PC/29

I acknowledge receipt of Weller Baines & Bishton's letter 16 July in connection with the Claimant's Statement of Case which was served 12 July.

In general I echo Mr Catchpole's sentiments that the clarification he requires will be given voluntarily, that is without the necessity for a formal order from me. Although, purely for a point of reference, I make this letter my Order for Directions No. 9.

The parties are, no doubt, aware that there is no specific provision for F. & B.P.'s under JCT Rules, as indeed, I have a note of having pointed out at the Preliminary Meeting. However, should this clarification not be given voluntarily then I will make an Order, require clarification, under my general authority to control the reference—I hope that this will not be necessary.

I refer now to paragraph 5 of Mr Catchpole's letter concerning the Claimant's claim for interest. If this interest is being claimed as 'Special Damages'—(*Hadley* v. *Baxendale*—2nd limb) then, of course, proof that the Claimant has incurred such loss must be provided. Alternatively, if the sum is being claimed as General Damages then the amount and the rates is left to my discretion under section 19A of the Arbitration Act 1950.

In any event I would point out that the judgment rate fell from 15 per cent to 8 per cent on 1 April 1993.

25.07.93 Jayrich Associates to Arbitrator, re Interest, PC/30

Thank you for your letter 19 July 1994.

We are grateful to you for pointing out the change in the judgment rate. However, having considered your comments we believe that interest should be claimed under two heads:

(1) a claim for damages for late payment of certificates;
(2) a Minter interest claim or, alternatively, a claim for Special Damages.

In due course we will be applying to you for consent to amend our Statement of Case to clarify this interest point and also to include any other clarification necessary as a result of the points raised by the Respondent, the answers to which are given on the attached letter.

cc Jeremy Catchpole

25.07.93 Jayrich Associates to Jeremy Catchpole, re F. & B.P.'s, PC/31

Further to your letter to the Arbitrator 16 July, and the Arbitrator's letter 19 July, we are happy to provide the particulars of our Statement of Case as requested by you. We adopt the paragraph numbering used in your letter to the Arbitrator.

(1) The Claimant's case is that whilst it was necessary to erect scaffolding to allow roof repairs, this had to be removed before replacement windows could be fitted. To minimise overall delay, the scaffolding was removed before the roof repairs were completed, necessitating the use of scaffold towers to complete this operation.
(2) The valuations of the Variations and Remeasured Items in paragraphs 11 and 12 were calculated using discounted rates in accordance with the Interim Declaratory Award. We suggest that the calculation of the figures given is a matter of expert evidence.
(3) The figures 16.8, 45 and 7 represent average numbers of operators, average hours worked per week and average rate per hour respectively. The method of calculation should now be clear.
(4) The Hudson formula has been used to calculate Overheads and Profit. The overhead profit percentage is based on figures contained in the Claimant's tender build up documents, copies of which you have received.
(5) Once you confirm that there are no other matters for which you require clarification we shall apply to the Arbitrator to amend our Statement, as agreed by you, to cover these

points of clarification and the matter of interest which we trust is now clear to you from the letter to the Arbitrator (PC/30) a copy of which is enclosed.

cc The Arbitrator

PC/32   15.08.93 Arbitrator to Parties cancelling Inspection Meeting, PC/32

As it is clear to me that the Respondent will not have served his schedule of alleged defects sufficiently in advance of the Inspection Meeting, scheduled for tomorrow, for the Claimant to study this schedule, I am cancelling this meeting.

Following receipt of this schedule we will find another convenient date for this visit.

The costs of and incidental to this cancelled meeting to be paid by the Respondent in any event.

For the purpose of identifying my Order for Directions this letter is to be taken as Order for Directions No 8.

PC/33   02.09.93 Arbitrator to Parties confirming telephone conversation with Redman, re appointment of new solicitor and abandonment of County Court Proceedings, PC/33

I confirm, having received a telephone call from Mr Redman of Jayrich Associates, informing me that he has agreed with Mr Crighton—the Respondent's newly appointed solicitor—to abandon the County Court action in respect of the unpaid Penultimate Certificate and the application is due to be heard shortly.

Mr Redman informed me that, following the outcome of this application, he would be applying to Amend his client's Statement of Case.

PC/34   16.09.93 Arbitrator to Parties, re Ad Hoc Arbitration Agreement and Amended Statement of Case, PC/34

I acknowledge receipt of Mr Redman's fax of even date confirming that the County Court have granted the Claimant's application that the action for non-payment of the Penultimate Certificate, No 12, be stayed to arbitation.

Having also received a fax from Mr Crighton, on the same matter, I enclose herewith the Ad Hoc Arbitration Agreement (4.4) extending my jurisdiction to cover this issue. Subject to receipt back of this Ad Hoc Arbitration Agreement, signed by both sides, I HEREBY CONSENT to the Claimant's request to Amend his Statement of Case, as previously indicated by the Respondent in his letter 25 July 1993.

As it is now necessary to amend the Statement of Case, in any event, in order to include this fresh issue, the Claimant has requested consent to include amendments covering his replies to the Respondent's request for Further and Better Particulars in addition to the interest point, which was raised earlier. This, of course, is acceptable and, indeed, sensible.

Under the circumstances the costs of this direction are to be costs in the reference.

PC/35   11.10.93 Letter from Respondent's Solicitor to Arbitrator, re meeting of Experts, PC/35

I have now had the opportunity of studying all the papers in the above reference.

I note item 9.00 of your Order for Directions No 2, re meeting of Experts and also your letter, to both parties 1 October, suggesting that you meet with the Experts to attempt to get them to agree on some of the technical issues and thus save hearing time.

I have discussed your proposal fully with the Claimaint's representative, Mr Redman, and we have arrived at the following joint agreement.

(1) We would like you to meet with the Experts, following close of pleadings, with a view to agreeing, where possible, quantum only (unless otherwise indicated), on the following issues:

Quantity Surveying Issue

For the Claimant: Joel Redman
For the Respondent: Miles Maclean

— Scott Schedule of alleged defective work.
— Disputed Remeasured work.
— Variations—under two separate heads
  (i) those covered by a written instruction but where quantum not yet agreed;
  (ii) (a) those which the Claimant says are variations but for which there is no written instruction;
       (b) those which the Respondent says are not variations at all as they form part of the original Lump Sum Contract.
— Extension of Time—agreement on 'figures as figures'.
— Loss and Expense Claim.

Building Surveying Issues

For the Claimant: David Sharkey
For the Respondent: Stanley Longdon

— Remedial works—basement including consequential losses
— Reinstatement of Gibbs ceiling by specialist firm
— Remedial works to defective fireproofing of doors

Financial Issues

For the Claimant: Jamal Hussein
For the Respondent: Mark Page

— Consequential losses related to collapsed ceiling

(2) In the case of Messrs Sharkey and Longdon, we instruct them to express an opinion concerning the reason for the collapse of the Gibbs ceiling.

(3) Mr Longdon to give his opinion, against that of Mr Carmel, concerning the reason for the failure of the fireproofing on the doors. (It is not envisaged that these two experts will meet under the chairmanship of the arbitrator.)

(4) Messrs Page and Hussein have yet to exchange Final Reports as Mr Page cannot finalise his claim for Loss of Profit until the final unit is relet. Work on restoring the Gibbs ceiling commenced on 3 October and is anticipated to be completed within 10 days or so following which the reletting programme will be intensified.

It is understood, therefore, that at this stage, Messrs Page and Hussein can do no more than consider each other's draft Reports and attempt to agree on the basis of the calculations which will apply once the final of these 15 units is relet.

(5) These Experts to meet 'open' with authority to agree quantum for the various issues with which they are concerned on the clear understanding that nothing said at these meetings should be taken as evidence or acceptance of liability of any issue for which quantum is agreed (other than noted above for variations).

(6) In conducting these meetings with the Experts the arbitrator may act inquisitorially.

(7) A note of each separate meeting of Experts shall be prepared recording the issues on which they agree and those on which they do not agree—all in accordance with item 9.02 of Order for Directions No 2.

The above is agreed on behalf of the Claimant

....

Joel Redman
cc M Maclean
D Sharkey
S Longdon
I. Ifram
J Hussein

PC/36   29.11.93 Meeting of Experts at Joel Redman's Office, PC/36

Note of matters discussed and agreed

This meeting followed joint instructions from Mr Redman and Mr Crighton, by their letter to the Experts dated 11 October 1993.

Those present at this meeting were, for the Claimant Mr David Sharkey, for the Respondent Mr Stanley Longdon and, as chairman, the arbitrator Mr D Emsee.

The object of the meeting was twofold

(i) to discuss the remedial works to the basement and alleged consequential losses arising from the flooding thereof on or about 15 April 1992.

(ii) To determine the *quantum only* of restoring the Gibbs ceiling by a specialist firm including architects fees.

Flooded Basement

Reference was made to the arbitrator's Interim Declaratory Award, 10 June 1993, in which he found the Reliable Building Company in breach of contract over the waterproofing of the basement. This being the case, Mr Sharkey agreed with Mr Longdon's suggested solution of extending the tanking 6 inches higher than it was at present.

A specification of these remedial works is attached hereto as Appendix A and the Reliable Building Company has undertaken to carry out the work in accordance with the agreed specification, at the convenience of the employer.

The Experts then considered the Respondent's claim for consequential losses.

(i) They agreed the value of the two 35lb industrial washing machines and two 50lb industrial driers, purchased by W Bliss on 17 April 1992, at a figure of £14,050 ex VAT. Plus a replacement de-humidifying system, which was also ruined in the flooding, at a cost of £750 ex VAT.

(ii) The balance of the claim for consequential losses involved ruined linen belonging to Sanctuary House Limited and clothing belonging to the residents.

Although a schedule of linen/clothing had been made at the time of the flood, and the Experts had a copy of that schedule signed by the Matron Hermione Glover available, they were unable to agree on the value of any of the residents' clothing, as there was insufficient description of each item and no indication of age or condition.

So far as the linen/staff clothes/uniforms belonging to Sanctuary House Limited was concerned, the Experts were able to agree on a figure of £1498 ex VAT for linen in accordance with the schedule on Appendix B to this report. In arriving at this figure the Experts examined the original list of linen/uniforms purchased in March 1992—just six weeks before the flood and compared this with the list of linen which it was alleged was ruined by the flooding. Both Experts agreed that the list of linen claimed to have been damaged appeared plausible when viewed in relation to the total amount of linen purchased in March 1992.

Reinstatement of Gibbs Ceiling

The experts were asked to agree whether the cost of £38,424, being the amount of the accepted tender for the restoration of the Gibbs ceiling, was reasonable.

The experts had liaised on this matter prior to the meeting and agreed to obtain an estimate from the specialist firm of Charles B Carter Limited of Norwich. This quotation was tabled.

It included three alternatives. The first two being based on reproducing the decorations and moulding as nearly as possible; the third alternative was for a plain ceiling. The question of what should have been replaced being a matter for the arbitrator.

It was only Alternative One which concerned the meeting today. This was for a replica ceiling matching, as nearly as possible, the original, restored using original type materials. Carter's quote for this was at £39,360 ex VAT, therefore, the two experts agreed that this showed that the actual cost of doing this work, of £38,424, was reasonable. They also agreed that the architect's fee of £5,500 (ex VAT), which had been charged, was also an acceptable figure.

Remedial Works to fireproofing on doors.

The experts were unable to agree on what remedial work was necessary as neither were experts in this particular specialist work. They agree that this would best be left to independent specialist expert opinion.

Signed by David Sharkey on behalf of the Claimant

Signed by Stanley Longdon on behalf of the Respondent

....

....

Date ....

Date ....

APPENDIX A: Specification of agreed Remedial Works to the Basement Waterproofing.

APPENDIX B: Agreed List of Linen/Clothing etc damaged by Flooding of the Basement on or about 15 April 1992.

(i) Residents' clothes/linen   £

List of Residents' Clothes/Linen

Total claimed   £384
(Not agreed)

(ii) SHL Linen/Staff Clothes Uniforms   £

List of Linen/Clothes etc

Total   £1498

11

PC/37 **29.11.93–30.11.93 Note of Meetings of Experts at Joel Redman's Offices, PC/37**

Experts present:

> Joel Redman for the Claimant
> Miles Maclean for the Respondent

The arbitrator, Mr D Emsee, who chaired this meeting, requested both parties to confirm their receipt of the joint letter from the parties' representatives, Messrs Redman and Crighton, addressed to all the Experts generally re the limit of the Experts' authority—this they did.
  The following matters were discussed:

1 Scott Schedule of Alleged Defective Work

The parties, under the chairmanship of the arbitrator, discussed each item on the Scott Schedule in turn and came to agreement on *quantum only* on a number of these items.

2 Disputed Remeasure Items

Each of the eight items was discussed but the experts were unable to agree on quantum for any of them. Each Expert will assess his own quantum based on his understanding leaving it to the arbitrator to determine which alternative he prefers once he has decided whether all or any of these items fall to be remeasured following agreement made at the 8 April 1991 site meeting.

3 Variations

As instructed Variations were classified under the following heads:

 (i) those covered by a written instruction but where quantum not yet agreed;
(ii)(a) those which the Claimant says are variations but for which there is no written instruction;
  (b) those which the Respondent says are not variations at all as they form part of the original Lump-Sum Contract.

  We were able to agree a division of all scheduled variations under one or other of the above categories. Following which a certain amount of progress was made in agreeing quantum for these variations.

4 Future Action

The experts would continue to meet up to the Hearing provided progress can be made in narrowing the issues.
  At the commencement of the Hearing an updated version of the Scott Schedule, on which are notes of those items which are agreed will he handed to the arbitrator.
  In addition a schedule of Variations will be prepared under the agreed categories with a note of those for which quantum is agreed subject to liability to be determined by the arbitrator other than for category against (a) above were once agreed between the experts the parties will be bound both as to liability and quantum.
  An updated schedule of these Variations and what is agreed, as set out above, will be handed to the arbitrator at the commencement of the Hearing.

5 The Claimant's Loss and Expense claim

Here virtually no common ground was found. It was agreed that the Experts would proceed to produce their own Reports on this head of claim.

6 The Claimant's Claim for Extension of Time

General principles only were discussed as per the parties' representatives instructions.
   A measure of agreement was reached as to the approach to be adopted in undertaking this exercise.

7 Experts' Reports

It was agreed that the experts would meet shortly to agree the heads under which each would prepare his Report. This would make a comparison of the Experts' viewpoints far simpler to make.

For the Claimant   For the Respondent

....
Joel Redman   Miles Maclean

Date ....   Date ....

03.12.93 Meeting of Accountants at Mr J Redman's Offices, PC/38   PC/38

Those present were:

   D Emsee, MSc, FRICS, FCIArb—Arbitrator

   Jamal Hussein, BSc(Econ), FCA, ACIArb, FBaE
   Regents House
   Upper Oxford Street
   London W1

   Mark Page, BA(Hons) (Oxon), ACA, MBaE
   Forensic Services Group Division
   Arthur Price, Accountants
   274 Fleet Street
   London.

   Both accountants acknowledge receipt of a Letter of Instruction, dated 11 October, signed jointly by the Claimant's representative Mr Redman, and the Respondent's solicitor Mr Crighton.
   The purpose of the meeting was to discuss the consequential losses alleged, by the Respondent, to flow from the collapsed Gibbs ceiling in the sitting-room of Sanctuary House.
   Each Expert produced his own draft report of the costs involved and these reports formed the basis of discussion.
   It had been understood that, when these meetings had been arranged, it was only the heads of claim and principal calculations which could be discussed as the restoration of the Gibbs ceiling had only been completed on 3 November, following which the reletting had commenced. Until the final unit has been relet Mr Page would be unable to finalise his figures.
   It became clear, after a short period, that the Experts could not agree on the basis of the calculation of these alleged losses, nor any component part of the make-up of such losses.

Reluctantly, as the Experts were so far apart, and their calculation of losses were based on entirely different premises, the only agreement that they reached was to submit separate reports, which it was agreed would be exchanged in accordance with item 9.02 of Order for Directions No 2, i.e. not later than 14 days before the hearing on the proviso that all 15 units had been relet before that date and Mr Page was in a position to finalise his claim.

In the event that all of the units had not been relet in order to meet the above date then Reports should be exchanged within 24 hours of the final unit being relet.

For the Claimant   For the Respondent

....
Jamal Hussein   Mark Page

Date ....   Date ....

CHAPTER 3

The Appointment

1. Invitation Letter from RICS (3.1 Arb)

THE ROYAL INSTITUTION OF CHARTERED SURVEYORS

Arbitration Service: Surveyor Court, Westwood Way, Coventry CV4 8JE
Telephone 071-222 7000, 0203 694757; Facsimile: 071-334 3802; Telex: 915443 RICS G;
DX: 702112 Coventry 6

D Emsee, MSc, FRICS, FCIArb
Toad Hall
Hunstanton Water
Norfolk

Dear Mr Emsee

Re: Reliable Builders Ltd v Sanctuary House Ltd

The President has received an application, the details of which are enclosed, for the appointment/nomination of an Arbitrator and I am instructed to enquire as to whether you would wish your name to be submitted for consideration by the President in making the appointment/nomination.

As you will appreciate, the President has a responsibility to ensure that neither party can reasonably object to an appointment/nomination which he has made. As part of the careful checks carried out by the Institution, I must therefore ask you whether there are any matters which should be disclosed to the President. Examples of matters which ought to be disclosed are contained in the RICS 'Guidance notes for surveyors acting as arbitrators or as independent experts in rent reviews'. The President may pass the information on to both parties for their comments before making an appointment/nomination.

While the President will, of course, give careful consideration and due weight to any representation made by the parties or their representatives he will reach his own decision as to who shall be appointed/nominated. Your attention is drawn to the policy statement PAGA/S(92)1 (if you do not already have a copy please contact the Arbitration Service).

I must also ask you to confirm each of the following:

    (a) that the subject-matter of the dispute falls within the sphere of your own normal professional practice (not merely that of your firm);
    (b) that you would be able to undertake the task with all reasonable expedition;
    (c) that having made enquiries within your organisation no possibility of conflict of interest exists;
    (d) that you comply with any special requirements of the lease (as specified on the reverse of the attached 'Case Details');

(e) that you are not currently engaged as arbitrator or as independent expert in another case where your duties and functions to the parties would conflict with your duties and functions to the parties in this case; and

(f) that you have appropriate professional indemnity insurance cover.

The President has asked me to stress that your letter should be signed personally and not on your behalf.

Yours sincerely
I. Cook
Arbitration Officer
Enc

2. Case Details (3.2 Arb)

CASE DETAILS

Our ref: D001001

Dispute: Reliable Builders Limited v Sanctuary House Limited

Name & Address of Applicant Party:	*Name & Address of Non-Applicant Party:*
Reliable Builders Limited Snape Yard Woodbridge Suffolk	Sanctuary House Ltd Registered Office: Matthews House Main Street Ipswich Suffolk
FAO Harry Hocking	
Applicant's *Representative:*	*Non-Applicant's* *Representative:*
Claims Consultant	William Bliss—Sanctuary House Ltd
Jayrich Associates 12 Church Close Ipswich Suffolk FAO J H Redman	

The undertaking as to fee is: Signed

The Terms of Reference for the appointment will be as follows:

Concerning non-payment of monies due under a contract for works at Sanctuary House, Woodbridge, Suffolk. *Plus* a Loss and Expense Claim for prolongation, disruption and uneconomic working and recovery of Liquidated and Ascertained Damages wrongfully deducted. The total claimed is approximately £380,000.

This appointment will be made under the terms and conditions of a JCT Intermediate Form of Building Contract 1984.

Special Requirements: None

Date of Print: 2 February 1993

3. Application Form

(1) General—other than (2) below (3.3/1 Arb)

Form AS2 (October 1992)

THE ROYAL INSTITUTION OF CHARTERED SURVEYORS

Arbitration Service

APPLICATION FOR THE APPOINTMENT/NOMINATION OF AN ARBITRATOR/INDEPENDENT EXPERT BY THE PRESIDENT OF THE ROYAL INSTITUTION OF CHARTERED SURVEYORS

(OTHER THAN COMMERCIAL PROPERTY RENT REVIEW AND AGRICULTURAL HOLDINGS ACT CASES)

All details must be typewritten

I/~~We~~ *H. HOCKING of RELIABLE BUILDERS LTD* hereby request the President of the Royal

Institution of Chartered Surveyors to | appoint | an | Arbitrator |

(delete as appropriate) to act in the case described overleaf
OR
~~The application for the appointment/nomination of an Arbitrator/Independent Expert to which the following details refer was made in a letter form:~~

    dated: *1 FEB 1993*   ref:

Applicant/Claimant (full names and address)

RELIABLE BUILDERS LTD,
SNAPE YARD,
WOODBRIDGE,
SUFFOLK

Applicant's Solicitors (name, address, telephone number and reference)

Applicant's Surveyors (name, address, telephone number and reference)

JAYRICH ASSOCIATES,
CLAIMS CONSULTANTS,
12 CHURCH CLOSE,
IPSWICH,
SUFFOLK

Other Party/Respondent (full names and address and reference)

SANCTUARY HOUSE LIMITED,
SANCTUARY HOUSE,
WOODBRIDGE,
SUFFOLK

Other Party's Solicitors (name, address, telephone number and reference)

JEREMY CATCHPOLE,
WELLER BAINES & BISHTON,
1 CHANCERY LANE,
LONDON W.C.2

Other Party's Surveyors (name, address, telephone number and reference)

NONE APPOINTED

To which of the above should communications on this matter be addressed (name of individual if known)?

Cl. *JAYRICH ASSOCIATES*, JOEL REDMAN
R. *WILLIAM BLISS AT REGISTERED OFFICE OF SANCTUARY HOUSE LTD*

Conflicts of Interest

If you think that there are any Chartered Surveyors who should not be considered for appointment/nomination because they do not fulfil the criteria referred to in the attached policy statement, please state their names here, together with full reasons supporting your views (continue on a separate sheet if necessary). It is emphasised that, while the President will give careful consideration to any representations, he will reach his own decision as to who shall be appointed/nominated.

N/A

Nature of Dispute

(including approximate sum of money in dispute and address of premises, if relevant; continue on a separate sheet if necessary)

> *Non-payment of monies due under an IFC '84 contract for Works at Sanctuary House, Woodbrige, Suffolk. Plus a Loss & Expense claim for prolongation, disruption and uneconomic working and recovery of Liquidated and Ascertained Damages wrongfully deducted.*
> *Total claim approx £380,000.*
Interest

Agreement to Refer

Which clause of the contract or other relevant agreement provides for the dispute to be referred to the decision of a surveyor appointed/nominated by the President of the Royal Institution of Chartered Surveyors? A copy of the signed contract or comparable document should accompany this application. If this does not incorporate provision for the settlement of disputes by an arbitrator/independent expert appointed/nominated by the President then a separate agreement making such provision, signed by both parties will be required before any appointment/nomination can be made, except in cases where the appointment/ nomination is made by order of the Court.

Notice of dispute sent 19 Jan 1993
IFC '84 contract, Article 5.

We accept that in some circumstances the appointment will be made by the President through one of his Vice-Presidents or duly appointed agents and this is the basis upon which the application is submitted to you and upon which the application will be entertained. We accept that in special circumstances (to be decided by the President) it may be inappropriate for the President to effect the appointment and in these circumstances the appointment may be effected by a Vice-President in his own name.

Fees

Except in cases where the President is designated by statute as the appointing authority or the appointment is to be made by Order of the Court a fee of £135.00 (inclusive of VAT), non-returnable must accompany all applications for appointments by the President.

We enclose a cheque for £135.00 (made payable to the RICS)/copy of the Court Order directing that this appointment be made and we undertake to be responsible for payment of the professional fees and costs of the Surveyor appointed, including any fees and costs due where a negotiated settlement is reached before the award or determination being taken up. FEE INCREASE: The fee payable as from 1st July 1993 will be £150.00 (inclusive of VAT)

Signed ......*Joel Redman*..............................

Dated ....1 Feb 1993. ....

To be returned to: The Arbitrations Section, RICS, Surveyor Court,
Westwood Way, Coventry, CV4 8JE
Tel: 071 222 7000 (or Local Calls: 0203 694757) Fax: 071 334 3802

(2) Commercial Property Rent Review (3.3/2 Arb)

Form AS1 (January 1994)

THE ROYAL INSTITUTION OF CHARTERED SURVEYORS

Arbitration Service

APPLICATION FOR APPOINTMENT/NOMINATION OF AN ARBITRATOR/ INDEPENDENT EXPERT BY THE PRESIDENT OF THE ROYAL INSTITUTION OF CHARTERED SURVEYORS
(COMMERCIAL PROPERTY RENT REVIEW)

All details must be typewritten

I/We   hereby request the President of the Royal

Institution of Chartered Surveyors to appoint/nominate an Arbitrator/Independent Expert

(delete as appropriate) to act in the case below
OR
The application for the appointment/nomination of an Arbitrator/Independent Expert to which the following details refer was made in a letter from:

   dated: ref:

___

Address of Premises for which Rent is to be Reviewed. It is essential for the computerised processing of applications that the correct full post code is quoted

Post Code

___

Type of Premises, and short description of premises (eg High Street Shop, Storage Warehouse, Retail Warehouse, Office Suite)

___

Present Rent

___

Date of Lease

___

Agreed or alleged date of review

___

Name and Address of Present Landlord

3.3/2 Arb 22

_____

Name and Address of Present Tenant

_____

Name of Original Landlord

_____

Name of Original Tenant

_____

Parent or Subsidiary Company of Landlord, if any

_____

Parent or Subsidiary Company of Tenant, if any

_____

Name, Address, Telephone Number and Reference of Present Landlord's Representative (eg solicitor, surveyor, company official) ie person or firm to whom communication should be sent

_____

Name, Address, Telephone Number and Reference of Present Tenant's Representative

_____

Conflicts of Interest

Please state below the names of any Chartered Surveyors who should not be considered for appointment/nomination because they do not fulfil the criteria referred to in the attached policy statement (continue on a separate sheet if necessary). It is emphasised that, while the President will give careful consideration to any representations, he will reach his own decision as to who shall be appointed/nominated. Please note that objections will not be entertained unless full reasons are given.

_____

Agreement to Refer

Which clause in the lease gives the President power to make this appointment/nomination?

`3.3/2 Arb 23`

....

NB: A copy of the duly-executed (not draft) lease must accompany this application.

We accept that in some circumstances the appointment will be made by the President through one of his Vice-Presidents or duly appointed agents and this is the basis upon which the application is submitted to you and upon which the application will be entertained. We accept that in special circumstances (to be decided by the President) it may be inappropriate for the President to effect the appointment and in these circumstances the appointment may be effected by a Vice-President in his own name.

Fees

Except for cases in which the appointment/nomination is to be made by Order of the Court, a fee of £150.00 (inclusive of VAT) which is solely for administrative costs must accompany all applications for appointment/nomination by the President. The fee is non-returnable whether or not the President makes the appointment (eg if the matter is settled by agreement). **I/We enclose** a cheque for £150.00 (made payable to the RICS)/a copy of the Court Order directing that this appointment/nomination be made.

I/We undertake to ensure that the professional fees and costs of the Surveyor appointed/ nominated are paid, including any fees and costs arising where a negotiated settlement is reached before the award or determination is taken up.

Signed ....

Dated ....

To be returned to: The Arbitrations Section, RICS, Surveyor Court,
Westwood Way, Coventry, CV4 8JE
Tel: 071 222 7000 (or Local Calls: 0203 694757) Fax: 071 334 3802

4. RICS Policy Guideline (3.4 Arb)

APRIL 1992 PAGA/S(92)1

**3.4 Arb
24**

THE ROYAL INSTITUTION OF CHARTERED SURVEYORS

APPOINTMENT OF ARBITRATORS AND INDEPENDENT EXPERTS, PARTICULARLY IN COMMERCIAL PROPERTY RENT REVIEW DISPUTES—POLICY STATEMENT ON ALLEGED CONFLICTS OF INTEREST

1 Introduction

The President of The Royal Institution of Chartered Surveyors is frequently called upon to appoint arbitrators and independent experts to settle disputes between parties where the nature of the dispute falls within the province of the profession. By far the greatest number of applications for such appointments relate to the periodic review of rents paid under leases of commercial property.

The President's role in appointing an arbitrator or independent expert is, on the face of it, a straightforward one. He is concerned to select a member with the appropriate expertise who is not precluded from taking the appointment due to a lack of independence. If, in a rent review dispute, the parties cannot agree the rent, the usual format of rent review clauses is that they have a period during which they attempt to agree upon the identity of such a person, but if this fails, they delegate the task to the President. Ideally, therefore, the President should be entirely free to exercise his discretion as regards both the requirement of expertise and that of independence.

In recent years, however, there has been an increasing tendency for the parties to attempt to influence the President's decisions by stating that specified surveyors or all surveyors from specified firms would not be acceptable, sometimes without stating reasons for the objection. Delays and difficulties are being caused because the system is being misused in some cases, whether through ignorance or the proper principles to be applied, or for tactical reasons.

2 The Central Problem

The parties rightly expect an independent expert or arbitrator to be experienced in the subject-matter of the dispute. The arbitrator takes evidence from the parties and will be in a better position to assess the weight to be given to that evidence if s/he is experienced in the type of property involved. It will be remembered that the arbitrator should not normally seek evidence through his/her own investigations. For the independent expert, who does have an investigatory role, the need for knowledge of the type of property involved is essential.

The parties are also rightly concerned that the arbitrator or independent expert appointed is truly independent. This concern, however, may sometimes lead to attempts to exclude from consideration a large number of prospective appointees, on the grounds that they have, or have in the past had, some connection, no matter how remote, with one of the parties. In some specialist fields, the President could find that he was being asked to disregard every specialist. The President cannot properly be placed in that position, if he is to perform his intended function under the terms of the ease of appointing a suitable person.

3 Guidelines

The following principles are put forward for the information of parties to rent review disputes and their professional representatives. The principles are based on recent legal advice.

(i) The President will give careful consideration and due weight to any objections or other comments made by the parties or their representatives. However, he cannot be bound by any such objections or representations and will reach his own decision as to who should be appointed.

(ii) It is inconceivable that the President would knowingly appoint a person with a real pecuniary or other interest in the outcome of the dispute. A very remote or indirect pecuniary interest would not, however, disqualify an appointee.

(iii) The President would not appoint someone whose appointment would raise a real possibility of bias in the eyes of a reasonably-minded person. The test is not what the party to the dispute or his/her representative believes, or what in fact would happen or has happened. The President, once he has made himself aware of all the relevant facts, must consider whether a reasonably-minded person could perceive a real possibility of bias if the member in question were to be appointed.

4 Disclosure

As part of the careful checks carried out by the Institution on behalf of the President, any prospective arbitrator or independent expert is supplied with details of the dispute, including the names and addresses of the parties and their representatives, and is requested to disclose to the President matters which may be relevant in deciding whether the appointment should be made. For example:

(a) If one of the parties is a company in which the appointee or his/her partner or his/her family have substantial shareholdings, bias would appear possible.

(b) If the appointee or his/her firm also acts for the landlords or tenants of nearby properties where rent reviews are due shortly, his/her decision might be thought to be influenced by the knowledge of the effect it will have on the imminent rent reviews.

Further examples are contained in the RICS 'Guidance notes for surveyors acting as arbitrators or as independent experts in rent reviews'*. It is emphasised, however, that the list is not exhaustive and, if in doubt, the prospective appointee is expected to disclose.

Upon receipt of such details, the President may take the view that the member concerned could not be seen to be independent, and will seek another prospective appointee.

In most cases, however, the President will not find it necessary to take this view initially, and will pass on the disclosures to the parties or their representatives, inviting comments within 7 days. At that stage, the President will consider and give due weight to any objections but he will not be bound by them and the final decision as to the appointment will be his alone.

5 After the appointment has been made

Once the President has made an appointment, his jurisdiction in the matter is at an end unless the lease (or, in a relatively few cases, statute) itself provides to the contrary. If, therefore, after the appointment of the arbitrator or independent expert, a party should bring to the attention of the appointee a matter claimed to constitute a real pecuniary or other interest in the outcome of the dispute or to give rise to a real possibility of bias, the arbitrator or expert would be expected to:

* Available from RICS Books at 12 Great George Street, Parliament Square, London SW1P 3AD or by post from RICS Books, Surveyor Court, Westwood Way, Coventry CV4 8JE. Telephone 0171-222 7000.

(a) obtain full details of the objection in writing;

(b) notify the other party in writing and invite his/her comments;

(c) consider whether the matters disclosed might affect his/her mind in coming to a decision or would raise a real possibility of bias in the eyes of a reasonably-minded person;

(d) if the answer to either of these questions is yes, unless both parties agree in writing that s/he should continue, s/he should seek the agreement of the parties to his/her resignation and replacement by the President of the RICS;

(e) if the answer to each of these questions is no, continue.

Equally, if the arbitrator or independent expert should discover a matter which might affect his/her mind in coming to a decision, or would raise a real possibility of bias in the eyes of a reasonably-minded person, s/he would be expected immediately to disclose it to the parties and then proceed as in (d) and (e) above.

5. Reply—willing to act (3.5 Arb)

D. EMSEE, MSc (Construction Law), FRICS, FCIArb

REGISTERED ARBITRATOR

Toad Hall, Hunstanton Water, NORFOLK
Telephone: 0999 590124; Facsimile: 0999 590690
7 February 1993

LETTER & FAX

Your ref: D0001001

Our ref: 4898.2

The Royal Institution of Chartered Surveyors
Arbitration Service
Surveyor Court
Westwood Way
Coventry CV4 8JE

For the attention of I Cook Esq

Dear Mr Cook

Dispute—Reliable Builders Ltd v *Sanctuary House Ltd*

Thank you for your letter 6 February offering to submit my name to the President for consideration as arbitrator in the above dispute.
  I confirm that I am willing and able to carry out this task should the President so decide.
  I also confirm that—

(a) The subject matter of the dispute falls within my normal professional experience.
(b) I will be able to undertake this task with reasonable expedition.
(c) No conflict of interest exists.
(d) There are no special requirements (on the reverse side of the 'Case Details') with which I am to comply.
(e) There is no conflict under item (e) of your letter.
(f) I do have appropriate professional indemnity insurance cover.

Yours sincerely

D Emsee MSc, FRICS, FCIArb

6.(1) Appointment (3.6/1 Arb)

THE ROYAL INSTITUTION OF CHARTERED SURVEYORS

The President's Office

I, G. Everest FRICS President of the Royal Institution of Chartered Surveyors, hereby nominate

> D Emsee MSc FRICS FCIArb
> Toad Hall
> Hunstanton Water
> Norfolk

as   Arbitrator

to determine a dispute between:

> Reliable Builders Limited
> Snape Yard
> Woodbridge
> Suffolk

and

> Sanctuary House Limited
> Registered Office
> Matthews House
> Mains Street
> Ipswich
> Suffolk

Concerning a dispute over monies owed and a Loss & Expense Claim arising out of works at Sanctuary House, Woodbridge, Suffolk.
This appointment is made in under the terms and conditions of a JCT Intermediate Form of Building Contract 1984.

Dated this: 20 Feb 1993   Signed ....
                                     President

Ref No: D0001001

                                                      NR1

6.(2) Covering letter (3.6/2 Arb)

THE ROYAL INSTITUTION OF CHARTERED SURVEYORS

Arbitration Service: Surveyor Court, Westwood Way, Coventry CV4 8JE
Telephone: 0171-222 7000, 01203 694757; Facsimile: 0171-334 3802; Telex: 915443
RICS G; DX: 702112 Coventry 6

Our Ref: D0001001
Your Ref: 4898.2

20 Feb 1993

D Emsee, MSc, FRICS, FCIArb
Toad Hall
Hunstanton Water
Norfolk

Dear Mr Emsee

Reliable Builders Ltd v *Sanctuary House Ltd*

Thank you for your recent letter agreeing to act in this case. The President has signed the necessary form, which I now enclose, together with a copy of the lease/contract as submitted by the applicant.

The Vice-President has asked me to draw your attention to the importance of making your award or determination as expeditiously as possible and of keeping the parties fully informed if any delay is anticipated.

It is *essential* that the award/determination should be available for collection by the parties at the time they are notified that it may be taken up upon payment of costs.

I have sent copies of the form of appointment to the parties/representatives and informed them that you will now be contacting them.

Please note that a copy of the 'Case Details' has not been sent to either party. In order to ensure that information before you is available to both parties, you should now send a copy to each side.

I would draw your attention to the 'Guidance Notes for Surveyors acting as Arbitrators or as Independent Experts in Rent Reviews' generally, and particularly in relation to fees for abortive work.

Please complete and return the enclosed 'Case History Report' form.

Yours sincerely
I. Cook
Arbitration Officer
Enc   CL2

7. Acknowledgement of appointment (3.7 Arb)

D. EMSEE, MSc (Construction Law), FRICS, FCIArb

REGISTERED ARBITRATOR

Toad Hall, Hunstanton Water, NORFOLK
Telephone: 01999 590124; Facsimile: 01999 590690

Your ref: D001001

Our ref: 4898.3.

The Royal Institution of Chartered Surveyors

Arbitration Service
Surveyor Court
Westwood Way
Coventry CV4 8JE

FAO I Cook Esq

Dear Mr Cook

In the matter of an Arbitration between Reliable Builders Limited and Sanctuary House Limited

I write to thank you for your letter 20 February 1993 with which you enclosed the appointment for the above dispute, dated 20 February 1993.

    You can be assured that I shall deal with this as expeditiously as the circumstances will allow. To this end I am writing this day to invite the parties to a Preliminary Meeting in the week beginning 8 March 1993.

    I confirm I have sent to the parties, a copy of the Case Details, as you requested.

Yours sincerely

D Emsee MSc FRICS FCIArb

8. Arbitrator's Appointment Letters

(1) To Parties (3.8/1 Arb)

THE CHARTERED INSTITUTE OF ARBITRATORS

Ref: 5/AO/299940000 May 1994

To: the parties

Dear Sirs

Re: Arbitration

We have received an application for the appointment of an arbitrator in the above matter together with our prescribed registration/appointment fee. A receipted invoice is enclosed where appropriate.

We confirm that the procedure for the appointment of an arbitrator by this institute has been initiated. The Parties will be notified of the name and address of the appointee in due course.

Yours faithfully

Franklin J.C. Laratta
Legal Adviser

aol/94/6

enc.

INTERNATIONAL ARBITRATION CENTRE
24 ANGEL GATE · CITY ROAD · LONDON EC1V 2RS
TELEPHONE: (+44) 071-837 4483 FACSIMILE: (+44) 071-837 4185
PRESIDENT: THE RT. HON. SIR THOMAS BINGHAM, MASTER OF THE ROLLS
FCIArb
SECRETARY: KERRY R.K. HARDING, MITD FRSA FCIArb

(2) To Nominee Arbitrator (3.8/2 Arb)

THE CHARTERED INSTITUTE OF ARBITRATORS

Ref: 5/AO/299940000
(to: nominee arbitrator)

1994

Dear Mr

Re: Arbitration

We have received an application for the appointment of an arbitrator in a dispute that has arisen between the above-noted parties. I enclose a copy of the application and of the information and documents we have received to date, together with a copy of our letter to the parties confirming receipt of the application.

You are being considered for this appointment. I would be grateful if you would let me know as soon as possible whether or not you are willing to accept this, and that you will be able to proceed with the reference reasonably promptly.

If you are unable to accept, please return the enclosures to us so that we may forward them to someone else.

Yours sincerely,

Franklin J.C. Laratta
Legal Advisor

enc.
ao3/94/5

INTERNATIONAL ARBITRATION CENTRE
24 ANGEL GATE · CITY ROAD · LONDON EC1V 2RS
TELEPHONE: (+44) 071-837 4483 FACSIMILE: (+44) 071-837 4185
PRESIDENT: THE RT. HON. SIR THOMAS BINGHAM, MASTER OF THE ROLLS
FCIArb
SECRETARY: KERRY R.K. HARDING, MITD FRSA FCIArb

(3) Appointment (3.8/3 Arb)

Ref: 5/AO ref

**3.8/3 Arb
33**

IN THE MATTER OF THE ARBITRATION ACTS 1950–1979
AND IN THE MATTER BETWEEN

claimant

AND

respondent

APPOINTMENT OF ARBITRATOR

Pursuant to an Application dated:

I HEREBY APPOINT:

of
to be the Arbitrator in the above matter.

Signed:

Chairman/Vice-President

Date:

(For and/or on behalf of
the President of the
Chartered Institute of
Arbitrators)

ACCEPTANCE OF ARBITRATOR

I HEREBY ACCEPT   the above appointment

Signed:

Arbitrator

Date:

(4) Covering letter re Appointment (3.8/4 Arb)

THE CHARTERED INSTITUTE OF ARBITRATORS

Ref: 5/AO

Dear Mr

Arbitration: v

We confirm that you have agreed to act as arbitrator in the above-noted matter and wish to thank you for doing so.

We enclose the original notice of your appointment together with a copy. Kindly endorse the copy with your acceptance and return it to our attention. The original is for your records.

The parties have been advised of your appointment. Accordingly, we would ask that you inform them of your acceptance and make any necessary arrangements with them for the conduct of the reference.

Yours sincerely,

Franklin J.C. Laratta
Legal Adviser

enc
AO/let4

INTERNATIONAL ARBITRATION CENTRE
24 ANGEL GATE · CITY ROAD · LONDON EC1V 2RS
TELEPHONE: (+44) 071-837 4483 FACSIMILE: (+44) 071-837 4185
PRESIDENT: THE RT. HON. SIR THOMAS BINGHAM, MASTER OF THE ROLLS
FCIArb
SECRETARY: KERRY R.K. HARDING, MITD FRSA FCIArb

(5) Informing parties of Appointment (3.8/5 Arb)

THE CHARTERED INSTITUTE OF ARBITRATORS

Ref: 5/AO
Dear Sirs,

Arbitration: v

The parties are informed that:

has been appointed arbitrator, having previously indicated to us that he is able and willing to accept such appointment. Subject, therefore, to his formal acceptance of the appointment, the arbitration can proceed. The arbitrator will be contacting the parties himself in due course.
   Upon his formal acceptance, the arbitrator will be seised of the matter and this Institute will not be able to enter into correspondence on matters within the arbitrator's province.

Yours faithfully,

Franklin J.C. Laratta
Legal Adviser

ao5/94/6

INTERNATIONAL ARBITRATION CENTRE
24 ANGEL GATE · CITY ROAD · LONDON EC1V 2RS
TELEPHONE: (+44) 071-837 4483 FACSIMILE: (+44) 071-837 4185
PRESIDENT: THE RT. HON. SIR THOMAS BINGHAM, MASTER OF THE ROLLS
FCIArb
SECRETARY: KERRY R.K. HARDING, MITD FRSA FCIArb

9. Letters notifying parties of appointment (JCT Rules) (3.9 Arb)

D. EMSEE, MSc (Construction Law), FRICS, FCIArb

REGISTERED ARBITRATOR

Toad Hall, Hunstanton Water, NORFOLK
Telephone: 01999 590124; Facsimile: 01999 590690

FAX AND POST   24 February 1993

Our ref: DE/3.9 Arb.

Reliable Builders Ltd   Sanctuary House Ltd
Snape Yard   c/o Matthews House
Woodbridge   Main Street
Suffolk   Ipswich
FAO Harry Hocking Esq   Suffolk
                                         FAO William Bliss Esq

Gentlemen

Works at Sanctuary House, Woodbridge, Suffolk

In the matter of an arbitration between Reliable Builders Ltd v Sanctuary House Ltd under the JCT Arbitration Rules (30 July 1988)

1. I have been appointed by the President of the Royal Institution of Chartered Surveyors (RICS) as Arbitrator in the above Arbitration, pursuant to an application to the RICS and my appointment dated 20 February 1993, received under cover of their letter 20 February 1993. The RICS specifically request me to send copies of the Case Details to each party. These are attached hereto.

2. I confirm that the arbitration is to be conducted in accordance with the JCT Arbitration Rules dated 18 July 1988.

3. I confirm that the **Notification Date** for the purpose of the JCT Arbitration Rules is the date of this letter namely 24 February 1993.

4. As the parties will appreciate, under these Rules, the Notification Date is the date on which I inform them of my appointment, after which the Preliminary Meeting has to be held within 21 days (Rule 4.1); from thence the entire timetable is geared to this date.

5. I propose holding a Preliminary Meeting with the parties on one of the following dates:

8, 9, 10, 13 or 16 March 1993 at 10.30 a.m.

I suggest that this meeting be held at:

The Fleet Arbitration Centre, Hulton House, 161/166 Fleet Street, London

unless the parties agree to hold it at the offices of one of their solicitors/representatives—please liaise over this and inform me of your joint decision. I will leave it to the Claimant's solicitor to make the necessary arrangements. I am holding all these dates and times so please let me know, as soon as possible but in any event within seven days, where this meeting is to be held, so I can issue the necessary direction and agenda. If you wish to contact me via my fax number in order to confirm this, by all means do so.

6. Please inform me, and the other party, of the names and status of those who are expected to attend the Preliminary Meeting, and I should like to have this information not later than seven days prior to the meeting date. Please note that I do like to see a senior representative from each party at this meeting not merely the parties' representatives.

7. At the Preliminary Meeting I shall expect the parties, or their representatives, as appropriate, to address me either on their joint decision as to which of Rules 5, 6 or 7 is to apply to the conduct of the arbitration or, if no joint agreement is reached, then to let me have their views on the appropriate Rule. In order to do this it is imperative that the parties or their representatives be fully conversant with the nature of the dispute or difference and that areas of agreement and disagreement are fully canvassed and identified to me. The parties should consider liaising before the Preliminary Meeting with a view to narrowing issues as far as possible. I shall also be asking the parties to assist me in estimating the likely length of any hearing, in the event that Rule 6 applies to the conduct of the arbitration.

8. If the Claimant wishes Rule 7 to apply, I would remind him of the requirements of Rule 4.2 which must be complied with in advance of the Preliminary Meeting and I look forward to receiving a copy of the written case and statement that at the Preliminary Meeting will be requesting the Respondent to agree that Rule 7 should apply.

9. I remind the parties that the JCT Arbitration Rules contain certain very strict timetables in connection with the delivery of statements. Failure to serve any statement in accordance with the prescribed or directed timetable under Rules 5 or 6, as applicable, can involve the parties in very serious consequences.

10. As required by Rule 3.1 of the JCT Arbitration Rules, can each party please notify the other and me of the address for service upon them to statements, documents and notices referred to in the Rules.

11. You will find enclosed a copy of my Terms and Conditions and I would appreciate it if each of you would sign your copy and return it to me forthwith, together with the deposit cheque, as specified, from the Claimant.

12. I also enclose herewith a checklist of possible matters for consideration at the forthcoming Preliminary Meeting.

13. Should either party not be familiar with these Rules I can recommend Neil F Jones's book 'A User's Guide to the JCT Arbitration Rules'.

Yours faithfully

D Emsee, MSc, FRICS, FCIArb
Registered Arbitrator

Note: Terms, Case Details and Checklist not faxed—with hard copy only.

10. Checklist for Preliminary Meeting (3.10 Arb)

CHECKLIST OF MATTERS FOR CONSIDERATION AT PRELIMINARY MEETING

1. Confirmation of parties to the dispute.

2. A copy of Notice of Arbitration required to be produced for the Arbitrator. (Failure to agree within 14 days of written notice).

3. The original contract is required to be produced for the Arbitrator's inspection.

4. If JCT Arbitration Rules have been amended since the Base Date in Appendix to Contract (or the date of Agreement in respect of the JCT Minor Works) do the parties wish to use the amended rules. If so a joint agreement in writing is required.

5. Outline of Claimants case followed by outline of Respondents reply. Following discussion of the issues, identify and record principal areas of agreement and disagreement.

6. Is there a possibility of joinder of parties?

7. Are parties briefing Counsel?

8. Is there to be an exclusion agreement under Section 3 of the Arbitration Act 1979? If so, parties to agree in writing. Does either party require a reasoned award? If so, party requiring it must so state in writing in accordance with Rule 11.1.—notice must be explicit as to extent of reasons.

9. Selection of appropriate Rule from Rule 5, Rule 6 or Rule 7.

10. If Rule 7 is agreed by the parties fix hearing date and give other appropriate directions to suit the case. (Arbitrator has power to order further documents to be supplied if he considers these are essential. If parties do not agree on Rule 7 Arbitrator to decide whether Rule 5 or 6—see Rule 4.3.1. If disputed facts or disputed experts opinions then Rule 6 more appropriate).

11. If Rule 5 is to apply consider whether in addition to the prescribed statements there should be one further statement following any Statement of Reply.

12. If Rule 6 is to apply consider whether any proofs of evidence whether of fact or expert opinion be appended to statements.

13. Consider whether specific issues in the dispute can be split off to Rules 5, 6 or 7 as appropriate. If so parties to expressly consent. Are there any preliminary issues which could be conveniently dealt with at a separate hearing (i.e. liability with Arbitrator directing parties to seek agreement on quantum)?

14. If Rule 5 or 6 is to apply consider whether timetable should be as prescribed by the Rules or otherwise directed?

15. In relation to service of statements by facsimile under Rule 3.2, if documentation voluminous consider agreeing that such documents should be sent separately by first-class post at the same time as the facsimile statement and that this be regarded as good service.

16. Copies of statements to be served under the Rules to be sent to Arbitrator at the same time as to the other party.

17. If either party fails to comply with timetable other party to notify Arbitrator immediately of non-service and/or late service.

18. Consider other directions including:

(a) Inspection under Rule 8, if an inspection of the premises where the works have been carried out is requested by the parties, or thought desirable by the Arbitrator, this will normally take place following the hearing unless the parties request otherwise. On such inspection the Arbitrator will wish to be accompanied by one representative of each party.

3.10 Arb 39

(b) Agreement as to correspondence, plans, photographs, figures, etc.

(c) If the parties intend to instruct experts, their number. Such experts to meet, without prejudice, to endeavour to narrow the issues and agree figures as figures so far as possible.

The experts shall prepare, date and sign a note of the facts and opinions upon which they are agreed and of the issues upon which they cannot agree.

A copy of such note to be exchanged and delivered to the Arbitrator within fourteen days of their final meeting, but in any case, not less than seven days before the hearing.

(d) Selective discovery—can one party satisfy the Arbitrator that other party is likely to have in his possession documents damaging to that other party's case which are not likely to appear in supporting documentation of that party's case.

(e) If Rule 6 to apply:
  (i) Consider limit on orality.
    — Witness of fact proofs of evidence, if agreed, to be exchanged simultaneously and copied to the Arbitrator. Exchanged proofs to be admitted as evidence-in-chief.
    — Opening advocates' submissions to the Arbitrator and the other party seven days before the hearing.
    Closing advocates submissions seven days after close of hearing and Claimants' submissions seven days thereafter.
    N.B. If the parties agree that closing submissions be in writing, as above, the parties to be notified under Rule 6.9.2 that the Award will be published within 28 days of the receipt by the Arbitrator of the Claimants written closing submission.
  (ii) Date, time, place and estimated length of pre-hearing review, if appropriate.
  (iii) Date, time, place and estimated length of hearing.
  (iv) Venue and who will be responsible for arranging accommodation for pre-hearing review and hearing, as appropriate.

19. All communication to the Arbitrator to be copied to the other party. All communications to the Arbitrator to be in writing—not by telephone—but may be served by fax, in which case a further copy must be sent forthwith by first-class post or actually delivered.

20. Liberty to apply.

21. Costs.

D Emsee, MSc, FRICS, FCIArb
24 February 1993

11. Arbitrator's Terms (3.11 Arb)

3.11 Arb
40

ARBITRATOR'S TERMS

WHEREAS a dispute has arisen between Reliable Builders Ltd and Sanctuary House Ltd over Works at Sanctuary House, Woodbridge, Suffolk.

The parties to the contract hereby agree to submit and do submit all disputes and differences arising out of and in connection with the contract between the parties for the above Works, shall be referred to arbitration under the Arbitration Acts 1950 and 1979 and to the arbitration and final decision of a person to be nominated by the President, or a Vice-President, of the Royal Institution of Chartered Surveyors and on the nomination of the said President, or Vice-President, we have jointly agreed to the appointment of

D EMSEE, MSc, FRICS, FCIArb

as the said Arbitrator.

We hereby jointly and severally agree as follows:

(1) A minimum non-returnable commitment fee of £400 plus Value Added Tax will be paid by the Claimant forthwith; this amount to be set off against fees and expenses, otherwise payable under this Schedule, should such fees and expenses equal or exceed the amount of this minimum fee.

(2) To pay the fees and expenses of the Arbitrator at the rate of £80 per hour, for all time engaged upon the duties of the reference, other than the Hearing (irrespective of whether the matter reaches a Hearing or Award), together with all expenses, disbursements and outgoings incurred by him. Such hourly rate will be subject to review annually on 1 January.

(3) To pay the fees and expenses of the Arbitrator at the rate of £80 per hour, for time spent at the Hearing, or Interlocutory Meetings, with a minimum charged per day of £320.

(4) Where the Arbitrator travels inter-city, air or rail travel shall be first class; where on suburban routes, second class. Travel time, other than that spent reading in connection with this arbitration, will be charged at half of the above quoted hourly rate.

(5) Once dates for a Hearing or Interlocutory Meetings have been fixed, a fee shall be payable for time set aside and not spent, calculated as a percentage of the time charge set out above, according to the period of notice before the first day fixed for the Hearing or meeting as follows:

More than 6 months	Nil
Between 3 months and 6 months	25%
Between 1 month and 3 months	50%
Between 1 week and 1 month	75%
1 week or less, or after commencement of Hearing	100%

If the period fixed for the Hearing exceeds 10 working days the fees payable for time set aside and not spent, as set out above, shall be reduced by the following percentages, counting from the first day fixed for the Hearing or from the date of cancellation, whichever is later:

From 11th to 20th day	25%
From 21st day to 52nd day	50%
From 53rd day onward	75%

For the avoidance of doubt set aside days are charged at eight hours per day and include one day pre-hearing reading and preparation and one day post hearing collation and drafting.

(6) All fees and expenses to be subject to the addition of Value Added Tax at the appropriate rate.

(7) The Arbitrator may deliver interim fee notes quarterly and these are payable by the Claimant, 14 days after delivery, unless otherwise directed. Interest will be charged, on any fees remaining unpaid 14 days after delivery, at the rate of 5% p.a. above NatWest base rate monthly rests.

(8) The parties shall lodge such security in respect of the Arbitrator's fees and expenses as he may, in his absolute discretion, direct and it is understood that this money belongs to the Arbitrator. In the event that such security is sought the paying party will be invoiced for the money received. However, should it subsequently transpire, at the completion of the reference, the Arbitrator is not beneficially entitled to the entire sum paid as security, then the payment will be refunded and a credit note issued.

(Note: Security will normally be required to be deposited by the Claimant—subject to an appropriate contribution from the Respondent, as the Arbitrator may direct, should there be a counterclaim of substance—in the full amount of the fee payable in respect of any Hearing upon that Hearing being **firmly** fixed.)

(9) Any money paid in advance as fees and expenses will be placed in the Arbitrator's normal bank account and any interest earned thereon will accrue for the benefit of the Arbitrator.

(10) All outstanding fees are payable on taking up the Award or 10 days after notification that the Award is ready for collection, whichever is earlier.

(11) In the event of a settlement of the issues by agreement between the parties before an Award is made, the fees and expenses properly payable to the Arbitrator, shall be paid by the party or parties responsible for doing so under the Terms of the settlement, within 10 working days, after notification of the amount irrespective of whether a Consent Award is required or published.

For the avoidance of doubt, should the responsible party fail to pay these fees and expenses, both parties remain jointly and severally liable for them.

(12) The Arbitrator will be entitled to make time charges up to the time his final Fee Claim is settled.

(13) The Arbitrator shall be empowered to take legal advice if he considers it necessary, the cost of such advice to be part of the 'costs of the Award'.

In this event the Arbitrator will
  (i) discuss with the parties the choice of legal advisor
  (ii) show the parties the advice received or tell them the substance of the advice if given orally and
  (iii) give the parties the opportunity of addressing him briefly upon it, if they so wish, before he finally decides the point.

(14) The Arbitrator shall have power to proceed with the arbitration *ex parte* should either party fail, after due notice and without reasonable cause, to properly comply with any of the Arbitrator's Directions or Orders.

(15) This Agreement is not effective until it is signed on behalf of both Claimant and Respondent.

Agreed by/on behalf of the Claimant

....

Status .... Date ....

Agreed by/on behalf of the Respondent

....

Status .... Date ....

24 February 1993

12. Letter notifying parties of appointment (Non–JCT Rules) (3.12 Arb)

D EMSEE, MSc (Construction Law), FRICS, FCIArb

REGISTERED ARBITRATOR

LETTER & FAX

ARBAPPT   199

Messrs   Messrs

Gentlemen

re: In the matter of an Arbitration
between
and

in connection with Works at

I have been appointed by the (Vice) President of the Royal Institution of Chartered Surveyors (RICS) as Arbitrator in the above Arbitration, pursuant to an application to the RICS and my appointment dated   199 , received under cover of this letter   199 .

I propose holding a Preliminary Meeting with the parties on one of the following dates:

I note the location of the parties and their representatives' offices. I shall be happy to hold the Preliminary Meeting at the offices of one of the parties' solicitors or any other location agreed between the parties. Alternatively, if the parties cannot agree and they prefer to hold the meeting in London then I suggest the Fleet Arbitration Centre Limited, 6th Floor, Hulton House, 161–166 Fleet Street, London EC4A 2DY—please liaise over this and inform me of your joint decision. I will leave it to the Claimant's solicitor to make the necessary arrangements. I am holding all these dates and times so please let me know, as soon as possible but in any event within seven days, where this meeting is to be held, so I can issue the necesssary direction and agenda. If you wish to contact me via my fax number in order to conform this, by all means do so.

Please inform me and the other party of the names and status of those who will be expected to attend the Hearing or Meeting, and I should like to have this information not later than seven days prior to the meeting date. Please note that I do like to see the parties in person, at this meeting, not merely the parties' representatives, or, if one party or other is a company then a senior representative from that company.

At the Preliminary Meeting, after seeing the Original Contract and relevant Arbitration Clause, I should expect to ascertain the wishes of the parties so as to enable me to issue directions as to the conduct of this reference.

At the Preliminary meeting I shall wish to hear from each party, informally, details of how they see this dispute so that, between us we can decide on the most cost-effective method of resolution, for example, whether to have Formal Pleadings or a Statement of Case procedure. Following which we will then work out our timetable up to the oral Hearing, should it be agreed that is what is required.

Would the parties please confirm that the names and addresses shown on this letter are the correct points of contact.

LETTER NOTIFYING PARTIES OF APPOINTMENT (NON-JCT RULES)

If the parties intend to be represented in the proceedings by a solicitor or Counsel, it is highly desirable that the solicitor be present at the Preliminary Meeting and (if Counsel is being instructed) that solicitor should have discussed with Counsel before the meeting, the nature of any direction desired and the dates on which Counsel will, or will not be available for a hearing.

3.12 Arb 43

Please would you ensure that all letters sent by you to me are copied to the other party. All communications to me to be in writing—not telephone. Fax may be used.

You will find enclosed a copy of my Terms and Conditions and I would appreciate it if each of you would sign your copy and return it to me forthwith, together with the deposit cheque, as specified, from the Claimant.

Finally, as requested by the RICS, I enclose a copy of the Case Details prepared by them in connection with the Claimant's application for the appointment of an arbitrator. (Note: Terms and Case Details not faxed—with hard copy only).

Yours faithfully

D Emsee, MSc, FRICS, FCIArb
Arbitrator

13. Letter notifying parties of appointment (Maybe JCT Rules) (3.13 Arb)

D EMSEE, MSc (Construction Law), FRICS, FCIArb

REGISTERED ARBITRATOR

LETTER & FAX

48FORM9   199

Messrs   Messrs
Solicitors   Solicitors

FAO   FAO

Gentlemen

re: In the matter of an Arbitration
between
and

I have been appointed by the President of the Royal Institution of Chartered Surveyors (RICS) as Arbitrator in the above Arbitration, pursuant to an application to the RICS and my appointment dated   199 , received under cover of their letter 199 .

From the information sent to me by the RICS, I cannot ascertain whether this contract is governed by the JCT Arbitration Rules or not. If it is, I have to confirm the Notification Date, which I will refrain from doing until I know whether the Rules apply or not.

As the parties will appreciate, under Rules, the Notification Date is the date on which I inform them of my appointment, after which the Preliminary Meeting has to be held within 21 days (Rule 4.1), after which the entire timetable is geared to this date.

If the Rules do not apply, of course, we have far more flexibility over our timetable.

I remind the parties that the JCT Arbitration Rules contain certain very strict timetables in connection with the delivery of statements. Failure to serve any statement in accordance with the prescribed or directed timetable under Rules 5 or 6, as applicable, can involve the parties in very serious consequences. I would be obliged if the two solicitors would liaise over this point, and if they decide that the Rules are applicable, then you will appreciate that I need to be addressed at the Preliminary Meeting, as to your joint decision as to which of the Rules 5, 6 or 7 is to apply to the conduct of the arbitration, or if you cannot agree then let me have your views on the appropriate Rule. In order to do this it is imperative that the representative's of the parties be fully conversant with the nature of the dispute or difference, and the areas of agreement and disagreement are fully canvassed and identified to me. The parties should consider liaising before the Preliminary Meeting, with a view to narrowing issues as far as possible. I shall also be asking the parties to assist me in estimating the likely length of any hearing, in the event the Rule 6 applies to the conduct of the arbitration.

If the Claimant wishes Rule 7 to apply, I would remind him of the requirement of Rule 4.2 which must be complied with in advance of the Preliminary Meeting, and I look forward to receiving a copy of the written case and statement that at the Preliminary Meeting he will be requesting the Respondent to agree that Rule 7 should apply.

LETTER NOTIFYING PARTIES OF APPOINTMENT (MAYBE JCT RULES)

I am assuming for the purpose of Rule 3.1 that the solicitors' addresses are those to be used for notification for service of statements, documents, notices, etc. referred to in the Rules. Again, please confirm.

A copy of my Terms and Conditions is enclosed; please sign your copy and return it to me forthwith.

I propose holding a **Preliminary Meeting** with the parties on one of the following dates:

I suggest that this meeting be held at the Fleet Arbitration Centre, Hulton House, 161/166 Fleet Street, London, unless the parties agree to hold it at the offices of one of their solicitors/representatives—please liaise over this and inform me of your joint decision. I will leave it to the Claimant's solicitor to make the necessary arrangements. I am holding all these dates and times so please let me know, as soon as possible but in any event within seven days where this meeting is to be held, so I can issue the necessary direction and agenda. If you wish to contact me via my fax number in order to confirm this, by all means do so.

Your faithfully

D Emsee, MSc, FRICS, FCIArb
Arbitrator

14. Setting up—Time sheets (3.14 Arb)

D EMSEE, MSc (Construction Law), FRICS, FCIArb

REGISTERED ARBITRATOR

JOB _____   Ref No. _____

ARBITRATION TIME SHEET

Date	Subject Matter	Time Expended Hrs/Mins

TOTAL C/F

Page No.

15. Setting up—Expense sheet (3.15 Arb)

D EMSEE MSc (Construction Law), FRICS, FCIArb

REGISTERED ARBITRATOR

Toad Hall, Hunstanton Water, NORFOLK
Telephone: 01999 590124; Facsimile: 01999 590690

Job _____   Ref No. _____

ARBITRATION/COST SHEET

Date	Expense Details				Cost £.00
	Telephone/Faxes/Typing/Postage/Photocopying (delete whichever appropriate)				
	To	Subject Matter	Time of Day	Duration Min/Sec	
	OTHERS				

CHAPTER 4

The Preliminary Meeting

1. Order for Directions No 1 (4.1 Arb)

IN THE MATTER OF THE ARBITRATION ACTS 1950 TO 1979

AND

IN THE MATTER OF AN ARBITRATION UNDER THE JCT ARBITRATION RULES (18 JULY 1988)

BETWEEN

RELIABLE BUILDERS LIMITED	Claimant
AND	
SANCTUARY HOUSE LIMITED	Respondent

ORDER FOR DIRECTIONS NO 1

---

1. **BY CONSENT** the Parties or their Representatives shall appear before me at a procedural meeting at the offices of the Claimant's surveyor, Standard House, Ipswich on 23 March 1993 at 10.30 a.m. The Claimant to be responsible for booking the accommodation.

2. The business of this meeting shall be in accordance with the attached agenda.

3. Parties to acknowledge receipt of this order.

4. Costs to be costs in the reference.

Date: 2 March 1993

**D Emsee MSc FRICS FCIArb
Arbitrator**

To: 1. Claims Consultant

    2. William Bliss

Representative of the Claimant
FAO Joel Redman
Respondent

2. Agenda for Preliminary Meeting

JCT Rules—Statement of Case (4.2/1 Arb)

IN THE MATTER OF THE ARBITRATION ACTS 1950 TO 1979

AND

IN THE MATTER OF AN ARBITRATION UNDER THE JCT ARBITRATION RULES (18 JULY 1988)

BETWEEN

RELIABLE BUILDERS LIMITED   Claimant

AND

SANCTUARY HOUSE LIMITED   Respondent

PRELIMINARY MEETING

To be held at 10.30 a.m. on 23 March 1993 at the offices of the Claimant's Surveyor, Swansea House, 48 Queen's Road, Norwich

AGENDA

1.00 Introductions

Confirmation of identity and status of Parties

2.00 Arbitration Agreement

2.01 A copy of Notice of Arbitration required to be produced for the Arbitrator.

2.02 Notification date—confirmation of.

3.00 Original Contract

Required to be produced for Arbitrator's inspection.

4.00 JCT Rules

Not aware of any amendments therefore original 1988 Rules applicable.

5.00 Identify items in Dispute

5.01 Outline of Claimant's case.

5.02 Outline of Respondent's case.

5.03 Discussion of issues.
Identify and record principal areas of agreement and disagreement.

6.00 Joinder
Is there any possibility of joinder of parties?

7.00 Selection of Appropriate Rule
Most cost-effective procedure?

7.01 **If RULE 7—SHORT PROCEDURE WITH HEARING is to apply**
Only suitable for 'quality' disputes requiring some summary decision.
Each side bears own costs.
Claimant must deliver Statement of Case 7 days *before* Preliminary Meeting.
The Claimant must request the Arbitrator, at the Preliminary Meeting, to agree Rule 7
(irregularities can be waived—see p. 127).

4.2/1 Arb
51

7.02 If **RULE 5—DOCUMENTS ONLY is to apply**
Unsuitable where a serious dispute over relevant facts.
Issues need to be framed with more precision than Rule 6.

Timetable
Rule 5.3 (see p. 94)
Clarification Rule 5.8 (see p. 95)

7.03 **Preliminary Issues**
Can either party identify one or more issues which, if decided particular way, could
dispense with all, or a substantial element of, the dispute?

Consider whether specific issues in the dispute can be split off to Rules 5, 6 or 7 as
appropriate. If so, parties to expressly consent.

7.04 Consider **limiting:**
Time allowed for examination-in-chief and cross examination of witness OR alterna-
tively the length of the hearing.
The issues on which the Arbitrator needs to be addressed.
Reading aloud from documents or authorities.

7.05 **General**
All applications for extension of time must be made to the Arbitrator, in writing, before
time expires—copy to other party.
All Statements under Rules shall set out factual and *legal* basis relied upon. (How
realistic is this timescale?)
Sealed offers—*modus operandi?*

7.06 **If RULE 6—FULL PROCEDURE WITH HEARING is to apply**
Need not *all* be oral.
For disputes which require examination/cross-examination of witnesses of fact.
7.06.1 Consider whether Scott Schedule desirable.
7.06.2 Consider whether any proofs of evidence/rebuttals, whether of fact or expert opinion
be appended to Statements.
OR alternative if not appended to Statements—see below.
Witnesses' proofs of evidence, if agreed, to be exchanged simultaneously and copied
to the Arbitrator. Exchanged proofs to be admitted as evidence in chief.
Rebuttals?
Date of exchange?
Except by the Arbitrator's leave (which will only be given in special circumstances) no
witness may be called at the Hearing unless a written proof of evidence has been
provided in accordance with the preceding paragraph and no evidence-in-chief may
be adduced by a witness to any issue which has not been included in the

proof of evidence of that witness, either specifically or in general terms to the supporting documentation to that party's Statements.

All Statements together with their supporting documentation served under these Rules shall, once proved, be admitted as documentary evidence, subject to proof.

7.06.3 Opening advocates submissions to the Arbitrator and the other party seven days before the Hearing.

7.06.4 Closing submission from Respondent seven days after closing of Hearing and Claimant's submission seven days after. The parties are hereby notified under Rule 6.9.2 that the Award will be published within 28 days of the receipt by the Arbitrator of the Claimant's written closing submission.

7.06.5 *Timetable*

If Rule 6 to apply then the timetable and requirements laid down in Rule 6.3 shall be followed, unless otherwise directed, viz:

Rule

(6.3.1) The Claimant shall, within 28 days after the date when Rule 6 becomes applicable, serve a *Statement of Case*.

(6.3.2) If the Claimant serves a Statement of Case within the time or times allowed by these Rules the Respondent *shall*, within 28 days after service of the Claimant's Statement of Case, serve a *Statement of Defence* to the Claimant's Statement of Case and a Statement of any *Counterclaim*.

(6.3.3) If the Respondent serves a Statement of Defence within the time or times allowed by these Rules the Claimant *may*, within 14 days after such service, serve a Statement of *Reply to the Defence*.

(6.3.4) If the Respondent serves a Statement of Counterclaim within the time or times allowed by these Rules the Claimant *shall*, within 28 days after such service, serve a *Statement of Defence* to the Respondent's *Counterclaim*.

(6.3.5) If the Claimant serves a Statement of Defence to the Respondent's Statement of Counterclaim within the time or times allowed by these Rules the Respondent *may*, within 14 days after such service, serve a Statement of Reply to the Defence.

(6.3.6) The Claimant with his Statement of Case and any Statement setting out a Reply to the Respondent's Statement of Defence and his Statement of Defence to any Statement of Counterclaim by the Respondent

and the Respondent with his Statement of Defence and any Statement of Counterclaim and any Statement setting out a Reply to the Claimant's Statement of Defence to any Counterclaim

shall include a list of any documents the Claimant or Respondent, as the case may be, considered necessary to support any part of the relevant Statement and a copy of the principal documents on which reliance will be placed identifying clearly in each document the relevant part or parts on which reliance will be placed.

Legal basis relied upon with Statement?—see Rule 3.4.

7.06.5 No provision for Further and Better Particulars—consider each party serving a Notice to Admit and/or Interrogatories.

If Further and Better Particulars prove necessary, at the discretion of Arbitrator, Requests are to be made within seven days of the delivery of the Statement ('Pleading') to which they refer.

Note: The criteria adopted to determine whether Further and Better Particulars are reasonable, are

1 Is it capable of answer?
2 Will it assist questioning party to understand the case against it or to investigate it?
3 Is it on the critical path and/or forms the logic necessary to reach the Award?

Consent is likely to be refused where—

1 Questions are oppressive and it appears that the intention is to distract the answering party from other matters.
2 They seek evidence.
3 They fail to go to an issue on the critical path.

4.2/1 Arb 53

Replies to Requests for Further and Better Particulars are to be made within seven days of the Request.

Note: The period for delivery of any subsequent Statement ('Pleading') shall be extended by the time which elapses between the delivery of a Request for Further and Better Particulars and the delivery of the answer thereto.

Pleadings (service of Statements) shall be deemed to be closed seven days after the delivery of the last of the above mentioned Statement ('Pleading') or seven days after the expiry of the period allowed delivery of any Statement ('Pleading') if no further Statement ('Pleading') has been delivered.

7.06.6. Experts

7.06.6.1 If Experts engaged, date for exchange of their reports/rebuttals, if not delivered with Statements.

7.06.6.2 Inspection access for experts—if necessary?

7.06.6.3 Experts could exchange draft reports *before* they *meet*.

7.06.6.4 Experts will meet, 'open' or 'without prejudice', to endeavour to narrow the issues.

7.06.6.5 What authority do they have?

7.06.6.6 The Experts to exchange draft reports within four weeks of the close of 'Pleadings' and to meet within two weeks of this exchange.

They shall endeavour to narrow the issues and to agree facts as facts, figures as figures, etc. as far as possible.

The Experts shall prepare, date and sign a note of the facts and opinions upon which they are agreed, and of the issues upon which they cannot agree. A copy of such note to be exchanged and delivered to the Arbitrator within 14 days of their meeting, but in any event, no later than 14 days before the Hearing.

7.06.6.7 'Without prejudice' removed in respect on matters agreed.

7.06.7 Discovery

There is no provision for discovery under JCT Rules as documents on which parties wish to rely will be included with their Statements.

However, if one party can satisfy the Arbitrator that the other party is likely to have in his possession documents which might be helpful to that party's case or damaging to that other party's case which are not likely to appear in supporting documentation of that party's case then the Arbitrator can order selective discovery under Rule 12.1.7.

7.06.8 Hearing

Rule 6.8 provides that after the receipt of the last of statements and documents referred to in Rule 6.3, the Arbitrator will notify the parties of the date of the Oral Hearing. This is generally too late.

Suggest change this, by agreement, to 'unless otherwise directed', then agree a date.

7.06.8.1 *Sitting*

Each sitting day will be from 10.00 a.m. to 5.00 p.m. with one hour's recess for luncheon.

7.06.8.2 *Estimated Duration*

Provisional Date? Total length in days?
Four-day sitting week.

7.06.8.3 *Venue/Accommodation*

Claimant will arrange suitable accommodation in consultation with the Respondent and the Arbitrator. In the absence of agreement between the parties the Claimant shall book accommodation at a venue to be directed by the Arbitrator.

7.06.8.4 *Hearing bundle*

Parties to deliver to the Arbitrator not less than seven days before the Hearing a Hearing bundle of documents properly paginated and annotated.

After delivery of this bundle the Arbitrator will wait 24 hours before reading it in order to give the parties the opportunity to check if, inadvertently, any 'without prejudice' material has found its way into the bundle. In which case, on being informed of this the Arbitrator's secretary will locate the document and return it, unread by the Arbitrator, to the parties.

A core bundle of principal documents?

What do the parties want the Arbitrator to read prior to the Hearing?

Nothing in the bundle is to be taken as read by the Arbitrator until adduced at the Hearing.

7.06.8.5 *Rules of Evidence*

Are the parties prepared to waive strict observance of the rules of evidence?

7.06.8.6 *Evidence on Oath*

All oral evidence shall be on oath or affirmation.

7.06.8.7 *Textbooks/Law Reports*

The Arbitrator to be notified if textbooks and/or Building Law Reports are to be referred to at the Hearing then, seven days before the Hearing, the party wishing to refer to such shall send the Arbitrator a copy of the Report or extract, with the passage on which that party wishes to place reliance, suitably highlighted.

7.06.9 Pre-Hearing Review

7.06.9.1 To consider all outstanding issues which need to be narrowed and clarified.
7.06.9.2 Provisional date/venue?

8.00 Counsel

Are parties briefing Counsel?

9.00 Exclusion Agreement

Is there to be an exclusion agreement under s.3 of the Arbitration Act 1979? Who will draft?

10.00 Reasoned Award

Does either party require reasoned award? If so party requiring it *must so state in writing*, and must say where and to what extent reasons are required, in accordance with Rule 11.1, i.e. the request should include a formulation of the question of law on which the parties might wish to appeal.

4.2/1 Arb
55

11.00 Settlement of Costs

The Arbitrator will exercise discretion under Rule 12.1.5 to settle the parties' costs, if not agreed. Basis shall be 'reasonable amount, reasonably incurred commercial man basis' Form of Bill may be prepared on a solicitor and client basis.

12.00 Service of Statements/Documents

12.01 In relation to service of Statements by facsimile under Rule 3.2, if documentation is voluminous consider agreeing that such documents should be sent separately by first class post or courier at the same time as the facsimile Statement and that this shall be regarded as good service.

12.02 Copies of Statements to be served under Rules to be sent to the Arbitrator at the same time as to the other party.

12.03 If either party fails to comply with timetable the other party to notify Arbitrator immediately of non-service and/or late service.

13.00 Inspection

Inspection under Rule 8, if an inspection of the premises where the works have been carried out is requested by the parties, or thought desirable by the Arbitrator, this will normally take place at a date to be agreed prior to the Hearing unless the parties request otherwise. On such inspection the Arbitrator will wish to be accompanied by one representative of each party.

14.00 Agreement of Common Ground

Agreement as to correspondence, plans, photographs, figures as figures, etc.

15.00 Communications

All communications to the Arbitrator to be copied to the other side, and to be in writing—not telephone—but may be served by fax, in which case a further copy must be sent forthwith by first-class post or delivered by hand.

16.00 Arbitrator's Terms and Costs

16.01 Have Terms been signed and returned by both parties?

16.02 Interim Fee Statements—to be paid by the Claimant.

16.03 Security for Costs—usually from Claimant but also Respondent if there is a substantial counterclaim.

16.04 Once Hearing days have been reserved any party responsible for cancelling may be held liable for the Arbitrator's cancellation charges.

16.05 If settlement takes place, any Hearing days reserved shall form part of the Arbitrator's fees to be paid as part of the settlement.

17.00 Insurance

17.01 Of documents in possession of arbitrator—consequential loss.

17.02 Of the arbitrator in a protracted reference.

18.00 Any other business

D Emsee MSc FRICS FCIArb
Arbitrator

Alternatives for Preliminary Meeting where Rules do not apply (4.2/2 Arb)

IN THE MATTER OF THE ARBITRATION ACTS 1950 TO 1979

AND

IN THE MATTER OF AN ARBITRATION

4.2/2 Arb
57

BETWEEN

Claimant

AND

Respondent

PRELIMINARY MEETING

To be held at   at   a.m. on   199

AGENDA

1.00 Introductions

Confirmation of identity and status of Parties

2.00 Arbitration Agreement

A copy of Notice of Arbitration required to be produced for the Arbitrator.

3.00 Original Contract

Required to be produced for Abritrator's inspection.

4.00 Identify Items in Dispute

4.01 Outline of Claimant's case.
4.02 Outline of Respondent's case.
4.03 Discussion of issues.
     Identify and record principal areas of agreement and disagreement.

5.00 Joinder

Is there any possibility of joinder of parties?

6.00 Conduct of the Reference

6.01 Documents only or attended Hearing?
6.02 Formal/Informal Pleadings/Statement of Case?

7.00 Proceedings

Most cost-effective procedure?

7.01 **If SHORT PROCEDURE WITH HEARING is to apply**
     Only suitable for 'quality' disputes requiring some summary decision.
     Each side bears own costs.

7.02 If DOCUMENTS ONLY is to apply

Unsuitable where a serious dispute over relevant facts.

Issues need to be framed with more precision than when attending Hearing.

Timetable

Date for Claimants' written Statement, evidence, witness proofs and experts' reports (if any).

Period for Respondent's written Statements, evidence, witness proofs and experts' reports (if any).

Period for Claimants' written response.

Period for Respondent's written Reply.

Where the Arbitrator considers that any document listed in any of the Statements requires further clarification by an interview with the parties or otherwise, or that some further document is essential for him properly to decide on the matters in dispute the Arbitrator may require such clarification or further document by notice in writing to the Claimant or the Respondent as appropriate and shall serve a copy of that notice upon the party not required to provide such clarification or further document. Such clarification by an interview with the parties or otherwise shall be obtained in accordance with the directions of the Arbitrator and such further document shall be supplied to the Arbitrator with a copy to the other party by the Claimant or Respondent forthwith upon receipt of the notice in writing from the Arbitrator.

7.03 Preliminary Issues

Can either party identify one or more issues which, if decided a particular way, could dispense with all, or a substantial element of, the dispute?

Consider whether specific issues in the dispute can be split—documents only/quantum/liability only. If so, parties to expressly consent.

7.04 Consider limiting:

Time allowed for examination-in-chief and cross examination of witness OR alternatively the length of the hearing.

The issues on which the Arbitrator needs to be addressed.

Reading aloud from documents or authorities.

7.05 General

All applications for extension of time must be made to the Arbitrator, in writing, before time expires—copy to other party.

All Statements of Case shall set out factual and *legal* basis relied upon. (How realistic is this timescale?)

Sealed offers—*modus operandi*?

7.06 If STATEMENT OF CASE PROCEDURE WITH HEARING is to apply

Need not *all* be oral.

For disputes which require examination/cross-examination of witnesses of fact.

7.06.1 Consider whether Scott Schedule desirable.

7.06.2 Consider whether any proofs of evidence/rebuttals, whether of fact or expert opinion by appended to Statements.

OR alternative if not appended to Statements—see below.

Witnesses' proofs of evidence, if agreed, to be exchanged simultaneously and copied to the Arbitrator. Exchanged proofs to be admitted as evidence in chief.

Rebuttals?

Date of exchange?

Except, by the Arbitrator's leave (which will only be given in special circumstances) no witness may be called at the Hearing unless a written proof of evidence has been provided in accordance with the preceding paragraph and no evidence-in-chief may be adduced by a witness to any issue which has not been included in the proof of evidence of that witness, either specifically or in general terms to the supporting documentation to that party's Statements.

All Statements, together with their supporting documentation, served under these Rules shall, once proved, be admitted as documentary evidence, subject to proof.

7.06.3 Opening advocates' submissions to the Arbitrator and the other party seven days before the Hearing.

7.06.4 Closing submission from Respondent seven days after close of Hearing and Claimant's submission seven days thereafter.

4.2/2 Arb 59

7.06.5 *Timetable*

The following timetable shall be followed, unless otherwise directed, viz:

7.06.5.1 The Claimant shall, within 28 days of the date of Preliminary Meeting, serve a *Statement of Case*.

7.06.5.2 If the Claimant serves a Statement of Case within the time 28 days directed the Respondent *shall*, within 28 days after service of the Claimant's Statement of Case, serve a *Statement of Defence* to the Claimant's Statement of Case and a Statement of any *Counterclaim*.

7.06.5.3 If the Respondent serves a Statement of Defence within the 28 days directed the Claimant *may*, within 14 days after such service, serve a Statement of *Reply to the Defence*.

7.06.5.4 If the Respondent serves a Statement of Counterclaim within the 14 days directed the Claimant *shall*, within 28 days after such service, serve a *Statement of Defence* to the Respondent's *Counterclaim*.

7.06.5.5 If the Claimant serves a Statement of Defence to the Respondent's Statement of Counterclaim within the 28 days directed the Respondent *may*, within 14 days after such service, serve a Statement of Reply to the Defence.

7.06.5.6 The Claimant with his Statement of Case and any Statement setting out a Reply to the Respondent's Statement of Defence and his Statement of Defence to any Statement of Counterclaim by the Respondent

and the Respondent with his Statement of Defence and any Statement of Counterclaim and any Statement setting out a Reply to the Claimant's Statement of Defence to any Counterclaim

shall include a list of any documents the Claimant or Respondent, as the case may be, considered necessary to support any part of the relevant Statement and a copy of the principal documents on which reliance will be placed identifying clearly in each document the relevant part or parts on which reliance will be placed.

7.06.5.7 No provision for Further and Better Particulars—consider each party serving a Notice to Admit and/or Interrogatories.

If Further and Better Particulars prove necessary, at the discretion of Arbitrator, Requests are to be made within seven days of the delivery of the Statement ('Pleading') to which they refer.

Note: The criteria adopted to determine whether Further and Better Particulars are reasonable, are

1 Is it capable of answers?

2 Will it assist questioning party to understand the case against it or to investigate it?

3 Is it on the critical path and/or forms the logic necessary to reach the Award?

Consent is likely to be refused where—

1 Questions are oppressive and it appears that the intention is to distract the answering party from other matters.
2 They seek evidence.
3 They fail to go to an issue on the critical path.

Replies to Requests for Further and Better Particulars are to be made within 7 days of the Request.

Note: The period for delivery of any subsequent Statement ('Pleading') shall be extended by the time which elapses between the delivery of a Request for Further and Better Particulars and the delivery of the answer thereto. Pleadings (service of Statements) shall be deemed to be closed seven days after the delivery of the last of the above mentioned Statement ('Pleading') or seven days after the expiry of the period allowed delivery of any Statement ('Pleading') if no further Statement ('Pleading') has been delivered.

7.06.6 *Experts*

7.06.6.1 If Experts engaged, date for exchange of their reports/rebuttals, if not delivered with Statements.
7.06.6.2 Inspection access for experts—if necessary?
7.06.6.3 Experts could exchange draft reports *before* they *meet*.
7.06.6.4 Experts will meet, 'open' or 'without prejudice' to endeavour to narrow the issues.
7.06.6.5 What authority do they have?
7.06.6.6 The Experts to exchange draft reports within four weeks of the close of 'Pleadings' and to meet within two weeks of this exchange.

They all endeavour to narrow the issues and to agree facts as facts, figures as figures etc. as far as possible.

The Experts shall prepare, date and sign a note of the facts and opinions upon which they are agreed, and of the issues upon which they cannot agree. A copy of such note to be exchanged and delivered to the Arbitrator within 14 days of their meeting, but in any event, no later than 14 days before the Hearing.
7.06.6.7 'Without prejudice' removed in respect on matters agreed.

7.06.7 *Discovery*

There is no provision for discovery under this procedure as documents on which parties wish to rely will be included with their Statements.

However, if one party can satisfy the Arbitrator that the other party is likely to have in his possession documents which might be helpful to that party's case or damaging to that other party's case which are not likely to appear in supporting documentation of that party's case then the Arbitrator can order selective discovery.

7.06.8 *Hearing*

7.06.8.1 *Sitting*
Each sitting day will be from 10.00 am to 5.00 pm with one hour's recess for luncheon.
7.06.8.2 *Estimated Duration*
Provisional Date? Total length in days?
four day sitting week.

7.06.8.3 *Venue/Accommodation*
> Claimant will arrange suitable accommodation in consultation with the Respondent and the Arbitrator. In the absence of agreement between the parties the Claimant shall book accommodation at a venue to be directed by the Arbitrator.

7.06.8.4 *Hearing bundle*
> Parties to deliver, to the Arbitrator, not less than seven days before the Hearing, a Hearing bundle of documents properly paginated and annotated. After delivery of this bundle the Arbitrator will wait 24 hours before reading it in order to give the parties the opportunity to check if, inadvertently, any 'without prejudice' material has found its way into the bundle. In which case, on being informed of this the Arbitrator's secretary will locate the document and return it, unread by the Arbitrator, to the parties.
>
> A core bundle of principal documents?
>
> What do the parties want the Arbitrator to read prior to the Hearing?
>
> Nothing in the bundle is to be taken as read by the Arbitrator until adduced at the Hearing.

4.2/2 Arb 61

7.06.8.5 *Rules of Evidence*
> Are the parties prepared to waive strict observance of the rules of evidence?

7.06.8.6 *Evidence on Oath*
> All oral evidence shall be on oath or affirmation.

7.06.8.7 *Text Books/Law Reports*
> The Arbitrator to be notified if text books and/or Building Law Reports are to be referred to at the Hearing then, seven days before the Hearing, the party wishing to refer to such shall send the Arbitrator a copy of the Report or extract, with the passage on which that party wishes to place reliance, suitably highlighted.

7.06.9 *Pre-Hearing Review*
    7.06.9.1 To consider all outstanding issues which need to be narrowed and clarified.
    7.06.9.2 Provisional date/venue?

8.00 Counsel

Are parties briefing Counsel?

9.00 Exclusion Agreement

Is there to be an exclusion agreement under s.3 of the Arbitration Act 1979? Who will draft?

10.00 Reasoned Award

Does either party require reasoned award? If so party requiring it *must so state in writing*, and must say where and to what extent reasons are required, i.e. the request should include a formulation of the question of law on which the parties might wish to appeal.

11.00 Settlement of Costs

The Arbitrator will exercise the discretion he has, by virtue of s.18(1) of the Arbitration Act 1950, to settle the parties' costs, if not agreed. Basis shall be 'reasonable amount, reasonably incurred commercial man basis' Form of Bill may be prepared on a solicitor and client basis.

12.00 Service of Statements/Documents

12.01 In relation to service of Statements by facsimile if documentation is voluminous consider agreeing that such documents should be sent separately by first class post or courier at the same time as the facsimile Statement and that this shall be regarded as good service.

12.02 Copies of Statements to be sent to the Arbitrator at the same time as to the other party.

12.03 If either party fails to comply with timetable the other party to notify Arbitrator immediately of non-service and/or late service.

13.00 Inspection

In an inspection of the premises where the works have been carried out is requested by the parties, or thought desirable by the Arbitrator, this will normally take place at a date to be agreed prior to the Hearing unless the parties request otherwise. On such inspection the Arbitrator will wish to be accompanied by one representative of each party.

14.00 Agreement of Common Ground

Agreement as to correspondence, plans, photographs, figures as figures etc.

15.00 Communications

All communications to the Arbitrator to be copied to the other side, and to be in writing—not telephone—but may be served by fax, in which case a further copy must be sent forthwith by first class post or delivered by hand.

16.00 Arbitrator's Terms and Conditions

16.01 Have Terms been signed and returned by both parties?

16.02 Interim Fee Statements—to be paid by the Claimant.

16.03 Security for Costs—usually from Claimant but also Respondent if there is a substantial counterclaim.

16.04 Once Hearing days have been reserved any party responsible for cancelling may be held liable for the Arbitrator's cancellation charges.

16.05 If settlement takes place, any Hearings days reserved shall form part of the Arbitrator's fees to be paid as part of the settlement.

17.00 Insurance

17.01 Of documents in possession of arbitrator—consequential loss.

17.02 Of the arbitrator in a protracted reference.

18.00 Any other business

D Emsee MSc FRICS FCIArb
Arbitrator

3. Notes for Preliminary Meeting (4.3 Arb)

NOTES FOR PRELIMINARY MEETING

1.00 Introductions—Parties present

1.01 Confirmation of identity and status of Parties.

2.00 Arbitration Agreement

See Original Contract and check relevant Arbitration Clause.
Check correct nominating body.

3.00 Identify Items in Dispute

3.01 Outline Claimants' Position

Brief ORAL statement to paint the picture—entirely informal.

3.02 Outline Respondents' Position

Brief ORAL statement to paint the picture—entirely informal.

4.00 Counsel

—To find out if parties are briefing Counsel—each need to know the others intentions.

5.00 Conduct of Reference

What is most cost-effective procedure?

5.01 Documents only OR attended Hearing

Preliminary issue can sometimes be dealt with on a documents only basis.
OR

Dispute turning on point of law, interpretation of document in technical sense, etc. appropriate for DOCUMENTS ONLY if little evidence from independent source, then ORAL probably better—easier to test the credibility of W's from Exam-in. C and X-exam.
If Documents only P's must expressly agree but subject to either Arbitrator of P's reserving right to revert to ORAL.

5.02 Formal or Informal Pleadings

A copy of each pleading to be sent to the Arbitrator concurrently with service on the other party.
Consider delaying reformulation of Pleadings (for any agreed amendments) until Pre Hearing Review (7.01.4 post).

5.02.1 Schedules

Scott Schedules alone (in defects and quantum; final account claims etc).
OR

Maybe Scott Schedule required as part of other Pleadings?

5.03 Timetable—if documents only

5.03.1 Date for **Claimants' written submissions**, evidence, witness proofs and expert reports (if any).

5.03.2 Period for **Respondents' written submissions**, evidence, witness proofs and expert reports (if any).

5.03.3 Period for **Claimants' written response**.

5.03.4 Period for **Respondents' written reply**.

5.04 Timetable—if Informal Pleadings

Simplest form letter from CLAIMANT to RESPONDENT setting out claim. Letter of reply from RESPONDENT stating grounds on which he denies liability.

(OR

even relying on previous correspondence between parties

then would almost certainly need 'hands-on' formulation of questions re formulative series of questions, gleaned from correspondence, which will be basis of arbitration (but this only if representative in person or lay advocates)).

5.04 Timetable—Formal Pleadings

Set dates, if any slippage, party responsible will pay the costs of deferring Hearing dates.

5.04.1 **Dates for Points of Claim**
(Delivered to R and the Arbitrator)

5.04.2 **Period for Defence and Counterclaim** (if any) (28 days of delivery of Points of Claim—by end week 7)

5.04.3 **Period for Reply and Defence of Counterclaim** (if any) (28 days of delivery of Points of Defence—by end week 11)

5.04.4 **Period for Reply to Defence to Counterclaim** (if any) (28 days of delivery of Defence of Counterclaim—by end week 15)

5.04.5 **Period for Requests for Further and Better Particulars** (Within seven days of the delivery of the Pleading to which it refers *Note*—the criteria adopted to determine whether FP/BP are reasonable are:

1. Is it capable of answer?

2. It will assist questioning party to understand case against it or to investigate it.

3. It is on the critical path that forms the logic necessary to reach the Award.

Consent is likely to be refused where

1. The questions are oppressive and it appears that the intention is to distract the answering party from other matters.

2. They seek evidence.

3. They fail to go to an issue on the critical path.

5.04.6 **Period for Response to Requests for Further and Better Particulars** (Answered within seven days of request)

N.B. The period for delivery of any subsequent Pleadings shall be extended by the time which elapses between delivery of a Request for Further and Better Particulars of the delivery of the answer thereto.

Pleadings shall be deemed to be closed seven days after the delivery of the last of the above mentioned Pleadings or seven days after the expiry of the period allowed for delivery of any Pleadings if no further Pleading has been delivered.

5.04.7 Exchange of Lists/Inspection

5.04.7.1 Informal

For Informal Pleadings and Statement of Case no provision made for discovery and inspection but would give necessary Direction for specific documents if not produced and I was satisfied were relevant.

4.3 Arb
65

5.04.7.2 Formal

(Only documents relevant to the matters in dispute, ie likely to advance own case or damage that of your opponents).

Rather than full/formal discovery consider following alternatives:

1. Documents on which party relies served with Pleadings *plus* a list of categories of other documents which other party is at liberty to call for.

2. Conference between solicitors where they could attempt to agree on which document they will allow inspection. Lists could be dispensed with and files open to inspection to respective solicitors to determine which documents they require copies of; then application to Arbitrator for Order for Directions by consent.

3 At close of Pleadings solicitors to list those matters which they consider are pertinent for discovery.

If none of these devices work then formal discovery as follows:

Parties to deliver to the Arbitrator and to the other a list of documents which are or have been in its possession, custody or power relating to the matter in question in this Arbitration and inspection shall be given on two days' notice thereafter. (Two weeks after close of Pleadings—say by end of week 17.)

(Note: Restrict amount by date or type

OR

solicitors can meet and agree on which documents they will allow inspection.)

5.04.8 Date for Hearing Bundle

Parties to deliver to the Arbitrator four weeks after exchange of lists—say end of week 21—a Hearing bundle of documents properly paginated and identified.

5.04.9 Late service

If either party fails to comply with the timetable the other party to notify the Arbitrator of non-service/late service.

N.B. In relation to service of Pleadings if documentation voluminous consider agreeing that such documents should be sent separately by facsimile and first-class post at the same time and this be regarded as good service.

[ALTERNATIVE TIMETABLE

5.04 Statement of Case

Include

1. Background and factual matrix. The Claims. The outline facts establishing each and the legal basis of each including ref to each contract term relied upon.

2. Outline statement of relevant law to each claim and copies of authorities.

3. List documents referred to in Pleadings (in smaller cases plus JCT attach all documents relied upon).

4. At least the heads of Witness Statements.]

5.05 Witnesses Proof of Evidence

Witnesses of fact, proofs of evidence shall be exchanged simultaneously. Exchanged proofs to be admitted as evidence-in-chief.

> Rebuttals?
> Date for exchange

Except, by my leave (which will only be given in special circumstances), no witness may be called at the Hearing unless a written proof of evidence has been provided in accordance with the preceding paragraph and no evidence-in-chief may be adduced by a witness to any fact which has not been included in the written proof of evidence of that witness.

5.06 Engagement of Experts

Do parties intend to use Experts—important that experts receive identical instructions. (If C engaged, then early appt to brief Expert.)

5.06.1 Exchange of Experts' Reports

Inspection access for experts—if necessary?

> Experts could exchange draft reports *before* they *meet*.

> Experts will meet, 'open' or 'without prejudice' to endeavour to narrow the issues and agree figures as figures so far as possible.

> What authority do they have?

> The Experts shall prepare, date and sign a note of the facts and opinions upon which they are agreed, and of the issue upon which they cannot agree. A copy of such note to be exchanged and delivered to the Arbitrator within 14 days of their final meeting but in any event not later than 14 days before hearing.

> 'Without prejudice' removed in respect of matters agreed upon?

5.07 Common Ground/Admissions

5.07.1 Correspondence, plans, photographs and other figures shall be agreed as such as far as possible.

5.07.2 Following service of Defence parties should consider serving on each other Notices to Admit (facts).
> Also directing interrogatories—to be answered under oath—to specific individuals amongst the parties.

5.08 Status of Hearing Bundle

5.08.1 Will it be Agreed?

5.08.2 Properly paginated and annotated as Claimant and Respondent Bundles—ensure both same pagination.

5.08.3 Core Bundle of principal documents?

5.08.4 What do you want the Arbitrator to read?

5.08.5 Date for delivery

5.08.6 Nothing in Bundles to be taken as read by the Arbitrator until adduced at Hearing.

6.00 Preliminary Issues

Can either party identify one or more issues which, if decided in a particular way could dispense with all or a subtantial element of the dispute?

7.00 Pre-Hearing Review—(Will be subject of separate direction)

Is this necessary? If so hold it after close of Pleadings/Discovery and exchange of Expert Reports.

Each party should be represented by whoever will be their advocate at the hearing.

Objective—to ascertain if issues have been narrowed and generally to review the case.

7.01 Will confirm current position with regard to:

7.01.1 Any outstanding directions.

7.01.2 Witnesses proofs.

7.01.3 Hearing bundle—this will not be evidence—see 5.08.6 *ante*).

7.01.4 Delivery to Arbitrator of finalised uncoloured copy of Pleading.

7.01.5 Identification of issues. Parties to prepare and agree list of issues and deliver list to Arbitrator not later than three days before meeting (or alternatively prepare with parties at Meeting).

7.01.6 Identification of witnesses.

7.01.7 Sealed offers—*modus operandi?*

7.01.8 To ascertain whether any Further Directions are sought.

7.01.9 To deal with any other outstanding matters.

8.00 If attended Hearing

8.01 Date

To be determined at the Pre-Hearing Review. Each sitting day will be from 10.00 a.m. until 5.00 p.m. with one hour's recess for luncheon.

8.02 Estimated Duration

(4-day sitting week).

8.03 Venue

8.04 Accommodation

Claimant will arrange suitable accommodation.

8.05 Limitation or orality

8.05.1 Opening advocates submissions to other party and Arbitrator seven days before Hearing.

8.05.2 Closing R's advocates submissions seven days after close to C and Arbitrator and C's advocates submission seven days thereafter.

8.06 Rules of Evidence

Are the parties prepared to waive strict observance of the rules of evidence?

8.07 Evidence on Oath

All oral evidence shall be on oath or affirmation.

8.08 Textbooks/Law Reports

The Arbitrator to be notified if textbooks and/or Building Law Reports are to be referred to at the Hearing then, seven days before the Hearing, the party wishing to refer to such shall send the Arbitrator a copy of the Report or extract suitably highlighted.

9.00 Inspection

If an inspection of the premises where the works have been carried out is requested by the parties or thought desirable by the Arbitrator this will normally take place following the Hearing unless the parties request otherwise. On such an inspection the Arbitrator would wish to be accompanied by one representative of each party.

10.00 Award

10.01 Reasoned or unreasoned?

If either party wishes a reasoned award any request for reasons shall be made before the close of the Hearing.

If reasoned award required the request should include a formulation of the question of law upon which the parties might wish to appeal.

10.02 Interim Award

Are there any preliminary issues which could be conveniently dealt with at a separate Hearing? Whether there is any advantage in dealing with liability separate from quantum?

10.03 Taxation of Costs

Possible for Arbitrator to tax parties costs but highly skilled job—only 'reluctantly' agree provided parties agree that it is done by reference to reasonable costs reasonably incurred on a commercial man basis, i.e. not standard basis under White Book. Form of Bill may be solicitor and own client basis.

11.00 Exclusion Agreement

Do the Parties wish to enter into an exclusion agreement under the 1979 Act s.3.
Who will draft?

12.00 Communications

All communications to the Arbitrator to be copied to the other party.

All communications to the Arbitrator to be in writing—not telephone—but could be served by Fax, in which case a further copy must be sent forthwith by first-class post or actually delivered.

13.00 Costs Thrown Away

Costs thrown away for hearing dates agreed between the parties paid by party causing postponement or cancellation.

14.00 Arbitrator's Terms

14.01 Have Terms been signed and returned?
14.02 Interim costs/security.

15.00 Any Other Business

4. Ad Hoc Arbitration Agreement (4.4 Arb)

IN THE MATTER OF THE ARBITRATION ACTS 1950 TO 1979

AND

IN THE MATTER OF AN ARBITRATION UNDER THE JCT ARBITRATION RULES (18 JULY 1988)

BETWEEN

RELIABLE BUILDERS LIMITED   Claimant

AND

SANCTUARY HOUSE LIMITED   Respondent

ARBITRATION AGREEMENT

We RELIABLE BUILDERS LTD and SANCTUARY HOUSE LTD hereby agree to submit and do submit all disputes and differences between us which have arisen out of, or in connection with, the contract between us for works and services at SANCTUARY HOUSE, WOODBRIDGE, SUFFOLK including the matters covered by the order, dated   1993, from District Judge   sitting   at County Court, to be determined by the Arbitration of D EMSEE of Toad Hall, Hunstanton, Norfolk.

Signed .... For Claimant
                                                              Reliable Builders Ltd

Signed .... For Respondent
                                                              Sanctuary House Ltd

                                                              Date ....

5. Standard Direction on Expert Evidence (4.5 Arb)

STANDARD DIRECTION ON EXPERT EVIDENCE

Direct that:

(i) On or before   the parties exchange the names, fields of expertise and witness statements of the experts whose opinions will be advanced as evidence.

(ii) (a) Thereafter the parties arrange for their respective experts in each field of expertise to meet together as soon as reasonably practicable and on so many occasions as may be necessary to prepare the report referred to hereafter;

(b) it will be the purpose of the meeting and the responsibiity of the experts to strive to reach agreement on as much as possible of the expert opinion relevant to the dispute;

(c) the meeting of experts is encouraged to call by unanimous agreement on the parties or either of them to obtain and provide any additional data or information the experts may need with a view to reaching agreement, a copy of any such call to be lodged by the claimant with the arbitrator/referee;

(d) either party shall be at liberty to apply for a direction that such call be complied with;

(e) the experts shall prepare a condensed joint report stating in the first part the matters upon which they have finally been able to reach agreement and stating in the second part the matters upon which they have not been able to reach agreement;

(f) the report shall be accompanied by annexures prepared by each expert stating in condensed form the opinion of the expert on each matter of disagreement including the reasons why the expert does not agree with the opinions of the other experts;

(g) the original report shall be sent to the claimant on or before   who shall forthwith lodge it with the arbitrator/referee and send a copy to each other party;

(h) evidence may not be received from an expert who has without adequate reason not participated in such meeting and report.

(iii) at the hearing

(a) as each field of expertise arises for consideration each expert in that field will verify by affirmation his/her witness statement, the joint report and his/her annexure to the joint report. After these documents have been admitted into evidence all the expert witnesses in that field shall participate in a continuation of their meeting at which they will discuss with each other the matters of disagreement;

(b) for the purpose of such discussion the experts will be seated facing each other at a table placed between the arbitrators/referee's table and the bar table;

(c) the discussion will be chaired by the arbitrator/referee who will guide the discussion and will intervene with the object of the matters of disagreement being examined and analysed so as to enable the arbitrator/referee to reach a determination upon them;

(d) the representatives of the parties will be at liberty with the permission of the arbitrator/referee to intervene in the discussion and, prior to the arbitrator/referee reaching a determination on any matters of disagreement, they will be permitted to question the experts and make submissions to the arbitrator/referee.

6. Order for Directions No 2—Consent Order following Preliminary Meeting—where JCT Rules apply (4.6 Arb)

IN THE MATTER OF THE ARBITRATION ACTS 1950 TO 1979

AND

IN THE MATTER OF AN ARBITRATION UNDER THE JCT ARBITRATION RULES (18 JULY 1988)

BETWEEN

RELIABLE BUILDERS LIMITED   Claimant

AND

SANCTUARY HOUSE LIMITED   Respondent

ORDER FOR DIRECTIONS NO 2

UPON hearing Representatives for both Parties on 23 March 1993 the following Directions are given by CONSENT (unless otherwise noted) and it is

HEREBY DIRECTED THAT

1.00 Parties

The **Parties** in this Arbitration are
1.01 Reliable Builders Limited of Snape Yard, Woodbridge, Suffolk as **Claimant**.
1.02 Sanctuary House Limited, Registered Office: Matthews House, Main Street, Ipswich, Suffolk as **Respondent**.

2.00 Contract

The **contract** governing this dispute is the JCT Intermediate Form of Building Contract (IFC '84) 1990 Edition.

3.00 Rules

3.01 The JCT Arbitration Rules (18 July 1988) govern this arbitration.
3.02 The Notification Date for the purpose of the arbitration shall be 24 February 1993
3.03 The Claimant has not previously informed me that he wished Rule 7 to apply.
3.04 It was agreed that Rule 6 would apply.

4.00 Joinder

There is to be no joinder of parties to this arbitration.

5.00 Timetable

5.01 The Timetable for service of Statements/Submissions (Pleadings) is to be as set out in Rule 6.3 but for the avoidance of doubt:
5.02 The Statement of Case shall be served no later than 5.00 p.m. 28 days after the publication of the award on the preliminary issues—see item 6.00 *supra*.

5.03 The Statement of Defence and Counterclaim shall be served no later than 5.00 p.m. 28 days after the service of the Statement of Case.

5.04 The Defence to the Counterclaim shall be served no later than 21 days after the service of the Statement of Defence and Counterclaim.

5.05 There is no provision for Replies other than those listed herein.

5.06 All statements shall set out the factual and legal basis relied upon and shall include a list of any documents the Claimant or Respondent considers necessary to support any part of the relevant statement and a copy of the principal documents on which reliance will be placed identifying clearly in each document the relevant part or parts of which reliance will be placed.

5.07 The Respondent's Statement of Counterclaim shall incorporate a Scott Schedule with full particulars of each item of alleged defective work separately listed and costed out.

The Claimant will complete his part of this Schedule with his Defence to the Counterclaim.

6.00 Preliminary Issues

6.01 It was agreed that there were a number of preliminary issues which it was considered could be conveniently dealt with at a separate hearing.

6.02 These items were identified as follows:

6.02.1 When and how was the contract formed?

6.02.2 What are the Terms and Conditions of the Contract?

6.02.3 What items are subject to remeasurement?

6.02.4 What rates are to be applied to the contract work generally and what is the status of the discount?

6.02.5 The genuineness of the Gibbs ceiling.

6.02.6 Is the contractor in breach of contract in respect of the waterproofing of the basement?

6.03 The actual wording of these preliminary issues to be determined by Counsel for the Claimant in consultation with the appointed advocate for the Respondent.

6.04 The timetable for the events leading to the determination of the Preliminary issues will be as follows. The references thus ( ) being to the main item numbers in this Order. Reference should be made to these items and any other item in the main body of this Order which may be equally applicable to the Preliminary issues in which case it will apply with equal force.

6.04.1 The Claimant's Statement of Case be served on the Respondent and copied to me no later than 5.00 p.m. 8 April 1993.

6.04.2 The Respondent's Statement of Case to be served on the Claimant and copied to me no later than 5.00 p.m. 6 May 1993.

6.04.3 There will be no provision for separate Replies to the Responses. Such Replies to be incorporated into the advocates written opening submissions.

6.04.4 The following documents to be delivered to me not later than 5.00 p.m. 12 May 1993.

(i) The Expert Reports (9.00)

(ii) The Agreed Bundle (12.00)

(iii) Proofs of Evidence (13.00)

(iv) Advocates opening submissions (17.00)

6.05 There will be a Hearing for the Preliminary issues of two-days duration, which time shall be divided equally to each side. This two-day Hearing will commence on 24 May 1993.

7.00 Service

7.01 Statements may be served by facsimile, first-class post or courier, but if by facsimile then a hard copy must follow by first-class post.

7.02 If either party fails to comply with the timetable set out above, the other party to notify me of non-service or later service.

8.00 Counsel

The Claimant intends to instruct Counsel. The Respondent will inform me and the other side, no later than 5.00 p.m. on 6 May 1993, by whom he will be represented, both for the Preliminary issues and for the Hearing on the substantive issues.

4.6 Arb 73

9.00 Experts

9.01 Each party intends to instruct 4 Experts. The parties will attempt to agree on joint instructions. A copy of the agreed instruction to be sent to me or, if no agreement, details of those points of instruction on which they do agree and details of those on which they do not.

9.02 These instructions to state that Experts will meet 'open' or 'without prejudice' and also what authority they have (if any) to bind their respective parties. In any event 'without prejudice' attaching to these discussions shall be removed in respect of matters agreed upon.

9.03 The Experts to consider exchanging draft reports before they meet but, in any event, not later than 8 weeks of the service of the last Statement or Reply to any Request for further and Better Particulars thereof (see 7.04.5 of Agenda) for the Preliminary Meeting and to meet within 2 weeks of this exchange.

9.04 The Experts shall endeavour to narrow the issues and to agree facts as facts, figures as figures etc. as far as possible.

9.05 They shall prepare, date and sign a note of the facts and opinions upon which they are agreed and of the issues upon which they are not. A copy of such note to be exchanged and delivered to me within 14 days of their final meeting but, in any event, no later than 14 days before the Hearing. Reports not exchanged will not be admitted.

10.00 Discovery/Inspection

10.01 There is no provision for discovery under JCT Rules as documents on which parties wish to rely will be included with their Statements.

10.02 However, if one party can satisfy me that the other party is likely to have in his possession documents which might be helpful to that party's case or damaging to that other party's case which are not likely to appear in supporting documentation of that party's case then I can order selective discovery under Rule 12.1.7.

11.00 Hearing

11.01 The parties having agreed to add the words 'unless otherwise directed' to Rule 6.8, there shall be a **Hearing** in this Arbitration the duration and dates for which are to be determined.

11.02 Each sitting day will be from 10.00 a.m. to 5.00 p.m. with one hour's recess for luncheon.

11.03 The Hearing shall be held, at a venue to be notified, in suitable accommodation arranged by the Claimant with the agreement of the Respondent.

11.04 Exchanged proofs of evidence shall be admitted as evidence-in-chief.

11.05 All oral evidence shall be on oath or affirmation.

11.06 The parties may, but have not yet agreed to, waive the strict rules of evidence.

11.07 Should either party be responsible for the postponement or cancellation of any Hearing days set aside then that party will be responsible for the costs thrown away by that postponement or cancellation.

12.00 Agreed Bundle

There will be an **Agreed Bundle** for the Hearing. It will be the Claimant's responsibility to ensure that this bundle is properly paginated and annotated and a copy delivered to me no later than 7 working days before the Hearing. The parties require me to read this bundle.

13.00 Proofs of Evidence

Proofs of evidence, of witness of fact, to be exchanged and a copy delivered to me no later than seven days before the Hearing and to be admitted as evidence-in-chief but a brief examination-in-chief will be permitted if requested.

Except, by my leave (which will only be given in special circumstances), no witness may be called at the Hearing unless a written proof of evidence has been provided in accordance with the preceding paragraph and no evidence-in-chief may be adduced by a witness to any issue which has not been included in the written proof of evidence of that witness, either specifically or in general terms to the supporting documentation to that party's statement.

14.00 Pre-Hearing Review

The Parties or their representatives shall appear before me for a **Pre-Hearing Review** on a date to be determined to finalise the date, time, venue and probable duration of the Hearing and to confirm that all interlocutory steps in this Arbitration have been or will be taken.

15.00 Common Ground

Correspondence, plans, photographs and figures shall be agreed as such as far as is possible and a statement of this common ground shall be included in the Agreed Bundle.

16.00 Law Reports/Authorities

Seven days before the Hearing the parties will provide me with copies of any additional Law Reports or authorities not included in their statements on which they wish to rely with the appropriate passage/passages suitably highlighted.

17.00 Advocates' Submissions

17.01 Advocates' opening submissions shall be reduced to writing and delivered to me and the other party at least seven days before the Hearing.

17.02 Advocates' closing submission shall be reduced to writing. The Respondents advocate's closing submission to be delivered to me and the other party not later than seven days after the close of the Hearing and the Claimants advocate's closing submissions to me and the other party not later than seven days thereafter.

18.00 Inspection

I am required to carry out an Inspection of the Works. This inspection will take place at 10.00 a.m. on 16 August 1993 when I will be accompanied by one representative from each side who will merely point out what it is I am to look at—nothing said on this visit will be evidence.

19.00 Reasoned Award

Both parties require a reasoned award and they are therefore required to so state, to me, in writing, and must say where and to what extent reasons are required (Rule 11.1), i.e. the request should include a formulation of the questions of law on which the parties might wish to appeal.

20.00 Exclusion Agreement

The parties agree to exclude their rights of appeal under s.3 of the 1979 Arbitration Act and the claimant's solicitor will be responsible for drafting the Exclusion Agreement, the finally jointly signed version of which is to be sent to me.

OR [delete as necessary]

The parties do not wish to enter into an exclusion agreement under s.3 of the 1979 Arbitration Act.

**4.6 Arb
75**

21.00 Taxing Parties' Costs

21.01 I will exercise my discretion under Rule 12.1.5 to tax the Parties **costs** in the event that they are not agreed.

21.02 The basis of the settlement will be on a 'reasonable amount, reasonably incurred commercial man basis'—not the standard basis as laid down in the White Book.

21.03 The Form of Bill may be that prepared on a solicitor and client basis with an appropriate breakdown, details of which will be covered by a separate direction.

22.00 Communications

All communications to me to be in writing, copied to the other party and may be sent by facsimile, in which case a further copy must be sent forthwith by first class post.

IT IS FURTHER DIRECTED THAT:

23.00 I may submit quarterly Interim Fee Accounts in accordance with my Terms and Conditions in which case these will be paid by the Claimant. I shall exercise the discretion I have by virtue of Clause 8) of my Terms and require Security for my Fees and Expenses in such sum I shall direct, one month before the Hearing.

24.00 Once the Hearing days are agreed and reserved by me, should either party be responsible for cancelling or postponing them, then that party may be held liable for costs thrown away and, in particular, my cancellation charges as set out in my Terms and Conditions.

Similarly, should these Hearing days be abandoned as a result of a settlement between the parties, such cancellation charges shall form part of my fees to be paid by the parties as part of the settlement.

25.00 Costs in the Reference.

26.00 Liberty to apply.

Date: 25 March 1993

To: Claims Consultant

William Bliss

D Emsee MSc FRICS FCIArb
Registered Arbitrator

Representative of the Claimant
FAO
Respondent

Order for Directions—Consent Order following Preliminary Meeting—Full Pleadings (4.7 Arb)

IN THE MATTER OF THE ARBITRATION ACTS 1950 TO 1979

AND

IN THE MATTER OF AN ARBITRATION

BETWEEN

Claimant

AND

Respondent

ORDER FOR DIRECTIONS NO

Upon hearing Solicitors for both Parties on   1993 the following Directions are given by CONSENT (unless otherwise noted) and it is

HEREBY DIRECTED THAT:

1.00 Parties

The **Parties** in this Arbitation are:
1.01   as **Claimant**
1.02   as **Respondent**

2.00 Contract

The **Contract** governing this dispute is

3.00 TIMETABLE

There shall be an attended Hearing preceded by an exchange of **Pleadings** as follows:
3.01 Points of **Claim** to be delivered to me and to the Respondent by   199 .
3.02 Points of **Defence and Counterclaim** to be delivered to me and to the Claimant within 56 days of delivery of the Points of Claim.
3.03 Points of **Reply and Defence of Counterclaim** (if any) to be delivered to me and to the Respondent within 56 days of delivery of the Points of Defence.
3.04 Points of **Reply to Defence to Counterclaim** (if any) to be delivered to me and to the Claimant within 42 days of delivery of the Defence to Counterclaim.
3.05 Any request for **Further and Better Particulars** shall be delivered within 14 days of delivery of the Pleading to which it refers and shall be answered within a further 14 days.
3.06 The period for delivery of any subsequent Pleading shall be extended by the time which elapses between delivery of a request for Further and Better Particulars and delivery of the answer thereto.
3.07 Pleadings shall be closed seven days after the delivery of the last of the above mentioned Pleadings or seven days after expiry of the period allowed for delivery of any Pleadings if no further Pleading has been delivered.
3.08 Pleadings shall incorporate a Scott Schedule, prepared by the Claimant in a form to be approved by the Respondent. A copy of this form to be sent simultaneously to the Arbitrator.

3.09 Pleadings may be served separately by facsimile and first-class post or courier at the same time and the receipt of the facsimile will be regarded as good service.

3.10 If either party fails to comply with the timetable set out above, the other party to notify me of non-service or late service.

4.00 Preliminary Issues

There were no preliminary issues which the parties considered should be conveniently dealt with at a separate hearing.

4.7 Arb
77

5.00 Counsel

Both/neither party intends to instruct **Counsel**.

6.00 Experts

6.01 Each party intends to instruct   Experts. The parties will attempt to agree on joint instructions. A copy of the agreed instruction to be sent to me or, if no agreement, details of those points of instruction on which they do agree and details of those on which they do not.

6.02 These instructions to state that Experts will meet 'open' or 'without prejudice' and also what authority they have (if any) to bind their respective parties. In any event 'without prejudice' attaching to these discussions shall be removed in respect of matters agreed upon.

6.03 The Experts to consider exchanging draft reports before they meet but, in any event, not later than 8 weeks of the service of the last Statement or Reply to any Request for Further and Better Particulars thereof (see 7.04.5 of Agenda) for the Preliminary Meeting and to meet within 2 weeks of this exchange.

6.04 The Experts shall endeavour to narrow the issues and to agree facts as facts, figures as figures etc. as far as possible.

6.05 They shall prepare, date and sign a note of the facts and opinions upon which they are agreed and of the issues upon which they are not. A copy of such note to be exchanged and delivered to me within 14 days of their final meeting but, in any event, no later than 14 days before the Hearing. Reports not exchanged will not be admitted.

7.00 Discovery/Inspection

By   199   each Party shall deliver to me and to the other a **list of Documents** which are or have been in its possession, custody or power relating to the matters in question in this Arbitration and **Inspection** shall be given on 2 days notice thereafter (or if No Direction re Discovery see 48 form 8).

8.00 Hearing

8.01 There shall be a Hearing in this Arbitration for which   hearing days have been reserved. The Hearing will commence on   199   and continue until   199 .

8.02 Each sitting day will be from 10.00 a.m. to 5.00 p.m. with one hour's recess for luncheon.

8.03 The Hearing shall be held at the   in suitable accommodation arranged by the Claimant with the agreement of the Respondent.

8.04 Exchanged proofs of evidence shall be admitted as evidence in chief.

8.05 All oral evidence shall be on oath or affirmation.

8.06 The parties agree [do not agree] to waive the strict rules of evidence.

8.07 Should either party be responsible for the postponement or cancellation of the Hearing days set aside then that party will be responsible for the costs thrown away by that postponement or cancellation.

9.00 Agreed Bundle

There will be an **Agreed Bundle** for the Hearing. It will be the Claimant's responsibility to ensure that this bundle is properly paginated and annotated and a copy delivered to me no later than seven working days before the Hearing. The parties require me to read this bundle.

10.00 Proofs of Evidence

Proofs of evidence, of witness of fact, to be exchanged and a copy delivered to me no later than six weeks of close of pleadings and to be admitted as evidence-in-chief but a brief examination-in-chief will be permitted if requested.

Except by my leave (which will only be given in special circumstances), no witness may be called at the Hearing unless a written proof of evidence has been provided in accordance with the preceding paragraph and no evidence-in-chief may be adduced by a witness to any fact which has not been included in the written proof of evidence of that witness.

11.00 Pre-Hearing Review

The Parties or their representatives shall appear before me for a **pre-Hearing Review** on a date to be determined to finalise the date, time, venue and probable duration of the Hearing and to confirm that all interlocutory steps in this Arbitration have been or will be taken.

12.00 Common Ground

Correspondence, plans, photographs and figures shall be agreed as such as far as is possible and a statement of this common ground shall be included in the Agreed Bundle.

13.00 Law Reports/Authorities

Seven days before the Hearing the parties will provide me with copies of any Law Reports or authorities not included in their Pleadings on which they wish to rely with the appropriate passage/passages suitably highlighted.

14.00 Advocates' Submissions

14.01 Advocates' opening submissions shall be reduced to writing and delivered to me and to the other party at least seven days before the Hearing.

14.02 Advocates' closing submissions shall be reduced to writing with the Respondent's submission being delivered to me and the other side within seven days of the close of the Hearing and the Claimant's submission to me and the Respondent within seven days thereafter.

15.00 Inspection

I am [not] required to carry out an **Inspection** of the Works.

16.00 Reasoned Award

[Neither]/both parties have requested a **reasoned award** and therefore are required to so state, to me, in writing, and must say where and to what extent reasons are required, i.e. the request should include a formulation of the question(s) of law on which the parties might wish to appeal.

17.00 Exclusion Agreement

The parties agree to exclude their rights of appeal under s.3 of the 1979 Arbitration Act and the Claimant's solicitor will be responsible for drafting the Exclusion Agreement, the finally jointly signed version of which is to be sent to me.

OR [*delete as necessary*]

The parties do not wish to enter into an Exclusion Agreement under s.3 of the 1979 Arbitration Act.

4.7 Arb 79

18.00 Taxing Parties' Costs

18.01 I will exercise my discretion, under Rule 12.1.5 to tax the Parties **costs** in the event that they are not agreed.

18.02 The basis of the settlement will be on a 'reasonable amount, reasonably incurred commercial man basis'—not the standard basis as laid down in the White Book.

18.03 The Form of Bill may be that prepared on a solicitor and client basis with an appropriate breakdown, details of which will be covered by a separate direction.

19.00 Communictions

All communications to me to be in writing, copied to the other party and may be sent by facsimile, in which case a further copy must be sent forthwith by first class post.

IT IS FURTHER DIRECTED THAT:

20.00 I may submit quarterly Interim Fee Accounts in accordance with my Terms and Conditions in which case these will be paid by the Claimant. I shall exercise the discretion I have by virtue of Clause (7) of my Terms and require Security for my Fees and Expenses in such sum as I shall direct, one month before the Hearing.

21.00 Once the Hearing days are agreed and reserved by me, should either party be responsible for cancelling or postponing them then that party may be held liable for costs thrown away and in particular my cancellation charges as set out in my Terms and Conditions.

Similarly, should these Hearing days be abandoned as a result of a settlement between the parties, such cancellation charges shall form part of my fees to be paid by the parties as part of the settlement.

22.00 Costs in the Reference.

23.00 Liberty to apply.

Date: 199

D Emsee MSc, FRICS, FCIArb
Arbitrator

Solicitors for the Claimant
FAO

Solicitors for the Respondent
FAO

Exclusion Agreement (4.8 Arb)

IN THE MATTER OF THE ARBITRATION ACTS 1950 TO 1979

AND

IN THE MATTER OF AN ARBITRATION

BETWEEN

Claimant

AND

Respondent

EXCLUSION AGREEMENT

WE the undersigned having referred to arbitration the dispute that has arisen from the contract made, on or about   199   for Works at   and D. Emsee having been appointed Arbitrator in this reference, HEREBY AGREE, pursuant to Section 3 of the Arbitration Act 1979, that the jurisdiction of the High Court under Sections 1 & 2 of the said Act, in respect of this Arbitration, shall be excluded.

For the avoidance of doubt this agreement excludes all supervisory powers of the Court and specifically; power to entertain an appeal; power to order the arbitrator to state further reasons; power to entertain a preliminary point of law and power to transfer to the High Court an arbitration involving an issue of fraud.

Signed by or on behalf of the Claimant by: ....
Dated this   day of   199

Signed by and on behalf of the Respondent by: ....
Dated this   day of   199

Typical Rent Review Letter—Notifying Parties of Appointment (4.9 Arb)

Sirs,

IN THE MATTER OF THE ARBITRATION ACTS 1950 TO 1979
AND IN THE MATTER OF AN ARBITRATION BETWEEN
[THE LANDLORD]
AND
[THE TENANT]
RE: [ADDRESS]

1 **APPOINTMENT/LEASE:** By letter dated   from the [Vice] President of the Royal Institution of Chartered Surveyors I am appointed as **Arbitrator** to determine the rent of the above property pursuant to the Lease dated ... made between   (1) and   (2). The RICS has sent to me a copy of the   [document], and I am told you have received a copy of the Case Details from which my appointment derives.

2 **TIME DELAY:** To mitigate costs I am deferring issuing procedural directions for **seven days** from the date of this letter so that the parties may have an opportunity to advise me if they wish to request me to defer proceeding with the matter in the event of the dispute nearing early resolution. If I do not hear from *both* parties that they wish me to defer proceeding within the time limit I shall proceed and issue procedural directions.

3 **COMMUNICATIONS:** This letter is written to the parties and, where appropriate, the parties' representatives which have been notified to the Royal Institution of Chartered Surveyors. Unless I am requested otherwise future correspondence, notices and matters pertinent to this arbitration will be sent to the representatives of the parties (where appropriate) only.

Save in an emergency all communications to me should be in writing **with confirmation that a copy has been sent simultaneously to the opposing party**. For the avoidance of doubt copies of correspondence between the parties should not be sent to me.

4 **FEES:** I will provide full details of my proposed level of fees if and when I proceed and issue procedural directions. In the event of the dispute having been resolved upon agreed terms prior to me issuing procedural directions my total costs will be on a relatively nominal basis based upon *quantum meruit.*

5 **RESOLUTION OF THE DISPUTE:** If, at any stage, the parties reach a settlement the parties should notify me, immediately. Any settlement should be comprehensive to include all matters referred to arbitration and must include agreement as to who is to pay my costs (apportioned, if appropriate).

Yours faithfully,

ARBITRATOR

DISTRIBUTION:

Follow up to the last Rent Review Letter (4.10 Arb)

Sirs,

IN THE MATTER OF THE ARBITRATION ACTS 1950 TO 1979
AND IN THE MATTER OF AN ARBITRATION BETWEEN
[THE LANDLORD]
AND
[THE TENANT]
RE: [ADDRESS]

1 [The parties have not jointly requested deferral of the procedure; accordingly] I request the parties to respond to the questions I raise in the following paragraphs within   [days] from the date of this letter.

2 **APPOINTMENT/LEASE:** I have previously referred to my appointment. A copy of the Lease has been sent to me. If either party wishes to verify the authenticity of the document I am to be advised immediately and I will send to the party a copy of my copy for verification.

3. **PARTIES' REQUESTED PROCEDURE:** So that I may decide whether to arrange a preliminary meeting at which the detailed procedure and timetable can be agreed or, failing agreement, decided by me, I need to know whether the parties wish to proceed by way of a hearing or solely upon written representations, written cross representations, written summary of contentions.

If either party or both parties wish to proceed by way of a hearing I shall hold a preliminary meeting.

If both parties wish to proceed solely by written representations I shall be pleased to learn whether the parties wish me to proceed with Directions without holding a preliminary meeting or whether they would find a preliminary meeting helpful. If this method is agreed I nevertheless reserve the right to direct a hearing if I consider this necessary or desirable.

If I have no response from both parties within the time limit I have imposed I shall proceed to an Order for Directions for a preliminary meeting.

4 **ISSUE OF LAW:** When replying please let me know whether or not there appears to be any dispute on the interpretation of the Lease or on any other legal matter.

5 **WITHOUT PREJUDICE MATTERS:** Please note that no 'without prejudice' correspondence or negotiations shall be disclosed to me, including any opening shot if without prejudice privilege is expressly reserved. For the avoidance of doubt I regard any part of a bona fide negotiation for a settlement, whether or not marked 'without prejudice', as privileged and inadmissible unless the privilege has been expressly and unambiguously removed. **I stress the importance of this direction**.

6 **BASIS OF MY COSTS:** My costs in this matter can, of course, be left to be determined in accordance with the provisions of the Arbitration Acts, but I have found that the parties usually prefer to know my proposed basis of costs and, if acceptable, to confirm their agreement. In this case my total costs will be on the basis of [a fixed cost of £   reflecting the circumstances plus] £   per hour calculated upon the time I personally spend on the reference. [Additional charges will be made for secretarial time and typing at the rate of £ per hour.] [I shall charge travelling time at half my hourly rate.] Additional charges for disbursements, if significant, will be made in respect of room hire, legal advice (if appropriate) and other relevant disbursements. In the event of the dispute being resolved upon agreed terms or a joint request to me to make an Award by Consent, my total costs will be based solely upon the above hourly rate, but in any event not less than £   . All these costs will be subject to the addition of V.A.T.

7 **AMOUNT OF MY COSTS:** If there is to be a hearing the amount of my total costs will be largely in the hands of the parties.

If the matter proceeds on documents only with written representations with or without a preliminary meeting and my Award is not reasoned I estimate my time involvement is unlikely to produce total costs exceeding £   plus V.A.T. for my Declaratory Award as to the amount of the rent. This assumes there are no unusual circumstances, interlocutory issues or issues of law to be resolved requiring significant time involvement. This is, of course, a without prejudice indication of the amount of my costs.

**4.10 Arb
83**

8 **APPLICATIONS:** Liberty is given to either party to apply. In the event of an application being made to me I recommend that in the first instance the applicant should meet/discuss the question with the opposing party. If there is agreement I would issue a consent order. If not it is likely it will be necessary for me to invite the silent party to address me before I issue a direction; this will take time and may add to costs.

Yours faithfully,

ARBITRATOR

DISTRIBUTION

Rent Review—Preliminary Meeting Agenda (4.11 Arb)

IN THE MATTER OF THE ARBITRATION ACTS 1950 TO 1979
AND IN THE MATTER OF A RENT REVIEW ARBITRATION

BETWEEN

[THE LANDLORD]

AND

[THE TENANT]

RE: [ADDRESS]

PRELIMINARY MEETING AGENDA

1. Confirmation of correct names and addresss of Parties (Claimant, Respondent); **Authenticity of copy documents submitted; additional documents**

2. Jurisdiction

3. Formulation of the dispute:

Identification of issues within the dispute, e.g. admissibility, points of law, points of valuation.

Agreed Statement of Facts—in particular: floor areas, improvements, comparable properties intend to be relied upon.

4. Methods of Representations:

A. Procedure for a hearing: Pleadings, Statement of Case/Reply thereto. Advocate, lay advocate, written openings and closings, written summary of issues. Witnesses, expert witnesses, sequential/simultaneous exchange of statements in like disciplines.

B. Procedure solely on written representations: exchange and delivery of (A) Schedule of Comparables intend to be relied upon, (B) Agreed Statement of Facts (? included in Statement of Case). (C) Statement of Case, (D) Reply to Statement of Case, (E) Summary of Contentions.

5. Extension of Time

6. Resolution of Issues of Law

Exclusion agreement, case state, legal advice, alternatives.

7. Discovery

8. Degree of Proof:

Admissibility of evidence and waiver.

9. **Inspection**

10. **Timetable**

11. **Reasoned Award**

12. **Interest**

13. **Costs:**

Interlocutory matters; costs of award; costs of the reference, interim award (Calderbank Letter); final award.

14. **Taxation of costs if not agreed**

15. **Transcript/shorthand note of the hearing**

16. **Copies of authorities intended to be relied upon**

17. **Completion of representations**

18. **Resolution of dispute**

19. **Cost of the preliminary meeting and subsequent order for directions**

20. **Other matters**

Rent Review—Order for Directions following Preliminary Meeting Documents only (4.12 Arb)

IN THE MATTER OF THE ARBITRATION ACTS 1950 TO 1979

AND

IN THE MATTER OF AN ARBITRATION

BETWEEN

Claimant

AND

Respondent

ORDER FOR DIRECTIONS NO ...

Upon [receiving procedural submissions without a preliminary meeting] [hearing the parties/representatives at a preliminary meeting held on   and] upon considering their submissions and in the exercise of my discretion

I HEREBY ORDER AND DIRECT THAT:

This Order is suspended for   days to allow time for objection—[*Author's note: this is appropriate if there has been no preliminary meeting and therefore no opportunity for a party's representative at the preliminary meeting to ask for time to obtain client's instructions.*]

Author's general note: any matter agreed should be preceded by 'by consent'.

    1. **PARTIES:** The Landlord shall be the Claimant and the Tenant shall be the Respondent.

    2. **ARBITRATION BY DOCUMENTS ONLY:** By consent the arbitration shall be on documents only with written representations.

    3. **HEARING:** I reserve the right to call a hearing if, within my discretion, I consider it appropriate.

    4. **EXCHANGE OF COMPARABLES:** Any comparable transactions intended to be referred to in either party's statement of case shall be exchanged by the parties in duplicate on or before   [date] with subsequent delivery to me. Any such comparable transactions shall include as many facts as possible relating thereto and, in particular, floor areas and plans (if any).

    5. **STATEMENT OF CASE:** Each party shall prepare a statement of case to be exchanged simultaneously, in duplicate, by the parties not later than   days after exchange of comparables with subsequent delivery to me.

    6. **AGREED FACTS:** As many facts as possible relevant to my award as to the amount of the rental value of the subject property shall be agreed between the parties and their agreement recorded and included within the parties' statement of case.

    7. **REPLY TO STATEMENT OF CASE:** Each party shall prepare a reply (if any) to the opposing party's statement of case to be exchanged simultaneously, in duplicate, by the parties not later than   days after exchange of statements of case with subsequent delivery to me.

    8. **SUMMARY OF CONTENTIONS:** Each party shall prepare a written summary of its main contentions, the summary not to exceed in length   [No.] sides of A4 paper, to be exchanged simultaneously, in duplicate, by the parties not later than   days after exchange of the reply to statement of case with subsequent delivery to me.

9. **ALTERNATIVE DELIVERY AND EXCHANGE PROCEDURE:** In the alternative and if both parties expressly agree I will effect exchange of documents after delivery to me; in which case they should be delivered to me in duplicate.

10. **CONTENTS OF STATEMENT OF CASE:** A party's statement of case shall be made by a named person and should contain, *inter alia*:

Identification of all of the issues within the dispute upon which a party places reliance and the contentions thereon;

Documentary evidence (if any) including statements of witnesses of fact and/or expert witnesses (if any) upon which a party places reliance;

Propositions of law (if any) upon which a party places reliance;

An honest rental valuation of the subject property together with valuation calculations upon which it is based; a statement setting out the valuation assumptions on the basis of which the valuation has been made; analyses of comparable transactions which are admitted.

11. **CONTENTS OF REPLY TO STATEMENT OF CASE:** Replies should not include any evidence other than evidence in rebuttal of the opposing party's statement of case and they should not introduce evidence on new matters.

12. **ISSUE OF LAW:** If an issue of law arises the other party must be informed of its subject matter in advance to allow the other party full opportunity to respond. The parties/ representatives shall formulate any issue(s) of law in writing in a form suitable for inclusion in my award.

13. **WITHOUT PREJUDICE MEETINGS:** (1) At a time convenient to the parties before exchange of statement of case the parties/their experts shall hold a without prejudice meeting or discussion to identify those matters upon which they are agreed and not agreed. They should prepare a list of those matters upon which they are agreed—and, if possible, those matters on which they are not agreed for inclusion in their statement of case.

(2) At a time convenient to the parties after exchange of reply to statement of case and before exchange of summaries of contentions the parties/their experts shall hold a without prejudice meeting or discussion to attempt to narrow the issues and identify the issues to be included in each party's summary of contentions.

14. **COMMUNICATIONS:** All communications to me shall be in writing and shall be copied to the opposing party and contain confirmation that a copy has been sent simultaneously to the opposing party.

15. **INSPECTION:** Inspection of the subject property shall be allowed at a date to be arranged.

16. **ACKNOWLEDGEMENT:** Parties to acknowledge receipt of this Order.

17. **COSTS:** Costs of this Order are costs in the reference.

18. Liberty is given to either party to apply.

DATE:

ARBITRATOR:

DISTRIBUTION:

Rent Review—Order for Directions following Preliminary Meeting but with a Hearing (4.13 Arb)

IN THE MATTER OF THE ARBITRATION ACTS 1950 TO 1979

4.13 Arb
88

AND

IN THE MATTER OF AN ARBITRATION

BETWEEN

Claimant

AND

Respondent

ORDER FOR DIRECTIONS NO . . .

Upon Hearing the parties/representatives at a preliminary meeting held on   and upon considering their submissions and in the exercise of my discretion I HEREBY ORDER AND DIRECT THAT:

[Author's general note—any matter agreed should be preceded by 'by consent'.]

1. **PARTIES:** The landlord shall be the Claimant and the tenant shall be the Respondent.
2. **HEARING:** There shall be a Hearing commencing at   [time] on   [date] at [venue] and continuing with an appropriate recess for lunch through to   [time] on the same day [and continuing in a like manner on   [date(s)] [with liberty to both parties to agree a continuation beyond   [time]] and, if not then concluded, it shall stand adjourned to such date as may then be agreed or determined by me.
3. **EXCHANGE OF COMPARABLES:** As many comparable transactions intended to be referred to in either party's statement of case shall be exchanged by the parties, in duplicate, on or before   [date] with subsequent delivery to me. Any such comparable transaction shall include as many facts as possible relating thereto and, in particular, floor areas and plans (if any).
4. **AGREED FACTS:** As many facts as possible relevant to my award as to the amount of the rental value of the subject property shall be agreed between the parties and their agreement recorded and included within the parties' statements of case.
5. **STATEMENT OF CASE:** There shall be no pleadings but each party shall prepare a statement of case [being a full presentation of the case/being a summary of contentions] to be exchanged simultaneously, in duplicate, by the parties not later than   days after exchance of comparables with subsequent delivery to me.
[6. **REPLY TO STATEMENT OF CASE:** Each party shall prepare a reply (if any) to the opposing party's statement of case to be exchanged simultaneously, in duplicate, by the parties   days after exchange of statements of case with subsequent delivery to me.]
[7. **CONTENTS OF STATEMENT OF CASE:** Each party's statement of case shall include: (A) the rental valuation contended for the subject property with any calculations intended to be submitted in support thereof being an honest opinion of the amount of the rent of the subject property in accordance with the terms of the lease (B) every valuation assumption on the basis of which the valuation has been made (C) full particulars of every comparable transaction intended to be relied upon (D) a summary of contentions of fact and law (if any) (E) a summary of expert and factual evidence intended to be adduced (F) propositions of law (if any) with a copy of a recognised full report of any authority intended to be relied upon.]

[8. **WITNESSES OF FACT:** Statements of witnesses of fact intended to be called by either party shall be exchanged not later than   weeks before the Hearing.]

[9. **EXPERT WITNESSES:** Statements of expert witnesses of the disciplines intended to be called by either party shall be exchanged not later than   weeks before the Hearing. [By consent expert witnesses shall be limited to no more than   [number] on each side.]]

[10. **OATH:** Evidence given at the Hearing shall be on oath or affirmation.]

11. **WITHOUT PREJUDICE MEETING:** After exchange of statements of case and not later than   weeks before the Hearing Date the parties' expert witnesses of the disciplines shall hold a without prejudice meeting or discussion to seek to narrow the issues. [They shall prepare a list of those matters upon which they are agreed—and, if possible, those matters on which they are not agreed to be delivered to be not later than   days before the date of the Hearing.]

12. **REPRESENTATION:** Each party shall inform the opposing party not later than   weeks before the Hearing date of the name and status of persons intending to appear and be called at the Hearing.

13. **DELIVERY OF DOCUMENTS:** I am to be supplied with any documents intended to be relied upon at the Hearing not later than   days before the Hearing Date.

14. **ISSUE OF LAW:** If an issue of law arises the other party must be informed of its subject matter in advance of the Hearing. If either party intends to refer to a legal authority a recognised full report of the case must be provided. The parties/representatives shall formulate any issue(s) of law in writing in a form suitable for inclusion in my award.

15. **DISCOVERY:** There shall be no order for discovery with liberty to either party to apply [for specific discovery].

16. **FINAL LEGAL SUBMISSIONS:** Any legal submissions on an issue(s) of law are to be reduced to writing after the close of the Hearing and served sequentially; the Respondent's to be served   days after the close of the Hearing; the Claimant's to be served   days thereafter.]

17. **FINAL SUBMISSIONS:** After the close of the Hearing final submissions shall be reduced to writing to include a summary of the issues within the dispute to be served simultaneously within   days after the close of the Hearing.

18. **COMMUNICATIONS:** All communications to me shall be in writing and shall be copied to the opposing party and contain confirmation that a copy has been sent simultaneously to the opposing party.

19. **ACKNOWLEDGEMENT:** The parties shall acknowledge receipt of this order.

20. **COSTS:** Costs of the preliminary meeting and this order are costs in the reference.

21. Liberty is given to either party to apply.

DATE:

ARBITRATOR:

DISTRIBUTION:

4.13 Arb
89

Rent Review Dispute—Typical Letter of Guidance to Parties (4.14 Arb)

Sirs,

IN THE MATTER OF THE ARBITRATION ACTS 1950 TO 1979
AND IN THE MATTER OF AN ARBITRATION BETWEEN
[THE CLAIMANT]
AND
[THE RESPONDENT]
RE: [ADDRESS]

1. **INTRODUCTION:**

2. **ACKNOWLEDGEMENT:** I remind you of my direction that you shall confirm to me that you have received the enclosed Order for Directions.

3. **GUIDANCE:** As [there has been preliminary meeting and] no hearing is proposed at this stage I introduce the following paragraphs as guidance to the parties which I hope may be of assistance.

4. **EXTENSION OF TIME LIMITS:** I shall pay particular regard to the fact that each party must be given a fair opportunity to present the case; to know the opposing case; to meet the opposing case. However, I trust both parties will recognise one of the accepted merits of arbitration is early resolution of a dispute which must include expediting the procedure. I would consent to a reasonable application of extension of time if reasons are given. However, if the reasonableness or otherwise of time delay became a dispute in itself I would invite representations thereon from both parties and thereafter make a decision. The parties are aware the Arbitration Acts 1950, Section 18, gives me a discretion as to costs and one of the factors I may take into account in exercising my discretion is unreasonable actions by one party.

In the event of a party/the parties seeking an extension of the time limits I recommend that, in the first instance, the parties themselves endeavour to agree any such extension and inform me accordingly to avoid a dispute on time limits. I would, of course, agree to a joint agreement for an extension.

5. **ELEMENT OF SURPRISE:** The purpose of my procedural directions is to (1) identify the issues in dispute, (2) enable the parties to assess their relative strengths at the earliest possible time, (3) get the cards on the table with a view to establishing the real issues, (4) eliminate the element of surprise, (5) keep costs to a minimum.

6. **EXCHANGE OF COMPARABLES:** The purpose of this direction is to ensure each party has an equal opportunity to consider all the comparable evidence intended to be introduced prior to service of statement of case.

7. **STATEMENT OF CASE, REPLY TO STATEMENT OF CASE:** I am appointed for my skill and expertise but limited to understand the parties' contentions. It would be misconduct for me to rely on any evidence not introduced; I must not rely on 'secret evidence'. It is for the parties to tell me their case; I am expected to receive the evidence of witnesses and submissions and to be guided by them in reaching my conclusion. With this in mind I shall not draw inferential conclusions if there is no evidence to support such a conclusion. The parties should not overlook that if a party's submission/evidence is not contested by the opposing party I shall regard such submission/evidence as accepted unless it falls short of establishing the contention in support of which it is made.

8. **SUMMARY OF THE CONTENTIONS:** My purpose of this direction is to ensure both parties clearly identify the issues within the dispute which I have to decide. This will ensure I do not overlook any matter upon which a party places reliance. I trust the parties will recognise the merit in the second without prejudice meeting/discussion I have directed.

9. **EVIDENCE:** As guidance to the parties I shall (A) weigh the evidence for each party against the factual material put before me, (B) in so far as there is no factual material on the evidence in question I will test the evidence against the relevant experience of the witness and the manner in which that experience and the evidence stand up to contradiction.

10. **MATERIAL AND ADMISSIBLE EVIDENCE:** I remind the parties they may impliedly waive rules of evidence.

Subject to the parties agreeing otherwise I am minded to take the view that no particulars of a transaction in a comparable property should be included in any representation unless **either** those particulars have been agreed between the parties **or** those particulars are within the personal knowledge of the writer or a member of his Firm **or** such particulars are confirmed by the person acting in the transaction to include all relevant information relative to the transaction **or** those particulars are accepted unchallenged by the other party.

4.14 Arb
91

11. **REASONS:** I shall not publish a reasoned award unless requested to do so. If the dispute is an issue of fact it is unusual for reasons to contain a detailed analysis of each party's case. If reasons are requested on issues of fact it would be helpful if the extent of reasons is identified, perhaps by reference to the issues identified in the summary of contentions. I remind the parties that if the dispute is one of fact only and a request from one party for a reasoned award is opposed by the other party and no question of law is involved I may take the view that the request for reasons is unjustified. In which case I am entitled to refuse to give reasons leaving the applicant to apply to the court if the applicant so wishes.

If no question of law is involved, I, in the exercise of my discretion, reserve my decision as to reasons after the parties have had an opportunity to address me.

12. **ALTERNATIVE DELIVERY AND EXCHANGE PROCEDURE:** In the event of the parties' joint agreement to this procedure I shall not look at any such document until after five working days after I have effected exchange of such documents to allow each party to consider the content of the opposing party's representations.

13. **INSPECTIONS:** I shall indicate to the parties a convenient date for my inspection. At my inspection I shall not receive evidence of any kind save that each party/representative may draw my attention to factual matters referred to in evidence. For the avoidance of doubt what I see at the inspection shall be evidence, what I hear shall not be evidence. The parties shall inform me not later than the stage of service of summary of contentions if they wish to accompany me during this inspection. If the parties agree that I shall make my inspection unattended and if one of the parties/an employee is in occupation of the subject premises I require the express approval of the opposing party for me to inspect in the presence of the occupant. I shall not inspect in the presence of one party without securing from the other agreement to that effect.

I shall wish to inspect the subject property in detail. If either party wishes me to inspect any of the comparable properties introduced in detail, I am to be advised and I shall expect that party to make the necessary arrangements for my inspection. If no request is made to me to make a detailed inspection of a comparable property I shall look at such areas of it as may be regarded as 'public areas' normally seen by visitors to the property.

14. **INTERIM AWARD:** In the absence of an application by either party for an interim award (an award with matters reserved) I shall, subject to my discretion, publish an award final on all matters except as to taxation of costs, if unagreed. I remind the parties of the possible merit, in appropriate circumstances, of an interim award in respect of one or more of the issues (but not all of the issues) within the dispute if such an interim award would be likely to achieve an expeditious and cost-effective resolution of the dispute.

15. **COSTS GENERALLY:** As arbitrator I have a duty to include in my award (or further award, as the case may be, if costs are unagreed) my decision as to how costs of the arbitration are to be borne. Costs include not only the costs of the award (my costs) but also costs of the reference (costs incurred by a party in preparing and presenting the case). It is nevertheless open for the parties to agree a division as to costs; in which case their agreement should be included in an agreed statement.

I remind the parties of the relevance of special circumstances in the exerise of my discretion, e.g. a valid *Calderbank* offer. In the event of any offer upon which a party intends to rely in my discretion as to costs no such offer shall be communicated to me until matters other than costs have been resolved. If, however, a sealed offer procedure is intended I will, on application, issue directions.

In the absence of joint agreement to the contrary and subject to being addressed by the parties on the matter I shall not take into account a valid offer which fails by any amount. This is, however, subject to the *de minimis* rule in that I have a discretion as to whether the offer fails by a negligible or non-negligible amount; if a close offer fails by a non-negligible amount I will consider costs as though such offer had not been made.

In the event of taxation of the costs of the reference being required I may be minded, within my discretion, to reserve taxation to myself as reasonable costs reasonably incurred in the conduct of the reference on a commercial basis without prejudice to me not being bound by the rules of the supreme court or any other rules.

16. **POINTS OF LAW:** If either party intends to seek and include in either the statement of case or replies to statement of case any legal opinion I am to be informed of the fact and the other party must be informed in advance, of its subject matter so as to have an equal opportunity of taking advance on the point arising.

If an issue of law arises and either party is unwilling to enter into an exclusion agreement they may agree that the issue is dealt with by way of 'a case stated' for the opinion of a solicitor or Counsel or whether issue of law shall be decided in some other manner.

17. **DISCOVERY:** My order for directions does not include an order for discovery. In the event of an application being served and subject to either party wishing to address me on the point, I may be minded to refuse an order for general discovery but would consider submissions requesting an order for specific discovery.

18. **APPLICATIONS:** I remind the parties of the merit of seeking the consent of the other party to any application to me.

19. **RESOLUTION OF THE DISPUTE:** The parties are at liberty to resolve their differences at any time prior to publication of my award. Any agreement should include provisions as to my costs and the parties' costs.

20. **LIBERTY TO APPLY:** This direction means that either party may apply to me for amended directions. I recommend that in the first instance the applicant party should inform the opposing party and consider the merit of a joint application by consent.

Yours faithfully,

ARBITRATOR

CHAPTER 5

Preliminary Issues

1. Statement of Case of the Claimant on the Preliminary Issues (5.1)

IN THE MATTER OF THE ARBITRATION ACTS 1950 TO 1979

AND

IN THE MATTER OF AN ARBITRATION UNDER THE JCT ARBITRATION RULES (18 JULY 1988)

BETWEEN

RELIABLE BUILDERS LIMITED   Claimant

AND

SANCTUARY HOUSE LIMITED   Respondent

STATEMENT OF CASE ON THE PRELIMINARY ISSUES
(CLAIMANT)

1. The Project

1.1   At all material times the Claimant carried on business as a building contractor.
1.2   At all material times the Respondent was the owner of Sanctuary House (formerly known as the Manor House) Woodbridge, Suffolk (Sanctuary House) and was concerned with its redevelopment and extension as a Nursing Home for the frail elderly.

2. Background to the Dispute

2.1   The Claimant successfully tendered for the Refurbishment and extension of Sanctuary House ('the works') in January 1991.
   The Respondent appointed Mr D'Iffy of The Architectural Partnership ('TAP') of Norwich who, at all material times, acted as the Respondent's agent in connection with this contract. In this Statement, reference to the Respondent is usually reference to his agent Mr D'Iffy.
2.2   By letter dated 7 January 1991, the Respondent invited the Claimant to tender for the works of refurbishment of The Old Manor House, Woodbridge, Suffolk (later renamed Sanctuary House).
2.3   With the letter of invitation to tender, 7 January 1991, was enclosed, *inter alia*, a Bill of Quantities relating to the works which had been prepared by the Respondent.
   The said letter stated that the successful tenderer would be bound by the appropriate conditions of the JCT Intermediate Form of Building Contract (IFC '84) 1990 Edition.

2.4 By letter 31 January 1991 the Claimant submitted the tender to carry out the work for the sum of £617,148.24 ex VAT.

2.5 On or about 16 February 1991, Mr D'Iffy on behalf of the Respondent, telephoned Mr Hocking of the Claimant, and stated that his tender was too high.

2.6 Between 20 February and 7 March 1991 there were several telephone calls, between Mr D'Iffy and Mr Hocking, during which various arithmetical errors on the original tender were corrected as well as some omissions and additions made. The net effect of all of these changes increased the tender figure to £622,171.95 ex VAT.

2.7 On 7 March 1991 Mr Hocking agreed to reduce the revised tender figure to £550,000.00 ex VAT on the understanding that if he did so he would be awarded the contract.

2.8 By letter, 20 March 1991, Mr D'Iffy confirmed the reduced contract sum and requested that Claimant to start work on the site on 2 April 1991 on the basis that he would be reimbursed all reasonable costs incurred if a contract was not entered into. The letter further stated that it was the intention to enter into a contract with the Claimant on the basis of the IFC '84 Form and the contract would be on a fixed-price lump-sum basis, not subject to remeasurement.

2.9 The Claimant acknowledged Mr D'Iffy's letter 20 March 1991, by his letter 28 March 1991, but questioned, in that letter, that the contract should not be on a fixed-price lump-sum basis.

2.10 A meeting was held between the parties on 8 April 1991 to discuss the lump-sum nature of the contract and the question of remeasurement. At the conclusion of that meeting, agreement apparently having been reached on the remeasure items, the parties signed the IFC '84 Contract. Subsequently, by letter 15 April 1991, to the Claimant, the Respondent wrote that

'Further to our meeting on-site on 8 April 1991 we confirm that the terms and conditions of the IFC '84 Contract, which we signed at the conclusion of that meeting, will apply except remeasurement will take place limited to those items listed on the attached sheet.

Please confirm, in writing, your agreement to this list which will be incorporated as a contract document.'

2.11 It is denied by the Claimant that the agreement alleged by the Respondent, in their letter 15 April 1991, was entered into by the parties. By letter 22 April 1991, the Claimant wrote to the Respondent stating that

'We acknowledge receipt of your letter dated 15 April 1991 and confirm our acceptance of the listed items that are to be remeasured. We must, however, reserve the right to ask for a remeasure on any item which we might find to vary from your draft Bill of Quantities.

We would only request such a remeasure if it seemed to us that it would make a significant difference in the value of that particular Bill of Quantity item.'

3. The Contract Period

The Claimant had commenced work on the site, initially under a letter of intent on 2 April 1991, as requested by the Respondent's letter 20 March 1991 and the works were virtually completed by 31 March 1992.

4. The Contract

4.1 On its true construction, the conduct of the Respondent after receipt of the Claimant's letter 22 April 1991, in failing to rebut that letter, was an acceptance, by the Respondent, that the works would be carried out by the Claimant on the following terms:

4.1.1 That the Articles and Conditions of the IFC '84 Contract would apply, including Recital 2nd B.

4.1.2 That the items on the list attached to the Respondent's letter 15 April 1991, would be remeasured.

4.1.3 That if, in the Claimant's opinion, the quantity set out for any item in the Bills of Quantity increased such as to make a significant alteration to the value of any item, that item would be remeasured.

4.2 Alternatively, if, which is denied, Recital 2nd A and not Recital 2nd B is incorporated into the contract between the parties, that the quantities in the Bills of Quantities were reasonably accurate.

5. The Claimant's Case

It is the Claimant's primary case that the errors in the quantities included in the Bills of Quantities, provided by the respondent with his invitation to tender, are such as to entitle the Claimant to a remeasure of the whole of the contract works.

6. Rectification

6.1 If, contrary to the Claimant's primary case which is set out in paragraph 4 above, the contract was contained solely in documents which do not include the Claimant's right to remeasurement as set out in paragraph 4.1.3 above, the Claimant will contend

6.1.1 that by reason of a common mistake by the parties and/or a mistake by the Claimant which the Respondent knew or ought to have known of the said contract documents do not represent:

6.1.1.1 the agreement which the parties made at their meeting 8 April 1991 and which is evidenced by the Claimant's letter 22 April 1991 which is set out in paragraph 2.11 above; and/or

6.1.1.2 the parties' common continuing intention and/or the Claimant's intention which is outwardly expressed in the Claimant's letter 22 April 1991 which is set out in paragraph 2.11 above.

6.1.2 And accordingly, the said contract should be rectified as to embody the agreement actually made between the parties or their true intentions at the time. The actual agreement and/or their true intentions are as set out in paragraph 2.11 above.

6.2 The Claimant will rely on the provisions of IFC '84 Clause 9.3 which expressly empowers the Arbitrator to rectify the contract so that it accurately reflects the true agreement made between the Claimant and the Respondent.

7. In the alternative, if, which is denied, the parties did not reach agreement on the basis set out in paragraph 4 herein, then the Claimant will contend that it was an implied term of the contract that the Claimant was entitled to be paid a *quantum meruit* for the additional contract works arising from a remeasure rather than a sum calculated in accordance with the rules set out in IFC '84 clauses 3.7.1 to 3.7.9.

The said term is to be implied in order to give effect to the presumed intention of the parties and/or to give the contract business efficacy.

Alternatively, the Claimant is entitled to be paid an additional sum for the additional contract works, remeasured as a result of paragraph 4.1.3 above calculated in accordance with the rules set out in clauses 3.7.1 to 3.7.9 of the said IFC contract and, or alternatively, the Claimant is entitled to the sum claimed in his Final Account, dated 30 October 1992 (submitted in Draft 3 June 1992).

8. Further, the agreement for a discount referred to in paragraph 2.7 herein, was lump sum discount and accordingly, any valuations to be carried out in accordance with the terms set out in paragraph 4 herein, are to be carried out by reference to the rates set in the Bills of

Quantities, as originally submitted by the Claimant, (were applicable), as adjusted by agreement between the parties—see paragraph 2.6 herein—but before the application of the lump-sum reduction referred to in paragraph 2.7 herein.

9. Disputes have arisen between the parties relating to the Works. In accordance with the contract for the Works D Emsee MSc FRICS FCIArb (the Arbitrator) was appointed on 20 February 1993 to resolve the disputes.

10. The parties agreed that the Arbitrator should determine preliminary issues in advance of the substantive issues. The preliminary issues were set out in the Arbitrator's Direction No 2 dated 25 March 1993.

5.1
96

11. The Claimant claims interest on any sums found to be payable to it pursuant to S.19A of the Arbitration Act 1950.

AND THE CLAIMANT CLAIMS:

   (i) A declaration that the terms of the agreement between the parties is as set out in para 4.1. hereof; alternatively, para 4.2 herein;

  (ii) Alternatively, insofar as is necessary and without prejudice to the Claimant's contentions in paragraph 4 above, an order that the written contract be rectified so as to embody the agreement actually made between the Claimant and the Respondent or their true intentions at the time of exercising the same in the respects set out above and to have the said agreement treated as being so rectified.

 (iii) A declaration that the Claimant is entitled to have the works measured and valued as set out in paras 5, 7 and 8 herein;

 (iv) Alternatively, a declaration that the Claimant is entitled to be paid on a *quantum meruit* basis as set out in paragraph 8 herein.

  (v) A declaration that the Claimant is entitled to the sums claimed under para 8 herein and/or an order that the Respondent do pay such sums;

 (vi) A declaration that the 'Gibbs ceiling is not genuine but a latter-day reproduction.

(vii) A declaration that the Claimant had complied with the terms of the contract concerning the waterproofing of the basement specifically clause 3.15a of the specification.

(viii) Interest pursuant under Section 19A of the Arbitration Act 1950.

Toby Belcher

SERVED this 8th day of April 1993

2. Statement of Case of the Respondent on the Preliminary Issues (5.2)

IN THE MATTER OF THE ARBITRATION ACTS 1950 TO 1979

AND

IN THE MATTER OF AN ARBITRATION UNDER THE JCT ARBITRATION RULES (18 JULY 1988)

BETWEEN

RELIABLE BUILDERS LIMITED   Claimant

AND

SANCTUARY HOUSE LIMITED   Respondent

STATEMENT OF CASE OF THE RESPONDENT ON THE PRELIMINARY ISSUES

The following paragraph references are to the Claimant's Statement of Case on the Preliminary Issues.

1. Paragraph 1 is admitted.
2. Paragraphs 2.1–2.10 inclusive are admitted.
3. Paragraph 2.11 save that the Claimant sent the letter 22 April 1991, in the terms stated, no further admission is made
4. Paragraph 3 is admitted.
5. Paragraphs 4–8 inclusive are denied.
6. Paragraphs 9 and 10 are admitted.
7. There are six preliminary issues to be addressed in this Statement of Case and each will be dealt with in turn. It should be stressed that this is not a Response to the Statement of Case served by the Claimant dated 8 April 1993 as on preliminary issues it is submitted that each side should be able to plead its own case.

8. First issue: how and when was the contract formed?

8.1   Following receipt of a tender, on 31 January 1991, from the Claimant (RBL), various negotiations took place which resulted, initially, in the tender price being adjusted upward to £622,171.95 ex VAT and then finally negotiated down to £550,000 ex VAT.
      The record of these negotiations is set out fully in the proofs of evidence of both Mr D'Iffy and Miss Hutch.
8.2   At a meeting, 8 April 1991, the figure of £550,000 was confirmed subject only to remeasurement, on completion, of specific items. These items were limited to a list compiled jointly by Mr D'Iffy, the Respondent's architect and Mr Hocking, the Managing Director of the Claimant company at the conclusion of the above meeting.
8.3   A contemporary note made by Mr D'Iffy at this meeting (produced as Appendix A to his proof of evidence) reads

      'Quants—remeasure to be agreed after meeting
      2–3% error acceptable
      Redesign drains.'

8.4 It was duly agreed at this meeting that

    8.4.1 there would be limited remeasurement
    8.4.2 all else in the contract would be subject to a lump-sum fixed price.

8.5 Mr D'Iffy, who, at this meeting was attended by his client, Mr Bliss, was satisfied that, following its conclusion, there were no outstanding matters of disagreement between the parties.

8.6 Mr D'Iffy is certain about this as it had been made clear to him, not only by his client but also by the representative of the clients banker, Mr Paul Goldstone, that certainty of cost was paramount. Thus Mr D'Iffy knew when he convened this meeting that its primary objective was to tie up any loose ends.

8.7 The Respondent's case then is that the contract was formed on the 8 April 1991 following the meeting attended by Mr Bliss, Mr D'Iffy and Miss Hutch for the Respondent and Mr Hocking, Mr Reeves and Mr Watts on behalf of the Claimant.

8.8 The Respondent could argue that the contract was actually formed before this 8 April meeting but for the purpose of this submission accepts that it was not. It is clear that following this meeting there was no doubt in the minds of any of the Respondent's representatives, who attended that meeting, that a bargain had been struck. It is therefore submitted that no matter what transpired following that meeting is of no avail—a deal had been concluded and the parties were bound by it.

8.9 The Respondent refers to the authority of the decision in *Whitworth Street Estates (Manchester) Ltd* v *James Miller & Ptnrs Ltd* [1970] AC 583 a copy of which is attached. Here it was held that once a contract has come into being, subsequent actions or statements made by the parties cannot affect the position of the parties to that contract.

8.10 In this regard see the Claimant's letter 22 April 1991 which attempts to impose terms different from those agreed at 8 April meeting. This attempt should not be allowed to succeed.

8.11 The Claimant's case is that the Respondent's conduct in failing to rebut the Claimant's letter, 22 April 1991, evidenced the agreement reached at 8 April 1991 meeting and this failure to rebut this letter was an acceptance of those terms by the Respondent. If that proposition is valid then it is equally valid to say that by allowing the Claimant to go on working after the 8 April meeting was also conduct evidencing acceptance of a previous offer, be it oral or written.

    Having said that, the Claimant does not point out any particular conduct which directly evidences that acceptance.

8.12 The Respondent therefore rebuts the conduct point and maintains that following the 8 April meeting, all outstanding matters having been disposed of, a contract was concluded and therefore both parties considered themselves bound.

9. Second issue: what are the terms and conditions of the contract

9.1 The contract documents are or are evidenced by, the following:

    9.1.1 Specification of Works—dated Nov 1990.
    9.1.2 Drawings—TAP/1 A, 2, 3B, 4C, 5, 6, 7A, 8, & 9
        MECH/ENG 1029/1, 2 & 3
        ELEC 78/1 & 2
        Site Level Drawing S1.70
        Drainage schematic D1 & 2
    9.1.3 Schedules Ironmongery, Finishes, Bathroom fittings, Joinery, Doors & Windows.
    9.1.4 The Respondent's letter 20 March 1990.
    9.1.5 The JCT Intermediate Form of Building Contract (IFC '84)—1990 Edition as signed at the conclusion of the 8 April 1991 meeting.

9.1.6 The Respondent's letter 15 April 1991.

9.2 On the issue of mistake the Respondent pleads to paragraph 6 of the Statement of Case as follows:

9.2.1 Subparagraph 6.1.1 is specifically denied. It is denied that there was any such common mistake between the parties and the Claimant has given no particulars thereof. As averred above the Claimant was made fully aware of the works which would be subject to remeasure, when agreement was reached at 8 April 1991 meeting.

9.2.2 As to allegation in the alternative of a 'mistake by the Claimant which the Respondent knew or ought to have known', that contention is denied as a matter of fact and it is denied that as a matter of law the same could ground any claim for rectification of the contract.

9.2.3 As to subparagraphs 6.1.1.1 and 6.1.1.2 even if the Claimant's letter 22 April 1991 was sent to the Respondent the same would not in any event evidence any agreement to the effect alleged in 6.1.1.1 and 6.1.1.2 and it is denied that any personal intention on the Claimant's part to seek further payment for the contract works had any relevance whatsoever to the Claimant's entitlement to any payment.

9.2.4 Subparagraph 6.1.2 is in the premises denied. There is no basis either in fact or in law for any claim to rectify the contract.

9.3 As to paragraph 6.2 of the Statement of Case it is admitted only that the Arbitrator has power to rectify the contract if there is a proper basis for doing so. It is denied (if it is contended) that the Arbitrator has power to award a *quantum meruit* outside the contract.

9.4 The Respondent will refer to the contract for its full terms, meaning and effect.

10. Third issue: what items are subject to remeasurement?

10.1 The Respondent's case is that the items subject to remeasurement are those, and only those, listed in the appendix to the Respondent's letter 15 April 1991 as agreed at the meeting 8 April 1991.

10.2 The Claimant's case is that he has reserved the right to remeasure anything where he considers there might be a substantial financial effect, presumably where there is likely to be a substantial financial advantage in his favour.

10.3 If this indeed was what had been agreed between the parties at the 8 April meeting why bother to agree a list of remeasure items at all? If the contract was entered into on 8 April, as the Respondent avers, the remeasure items are limited to those listed with the Respondents letter 15 April 1991.

10.4 The only evidence concerning total remeasure comes from Mr Hocking where he steadfastly maintains that was always his position. However, it was not a position ever accepted by the Respondent, indeed quite the opposite. In order to placate the Claimant over his request for total remeasurement the Respondent, against his better judgment and interest agreed to a very limited remeasurement at the 8 April meeting. Where is the evidence that the Respondent ever agreed to anything else?—there is none, and therefore the Respondent's view must prevail.

10.5 The point made in the Claimant's Statement of Case, para. 5, is irrelevant. The scope of the preliminary issues does not extend to an analysis of the errors in the original tender or how they came to be corrected.

10.6 For these reasons and the fact that the agreement claimed by the Claimant to have been made, is too uncertain to be meaningful, we ask the Arbitrator to reject the Claimant's view of this issue and find for the Respondent.

10.7 Specifically the Respondent pleads to paragraph 7 of the Statement of case as follows:

10.7.1 It is denied that any such term could possibly be implied into the IFC '84 contract.

10.7.2 The IFC '84 contract sets out in express terms what are the parties' rights with respect to variations. By the said express terms any genuine variation to the contract works as defined by reference to the contract documents will be subject to valuation by the rules contained in Clauses 3.7.1 to 3.7.9 of the contract conditions. There is no room or need for any implied term with respect to variations or their valuation.

10.7.3 Further, as to the Claimant's alternative contention, it is denied that the Claimant could possibly be entitled to payment for the alleged, or any, additional contract works, resulting from remeasure, calculated in accordance with clauses 3.7.1 to 3.7.9 by reason of any implied terms, since the valuation rules and the definition of variations are expressly set out in the contract.

10.7.4 It is denied that the contract can be divided up in the way alleged by the Claimant. There is no justification at all for the contention that any work beyond that agreed to be remeasured at 8 April 1991 meeting was agreed to be paid for on a *quantum meruit* basis and no particulars whatever of any such agreement have been provided. (In this pleading it is assumed that by *quantum meruit* the Claimant means 'reasonable sum' within the contract and is not referring to a *quantum meruit* in the strict sense of a quasi-contractual remedy.)

10.7.5 The Claimant's case relies entirely on the contention that the contract includes agreement to remeasure as set out in the Claimant's letter 22 April 1991 which letter does not form part of the contract documents.

12. Fourth issue: what rates are to be applied to the contract work in general and what is the status of the discount?

12.1 There is no dispute that a discount was agreed between the parties following submission of RBL's tender and before acceptance of that tender.

12.2 The Claimant suggests that this was a lump-sum discount which should be applied to the final account and not effect the individual rates which make up the tender figure.

12.3 The Respondent assumed, in running this contract, that this discount would be treated, as it normally is in such cases, by application of a percentage reduction across all of the rates.

12.4 It is hard to reconcile the Claimant's view with his insistence that this is, in effect, a remeasurement contract. How can you apply a lump-sum discount to the final account, to reflect what was agreed at tender stage, other than on a percentage basis?

12.5 In para 7 of the Claimant's Statement of Case, he contends that if the parties did not reach agreement then he claims to be paid on a *quantum meruit* basis.

If there is no agreement there is no contract and therefore no arbitration agreement. This means that the Claimant cannot pursue this argument in this Arbitration—the Arbitrator simply does not have jurisdiction to deal with it.

12.6 The Respondent maintains that the parties pursued this arbitration on the basis that there was agreement and they cannot now resile from that position. The act of participating in the arbitration is sufficient to estop the Claimant from denying that there is no contract and *ipso facto* no arbitration clause.

13. Fifth issue: the Gibbs ceiling—is it genuine?

13.1 The Gibbs ceiling is probably genuine on scientific data. In particular, the following matters show that the ceiling was installed at least 150 and probably more than 200 years ago:

13.1.1 The erosion of ferrous materials is inconsistent with a younger ceiling.

13.1.2 The successive decorations of the ceiling show that it has been in use for that time.

13.1.3 The formation of white lead sulphide in the materials of the ceiling is inconsistent with a younger ceiling.

14. Sixth issue: is the builder in breach of contract over the waterproofing of the basement?

14.1 The contract, by clause 3/15a, required tanking by the contractor to the concrete floor and existing walls to a height to be determined as 150 mm above the highest recorded level of the water table immediately adjacent to the property.

14.2 The mere fact that, on 13 April 1992, the basement flooded, establishes that the tanking as installed by the Claimants, was not as high as the water table on that date, much less 6 inches higher than that level, as required by the contract. No admissions are made as to the height of the water table on that date but, if it be contended by the Claimants that it was a record height, the Claimants are put to proof of that fact and also that the water table was 6 inches or more higher than any previously recorded level.

14.3 In the premises the Claimants were in breach of the requirement of clause 3/15a of the contract.

A short note on authorities

The Respondent does not consider that the Arbitrator would be assisted by a further citation of cases relating to offer and acceptance.

Counsel noted the Arbitrator's helpful suggestion that the parties should consider whether this might be a 'Battle of the Forms' situation but this is not the Respondent's view.

Nor is it Counsel's view that the Arbitrator will be assisted by consideration of the *Cleveland Bridge* case. This case merely goes to show that where there is no agreement there is an entitlement to *quantum meruit*. There is nothing between the parties on that question of law.

Reasons

The Respondent asks for a reasoned award on the preliminary issues. The legal issues are those embodied in this Statement of Case.

Bernadette O'Brien

Served this 6th day of May 1993 by Jeremy Catchpole, 1 Chancery Lane, London EC4. Solicitor to the Respondent

Order for Directions No 3—Amendment of Pleadings (5.3 Arb)

IN THE MATTER OF THE ARBITRATION ACTS 1950 TO 1979

AND

IN THE MATTER OF AN ARBITRATION UNDER THE JCT ARBITRATION RULES (18 JULY 1988)

**5.3 Arb
102**

BETWEEN

RELIABLE BUILDERS LIMITED   Claimant

AND

SANCTUARY HOUSE LIMITED   Respondent

ORDER FOR DIRECTIONS NO 3

WHEREAS

1.00 The Claimant served his Statement of Case for the Preliminary Issues, as directed, on 8 April 1993 and

2.00 The Respondent served his Statement of Case for the Preliminary Issues, as directed, on 6 May 1993.

3.00 The Claimant, by letter dated and faxed to me on 8 May, requests consent to amend his Statement of Case to cite further authority in connection with the Gibbs ceiling.

4.00 Consent to amend is HEREBY GRANTED on condition that should the Respondent also wish to amend his Statement of Case, he has consent to do so.

5.00 Should the Claimant's Request and subsequent Consent to Amend cause either of the hearing dates set aside to be postponed or cause the Respondent any additional expense, such costs will be paid by the Claimant in any event.

6.00 Costs of and incidental to this direction to be paid by the Respondent in any event.

Date: 8 May 1993   **D Emsee MSc FRICS FCIArb
                            Registered Arbitrator**

To: Jayrich Associates   Representatives of the Claimant
                                  FAO Joel Redman

        Weller, Baines & Bishton Solicitors for the Respondent
                                  FAO Jeremy Catchpole

Order for Directions No 4 (5.4 Arb)

IN THE MATTER OF THE ARBITRATION ACTS 1950 TO 1979

AND

IN THE MATTER OF AN ARBITRATION UNDER THE JCT ARBITRATION RULES (18 JULY 1988)

BETWEEN

RELIABLE BUILDERS LIMITED   Claimant

AND

SANCTUARY HOUSE LIMITED   Respondent

5.4 Arb 103

ORDER FOR DIRECTIONS NO 4

WHEREAS

1.00 There is to be a Hearing of the Preliminary Issues on 24 and 25 May 1993 commencing at 10.00 a.m.

2.00 The venue for this Hearing will be the offices of the Respondent's solicitor, Messrs. Weller, Baines & Bishton, 42 South Square, Gray's Inn, London WC1.

3.00 Costs in the Reference.

Date: 14 May 1993   **D Emsee MSc FRICS FRIArb**
                          Registered Arbitrator

To: Jayrich Associates   Representatives of the Claimant
                                 FAO Joel Redman

       Weller, Baines & Bishton Solicitors for the Respondent
                                  FAO Jeremy Catchpole

Claimant's Proofs of Evidence—Harold Hocking (5.5)

IN THE MATTER OF THE ARBITRATION ACTS 1950 TO 1979

AND

IN THE MATTER OF AN ARBITRATION UNDER THE JCT ARBITRATION RULES (18 JULY 1988)

BETWEEN

RELIABLE BUILDERS LIMITED   Claimant

AND

SANCTUARY HOUSE LIMITED   Respondent

PROOF OF EVIDENCE OF HAROLD HOCKING

1. My full names are HAROLD EDWIN HOCKING. I am the managing director of Reliable Builders Limited of Snape Yard, Woodbridge, Suffolk.

This company was established in 1923 and I have been managing director since 1983.

2. We do all sorts of building work, including substantial works of refurbishment and employ around 25 trades-people and our annual turnover is approximately £1M.

3. Just before Christmas 1990 we received a telephone call from Miss Hutch of The Architectural Practice in Norwich inquiring whether we were prepared to tender for a refurbishment job in Woodbridge. The formal invitation came by letter 7 January 1991 although the letter was not received until Thursday 10 January. We were to return our tender not later than 31 January 1991. The tender documents requested a fixed-price tender but did not specify 'lump sum'. We were not left with much time to price the Bill of Quantities which was included with the invitation to tender as we had to get prices in from various subcontractors. The documents, accompanying the invitation to tender, did not provide information such as levels to enable earthwork quantities to be checked. Also, there was no time to check the quantities, or prepare our own. All we could do was to visit the site.

4. With the assistance of Mr Redman, a consultant surveyor who we employ from time to time, I personally priced the Bill of Quantities and by letter on 31 January 1991, I sent in a quotation in the sum of £617,148.24 ex VAT.

5. In the letter comprising the invitation to tender was a paragraph which read:

'The enclosed Bill of Quantities is for guidance only. Sanctuary House Limited will not be liable for the accuracy of dimensions or quantities.'

6. I heard nothing from Mr D'Iffy until 16 February 1991 when he telephoned me to say that my price was too high. He pointed out that some of my rates, compared with other tenderers, were too high and asked if I was prepared to adjust them. I said that I would not, but did say, that I was prepared to negotiate as we were short of work.

7. Mr D'Iffy telephoned again on 20 February 1991 and several times between that date and 7 March. During these calls we agreed on corrections of arithmetical errors in my tender as well as omitting some items tendered for and pricing some previously not priced. The outcome of these adjustments was to increase our tender to £622,171.95 ex VAT. However, Mr D'Iffy made it clear that if we were prepared to reduce our price to around £540,000.00 the

job was ours. We could not drop as far as that but, on 7 March, I did agree a figure of £550,000.00 ex VAT.

8. When I am asked to enter into a lump-sum contract I always take the quantities off the plans myself and even then expect the normal treatment that any variations in the final specification would involve a variation in the price. When Mr D'Iffy put it to me about reducing my price I recall I had to think about it carefully and phone him back before agreeing to lower the price. I did so because I was entitled to expect, and did expect, the figures in the Bill of Quantities to be accurate or reasonably accurate. I also expected that any variations in the work or quantities would be subject to remeasure. The only reference to the form of contract in the invitation to tender, was to the IFC '84 Contract. There was no mention of a 'lump sum'. The first time I saw this expression was in the architect's letter dated 20 March 1991.

9. I received confirmation of the agreed contract figure by letter dated 20 March 1991 from Mr D'Iffy. In that letter it said that the contract 'would be on a fixed-price lump-sum basis not subject to remeasurement'. The letter also instructed me to proceed with the work commencing on Tuesday 2 April and said that we would be reimbursed all reasonable costs incurred in the unlikely event that we did not enter into a contract.

10. I was not prepared to accept that there should be no remeasurement so I wrote to Mr D'Iffy on 28 March 1991, explaining that I would not agree there being no remeasurement.

11. On receipt of my letter 28 March, Miss Hutch telephoned me and said that Mr D'Iffy thought that the matter should be resolved at a meeting and suggested that we discussed it at the site meeting scheduled for 8 April 1991.

12. I attended this meeting at which Mr D'Iffy, amongst others, was present. When the main site meeting was concluded, Mr D'Iffy and I stayed behind to compile a list of the main items for which I required remeasurement—this list was mainly confined to earthworks, about which we were already concerned.

13. In any event I did not agree to remeasurement being limited to those items. I specifically stated, earlier at the meeting, that I reserved the right to request a remeasure if any of the quantities proved incorrect. Neither Mr D'Iffy nor Mr Bliss the Client, who was also at the meeting, raised any objections. I expressed the same reservations to Mr D'Iffy when we met alone following the meeting.

14. After we had agreed the main items to be remeasured, Mr D'Iffy suggested that we might as well sign the IFC '84 contract, which had been prepared earlier. When he invited me to sign, I asked about what we had just agreed. Mr D'Iffy said it would be covered as he would write shortly and confirm the substance of the agreement which we had reached on the remeasurement.

15. On 22 April 1991 when I returned to work after an extended Easter holiday I received the Respondent's letter dated 15 April in which the items, which we had agreed at 8 April meeting, would be remeasured, were listed. I immediately wrote back confirming our right to remeasure any items which we might find to vary from the Bill of Quantities.

16. The architect did not reply to my letter 22 April and we continued work on the basis of the understanding reached at the 8 April meeting as expressed in my letter 22 April. Both parties subsequently administered the contract applying the terms of the IFC '84 Contract.

17. As we got into the contract it became more and more obvious to me and my staff that the quantities were inaccurate—they were generally substantially undermeasured. In particular:

17.1 The actual floor area of the extension is approximately 12 per cent more than the Respondent's area in his Bill. This item is not included in the limited remeasurement list agreed with the Respondent.

17.2 The steel reinforcement used on-site was approximately twice that of the measured quantity in the Bill. This item was not included on the limited remeasurement list agreed at 8 April meeting.

17.3 The area of retiling to the main roof is approximately 30 square metres more than that allowed in the Bill. Again this item was not included on the list of items to be remeasured.

18. From these, and other examples, it is clear to me that the errors and inaccuracies in the Bill of Quantities were such that a total remeasurement was appropriate.

19. Where items, on the list agreed on 8 April, have been remeasured, the Respondents have applied a reduction in our price of a percentage discount equal to that which reflects the reduction in my original tender price to £550,000.00 which I was persuaded to accept. I accepted the lump-sum reduction of the contract price in order to obtain the job on the understanding that it was a 'one-off' discount. I naturally assumed that variations and remeasurement would be reimbursed at reasonable rates and not reduced by the initial discount.

20. From the beginning of the contract there were regular progress meetings which I attended together with Bill Reeves, our contract administrator, John Watts, the site foreman and occasionally Joel Redman our outside surveyor. On the Respondent's side Miss Hutch was always in attendance and occasionally Mr D'Iffy. We were assured on a number of separate occasions, both by Miss Hutch and Mr D'Iffy, that we would be paid and treated fairly when valuing variations to the contract.

21. Finally I deal with the works of waterproofing in the basement, which RBL carried all in accordance with the requirements of the contract specification which were as follows:

Cl 3/9d: Provide and lay new 150 mm concrete floor to basement in type 1 concrete and finish to receive tanking as appropriate.

Cl 3/15a: Provide tanking to new concrete floor and existing walls to basement to a height to be determined as 150 mm above the highest recorded level of the water table immediately adjacent to the property.

22. There really was no time to sort out the height the water table was during the tender period so we put a provisional sum against this item. When Mr D'Iffy was trying to get me to reduce our price, he wanted me to firm up the price of this work. I remember speaking to Mr Redman about this and we decided that some tanking was required, but probably not for the full height of the basement.

23. However, I was worried about confirming a price which had simply been guessed at and which might leave us with a loss. Mr Redman suggested that the safest thing to do would be to price the tanking for half the height and waterproof rendering for the rest, which is how he had arrived at the provisional sum. I decided to take a chance and confirm this as a fixed price for this work.

24. Once the work started I thought that I should try to find out more about the water table and wrote to Woodbridge District Council and they told me to speak to their Building Control Officer. I asked John Watts to do this and I understand that he agreed the height of the water table with the Building Control Officer.

25. Mr Reeves was told to sort out the detail but he came back to me and said that it would be best simply to tank the whole height of the basement. I realised that this would have cost more than we had allowed for and so I told him to tank only up to 6 inches above whatever level he had been given by the Building Control Officer. Mr Reeves said that this would be 1.35 metres above the floor of the basement and I told him to go ahead on that basis.

26. I believe that we did what the specification required.

Signed .... Dated ....

Claimant's Proofs of Evidence—John Watts (5.6)

IN THE MATTER OF THE ARBITRATION ACTS 1950 TO 1979

AND

IN THE MATTER OF AN ARBITRATION UNDER THE JCT ARBITRATION
RULES (18 JULY 1988)

BETWEEN

RELIABLE BUILDERS LIMITED   Claimant

AND

SANCTUARY HOUSE LIMITED   Respondent

PROOF OF EVIDENCE OF JOHN WATTS

I, JOHN WATTS of 10 Edwina Villas, Norwich

WILL SAY as follows:

1. I am a site foreman employed by the Claimant, Reliable Builders Limited, for whom I have worked for the past 21 months.

2. I was taken on by the Claimant Company to finish a hospital job in Norwich and then be foreman on the Sanctuary House site in Woodbridge for the Respondent, Sanctuary House Limited.

3. Once the Sanctuary House scheme started in April 1991 this was the only job that I did for the Claimant company and I was on-site every day during this contract.

4. I went to the meeting on 8 April 1991 with Mr Hocking and Bill Reeves from Reliable Builders and Mr Bliss, from Sanctuary House and his architect Mr D'Iffy.

5. We had started work on the site, about a week earlier, on 2 April and I noticed differences between the quantities in the Bill provided by the Architect and the actual quantities on-site—I was particularly worried about the earthworks. The meeting on 8 April had been called to sort this out and other matters but I believe it was also meant to be an ordinary site meeting as well.

6. Mr Hocking had asked me to go to the meeting so I would know, for myself, what was agreed.

7. The meeting started with some discussion about what were the terms and conditions of the contract. I was told that this had not been made clear when we were asked to tender.

8. Following this discussion Mr Hocking said he was happy to stick to the rates that he had quoted in his tender but because of the errors in the quantities he reserved the right to remeasure all or any items of the contract, where there was a big difference between the Bill and the actual work on-site. Mr D'Iffy, the architect, after discussing this in private with his client Mr Bliss, reluctantly agreed to a remeasure. I took this to mean a total remeasure and this is certainly what I took Mr Hocking to have agreed to.

9. At the end of the meeting everyone left except Mr D'Iffy and Mr Hocking who stayed

behind to agree some details. I am not sure exactly what these were. I had to get back to site as there were various things that needed my attention. As we left the meeting, Frances Hutch, told me that she was surprised that Mr Bliss had agreed the remeasure.

10. During this contract I worked with Miss Hutch on a daily basis. In this time there were many variations in quantities which I was prepared to agree with her or, at least, believing that there was to be a total remeasure, leave to the Final Account stage. I remember saying to her immediately after the meeting 8 April, 'now I've got no worries with variations because we are on a remeasure'. She did not disagree with me nor did she ever say anything to the contrary when this matter was discussed at various site meetings.

11. I have been asked to comment on our claim for an Extension of Time. Frankly, I cannot see why the architect refuses it. I suppose it is because a lot of it, the delay that is, was down to him and Miss Hutch.

I was always findings bits and pieces of detail missing from their drawings or specification and would often have to stop work on something or other waiting for this information. Then there were the variations—this architect was always changing things.

The other thing that messed us about, quite a lot, was Mr Bliss's workmen. They came to fix the kitchen and sent the equipment etc long before they came themselves. This meant storage, because the kitchen area was not ready. We were trying to finish off various rooms and I seem to remember having to move this equipment at least twice, if not three times. All in all we were properly messed about on this job.

12. The other matter I was asked to comment on was the tanking of the basement. I remember when this was discussed quite early on in the job. All I did was to get the highest water-table figure from the Building Control Officer, Woodbridge District Council, as instructed by Mr Hocking. I gave this to Mr Reeves and he later told me what height to tank to and then put waterproof rendering above.

13. This Statement is true to the best of my information and belief.

Signed .... Dated ....

Claimants Proofs of Evidence—William Reeves (5.7)

IN THE MATTER OF THE ARBITRATION ACTS 1950 TO 1979

AND

IN THE MATTER OF AN ARBITRATION UNDER THE JCT ARBITRATION RULES (18 JULY 1988)

BETWEEN

RELIABLE BUILDERS LIMITED   Claimant

AND

SANCTUARY HOUSE LIMITED   Respondent

PROOF OF EVIDENCE OF WILLIAM REEVES

I, WILLIAM REEVES of 28 Riverside Mansions, Ipswich, WILL SAY as follows:

1. I am a Contracts Administrator employed by Reliable Builders Limited and have been in that position for the past 10 years.

2. On 8 April 1991 I attended a site meeting at the Sanctuary House project in Woodbridge, Suffolk.

3. This was the first scheduled site meeting but as my managing director, Mr Hocking, was concerned about errors in the quantities on which we had based our Tender, he had agreed with Mr D'Iffy, the Respondent's architect, that we could discuss this matter at that meeting.

4. Apart from me and Mr Hocking, for our side John Watts, our site foreman, was there as was also Joel Redman, an outside surveyor who we use for valuations and the like.

Representatives for the Respondent included Mr Bliss, the Employer, Mr D'Iffy, his architect and Miss Frances Hutch, the Job Architect.

5. After dealing with general matters the discussion then moved on to deal with the question of remeasurement which Mr Hocking said should be a total remeasure. The Respondents said they did not see why a remeasure was necessary, as the size of the building had not changed. We pointed out that the initial quantities of topsoil and reduced levels appeared to be quite different from the quantities for these items included in the Bill of Quantities that they had sent with their invitation to tender. We discussed a number of items which were connected with our work on this contract. In doing so it seemed clear from the amount of variation that the argument for remeasure was overwhelming and it was clear to me that the Respondents agreed.

6. I then left the meeting with Mr John Watts and Miss Frances Hutch. As soon as we got outside Miss Hutch remarked that she had been in the meeting, with the Respondent and his representative, prior to the one we had just had where it was impressed upon him and Mr D'Iffy that they should not agree to remeasure but within an hour they had agreed to the remeasure. At the meeting when this was discussed there was no mention of remeasurement being limited in any way and my understanding was that a total remeasure was agreed.

7. The other Preliminary Issue matter which I can comment on is the waterproofing of the basement.

When we received the tender documents I pointed out to Mr Hocking that they were rather vague concerning this item. As the cellar was not very large and we were pressed for time, having not been given long to put our price together, we agreed to include a Provisional Sum to cover this work.

Later, at the meeting on 8 April 1991, this was one of the items which I understand Mr Hocking firmed up. As we had allowed tanking to about half the height of the basement with waterproofing rendering above when we worked out the Provisional Sum, Mr Hocking was apparently happy to firm up at that figure.

When it came to doing the work Mr Watts, our site foreman, came to me and said that he had obtained the highest recorded water-table level, from the Building Control Officer, at Woodbridge District Council. The figure he gave to me, which he had apparently been given by this B.C.O. was 750 mm below ground.

I subsequently instructed him to tank to 6 inches above this height, i.e. 2.15 metres above datum and waterproof render above.

Having complied with the contract specification I cannot see how we can be liable for any damage caused by subsequent flooding.

8. This statement is stated to the best of my belief and information.

Signed .... Dated ....

Claimant's Proofs of Evidence—Joel Redman (5.8)

IN THE MATTER OF THE ARBITRATION ACTS 1950 TO 1979

AND

IN THE MATTER OF AN ARBITRATION UNDER THE JCT ARBITRATION RULES (18 JULY 1988)

BETWEEN

RELIABLE BUILDERS LIMITED   Claimant

AND

SANCTUARY HOUSE LIMITED   Respondent

5.8
111

PROOF OF EVIDENCE OF JOEL REDMAN

1. My full names are JOEL LIONEL REDMAN. I am a chartered surveyor having qualified in 1963 and have been in private practice on my own for some 12 years.

As well as my professional work I also work with building contractors doing estimating and post-contract valuations as well as final account work on a variety of contracts. My office is not far from the Claimant's offices in Norwich and I have worked, on a number of jobs, with them over a number of years.

2. Mr Hocking, the managing director of the Claimants, on or about the beginning of April 1990, asked me to act for them to agree the interim valuations and also to deal with any remeasurement work on the final accounts.

3. From the beginning of the contract I dealt with all the valuations on behalf of the Claimant. The valuation meeting were attended by Miss Hutch, the job architect, on behalf of the Respondent and occasionally Mr D'Iffy also attended but not more than once or twice. It was clear to me, from the early valuations that contract variations and other changes were occurring which would have an effect on the original quantities. On the occasions when I mentioned this to Miss Hutch, she was anxious to assure me that we would be treated reasonably and fairly in dealing with this final account.

4. The contents of this Statement are true to the best of my information and belief.

Signed .... Dated ....

Claimant's Proofs of Evidence—Solomon Ambrose—Expert: Ceiling (5.9)

IN THE MATTER OF AN ARBITRATION BETWEEN RELIABLE BUILDERS LTD AND SANCTUARY HOUSE LTD

REPORT OF SOLOMON AMBROSE, ARCHITECT FOR MESSRS JAYRICH ASSOCIATES

5.9
112

May 1993

Solomon Ambrose, Architect, acting as Expert Witness concerning the authenticity of a ceiling reputedly designed by James Gibbs, Architect, and constructed by his Italian team of Plasterers *circa* 1724.

My name is Solomon Ambrose. I read Architecture at University College, London, and qualified in 1962 after spending a pre-graduate year as a French Government Scholar at les Ecoles des Beaux Arts, Paris, under the direction of Professor Beaudoin. On returning to England I was invited to join the practice of R C White Cooper, Tutor at U.C.L. and a well-known classicist. Since, I have practised on my own account in Gray's Inn and central London and for many years I have specialised in the refurbishment of period and listed buildings.

I was invited by Messrs Jayrich Associates to make a detailed inspection of a collapsed ceiling, reputedly by the eighteenth century Architect James Gibbs and his team of plasterers who had carried out much superb work at such illustrious houses as Stowe, Buckingham-shire, Tring Park, Hertfordshire and Ditchley, Oxfordshire. The brothers Bagutti, Serena and Vassalli were highly sought by patrons and architects alike for their high quality and beautiful craftsmanship. My specific remit was now to look at the construction and artistry and confirm the authenticity of the original ceiling.

The contractor had swept up some of the collapsed ceiling when I visited the house but now the original construction of the ceiling was clearly visible. Authenticity should not solely revolve round the rather subjective artistic appraisals. I was able to see exactly how the work had been executed which in itself not only indicated to me when the work had been carried out but, in fact, who had carried it out. Plasterers capable of doing such intricate and superb work had their own individual secrets regarding construction which, to any expert in this field, would have been clearly identifiable.

I first raked through the remains on the floor. I found a short length of oak lath which had been split from the log. Hardwood was used for laths in high-class work at this period but I was disappointed to see a ferrous nail at one end of it. This was not typical of the calibre of work, that one would expect to find in this period, as rust could bleed through and spoil the appearance of the ceiling.

I cast around again, looking at the plaster mix and stratification. The first thing I was able to establish was that it was three-coat work described at the time as lath, lay, float and set. The 'pricking up' is the name given in this case to the first coat which is 'laid' over the laths. I could see deep scratches cut diagonally about 50 mm apart, obviously done with a purpose-made scratching tool. I could also clearly see the float coat made up of fine stuff and small tufts of fine hair. This hair was undoubtedly human, no doubt swept up from the barber's floor, and would seriously affect the dating of the ceiling by, say, 175 years as, historically, human hair replaced ox or horse hair as the use of these animals declined.

The presence of this human hair immediately cast doubt on the date of the ceiling. I then had to establish whether I was looking at a fine replica ceiling carried out not by the Italian team, but by a very competent late Victorian plasterer. The setting coat was very fine stuff made from, it would appear, lime dissolved in water and a little silver sand; here again, a little hair protruded. Plasterers' putty was not traditionally used with hair as it was generally too thin to require reinforcement.

I then examined some pieces of moulding or ornaments. I was able to locate some actual bas-relief decoration from the debris and found a piece of decoration which was made of 'Carton pressé', consisting of pulped newsprint which had been forced into moulds to create some of the ornamentation. On the face of my sample there were traces of plaster of Paris which was the traditional way of sharpening up details in 'Carton pressé' work. This form of construction was lighter, more easily transported, easier to fix and less expensive in a country district where skilled workman to cast ornaments were not easily obtainable and therefore it was used extensively by the Victorians.

5.9
113

Conclusion

In conclusion, my professional view is that the ceiling, which recently collapsed, was not erected by the Italian brothers Bagutti, Serena and Vassalli and is not *circa* 1724 as previously supposed but a replica of the original ceiling designed by James Gibbs. I have come to this conclusion based on my analysis of the methods of construction employed which are not contemporary with current practices used by plasterers in the early eighteenth century.

Solomon Ambrose
11 May 1993

Claimant's Proofs of Evidence—David Sharkey—Expert: Basement (5.10)

IN THE MATTER OF AN ARBITRATION BETWEEN RELIABLE BUILDERS LTD AND SANCTUARY HOUSE LTD

REPORT OF DAVID ROBERT SHARKEY, BSC, SANCTUARY HOUSE WOODBRIDGE SUFFOLK FOR: JAYRICH ASSOCIATES

REF: DRS/ATC/3477
DATE: MAY 1993

5.10
114

Introduction

This is a report prepared by David Robert Sharkey BSc ARICS of Worthingtons, Chartered Building Surveyors of 2 St John's Green, Ipswich, Suffolk. Mr Sharkey is an Associate of the practice and has been employed by them since he qualified eight years ago. He gained his BSc in building surveying at Salford University and undertook a two-year period of pre-qualification practical training in the building surveying department of Beeley & Hayker in London. His experience includes acting as Contract Administrator under the most commonly used standard form of contract, including the JCT Intermediate Form of Contract. The projects on which he has been engaged include refurbishment, maintenance and repair work, mostly to domestic buildings throughout Suffolk and Norfolk. Mr Sharkey will say as follows:

Instruction

I have been instructed by Jayrich Associates, Construction Claims Consultant representing Reliable Builders Limited to provide advice and opinions relating to the flooding of the basement at Sanctuary House, Woodbridge, Suffolk on 13 April 1992.

I inspected the property on Tuesday 30 March 1993 and again on Friday 2 April 1993. I have also seen and considered the following documents:

1. A specification of refurbishment works to Sanctuary House prepared by The Architectural Partnership of Norwich dated November 1990.
2. Drawings Nos. TAT/1A, 2, 3B, 4C, 5, 6, 7A, 8 and 9 also prepared by The Architectural Partnership. These appear to be the contract drawings.
3. Drawing No. S1.70 showing site levels as existing before the works commenced.
4. A letter from Reliable Builders Limited to Woodbridge District Council dated 2 April 1991 and a reply dated 11 April 1991.

Background

I understand that Reliable Builders were engaged to carry out extensive refurbishment works and the construction of an extension to Sanctuary House, Woodbridge for Mr and Mrs Bliss trading as Sanctuary House Limited under a JCT Intermediate Form of Contract. The contract documents included the specification of works and drawings prepared by The Architectural Partnership.

The specification includes the following clauses in connection with works to the basement:

3/2b: Break up existing concrete/brick paving floor to basement and clear and cart away.

3/8h: Excavate as necessary for new basement floor construction and clear and cart away debris.

3/9c: Provide minimum 150 mm hard core bed beneath new basement floor slab.

3/9d: Provide and lay new 150 mm concrete floor to basement in type 1 concrete and finish to receive tanking as appropriate.

3/15a: Provide tanking to new concrete floor and existing walls to basement to a height to be determined as 150 mm above the highest recorded level of the water table immediately adjacent to the property.

3/21g: Lay 50 mm screed to basement floor.

The detailed specification for hard core, concrete and screeding is given in the preambles and standard work descriptions section of the specification.

The drawings show the basement room which is beneath the television room at the rear of the building. The section on Drawing No. TAT/7a shows the new hard core and concrete floor and a note at the side states 'tanking to walls and floor as specification item 3/5a'. This item in the specification deals with the removal of redundant pipework throughout the property. The drawing reference is clearly wrong and is probably a graphical error and should read 3/15a.

The basement staircase is shown on the drawings but there is no reference either on the drawings or in the specification to any works to be carried out to this staircase.

5.10
115

The Tender

I understand that Reliable Builders were given very little time to price for the works and so did not have time to fully investigate the question of the water table. They therefore priced item 3/15a in the specification as a provisional sum. After their tender was submitted various discussions took place during which corrections were made to arithmetical errors and various additions and omissions were made. Mr Hocking of Reliable Builders says that he was pressed to amend his pricing of this item from a provisional sum to a firm price. He says that he consulted with Mr Redman his outside surveyor, who assisted him with pricing and they agreed to do so. He says that at the time he was given no indication that there had been a problem with the basement flooding in the past. However, he says that he assumed that some tanking was required, at least to the lower parts of the walls, otherwise the item would not have been included. He also says that he assumed that it was only to be partial tanking, otherwise the specification would have stated that the basement was to be tanked for its full height. He says that at Mr Redman's suggestion they agreed to price the tanking half the height of the wall only, but to allow for waterproof rendering to the remainder as this would give them a margin for error.

Investigations by Reliable Builders

Once the job started on-site Mr Hocking realised that he should make further enquiries about the water table. He therefore wrote to Woodbridge District Council on 2 April 1991 as follows:

'As you know we are carrying out work to the above property. We need to establish the highest level of water table at this location and I would be grateful for any information you can provide.'

The reply from Woodbridge District Council was as follows:

'This council does not keep records of the information you requested and you should make your own investigations on-site. Our Building Control Office will be pleased to discuss any temporary works you may need to carry out to prevent ground water damaging trenches or any other temporary or permanent work.'

I understand from Mr Hocking that the site foreman, John Watts, raised the question of the water table level with the Building Control Officer when he visited the site some time later in April and that the Building Control Officer volunteered the information that the highest level of the water table he had known in the area was about 750 mm below ground level. Mr Hocking says that he instructed his foreman to act on this information and ensure that any tanking finished no lower than 600 mm below ground level. He then left it to his contracts manager, Bill

Reeves, to decide exactly how the tanking was to be detailed. Mr Reeves says that he investigated a number of possibilities and decided that given the depth of tanking required that Bituthene deep sheet tanking system would be most appropriate. However, he was concerned that the information regarding the water-table level was rather vague and suggested to Mr Hocking that they tank for the full height of the walls. Mr Hocking realised that this would be more expensive than the amount which he had allowed for in his tender and they therefore agreed to Bituthene tanking to 1.35 metres above basement floor level and waterproof rendering above.

Situation On-site

5.10
116

From the site level Drawing No. S1.70 it can be seen that the grounds to the property are remarkably flat, varying from a minimum of 2.695 metres above datum to 2.955 metres above datum. Assuming that the maximum level of the water table is 750 mm below ground level, its height in relation to the datum could be anything between 1.945 metres above datum to 2.105 metres above datum. Using the same datum I calculate from measurements taken on-site, that the top of the tanking is at 2.145 metres above datum. Using the above figures therefore, the maximum water table could be anything from 40 mm below to 200 mm below the top of the tanking. Immediately outside the basement the paving is 2.835 metres above datum. However, this is about 100 mm above the general ground level immediately adjacent. Again, using a figure of 750 mm below ground level for the water table, this would indicate that it is at 1.985 metres above datum, i.e. 160 mm below the top of the tanking.

It is clearly impossible to establish the highest recorded level of the water table without detailed records. However, the best information available seems to be that it is anything between 1.945 and 2.105 metres above datum and that the top of the tanking is therefore anything from 40 mm to 200 mm above it. However, immediately adjacent to the basement the tanking appears to be 160 mm above the water table. The specification required it to be a minimum of 150 mm above the water table.

Whether or not the tanking extends above the water table, I was initially surprised that a sudden flood was apparently caused. Although waterproof rendering cannot be regarded as tanking, it seems unlikely that even if the water table rose above the Bituthene tanking a sudden flood of water would enter the basement and flood to a depth of 60 mm overnight. I understand from Mr Reeves that he inspected the basement on Tuesday 14 April 1992 and that water was pumped out at various times over the following few days whilst inspections were carried out. By Thursday 16 April all fittings in the room had been removed and some opening up begun. This continued on Friday 17 April, which was Good Friday and from time to time over the rest of the Easter weekend. The detailing at the junction of the tanking and the waterproof rendering was recognised as the most likely point of entry and the timber capping which coincides with this joint was replaced with quarry tiles bedded in mortar with a waterproof additive. I understand that no further flooding has occurred, that the interior has now dried out and that the basement has been in full use again since early June 1992.

Based on the above, the most likely cause of the flooding seems to be a defect in the junction detail between the Bituthene and the waterproof rendering which has since been remedied. Since the rendering above the Bituthene is waterproof it seems to me even if the top of the Bituthene is not at least 150 mm above the highest recorded level of the water table, or if the water table raises above this height, that further flooding is very unlikely to occur.

....
D R Sharkey BSc ARICS   Date

Respondent's Proofs of Evidence—Maximilian D'Iffy (5.11)

IN THE MATTER OF THE ARBITRATION ACTS 1950 TO 1979

AND

IN THE MATTER OF AN ARBITRATION UNDER THE JCT ARBITRATION RULES (18 JULY 1988)

BETWEEN

RELIABLE BUILDERS LIMITED   Claimant

AND

SANCTUARY HOUSE LIMITED   Respondent

PROOF OF EVIDENCE OF MAXIMILIAN D'COURCY D'IFFY

I, MAXIMILIAN D'COURCY D'IFFY of the Old Water Mill, Brightlingsea, Essex, WILL SAY as follows:

1. I am 59 years old and have been in practice since I qualified as an Architect at the AA in 1956.

2. I am presently the senior partner of The Architectural Practice (TAP) of Norwich of which I was a founding partner when it was established in 1963.

3. The practice is engaged on a wide variety of commissions but specialises in conversions and refurbishment of quality buildings.

4. I have a particular interest in historic buildings and am an active member of the Georgian Group as well as a friend of English Heritage.

5. My practice was first approached by Mr and Mrs Bliss when they were considering buying the old Manor Hall, as Sanctuary House used to be called. We carried out a building survey for them, prior to purchase, and were able to assure them that the house was in reasonably good order. We had the added advantage of having worked for the previous owners so that we were reasonably familiar with the property and its condition.

6. We were aware from the beginning that the Blisses intended to convert the Manor Hall into a high-quality nursing home and our view was that the building would convert very nicely. In order to provide all the necessary facilities we had to design a back extension into which we were able to accommodate the kitchen, a small self-contained medical centre, an assisted bathroom and on the upper floors, fifteen superior bed-sitting rooms with *en suite* bathrooms.

7. The whole enterprise was very costly and we provided the Blisses with costings to incorporate into their business plan for presentation to their financial backers. We actually met, on a number of occasions, the bank executive assigned to this project, a Mr Paul Goldstone. He impressed upon us the need to keep a tight control on the finances and certainty of cost. Provided it was within budget, was even more important than an open-ended situation even if it might actually save money in the long run.

8. I had this very much in mind when I discussed the tender received from Reliable Builders Limited (RBL) at the end of January 1991. Unfortunately RBL's tender, although the lowest was still more than £77,000, or approximately 14 per cent, over budget. I knew that there was no way that the bank would be prepared to lend this additional money and therefore had a

number of conversations with RBL's managing director, Harry Hocking, with a view to knocking down their price.

9. We carried out an exercise of comparison between RBL's tender and the next two lowest and discovered a number of anomalous rates where RBL appeared to be too high. We were able to carry out this exercise because we had provided the tenderers with a Tender Budget of approximate quantities. We have found, over the years, that small local builders are more likely to tender if you give them indicative quantities, although we are always careful to mark them 'For Guidance Only'. I asked Mr Hocking if he was prepared to adjust those of his rates which were clearly out of line, if we awarded him the contract, but he refused to do so. He did, however, make it clear that he was short of work and would be prepared to negotiate.

10. I had several telephone conversations with Mr Hocking, following receipt of their tender. During these we corrected one or two arithmetical errors in their tender as well as omitting some items which they had priced and priced some items which we had included as provisional sums. Unfortunately the overall effect was to increase the tender figure by almost £5000.

11. I tried to get RBL's price down to the Blisses budget figure of £540,000 but the closest I could get was £550,000, and I noted in my diary on 7 March 1991 that we had agreed on this figure. I was a little relieved but I was also very concerned at how small a contingency sum we had left to cope with other unforeseen problems.

12. The tenders came in around the end of January 1991 and these negotiations took until the end of March. When we wrote to RBL, confirming the revised tender figure and emphasising that this was a fixed-price lump-sum contract with no remeasurement. We really could not afford any misunderstanding on this score.

13. We were therefore a little alarmed when Hocking replied to that letter confirming the revised figure but questioning the fixed-price nature of the contract. RBL had started work on-site, immediately after the Easter Holiday, 2 April, and the first site meeting was scheduled for 8 April so I telephoned Hocking and suggested that we sort this matter out at that meeting.

14. After some preliminary matters had been dealt with we got on to this question of fixed price. Mr Hocking reiterated what he said before, that was that he did not see how this could be fixed price as they had not had a chance to check our quantities or to prepare their own. I explained that this was a spec. and drawings job and it was for the tenderers to prepare whatever quantities they saw fit. Hocking said that they had already identified discrepancies in the earthwork quants, having by then done around 25 per cent of the topsoil removal and some reduced level dig.

15. Hocking was insistent that the job be remeasured on completion but this was totally unacceptable to my client, Mr Bliss, who was also in attendance. We were in a weak negotiating position with RBL already working on-site; we could not afford the cost of the delay if we failed to come to terms with RBL and had to go out to tender again.

16. After a private consultation with my client we agreed on a very limited remeasure—mainly the earthwork items about which Hocking seemed concerned. At the same time we agreed to remeasure the drainage system, as Miss Hutch, my assistant, was confident that she could recover some of the extra cost with a redesign.

17. I agreed to stay behind after the main meeting broke up in order to agree the precise list of items subject to an end remeasure. This we did and I confirmed the list to RBL by letter 15 April 1991.

18. Mr Hocking acknowledged this list with a comment about reserving the right to ask for remeasurement of any item which they found to be substantially more than our Tender Budget but would only ask for this if it meant a significant financial effect. We took this to mean that they would only ask for remeasurement of any work involved in any variations that we might order if there was a substantial financial effect. In other words they would absorb small changes.

19. When Mr Hocking and I had compiled the list of items which we agreed would be

remeasured on completion, I invited him to sign the IFC '84 Contract, which I had already prepared. We both signed. Mr Hocking asked how we would deal with remeasure items and I told him that I would write to him and confirm the list. I do not recall Mr Hocking expressing any further reservations at that stage, indeed, had he done so I would not have left the matter there. Subsequently I wrote to RBL, 15 April 1991, with the agreed list and assumed that was the end of the matter. I was a little concerned, therefore, to receive a letter, dated 22 April 1991, repeating his reservation about further remeasurement. I told my Associate, Miss Hutch, not to bother to reply as we had already full aired the matter at the 8 April site meeting and afterwards at my meeting with Mr Hocking.

20. At that point I dropped out of direct contact with RBL, the day-to-day running of this contract being in the hands of my associate, Frances Hutch.

5.11
119

21. RBL did not turn out to be very efficient. They were always short of labour. In the event they finished around three months late. As a result I advised my client that he could deduct the liquidated damages that we had provided for in the spec. It was my job to advise on such matters as the Architect named in the contract.

22. Both Mr Bliss and I were concerned about the quality of some of RBL's work so, following an inspection with Mr Bliss and RBL's contract administrator, Bill Reeves, I advised Mr Bliss to make a further reduction in the Final Certificate to cover defective work. In the end, I understand that, following consultation with Mr Goldstone, Mr Bliss did not pay this certificate at all.

23. The whole business of the remeasurement was raised again when we started discussing RBL's final account following completion of the project. We made several attempts to make them see sense but at the end of the day had little choice but to reluctantly agree to go to arbitration.

24. In the meantime disaster had struck. Firstly, only days after the work was completed, the basement flooded and then, on Christmas Eve, our precious Gibbs ceiling in the lounge, on which we had spent a considerable sum restoring, collapsed and the health authority subsequently insisted on evacuation and a complete closure of the floor above.

25. I cannot comment on the reasons why these two defects should have occurred as Miss Hutch dealt with the day-to-day supervision of this project.

26. The information contained in this Proof of Evidence is true to the best of my knowledge and belief.

....
Maximilian D'Courcy D'Iffy FRIBA
Dated the .... day of 1993

APPENDIX A—MAXIMILIAN D'COURCY D'IFFY'S PROOF OF EVIDENCE

Handwritten Note of Meeting 9 April 1991

'Quants—remeasure to be agreed after meeting.
2–3% error acceptable
Redesign drains.'

Fair copy of the above Handwritten Note

Quants—remeasure to be agreed after meeting
2–3% error acceptable
Redesign drains

Respondent's Proofs of Evidence—Frances Hutch (5.12)

IN THE MATTER OF THE ARBITRATION ACTS 1950 TO 1979

AND

IN THE MATTER OF AN ARBITRATION UNDER THE JCT ARBITRATION RULES (18 JULY 1988)

5.12
120

BETWEEN

RELIABLE BUILDERS LIMITED   Claimant

AND

SANCTUARY HOUSE LIMITED   Respondent

PROOF OF EVIDENCE OF FRANCES HUTCH

I, FRANCES KIMBER HUTCH of The Look-out, Hollesley Bay, Suffolk, WILL SAY as follows:

1. I am presently an Associate partner in The Architectural Practice (TAP) in Norwich. One of my duties during 1990 was to act as Job Architect for the contract being carried out, by Reliable Builders Limited, at Sanctuary House, Woodbridge, Suffolk.

2. I have been with TAP ever since I left the Anglia Polytechnic having completed the degree course in architecture.

3. As Job Architect I was involved with the contractual side of the contract, although the ultimate responsibility rested with my principal, Mr M D'Iffy, who was named in the specification as the Architect.

4. I was present at a meeting on-site on 8 April 1991 when the contract was discussed with RBL.

5. From my job diary, in which I record relevant events on the contract and, attached to this Proof of Evidence, is a copy of the page for 8 April 1991 on which I recorded my attendance at the meeting.

6. From my note it can be seen that two main matters were discussed at the meeting, 8 April 1991.
    (i) General contractual matters and
    (ii) the question of remeasurement.

7. I was present at this meeting more as an observer than a participator as the main role, from our side, was taken by my principal, Mr M D'Iffy. I therefore took little part in the discussion.

8. There was, I recall, some dispute as to whether or not the contract was a lump-sum one—Mr D'Iffy was quite sure that it was and Mr Hocking, of RBL, believed that it was not and therefore was subject to remeasure.
    The meeting had been called to clarify the issue although, I had noted in my diary that it was also the date scheduled for the first site meeting.

9. My understanding was that RBL were unhappy to accept a lump-sum contract as they had based their tender on the rough quantities that we had provided to assist the tenderers and RBL were not happy with these quantities, believing them to be substantially understated. As a result they did not want to take the risk on these quantities by agreeing to a lump sum.

10. Mr D'Iffy and Mr Hocking therefore agreed that there would be a partial remeasurement of the works, mainly the earthworks but specifically items on a list to be compiled between them at the conclusion of the meeting.

11. We included drainage on this list as we considered that we could produce a better drainage design than the one originally drawn and included with the tender and as a result we could reduce the quantities included in the draft bill, although, of course, we could have achieved the same effect through a variation order. By redesigning the drainage we thought to produce a saving to set against any additional costs incurred in agreeing the limited remeasurement settled upon.

5.12
121

12. As I have said, the detail of what was to be the subject of remeasure was worked out between Messrs D'Iffy and Hocking, everything else was to be part of the lump-sum price and not subject to remeasurement. On that score I am certain. As far as we were concerned RBL were perfectly happy, at the time, with the arrangement arrived at as a result of the 8 April meeting.

13. Our side was not particularly happy with the deal that had been struck, at the 8 April meeting, as we were aware that SHL were on a very tight budget and could not afford to take the risk on any substantial remeasure. We had gone into the meeting thinking that a lump-sum price had been agreed and came out having agreed to a partial remeasure. When Mr D'Iffy returned to the office later that afternoon he told me that Mr Bliss, the M.D. of the client company, was not at all pleased with the outcome. However, when I left the meeting I thought at least the principles had been sorted out and the way forward was clear-cut.

14. There was no discussion of the calculation of RBL's rates or how the agreed reduction in the tender price would be applied to these rates, whilst I was at the meeting.

15. On 15 April I confirmed, by letter to RBL, the agreement made at 8 April meeting. RBL replied 24 April accepting the list of remeasure items but reserving the right to ask for remeasure of any items which prove to be substantially in excess of the quantity for the same item in the Tender Bill. I did not reply to this letter as I took this reference to be to any possible variations which would in any event get remeasured. We heard no more on this matter until after the end of the job when RBL started submitting what they believed they were entitled to remeasure. We merely reiterated our former position and referred RBL to the earlier exchange of correspondence.

16. Similar problems occurred over the lump-sum reduction which we had agreed at tender stage. For the duration of the contract I had rounded this up to 12 per cent and deducted this from each valuation. When it came to the Final Account RBL insisted that the discount should be taken off as a lump sum rather than applied to each individual rate. I have been involved in many contracts where a sum has been negotiated off the tender amount before acceptance and in every instance we have calculated this as a percentage and applied this percentage as a reduction to all the rates when doing interim valuations or pricing variations.

17. As a practice we had worked for the previous owners of Sanctuary House, or the Manor Hall as it was then known. We were therefore aware that the water table in this part of Woodbridge is very high and the cellar, or basement of the Manor Hall had a propensity to flood fairly regularly.

18. As this area was required for the nursing home laundry we specified tanking 6 inches above the highest historic water table ever recorded in the vicinity. Of course we left it to the successful tenderer to ascertain what was this level. Despite this requirement the basement flooded, on 13 April 1992, shortly after the contract works had been completed. Two washing machines, two industrial dryers and a dehumidifier were ruined as was a large quantity of the residents linen and clothing belonging to SHL.

19. The information contained in this Proof of Evidence is true to the best of my belief and knowledge.

5.12
122

Frances Kimber Hutch

Dated the .... day of 1993

Respondent's Proofs of Evidence—William Bliss (5.13)

IN THE MATTER OF THE ARBITRATION ACTS 1950 TO 1979

AND

IN THE MATTER OF AN ARBITRATION UNDER THE JCT ARBITRATION RULES (18 JULY 1988)

BETWEEN

RELIABLE BUILDERS LIMITED   Claimant

AND

SANCTUARY HOUSE LIMITED   Respondent

PROOF OF EVIDENCE OF WILLIAM HUBERT BLISS

I, WILLIAM HUBERT BLISS of Sanctuary House, Woodford, Suffolk, WILL SAY as follows:

1. In the late summer of 1990 I was made redundant from my post of Administrator of the West Anglian Health Authority. This was the result of one of the many government reorganisations of the National Health Service.

2. A year earlier I had married a ward sister. Constance, my wife, had always been interested in the idea of running our own nursing home so, with my substantial redundancy payment, this seemed to us to be the ideal opportunity.

3. We settled on East Anglia and with the property market being in severe depression quickly found the ideal property at a very reasonable price.

4. I had prepared a rough budget and discussed this with my bank who had, in principle, agreed to finance the venture. The price we agreed with the seller of the Old Manor Hall, Woodbridge, was within our budget, despite having to pay £15,000 over our original offer, due to the amount of interest being shown in this property, so we made an offer 'subject to survey'.

5. I was introduced, by our estate agent, to a local firm of Architects who apparently specialised in the refurbishment of listed buildings, which the Old Manor Hall was, being Georgian. We asked this practice, The Architectural Practice (TAP) of Norwich, to do a building survey for us and at the same time comment on the suitability of the property for the purpose of a nursing home.

Their report was very positive on both fronts. Unbeknown to us this firm had done work for the current owners of The Hall and therefore were relatively familiar with property. We completed the purchase.

6. After a few months of detailed planning the plans were finalised and a budget agreed with the bank. With my wide experience as a health administrator I was confident about my budget figures. The only thing I could not completely control was the building cost.

7. We told TAP that we could live with £540,000 and even introduced them to Paul Goldstone, the bank executive in charge of our account, so that he could impress upon them the need to tightly control costs.

8. Unfortunately when the tenders came in, in early '91, they were considerably in excess of Budget. I made it clear to Mr D'Iffy, the architect from TAP, that he would have to look for savings to bring the figure down to our budget. However, in the end we had to agree on a

figure £10,000 higher and this we did by almost wiping our contingency sum for unforeseen expense during building.

9. No sooner had the architect told me that we had agreed on the building cost, then he informed me that the builder was wavering. I was so anxious that we got this right that I insisted on attending a meeting with the architect and the builder, who had by then already started on site. I told D'Iffy that I was surprised that he had let the builder start before terms had been agreed but he told me that as far as he was concerned the terms had been agreed.

10. In the event I was forced, at this meeting in early April, to be guided by Mr D'Iffy, and agree to a limited amount of remeasurement. The significance of this was lost on me, I merely reiterated, what I and my bankers had said many times before, we must stay within budget.

11. The builders, ironically called Reliable Builders Ltd (RBL), were hopeless. Not only were they three months late in finishing the job, which meant that we were unable to fill our rooms before Christmas, as we had planned, but the quality of their work was poor.

Only a week or two after we had moved our residents in, the basement flooded ruining not only our washing and drying equipment but also a considerable quantity of the residents linen as well as a considerable amount of clothing which we provide for our employees. A bad start, particularly on top of the delay to which these residents had been subjected in moving in.

12. Things then settled down, although there were still a large number of irritating items which needed attention by the builder, until on Christmas Eve the wonderful Gibbs ceiling in the lounge collapsed. Thank heavens this occurred in the late evening when all the residents were in bed so no one was injured.

The health authority got involved and the listed building people and the long and short of it is that we were forced to evacuate the entire floor above the lounge and have had to keep it empty ever since.

The weekly loss of revenue is in excess of £6000. The bank have been helpful but for how much longer?

13. When it came to paying the builder his penultimate certificate it arrived shortly after we had carried out a final inspection visit. Both Mr D'Iffy and my banker, Mr Goldstone, had accompanied us on this inspection and we had identified a very large number of defects. A day or so after this visit the basement flooded (referred to in 11 above) which I took to be the responsibility of the builder who was supposed to have made it waterproof.

All in all, and after discussing this with my banker and the Architect, we all agreed that I would be quite within my rights not to pay this certificate. In any event, Mr Goldstone made it clear that the bank were not at all happy with the current state of affairs and would be unlikely to make the funds available to pay this certificate.

14. The builder's response to this was to sue us for the money in the County Court. For one reason or another this matter did not progress very fast and was still not resolved when further disputes arose and we found ourselves in arbitration with this builder.

I must stress that at all times I have been advised by my professional team, including my bankers, and have only refrained from paying this builder as a result of this advice.

The information contained in this Proof of Evidence is true to the best of my knowledge and belief.

....
William Hubert Bliss BSc MBA (Business Administration) BIM

Dated the .... day of 1993

Respondent's Proofs of Evidence—Simon Rector—Expert: Ceiling (5.14)

SIMON RECTOR, FRIBA ACIArb AADip FSA MBAE

Advice on the age of a ceiling reputed to date from *circa* 1724 and to be the work of craftsmen employed by James Gibbs (*circa* 1682–1754)

Instructions

1. I, Simon Rector, of 9 Astragal Street, London W1, am instructed to advise on the probable date of construction and on the authenticity of a ceiling, now wholly destroyed, at Sanctuary House in Woodbridge, Suffolk.

5.14
125

Experience

2. I qualified as an architect in 1959 after five years at the AA School of Architecture and gained initial experience in the office of Modillion, Cornice & Dentil, a practice largely working for Banks and County Landowners. Thereafter I was with the Ministry of Works for eight years, specialising in maintenance and repair of historic buildings.

3. After further employment with the National Trust and the DOE I entered practice on my own account and now have offices in London and Yorkshire. I am principally concerned with repair and refurbishment of ecclesiastical, civic and major domestic properties of the eighteenth and nineteenth centuries.

Background to the Action

4. The ceiling in the Saloon at Sanctuary House has recently been destroyed, having separated from its supporting structure, I am advised, during renovation work to the house. The nature and quality of its replacement will depend on the age and historical value of the original ceiling, which is in dispute.

5. It is argued that the original was constructed under the direction of James Gibbs and executed by the craftsmen whom he customarily employed. By contrast, the alternative argument is that it is a mid/late Victorian copy of the original, and of little historical value.

6. The design is not unlike the lower figure of Plate 58 of Gibbs work 'Rules for drawing the several parts of architecture' ('Rules') published in 1732; and the details of the work are consistent with an attribution to Gibbs (see Appendix A).

The Evidence

The Underlying Construction

7. In my examination of fragments of the ceiling I noted that the oak laths on which it had been formed were fixed with ferrous 'cut nails', whose ultimate deterioration, in my opinion, largely contributed to the ceiling's failure.

8. While copper nails were preferred for high-class work the use of iron was not uncommon in provincial buildings on grounds of economy; and even in the better class of work the substitution of iron for copper was not unknown where surveillance of the preparatory construction was deficient.

9. The erosion evident in the nails could hardly, in my view, come about in less than 150 years, a figure which I consider conservative.

10. The growth date of the timber used for the laths would in principle be determinable by dendrochronology, but the exercise was not considered cost-effective, given that it could establish the timber's age but not the date of its incorporation into the works.

The Plasterwork: Materials

11. Obviously three-coat work had been adopted, whose workmanship was regular and consistent through all the samples I examined. It was reinforced with hair which proved to be human rather than the more usual 'ox hair' or horsehair. This feature is, curiously, more frequent as the workplace becomes more distant from London. It has been suggested that 'provincial' builders aspired to a 'refinement' that the capital could disdain: in practice a more utilitarian motive is likely, in that human hair was thought more delicate and amenable to detailed work.

12. Major features had been formed in papier maché whose use as an early form of 'prefabrication' seems to have been introduced from France in the wake of Marlborough's campaigns. Although the earliest used cited in the OED dates from 1753 ('Mrs Delany, Life & Corr. (1986) III. 262 'The ceiling ornamenting with papier machée'), an account book from Shewin House, Barsetshire shows that it was used there *ca* 1720, under the description 'carton pressé'.

The Paintwork: Materials

13. The ceiling was originally painted: Gibbs 'Rules' says in the text to Plate 58: 'Flat Cielings may be divided into Pannels and adorned with Fret-work and Painting'. Samples of the paint were analysed and it was found that four layers of decoration had been applied over the original paintwork.

14. All save the last application, which contained titanium dioxide, were consistent with what would be looked for in paint of either the eighteenth or nineteenth Centuries. The absence of alien materials in the underlying layers does not, of course, assist any positive establishment of the date of the ceiling. More significant, it may be thought, is the number of times the work has been redecorated, which is hardly indicative of a mid-to-late nineteenth Century date for its construction.

15. Also of significance, and to me very persuasive of the earlier date for the ceiling, is the extent to which lead sulphide has formed from the original white lead pigment of the lowest layer of paint. The conversion of the white lead is almost complete, a process that I am advised by the analytical laboratory could hardly have reached that state in less than two centuries.

Workmanship and Style

16. The ceiling's decoration incorporated what Gibbs termed 'Frets or *Guilochi's*', in this instance 'the *Vitruvian* Scroll, adorned with Leaves and Sprigs' (cf Plate 59). When the successive accretions of paint had been eliminated, the workmanship of these 'frets' can be recognised as of a very high standard requiring considerable, I would say 'exceptional', skills in their modelling.

17. Skilled though the craftsman of the Victorian era was in the production of the details customary in that period, I believe it unlikely that he could readily have acquired the techniques used by his predecessors in a wholly different decorative mode, particularly in the formation of so delicate a detail as this.

18. Today such details are reproducible with the aid of silicone rubber which can make light of 'undercuts' and 're-entrants'; but no such technique was available to the Victorian craftsman. In parenthesis I would remark that the self-confidence of that era was such that it is, in my experience, extremely rare to find an architect, client or builder who was prepared simply to reproduce the earlier age's work without, to a greater or lesser extent, 'improving' on it.

19. The quality of the work on this feature persuades me that it is by the hand of a

craftsman contemporary with Gibbs and familiar with Gibbs designs. It is possible that it was indeed, as the tradition of the house has it, the work of Vassalli and Serena.

20. Those itinerant masters would not themselves have undertaken the underlying construction of the work that was to receive their skills as the 'icing on the cake'. The construction, which formed the 'bread and butter' so to speak, would be done by competent local craftsmen in whatever manner and largely with whatever materials local customary practice dictated.

Conclusion

21. The views set out above in respect of the ceiling's style and craftsmanship as indications of its date are necessarily subjective, though perhaps not on that account to be wholly disregarded.

22. The indications afforded by the erosion of the iron nails, the successive redecorations of the paintwork and the extent of the conversion of white lead sulphide, are all, by contrast, objective considerations. Of those, the last is to my mind virtually conclusive of the ceiling's age as not later than the end of the eighteenth Century, and probably earlier.

23. Stylistically I would attribute it to Gibbs' middle life, the period of St Martin-in-the-Fields and the Cambridge Senate House, about 1720–30; and probably before publication of his 'Book of Architecture' in 1728.

24. For the reasons I have given I do not see it as a tenable proposition that the ceiling was constructed in the latter half of the nineteenth Century.

25. It was, to my mind, until its catastrophic collapse, a reputable example of a Gibbs ceiling, whose outward face, though not its underlying construction was almost certainly executed by one of his customary team of Italian craftsmen, and quite possibly by Vassalli and Serena, as the tradition maintains.

Simon Rector, FRIBA, ACIArb, AADip, FSA, MBAE
Date: 11th May, 1993

APPENDIX

INDEX OF PLASTERERS

ARTARI, Albert, an Italian stucco worker employed with Bagutti in certain churches and buildings designed by James Gibbs. In the Church of St. Martin-in-the-Fields (1721), the ceiling is "divided into Pannels enrich'd with fretwork by Signori Artari and Bagutti, the best fretworkers that ever came into England" (Gibbs, *A Book of Architecture*, p. v). They were also employed at Marylebone Chapel and in "a room built by the Hon. James Johnston, Esq., at Twickenham (Plate lxxxi., *ibid.*) and at the Senate House, Cambridge (1725) (Willis and Clark, *Architectural History of Cambridge*). Artari was employed at the Radcliffe Library, Oxford (shortly after 1737); at Sutton Scarsdale, Derbyshire (shortly after 1724); and at Houghton Hall, Norfolk (Fig. 137).

BAGUTTI, an Italian stucco worker, employed by James Gibbs (see ARTARI). Bagutti was employed at Mereworth for the stucco work of the rotunda (finished in 1725) (Colin Campbell, *Vitruvius Britannicus*), and Cassiobury (where Virtue speaks of the "admirable execution of a ceiling in stucco"). Bagutti (misspelt Pargotti) is described by Defoe as "an Italian said to be the finest artist in those particular works now in England" (*Tour through England*). He worked with Artari at the "ceiling in the new building" at the Senate House, Cambridge (1725).

BROMFIELD, Joseph (of Shrewsbury), employed for the stucco work of the library ceiling at Hartlebury Castle, Worcestershire, added in 1782, of which the original drawings are preserved and signed by one James Smith of Shifnall. He appears as a subscriber to George Richardson's *Book of Ceilings*, 1774.

CLARK, Thomas, of Westminster, with "great accuracy followed the antique manner" at Holkham.[1] In 1753 he was employed at the Horse Guards, Whitehall, and in the following year at the New Building of the Foot Guards.[2] Between 1778 and 1780 the firm of Thomas & Charles Clark were employed (with William Collins) upon the works at the New Buildings, Somerset House. The surviving partner, Charles Clark, in *The Plasterers' Bill for Works done at the New Buildings, Somerset House* (1783), speaks of Thomas Clark as "one of the most skilful masters of the trade."[3]

COBBE, John, paid in 1601 for the "frettishing" of the ceiling of the great chamber and long gallery at St. John's College, Cambridge (Willis and Clark, *Architectural History of Cambridge*, vol. ii. p. 260).

COLLINS, William, a plasterer employed by Sir William Chambers on several buildings and also at Somerset House (1778–80), where his employment was resented by the firm of Clark.

---

[1] Brettingham's *Plans, Elevations, etc., of Holkham*, p. vi.
[2] Minutes, Rebuilding of the Horse Guards, January 1753–June 1760.—*P.R.O.*
[3] P. 6.

Respondent's Proofs of Evidence—Stanley Longdon—Expert: Basement (5.15)

SANCTUARY HOUSE, WOODBRIDGE, SUFFOLK

I am STANLEY ARTHUR LONGDON, FRICS, ACIArb, a Chartered Building Surveyor of The Meads, Green Lane, Stowmarket, Suffolk. I qualified as a chartered surveyor in 1961 when in private practice as a surveyor with the long established practice of West & Barnfield, Chartered Architects and Surveyors in Bury St Edmunds, Suffolk. After some years as their Building Surveys Manager I joined Suffolk County Council as a Senior Grade Building Surveyor and over the years I was appointed in various departments of the Council. Following an internal reorganisation I left the council and have been in private practice on my own account under the title S A Longdon & Co for the last three years. During my days with West & Barnfield I was associated with a number of high-class conservation projects to country houses throughout the area.

5.15
129

I was recently commissioned by Max D'Iffy to give my expert opinion on a number of technical matters relating to the disastrous flooding of the basement at Sanctuary House, Woodbridge, Suffolk which occurred on Monday 13 April 1992.

I attended at the subject property on 14 April 1992 and undertook a detailed investigation of the basement. The building is of classic proportions and design, generally of the Georgian vintage with a tastefully designed new extension at the rear. The main building is understood to have been refurbished throughout under the supervision and to the design of Max D'Iffy and his colleagues.

For the purposes of this report the front of the building has been termed north and all other references given will have been in relation to this nomenclature, which is not necessarily the actual orientation of the building but is given for reference purposes only.

As is my normal custom, I am obliged to state that I have not inspected woodwork or any other parts of the property which are hidden, unexposed or inaccessible and therefore cannot be commented on with any degree of intimacy, so I am therefore unable to confirm or deny that any such parts are free from defect. This paragraph should be noted and borne in mind throughout this report.

Dealing now with the basement, this is not extensive and is situated more or less under the right-hand part of the house. It is approached via a set of brick and stone steps which are a fine example of the original features in this property.

The provision of a horizontal damp-proof course as appropriate, is always necessary in buildings to prevent water ingress by any means including rising dampness. This property is no exception and it is therefore no surprise to find that the architect had specified tanking to within 6 inches of the highest historic water table ever recorded in the vicinity.

According to the information provided to me, the builder put in a Bituthene tanking on the walls of the basement up to a level of 4 feet 6 inches (approximately 1.35 metres). The Bituthene was protected by a blockwork wall of similar height surmounted by a timber capping. Above this height the walls were finished with plaster. In addition, I understand that within the general building work of a maintenance nature which was carried out at the same time as the upgrading, a damp-proof course of horizontal nature was provided to all the walls. I would add that this is the same specification, at least in principle, as I would always recommend to properties of this nature. The specification in my opinion is quite clear and the builder should have no difficulty in understanding that he should provide a watertight basement.

The cause of the flooding on 13 April 1992 is I am told, something of a mystery. However, I have carried out my own careful research into this case and I have discovered that Mr D'Iffy has been associated with this building under its former name of The Old Manor Hall. During his many years experience with this property work has been carried out to the house and its garden. Mr. D'Iffy has told me that the water table varies with seasonal fluctuation and has been as high as two feet six inches (760 mm) below ground level. He has gleaned this information from his experience, having carried out various works to the property over the years during which he has had excavations dug around the house and grounds for drain repairs, new foundations to outbuildings, etc. The highest level of ground water has generally been experienced in February and March each year, which is logical after all the winter rains which are a feature of this part of the country.

I have carried out some careful measurements and calculations and clearly if one measures from the ground level down to the top of the Bituthene, then the high level of water table at two feet six inches (760 mm) below ground level is level with the top of the Bituthene. The specification requests that the tanking is taken up to six inches above this level and this has not been done. The tanking has not therefore, in my opinion been taken up to six inches above the highest historic water table ever recorded in the area.

5.15
130

I have also undertaken some careful research into the rainfall in this area over the last few years. The Meteorological Office has provided statistics for a measuring station located only two miles from the site on the other side of Woodbridge. These show that in the two winters of 1990/91 and 1991/92 the average rainfall in the area was 2.3 per cent and 5.7 per cent below the average for many previous years. It has been pointed out to me that between 5 and 11 April 1992 there was a great deal of rain produced mainly by three violent storms which occurred during this period. However, I would say that in my opinion this is not so unusual and is unlikely to have caused the water table to rise above its greatest height even in the past. However, it might have caused the water table to rise to its maximum historical height and because the tanking was not to the correct height this has caused the flooding.

Conclusion

In conclusion therefore, it is my opinion that the builder did not construct the basement tanking as per the specification. The basement tanking is level with the highest water table level ever recorded, whereas it should be six inches above this level. The tanking should, in my opinion, be extended in height by at least six inches all round the basement.

Stanley Arthur Longdon FRICS ACIArb

10 May 1993

Respondent's Closing Submissions (5.16)

IN THE MATTER OF THE ARBITRATION ACTS 1950 TO 1979

AND

IN THE MATTER OF AN ARBITRATION UNDER THE JCT ARBITRATION
RULES (18 JULY 1988)

BETWEEN

RELIABLE BUILDERS LIMITED   Claimant

AND

SANCTUARY HOUSE LIMITED   Respondent

RESPONDENT'S SKELETON CLOSING SUBMISSIONS ON THE PRELIMINARY ISSUES

These written Submissions do not repeat either the Oral Closing or the written Submissions made in the Respondent's Statement of Case. Each issue is addressed in turn and in regard to the evidence which the Arbitrator has already heard.

1. When and How was the Contract Formed

1.1 The Claimant avers that the IFC '84 Contract signed at the conclusion of the meeting on 8 April 1991 does not reflect the common intention of the parties as it did not include a reference to the items which it had been agreed earlier, at that meeting, would be remeasured.

1.2 In consequence the Claimant seeks rectification of that contract to incorporate his letter 22 April 1991 which he purports reflects this common intention.

1.3 The Respondent denies that the Claimant's letter 22 April 1991 is a true representation of what was agreed and submits that the architect's letter 15 April 1991 represents the common intention of the parties.

1.4 If any rectification is to be made therefore it should include the letter of 15 April 1991 only and not the letter 22 April 1991 in which the Claimant sought to reopen the negotiations.

1.5 To the extent that the Arbitrator decided that rectification may be necessary I will now address this question.

2. Rectification

2.1 The evidence given during the arbitration hearing on this point more than confirms the Respondent's contention that the Claimant comes nowhere near providing the 'convincing proof' required before a claim for rectification can succeed. The Respondent repeats its submissions as to rectification made in pages 10 to 16 of its opening submissions.

2.2 The Claimant appears to put its case in two ways:

2.2.1 It is alleged that there was a common continuing intention that the Claimant should be paid for the work covered by the contract and in addition be permitted

'to ask for a remeasure of any item which we find are substantially more than your draft Bill of Quantities.'

2.2.2 That even if there was no such common continuing intention outwardly expressed, there was a unilateral mistake on the part of the Claimant of which the Respondent had knowledge at the date of execution of the IFC '84 contract so that it would be inequitable to permit the Respondent to rely upon the terms of that contract.

5.16
132

3. Common Intention of Agreement

3.1 Following the main site meeting 8 April 1991, Mr D'Iffy and the Claimant met and agreed a list of items which would be subject to remeasure. This is common ground.

3.2 This list was subsequently confirmed by letter 15 April 1991 and was confirmed by the Claimant, in his letter 22 April 1991, when he said:

'We ... confirm our acceptance of the listed items that are to be remeasured.'

3.3 There is accordingly no evidence, convincing or otherwise, to support any conclusion to the effect that at the date when the contract documents were executed, both the Claimant and the Respondent were under a common misapprehension that the Claimant was to receive payment additional to that stated in the contract and the Respondent's list in his letter 15 April 1991 for the works stated in the contract.

3.4 The subsequent correspondence relied upon by the Claimant does not remotely establish that conclusion. The Claimant's letter 22 April 1991 merely evidences his intention to reopen negotiations following the previous agreement.

3.5 The Claimant had, by his reply, as has been shown, outwardly signified his agreement to the terms of the IFC '84 contract as amended by the list in the letter 15 April 1991. The letter of 22 April 1991 cannot on its own terms be said to signify a common intention: it is merely a declaration that:

'We ... reserve the right to *ask* for a remeasure ...'

And later in that letter:

'We will only ask for this to be done ...'

3.6 These words 'ask' and 'request' do not evidence anything to overturn that which had been agreed by execution of the contract documents on 8 April 1991 or the agreement as to remeasure reached on that date. The Claimant says that this agreement is to be spelt out from the absence of a reply to the 22 April 1991 letter. That cannot constitute 'convincing proof' of any such conclusion.

3.7 There is no subsequent correspondence which hints at an agreement continuing before and after the execution of the IFC '84 contract or with which the terms of that contract are inconsistent.

3.8 Altogether, the Respondent contends that it is perfectly clear from the evidence given in the arbitration that the Claimant can come nowhere close to discharging the burden of presenting convincing proof that despite the clear words of the contract executed the Claimant and Respondent had in fact agreed that the Claimant was to receive additional payment for the contract works in the terms of his letter 22 April 1991 rather than what had been agreed and was evidenced by the 15 April 1991 letter.

4. Unilateral Mistake

4.1 The alternative way in which the Claimant presents its claim for rectification is equally unsupportable on the evidence. To succeed on this alternative footing, the Claimant must establish that the Respondent knowingly acquiesced in the Claimant signing a document which did not reflect the true agreement between the parties. There is simply no evidence at all in support of that conclusion. In its opening submission (see paragraph 4.4.5 thereof) the Claimant appears to place reliance on the Claimant's letter 22 April 1991.

4.2 The Respondent repeats its submissions in relation to the 22 April 1991 letter made above. That letter does not in terms refer to any mistake on the part of the Claimant but even if the Arbitrator were to find that the Claimant had made a mistake (which is not at all accepted by the Respondent) the letter of 22 April 1991 would not in any event show that the Respondent acquiesced knowingly in the mistake alleged. Yet that state of knowledge is an essential requirement of recovery under this head: see Respondent's opening submissions, pages 8 and 9.

4.3 Altogether the Claimant can come nowhere near discharging its burden of proof in relation to the alternative basis upon which it seeks rectification.

4.4 It is not for the Respondent to speculate as to why the Claimant should seek the additional payments in dispute under this head. However, the Respondent contends that on the evidence as a whole it is highly likely that the Claimant has sought to resile from an agreement made with the Respondent.

4.5 Mr Hocking is an experienced contractor and it cannot be said that he did not appreciate what he was doing when he signed the contract despite it not making specific reference to the list of remeasure items which he and Mr D'Iffy had agreed, a short while earlier.

4.6 So there can be no question of the Respondent having knowledge of the Claimant's mistaken view of things so as to establish the Claimant's alternative claim for rectification.

5. Therefore the First Issue can be answered as follows:

The Contract was formed at the meeting 8 April when all the essential terms were agreed.

6. What are the terms and the conditions of the Contract?

The Contract documents comprise:
  (i) The JCT Intermediate Form of Building Contract—IFC '84—1990 Edition as modified by:
  (ii) Invitation to tender with attachments and the documents referred to therein.
  (iii) The Claimant's quotation, 21 January 1991.
  (iv) The Respondent's letter 20 March 1991 together with the documents referred to therein.

The following are *not* part of the Contract Document.
  (i) The Claimant's letter 28 March 1991 and the note of the Respondent's telephone call reply, 7 April 1991—listing matters to be discussed at 8 April meeting.
  (ii) Letters 15 April and 22 April. These merely reflect the parties' respective contentions as to outcome of 8 April meeting.

Therefore Respondent submits that
The Terms and Conditions of the Contract are those set out in the body of the Contract Documents in items (i)–(iv) above.

7. What, if any, items of Contract works are subject to remeasurement?

7.1 The Respondent's view is that it is the list of items identified in TAP's letter 15 April evidencing the agreement reached at the 8 April 1991 meeting.

7.2 There was a disparity in the oral evidence. The Claimant's contend that they reserved the right to a complete remeasure, as evidence by their account, 22 April 1991, of 8 April meeting. See para 11 of Mr Hocking's written statement:

> '... I received the Respondent's letter dated 15 April in which the items, which we had agreed at 8 April meeting, would be remeasured, were listed.'

7.3 Therefore there can be no dispute as to contents of this 15 April letter i.e. there is to be only partial remeasurement of specific items.

7.4 William Reeves, in his written statement, did not say that RBL had reserved the right to remeasure the *whole* job. What he said in para 5 was:

> '... it seemed clear, from the amount of variation, that the argument for remeasurement was overwhelming.'

7.5 This evidence is as consistent with an agreement for partial remeasurement as it is for complete remeasurement.

7.6 It is common ground that the items to be remeasured were specifically agreed at the 8 April 1991 meeting and, a list of these items was attached to TAP's letter 15 April 1991.

7.7 John Watt's evidence is that he took the agreement to mean total remeasurement not that total remeasurement was agreed. The reservation of the right to remeasure, that Mr Hocking refers to, would be unnecessary if, indeed, a complete remeasure had been agreed.

7.8 The Tender Budget is clearly not a Bill of Quantities within the meaning of the IFC '84 Contract. It has not, for example, been prepared in accordance with the Standard Method of Measurement. Therefore the items which would be adjusted under the Contract, if the Tender Budget was a Bill of Quantities, do not apply here.

7.9 Much has been made of the lack of reply to 15 April letter, i.e. failure to reply meant that the contents were agreed. The reason why no reply was given was that TAP considered that the letter reflected their understanding of the meeting. Whether this interpretation was right or wrong is not to the point. Such interpretation does not fix Miss Hutch with an understanding of that meeting different from her written Statement.

7.10 Why was it necessary to make adjustments to the tender prior to acceptance if this was a remeasure contract such as would have been adjusted automatically?

8. What rates are to be applied to the Contract works in general (including additional and/or varied works)? In particular, are the contract rates to be reduced by the same percentage that the negotiated discount bears to the revised tender price, alternatively, how is a discount to apply to the rates and the subcontract sum?

8.1 The only effective use of the negotiated discount is as an application to all rates pro rata and in proportion, in accordance with ordinary quantity surveying practice.

9. Genuine Gibbs Ceiling?

9.1 Mr Rector gave three main reasons for concluding that the ceiling was genuine Gibbs viz:

    (i) Erosion of nails
    (ii) Successive decorations
    (iii) The formation of white lead sulphide.

9.2 These are analytical, scientific considerations. They are not 'aesthetic' matters as to which a wider variation of expert opinion might have been expected. Moreover, if these considerations are relevant they establish a date *after which* this ceiling could not have been constructed. On the evidence of the nails, the date is at least (conservatively says Mr Rector)

150 years ago. The conversion of white lead sulphide is even more conclusive: that puts the date of the ceiling back 200 years. Either of these dates are completely inconsistent with a 'late Victorian'.

9.3 Mr Ambrose's conclusions rest entirely on two facts, viz:

(i) Human hair had been used, not horse hair or ox hair.
(ii) 'Carton pressé' was used.

9.4 These two facts, as facts, are not in dispute (at least if 'carton pressé' is to be taken to include some form of papier mâché prefabrication or moulding). The learned Arbitrator will, of course, look for some fact which *excludes* the earlier (or, for that matter, the later) date of the ceiling. If such a fact (or facts) can be found then the issue is decided. As Sherlock Holmes was supposed to have said: exclude the impossible and what you are left with, however improbable, must be the truth.

9.5 Put another way, there is no necessity, and it is undesirable, to come to a conclusion on a balance of probabilities if there are facts which logically exclude all but one conclusion.

9.6 It was for that reason that Mr Ambrose was asked in cross-examination whether or not human hair and 'carton pressé' were in use at all in the 1720s. If he had said no, and if the evidence satisfied the Arbitrator, that would have been an end of the matter, against the Respondents and in favour of the Claimants.

9.7 Mr Ambrose's answers are inconclusive. As to human hair, he simply says that by the beginning of the nineteenth century it was 'extensively used', but he does not say that it was unavailable in the early eighteenth century. As to 'carton pressé' he says that this technique 'became progressively popular in the latter half of the eighteenth century and sporadically in the nineteenth century', but fails to answer the precise question: indeed, his evidence suggests that it was more of an eighteenth- than a nineteenth-century technique.

9.8 Since Mr Ambrose fails to identify any feature of this ceiling which *must* be late nineteenth century, so far the question remains open as to the date of this ceiling.

9.9 One must therefore look to see if Mr Rector's scientific observations (at least (i) and (iii), even if one regards successive layers of decoration as inconclusive) have been answered by Mr Ambrose.

9.10 To these observations Mr Ambrose gives no answer at all. He is 'disappointed' to find ferrous metals have been used, but he does not suggest that ferrous metals were not available in the 1720s, i.e. he does not challenge Mr Rector's assertion that they were.

9.11 Likewise, with white lead (or lead white). Far from excluding this as a substance available to craftsmen of the Gibbs period, he actually confirms that 'up to *circa* 1850 the only source of white pigment was white lead'. As to the formation of lead sulphide, on which Mr Rector lays such store, Mr Ambrose has no answer whatever: he simply does not deal with it.

9.12 The Respondents therefore submit Mr Rector's scientific observations not having been challenged at all by Mr Ambrose, there is no reasonable conclusion other than the ceiling was of the age of Gibbs or thereabouts, and since there is no contention by the Claimants that it was of that period but not of Gibbs (the Claimant's case being unequivocally based on a late nineteenth-century ceiling), the only reasonable or indeed possible conclusion is that the ceiling was Gibbs.

10. Is the builder in breach of contract for waterproofing of the basement?

10.1 The contractual requirement is clear, if rather onerous on the contractor. Clause 3/15a required tanking to 'a height to be determined as 150 mm above the highest recorded level of the water table immediately adjacent to the property'.

10.2 The contractor clearly undertook this obligation, regardless of the difficulties of determining such historical data. Miss Hutch confirms that the Respondents 'left it to the successful tenderer to ascertain what was this level'. Contractors often take on difficult or even near-impossible obligations to get the contract, but that does not alter their contractual liability: they simply take on the risk. This can be well illustrated by the provisions of the ICE conditions where the contractor undertakes to satisfy himself, before starting work, of underground conditions of which, in many cases, no one can possibly be certain.

10.4 In this case the contractor's obligation was not unduly hard or unfair: if he could not to his own satisfaction ascertain the highest recorded water table with any certainty, he had only to build in a safety factor, tank to a higher level, and include the costs of that in his price.

10.5 The basement flooded. Therefore, the water table rose to a point where it was at least as high as the tanking. Therefore the tanking did not comply with the requirement that it should be six inches higher than the highest recorded level, unless, of course, it is contended that the 13 April 1992 level was an all-time record at least six inches higher than any previously recorded level. No such suggestion is made by the contractor/Claimant. Mr Longdon gives his opinion that even the rain and storms between 5 and 11 April 1992 were not so unusual as to have caused a record high water table. By contrast, Mr Sharkey says that 'it is clearly impossible to establish the highest recorded level of the water table' and both experts accept that the cause of the flood was something of a mystery. Mr Sharkey himself leaves open the question of 'whether or not the tanking extends above the water table ... even without the 6 inches safety margin provided for in the contract'.

10.6 In construction contracts, mysteries frequently occur. The question is: on whose shoulder falls the risk? Given the terms of the contract, the risk falls squarely on the contractor unless he can establish

   (a) the highest recorded level of the water table and
   (b) that he tanked to six inches above the level.

Since the contractor cannot establish (a) as his expert admits, he is of course unable to establish (b).

10.7 On a more practical consideration of the facts, furthermore, the contractor clearly made no attempt to comply with clause 3/15a. Mr Hocking asked the Building Control Officer about the level of the water table, and was given some informal information: that is clearly not good enough for clause 3/15a. Worse, Mr Hocking consulted his outside surveyor, Mr Redman, who knew nothing about the water table and who suggested that half the height of the wall should be tanked and the rest waterproof rendered. This suggestion was for economic reasons, as waterproofing is cheaper than tanking.

10.8 This was clearly a risky compromise solution. Waterproof rendering is not specified anywhere in the contract. Tanking is. If there were no risk of the water table rising above Mr Hocking's intended tanking level, why provide waterproof rendering at all?

10.9 The only possible conclusion is that Mr Hocking has not ascertained the historical data necessary to determine the highest recorded level of the water table, and therefore, and at a saving to RBL, decided to install a 'fail-safe' waterproof rendering (not specified) above the tanking, in case the tanking level was not in accordance with the contract specification, which in turn clearly shows that the contractor did not know what the tanking level should be.

Bernadette O'Brien
1 June 1993.

Claimant's Closing Submissions (5.17)

IN THE MATTER OF THE ARBITRATION ACTS 1950 TO 1979

AND

IN THE MATTER OF AN ARBITRATION UNDER THE JCT ARBITRATION
RULES (18 JULY 1988)

BETWEEN

RELIABLE BUILDERS LIMITED   Claimant

AND

SANCTUARY HOUSE LIMITED   Respondent

CLAIMANT'S CLOSING SUBMISSIONS ON PRELIMINARY ISSUES

GENERAL INTRODUCTION

1. The Claimant's Opening Submissions addressed the legal principles which are relevant to the issues which arise in this arbitration. They did so in general terms. The purpose of these submissions is not to reiterate the general submissions made in the Opening, nor to cite once again all the authorities upon which the Claimant relies. Reference should be made to the Opening for those. In any event, the Claimant suggests that there is little between the parties about their understanding of the legal principles which are to be applied (certainly so far as the law of rectification is concerned). The argument is more about how those principles are to be applied here. To a large extent that will depend upon how the Arbitrator resolves the factual issues.

2. These submissions are in addition to and not in substitution of oral submissions made at the hearing.

As it was agreed at the hearing that to avoid confusion over the parties respective Statements of Case on the Preliminary Issues, we should also follow the Respondent's format and deal with the six issues: their Closing Submissions also follow that agreed format.

3. These submissions address first the issue of 'When and How the Contract was Formed'. Under this head fall the issues concerning the construction of the contract and rectification. Following which, the Terms and Conditions of the Contract, are considered then the issues of What items are Subject to Remeasurement and What Rates, are dealt with. Then follows the genuinness of the Gibbs ceiling. Finally I deal with the issue of whether or not the Claimant was in breach of contract over the Waterproofing of the Basement.

ISSUE 1—WHEN AND HOW WAS THE CONTRACT FORMED?

The Construction of the Contract

Introduction

4. It is suggested that at the heart of the case as a whole is the fact that the IFC '84 Form, taken in isolation, did not represent the true intentions of the parties with regard to the definition of the contract works.

The Claimant approaches the matter by identifying two sub-issues.

In *Sub-Issue 1*: Whether the contract is to be found

(a) solely in the IFC '84 Form or
(b) whether it is also to be found in the Respondent's letter 15 April 1991 and the Claimant's letter 22 April 1991 referred to in paragraph 2.1 of the Statement of Case.

Sub-Issue 2: If (b), whether all the contract documents when read together have the effect for which the Claimant contends.

5. These issues correspond to the first question addressed by the Respondent in their opening submissions 'the construction of the contract'.

6. The Claimant contends that the contract is to be found in the letters referred to as well as in the IFC '84 Form. Paragraph 2.11 of the Statement of case makes reference to the two letters.

(i) The Respondent's letter 15 April 1991.
(ii) The Claimant's reply to that letter 22 April 1991.

7. The Claimant's letter 22 April 1991 states, *inter alia*:

'We acknowledge receipt of your letter dated 15 April 1991 and confirm our acceptance of the listed items that are to be remeasured. We must, however, reserve the right to ask for a remeasure on any item which we might find to vary from your draft Bill of Quantities. We would only request such a remeasure if it seemed to us that it would make a significant difference in the value of that particular Bill of Quantity item.'

8. The real issue is thus whether the letters of 15 April and 22 April 1991 are contract documents.

9. The importance of this question is this: the Claimant contends that when these letters and the IFC '84 Form are construed together, the true construction is that the Claimant agreed to carry out the works which it had tendered to carry out in January 1991 for the sum stated in the IFC '84 Form, subject to the remeasurement detailed in the Claimant's letter 22 April 1991.

Sub-Issue 1

10. The first question is whether the letters are contractual documents. It seems to be common ground between the parties that the object sought to be achieved when construing any contract is to ascertain the intentions of the parties as expressed by the words they have used in the contract. The intention of the parties is the meaning of the words they have used. There is no intention independent of that meaning. However, this begs the question 'which words?' or, to put the same question in another way, 'which are the documents to be construed?'

11. The parties signed an IFC '84 contract which defined the works which were to be carried out for the Contract Sum. Clause 1.1 of this contract defined the contractor's obligations. Clause 1.2 expressly provided which documents were to prevail in the event that

'the work stated or shown on the Contract Drawings is inconsistent with the description, if any, of that work in the Specification . . .' It may be said that it is plain that the parties intended to express or record their contractual intentions in the IFC '84 Form and nowhere else. For the reasons which follow, the Claimant submits that this is not so.

12. No evidence from outside the contractual document may normally be adduced to contradict, vary, add to or subtract from the written terms. This principle is sometimes referred to as the 'parol evidence rule'. However, there are exceptions. One such is that extrinsic evidence may be admitted to identify the subject-matter of the contract: see *Chitty on Contracts*, 26th ed., Vol 1, para 873 (27th ed., Vol 1, para 12–108), and *Scarfe v Adams* [1981] 1 All ER 843.

It is submitted that a comparison between the signed contract document and the amendment to that document, agreed prior to signature and evidenced by the Claimant's letter 22 April 1991, reveals a discrepancy which may properly be regarded as more than a mere inconsistency, so that the uncertainty which is thus produced is properly to be resolved by the admission of extrinsic evidence. Such a discrepancy does exist as became apparent at the hearing.

5.17
139

13. There is another exception of the rule which is relevant. Although drafts of the contract and preparatory negotiations may not in general be relied upon in interpreting the contract which the parties eventually make, a concluded antecedent agreement may be relied upon in interpreting a later instrument made pursuant to the agreement: *Lewison, Interpretation of Contracts*, para 2.05 and the authorities cited there.

The Claimant submits that following the meeting between Messrs Hocking and D'Iffy at the conclusion of the 8 April 1991 meeting, and immediately prior to the signing of the contract, there was a concluded agreement and that it is permissible to have regard to that agreement when construing the IFC '84 Form. It may be objected that even if it be found that the parties were *ad idem* at 8 April 1991 at the latest, they had not made a binding contract/concluded agreement which would have been legally enforceable *inter alia* because it was anticipated that their agreement was to be reduced into a JCT standard form. The Claimant's response to such a suggestion will be that this does not mean that there was not a 'concluded agreement' (in the sense being considered here) at an earlier date. Apart from anything else, in the law of rectification (a quite separate issue which will be addressed below) the courts have moved away from the requirement that there be an antecedent agreement prior to the written document which the parties sign: rather there should be a common continuing intention (see below). The Claimant submits that a similar approach should be adopted at this stage.

Sub-Issue 2

14. Sub-Issue 2 only arises if Sub-Issue 1 is resolved in the Claimant's favour. In that event, the next question which falls to be considered is whether the IFC '84 Form and the letters are to be construed in the way in which the Claimant contends.

15. The Claimant submits that the key to this question is the Claimant's letter dated 22 April 1991. As will now be plain, there is a clear issue of fact between the parties concerning this letter. The Claimant contends that this letter confirms the true agreement made between the parties at the meeting 8 April 1991, i.e. that he reserved

'the right to ask for a remeasure on any item which we might find to vary from your draft Bill of Quantities.'

16. Recall the cross-examination of Mr Hocking.

1. Did he accept that agreement was reached at the 8 April meeting—Yes he did.
2. Is that what you want us to accept?—Yes it is.
3. It is plain that agreement was reached but that you wish to avoid the consequences—No.

4. If 8 April meeting agreement included reservation about remeasurement why not say so in your letter 22 April?—Thought I had.

5. But you agreed there was no reference to 8 April in your letter—Yes, I agree.

6. Why not say, in your letter 22 April, that they had gone back on what they had agreed at 8 April meeting, if this is what you believed?—My letter was no different to what I had said on 8th.

Rectification

Introduction

5.17
140

17. If sub-Issue 1 is resolved in the Respondent's favour, the next question is whether the IFC '84 Form should be rectified. It is the Claimant's case that the true agreement between the parties was that the Claimant would carry out for the sum of £550,000 ('the Contract Sum') the works which it had tendered to carry out for that price (the price having been negotiated down from the revised tender figure of £622,171.95) subject to the right of remeasurement, as set out in para 15 above.

The Law

18. Before turning in detail to the circumstances in which rectification is an appropriate remedy, one preliminary point may be made. It is often said (correctly) that the court requires 'convincing proof' that the parties' written agreement does not accurately reflect their true intentions. In this context two perhaps obvious points should not be forgotten.

First, where one party claims rectification and the other party seeks to resist such a claim, the court or arbitrator will almost inevitably be faced with conflicting factual evidence which is likely to revolve around what was or was not agreed prior to the written contract being signed. The fact that the parties are at odds on this does not preclude an order for rectification if the claimant satisfies the court or arbitrator that his factual evidence is to be preferred and it is sufficient to lay the factual basis for an order for rectification.

Second, the standard of proof which the Claimant must discharge if he is to satisfy the court or arbitrator is the normal civil standard of proof: the balance of probabilities. The requirement that there shall be 'convincing proof' does not increase the standard of proof which the Claimant has to meet. In particular, it does not require the Claimant to meet the criminal standard of proof or something in between the civil and criminal standards of proof (*Phipson on Evidence*, passim). It is simply a reflection of the courts' historical disinclination to interfere with written agreements which the parties have signed and the courts' informal presumption that the parties intended the written agreement to record their mutual rights and obligations. The Claimant does not understand that the submissions in this paragraph are controversial.

19. The jurisdiction to rectify depends on the following conditions (this analysis follows that in *Emmet on Title* which, it is suggested, provides the clearest guidance to the principles to be applied. However, it does not differ from the approach adopted in the many other textbooks which deal with the subject):

Condition 1: Common mistake (*Chitty*, 26th ed., Vol 1, para 375; 27th ed., Vol 1, para 5–041)

Either there must have been a prior concluded agreement between the parties going beyond mere negotiations.

Or there must have been a common continuing intention of the parties, which intention has some outward expression, even though no prior concluded contract exists.

See *Joscelyne v Nissen* [1970] 2 QB 86

Condition 2: The written contract must fail to represent the prior concluded or common intention because of a mistake of both parties. However, there are two exceptions to this requirement, where there may be rectification despite the mistake being made by only one of the parties:

First where the other party has taken advantage of the mistaken party in a way fraudulent to the eyes of equity.

Second, if one party to a transaction knows that the instrument contains a mistake in his favour but does nothing to correct it, he will be precluded from resisting rectification on the ground that the mistake is unilateral and not common.

A Roberts & Co Ltd v Leicestershire CC [1961] Ch 555
Thomas Bates Ltd v Wyndam's Ltd [1981] 1 WLR 505

5.17

141

Condition 3: It must be shown that the written contract was intended to represent the agreement or common intention of the parties.

Condition 4: The case must be one for the exercise of equity's discretion.

Snell's Equity, Twenty-Ninth Edition, pp 626–633
Emmet on Title, Nineteenth Edition, para 3.011
Keating on Building Contracts, 5th ed., pp 266–269; 6th ed., pp 288–291.

20. The requirement of 'convincing proof' is not a fifth condition. It is simply a description of the evidence which the Claimant must adduce if he is to satisfy conditions 1 to 4.

21. The circumstances in which rectification is available are more succinctly stated by Lord Diplock in *American Airlines Inc v Hope* [1974] 2 Lloyd's Rep 301 (cited in *Keating*, 5th ed., page 266; 6th ed., page 288).

'Rectification is a remedy which is available where parties to a contract, intending to reproduce in a more formal document the terms of an agreement upon which they are already 'ad idem', use, in that document, words which are inapt to record the true agreement reached between them. The formal document may then be rectified so as to conform with the true agreement which it was intended to reproduce and enforced in its rectified form.'

22. It is suggested that this short quotation provides a useful overview which should not be lost sight of. For, as will become clear below, to some extent the identification of four apparently distinct conditions is somewhat artificial.

The Evidence

23. The Claimant's submissions follow the same pattern as has been followed in the passage above which deals with the law.

24. *The first condition* for common mistake is that either there must have been a prior concluded agreement between the parties going beyond mere negotiations or there must have been a common continuing intention of the parties, which intention has some outward expression, even though no prior concluded contract existed.

25. The Claimant contends that the true agreement between the parties and/or their common intention is the one pleaded in paragraph 2.11 of the Statement of Case.

26. The 'convincing proof' of such an agreement or the outward expression of such intention is to be found first in the correspondence from the Respondent's architect, 15 April 1991 and the Claimant's reply to that letter 22 April 1991 which was not resiled from by the Respondent until this dispute arose.

Consider the unconvincing answers given by this architect in cross-examination when asked why he had not replied to the Claimant's letter.

1. Re RBL's letter 22 April, where they said 'must reserve right to remeasure'. Why not reply?—Because all had been agreed at 8 April meeting.
2. As letter, 22 April, was different from agreement, 8 April, why not reply and say 'no' to remeasure. We already have agreement—Possibly we should have.
3. What do you think the second paragraph of RBL's letter 22 April means? I.e. We would only ask for (remeasure) where significant alteration in value of item etc.—Thought this referred to variations therefore not inconsistent with our agreement.

27. The 'convincing proof' therefore is to be found in the absence of a response to the Claimant's letter 22 April 1991.

It is inconceivable that the reason for not replying, as given in evidence by Mr D'Iffy was that he thought Mr Hocking was referring to variations, therefore, his (Mr Hocking's) letter 'was not inconsistent with our agreement.'

We have evidence from Mr Bliss and Mr D'Iffy concerning the tightness of the budget for this job; £10,000 of which had already been eaten into by having to agree a higher than expected contract sum. At the slightest hint of an open-ended commitment to expend further monies you would have expected Mr D'Iffy to reply immediately confirming, what he says, was his understanding of the agreement reached.

He did not do so I submit, because Mr Hocking's letter 22 April 1991 truly reflected that agreement. It is only now that there is a dispute about the amount of remeasure and the additional cost thereof, that Mr D'Iffy seeks to resile from that previous agreement.

28. The *second condition* is that the written contract must fail to represent the prior concluded agreement or common intention because of a mistake of both parties. However, there are two exceptions to this requirement, where there may be rectification despite the mistake being made by only one of the parties; first, where the other party has taken advantage of the mistaken party in a way fraudulent to the eyes of equity; second, if one party to a transaction knows that the instrument contains a mistake in his favour but does nothing to correct it, he will be precluded from resisting rectification on the ground that the mistake is unilateral and not common.

29. In summary, for the reasons which follow, it is suggested that the finding whether or not condition 2 is satisfied is likely to turn on the finding in respect of condition 1.

30. If it is found that the Claimant has satisfied condition 1, the logical consequence is that the written agreement must fail to represent the parties' prior agreement/continuing intention because of a mistake. For if the parties intended/agreed one thing, it is hardly likely that they would have intended their written contract to say something quite different. Given that, the IFC '84 Form was signed under time pressure, at the end of 8 April site meeting when RBL had already been on-site for a week and SHL were anxious to tie them down to a contract sum, which was within their budget, it is easy to conceive how a common mistake occurred.

31. Of course, the Respondent says there was no mistake at all. There is, however, the same relationship between the Respondent's case on conditions 1 and 2 contention, as there is between the Claimant's case on these conditions: in effect the Respondent says there was no mistake *because* it was agreed at the contract signing meeting that all the works would be carried out for the contract sum subject only to the limited remeasure listed in the Respondent's letter 15 April 1991. Similarly, if condition 1 is resolved in the Respondent's favour, the logical consequence must be that there was no mistake.

32. If it be right that there was a common mistake, it follows that at some time since then the Respondent has decided to try to turn that mistake to its own advantage by contending, wrongly, that the IFC '84 Form, together with his letter 15 April 1991, accurately records the parties' agreement.

33. Alternatively, it is submitted that there was a unilateral mistake by Mr Hocking which the Respondent knew about. The Respondent realised at the time that by signing the IFC '84 Form the parties were apparently making an agreement which did not represent what had

been previously agreed and/or what was intended by the parties. The Claimant did not fully appreciate the significance of this. The Respondent knew that the Claimant had not understood the full significance of his action, but said nothing.

34. Once condition 1 is satisfied, the question whether there was a mistake and, if so, whether the mistake was common or unilateral is a matter of inference. For the Claimant's purposes, it matters not whether the Arbitrator concludes that the Respondent was a party to the mistake and subsequently sought to take advantage of it or whether the Arbitrator finds that the Respondent was not a party to the Claimant's mistake, but was aware of it. Either finding leads to the same conclusion.

35. In this context, a finding that Mr Hocking knew at the time he signed the IFC '84 Form that this contract did not include a right to remeasurement as agreed, does not preclude rectification.

36. The *third condition* is that it must be shown that the written contract was intended to represent the agreement or common intention of the parties. There is no suggestion on either side that it was intended to do anything else. The question is what they had agreed/what their common intention was prior to signing the contract.

37. So far as *condition four* is concerned, there is no suggestion, so far as the Claimant is aware, that if conditions 1 to 3 are satisfied, rectification should not be granted.

38. In summary, adopting Lord Diplock's analysis in *American Airlines*, the parties were *ad idem* about what work was to be done for the sum which had been quoted but that they used in IFC '84 words which were inapt to record the true agreement reached between them.

39. *In summary on this First Issue—When and How was the Contract Formed?* The Claimant contends that:

    (i) Agreement was reached at the site meeting on 8 April 1991

    (ii) (a) The terms are those of the JCT Intermediate Form of Building Contract—IFC '84 together with the specification and to include the remeasurement of items listed with the Respondent's letter 15 April 1991.

        (b) The Claimant has the right to remeasure any item which substantially departs from the quantities given at tender stage.

40. SECOND ISSUE—WHAT ARE THE TERMS AND CONDITIONS OF THE CONTRACT?

The Claimant accepts the Respondent's list as scheduled in the Respondent's Statement of Case for the Preliminary Issues, as scheduled in 9.1.1–9.1.6 provided the Claimant's letter to the Respondent's Architect, Mr D'Iffy, 22 April 1991, is also included.

41. THIRD ISSUE—WHAT, IF ANY ANY ITEMS OF CONTRACT WORKS ARE SUBJECT TO REMEASUREMENT?

42. (i) The contract sets out the items which are subject to variation plus the agreed list of remeasure items.

43. (ii) The draft Bill of Quantities entitled 'Tender Budget' was the Bill of Quantities as defined by the recitals in IFC '84. Accordingly any difference in quantities set out in this document is to be treated as a variation as detailed in Condition 1.4 of the Contract.

44. The following support this right of remeasurement.

45. (i) The Claimant relied on the quantities given at tender stage and the Respondent knew that tenderers would rely on these quantities. The tender period was too short for these quantities to be checked.

46. (ii) Prior to 8 April 1991 meeting Mr Hocking was aware that quantities already inaccurate. By the 8 April meeting RBL were working on-site so therefore were in a strong negotiated position.

47. The Respondent was in a weak negotiating position given the delay which would follow if another contractor had to be found.

48. Mr Hocking has already agreed to a lump-sum reduction and could not afford to take any risk over inaccuracies in quantities.

49. Mr D'Iffy, prior to 8 April meeting, had already formed a view that remeasurement would have little effect and could be to Respondent's advantage.

50. There was reference, at the Hearing of the Preliminary Issues, as to the order in which items were discussed at the 8 April meeting, i.e. reservation about total remeasurement first and then agreement only to remeasure certain items. Mr D'Iffy's failure to respond to Claimant's letter 22 April 1991 is best evidence of what was agreed at 8 April meeting.

5.17
144

51. FOURTH ISSUE—WHAT RATES ARE TO BE APPLIED TO THE CONTRACT WORKS IN GENERAL AND WHAT IS THE STATUS OF THE DISCOUNT?

52. In particular are the contract rates to be reduced by the same percentage that the negotiated discount bears to the original tender figure, as adjusted?

53. How is the percentage negotiated discount to apply to the contract rates and the contract sum?

54. (i) RBL were not prepared to reduce their individual rates but did reduce their price overall therefore the only reasonable construction was that this was a lump-sum reduction and not a reduction of the individual rates.

55. (ii) For the purpose of the monthly valuation only an overall reduction of 12 per cent was applied whereas the actual reduction was approx. 11.6 per cent. If Mr D'Iffy is right then RBL voluntarily reduced their rates by a further 0.4 per cent.

56. (iii) The use of 12 per cent reduction for the monthly valuations is more consistent with Mr Hocking's account than Mr D'Iffy's.

57. FIFTH ISSUE—GIBBS CEILING

The two experts in this matter are at odds. On the one hand Mr Simon Ambrose says that the ceiling is only a replica—it is not a Gibbs ceiling, *circa* 1724, and on the other hand Mr Simon Rector, says the opposite.

58. My submission is that Mr Rector is wrong.

59. Mr Rector in evidence relies upon three items to reach the view that the ceiling is *circa* 1724.

  (i) Paint conversion.
  (ii) The 'Four' coats of paint.
  (iii) The erosion of nails.

60. (i) Paint conversion

Paint 'conversion' has occurred but would not have done so if it were less than two centuries old.

61. However, it is not open to the Arbitrator to accept such evidence at all. In cross-examination Mr Rector admits, quite candidly, that he was *not* competent to give such evidence. He had relied upon adduce by an unnamed analytical laboratory, merely repeating

what he had been told by the laboratory. Such hearsay evidence is inadmissible in law save where a notice is served under the Civil Evidence Acts 1968 and 1972. No such Notice was given.

62. I submit therefore that the paint conversion point must go.

63. (ii) Four coats of paint

Mr Rector says it is significant that four layers of decoration had been applied, since the original paintwork, and goes on to say that the number of layers is hardly indicative of a mid–late-nineteenth century date for its construction. But, in cross-examination, Mr Rector admitted that the 'mere number of coats was no real guide to a product's age ... it is an indication merely'.

5.17
145

64. Mr Rector appears to seriously back away from his earlier remark that the four coats is *significant* evidence of age.

65. I submit that the number of coats of paint was no evidence at all. The ceiling could have received any number of coats in 70–100 years.

66. (iii) Erosion of nails

Mr Rector had tried, with points 1 and 2 above, to indicate age but, in my view, substantially fails.

67. He then tried to age the ceiling by saying that the ferrous cut nails have eroded and as such erosion could hardly occur in *less* then 150 years, therefore the ceiling is Gibbs.

68. I submit that if Mr Rector could show that the whole of the ceiling, or even a major part of it, was installed in this way he *may* get home.

69. Rector admitted in cross-examination that mere fragments only, of the ceiling, were examined. He also admitted that he could not be confident that the whole of the work was installed using ferrous cut nails. Is it enough from these fragments to say that the whole of the ceiling was nailed in this way, I submit that Mr Rector went too far.

70. Finally I ask the arbitrator to turn to Mr Ambrose for greater assistance, in considering this matter.

71. In particular, he commented about the ceiling containing not only the traditional horse hair but human hair as well. It is there, he says, quite simply because horse hair, at this late date, was not available in sufficient quantities.

72. But Mr Rector has given no thought to the hair type at all. Candidly, he says, it is a topic he 'never thought to concern myself with' although he admits to having been surprised by the proposition of his opposing expert as to the shortage of horse hair, believing that horses were still in common use.

73. In effect, Mr Rector offers little assistance or resistance to Mr Ambrose's important point.

74. You may recall, Sir, my concluding question, in cross-examination which was ...

'If your observation about the nails and the paint are unsupported, you are left with nothing by way of objective considerations to base your conclusions upon, do you agree?'

75. To which Mr Rector replied that it was a 'portmanteau' of a question which he said at first was not capable of a concise answer, but went on to make some attempt to answer.

76. I submit that if Mr Rector's hearsay evidence goes, and if his observations about four coats of paint is weak, he is left only with a few fragments of nails which had eroded.

77. This by no means supports his contention that the fragments were 150 years old, either by offering evidence of tests or reasons why he can give such conclusive evidence; there is nothing whatsoever to corroborate his somewhat offhand remark.

78. The concise response to Mr Rector's expert evidence is to reject his proposition and find that the work is as described by his opponent expert.

79. I now deal finally with the flooded basement issue.

80. Flooding of the Basement

81. The Respondent says it is all the fault of the contractor because he, the contractor, did not comply with the architect's specification. The contractor, on the other hand, says that he constructed the basement precisely in accordance with what the architect required in his written specification.

82. A surveyor, Mr Longdon, has been engaged by the Respondent to lend support to the complaint against the contractor and that his report said that the Bituthene tanking to the walls of the basement had not been carried high enough in the verticals. He says that it is 6 inches too low; he also says that the Respondent's architect made it clear what level was required.

83. It is common ground that the architect specified the required height. His specification required the tanking (to) 'existing walls to a height to be determined as 150 mm above the highest recorded level of the water table immediately adjacent to the property'.

84. Notice that the architect has not given a datum for the tanking height. Instead he relied upon the contractor to find the highest ever level and then plot the datum from that. The Claimant builder has no complaint about that burden. Indeed, if it becomes clear that it can be shown that the builder did indeed plot the correct datum and carry the tanking up to the level plus 150 mm then no complaint could lie at the builders feet.

85. My closing submission would demonstrate that the builder did all he was asked and did it properly.

86. There are, I submit, three key questions to be faced.

(i) What *is* the highest recorded level of the water table?

(ii) Having established *that* level, what level ought the tanking to have been carried up to?

(iii) Did the contractor carry the tanking to that level?

87. On the question of the highest recorded level, according to Mr Longdon's investigation with the architect, that level was 760 mm (two feet six inches) below ground level and the Building Control Officer (BCO) apparently says almost the same thing.

88. It is, Sir, I submit, fair to conclude that the highest level is 760/750 mm below ground. Mr Longdon, in any event does not contradict this conclusion.

89. I now go on to deal with the second question, that is: What level ought the tanking to have been carried up?

90. If the architect specified a level of 150 mm above the highest level then the tanking ought to be no lower than 600 mm below ground.

91. Did he ask the contractor to carry the tanking to that level at least?

92. Mr Longdon for the Respondent, says no. He says that the tanking is at 750 mm below the ground but his own expert David Sharkey says that the tanking does meet the 600 mm datum at least.

93. Mr Sharkey has carried out and reported to the Learned Arbitrator a very detailed survey not only of the house grounds as a whole but of the ground levels adjacent to the basement. But, by contrast, Mr Longdon while saying he has carried out some careful measurements and calculations, leaves his report bare of such detail.

94. Concentrate on Mr Sharkey's report. The ground level immediately outside the basement is paved (but no mention of this paving was made by Mr Longdon) and is at 2.835 meters datum. Deducts 100 mm for paving and a further 750 mm for the water table. The result is datum of 1.985.

95. Is submitted that the tanking ought to be 150 mm higher than this datum which is 2.135.

Mr Sharkey confirms that this datum level is *higher* than this for the tanking and that it is at 2.145. In other words, the contractor has done all that he was required to do.

96. But why the discrepancy between the two experts?

97. Mr Longdon, in cross-examination, said 'I simply measured down from the ground level'. He makes no mention of paving and may well have overlooked that important item. In any event, it is submitted, that the thoroughness of Mr Sharkey's commentary provides an element of confidence which is absent from the opposing surveyor.

98. The Learned Arbitrator is also reminded that the burden of proof regarding the issue rests on the Respondent. It is he who says the builder fell into error. In which case, the Respondent must prove it.

99. If it is that two expert witnesses directly contradict each other such that the Arbitrator cannot decide which witness he prefers, I respectfully point out, that the Arbitrator must now ask which party has the burden of proof. That party must prove his allegations. If the scales remain even between the two parties then the party with the burden should fail to get home.

100. I submit that the Respondent had failed to prove his allegation and that the builder had done all that he had been asked to do.

Toby Belcher
6 June 1993

5.17
147

Interim Declaratory Award (5.18 Arb)

IN THE MATTER OF THE ARBITRATION ACTS 1950 TO 1979

AND

IN THE MATTER OF AN ARBITRATION UNDER THE JCT ARBITRATION RULES (18 JULY 1988)

BETWEEN

RELIABLE BUILDERS LIMITED   Claimant

AND

SANCTUARY HOUSE LIMITED   Respondent

INTERIM DECLARATORY AWARD

1.00 Background to the Dispute

1.01 Reliable Builders Limited (RBL) the Claimant, is a long-established construction company, founded in 1924 which, on 31 January 1991, submitted a tender for the refurbishment and extension of Sanctuary House (as it was to become known) in Woodbridge, Suffolk. Sanctuary House had been purchased, by the Respondent company (SHL), for the specific purpose of converting it into a nursing home, catering for the middle to top of the nursing home market.

1.02 SHL engaged the services of The Architectural Practice of Norwich (TAP) to undertake the design work, the calling of tenders and the supervision of the works of conversion and extension.

The principal of this practice, Mr Max D'Iffy, was familiar with this property, having worked on it for the previous owners. Mr D'Iffy had the added advantage that he, and his practice not only had experience of designing nursing homes but also was experienced at work of refurbishment on listed and schedule buildings.

Although Mr D'Iffy was the Architect 'named' in the Contract—the day-to-day work was carried out by his assistant, an Associate Partner, Miss Frances Hutch.

1.03 The Contract governing this project is as set out in 3.01 below.

So far as the works themselves are concerned, the only variation in the lump-sum price, which is permitted under this standard Contract, is for variations ordered by the Employer under the terms of this Contract.

1.04 The invitations to tender were sent out on 7 January 1991 and returned 31 January 1991.

TAP had sufficient experience of this sort of job in the past to know that the small local builder invited to tender would probably only put in a genuine tender if some sort of Bill of Quantities was provided. TAP did not consider that the size or complexity of the project warranted the full-blown services of a professional quantity surveyor but they did engage one to prepare, what was described on its cover, as follows:

Tender Budget—Nov '90.
Draft Bill of Quantities—For Guidance Only
Sanctuary House Limited are not liable for any
inaccuracies in quantities or dimensions.

1.05 In addition to sending out this Tender Budget with the Invitation to Tender, there was, *inter alia*, a document, described on its cover, as follows:

Specification of Works—dated Nov. 1990

1.06 Included on page 2/7 of this Specification, under the main heading of the Employer's Requirements—was the following note:

LUMP-SUM PRICE

'The Contractor is reminded that under no circumstances will substructures or any work to the buildings or external works be remeasured or payment increased due to additional costs incurred in substructure works of buildings, above those shown in the Bill of Quantities.'

5.18 Arb 149

1.07 The letter of Invitation, 7 January 1991, asked tenderers to submit their tenders not later than Thursday 31 January 1991, 'accompanied by your priced Bill of Quantities'.

1.08 The letter of Invitation to Tender also included the following clause:

'The successful tenderer will be bound by the appropriate conditions of the standard JCT Intermediate Form of Building Contract (IFC '84) 1990 Edition.'

1.09 Condition 1.2 of the Conditions of this contract provides, *inter alia*, as follows:

'Where and to the extent that quantities are contained in the Specification . . . , and there are no Contract Bills, the quality and quantity of the work included in the Contract Sum for the relevant items shall be deemed to be that which is set out in the Specification . . .'

Condition 1.5 headed Contract Bills and SMM reads

'Where the Contract Documents include Contract Bills, the Contract Bills unless otherwise expressly stated therein in respect of any specified item or items are to have been prepared in accordance with the Standard Method of Measurement of Building Works, 6th Edition published by the Royal Institution of Chartered Surveyors and the National Federation of Building Trades Employers.'

1.10 Mr Hocking, the managing director of RBL, dealt with all tender enquiries although not with the detailed preparation of their tender. Following an expression of interest, as a result of a telephone call from TAP sometime just before Christmas 1990, documents were sent to RBL on 7 January 1991 although these were not received until 10 January and, as a result, they were

'not left with much time to price the bills of quantities which was included with the invitation tender as we had to get prices in from various subcontractors.'

1.11 Mr Hocking went on to say, in his proof, that the tender documents

'did not provide information such as levels to enable earthwork quantities to be checked.' Furthermore 'there was no time to check the quantities, or prepare our own. All we could do was to visit the site.'

1.12 It is common ground that a drawing entitled 'Site Level Drawing S1.70' was, *inter alia*, included with the 7 January letter of Invitation to Tender.

1.13 Under cross-examination Mr Hocking did not deny that RBL had received details of levels with the tender documentation.

RBL chose not to carry out any independent check on the levels and relied on the quantities scheduled in the Tender Budget, despite the warning that these were 'For Guidance Only'. Even when Mr Hocking started getting concerned, as early as 7 April 1991, barely one week into the contract when less than 25 per cent of the topsoil stripping had been carried out, he did not attempt to undertake an independent check on the quantities although the information was available to him as, indeed, it had been at tender stage.

1.14 RBL submitted their Tender, dated 31 January 1991, in the form of a handwritten summary sheet, under cover of the following letter, the entirety of which was as follows:

'Further to your invitation to tender for the above works we have pleasure in quoting a figure of £617,148.24 ex VAT as per the attached summary sheet.

If you require any additional information, please contact the undersigned.'

No reservation was made about the lack of time to check the quantities or the reservation of the right to remeasure works on completion.

5.18 Arb 150

1.15 Mr D'Iffy had been hoping for a price within his client's budget figure of £540,000 and as a result, following receipt of RBL's tender, various telephone conversations took place between Mr D'Iffy and Mr Hocking.

A note made by Mr D'Iffy on RBL's letter 31 January 1991 reads, *inter alia*,

'Need the work, will talk price less 10 per cent.'

1.16 TAP carried out an exercise comparing RBL's rates with those of other tenderers with a view to persuading RBL to reduce some of their individual rates and in this manner he hoped to bring down their tender nearer to SHL's target figure. On 16 February, Mr D'Iffy telephoned Mr Hocking but he was not prepared to reduce these individual rates.

There is some dispute as to who made what offer or counteroffer during these various telephone conversations which took place between 20 February and 7 March but it is common ground that it was on 7 March that a figure of £550,000 ex VAT, was agreed.

This agreement was confirmed by TAP, by letter dated 20 March 1991, to RBL as follows:

'Further to your recent telephone conversations, we write to confirm that, it is our client's intention to enter into a contract with your company in accordance with the tender that you submitted on 31 January last but in the agreed revised sum of the sum of £550,000 ex VAT.

As specified, the contract is the JCT Intermediate Form—IFC '84, and my assistant, Miss Hutch, will prepare a document for your signature, and forward it to you shortly. This is, of course, a fixed-price lump-sum contract, not subject to remeasurement.'

In the meantime, we are pleased to confirm that, you should proceed with the works commencing Tuesday 2 April, and that you will be reimbursed all reasonable costs incurred in the unlikely event that a contract is not entered into.'

1.17 RBL replied to this letter, 28 March 1991, and said, *inter alia*,

'Thank you for your letter 20 March ... We note that you consider our quotation as a lump sum at a fixed price of £550,000 ex VAT. We would point out that our tender was compiled on the basis of the quantities which you sent to us with your invitation to tender. We did not have time to prepare our own Bill nor the opportunity to check yours, so we cannot see how the contract can be a fixed price.'

'With regard to the main superstructure items in your Bill, we have no reason to beleive [*sic*] that these are not correct and we will check them and do not intend to argue over minor percentages either way. Our concern is more for the earthworks and the effect of soft spots, deeper topsoil and the effect it would have on the muck away and the imported sub-base filling. We will of course have your interest at heart as well as our own and will try to keep all costs to a minimum, but we hope that you, or your site agent, if you use one, will agree the formation levels as they are formed. To this end the earthworks and infilling quantities can be agreed and will be paid for accordingly.'

1.18 TAP telephoned RBL, in reply to this letter and suggested that the question of the fixed-price lump-sum nature of the contract would best be resolved at a meeting and went on to suggest that the site meeting, scheduled for the following day, 8 April, would be a convenient opportunity for this.

1.19 Present at that meeting were the following:

For RBL	For TAP/SHL
Harry Hocking—M/D	William Bliss C/M SHL
William Reeves	Max D'Iffy Snr Ptnr TAP
Cont. Administrator	Frances Hutch Job Arch TAP
John Watts	
Site Foreman	
Joel Redman—Surveyor	

5.18 Arb
151

1.20 It is common ground that, at the conclusion of the meeting, Messrs D'Iffy and Hocking agreed a list of items which would be subject to remeasure and this list was sent to RBL with TAP's letter 15 April 1991.

It is also common ground that, following agreement of this list, Mr D'Iffy then invited Mr Hocking to sign the standard form of contract, IFC '84, which had been prepared previously.

This contract made no reference to the list of items which would be remeasured, on which it is alleged by Mr D'Iffy, total agreement had been reached.

It is further common ground that, in inviting Mr Hocking to sign the standard IFC '84 Form of Contract, Mr D'Iffy said that he would write shortly and confirm the substance of the agreement that he had just reached with Mr Hocking over the list of items subject to remeasurement.

Subsequently TAP wrote, on 15 April 1991, to RBL, in the following terms:

'Further to our meeting on-site on 8th April 1991, we confirm that the IFC '84 Terms will apply except that remeasurement will take place, limited to items agreed at that meeting and listed on the attached sheet.

Please confirm, in writing, your agreement to the list which will be incorporated into the contact documents.'

1.21 RBL's reply, 22 April 1991, to this letter was as follows:

'We acknowledge your letter 15 April and confirm our acceptance of the items listed which are to be remeasured.

We must however reserve the right to ask for a remeasure of any items that we find are substantially more than your Bill of Quantities. We will only ask for this to be done if we feel that the financial effect is a significant increase in the value of a particular Bill item.'

1.22 TAP did not reply to this letter for reasons dealt with later.

1.23 In November 1992 the following exchange of correspondence took place, in which were made, *inter alia*, the following statements:

TAP to RBL 2 Nov 1992
'We are in receipt of your remeasures for the above project and would refer you to our letter of 15 April 1991.

We are currently analysing your figures and we will advise you of our findings in due course.'

RBL to TAP 9 Nov 1992
'We note your reference to your letter 15 April 1991, but, in turn, would refer you to our reply dated 22 April 1991 and also our concern, mentioned on numerous occasions, both to your Mr D'Iffy and to Miss Hutch, over the original quantities compared to the revised design layout and the scheme as being built.'

RBL to TAP 18 Nov 1992
'. . . we are still very concerned about the interpretation of the tender reduction in respect of the additional subcontract works.

We would therefore appreciate a further site meeting, if possible for Monday 23 November, to resolve this matter ...'

TAP to RBL 20 Nov 1992

'The original intention was that this is a lump-sum contract based on your tender figure—as adjusted—and subsequently reduced by agreement by 12 per cent.

At our meeting together on 8 April 1991 we agreed to a limited remeasurement based on your tender rates, less 12 per cent. The list of items which we agreed would be remeasured were sent to you with our letter 15 April 1991.'

RBL to TAP 25 Nov 1992

'We note that you believe that the original tender documents should form a lump sum without variations despite our telling you, at the time, that this was not acceptable to us.

As we pointed out, quantities could change for reasons beyond our control.'

'We were led to believe that the design and layout of the works was final and that the quantities set out in your Tender Budget, which accompanied your invitation to tender, were accurate within minor amounts either way. We refer to our reservations stated in our letter 28 March 1991 and 22 April 1991.

Since then ... all elements have been revised ... to incorporate various changes which have resulted in major increases in each element.

For many months you have refused to accept these changes ... we cannot allow this matter to drift on.

On the question of discount we cannot accept that the percentage reduction applies to the rates for all additional work. We were led to believe that in agreeing to a reduction of £72,171.95 to get the job, the overall contract value would not materially change. It was your surveyor, not ours, who decided to convert this reduction into a percentage.

Of course, we stand by the reduction in the tender figure but we require the full rates for our tender to be applied to all additional works.'

TAP to RBL 27 Nov 1992

'We only agree to remeasure those items listed following the 8 April meeting and rates for this remeasure are subject to the 12 per cent adjustment.

The quants. sent to you, at tender stage, were indicative only—it was for you to assess the quantities of work to be done. We do not agree that the design has radically altered since tender stage.'

RBL to TAP 10 Dec 1992

'Both Mr D'Iffy and Miss Hutch have constantly assured us that we would be treated fairly over our final account but that does not seem to be the case ...

'... We must reiterate our previous position; we cannot accept that your quantities were only indicative. At the tender stage you requested us to accept these as the basis for a lump-sum agreement but we said that this was not acceptable due to the lack of detail and the shortness of time before we had to start on-site. You led us to believe that your quantities were reasonably accurate within minor percentages and your letter 27 November is the first time we have heard it suggested that these quantities were indicative only.'

TAP to RBL 11 Dec 1992

'We refer to your letter 10 December. We have clearly stated our position on a number of occasions and cannot usefully add to what we have already said.'

1.24 Following this exchange of correspondence the parties were unable to agree and following a Notice of a Dispute the Claimant applied, on 1 February 1993, to the Royal Institution of Chartered Surveyors for the appointment of an arbitrator, in accordance with Art. 5 of IFC '84.

1.25 The interlocutory stage that lead from my appointment to the hearing of the Preliminary Issues is covered in the recitals to this Award.

1.26 In the event both parties submitted their own Statement of Case covering the Preliminary Issues. (See 5.05 below).

WHEREAS

2.00 The works

2.01 On or about 7 January 1991 the Respondent (SHL) invited the Claimant (RBL) to tender for the Refurbishment and Extension of a Georgian period residential property, The Old Manor House (now known as Sanctuary House), situated in Woodbridge, Suffolk. The completed project was to be used for a nursing home for the frail elderly.

2.02 The Claimants submitted their Tender on 31 January 1991 in the sum of £617,148.24 ex VAT. After an exchange of telephone conversations, and some correspondence, a revised price of £550,000 ex VAT was agreed. On 20 March 1991 a letter of intent was sent to RBL, who started work on the site on 2 April 1991.

**5.18 Arb
153**

3.00 The contract

3.01 The Form of Contract is the JCT intermediate Form of Building Contract (IFC '84) 1990 Edition signed, by both parties on 8 April 1991.

3.02 Article 5 of IFC '84 is an Arbitration Clause.

4.00 Appointment

4.01 Disputes having arisen I, DAVID EMSEE of Toad Hall, Hunstanton Water, Norfolk, was appointed by the President of the Royal Institution of Chartered Surveyors, by appointment dated 20 February 1993.

4.02 The reference is governed by the JCT Arbitration Rules (1988) and I informed the parties that the Notification Date under these Rules was 24 February 1993.

5.00 Interlocutories and Hearing

5.01 A Preliminary Meeting took place, between me, the parties and their representatives, on 23 March 1993 at the Claimant's surveyors offices in Ipswich, Suffolk.

The Claimant had not informed me that he wished Rule 7 to apply. The Respondent informed me, by letter 28 February 1993, that he would only attend the Preliminary meeting 'without prejudice'. It subsequently transpired that the reason for this reservation was a jurisdictional point.

Agreement was reached, at the Preliminary meeting that Rule 6 should apply.

5.02 It was also agreed that I should determine some preliminary issues in advance of the substantive issues and although a timetable was agreed for service of the Statements on the substantive issues, this timetable was not to be activated until 28 days after the publication of the award on the preliminary issues.

5.03 The matters to be determined as preliminary issues were set out in my Order for Direction No 2, dated 25 March 1993.

5.04 A timetable was agreed for the exchange of the Statement of Case and Statement of Defence of the Preliminary Issues and a hearing date set for 24 May 1993. By consent, only two days were set aside to hear these issues and the time available to be shared equally between both parties.

5.05 In the event the Respondent's Counsel decided to also serve a Statement of Case.

He took the view that, on preliminary issues, each side is entitled to plead its own case, not be forced to counter the other sides arguments. I concurred with Counsel's submission on this and accepted the Respondent's Statement of Case contrary to my original direction.

5.06 Various other directions were given By Consent restricting orality at this hearing including one concerning exchange of witness proofs and their admission as evidence in chief. I further directed that:

> 'Except, by my leave (which will only be given in special circumstances) no witnesses may be called at the Hearing unless a written proof of evidence has been provided in accordance with (the preceding paragraph) and no evidence-in-chief may be adduced by a witness to any issue which has not been included in the written proof of evidence of that witness either specifically or in general terms to the supporting documentation to that party's statement.'

5.18 Arb 154

5.07 The Respondent's Counsel requested a Reasoned Award and, in accordance with the provisions of Rule 11.1, made that request in writing, at the beginning of the Hearing on the Preliminary Issues, when he defined the extent to which he required those reasons to be given.

5.08 Both parties confirmed that they did not wish to enter into an Exclusion Agreement under s.3 of the 1979 Arbitration Act.

5.09 The day before the Hearing, 23 May 1993, the Claimant made application to introduce one piece of fresh evidence and a witness proof, for a new witness which he now wished to call.

5.09.1 The Respondent objected to both applications and cited their grounds in their faxed letter 23 May.

5.09.2 I dealt with these applications at the commencement of the Hearing the following day.

5.09.3 In the event I decided that, provided that there was no prejudice to the Respondent I would admit the fresh evidence and allow the additional witness.

5.09.4 I accepted the Claimant's plea that this new witness had, until quite recently, been living overseas and that, as a result, the Claimant had believed that it would not be possible to call him. He admitted that he was aware that it was permissible to take evidence by affidavit, under such circumstances, but, in the interests of keeping down the parties costs, he had decided against that course of action.

5.09.5 I permitted the Respondent's Counsel to read the new proof before I saw it myself and invited him to address me on its admission.

5.09.6 After hearing Counsel for both sides I directed that the fresh evidence be admitted—although, in the event, it was never referred to—and the additional witness proof and witness also be admitted. I did however reserve the right to penalise the Claimant on costs if the introduction of this fresh evidence, or his additional witness, clearly added to the costs of the reference.

AND NOW

I, the said, D. EMSEE, having considered the submissions made by, and on behalf of, both parties,

DO HEREBY MAKE AND PUBLISH THIS MY INTERIM DECLARATORY AWARD

6.00 The Claimant claimed:

6.001   (i) A declaration that the terms of the agreement between the parties is as set out in paragraph 5.1 hereof; alternatively, paragraphs 5.2 herein,

6.002   (ii) Alternatively, insofar as is necessary and without prejudice to the Claimant's contentions in paragraph 5 above, an order that the written contract be rectified so as to embody the agreement actually made between the Claimant and the Respondent or their true intentions at the time of exercising the same in the respects set out above and to have the said agreement treated as being so rectified.

6.003   (iii) A declaration that the Claimant is entitled to have the works measured and valued as set out in paragraphs 5, 7 and 8 herein; (the Claimant's Statement of Case).

6.004   (iv) Alternatively, a declaration that the Claimant is entitled to be paid on a *quantum meruit* basis as set out in paragraph 8 herein; (The Claimant's Statement of Case).

6.005   (v) A declaration that the Claimant is entitled to the sums claimed under paragraph 8 herein (the Claimant's Statement of Case) and/or an order that the Respondent do pay such sums.

6.006   (vi) A declaration that the 'Gibbs ceiling is not genuine but a latter date reproduction.

6.007   (vii) A declaration that the Claimant had complied with the terms of the contract concerning the waterproofing of the basement specifically clause 3.15a of the Specification.

6.008   (viii) Interest pursuant to Section 19A of the Arbitration Act 1950.

6.01 Paragraphs 4–8 inclusive of the Claimant's Statement of Case, referred to above, read as follows:

6.02 Paragraph 4.1

On its true construction, the conduct of the Respondent after receipt of the Claimants' letter 22 April 1991, was an acceptance, by the Respondent, that the works would be carried out by the Claimant on the following terms:

4.1.1 That the Articles and Conditions of the IFC '84 Contract would apply, including Recital 2nd B.

4.1.2 That the items on the list attached to the Respondent's letter 15 April 1991, would be remeasured.

4.1.3 That if, in the Claimant's opinion, the quantity set out for any item in the Bills of Quantity increased such as to make a significant alteration to the value of any item, that item would be remeasured.

Paragraph 4.2

Alternatively, if, which is denied, Recital 2nd A and not Recital 2nd B is incorporated into the contract between the parties, that the quantities in the Bills of Quantities were reasonably accurate.

Paragraph 5

It is the Claimant's primary case that, the errors in the quantities included in the Bills of Quantities, provided by the Respondent with his invitation to tender, are such as to entitle the Claimant to a remeasure of the whole of the contract works.

5.18 Arb
155

Paragraph 6

6.1 If contrary to the Claimant's primary case, which is set out in paragraph 4 above, the contrast is contained solely in documents which do not include the Claimant's right to remeasurement, as set out in paragraph 4.1.3 above, the Claimant will contend:

6.1.1 That by reason of a common mistake by the parties and/or a mistake by the Claimant which the Respondent knew, or ought to have known of the said contract documents do not represent

6.1.1.1 the agreement which the parties made at their meeting, 8 April 1991 and which is evidenced by the Claimant's letter 22 April 1991, which is set out in paragraph 2.11 above: and/or

6.1.1.2 the parties common continuing intention and/or the Claimant's intention which is outwardly expressed in the Claimant's letter 22 April 1991 set out in paragraph 2.11 above.

6.1.2 And accordingly the said contract should be rectified so as to embody the agreement actually made between the parties or their true intentions at the time. The actual agreement and/or their true intentions is set out in paragraph 2.11 above.

6.2 The Claimant will rely on the provisions of IFC '84, clause 9.3, which expressly empowers the Arbitrator to rectify the contract so that it accurately reflects the true agreement made between the Claimant and the Respondent.

Paragraph 7

In the alternative, if, which is denied, the parties did not reach agreement on the basis set out in paragraph 4 herein, then the Claimant will contend that it was an implied term of the contract that the Claimant was entitled to be paid a *quantum meruit* for the additional contract works arising from a remeasure rather than a sum calculated in accordance with the rules set out in IFC '84 clauses 3.7.1 to 3.7.9.

The said term is to be implied in order to give effect to the presumed intention of the parties and/or to give the contract business efficacy. Alternatively, the Claimant is entitled to be paid an additional sum for the additional contract works remeasured as a result of paragraph 4.1.3 above, calculated in accordance with the rules set out in clauses 3.7.1. to 3.7.9. of the said IFC contract.

And, on either alternative, the Claimant is entitled to the sum claimed in his Draft Final Account, dated 30 October 1992.

Paragraph 8

Further, the agreement for a discount, referred to in paragraph 2.7 herein, was a lump-sum discount and accordingly, any valuations to be carried out in accordance with the terms set out in paragraph 4 herein, are to be carried out by reference to the rates set out in the Bills of Quantities submitted by the Claimant (where applicable) as adjusted by agreement between the parties—see para. 2.6 herein—but before the application of the lump-sum reduction referred to in para. 2.7 herein.

6.03 Miss O'Brien for the Respondent, in her Statement of Case on these Preliminary Issues, set out six issues which she requested me to determine.

6.03.1 How and when was the contract formed?

Sub-Issue 1. Whether the contract is to be found:
(i) solely in the IFC '84 Form or,
(ii) whether it is also to be found in the letters to which the Claimant refers in subpara. 2.11 of its Statement of Case?

5.18 Arb
156

Sub-Issue 2. If (ii) in 6.03.1 above, whether all the contract documents when read together will have the effect for which the Claimant contends?

Sub-Issue 3. If (i) in 6.03.1 above, whether the contract should be rectified?

6.03.2 What are the Terms and Conditions of the contract?

6.03.3 What items are subject to remeasurement?

6.03.4 What rates are to be applied to the contract work in general and the status of the discount?

6.03.5 The Gibbs Ceiling—is it genuine?

6.03.6 Is the builder in breach of contract over the waterproofing of the basement?

6.04 Mr Belcher, for the Claimant, agreed that, for convenience, I should determine the six discreet issues defined by Miss O'Brien as set out in 6.03 above and I would not be required to deal separately with the points of claim in his Statement of Case but would consider them in conjunction with the Respondent's issues.

5.18 Arb
157

Each of the Preliminary Issues were then considered, in turn, with Mr Belcher opening for the Claimant.

7.00 First issue

How and when was the Contract formed?

7.01 Mr Belcher, in his Opening Submissions, posed three sub-issues to Miss O'Brien's First Issue for me to consider.

7.02 Sub-Issue 1

Whether the Contract is to be found

7.02.1 solely in the IFC '84 Form or

7.02.2 whether it is also to be found in the letters to which the Claimant refers in subparagraph 2.11 of its Statement of Case.

7.03 Sub-Issue 2

7.03.1 If (7.02.2), whether all the contract documents when read together will have the effect for which the Claimant contends.

Claimant contends:

7.03.2 That a true construction of the contract is contained in all the documents which are pleaded and not exclusively in IFC '84 contract.

7.04 Sub-Issue 3

If (7.02.1) whether the written contract should be rectified.

7.05 Sub-Issues 1 & 2

7.05.1 I consider these two issues together. In summary, in his Closing Submissions, Mr Belcher suggested that at the heart of the case as a whole is the fact that the IFC '84 Form, taken in isolation, did not represent the true intentions of the parties, first, with regard to the definition of the contract works.

7.05.2 Firstly, I consider the facts surrounding the formation of this contract and then consider the law relating to the facts found which Counsel have succinctly put to me.

7.06 The key players at the 8 April 1991 meeting were Mr Hocking for the Claimant and Messrs Bliss and D'Iffy for the Respondent.

All, who were present, are clear that two main issues were dealt with:

(i) General contractual matters.

(ii) the whole question of the extent of the remeasure.

Mr Hocking, and his two colleagues, all steadfastly maintain that, throughout the meeting, he reserved his position to remeasure any item if the quantities proved incorrect. Mr Hocking averred that this reservation was only tempered by his conceding that a 2–3 per cent variation would be acceptable—i.e. for this he would not seek a remeasure.

Mr D'Iffy and Miss Hutch accept both that the reservation was made and also the proviso re the 2/3 per cent variation. However, the crucial difference between the parties is at what stage in the meeting was this reservation made?

The Claimant says that he never waivered from his line. He reserved the right, throughout, to seek remeasurement where it was obvious that the quantities—provided by the Respondent at the time of tender—entitled 'Tender Budget'—were incorrect.

Mr Reeves, for the Claimant, said that Mr Hocking *started* the discussion with the total remeasurement point and

'We discussed a number of items which were connected with our work on this contract. In doing so it seemed clear from the amount of variation that the argument for remeasure was overwhelming and it was clear to me that the Respondent agreed.'

7.07 Another of the Claimant's witnesses Mr John Watts suggested that a discussion of the Terms and Conditions of the Contract preceded Mr Hocking's reservation about the right to remeasure all, or any, items of work with which RBL were concerned. He went on to suggest that he took the agreement to remeasure to mean a

'total remeasure . . . this is certainly what I took Mr Hocking to have agreed to'.

7.08 In the event, Mr Joel Redman, for whom, the Claimant had sought special leave, at the commencement of the Hearing, to introduce, was not called.

7.09 Mr Belcher conceded that it was common ground that the contract was formed at the 8 April 1991 meeting, when the parties met to discuss the Claimant's concern over remeasurement. This was also confirmed, more than once, by Mr Hocking, under cross-examination.

7.10 The Respondent's witnesses, on the other hand, were clear as to the line they adopted at this meeting which—although a scheduled site meeting—was dedicated to resolving the question of what items would be remeasured.

7.11 The Respondent was locked into a tight budget with his bankers and was naturally anxious to tie down his building contractor to a lump-sum fixed-price contract.

RBL, being already on-site by the 8 April meeting, TAP/SHL had little choice but to accommodate, to some extent, their demands for remeasure.

RBL say, that by the time of this meeting they had already detected some significant differences in the quantities. However, Mr D'Iffy, for the Respondent, was anxious not to agree an open-ended remeasure but conceded a limited remeasure. For this reason, Messrs Hocking and D'Iffy met alone at the end of the 8 April meeting and actually agreed which items were to be the subject of remeasurement.

7.12 I prefer the Respondent's version of what happened at this 8 April meeting and I believe Mr Hocking made his reservations known at the early part of the meeting, as confirmed by his own witness Mr Reeves. This was unacceptable to the Respondent who then, reluctantly, agreed to partial remeasure, the precise nature of which was to be agreed between Messrs Hocking and D'Iffy.

If, Mr Hocking had, as he avers, made it clear that he maintained his right to total remeasurement, if necessary, why then agree a specific list of items to be remeasured?

Such a course of action, in agreeing this list, is inconsistent with common sense, indeed, it could be said that Messrs Watts and Reeves's evidence is not inconsistent with my reading of events.

7.13 The Respondents are quite clear what they agreed at the 8 April meeting. That is why the 22 April 1991 letter, from RBL was not replied to—it merely recorded what Mr D'Iffy believed they had agreed. He had sent a list of the items that he and Mr Hocking had agreed, following 8 April meeting, would be remeasured. Mr Hocking confirmed his acceptance of that list but then went on to . . .

> 'reserve the right to ask for a remeasure on any item which we find are substantially more than your Bill of Quantities. We will only ask for this to be done if we feel that the financial effect is a significant increase in the value of a particular Bill item.'

**5.18 Arb
159**

This last point, Mr D'Iffy took to refer to the 2/3 per cent variation that Mr Hocking had suggested at 8 April meeting, he would be prepared to absorb.

The earlier part of the reservation he took to mean that Mr Hocking required any work which was the subject of a change order, to be remeasured. This, of course, he did not object to. Indeed, it is what the contract conditions already provide. Had he read this reservation as being a repeat of the line taken by Mr Hocking at the beginning of 8 April meeting, that he could have a total remeasure if the quantities included in the Tender Budget varied by more than 3 per cent, then I am certain, from the evidence I heard, that Mr D'Iffy would have replied immediately to that letter, making it clear what was his understanding of the agreement reached on 8 April.

SHL were locked into a tight budget for this project; a Budget made tighter by the £10,000 tender excess on building costs and their concession to partial remeasurement. As a result they were anxious to tie down the contractor, as much as possible, in order to minimise their risk. On this point the Respondent's witnesses evidence was consistent and convincing.

7.14 I believe Mr Hocking misunderstands the status of Bill of Quantities. He stated, in evidence-in-chief, that Bills of Quantities and lump-sum prices do not go together. However, this is not the case.

The most commonly used form of lump-sum contract, for building works, is the JCT '80 Form with Quantities. In such contracts the Bills are prepared in accordance with the Standard Method of Measurement and errors in quantities would be adjusted post contract. In this contract, however, there was no Bill of Quantities merely a 'Tender Budget' the purpose of which was to provide guidance as to the scope of the works and, in the absence of the tenderer providing his own Bills of Quantity, as requested in the Invitation to Tender, could be used as a schedule of rates, where appropriate, to value variations.

7.15 I believe the parties were *ad idem* on the 8 April, and that Mr Hocking dropped his demand for total remeasure, albeit perhaps reluctantly, in favour of the partial remeasure—as evidenced by the list sent with the letter 15 April 1991—which list even included the drainage on which the Respondent was hoping to effect a saving to offset some of the extra cost he might incur by agreeing to remeasure the main earthwork items.

It should be stressed, however, that the 'partial remeasure' in effect covered all the topsoil about which Mr Hocking was already concerned on 7 April as well as the 'reducing levels' and cart away. Although he said he was also concerned about the possibility of soft spots, he agreed that, at 7 April, none had been found.

Thus, the remeasure items agreed to at 8 April meeting must have gone most of the way to removing the anxiety that Mr Hocking felt about some of the quantities contained in the 'Tender Budget'.

It may well be that, in restating his former position in his letter 22 April 1991, Mr Hocking did mean something different to what Mr D'Iffy read the words to mean. However, this mistake, if mistake it was, was irrelevant. The deal had been struck on 8 April and this was a post-contract event but not an agreed variation.

7.16 I admit the letters of 15 April 1991 and 22 April 1991, not as extrinsic evidence attempting to contradict/vary/amend the agreement raised on 8 April 1991 but, as a written record of the oral agreement made at that meeting.

7.17 Accordingly on the first two Sub-Issues I find:

THAT THE CONTRACT WAS FORMED AT THE 8 APRIL 1991 MEETING WHEN THE PARTIES AGREED THAT IT WOULD BE SUBJECT TO REMEASUREMENT LIMITED TO THOSE ITEMS LISTED IN THE APPENDIX TO TAP'S LETTER TO RBL DATED 15 APRIL 1991.

5.18 Arb 160

7.18 I now turn to the law governing my findings of fact as referred to me by both Counsel in their submissions.

7.18.1 I consider Sub-Issue 1 of Issue 1 of Mr Belcher's closing submissions.

'Whether the contract is to be found solely in the IFC '84 Form or whether it is also found in the letters of 15 & 22 April 1991.

7.18.2 I have found that the contract was formed at the 8 April 1991 meeting. Mr Belcher submits that where there is a discrepancy, which is more than a mere inconsistency, between the contract document and the parties' true intentions, extrinsic evidence may be admitted to identify the subject matter of the contract. Mr Belcher also contends that the contract is to be found in the two letters listed above as well as the IFC '84.

7.18.3 Miss O'Brien submits that the Mr D'Iffy's letter of 15 April 1991 alone represents the true intentions of the parties, on this issue, and that if the contract is to be found anywhere, other than in the IFC '84 Form, it is in this letter.

7.18.4 On the facts found I accept Miss O'Brien's submission. I do not find that this letter was a step in the negotiations as submitted by Mr Belcher and I therefore distinguish this case from that of *Davis* v *Fareham* to which Mr Belcher referred me in any event it is post contract and therefore irrelevant. In my view the point at which the parties agreed this list at the 8 April meeting was the point that they were *ad idem*.

Accordingly I hold on this Sub-Issue I of Issue 1:

THAT THE CONTRACT IS TO BE FOUND IN THE IFC '84 FORM AND IN THE 15 APRIL 1991 LETTER REFERRED TO ABOVE.

7.19 I now consider Sub-Issue 2 of Issue 1; whether this contract should be rectified?

7.19.1 I have considered the authorities and cases referred to me in both Counsel's submissions.

7.19.2 Mr Belcher points out that I require convincing proof that the contract documents do not accurately reflect the parties' true intentions. He suggests that 'convincing proof' does not increase the normal standard of proof in civil matters, i.e. on the balance of probabilities.

7.19.3 Miss O'Brien on the other hand, refers me to the cases of *Joscelyne* v *Nissen* and the *Nai Genova* on this point.

7.19.4 In *Joscelyne* I find

'jurisdiction to rectify an agreement if there is a common continuing intention in regard to a particular provision of the agreement, but that an outward expression of accord and convincing proof that the concluded instrument did not represent the parties' common intention were required'.

7.19.5 From the *Nai Genova* Miss O'Brien says that the burden of proof is not raised above the normal standard required but that the proof has to be clear and convincing or, as Lord Justice Bingham said in *Thomas Bates* v *Wyndham's* 'convincing proof is required in order to counteract the cogent evidence of the parties' intention displayed by the instrument itself . . . .'

7.19.6 Mr Belcher cites the conditions which must subsist in order to justify rectification. Firstly, where the written agreement does not reflect the parties' true intention due to a mistake, common or unilateral. Here he refers me to *Chitty on Contracts* (26th ed., Vol 1, para 375; 27th ed., Vol 1, para 5–041) which says that an exception to the general rule that the mistake has to be one of both parties is where one party knows of the mistake in his favour but does nothing to correct it.

In which case he will be precluded from resisting rectification on the ground that the mistake is unilateral and not common.

7.19.7 Mr Belcher points me to the authorities which demonstrate that it is not necessary that there was a pre-existing agreement or a common continuing intention. He also refers me to *Chitty on Contracts* (26th ed., Vol 1, para 383; 27th ed., Vol 1, para 5–020) and paragraph 8 of Miss O'Brien's closing submission which I considered, in addition to the case of *Roberts* v *Leicestershire CC* in his own opening. In this case one party inserted in the draft, sent to the other party for signature, a term regarding the time for completion which was different from the term which had been included in the other party's tender. So one party, in effect, altered the term and proffered it to the other party for signature.

7.19.8 It was held, in this case, that the parties were not as one as to the date for completion to be inserted in the contract so the company was not entitled to rectification on the ground that the 30-month period for completion was inserted in the contract by a common mistake, but that a party is entitled to rectification if he proves, beyond reasonable doubt, (but this expression 'beyond reasonable doubt' is altered by the judgment in the *Nai Genova* to the normal standard in civil cases—the balance of probability).

'that he believed a particular term to be included in the contract, and that the other party concluded the contract with the omission or a variation of that term in the knowledge that the first party believed that term to be included'.

Here the ingredients were a mistake by one party and actual knowledge by the other.

7.19.9 Mr Belcher then asked me, once more, to consider one of the cases cited by the *Nai Genova*. In this case Miss O'Brien referred me to the passage in this judgment by Lord Justice Slade, with which the other two Lord Justices agreed, where he reviews the relevant authorities relating to rectification. I read this judgment and noted particularly Lord Justice Slade's comments that

'. . . One significant feature of all the authorities is where there is a unilateral mistake there has to be actual knowledge.'

7.19.10 Mr Belcher submitted, on the authority of the *Roberts* case, whether the mistake became known at the time of executing the contract or whether there was no common continuing intention at all but simply a mistake by one party known to the other, the result is the same; there can be rectification. Thus, the *Roberts* case shows, in so far as unilateral mistake is concerned, one does not have to find a common continuing intention right up to the time the contract was signed—the essential point being a mistake by one party known to the other.

7.19.11 I then reconsidered Miss O'Brien's submissions, in particular those relating to rectification and unilateral mistake. She submits that here we are considering that branch of law concerned with equitable estoppel. She referred me to Lord Justice Slade's judgment in the *Nai Genova* where his Lordship restated the principles of this branch of law by quoting from *Snell's Equity* 28th edn. (1982), p. 614, as follows:

> 'By what appears to be a species of equitable estoppel if one party to a transaction knows that the instrument contains a mistake in his favour but does nothing to correct it, he (and those claiming under him) will be precluded from resisting rectification on the ground that the mistake is unilateral and not common.'

7.19.12 Miss O'Brien also referred me to a later passage in the same judgment which said:

> 'Basically it appears to us that it must be such as to involve the lessee in a degree of sharp practice.'

7.19.13 Miss O'Brien then reviewed the authority in *Keating*, 5th ed., p. 276; 6th ed., pp. 289 and 290.

> 'For a claim for rectification in these circumstances to succeed, it must be shown, firstly, that one party was mistaken as to the contents of the document; secondly, that the other party had actual knowledge of the mistake on the part of the first party; thirdly, that the other party did not draw the first party's attention to the mistake; and fourthly, that the mistake was one calculated to benefit the second party. In these circumstances, it is inequitable to allow the second party to resist rectification on the ground that the mistake was not a mutual mistake . . . It appears that the basis of the Court's approach is that the Plaintiff in such circumstances must prove conduct of the Defendant such as to make it inequitable that he should be allowed to object to the rectification of the document.'

7.19.14 Miss O'Brien submits that the burden on the Claimant is substantial. Not only was it necessary to show that Mr Hocking was mistaken about the effect of the documents that he was signing but also that Mr D'Iffy knew that he was mistaken and permitted Mr Hocking to execute the documents—in effect an element of sharp practice.

7.19.15 As I stated earlier whilst I am not prepared to impute any motive of dishonesty to Mr D'Iffy I do not find that the Claimant has adduced convincing evidence that the tests set out in the authorities above, *Snell*, *Keating* and the *Nai Genova* are satisfied.

7.20 Accordingly I reject the proposition that there was a unilateral mistake of which the other party was aware.

I now turn to the Claimant's alternative submission for rectification, that of a common mistake between the parties such that the IFC '84 Form taking in isolation does not represent the true intentions of the parties with regard to the definition of the contract works.

7.20.1 The conditions for rectification for common mistake are fully set out in Mr Belcher's submissions and I will therefore not repeat them here other than to say that I find that condition 1 is satisfied—that there must have been a prior concluded agreement between the parties going beyond mere negotiations.

7.20.2 I find condition 2 satisfied—the written contract must fail to represent the prior concluded agreement or common intention because of a mistake of both parties.

7.20.3 Condition 3—it must be shown that the written contract was intended to represent the agreement or common intention of the parties.

I believe this condition to be satisfied in that the contract was signed immediately following the agreement on the list of remeasure items as scheduled in Mr D'Iffy's letter 15 April 1991 letter.

7.20.4 Condition 4—the case must be one for the exercise of equity's discretion. Both Counsel accepted that provided conditions 1–3 were satisfied, rectification should be granted.

7.20.5 Mr Belcher submits that if I find that there is a prior concluded agreement going beyond mere negotiations then the logical consequence is that the written agreement must fail to represent the parties' prior agreement/continuing intention because of a mistake. For if the parties intended/agreed one thing, it is hardly likely that they would have intended their written contract to say something quite different. The written contract in this case did not contradict the parties' intentions, it was merely silent on an important condition, i.e. the question of remeasurement.

7.20.6 In summary, I quote Mr Belcher's words in adopting Lord Diplock's analysis in *American Airlines*, the parties were *ad idem* about what work was to be done for the sum which had been quoted but that they used in IFC '84 words which were inapt to record the true agreement reached between them.

7.21 Accordingly I hold on Sub-Issue 3 of Issue 1 that

THE AGREEMENT BETWEEN THE CLAIMANT AND THE RESPONDENT ON THE IFC '84 FORM 8 APRIL 1991 IS RECTIFIED TO INCLUDE, AS A CONTRACT CONDITION, THE LIST OF ITEMS SUBJECT TO REMEASUREMENT AS SET OUT IN THE LETTER DATED 15 APRIL 1991, FROM THE RESPONDENT'S ARCHITECT, MR D'IFFY, ADDRESSED TO THE CLAIMANT.

This disposes of First Issue.

8.00 Second issue

What are the Terms and Conditions of the Contract?

8.01 The invitation to Tender for the works was sent to RBL by TAP, dated 7 January 1991. To this Invitation was attached a list of tender documents as follows:

(1) Specification of Works—dated November 1990—including Preambles and Preliminaries.
(2) Drawing Nos: TAP/1A, 2, 3B, 4C, 5, 6, 7A, 8 & 9; MECH/ENG 1029/1, 2 & 3; ELEC 78/1 & 2; Site Level Drawing S1.70; Drainage—Schematic D1 & 2.
(3) Schedules: Ironmongery, Finishings, Bathroom Fittings, Joinery, Doors & Windows.
(4) Tender Budget—November 1990.
(5) 'Draft Bill of Quantities—For Guidance Only. Sanctuary House Limited are not liable for any inaccuracies in quantities or dimensions.'
   This invitation included, *inter alia*, the following:
(6) 'The successful tenderer will be bound by the appropriate conditions of the standard JCT Intermediate Form of Building Contract (IFC '84) 1990 Edition.'

8.02 Mr Hocking, in cross-examination, said that there was insufficient time to verify the quantities contained in the 'Tender Budget' and as a result they based their tender on the quantities contained therein. This, despite being instructed to send in their Bills of Quantities with their tender and despite the warning on the documents accompanying the 'Tender Budget', that it was for 'guidance only'. (See 1.04 and 1.07 above.)

I accept that, TAP caused confusion by also labelling the 'Tender Budget' as a 'Draft Bills of Quantities'.

8.03 Mr Hocking averred, in cross-examination, that it was not clear to him that this was a lump-sum contract not subject to remeasure, despite page 2/7 of the Specification of Works—Employers Requirements, sent to RBL as part of the tender documents, which makes this clear. (See 1.06 above.)

Mr D'Iffy confirmed, in evidence, that the 'Tender Budget' was not prepared in accordance with the provisions of condition 1.5 of the Conditions of Contract and it was never the intention that this clause would apply.

8.04 In TAP's letter to RBL, 15 April 1991, in scheduling the agreement reached at the 8 April meeting, Mr D'Iffy, confirmed that the terms and conditions of IFC '84 would apply 'except that limited remeasurement will take place and the items that will be remeasured are listed on the attached sheet.'

In replying to this letter, 22 April 1991, Mr Hocking accepted the list.

8.05 In referring to RBL's 22 April 1991 reply to TAP's letter 15 April 1991, Mr D'Iffy confirmed, in his proof, (paragraph 18) that he believed Mr Hocking's reference to 'remeasure' referred to variations and suggested that this was confirmed by Mr Hocking's own proof (paragraph 15) where he said that he confirmed RBL's right to remeasure any items which we might find to vary from the Bills of Quantities.'

8.06 I prefer the Respondent's evidence on this issue and I am clear that the 'Tender Budget' was never intended to be a contract document. When submitted with RBL's tender it became their 'Bills of Quantities' as required by the Invitation and in that regard was only contractually binding as a Schedule of Rates.

8.07 Accordingly on the Second Issue I find

THAT THE CONTRACT DOCUMENTS COMPRISE, OR ARE EVIDENCED BY, THE FOLLOWING:

(1) **Letter RBL to TAP 31 January 1991.**
(2) **Letter TAP to RBL dated 20 March 1991 including the contract referred to therein as follows:**
    The JCT Intermediate Form of Building
    Contract (IFC '84) 1990 Edition.
(3) **Letter TAP to RBL dated 15 April 1991 together with 'Agreed list of Items Subject to Remeasurement' attached thereto—two pages.**
(4) **The 'Tender Budget' dated November 1990 as a Schedule of Rates only as amended by letter TAP to RBL dated 20 March 1991.**
(5) **The Invitation to Tender, 7 January 1991, together with the documents referred to therein, as set out in para. 7.01 above.**

9.00 Third issue

What items are subject to remeasurement?

9.01 Most of the argument on this issue has been rehearsed in the earlier part of this Award.

RBL, in the week before 8 April 1991 meeting, had identified areas of potential under-measurement in earthworks, in particular topsoil and reduced levels, such that they approached the meeting with the request that the whole contract be remeasured.

TAP on the other hand, were anxious to maintain certainty of costs as their client, SHL, was tied into a tight fixed budget. However, they compromised and agreed on limited remeasurement which included the bulk of the items about which RBL were concerned.

A specific list of items, which would be remeasured, was drawn up and agreed between RBL and TAP at the close of the meeting on 8 April.

9.02 TAP subsequently attached a copy of this list to their letter 15 April 1991 and at the same time confirmed that the terms and conditions of the standard JCT contract IFC '84 would apply.

9.03 RBL, in their letter 22 April 1991, accepted the list but added the confusing caveat reserving the right to remeasure other items.

They did not, however, refer to the stand that they say they adhered to at 8 April meeting on remeasure.

The wording of their letter is such that the reservation could well have been being raised there for the first time.

9.04 The issue was clouded by RBL's comments at 8 April meeting to the effect that 2–3 per cent error in quantities was acceptable to them.

Mr D'Iffy's handwritten note of this meeting says

> 'Quants—remeasure to be agreed after meeting
> 2–3 per cent error acceptable.
> Redesign drainage'

9.05 All witnesses acknowledged that the '2–3 per cent' comment was made by Mr Hocking. However, despite this concession the ultimate agreement was to remeasure all of the earthworks, amongst other items, which would seem to supersede RBL's offer to carry errors up to 2–3 per cent.

5.18 Arb 165

Certainly that is the sort of comment one would expect to be made by someone concerned about errors in quantities, e.g. 'I am not worried about minor variations, i.e. 2–3 per cent.'

However, my own belief is that this 2–3 per cent comment was made *before* the final resolution of RBL's concern and the agreement to total remeasure of the excavation items.

Even the Claimant's own witness, Mr Watts, admitted that it was possible that Mr Hocking raised the question of total remeasure at the commencement of the meeting only to drop this in favour of limited remeasure, on an agreed list of items, at the end. Mr Reeves, the Claimant's other witness also stated 'unequivocally' that this matter was raised at the *start* of the meeting.

9.06 It is significant that TAP included drainage on the list of agreed items to be remeasured as they were confident that they could save money on this element.

Why bother to identify specific items if, as averred by RBL, it was accepted by TAP that RBL had reserved the right to remeasure any item of their work where the quantity exceeded that in the 'Tender Budget' by more than 2–3 per cent?

9.07 Mr Belcher suggests that the Respondent knew that the Claimant would rely on the Tender Budget quantities. I cannot accept that contention; was it not to guard against this very possibility that the wording 'For guidance only', referring to the quantities in the Tender Budget, were included in the handwritten schedule of conditions attached to the Invitation to Tender?

I agree that, prior to the 8 April meeting, Mr Hocking was aware that some of the quantities, in the Tender Budget, were inaccurate. We heard evidence that, by that date, RBL had stripped about 25 per cent of the topsoil and started on reducing levels—also, they had not at that stage, found any soft spots.

Again, this is consistent with the compromise agreement reached on the remeasurement of earthworks.

9.08 Mr Hocking averred, in his letter 25 November 1992, that 'We were . . . led to believe . . . that the quantities set out in your Tender Budget were accurate within minor amounts either way'. No evidence was adduced as to how and when he was lead to believe this. RBL only started work on-site, 2 April 1991, and by 8 April were already aware that there were inaccuracies in the earthwork quantities.

If RBL had somehow gained the impression that the quantities in the Tender Budget were accurate but had discovered that the earthwork element was not then this is further proof that the remeasurement mainly of the earthwork section was a reasonable compromise.

9.09 The Respondent may well have been in a weak negotiating position at the 8 April meeting, as was suggested, with RBL already working on-site but I believe that is why they were unable to insist that RBL stuck to the Contract and carried the entire risk on quantities and instead came to the compromise of partial remeasurement.

9.10 If Mr D'Iffy had formed the view, as Mr Belcher suggests, that the remeasurement would have little effect and could possibly be to TAP's advantage, then why did he not readily accede to Mr Hocking's request for a total remeasure?

In evidence Mr D'Iffy agreed that although such a remeasure might be to the advantage of SHL he could not say whether it was an advantage or a disadvantage. Again I come back to SHL's preference for certainty in view of their own contractual commitment to their bankers.

I cannot accept Mr Belcher's interpretation that Mr D'Iffy's acceptance of 22 April 1991 letter is evidence of the fact that he had agreed to Mr Hocking's reservation to a remeasure of any items where the quantities varied by 2 or 3 per cent. I find the Respondent's witnesses more persuasive on this point.

9.11 If Mr Hocking had really believed that he had reserved the right, at 8 April meeting, to a total remeasure then I suspect that he would have said that was what had been agreed. Instead, he said, 'we *must* reserve the right' not, we *reserved* the right etc.

Miss O'Brien refers me to paragraph 15 of Mr Hocking's proof where he says, *inter alia*, that

> '... I received the Respondent's letter dated 15 April, in which the items which we had agreed at 8 April meeting, would be remeasured, were listed.'

Note, he does not say alleged or purported agreement. Again, I believe, that this confirms that agreement was reached at 8 April meeting on partial remeasurement.

9.12 RBL's evidence defies logic. However, I do not find that the 2–3 per cent margin of error became a term of the Contract and therefore should be ignored in deciding which items to remeasure.

9.13 In addition, I find the Respondents witnesses' evidence of what happened at 8 April meeting and their interpretation of the subsequent correspondence most convincing.

9.14 Accordingly I find on the Third Issue

THAT THE ITEMS SUBJECT TO REMEASUREMENT, EXCLUDING MATTERS COVERED BY ARCHITECTS INSTRUCTIONS AND/OR DEFINED AS VARIATIONS, IS LIMITED TO THE AGREED LIST ATTACHED TO TAP'S LETTER 15 APRIL 1991.

10.00 Fourth issue

What Rates are to be applied to the Contract Work in General and what is the Status of the Discount?

10.01 It is common ground that after negotiations with TAP, RBL reduced its revised tender price by 11.6 per cent from £622,171.95 to £550,000. both ex VAT (see paragraph 7 Hocking's proof).

10.02 Mr Hocking avers that he was persuaded to accept a lump-sum reduction on his tender which was a 'one-off discount' in order to obtain the job.

10.03 It was put to Mr Hocking that Mr D'Iffy suggested that the reduction would only apply to valuations and they would call it 12 per cent and to this Mr Hocking agreed.

In his proof of evidence (paragraph 19) Mr Hocking said that

> 'I naturally assumed that variations and remeasurement would be reimbursed at reasonable rates and not reduced by the initial discount.'

10.04 Mr D'Iffy, following receipt of RBL's tender, at a figure higher than SHL's target price, carried out a comparative study of rates between those submitted by RBL and other tenderers.

10.05 As a result, on 16 February 1991, Mr D'Iffy spoke to Mr Hocking by telephone and noted, on RBL's letter 31 January 1991, that RBL

> 'need the work ... will talk price ...'

5.18 Arb 166

Mr D'Iffy, during this telephone conversation requested RBL to consider reducing those of their rates which appeared high. Mr Hocking was not prepared, at that stage, to change these individual rates, however, Hocking did agree that he was prepared to negotiate.

10.06 Between 20 February and 7 March further telephone calls were made by Mr D'Iffy to Mr Hocking. In the event they agreed to correct some moneying out errors, deleted some items that RBL had priced and added some items for which they had not priced.

The effect of all of these changes was to increase the initial tender figure from £617,148.24 to £622,171.95.

10.07 During a telephone conversation on 7 March 1991 the parties agreed to reduce the revised contract price to £550,000 ex VAT. This was, in effect, a reduction of 11.6 per cent.

5.18 Arb 167

10.08 Both Mr Hocking and Mr D'Iffy gave evidence as to how they understood this discount would be applied. Mr Hocking was of the opinion that it would merely be a lump-sum deduction from the end of the Final Account and Mr D'Iffy took the view that each rate would be reduced pro rata.

I am of the same view as Mr D'Iffy. A reduction of each rate making up the tender price would seem to be the only sensible way to treat such a discount.

10.09 For the purpose of valuations this discount was rounded off to 12 per cent. Despite Mr D'Iffy saying that RBL were willing to give him almost a further ½ per cent, I do not accept that this was RBL's intention.

Even if the reduction had been a 'one-off lump sum' I believe that Mr Hocking would have expected the correct discount of 11.6 per cent to be applied to the Final Account total, not the 12 per cent which, I believe, was used for convenience of calculation against valuations.

10.10 Accordingly I find on the Fourth Issue

THAT THE RATES TO BE APPLIED TO THE CONTRACT WORK GENERALLY WILL BE THE RATES AS SCHEDULED IN THE TENDER BUDGET DATED NOVEMBER 1990 ADJUSTED BY THE AGREEMENT, 7 MARCH 1991, IN EFFECT A DISCOUNT OF 11.6 PER CENT.

THE STATUS OF THE DISCOUNT THEN IS SUCH AS TO REDUCE EACH OF THE INDIVIDUAL RATES MAKING UP RBL'S PRICED TENDER AS AMENDED.

11.00 Fifth issue

The Gibbs Ceiling—is it genuine?

11.01 I carefully consider the two experts' reports on this issue, as well as reviewing their evidence and counsel's submissions.

11.02 On balance I preferred Mr Rector's view, although neither expert was able to positively identify a feature, either of the plasterwork itself and/or the decoration or the underlying construction, which would place this work either in the early eighteenth century, as claimed by Mr Rector or in the late nineteenth century as suggested by Mr Ambrose.

11.03 The ferrous nails point made by Mr Ambrose was not strong and I was more inclined towards Mr Rector's explanation. Master craftsmen such as Bagutti, Vassalli and Serena were likely to limit their talent to 'icing the cake' particularly for a project in such an out-of-the-way place as Woodbridge. The underlying construction having been completed and well-dried out long before they appear on the scene. If this was the case both points about ferrous nails and even the hair point become less significant.

11.04 I then considered the evidence concerning the decorative work itself—indeed, the very work that these 'Masters' were engaged to undertake. Here Mr Rector adduced considerable convincing evidence and Mr Ambrose very little. Mr Ambrose concentrated on the 'carton pressé' or 'carton pierre' as he preferred to call it.

11.05 However, Mr Rector was able to show that such was used in a stately home; Shewin House, Barcestershire, in the 1720s, which weakened Mr Ambrose's point.

11.06 Finally, I was more convinced by Mr Rector's evidence on the conversion of the white lead pigment to lead sulphide and the length of time that such a process would take. Mr Belcher suggested that I cannot admit this evidence as it is hearsay. Experts are expected to give opinion evidence and to quote the source of any research on which they may have based their opinion. Mr Rector did that. In addition Mr Ambrose dealt with the same point. He did not refute Mr Rector's point but instead opined—without any substantiation whatsoever—that the wet process involved in the fireproofing above the ceiling, carried out by RBL may have accelerated the conversion process.

5.18 Arb
168

11.07 Here we are talking of months between the installation of the fireproofing and thus the possible dampening of the plaster, and the ceiling's collapse. Compare this with the 200 years or so that Mr Rector says it would take for this conversion process to have occurred and without scientific evidence to support his theory I find Mr Ambrose's hypothesis untenable.

11.08 Accordingly I find on the Fifth Issue

THAT THE CEILING IN THE SITTING ROOM OF SANCTUARY HOUSE, WHICH COLLAPSED ON CHRISTMAS EVE 1992 WAS ERECTED IN THE EARLY EIGHTEENTH CENTURY AND WAS DESIGNED BY THE ARCHITECT JAMES GIBBS, OR UNDER HIS SUPERVISION. IN ADDITION THE DECORATIVE PLASTERWORK WAS EXECUTED BY MASTER CRAFTSMEN SUCH AS BAGUTTI, VASSALLI AND SERENA.

12.00 Sixth issue

Is the builder in breach of contract over the waterproofing of the basement?

12.01 Here I had to consider the issue of whether the contractor was in breach of contract in that he did not tank to a height of 150 mm above the highest recorded level of the water table immediately adjacent to the property.

12.02 The difficulty here arises in that there are no records of the highest water table immediately adjacent to the property.

12.03 As a result the best evidence each expert was able to adduce followed their enquiries from persons who were likely to hold such records.

12.04 RBL made enquiries from the Building Control Officer, who 'volunteered' the information that the highest level of the water table he had known in the area was *about* 750 mm below ground level. Thus, the builders relied upon one person's rather vague knowledge, i.e. 'about 750 mm below ground level'. How reliable was this one person's knowledge?

12.05 In any event this level was to some extent confirmed by enquiries that Mr Longdon made from the architect, Mr D'Iffy who, from his experience gained from working previously at Sanctuary House, and surrounding properties, suggested a level of 760 mm below ground for the level of the water table.

12.06 I then considered this in relation to the ground level. Mr Longdon admits that he did not actually take measurements of the ground level. He said that the ground there was 'pretty level' but if very modern equipment was used he expected that it would indicate small differences in ground levels. More inexactitude.

12.07 Mr Sharkey based his conclusions on precise measurements of the ground level adjacent to the basement after assuming a depth for the paving. Again introducing a potential variation.

12.08 Mr Sharkey also says that working on his measurements the water table could be anything from 1.945 metres above datum to 2.105 metres above datum—a variance of 160 mm. Thus, taking Mr Sharkey's worst case, the higher level of 2.105 would put the top of the tanking at only 40 mm above this level—clearly not the 150 mm which the contract called for.

12.09 Bearing in mind all of the other inexactitudes which I identified it seems clear that RBL has not discharged the burden of proof that they did tank, at least, to a height of 150 mm above the highest recorded water table level.

12.10 I accept that Miss O'Brien's submission that RBL clearly undertook the obligation of ensuring that the level of tanking that they installed was 150 mm above the highest recorded level of water table immediately adjacent to the property—this regardless of any difficulties that the contractor may experience in determining what the level might be. Contractors often take on difficult or near impossible obligations but the degree of difficulty does not alter the contractual obligations which they assume.

5.18 Arb
169

12.11 If RBL were in any doubt about the level to which they should tank they should have played safe and tanked to a sufficiently high level to ensure compliance. This they did not do.

12.12 Whatever was the cause of the eventual flooding, the fact remains that the Claimant has not discharged the burden of proof and

12.13 Accordingly on this Issue I find that

THE BUILDER IS IN BREACH OF CONTRACT CONCERNING THE WATERPROOFING OF THIS BASEMENT; SPECIFICALLY IN BREACH OF CLAUSE 3/15A OF THE SPECIFICATION.

13.00 Costs

13.01 I did not invite Counsel to address me on costs at the close of the Hearing but as and when I come to consider costs, following submissions from the parties, I would expect the costs of such a Hearing on Preliminary Issues would be 'Costs in the Reference' the object of which is to shorten the overall proceedings and to save both parties' costs, but I stress this is not to pre-judge the issue.

13.02 However, there were two issues I will have to consider when I come to deal with Costs.

13.03 The first was the Claimant's late arrival which delayed the start of the proceedings by an hour or so and the second was the requested late introduction of new evidence and the Claimant's new witness, Joel Redman.

13.04 On the first point, whilst I counsel any party to leave adequate travel time when attending a hearing, particularly when the parties are represented at no little expense, I accept that the weather conditions coupled with the heavier traffic due to this problem were exceptional and therefore the Claimant's delay was beyond his control.

13.05 On the second point I warned the Claimant at the time that if I allowed his very late application for the introduction of fresh evidence and his new witness, I might well penalise him on Costs.

13.06 When I come to consider Costs I shall hear submissions on both points.

13.07 Accordingly I hereby direct

THAT COSTS OF THE HEARING, INCLUDING COSTS INCIDENTAL THERETO, BE RESERVED.

14.00 Fit for Counsel

I thank both Counsel for their courtesy and kind assistance.

Given under my hand at Hunstanton this 10 June 1993

In the presence of
Name ....
Address ....
....
....
....
Occupation ....

....
D Emsee MSc FRICS FCIArb
Arbitrator

CHAPTER 6

Pleadings

Typical Request for Interrogatories (6.1 Arb)

IN THE MATTER OF THE ARBITRATION ACTS 1950 TO 1979

AND

IN THE MATTER OF AN ARBITRATION UNDER THE JCT ARBITRATION RULES (18 JULY 1988)

BETWEEN

RELIABLE BUILDERS LIMITED   Claimant

AND

SANCTUARY HOUSE LIMITED   Respondent

INTERROGATORIES

Interrogatories on behalf of the above-named Claimant for the examination of the above-named Respondent:

1.   Do you accept that you received the letter of 22 April 1991 written by the Claimant to yourself?

2.   If the answer to interrogatory 1 is yes, do you accept that you did not reply to it?

3.   If the answer to interrogatory 2 is that you accept you did not reply to the letter, do you allege that you made any complaint or statement (written or oral) in response to receipt of the letter of 22 April to the effect that its content was inconsistent with the agreement you now allege of 8 April, and if so, what complaint or statement did you make, to whom and when?

William Bliss, a Director of the above-named Respondent company, is required to answer all the above interrogatories.

Served this, etc.

Typical Order re Notice to Admit (6.2 Arb)

IN THE MATTER OF THE ARBITRATION ACTS 1950 TO 1979

AND

IN THE MATTER OF AN ARBITRATION

BETWEEN

Claimant

AND

Respondent

ORDER FOR DIRECTIONS

WHEREAS

1.00 The Respondent has requested the Claimant, by letter—to admit the facts set out in that letter and

WHEREAS

2.00 The Claimant has refused to admit the facts and the Respondent has requested me to allow him to serve a Notice to Admit Facts on the Claimant.

3.00 I HEREBY DIRECT that the respondent has consent to serve such Notice forthwith and that the Claimant shall Reply not later than 5.00 p.m.   199 .

4.00 The costs of proving any facts listed in the Respondent's letter   which, for no good reason, are not admitted by the Claimant in his Reply, shall be paid by the Claimant in any event.

5.00 The costs of the Respondent's application in connection with this Order and the costs of this Order to be paid by the Claimant in any event.

Date: 1993 **D Emsee MSc FRICS FCIArb**
                         Registered Arbitrator

To: Representatives of the Claimant
                       FAO

                       Representatives of the Respondent
                       FAO

Typical Order to Amend Pleadings (6.3 Arb)

IN THE MATTER OF THE ARBITRATION ACTS 1950 TO 1979

AND

IN THE MATTER OF AN ARBITRATION

BETWEEN

Claimant

AND

Respondent

ORDER FOR DIRECTIONS NO

Following hearing Mr   for the Claimant and Mr   solicitor for the Respondent, at the Interlocutory Meeting on   1993 the following Directions are given BY CONSENT (unless otherwise directed) and it is

HEREBY DIRECTED that:

due to the very recent change in the Respondent's representation, the dates shown in Order for Directions No   , and subsequent Orders, are now superseded by this Order, where appropriate.

   Numbered item references—unless otherwise noted—are to those items in Order for Directions No   .

1.00 Timetable

The Respondent will be permitted to re-serve his Defence and Counterclaim. Service to be not later than 5.00 p.m.   1993.

   In the serving this Defence and Counterclaim the Respondent to take into account the Claimant's previous Request for Further and Better Particulars, dated   1993 and the Replies given previously by Mr   dated   1993.

   As a result of the re-service of the Defence and Counterclaim the Claimant is HEREBY GRANTED CONSENT to serve an Amended Statement of Case not later than 14 days after the re-service of the Defence and Counterclaim.

   The Claimant will serve his Reply to the Defence and Defence to the Counterclaim not later than 5.00 p.m.   1994.

   Again, the Respondent will be permitted to serve a Reply to the Defence, if he so wishes, not later than 5.00 p.m.   1994.

   Items 5.02 and 5.03 remain unaltered but for the avoidance of doubt the Respondent will price up all the items on the Scott Schedule before passing it to the Claimant for his comments.

2.00 Hearing

The dates set aside for the Hearing—item 14.00 are hereby cancelled and new dates will be set, by agreement, with the parties not later than 5.00 p.m. 1993.

The parties to inform me of their joint view as to the number of days that I am to set aside for the Hearing, preliminary reading and drafting of the Award. Also the approximate number of witnesses of fact and expert witnesses they would like to call and whether they intend to use Counsel at the Hearing.

Following this I will let the parties know what dates I have available and we will, once more, make a firm fixture.

6.3 Arb 174

3.00 Costs Thrown Away

By the Respondent's conduct of the reference to date a number of Orders have been given by me concerning 'costs thrown away' and to be paid by the Respondent in any event.

As a condition of granting consent to the Respondent to re-serve his Defence and Counterclaim, the Respondent is to pay to the Claimant FORTHWITH all of his reasonable costs incurred which have become abortive as a result of the Respondent's conduct in this reference.

These costs include, but are not necessarily confined to, those incidental to and consequential on the following:

   (i) Any abortive 'Pleading' including Further and Better Particulars.
   (ii) Order for Directions No X
   (iii) Order for Directions No Y
   (iv) Late service to Defence and Counterclaim—see my letters to   199 .
   (v) Cancellation of Inspection Meeting   1993—see my letter
        1993.
   (vi) Interlocutory Meeting prior to Inspection on   1993.
   (vii) Cancellation of the Hearing Dates   1993.

These costs to be taxed by me, on a commercial basis, if not agreed.

In addition, the Respondent is to pay FORTHWITH my costs thrown away by the same events as per the attached Fee Statement.

Should the Respondent fail to pay within 14 days of the request for payment the amounts ordered by me in this Direction then, on application of the Claimant, I will encapsulate this Direction into an Interim Award.

4.00 Costs of and incidental to this Order to be paid by the Respondent in any event.

Date: 1993 **D Emsee MSc FRICS FCIArb**
                              Registered Arbitrator

To: Representative for the Claimant
                                 FAO

                                 Solicitor for the Respondent
                                 FAO

CHAPTER 7

The Interlocutory Period

Order for Directions No 5—Setting Hearing Dates (7.1 Arb)

IN THE MATTER OF THE ARBITRATION ACTS 1950 TO 1979

AND

IN THE MATTER OF AN ARBITRATION UNDER THE JCT ARBITRATION
RULES (18 JULY 1988)

BETWEEN

RELIABLE BUILDERS LIMITED   Claimant

AND

SANCTUARY HOUSE LIMITED   Respondent

ORDER FOR DIRECTIONS NO 5

WHEREAS

1.00 At the Preliminary Meeting, held on 23 March 1993, it was agreed to defer setting the Hearing dates until after the determination of the Preliminary Issues

AND WHEREAS

2.00 I published my Award on the Preliminary Issues on 10 June 1993, following which I received a Request, dated 15 July 1993, from the Claimant, to set aside time for hearing this dispute.

3.00 After consultation with both parties the following dates are now set aside

BY CONSENT

The Hearing will commence on Wednesday 7 March 1994 and continue on the following dates, 8, 9, 10, 14, 15, 16, 17, 21, 22, 23, 24, 28, 29, 30, 31, April 6, 7, 11 and 12. The venue is still to be determined and will be arranged by the Claimant, in consultation with the Respondent, not later than 3 December 1993.

4.00 As the Hearing dates listed above are now reserved by me, should either party be responsible for cancelling or postponing them, then that party may be held liable for 'costs thrown away' and, in particular, my cancellation charges as set out in Terms and Conditions.

5.00 Costs in the Reference.

6.00 Liberty to Apply.

Date: 16 July 1993 **D Emsee MSc FRICS FCIArb**
Registered Arbitrator

To: Jayrich Associates   Representatives for the Claimant
FAO Joel Redman

Weller Baines & Bishton   Solicitors for the Respondent
FAO Jeremy Catchpole

**7.1 Arb
176**

Order for Directions No 6—Timetable for Costs of Preliminary Issues (7.2 Arb)

IN THE MATTER OF THE ARBITRATION ACTS 1950 TO 1979

AND

IN THE MATTER OF AN ARBITRATION UNDER THE JCT ARBITRATION RULES (18 JULY 1988)

BETWEEN

RELIABLE BUILDERS LIMITED   Claimant

AND

SANCTUARY HOUSE LIMITED   Respondent

ORDER FOR DIRECTIONS NO 6

Following an application, dated 2 July 1993, from the Respondent for me to hear the issue as to whether the costs of dealing with the Preliminary Issues should be paid forthwith by the Claimant

I HEREBY DIRECT as follows:

1.00 Timetable

1.01   Sanctuary House Limited (SHL) shall prepare a Statement of Case to be served on Reliable Builders Limited (RBL), copied to me, not later than 5.00 p.m. on Wednesday 28 July 1993.

1.02 RBL shall prepare their Statement of Case, to be served on SHL, copied to me, not later than 5.00 p.m. Wednesday 11 August 1993.

1.03 There will be no provision for a separate Reply to RBL's Statement of Case to be served by the Claimant. Any such Reply may be incorporated in Counsels' written opening submissions, which shall be exchanged and delivered to me not later than Wednesday 18 August 1993.

1.04 All Statements shall include a list of any documents the Claimant, or Respondent, considers necessary to support any part of the relevant Statement and a copy of the principal documents on which reliance will be placed, identifying clearly in each document, the relevant part or clearly on which reliance will be placed. Statements will include copies of authorities on which the parties wish to rely, again, with relevant passages highlighted as above.

2.00 Service

2.01 Statements may be served by first-class post or courier.

2.02 If either party fails to comply with the timetable set out above, the other party to notify me of non-service or late service.

3.00 Counsel

Both parties intend to instruct Counsel.

4.00 Hearing

4.01 There shall be a Hearing for this issue on Tuesday 31 August 1993. The Hearing will commence at 4.45 p.m. and be completed that day.

4.02 The Hearing shall be held at the offices of Weller Baines & Bishton 42 South Square Grays Inn London WC1.

4.03 It is agreed that the time for this Hearing will be divided equally between the parties as they see fit. However, the intention is to complete all submissions—including the closing submissions of Counsel—on this issue during this one day Hearing.

5.00 Costs to be costs in the reference.

6.00 Liberty to Apply.

Date: 19 July 1993	**D Emsee MSc FRICS FCIArb** **Registered Arbitrator**
To: Jayrich Associates	Representatives for the Claimant FAO Joel Redman
Weller Baines & Bishton	Solicitors for the Respondent FAO Jeremy Catchpole

Respondent's Statement of Case—Cost of Preliminary Issues (7.3)

IN THE MATTER OF THE ARBITRATION ACTS 1950 TO 1979

AND

IN THE MATTER OF AN ARBITRATION UNDER THE JCT ARBITRATION RULES (18 JULY 1988)

BETWEEN

RELIABLE BUILDERS LIMITED   Claimant

AND

SANCTUARY HOUSE LIMITED   Respondent

7.3
179

STATEMENT OF RESPONDENT'S CASE—COSTS OF THE PRELIMINARY ISSUES

Background

1. There were five preliminary issues. They arose out of the Claimant's insistence that preliminary issues be tried. This was resisted by the Respondent, who submitted that at the end of the day the preliminary issues which were proposed by the Claimant would not take the matter much further. However, the issues were ordered and the Respondent was successful as regards each issue.

The First Preliminary Issue—The Contract when and how was the Contract formed?

2. The Respondent's case was that the contract was formed on 8 April 1991 following the meeting attended by Mr Bliss, Mr D'Iffy and Miss Hutch on behalf of the Respondent and Mr Hocking, Mr Reeves and Mr Watts on behalf of the Claimant. (See Statement of the Respondent's case on the Preliminary Issues—5.2)

In this the Respondent succeeded (see para 7.21 of the INTERIM DECLARATORY AWARD). The contention of the Claimant that the contract was formed at a later date did not succeed.

The Second Issue—What are the Terms and Conditions of the Contract?

3. Again, the Respondent succeeded, see paragraph 8.07 of the INTERIM DECLARATORY AWARD.

The Third Preliminary Issue—What items are subject to Remeasurement?

4. As regards this issue the Respondent's case was that the items subject to re-measurement were those set out in the Respondent's letter dated 15 April 1991. See paragraph 16 of the Respondent's Statement of Case on the Preliminary Issues. Again the Respondent succeeded on this issue, see paragraph 9.14 of the INTERIM DECLARATORY AWARD.

The Fourth Preliminary Issue—The Rates to be applied to the Subcontract Work in general and the Status of the Discount

5. The Respondent submitted in paragraph 24 of the Statement of Case that a discount was agreed and that such discount ought to be applied as a percentage pro rata to all the rates set out in the schedule. This was accepted by the Arbitrator in paragraph 10.10 of his Award. Again, the Respondent succeeded.

The Fifth Preliminary Issue—Whether the 'Gibbs Ceiling was Genuine

6. It was only the Claimant casting doubts on the genuineness of this ceiling which caused this to be considered as a Preliminary Issue. In the event the Arbitrator confirmed the Respondent's view that it was—see item 11.08 of the INTERIM DECLARATORY AWARD.

The Sixth Issue—Was the Claimant in Breach of Contract over the Waterproofing of the Basement?

7. The Respondent's case was that the Claimant, having undertaken the obligation to ensure that the level of tanking in the basement was installed 150 mm above the highest recorded level of water table immediately adjacent to the property, had to discharge this obligation regardless of the difficulty of establishing what this water table level was.

The Arbitrator found that the Claimant failed in this obligation and accordingly found in favour of the Respondent—see item 12.13 of the INTERIM DECLARATORY AWARD.

Submissions

8. On all issues save that which was not pursued the Respondent was successful. Costs ought therefore to follow the event.

9. The only question is whether the Respondent ought to anticipate submissions to contrary effect. The Arbitrator's comments in paragraph 13.00 of his Award were made without argument being heard. It was neither party's intention to address the Arbitrator on the question of costs prior to receipt of the Award.

It is anticipated that it will be submitted that these costs ought to be determined at the end of the arbitration. In other words it is to be suggested that costs should be in the reference.

10. This would be contrary to the justice of this case. Where preliminary issues are ordered the normal practice is for the costs of those issues to follow the event of the preliminary issues. There is good reason for this. The time set aside for the preliminary issues is severable from the rest of the action. The costs of this arbitration have been increased by unnecessary argument which the Claimant lost.

If the Claimant recovers a sum of money by Award, he will not have done so because of the preliminary issues upon which he lost and the unnecessary costs incurred in dealing with those issues. It is submitted that the normal rule that costs follow the event is applied in the case of preliminary issues to the costs of the preliminary issues following the event of the preliminary issues.

This would obtain in the event of an unsuccessful interlocutory application, for example, if the Claimant lost a discovery summons, then he would be liable to pay the costs of the application.

In this case the costs should be paid forthwith because the issues were demanded to be tried by the Claimant at considerable cost and it would not be right to keep the Respondent out of those unnecessary costs for the duration of the arbitration.

11. Given that this application relates to discretion, a bundle of authorities is not relied upon in support of this Statement of Case, but the position is reserved so far as a Reply is concerned.

Bernadette O'Brien

SERVED this twenty-eighth day of July 1993
by Weller Baines & Bishton 42 South Square, Grays Inn, London WC1
Solicitors for the Respondent

7.3
181

Order for Directions No 7—Non-Service of Defence (7.4 Arb)

IN THE MATTER OF THE ARBITRATION ACTS 1950 TO 1979

AND

IN THE MATTER OF AN ARBITRATION UNDER THE JCT ARBITRATION RULES (18 JULY 1988)

BETWEEN

RELIABLE BUILDERS LIMITED   Claimant

AND

SANCTUARY HOUSE LIMITED   Respondent

ORDER FOR DIRECTIONS NO 7

**7.4 Arb
182**

WHEREAS

1.00 By my Order for Directions No 2, item 5.02, I directed that the Claimant serve its Statement of Case after the publication of my Award on the Preliminary Issues.

2.00 The Award was published on 10 June 1993 and the Claimant served its Statement of Case, on 12 July 1993, following a grant of an extension of time of four days.

3.00 Item 5.03 of the above Order directed that the Statement of Defence and Counterclaim be served 28 days after the service of the Statement of case, that is, not later than 9 August 1993. This Statement has not been served.

4.00 On 9 August 1993 the Claimant informed me of this non-service. On the same day the Respondent's solicitor requested an extension of time to which, by faxed letter, the Claimant objected.

5.00 Rule 6.7 give me discretion to extend the time for service providing such application is made before the expiry of the relevant time for service. The Respondent's application was made after the expiry of the relevant time and, in any case, gave me no good reason for the extension.

6.00 ACCORDINGLY under the provisions of Rule 6.4
I HEREBY DIRECT that I propose to proceed on the basis that the Respondent will not be serving a Defence or Defence and Counterclaim unless he does so by not later than 5.00 p.m. 17 August 1993.

7.00 Should the above Statement be subsequently served later than 5.00 p.m. 17 August 1993, it shall be of no effect, unless I am satisfied that there was good and proper reason why such Statement was not served by the time directed.

8.00 Costs of, incidental to and consequent on, this Order be paid by the Respondent in any event.

Date: 10 August 1993   **D Emsee MSc FRICS FCIArb**
                        Registered Arbitrator
To: Jayrich Associates Representatives for the Claimant
                        FAO Joel Redman
Weller Baines & Bishton Solicitors for the Respondent
                        FAO Jeremy Catchpole

Claimant's Statement of Case—Costs of Preliminary Issues (7.5)

IN THE MATTER OF THE ARBITRATION ACTS 1950 TO 1979

AND

IN THE MATTER OF AN ARBITRATION UNDER THE JCT ARBITRATION RULES (18 JULY 1988)

BETWEEN

RELIABLE BUILDERS LIMITED   Claimant

AND

SANCTUARY HOUSE LIMITED   Respondent

COSTS OF THE PRELIMINARY ISSUES—STATEMENT OF THE CLAIMANT'S CASE

1. It is the Claimant's case that the appropriate, and usual order for the costs of the Preliminary Issues would be that costs be reserved to be reconsidered at the time that an order is made regarding the costs of the entire reference. In the Claimant's submission, there is no reason why this normal approach should not be taken in this case. Indeed, it is the Claimant's submission that the learned Arbitrator's judicial discretion in respect of costs would not be exercised in any other manner.

2. In its Statement of Case, the Respondent suggests the Preliminary Issues only arose because of the insistence of the Claimant, and implies that the costs of the Preliminary Issues were wasted because of this insistence. This characterisation of the situation is disputed.

Background

3. Following the production of the different versions of the Final Account it was apparent that there were significant differences between the parties as to the terms of the Subcontract between them. It was of obvious interest to both parties that this dispute be resolved at an early stage so as to limit the debate that would otherwise develop as to the basis upon which valuations were to be made. Resolution of these contractual issues was always likely to reduce the eventual costs of the proceedings.

4. The background to the decision to resolve the Preliminary Issues is set out in detail in the Interim Declaratory Award at paragraph 5.02. As recorded there, there was no dispute that it was appropriate to resolve certain contractual issues at the outset, although the definition of those issues did become the subject of future debate. The Respondent's principal objection to the hearing of the issues was as to the timing of the resolution of such issues. The Claimant therefore takes issue with the statement in paragraph 1 of the Claimant's Statement of Case that the Respondent resisted the application to have Preliminary Issues tried.

Usual Practice as to Costs of Preliminary Issues

5. The normal judicial practice is that an order regarding the costs of Preliminary Issues is made at the end of the proceedings following the disposal of the entire action or reference. The tribunal is then able to decide whether the costs of the Preliminary Issues should form part of the costs of the subsequent proceedings in following the event, or whether some other order is appropriate.

6. This approach is both just and practical. The purpose of Preliminary Issues is to save time and costs. By definition Preliminary Issues are only tried if the tribunal is of the view that some useful purpose can be served by determining these issues at the outset rather than as part of a hearing dealing with all issues. Some Preliminary Issues are of themselves decisive as to the outcome of the case, or are decisive if they are decided in a particular way. In this case the Preliminary Issues were not in themselves decisive of the outcome, but their resolution was expected to limit substantially the scope for subsequent debate between the parties.

7. In a case such as the instant case it is very likely that the Plaintiff or Claimant will lose on one or more of the Preliminary Issues but be ultimately successful in the proceedings. To make a separate order regarding the costs of Preliminary Issues before the determination of the amount, if any, due to the Plaintiff/Claimant (or to a Counterclaimant) would unfairly penalise that Plaintiff/Claimant. If there had been no trial of Preliminary Issues and these issues had been resolved at a hearing of all issues, the Plaintiff/Claimant would likely recover all the costs of these issues regardless of its success or failure on the individual issues as long as its Claim was successful as a whole.

8. Thus, the Plaintiff/Claimant would be being unfairly penalised for having achieved an increase in the efficiency in the proceedings if a separate costs order were to be made against it in respect of Preliminary Issues it had lost. This injustice is particularly acute as the fact that an order was made for the hearing of Preliminary Issues indicates the tribunal felt that some improvement in the judicial or arbitral process could be achieved by dealing with these issues in advance.

9. The consequences of a determination of Preliminary Issues, their utility and the success of a Plaintiff/Claimant can only be fairly judged once the claim has been finally determined. It would be unfair and premature to adopt any other approach in exercising the discretion as to the award of costs.

10. Accordingly, the Claimant seeks an order that the costs of the Preliminary Issues be reserved.

Authorities

11. The Claimant is endeavouring to obtain a transcript of an application for the costs of a trial of certain Preliminary Issues in the High Court during which the appropriate basis for exercise of the discretion was referred to. This transcript is not yet available but will be supplied as soon as possible. The Claimant craves the learned Arbitrator's indulgence for this further delay but submits that as long as the Respondent has adequate time to comment on further material on this issue, it would be appropriate for all such material to be placed before the Arbitrator before the hearing as to costs on these Preliminary Issues.

Toby Belcher

SERVED this eleventh day of August 1993
by Jayrich Associates, Swansea House, 48 Queens Road, Norwich, Norfolk NR2 LO6
Claimant's Representatives

Respondent's Opening Submissions—Costs of Preliminary Issues (7.6)

IN THE MATTER OF THE ARBITRATION ACTS 1950 TO 1979

AND

IN THE MATTER OF AN ARBITRATION UNDER THE JCT ARBITRATION RULES (18 JULY 1988)

BETWEEN

RELIABLE BUILDERS LIMITED   Claimant

AND

SANCTUARY HOUSE LIMITED   Respondent

7.6

185

RESPONDENT'S WRITTEN OPENING RELATING TO THE COSTS OF THE PRELIMINARY ISSUES

The Question to be Decided

1. The question before the Arbitrator is whether he should reserve the costs relating to the preliminary issues or whether he should make an immediate order.

2. The options open to the Arbitrator are as set out on page 121 of the report of the *Surrey Heath* case (48 BLR) namely:

    (i) Make the costs in the cause;
    (ii) Reserve the costs to the trial;
    (iii) Award the costs or a proportion of the costs to one or other party.

3. Of the three options, no party is asking for the costs to be in the cause and therefore it would be inappropriate for the Arbitrator to make such an order. The contest is between whether the costs should be disposed of immediately or whether they can be better dealt with following the main hearing and after all questions of liability and quantum have been disposed of.

The Respondent's Case

4. The Respondent's case is simple. The preliminary issues were a separate event with identifiable time and costs relating to them. It is correct for the Arbitrator to direct his mind to look overall to determine what were the matters principally argued at the hearing of the preliminary issues and who succeeded on those matters.

5. In this case all the preliminary issues were won by the Respondent, save the one issue which the Claimant abandoned. This is not a case of partial success, where it might be argued that the relative importance and impact of the preliminary issues between one and another should be assessed at the end of the day. The preliminary issues were clearly an 'event' in the sense as ordinarily understood and costs should follow them.

6. Given the relative simplicity of the Respondent's case, it is necessary to pass on to the

Claimant's case to see what is being said as to the reasons why costs should not follow the event.

The Claimant's Case Examined

7. '... the appropriate, and usual order for the costs of the Preliminary Issues would be that the costs be reserved to be reconsidered at the time that an order is made regarding the costs of the entire reference ...'

8. It is not the 'usual' order for such costs to be reserved. The *Surrey Heath* case is an example where that course was not followed. In fact the reverse is usually the case; preliminary issues are an event and costs follow them. In *Surrey Heath* it appears that the successful Defendant did not win all the issues, but still got an order relating to part of the costs. Judge Fox-Andrews QC asked the right question (see report p. 122).

9. It is not appropriate to make an order reserving the costs. No reason has been given as to why the Arbitrator is going to be any the wiser as to who should bear the costs of the preliminary issues at the end of the hearing. The assumption implicit in this submission by the Claimant is that if it gets a monetary Award in its favour at the end of the day, then the Arbitrator might be persuaded to exercise his discretion not to give the Respondent the costs of the preliminary issues. This would not be an appropriate outcome in this case.

10. If the Claimant does get a monetary Award, the preliminary issues were nevertheless the result of the Claimant's misconceived view of events and the law. It is no answer to a request that the costs of the exercise be paid by the losing party to say that time has been saved. The time which has been saved is only time which would have been wasted by contingent analysis of matters which the Arbitrator has held the Claimant had not succeeded in establishing. It would be unfair to require the Respondent to pay for any part of the steps which were taken to dispose of the Claimant's misconceived contentions.

11. '... it is the Claimant's submission that the learned Arbitrator's judicial discretion should not be exercised in any other manner ...'

This is a surprising and unjustified submission. It is quite open to the Arbitrator to regard the preliminary issues hearing as an 'event'. The submission suggests that the Arbitrator *must* act in a certain way. This is unwarranted.

12. '... the Claimant suggests the Preliminary Issues only arose because of the insistence of the Claimant, and implied that the costs of the Preliminary Issues were wasted because of this insistence. This characterisation of the situation is disputed.'

Weller Baines & Bishton have an attendance note of the Preliminary Meeting before the Arbitrator on 23 March 1993. At this meeting the Claimant submitted two questions which it said should be decided (see para 15 of the note). However, the Respondent submitted that the legal points identified by the Claimant were not the most significant difference and the real difference related to quantity surveying matters (see Weller Baines & Bishton's letter dated 22 March 1993 and paras 24 and 25 of the note of meeting 23 March 1993).

However, the Claimant was of the view that a decision on legal points would assist settlement and would get money payable to it immediately (para 32). The Respondent reiterated that the real dispute related to quantity surveying (paras 39, 44 and 48 of the note) but eventually agreed to the preliminary issues (para 53). The record speaks for itself.

13. 'To make a separate order regarding the costs of preliminary issues before the determination of the amount, if any, due to the Plaintiff/Claimant ... would unfairly penalise the Plaintiff/Claimant ...'

Why?

This is not a case where some issues were won by the Claimant. They won none of them. It is impossible to contend that the Claimant would be unfairly penalised by paying the costs of issues they have lost.

14. 'If there had been no trial of Preliminary Issues and these issues had been resolved at a hearing of all issues, the Plaintiff/Claimant would likely recover all the costs of these issues regardless of its success or failure on the individual issues as long as its Claim was successful as a whole . .'

This submission is misconceived. If the costs relating to the preliminary issues had been identifiable at the hearing then a special order could be made in respect of them. Furthermore to the extent that the hearing was prolonged by looking at the contingent claims, based upon the Claimant's view of events, i.e. that it was a completely remeasurable contract, then those costs could be the subject of a special order. The logic of the submission being made is that all the costs of going into a complete remeasurement of the account should be paid for the Respondent, notwithstanding that it was unnecessary if the Claimant was successful in getting a money Award after a full hearing. That logic is faulty.

15. 'Thus, the Plaintiff/Claimant would be being unfairly penalised for having achieved an increase in efficiency . . .'

This is a confused statement. The hearing may be more efficient than otherwise it would have been (whether there was a net saving in time and money in taking these preliminary issues may be the subject of debate) but this is only because the Claimant's misconceptions have been disposed of.

16. It cannot be right for the Respondent to pay for the costs of disposing of the Claimant's misconceptions on the grounds that the Claimant may get a money Award in its favour at the end of the day. This remark made on behalf of the Claimant suggests that the efficiency to which it refers is entirely neutral. This is not in this case.

17. The misconceptions of the Claimant may have made for inefficiency in conducting the reference. It cannot be right to require the Respondent, at the end of the reference, to pay for disposing of those misconceptions and avoiding the inefficiency. So to do would not encourage the taking of preliminary issues for the efficient and speedy disposal of matters and would encourage bad points to be taken.

18. The Arbitrator will learn nothing at the end of a full hearing to assist him in determining the costs of the preliminary issues. Therefore it is appropriate that an order relating to them be made now and that the costs should be taxed and paid forthwith for the reasons set out in the Statement of Case.

7.6
187

Authorities

19. The *Surrey Heath* case reported at 48 BLR 121–125 provides a debate relating to the costs of preliminary issues. It is noteworthy in that case that the Judge granted the Order notwithstanding that the Plaintiff won some issues. There is surprisingly little reported authority regarding the question of costs of preliminary issues. Probably because in the majority of cases the issues determine the action.

Bernadette O'Brien

SERVED this eighteenth day of August 1993
by Weller Baines & Bishton 42 South Square, Grays Inn, London WC1
Solicitors for the Respondent

Order for Directions No 10—Determination of Costs of Preliminary Issues (7.7 Arb)

IN THE MATTER OF THE ARBITRATION ACTS 1950 TO 1979

AND

IN THE MATTER OF AN ARBITRATION UNDER THE JCT ARBITRATION RULES (18 JULY 1988)

BETWEEN

RELIABLE BUILDERS LIMITED   Claimant

AND

SANCTUARY HOUSE LIMITED   Respondent

**7.7 Arb
188**

ORDER FOR DIRECTIONS NO 10

1.00 FURTHER to the Respondent's application for the Costs of the Preliminary Issue, dated 2 July 1993

AND

2.00 Having received and considered submissions and authorities from Counsel for each side, as directed by my Order for Directions No 6.

AND FURTHER,

3.00 Having heard Counsel for each side and considered these submissions and authorities at an Oral Hearing on Tuesday 31 August 1993 at Weller Baines & Bishton's offices at 42 South Square, Grays Inn, London WC1.

I HEREBY REJECT THE CLAIMANT'S APPLICATION AND DETERMINE THAT THE COSTS OF THE PRELIMINARY ISSUES SHALL BE PAID FORTHWITH BY THE CLAIMANT IN ANY EVENT.

4.00 Such costs, if not agreed, to be settled by me, on a 'reasonable costs, reasonably incurred basis', by a procedure to be confirmed by a further direction.

5.00 Fit for counsel.

6.00 The costs of and incidental to this order to be paid by the Claimant in any event.

Date: 16 July 1993 **D Emsee MSc FRICS FCIArb
Registered Arbitrator**
To: Jayrich Associates Representatives for the Claimant
FAO Joel Redman
Weller Baines & Bishton Solicitors for the Respondent
FAO Jeremy Catchpole

Amended Statement of Case (7.8)

IN THE MATTER OF THE ARBITRATION ACTS 1950 TO 1979

AND

IN THE MATTER OF AN ARBITRATION UNDER THE JCT ARBITRATION RULES (18 JULY 1988)

BETWEEN

RELIABLE BUILDERS LIMITED   Claimant

AND

SANCTUARY HOUSE LIMITED   Respondent

AMENDED STATEMENT OF CASE

1. The Project

1.1 At all material times the Claimant carried on business as a building contractor.

1.2 At all material times the Respondent was the owner of Sanctuary House (formerly known as the Manor House) Woodbridge, Suffolk ('Sanctuary House') and was concerned with its redevelopment as a Nursing Home for the elderly and infirm.

2. Background to the Dispute

2.1 In January 1991 the Claimant successfully tendered for the refurbishment and extension of Sanctuary House ('the Works'—as more particularly described in the documents referred to in paragraph 3.1 below). The Works were carried out and completed in the manner described in paragraph 6 below. (Outline Narrative)

2.2 Disputes have arisen between the parties relating to the Works. In accordance with the contract for the Works the Arbitrator was appointed on 20 February 1993 to resolve the disputes.

2.3 The parties agreed that the Arbitrator should determine preliminary issues in advance of the substantive issues. The preliminary issues were set out in the Arbitrator's direction no. 2 dated 25 March 1993.

2.4 Each party having submitted its Statement of Case in respect of the preliminary issues, the preliminary issue hearing took place over 2 days commencing on 24 May 1993. Written closing submissions were then submitted by each party.

2.5 The Arbitrator's Interim Declaratory Award was published on 10 June 1993.

2.6 The full background to the dispute is set out in paragraphs 1 to 5 of the Arbitrator's Interim Declaratory Award. To avoid unnecessary repetition, the Claimant does not replead its Statement of Case on the preliminary issues by the usual process of amendment and deletion. This Statement of Case relates to the substantive issues and adopts the findings of the Arbitrator on the preliminary issues, as paraphrased below in italics.

3. The Contract

3.1 *The contract was formed at a meeting on 8 April 1991 ('the Contract') and is contained in or evidenced by the following documents:*

1. The 'Tender Budget' dated November 1990 as a Schedule of Rates only as amended by letter TAP to the Claimant dated 20 March 1991.
2. The Invitation to Tender, dated 7 January 1991, together with the documents referred to therein as follows:
    (i) Specification of Works—dated November 1990—including Preambles and Preliminaries.
    (ii) Drawing Nos.: TAP/1A, 2, 3B, 4C, 5, 6, 7A, 8 & 9; MECH/ENG 1029/1, 2, and 3; ELEC 78/1 & 2; Site Level Drawing S1.70; Drainage—Schematic D1 and 2
    (iii) Schedules: Ironmongery, Finishings, Bathroom Fittings, Joinery, Doors and Windows.
3. Letter Claimant to TAP dated 31 January 1991.
4. Letter TAP to the Claimant dated 20 March 1991 including the JCT Intermediate Form of Building Contract (IFC '84) 1990 Edition referred to therein.
5. Letter TAP to the Claimant dated 15 April 1991 together with 'Agreed list of Items Subject to Remeasurement' attached thereto.

4. Express Terms

7.8
190

4.1 TAP and the Claimant orally agreed the Contract sum to be £550,000 excluding VAT, in consideration for which the Claimant agreed to carry out and complete the Works. (See paragraph 1.16 of the Arbitrator's Interim Declaratory Award).

4.2 The Conditions of Contract extracted from IFC '84, *inter alia*, include the following:

Clause 1.7—Provision of Information

The Architect/The Supervising Officer without charge to the Contractor shall provide him with 2 copies of such further drawings or details as are reasonably necessary to enable the Contractor to carry out and complete the Works in accordance with the Conditions.

Clause 2.3—Extension of Time

Upon it becoming reasonably apparent that the progress of the Works is being or is likely to be delayed, the Contractor shall forthwith give written notice of the cause of the delay to the Architect/the Contract Administrator, and if in the opinion of the Architect/the Contract Administrator the completion of the Works is likely to be or has been delayed beyond the Date for Completion stated in the Appendix or beyond any extended time previously fixed under this clause, by any of the events in clause 2.4 then the Architect/the Contractor Administrator shall so soon as he is able to estimate the length of delay beyond that date or time make in writing a fair and reasonable extension of time for completion of the Works.

The relevant events referred to in clause 2.3 and contained in clause 2.4 include *inter alia:*

Clause 2.4.5: Compliance with the Architect's/the Supervising Officer's instructions under clauses: . . . 3.6 Variations, or . . .

Clause 2.4.7: the Contractor not having received in due time necessary instructions, (including those for or in regard to the expenditure of provisional sums) drawings, details or levels from the Architect/the Contract Administrator for which he specifically applied in writing . . .

Clause 2.4.8: the execution of work not forming part of this Contract by the Employer himself or by persons employed or otherwise engaged by the Employer as referred to in clause 3.11 or the failure to execute such work.

Clause 2.6—Certificate of non-completion

If the Contractor fails to complete the Works by the Date for Completion or within any extended time fixed under clause 2.3 then the Architect/the Contract Administrator shall issue a certificate to that effect.

Clause 2.7—Liquidated damages for non-completion

Subject to the issue of a certificate under clause 2.6 the Contractor shall, as the Employer may require in writing not later than the date of the final certificate for payment, pay or allow the Employer liquidated damages at the rate stated in the Appendix for the period during which the Works shall remain or have remained incomplete, and the Employer may deduct the same from any monies due or to become due to the Contractor, under this Contract (including any balance stated as due to the Contractor in the final certificate for payment) or may recover the same from the Contractor as a debt.

Clause 3.5.1—Architect/Contract Administrator's Instructions

All instructions of the Architect/the Contract Administrator shall be in writing. The Contractor shall forthwith comply with such instructions issued to him which the Architect/the Contract Administrator is empowered by the Conditions to issue; save that where such instruction is one requiring a Variation within the meaning of clauses 3.6.2 the Contractor need not comply to the extent that he makes reasonable objection in writing to the Architect/the Contractor Administrator to such compliance.

7.8
191

Clause 3.6—Variations

The Architect/the Contract Administrator may subject to clause 3.5.1 issue instructions requiring a Variation and sanction in writing any Variation made by the Contractor otherwise than pursuant to such an instruction. No such instruction or sanction shall vitiate the Contract. The term Variation as used in the Conditions means:

Clause 3.6.1
the alteration of modification of the design or quality or quantity of the Works as shown upon the Contract Drawings and described by or referred to in the Specification/Schedules of Work/Contract Bills including
— the addition, omission or substitution of any work,
— the alteration of the kind or standard of any materials or goods to be used in the Works,
— the removal from site of any work executed or materials or goods brought thereon by the Contractor for the purposes of the Works other than work materials or goods which are not in accordance with this Contract,

Clause 3.7—Valuation of Variations

The amount to be added to or deducted from the Contract Sum in respect of instructions requiring a Variation and of instructions on the expenditure of a provisional sum may be agreed between the Employer and the Contractor prior to the Contractor complying with any such instruction but if not so agreed there shall be added to or deducted from the Contract Sum an amount determined by a valuation made by the Quantity Surveyor in accordance with the following rules in clauses 3.7.1 to 3.7.9.

All work executed by the Contractor for which an Approximate Quantity is included in the Contract Documents shall be measured and valued by the Quantity Surveyor in accordance with the rules in clauses 3.7.1. to 3.7.9.

Clause 3.8—Instructions to Expend Provisional Sums

The Architect/the Contract Administrator shall issue instructions as to the expenditure of any provisional sums.

Clause 4.2—Interim Payments

Subject to any agreement between the parties as to stage payments, the Architect/the Contract Administrator shall, at intervals of one month . . . certify the amount of interim payments to be made by the Employer to the Contractor within 14 days of the date of the certificate.

The amount of the interim payment to be certified shall be the total of the amounts in clauss 4.2.1 and 4.2.2 . . . less any sums previously certified for payment. These amounts are:

> *Clause 4.2.1*
> 95% of . . . (a) the total value of the work properly executed by the Contractor, including any items valued in accordance with clause 3.7 (Valuation of Variations) . . . (b) the total value of the materials and goods which have been reasonably and properly . . . delivered to the Works . . .

> *Clause 4.2.2*
> 100% of any amounts payable to the Contractor to to be added to the Contract Sum under Clauses . . . 4.11 (Disturbance of Progress) . . .

Clause 4.5—Computation of Adjusted Contract Sum

Not later than 6 months after Practical Completion of the Works the Contractor shall provide the Architect/the Contract Administrator, or if so instructed by the Architect/the Contract Administrator, the Quantity Surveyor with all documents reasonably required for the purposes of the adjustment of the Contract Sum. Not later than 3 months after receipt by the Architect/the Contract Administrator or the Quantity Surveyor as the case may be of the aforesaid documents a statement of all the final Valuations under clause 3.7 (Valuations of Variations) shall be prepared by the Quantity Surveyor and a copy of such statement and a copy of the computations of the adjusted Contract Sum shall be sent forthwith to the Contractor . . .

The adjustment of the Contract Sum shall be in accordance with clause 3.7.

Clause 4.6—Issue of Final Certificate

The Architect/the Contract Administrator shall, within 28 days of the sending of such computations of the adjusted Contract Sum to the Contractor . . . issue a final certificate certifying the amount due to the Contractor or to the Employer as the case may be. The amount to be certified shall be the Contract Sum adjusted as stated in clause 4.5 less any sums previously certified for payment. The amount so certified shall as from the twenty-eighth day after the date of the final certificate be a debt payable as the case may be by the Employer to the Contractor . . .

Clause 4.11—Disturbance of regular progress

If, upon, written application being made to him by the Contractor within a reasonable time of it becoming apparent, the Architect/the Contract Administrator is of the opinion that the Contractor has incurred or is likely to incur direct loss and/or expense, for which he would not be reimbursed by a payment under any other provision of this Contract, due to

7.8
192

(a) ...

(b) the regular progress of the Works or pay of the Works being materially affected by any one or more of the matters referred to in clause 4.12, then the Architect/the Contract Administrator shall ascertain, or shall instruct the Quantity Surveyor to ascertain, such loss and expense incurred and the amount thereof shall be added to the Contract Sum provided that the Contractor shall in support of his application submit such information required by the Architect/the Contract Administrator or the Quantity Surveyor as is reasonably necessary for the purposes of this clause.

The provisions of this clause 4.11 are without prejudice to any other rights or remedies which the Contractor may possess.

The matters referred to in 4.12 include *inter alia*:

Clause 4.12.1
the Contractor not having received in due time necessary instructions, (including those for or in regard to the expenditure of provision sums) drawings, details or levels from the Architect/the Contract Administrator for which he specifically applied in writing ...

Clause 4.12.3
the execution of work not forming part of this Contract by the Employer himself or by persons employed or otherwise engaged by the Employer as referred to in clause 3.11 or the failure to execute such work:

7.8
193

Clause 4.12.7
the Architect's/the Contract Administrator's instructions issued under clauses
1.4 (Inconsistencies) or
3.6 (Variations) or ...
...

4.3 The following express terms were included in the Contract documents:

The Date for Completion was to be 10 December 1991
Liquidated damages at the rate of £9,125.00 were payable for every week (or part week) delay.

5. Implied Terms

5.1 There were implied terms of the Contract *inter alia* as follows:
5.1.1 The Respondent by itself, its servants, or agents would not hinder or prevent the Claimant in and about the performance of the Works.
5.1.2 The Respondent by itself, its servants, or agents would take all steps reasonably necessary to enable the Claimant to discharge its obligations under the Contract and to execute the Works in a regular and orderly manner.

6. Outline Narrative

6.1 From the time the contract commenced on 2 April 1991 the Works were delayed and disrupted.
6.2 The Works were not completed on 10 December 1991.
6.3 The Works were completed on 31 March 1992 after a delay of 16 weeks.
6.4 The Respondent wrongfully deducted liquidated damages totalling £146,000 from payments due on Interim Certificates numbered 7, 8, 9 and 10. Interim Certificate number 12 was issued on 13 April 1992 and to date has not been paid.
6.5 The Respondent wrongfully deducted £32,000 in respect of alleged defects to the Works.

6.6 The Claimant submitted its draft Final Account which included its loss and expense claim as well as all necessary supporting documentation to TAP on 3 June 1992.

6.7 TAP, on behalf of the Respondent, refused (on 18 August 1992) to pay the balance stated in the Claimant's draft Final Account and has failed to issue a Final Certificate.

6.8 The Claimant submitted its Final Account to TAP on 30 October 1992. A Final Certificate has not been issued and payment has not been made.

7. Delay

7.1 From the date of commencement of the Works progress was delayed by late provision of information by TAP and/or the carrying out of Works by contractors employed by the Respondent direct and/or variations required by TAP.

7.2 There were five principal elements of the Works which were affected by delays. In addition a number of other elements of the Works were affected, full particulars of which are given in Appendix C. The combined effect of delays to individual parts of the Works caused an overall delay of 16 weeks. A summary of the principal elements of the Works, delayed and prolonged is set out below. (The periods of delay referred to below are calculated by reference to the Claimant's original programme for the Works at Appendix B).

7.2.1 Removals/Demolitions and Form New Openings

Soon after the Works commenced on 2 April 1991, the Claimant discovered that TAP's drawings and/or the Respondent's survey were inaccurate as some internal walls due to be demolished which were identified as non-load-bearing were in fact load-bearing. Removal and demolition work ceased until revised drawings were produced by TAP. It was apparent from the revised drawings that additional work was required. The delay caused by the need to reissue drawings and the additional work was four weeks. This had a direct effect of delaying the completion date by four weeks.

7.2.2 Works to the lift-shaft

TAP issued an Architect's instruction (variation) on the day works commenced on the new lift-shaft (14 April 1991), which altered the specification for the required brickwork and introduced a concrete ring beam at each floor level. The time it took (one week) for delivery of new bricks of the required type and the additional work required as a result of the issue of the Architect's instruction caused a delay to this section of the works by five weeks. This had a direct effect of delaying the completion date by one week.

7.2.3 Roof Repairs and Replacement Windows

1. Scaffolding was erected in accordance with the programme to allow roof repairs to be carried out and replacement windows fitted. TAP intended that the existing roof slates should be reused. However—as a proper survey would have revealed—many slates had delaminated and were extremely delicate. The additional care required in the removal of the slates extended the period programmed for this part of the works by two weeks. This had a direct effect of delaying the completion date by two weeks.
2. In addition, extensive dry rot was discovered in the roof structure. This had not been foreseen by TAP which initially instructed that timbers be replaced on a piecemeal basis. This approach, which proved to be unworkable had to be abandoned and, on the instructions of TAP, all the roof timbers were replaced by the Claimant. The additional work required caused a delay to this part of the works of eight weeks. This had a direct effect of delaying the completion date by eight weeks.

3. To minimise overall delay, the scaffolding was removed before roof leadwork was complete in order that the windows could be installed. The lead work was completed using scaffold towers.
4. The delay caused by the extra care required in the removal of roof slates and the piecemeal approach initially taken on the instructions of TAP in the replacement of roof timbers made it necessary for scaffolding to be kept in place for six weeks longer than originally anticipated. Replacement windows, which could not be fitted until scaffolding was removed, were therefore six weeks late in fitting.

7.2.4 First Fix and Second Fix

1. The carpentry first fix in the old part of Sanctuary House could not commence until the building was watertight and therefore did not start until the replacement windows were installed some six weeks late. The additional work referred to in paragraph 7.2.1 above in turn caused additional work to be required in the first carpentry fix. As a result this work was prolonged by one week, in turn delaying the start date for the mechanical and electrical first fix by one week. Overall the mechanical and electrical first fixes commenced seven weeks late. This had a direct effect of delaying the completion date by one week.
2. The subcontractor employed to carry out the mechanical and electrical fixing had one gang which would only commence first fix operations on the new part of Sanctuary House (the extension) once it had completed its work on the old part of Sanctuary House. The delay to works on the old part of the building was thus carried over to works on the new extension.
3. As a result of the additional work and delays on earlier parts of the works including the delays and additional work described above, the carpentry second fix in the old part of Sanctuary House commenced eight and a half weeks late. The start date for the commencement of the mechanical and electrical second fix was similarly delayed.
4. Due to a change in the specification for the mechanical and electrical works issued by TAP after the mechanical and electrical second fix works had commenced, it was necessary for the subcontractors to redesign these works. The change in specification also necessitated additional work. The mechanical and electrical works on the old part of Sanctuary House having commenced eight and a half weeks late were completed 10½ weeks late.
5. As with the first fix, the subcontractors could not commence mechanical and electrical second fix work on the new extension until their works on the old part of Sanctuary House were complete. The 10½ week delay was thus carried forward to second fix works on the new extension (which should have commenced at the same time as second fix works on the old part of Sanctuary House). The five-week period to complete the second fix mechanical and electrical works on the new extension when added to the 10½ weeks delayed start gives a 15½ week-period of delay.

7.2.5 Decorating and Commissioning Works

1. As the decorating works (followed by commissioning and snagging) could not commence until the second fix works were substantially complete, the 15½ week-delay to the second fix works delayed completion of decoration by 15½ weeks.
2. Further delays to the decorating work was caused by the late provision of colour schedules by TAP which were then subsequently altered by the Respondent. As a result the period allowed for decorating works in the original programme was increased by three days.

Overall, the Works were delayed for the reasons described above, and more particularly set out in Appendix C, by a period of 16 weeks.

8. The Claim for an Extension of Time

8.1 The Claimant is entitled to an extension of time of 16 weeks from 10 December 1991 to 31 March 1992. This claim is made pursuant to Clause 2.3 of the Contract (see paragraph 4.2 above) based on delays of which particulars are given in paragraph 7 and Appendix C all of which were known by the Respondent and TAP.

9. Return of Liquidated Damages withheld by the Respondent

9.1 By reason of the matters stated in paragraphs 7 and 8 above the Claimant is entitled to an extension of time of 16 weeks as a consequence of which liquidated damages of £146,000.00 withheld by the Respondent are payable to the Claimant.

10. Loss and Expense

10.1 The Claimant has suffered loss and expense particulars of which were delivered to the Respondent with the Claimant's draft Final Account on 3 June 1992. The Claimant's loss and expense claim is made under the following headings:

7.8
196

10.1.1 Prolongation

The claim for prolongation costs is based on the 16-week extension of time to which the Claimant is entitled. Due to the prolonged contract period the Claimant incurred additional costs as follows:

1. *Staff.* During the extended contract period the Claimant continued to employ a site agent, trade foreman, ganger, quantity surveyor and other labourers. Full particulars of periods of working and wages are given in Appendix D. The total cost to the Claimant in respect of staff for the 16-week period was £24,320.00.

2. *Site Accommodation.* During the extended contract period the Claimant continued to hire site accommodation including three site huts (for use as the office, store and mess room) and a toilet. Full particulars of periods and rates are given in Appendix D. The additional accommodation cost incurred by the Claimant during the 16-week period was £2,080.00.

3. *Site Expenses.* Site expenses for various items including telephone, electricity, petty cash, small tools and propane were incurred by the Claimant during the 16-week overrun. Full particulars are given in Appendix D. The total cost to the Claimant was £3,072.00.

4. *Transport.* Van hire was continued during the 16-week overrun, to ferry the Claimant's workers to and from the Claimant's yard. Particulars of the associated hire and fuel costs are given in appendix D and total £2,080.00.

Prolongation costs incurred by the Claimant calculated by addition of the figures stated in subparagraphs 1, 2, 3 and 4 above total £31,552.00.

10.1.2 Uneconomic Working

The Claimant was unable to make the best use of its labour either in the manner planned or in the most economic manner for the reasons described below:

1. *Late Provision of Information.* TAP were required to provide the Claimant with information in order that the Works could be completed within the original programme dates.

On various occasions such information was provided late. Specific examples of TAP's late provision of information are given in paragraph 7. Full particulars of TAP's late provision of information are given in Appendix C.

2. *Variations.* The number and timing of variations described in paragraph 7 and in Appendix C disturbed the Claimant's planned use of labour. (A full list of variations is contained in Appendix F).

3. *Interference by the Respondent's other contractors.* Particulars of the manner in which the Claimant's works were disturbed by the works carried out by the Respondent's other contractors are given in Appendix C.

As a result of the disturbance to the Claimant's programme for the Works the Claimant's labourers were unable to operate efficiently or achieve the output required by the Claimant so as to justify the cost of labour as calculated in the Claimant's tender. The Claimant has therefore incurred additional labour costs, the calculation of which is set out in Appendix D. The total claimed in respect of uneconomic working is £50,743.24.

10.1.3 Additional Staff and Equipment due to Disruption

As a result of TAP's late provision of information and the number, timing and lateness of variations (particulars of which are given in paragraph 7 and in Appendix C), sections of the Works, as well as being delayed, were also disrupted in that the programmed time periods were extended.

As a result of this disruption the Claimant had to retain staff on-site for extended periods to complete bricklaying and finishing operations. Equipment was also hired for extended periods in order to complete the bricklaying and finishing operations. Particulars of staff costs, equipment, hire costs and periods of prolongation are given in Appendix D.

The costs incurred by the Claimant as a result of disruption to the Works totalled £15,334.00.

10.1.4 Overheads and Profits

The Claimant is entitled to an extension of time and loss and expense. For the reasons described in paragraph 10.1 above which give rise to this entitlement, the Claimant was unable to deploy its site team and head office staff on new or other contracts. Accordingly the Claimant is entitled to recover lost profits and overheads. A *The 'Hudson* formula' is used to calculate the Claimant's lost overheads and profit as set out in Appendix E. The total claimed under this head is £36,666.66.

10.1.5 Inflation Costs

The Claimant is entitled to its inflation costs incurred as a result of the 16-week extension to the contract period. These inflation costs are calculated based on the difference between the provision allowed for inflation in the Claimant's original tender (based on the appropriate Building Cost indices) and the actual effect of inflation on the final account sum (based on the appropriate Building Cost indices). The total claimed under this head is £5,571.30, as particularised in our quantum Expert's Report, Joel Redman, section 7.

10.2 By reason of the matters set out above and the particulars given or referred to the regular progress of the Works and/or parts thereof was materially affected, and the Claimant is entitled to loss and expense pursuant to Clause 4.11 of the Contract.

10.3 The Claimant's claim for loss and expense is summarised as follows:

Prolongation	31,552.00
Uneconomical Working	50,743.24
Additional Staff and Equipment	15,334.00
Overheads and Profit	36,666.66
Inflation Costs	5,571.30
TOTAL	£139,867.20

10.4 Interest

The loss and expense set above was funded through the Claimant's overdraft facility with its Bankers. Interest was paid on this overdraft by the Claimant at 3 per cent above the bank's rate and compounded each quarter. The sums comprising the loss and expense to the Claimant were incurred progressively during and after the contract period. Accordingly, as part of its loss and expense claim, the Claimant is entitled to recover the interest charges it incurred on sums accumulating from 19 October 1991 to 28 January 1993 totalling £22,940.47 and thereafter (subject to any change in the bank's rate) at 9 per cent per annum compounded at quarterly intervals. The calculation of interest is set out in appendix H.

7.8
198

11. Variations, Provisional Sums and Contingencies

11.1 Variations

11.1.1 TAP issued instructions to the Claimant requiring alterations and additions to the scope of the Works and/or the quality of materials and/or the quality of material requested for the Works. The instructions constituted variations within the meaning of clause 3.6 of the Contract and as such stood to be agreed or valued in accordance with clauses 3.7.

11.1.2 The variations in respect of which the Claimant is entitled to payment in accordance with clause 3.7 of the Contract are set out in Appendix F. The calculations for the valuations given are based on the rates scheduled in the Tender Budget discounted by 11.6 per cent in accordance with the Arbitrator's Interim Declaratory Award.

11.1.3 The omissions and additions required to the Contract sum as a result of variations to the Contract (before the claim for loss and expense set out above) are as follows:

Omissions	£63,351.04
Additions	£142,035.27

11.2 Provisional sums

11.2.1 In accordance with TAP's instructions, the Claimant expended Provisional Sums as set out in Appendix G. The omissions and additions required to the Contract sum for expenditure of provisional sums (before the claim for loss and expense set out above) are as follows:

Omissions	£76,750.00
Additions	£107,011.87

11.3 Contingencies

11.3.1 The following contingency sums require to be omitted from the Contract sum:

Specification Items 1.30	£5,600.00
Specification Items 1.30	£8,000.00
TOTAL	£13,600.00

12. Remeasureable Sum

12.1 During the meeting on 8 April 1991 at which the Arbitrator found the Contract was made, Mr Hocking of the Claimant and Mr D'Iffy of TAP agreed a list of items (principally earth works and infilling) which were to be subject to remeasurement, despite the otherwise 'lump-sum' nature of the Contract.

12.2 Accordingly (although the Claimant contended that any item contained in the Bills of Quantity, the value of which significantly increased, should be remeasured) the Arbitrator found that:

> The [only] *items subject to remeasurement, excluding matters covered by Architects instructions, and/or defined as variations, are limited to the agreed list attached to TAP's letter dated 15 April 1991* [which was a copy of the list agreed at the meeting on 8 April 1991]

12.3 The following items were included in the list attached to TAP's letter dated 15 April 1991. These items, which may be treated in the same way as would provisional sums, have been remeasured in accordance with the Contract. The figures stated against each item are the amounts by which the remeasured sum exceeds the sum included for that item in the Claimant's tender dated 31 January 1991. The valuations are based on the rates scheduled in the Tender Budget dated November 1990 <u>discounted by 11.6 per cent in accordance with the</u> <u>Arbitrator's Interim Declaratory Award</u>.

Removal of topsoil and reduced level dig	1,440.00
Trench excavation and cart away	450.00
Landscaping cut fill and cart away	2,167.00
Brickwork to foundations	630.00
External Works	2,223.00
Main Driveway	749.00
Car Parking	1,680.00
Guttering change UPVC to cast	1,600.00
TOTAL	£10,939.00

12.4 The Remeasured sum to be added to the Contract sum is therefore £10,939.00.

13. Final Account: Calculation of total sum due to the Claimant under the Contract

13.1 As stated above, the Claimant's final account was submitted to the Respondent in draft form on 3 June 1992 and final form on 30 October 1992.

13.2 <u>Variations and items to be remeasured were originally calculated based on the</u> <u>undiscounted rates contained in the Tender Budget as the Claimant contended that, the</u> <u>discount applied to its tender price was a lump-sum discount. However the Arbitrator found</u> <u>that:</u>

> <u>The rates to be applied to the Works generally will be the rates as scheduled in the</u> <u>Tender Budget dated November 1990 discounted by 11.6 per cent.</u>

<u>Accordingly, variation and remeasurement items have now been recalculated based on</u> <u>discounted rates in accordance with the Arbitrator's Interim Declaratory Award as described</u> <u>above in paragraphs 11 and 12.</u>

13.3 The total sum which the Claimant is entitled to be paid prior to allowing for sums certified and paid by the Respondent and before the addition of the claim for loss and expense is calculated as follows:

	£—Omit	£—Add
Contract Sum		550,000.00
Provisional Sums	76,750.00	107,011.87
Variations	63,351.00	142,035.27
Contingencies	13,600.00	
Remeasured sum		10,939.00
	153,701.04	809,986.14
		(153,701.04)
TOTAL		£656,285.10

14. Adjustments

14.1 The Respondent has paid sums certified on interim certificates issued by TAP up to and including interim certificate 11 with the exception of the following sums which have been withheld by the Respondent.

1. £146,000.00 wrongfully withheld as liquidated damages.
2. £32,000 wrongfully withheld for allegedly defective work.
3. £9,200 withheld by way of the second moiety of retention.

The Claimant is entitled to be paid the sums withheld by the Respondent.

14.2 Interim Certificate 12 dated 13 April 1992 valued at £10,954 was not paid by the Respondent. The Claimant is entitled to be paid this sum. The gross value of the Works up to and including interim certificate 12 was £610,450.00.

14.3 The amount due to the Claimant pursuant to the Contract, before the addition of the amount claimed for loss and expense and the sums withheld by the Respondent as listed above, is calculated as follows:

Total due	656,285.10
Less gross value	610,450.00
TOTAL	45,835.10

15. Respondent's Breaches of Contract

15.1 Extension of Time

15.11 In breach of Clause 2.3, TAP failed to respond to the Claimant's applications for an extension of time and failed to grant an appropriate extension of time.

15.2 Loss and Expense

15.2.1 In the alternative to the claims made pursuant to the express terms of the Contract as set out in paragraphs 8, 9, and 10 above the Claimant contends that the Respondent was in breach of Contract as follows:

1. In breach of the implied term at subparagraph 5.1.1 above the Respondent and/or TAP hindered or prevented the Claimant from performing the Works in accordance with the Contract.
2. In breach of the implied term at subparagraph 5.1.2 above the Respondent and/or TAP did not take all steps reasonably necessary to enable the Claimant to discharge its obligations under the Contract and/or to execute the Works in a regular and orderly manner.
3. In breach of clause 1.7 the Respondent and/or TAP failed to issue further drawings or details as were reasonably necessary to enable the Claimant to complete the works in accordance with the conditions of the Contract.

7.8
200

Particulars of Breach. The Claimant repeats the particulars in paragraph 7 above and those contained in Appendix C.

15.2.2 By reason of the said breaches of Contract the Claimant has suffered loss and damage.

Particulars of Damage

Prolongation:	The Claimant repeats the particulars in paragraph 10.1.1
Uneconomic working:	The Claimant repeats the particulars in paragraph 10.1.2
Additional Staff and equip.	The Claimant repeats the particulars in paragraph 10.1.3
Loss of overheads and profit:	The Claimant repeats the particulars in paragraph 10.1.4
Inflation Costs:	The Claimant repeats the particulars in paragraph 10.1.5
Interest	The Claimant repeats the particulars in paragraph 10.4

15.3 Non-payment and late payment of interim certificates issued by TAP.

15.3.1 In the alternative to the claim made for payment of Interim Certificate 12 as part of the sum due to the Claimant pursuant to the Contract as set out in paragraph 14.2 above, the Claimant contends that in breach of clause 4.2 the Respondent has not paid the amount due on TAP's Interim Certificate 12.

15.3.2 Without prejudice and in the alternative to the claim made pursuant to the Contract in paragraph 9.1 above, for payment to the Claimant of liquidated damages withheld by the Respondent the Claimant contends that, in breach of clause 4.2, the Respondent wrongfully deducted liquidated damages from amounts certified under Interim Certificates 7, 8, 9 and 10. If, which the Claimant denies, the Respondent may otherwise have become entitled to an allowance by the Claimant for liquidated damages, such entitlement did not arise as in breach of clauses 2.3 and 2.7. TAP failed to grant an appropriate extension of time and failed to issue, as a necessary precondition of the right to deduct liquidated damages, a certificate of non-completion (there being no grounds upon which such a certificate could legitimately have been issued).

15.3.3 Without prejudice and in the alternative to the claim made pursuant to the Contract in paragraph 14 above, for payment to the Claimant of sums withheld by the Respondent for allegedly defective Work, the Claimant contends that in breach of clause 4.2 the Respondent wrongfully withheld payment of the sum of £32,000 there being no provision in the Contract by which this sum could lawfully have been withheld.

15.3.4 The Respondent was informed by the Claimant at the meeting on 8 April 1991 (at which the Arbitrator found that the Contract was made) and therefore had knowledge that the Claimant's financial position was such that it would incur finance charges, including interest, as a result of having to operate an overdraft if payment of all or any amount of the sums certified for payment on interim certificates were not paid within 14 days of the certificate or at all as required by the Contract.

15.3.5 By reason of the matters stated above in (paragraph 15.3) the Claimant has suffered loss and damage.

Particulars of Claims

(a) Non-payment of sums due under Interim Certificates
Architects Certificate No. 12 dated 13 April 1992 for £10,954. Payment was due on 22 April 1992.
Sums wrongfully withheld as liquidated damages from amounts certified under Interim Certificates 7, 8, 9 and 10 totalling £146,000 as set out in part A of Appendix I.
£32,000 wrongfully withheld by the Respondent in respect of allegedly defective work.

(b) Interest on liquidated damages withheld.

Interest in respect of sums wrongfully withheld as liquidated damages from amounts certified under Interim Certificates 7, 8, 9 and 10 (over and above the interest claimed for late payment of the full amounts due under these certificates as set out in (c) below) totalling £17,808.72, which continues to accrue from 28 January 1993 at 9 per cent per annum compounded at quarterly intervals, subject to any change in base rates. Particulars are given in Appendix I, part A.

(c) Late Payment of Interim Certificates

The interest claimed for late payment of sums certified under interim certificates 1 to 12 totals £4,268.56 accruing at 9 per cent per annum from 28 January 1993 (subject to any change in base rate) and compounded at quarterly intervals. Particulars are given in Appendix I, part B.

15.4 *Failure to Issue Final Certificate*

15.3.4.1 In the alternative to the claim made for sums due to the Claimant pursuant to the Contract at paragraphs 11 to 14 above the Claimant contends the Respondent was in breach of Contract as follows:

1. In breach of clause 4.5 TAP failed to prepare a statement of all final valuations or compute the adjusted contract sum within three months of receipt of the Claimant's draft Final Account (and other documents) on 3 June 1992.
2. In breach of clause 4.6 TAP failed to issue a Final Certificate or the Respondent make payment of any of the sums which should have been included within the Final Certificate, had it been produced.

15.3.4.2 By reason of the matters aforesaid (in paragraph 15.3.4) the Claimant has suffered loss and damage in that the Respondent has failed to pay the sum due to the Claimant under the Contract.

Particulars. The Claimant repeats the particulars in paragraphs 11 to 14 above.

16. Interest

16.1 ~~The Claimant is entitled to interest in lieu of damages at the judgment rate (15%) for late payment of interim certificates and on other damages from 2 July 1992.~~ In addition, or as an alternative to the interest which has been claimed above as special damages, the Claimant claims interest on all sums found due to the Claimant as damages for breach of contract, alternatively pursuant to the Contract, alternatively pursuant to Section 19A of the Arbitration Act 1950. Interest is claimed at whatever rate and from whatever date the Arbitrator deems just and equitable.

AND THE CLAIMANT CLAIMS

1. A declaration that the Claimant is entitled to an extension of time of 16 weeks to 31 March 1992. (as per paragraph 8.1 above).
2. A declaration that the Claimant is entitled to a refund of the sum of £146,000 wrongfully deducted by way of liquidated damages. (as per paragraph 9.1 above) or alternatively damages (including interest as special damages) as per paragraph 15.3.5(a) and (b).
3. A declaration that the Claimant is entitled to a refund in respect of sums wrongfully withheld in respect of alleged defects (as per paragraph 14.1 above) or alternatively damages as per paragraph 15.3.5(a).
4. The amount due under the Contract (as per paragraph 14.3 above) totalling £45,835.10 or alternatively damages as per paragraph 15.3.4.1.
5. The release of the second moiety of the retention fund as per paragraph 14.1 above.

6. Loss and Expense totalling £139,867.20 as per paragraph 10.3, together with £22,940.47 interest thereon which (subject to any change in base rates) continues to accrue at 9 per cent per annum from 28 January 1993 and compounded at quarterly intervals as set out in paragraph 10.4, or alternatively damages as per paragraph 15.2.2.

7. The sum of £10,954 in respect of Interim Certificate 12 either pursuant to the Contract (as per paragraph 14.2 above) or alternatively as damages for breach of Contract (as per paragraph 15.3.5(a) above) together with interest as special damages for non-payment of Interim Certificate 12 and late payment of other Interim Certificates (as per paragraph 15.3.5(c) above).

8.7 Interest as per paragraph 16 above.

9.8. Costs.

10.9. Further or other relief.

Served this 12th day of July 1993 by Jayrich Associates on behalf of the Claimant.

Re-served this 9th day of September 1993

7.8
203

IN THE MATTER OF THE ARBITRATION ACTS 1950 TO 1979

AND

IN THE MATTER OF AN ARBITRATION UNDER THE JCT ARBITRATION RULES (18 JULY 1988)

BETWEEN

RELIABLE BUILDERS LIMITED   Claimant

AND

SANCTUARY HOUSE LIMITED   Respondent

APPENDIX A

List of Documents referred to or relied on:

1. Letter Claimant to TAP dated 31 January 1991.

2. Letter TAP to the Claimant dated 20 March 1991 including the contract referred to therein as follows:
   The JCT Intermediate Form of Building Contract (IFC '84) 1990 Edition.

3. Letter TAP to the Claimant dated 15 April 1991 together with 'Agreed list of Items Subject to Remeasurement' attached thereto—two pages.

4. The 'Tender Budget' dated November 1990 as a Schedule of Rates only as amended by letter TAP to the Claimant dated 20 March 1991.

5. The Invitation to Tender, dated 7 January 1991, together with the documents referred to therein (as set out in para. 7.01 of the Arbitrator's Interim Declaratory Award).

6. The Claimant's letter to TAP dated 22 April 1991.

7. The Claimant's letter to TAP dated 10 April 1991.

8. The Claimant's letter to TAP dated 25 October 1991.

9. The Claimant's letter to TAP dated 1 January 1992.

10. The Claimant's letter to TAP dated 15 March 1992.

11. The Claimant's letter to TAP dated 15 October 1991.

[The above letters are examples only]

IN THE MATTER OF THE ARBITRATION ACTS 1950 TO 1979

AND

IN THE MATTER OF AN ARBITRATION UNDER THE JCT ARBITRATION RULES (18 JULY 1988)

BETWEEN

RELIABLE BUILDERS LIMITED   Claimant

AND

SANCTUARY HOUSE LIMITED   Respondent

APPENDIX B

CLAIMANT'S ORIGINAL PROGRAMME

**7.8
205**

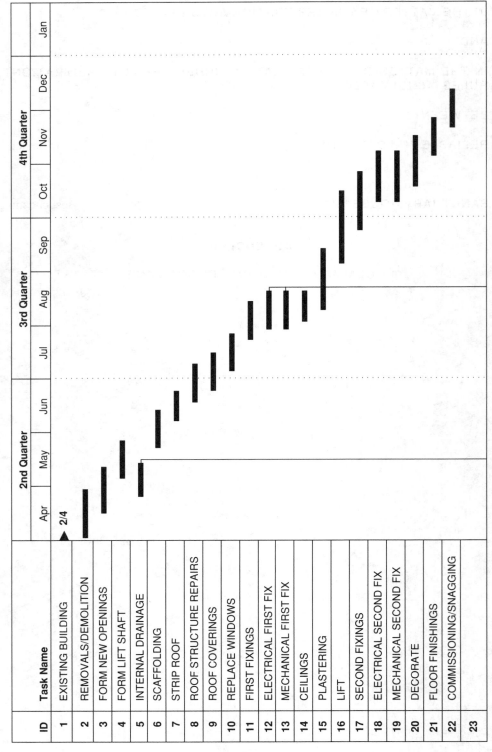

7.8
206

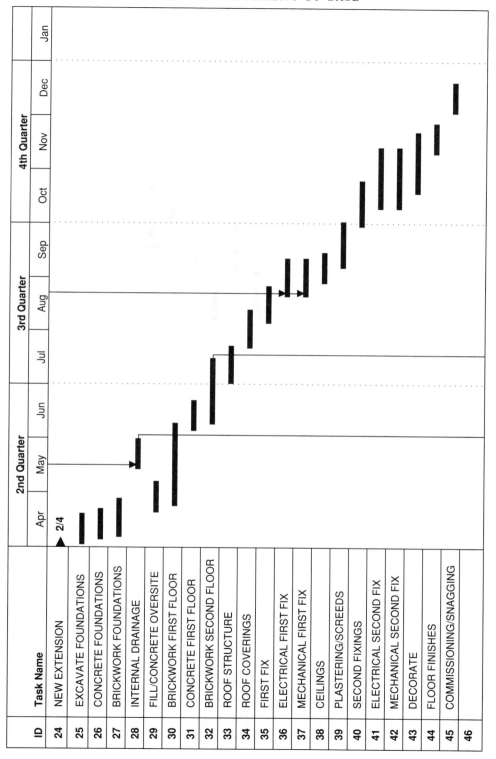

ID	Task Name
24	NEW EXTENSION
25	EXCAVATE FOUNDATIONS
26	CONCRETE FOUNDATIONS
27	BRICKWORK FOUNDATIONS
28	INTERNAL DRAINAGE
29	FILL/CONCRETE OVERSITE
30	BRICKWORK FIRST FLOOR
31	CONCRETE FIRST FLOOR
32	BRICKWORK SECOND FLOOR
33	ROOF STRUCTURE
34	ROOF COVERINGS
35	FIRST FIX
36	ELECTRICAL FIRST FIX
37	MECHANICAL FIRST FIX
38	CEILINGS
39	PLASTERING/SCREEDS
40	SECOND FIXINGS
41	ELECTRICAL SECOND FIX
42	MECHANICAL SECOND FIX
43	DECORATE
44	FLOOR FINISHES
45	COMMISSIONING/SNAGGING
46	

7.8
207

7.8
208

ID	Task Name	2nd Quarter			3rd Quarter			4th Quarter			
		Apr	May	Jun	Jul	Aug	Sep	Oct	Nov	Dec	Jan
47	EXTERNAL WORKS	2/4									
48	EXTERNAL DRAINAGE										
49	CAR PARK										
50	DRIVEWAY										
51	WALLS AND GATES										
52	LANDSCAPING										
53	PLANTING										
54	GARAGE										

IN THE MATTER OF THE ARBITRATION ACTS 1950 TO 1979

AND

IN THE MATTER OF AN ARBITRATION UNDER THE JCT ARBITRATION RULES (18 JULY 1988)

BETWEEN

RELIABLE BUILDERS LIMITED   Claimant

AND

SANCTUARY HOUSE LIMITED   Respondent

APPENDIX C

PARTICULARS OF DELAYS AND PROLONGATION

[Extracts Only]

Task Name	Delayed Completion (in weeks)	Prolongation (in weeks)	Reason for Delay/Prolongation
Removals/ Demolition	23	19	(1) Erroneous survey information (2) Late provision of revised drawing nos. DWG 00004/B and DWG 00005/B (3) Additional work arising as a result of Issue of Architects instructions nos. 4f, 4g, 4h, 5a, 5c, 6b, 6c, 10b
Form New Openings	4	4	(1) Erroneous survey information (2) Late provision of revised drawing nos. DWG 00004/B and DWG 00005/B (3) Additional work arising as a result of Issue of Architects instructions nos. 4g, 6a, 6g
Form Lift-shaft	4	4	(1) Additional work arising as a result of Issue of Architects instructions no 2a.
Ceilings/Plastering	7	1 day	(1) Delays to preceding trades as set out above. (2) Delay and disruption due to requirement to store and move equipment needed by Wonder Units Ltd.

Task Name	Delayed Completion (in weeks)	Prolongation (in weeks)	Reason for Delay/Prolongation
Plastering Screed	8	4	(1) Delays to preceding trades as set out above. (2) Delay and disruption caused by Respondent's contractor Alert Alarms. It was not possible to commence this task until a wiring diagram for the nurse call alarm system was provided on 3/10/91. Further delay and disruption was caused by the need to work alongside Alert Alarms labourers.
Floor Finishes	16	3 days	(1) Delays due to preceding trades as set out above. (2) Delay and disruption caused by Respondent's subcontractor Wonder Units delay in fitting kitchen units.

7.8
210

IN THE MATTER OF THE ARBITRATION ACTS 1950 TO 1979

AND

IN THE MATTER OF AN ARBITRATION UNDER THE JCT ARBITRATION RULES (18 JULY 1988)

BETWEEN

RELIABLE BUILDERS LIMITED   Claimant

AND

SANCTUARY HOUSE LIMITED   Respondent

APPENDIX D

PARTICULARS OF OVERALL PROLONGATION, UNECONOMIC WORKING AND DISRUPTION COSTS

7.8
211

1. Prolongation Costs based on 16-Week Extension of Time.

1.1 Staff	Weekly wages
Site Agent	410.00
Foreman	360.00
Ganger	300.00
QS (Part Time)	240.00
Indirect Labour (Cleaning)	210.00
	1,520.00

Total for 16 weeks £24,320.00

1.2 Site Accommodation	Weekly Hire charge (inc. VAT)
Office	30.00
Store	30.00
Toilet	30.00
Mess Room	40.00
	130.00

Total for 16 weeks £2,080.00

1.3 Site Expenses	Average Weekly Expenditure (inc. VAT)
Telephone	35.00
Electricity	30.00
Petty cash	50.00
Small Tools	50.00
Propane	27.00
	192.00

Total for 16 weeks £3,072.00

1.4 *Transport* Weekly costs (inc. VAT)
Van 80.00
Fuel 50.00
130.00

Total for 16 weeks £2,080.00

2. Uneconomic Working

2.1 Actual Average Weekly Labour Costs
Ave. No. of operators × ave. hrs. worked per week × ave. rate per hr.
16.8 × 45 × 7 = £5,064.23

Total labour cost for 52-week contract period = £263,339.96

2.2 *Labour included in tender rates*
Contract sum 550,000.00
Less:
Preliminaries and contingencies 76,000.00
Provisional sums 76,750.00 (152,750.00)
397,250.00

Assume 45% labour content—0.45 × 397,250.00 = £178,762.50

2.3 *Labour recovered through variations*
£35,407.90

2.4 *Disturbance of labour costs*
Actual costs of labour 263,339.96
Less:
Labour costs included in tender rates 178,762.50
Labour costs recovered through variations
(having accounted for 'omits') 33,834.22 (212,596.72)
Total £50,743.24

3. Disruption

3.1 Staff:
Finishings Foreman—13 weeks @ 340.00 per week = 4,420.00
Bricklayer Foreman—12 weeks @ 340.00 per week = 4,080.00
£8,500.00

3.2 Plant and equipment
Dumper 10 weeks @ 40.00 400.00
Forklift 20 weeks @ 80.00 1,600.00
5/3½ mixers 2 No 12 weeks @ 35.00 420.00
Standing scaffolding 18 weeks @ 46.00 828.00
Alterations to scaffolding 480.00
Transformers 2 No 15 weeks @ 20.00 300.00
Extension leads 5 No 15 weeks @ 5.00 75.00

7.8
212

Ladders and trestles Item		10 weeks	@	20.00	200.00
Sanders	2 No	10 weeks	@	20.00	200.00
Drills 2 No		15 weeks	@	15.00	225.00
Steam stripper	1 No	3 weeks	@	12.00	36.00
Space Heaters	1 No	6 weeks	@	32.00	192.00
Dehumidifier	1 No	6 weeks	@	33.00	198.00
Skill saws	2 No	12 weeks	@	20.00	240.00
Core drill	1 No	10 weeks	@	9.00	90.00
Kango	1 No	15 weeks	@	40.00	600.00
Paint strippers	3 No	10 weeks	@	30.00	300.00
Angle grinder	2 No	15 weeks	@	30.00	450.00
					£6,834.00

3.3   Total disruption cost: £8,500 + £6,834.00 = £15,334.00

7.8
213

IN THE MATTER OF THE ARBITRATION ACTS 1950 TO 1979

AND

IN THE MATTER OF AN ARBITRATION UNDER THE JCT ARBITRATION RULES (18 JULY 1988)

BETWEEN

RELIABLE BUILDERS LIMITED   Claimant

AND

SANCTUARY HOUSE LIMITED   Respondent

APPENDIX E

7.8
214

CALCULATIONS OF OVERHEADS AND PROFIT BASED ON THE HUDSON FORMULA

$$\text{Overhead Profit Percentage} \times \frac{\text{Contract Sum}}{\text{Contract Period}} \times \text{Period of Delay} = \text{Overheads and Profit}$$

$$0.15 \times \frac{55,000}{36} \times 16 = \underline{£36,666.66}$$

AMENDED STATEMENT OF CASE

IN THE MATTER OF THE ARBITRATION ACTS 1950 TO 1979

AND

IN THE MATTER OF AN ARBITRATION UNDER THE JCT ARBITRATION
RULES (18 JULY 1988)

BETWEEN

RELIABLE BUILDERS LIMITED   Claimant

AND

SANCTUARY HOUSE LIMITED   Respondent

APPENDIX F

LIST OF VARIATIONS

A.I. No.	Date	Description	Omit	Add
1a	06.04.91	10 No. Building Cards	—	—
1a	06.04.91	Drawing Issue	24,108.00	37,192.00
1c	06.04.91	Specification Issue	—	—
2a	14.04.91	Revisions to lift-shaft	2,400.00	4,271.00
3a	20.04.91	Dip & strip carved brackets		156.23
3b	20.04.91	Label & strip moulded work		371.00
4a	24.04.91	Deliver sound brackets		51.00
4b	24.04.91	Amendments to extension foundations	854.00	4,080.00
4c	24.04.91	Omit: Rebuilding of gable wall	279.00	540.00
4d	24.04.91	Omit: Honey comb dwarf wall	193.00	
4e	24.04.91	Joists to kitchen floor		664.59
4f	24.04.91	Repairs to timber frame		190.00
4g	24.04.91	Reissue of window details	1,413.00	16,156.00
4h	24.04.91	Reuse existing cornice		255.00
4k	24.04.91	Strip door hoods & timber mouldings		564.00
5a	30.04.91	Repairs to timber frame: North elev.		1,312.67
5b	30.04.91	Renew tiled cill		360.00
5c	30.04.91	Refurb works to gable elevation		1,813.12
6a	30.04.91	Work to existing windows		579.00
6b	30.04.91	Replace lead apron to W/3/3		421.00
6c	30.04.91	Additional span to garage roof		67.50
6d	30.04.91	Extension & utility room floor levels		
6e	30.04.91	Extension floor slab		
6f	30.04.91	Remedial to soffit of lintel D/G/4		150.00
6g	30.04.91	Lintel to door D/G/5		110.00
6h	30.04.91	Seal off storm water drain		3.76
6i	30.04.91	Omit: storm water manhole No. 2	394.00	
6j	30.04.91	Seal off foul water manhole		20.00
6k	30.04.91	Revised storm water drain	160.59	76.61
6l	30.04.91	Modify rainwater fully; kitchen		93.24
6m	30.04.91	Modify rainwater gully, extension		138.15
6n	30.04.91	Construct storm water manhole No. 2		589.25
6o	30.04.91	Construct new soakaway		726.38
6p	30.04.91	Adjust gully for kitchen waste		96.25
8a	17.05.91	Remove rubble inserts to fireplaces		384.00
9a	28.05.91	Lead soakers to apron flashing		519.00

7.8
215

A.I. No.	Date	Description	Omit	Add
9b	28.05.91	Work around W/2/3		224.06
9c	28.05.91	New lintel & brickwork		232.21
10a	05.06.91	Feathered lining to W/1/7		33.00
10b	05.06.91	Work to eaves of north elevation		490.75
10c	05.06.91	Work to fireplaces		
10e	05.06.91	Work to fireplace No. 1		44.00
10f	05.06.91	Work to fireplace No. 3		15.00
10g	05.06.91	Stairwell fascia		12.00
10h	05.06.91	Work to chimney; east elevation		210.50
10i	05.06.91	Replace stepped weathering		197.96
11a	17.06.91	Needle up stone chimney breast		409.00
11b	17.06.91	Remove partition between windows; beds 2		57.10
11c	17.06.91	Drawing issue; tie rods		698.00
12a	24.07.91	Omit: plasterboard; Add: hardboard		
12b	24.07.91	50 mm wood wool slabs		60.00
12c	24.07.91	Remove vent & patrass & make good		101.20
12d	24.07.91	Replace stone quoin		168.00
12e	24.07.91	Supply & fit register plate		36.30
13a	13.08.91	Replace lead flat, fit fascia, form drips		564.00
13b	13.08.91	Apron flashing to be dressed over		230.00
13c	13.08.91	Redress ends of roof valley gutter		160.00
13d	13.08.91	Renew apron flashing		162.00
13e	13.08.91	Work to W/2/1 & W/2/3		580.90
14a	13.09.91	Drawing issue (Revised)	5,161.00	7,112.00
14b	13.09.91	Architrave & dado details	1,211.00	1,427.80
15a	13.09.91	Drawing issue (Revised)	2,112.00	3,150.00
16a	17.10.91	Amend sink specification	225.00	357.45
16b	17.10.91	Revised Spec. M&E		
18a	18.10.91	Pay Reject Tiles invoice		158.63
18b	18.10.91	Colour tiles		41.80
18c	18.10.91	Work to attic bedroom		499.00
19a	18.10.91	Renew abutments to W/3/4		172.00
19b	18.10.91	Remove render step		50.00
19c	18.10.91	Replace incorrect lead covering		
19d	18.10.91	Replace door D.3.3		132.00
19e	18.10.91	Fit new skirting in attic No. 2		25.00
19f	19.10.91	Timber fillet to D.G.13		15.00
22a	28.10.91	Work by electrician		
22b	28.10.91	New architraves		60.50
22c	28.10.91	Issue of colour schedule		
23a	30.10.91	Removal of asbestos panelling		231.85
23b	30.10.91	Amend bath spec		33.06
23c	30.10.91	Insulate roof space		23.00
23d	30.10.91	Form access to above roof space		184.16
24a	11.11.91	Dimensions of gas hob		
25a	21.11.91	Renew tiled roof slopes		184.60
25b	21.11.91	Work to garden walls		2,626.63
25c	21.11.91	Stone dust rendering		23.00
25d	21.11.91	Wrap soil stack with glass wool		13.00
26b	21.11.91	Stone strings and gable to South elevation		742.00
26c	21.11.91	Obscure glass		255.00
26d	21.11.91	Glazing bars		298.00
26e	21.11.91	Form bulkhead in first-floor bathroom		74.28
26f	21.11.91	Case heating pipework		28.00
26g	21.11.91	Replace architrave; D.G.1		33.00
26h	21.11.91	Drawing issue Extension (Revised)	7,118.00	9,242.00
26i	21.11.91	Drawing issue Extension (Revised)	2,620.00	3,114.00
27a	22.11.91	Shelving in airing cupboard		105.30
29a	04.12.91	Omit: sheathing & floor finishes	1,656.00	
29b	04.12.91	Variety floors quote		2,905.63
30a	06.12.91	Lead flashings to dormers		518.00

A.I. No.	Date	Description	Omit	Add
30b	06.12.91	Dormer cornices		376.00
30c	06.12.91	Remove casing beads		212.00
30d	06.12.91	Gable wall, smooth finish rendered		257.00
31a	09.12.91	Drawing issue, joinery only		2,448.80
31b	09.12.91	Drawing issue		2,811.00
32a	13.12.91	Renew ceiling in lobby	24.20	84.26
32b	13.12.91	Repair rotten dado in lobby		35.20
32c	13.12.91	Omit: painting to stair handrail	70.00	
32e	13.12.91	Case vertical heating pipes		35.46
32f	13.12.91	Ceilings to basements		949.00
33a	13.12.91	Plaster as specification		
33b	13.12.91	New abutments to gable chimneys		256.56
33c	13.12.91	Remove rubble from fireplace		179.00
33d	13.12.91	Weather chimney stack		50.00
33e	13.12.91	Increase tile eaves overhang		171.77
33f	13.12.91	Paint chimney support metal work		31.14
34b	13.12.91	Plywood panel		22.00
35a	17.12.91	Patrass for entry phone		98.28
35b	17.12.91	Toilet roll holders	108.90	154.99
35c	17.12.91	Lead hood to W/1/10		170.00
35d	17.12.91	Lead slate to v.p.		80.00
35e	17.12.91	Work to attic window W/3/4		20.00
35f	17.12.91	New lead saddle		70.71
35g	17.12.91	Additionial undercoat; bed 2		35.20
36a	20.12.91	25×50 mm skirting in kitchen worktop		104.15
36e	20.12.91	Marble mantle shelf to living-room		118.56
36f	20.12.91	Remake back gutters; attic bed 2		412.00
36g	20.12.91	Work to chimneys		512.00
36h	20.12.91	Picture rail in bed 1		80.00
36j	20.12.91	Marble hearth to bed 2		29.00
37a	06.01.92	Reissue of colour schedule	100.80	189.00
38a	06.01.92	Batten sect & wardrobe rail: attic b/r		130.56
38b	06.01.92	John Try account; carved sections		84.38
38c	06.01.92	Treat ends to cills & trim of windows		10.00
38d	06.01.92	New rainwater pipe		84.00
38e	06.01.92	Work to rainwater gutter outlet		46.00
38f	06.01.92	Fixing of ceiling lighting fittings		175.00
39a	08.01.92	Remove loose rendering & re-render		41.20
39b	08.01.92	Remove paint from copings & M G		153.00
39c	08.01.92	Work to front entrance door D.G.1		29.00
39d	08.01.92	Extend short worktop		70.00
39e	08.01.92	Repoint stonework north elevation		195.00
39f	08.01.92	Stain new floorboards to match existing		209.00
39h	08.01.92	Cut & remake external putties		904.50
39i	08.01.92	Repoint leaded lights W.G.10, 11		21.00
39j	08.01.92	Rake out & repoint mortar; basement 2		180.00
40a	14.01.92	Work to staircase		342.00
41a	15.01.92	Revised redecoration		904.00
41b	15.01.92	Take up & relay stone paving		221.00
41c	15.01.92	Refix door & frame D.G. 14		46.00
41d	15.01.92	Remove hearth & make good; att rm		65.88
41e	15.01.92	Work to garden steps		95.00
41f	15.01.92	Leave clean stone on-site		
41g	15.01.92	Coir matting to lobby & garden entrance		105.16
41h	15.01.92	Adjust bottom of doors & fit threshold		81.75
41i	15.01.92	Fireplace installation		125.00
42b	27.01.92	Relocate bracket fitting		40.00
43a	29.01.92	Dining-room decorations		512.00
44a	03.02.92	Make good & point open joints		56.76
44b	03.02.92	Complete rendering to roof space		70.00
44d	03.02.92	Repairs to stone string: South elevation		84.60

7.8
217

A.I. No.	Date	Description	Omit	Add
44e	03.02.92	Roof level inspection		
45a	05.02.92	Letter plate		153.48
45b	05.02.92	Tool back stone dust rendering		109.00
45c	05.02.92	General trim lead		
45d	05.02.92	Redress wings of lead hood		
45e	05.02.92	Redress lead apron		
45g	05.02.92	New door D/G/1 omit letter plate		430.76
45h	05.02.92	Fit chubb mortise lock		50.00
46a	06.02.92	Wks roof level-E VALLEY		170.00
46b	06.02.92	Wks roof level-W VALLEY		181.50
46a	06.02.92	Wks Dormer gable STH ELEV		192.50
47a	13.02.92	Preparation of floors		725.00
49a	13.02.92	Smoke detectors		63.90
50a	24.02.92	Additional security devices		648.21
51a	24.02.92	Lay paving slabs		271.00
53a	28.02.92	Works to bedroom 1		47.30
53b	28.02.92	Works to airing cupboard and living-room		14.30
53c	28.02.92	Key for shutter catches		10.00
53d	28.02.92	Mortise lock		30.08
53e	28.02.92	Additional shelf		30.00
54a	28.02.92	Key for shutter catches		5.00
54b	28.02.92	Amend furniture W/3/4	41.05	13.45
54c	28.02.92	New nosing		37.00
54d	28.02.92	Renew rotten stonework		62.28
54f	28.02.92	Rake out and repoint garden wall		541.80
56a	28.02.92	New moulded plinth blocks		64.90
57c	03.02.92	Paint finish for doors		
57d	03.03.92	Omit top coat, add wallpaper	16.50	56.00
57e	03.03.92	Margins to fielded panels		1,606.00
57f	03.03.92	Redecoration on shutter cases		212.00
57g	03.03.92	Change garage roof tiles		518.00
58b	06.03.92	Install socket outlet		9.00
58d	06.03.92	Fit security bolts		30.80
58e	06.03.92	Fit coat peg rail		29.02
59a	06.03.92	Sash locks to windows	368.00	606.00
60a	09.03.92	Revised Glazing		954.00
60c	09.03.92	Revised call system		1,208.00
61a	13.03.92	Plinth for safe		171.00
61c	13.03.92	Pavings garage forecourt		1,200.00
61d	13.03.92	Service shutter		800.00
61e	13.03.92	Fit Preservation Trust plaque		15.00
61f	13.03.92	Security window locks		170.00
61g	13.03.92	Front door lock		70.00
62a	17.03.92	North Slopes Roof repairs		158.00
62b	17.03.92	North Slopes Roof repairs		172.00
63a	20.03.92	Change colours dining-room		322.00
63b	20.03.92	Make good rendering/decorate		110.00
64b	20.03.92	Room plaques		210.00
64c	20.03.92	Revise ceiling finish		151.00
65	23.03.92	Kitchen floor tiles		508.00
66	28.03.92	Attendance on Direct Contractors		270.00
67	28.03.92	New servery hatch		981.00
68	11.04.92	Attendance Direct Contractors		321.00
69	28.04.92	Fire Officer's requirements		588.00
70	30.04.92	Change colours bed 1		278.00
71	06.05.92	Wallpaper dining-room		351.00
72	08.05.92	Fire blankets in kitchen		208.00
		TOTAL OMITS/ADDS	63,351.04	142,035.27

IN THE MATTER OF THE ARBITRATION ACTS 1950 TO 1979

AND

IN THE MATTER OF AN ARBITRATION UNDER THE JCT ARBITRATION RULES (18 JULY 1988)

BETWEEN

RELIABLE BUILDERS LIMITED   Claimant

AND

SANCTUARY HOUSE LIMITED   Respondent

APPENDIX G

PROVISIONAL SUMS

7.8
219

A.I. No.	Date	Description	Omit	Add
2(b)	14.04.91	Acceptance of G Goslings tender	18,200.00	27,853.77
2(b)	14.04.91	Acceptance of G Goslings tender	1,200.00	1,506.98
2(c)	14.04.91	Acceptance of R T Browns tender	16,000.00	18,225.26
2(c)	14.04.91	Acceptance of R T Browns tender	3,600.00	4,293.54
20(a)	21.10.91	Settle Boulton and Paul Invoice	—	1,971.78
21(a)	25.10.91	John Lewis Quotation	—	2,903.72
55(a)	28.02.92	Adjustment of Provisional Sums	15,750.00	18,217.72
55(a)	28.02.92	Adjustment of Provisional Sums	12,000.00	19,251.54
55(a)	28.02.92	Adjustment of Provisional Sums	10,000.00	12,787.56
		TOTAL OMITS/ADDS	76,750.00	107,011.87

THE INTERLOCUTORY PERIOD

IN THE MATTER OF THE ARBITRATION ACTS 1950 TO 1979

AND

IN THE MATTER OF AN ARBITRATION UNDER THE JCT ARBITRATION
RULES (18 JULY 1988)

BETWEEN

RELIABLE BUILDERS LIMITED   Claimant

AND

SANCTUARY HOUSE LIMITED   Respondent

APPENDIX H

**7.8
220**

CALCULATION OF 'MINTER' INTEREST

Costs comprised within the Claimant's loss and expense accumulated as follows:

Date	Loss and Expense Head	Cumulative Amount
19.10.91	Disruption/Uneconomic Working	£66,077.24
28.11.91	Inflation Costs	£5,571.30
03.02.92	Prolongation Costs/Head Office	£139,867.20

The following table shows the applicable dates, interest rate and principal sums upon which
the calculation of the Claimant's entitlement to interest is based.

From	To	Days	Principal	Rate %	Amount
19.10.91	28.11.91	39	66,077.24	13.5	953.14
29.11.91	31.12.91	33	71,648.54	13.5	874.50
01.01.92	03.02.92	34	73,459.18	13.5	923.77
04.02.92	31.02.92	57	141,694.84	13.5	2,987.24
01.04.92	05.05.92	35	145,605.85	13.5	1,884.90
06.05.92	30.06.92	91	145,605.85	13.0	4,719.22
01.07.92	15.09.92	79	152,209.97	13.0	4,282.73
16.09.92	18.09.92	3	152,209.97	15.0	187.65
19.09.92	22.09.92	4	152,209.97	13.0	216.84
23.09.92	30.09.92	8	152,209.97	12.0	400.33
01.10.92	16.10.92	16	157,297.52	12.0	827.42
17.10.92	13.11.92	29	157,297.52	11.0	1,374.73
14.11.92	31.12.92	48	157,297.52	10.0	2,068.57
01.01.93	28.01.93	28	161,568.24	10.0	1,239.43
				Total	**£22,940.47**

and from the 28.01.93 (subject to any change in base rates) accruing at 9% per annum
compounded at quarterly intervals.

IN THE MATTER OF THE ARBITRATION ACTS 1950 TO 1979

AND

IN THE MATTER OF AN ARBITRATION UNDER THE JCT ARBITRATION RULES (18 JULY 1988)

BETWEEN

RELIABLE BUILDERS LIMITED   Claimant

AND

SANCTUARY HOUSE LIMITED   Respondent

APPENDIX I

PART A

Liquidated damages were wrongfully deducted from interim certificates 7, 8, 9 and 10. These certificates and others were also paid late; the interest claimed for which is included in Part B below. Interest in respect of sums withheld on interim certificates has been calculated from the date of partial payment of the sums due on these interim certificates.

Certificate	Date Damages Deducted	Amount of Damages
7	12.12.91	36,500.00
8	12.01.92	45,625.00
9	01.02.92	45,625.00
10	15.03.92	18,250.00
	Total	**£146,000.00**

Calculation of Compound Interest on Sums Wrongfully Deducted as Liquidated Damages from Interim Certificates

Amount	Days	Interest Date	Total £
36,500.00	19	13.5	256.50
36,756.50	12	13.5	163.13
83,381.50	20	13.5	616.79
129,006.50	43	13.5	2,051.73
147,256.50	16	13.5	871.43
150,959.58	5	13.5	279.17
150,959.58	56	13.0	3,010.91
150.959.58	78	13.0	4,193.78
150,959.58	2	15.0	124.07
150,959.58	4	13.0	215.06
150,959.58	8	12.0	397.04
159,179.61	17	12.0	889.65
159,179.61	29	11.0	1,391.48
159,179.61	48	10.0	2,093.32

163,554.06	28	10.0	1,254.66
		Total	17,808.72

and from the 28.01.93 (subject to any change in base rates) accruing at 9% per annum compounded at quarterly intervals.

PART B

Calculation of Compound Interest for Late Payment of Interim Certificates

Certificate No.	Amount	Days Late	Interest Rate	Total £
1	32,800.00	8	14.5	104.24
2	41,200.00	10	14.5	163.67
3	53,800.00	17	14.0	350.81
4	76,800.00	16	14.0	471.32
5	88,600.00	14	13.5	458.78
6	91,800.00	14	13.5	475.35
7	56,896.00	13	13.5	273.56
8	47,200.00	13	13.5	226.94
9	45,700.00	5	13.5	84.51
10	36,800.00	18	13.5	244.99
11	27,900.00	23	13.5	237.34
12	10,954.00	8	13.5	32.41
	10,954.00	91	13.0	355.02
	11,341.43	79	13.0	319.11
	11,341.43	3	15.0	13.98
	11,341.43	4	13.0	16.15
	11,341.43	8	12.0	29.82
	11,720.49	16	12.0	61.65
	11,720.49	29	11.0	102.43
	11,720.49	48	10.0	154.13
	12,038.70	28	10.0	92.35
			Total	4,268.56

and from 28.01.93 (subject to any change in base rates) accruing at 9% per annum compounded at quarterly intervals.

Order for Directions No 11—Consent to re-serve Defence and Counterclaim (7.9 Arb)

IN THE MATTER OF THE ARBITRATION ACTS 1950 TO 1979

AND

IN THE MATTER OF AN ARBITRATION UNDER THE JCT ARBITRATION RULES (18 JULY 1988)

BETWEEN

RELIABLE BUILDERS LIMITED   Claimant

AND

SANCTUARY HOUSE LIMITED   Respondent

**7.9 Arb
223**

ORDER FOR DIRECTIONS NO 11

Upon receiving and considering a Request, dated 14 September 1993, from Mr Crighton, to be permitted to re-serve the Respondent's Statement of Defence and Counterclaim and also consider the Claimant's objections to their Request in his letter dated 15 September 1993

I HEREBY DIRECT THAT

due to the very recent change in the Respondent's representation, the dates shown in Order for Directions No 2, and subsequent Orders, are now superseded by this Order, where appropriate.

(Numbered item references—unless otherwise noted—are to those items in Order for Directions No 2)

1.00 Timetable

The Respondent will be permitted to re-serve his Defence and Counterclaim. Service to be not later than 5.00 p.m. 8 October 1993.

In the re-serving this Defence and Counterclaim the Respondent to take into account the Claimant's previous Request for Further and Better Particulars, dated 28 August 1993.

As a result of the re-service of the Defence and Counterclaim the Claimant is HEREBY GRANTED CONSENT to serve an Amended Statement of Case not later than 14 days after the re-service of the Defence and Counterclaim.

The Claimant will serve his Reply to the Defence and Defence to the Counterclaim not later than 5.00 p.m. 28 days after the date of service of that pleading.

Again, the Respondent will be permitted to serve a Reply to the Defence to the Counterclaim, if he so wishes, not later than 5.00 p.m. 28 days after the date of service of that pleading.

2.00 Hearing

The dates set aside for the Hearing—item 3.00 Order for Directions No 5—are hereby cancelled and new dates will be set, by agreement, with the parties not later than 5.00 p.m. 6 December 1993.

The parties to inform me of their joint view as to the number of days that I am to set aside for the Hearing, preliminary reading and drafting of the Award. Also the approximate number of witnesses of fact and expert witnesses they would like to call and whether they intend to use Counsel at the Hearing.

Following this I will let the parties know what dates I have available and we will, once more, make a firm fixture.

3.00 Costs Thrown Away

By the Respondent's conduct of the reference to date a number of Orders have been given by me concerning 'costs thrown away' and to be paid by the Respondent in any event.

Accordingly the Respondent is to pay to the Claimant FORTHWITH all of his reasonable costs, reasonably incurred, which have become abortive as a result of the Respondent's conduct in this reference.

These costs include, but are not necessarily confined to, those incidental to and consequential on the following:

(i) Any abortive 'Pleading' including Further and Better Particulars.
(ii) Order for Directions No 7.
(iii) Order for Directions No 8.
(iv) Order for Directions No 11 (this Order).
(v) Late service of Defence and Counterclaim—see my letter 10 August 1993.
(vi) Cancellation of Inspection Meeting 16 August 1993—see my letter 12 August 1993.
(vii) Cancellation of the Hearing Dates as scheduled at item 3.00, Order for Directions No 5.

These costs to be taxed by me, on a commercial basis, if not agreed.

In addition, the Respondent is to pay FORTHWITH my costs thrown away by the same events as per the attached Fee Statement.

Should the Respondent fail to pay within 14 days of the request for payment the amounts ordered by me in this Direction then, on application of the Claimant, I will encapsulate this Direction into an Interim Award.

4.00 Costs of and incidental to this Order to be paid by the Respondent in any event.

Date: 16 September 1993	**D Emsee MSc FRICS FCIArb** **Registered Arbitrator**
To: Jayrich Associates	Representatives for the Claimant FAO Joel Redman
Kalmsyde & Joyoff	Solicitors for the Respondent FAO James Crighton

7.9 Arb
224

Order for Directions No 12—Seven-Day Notice to Respondent re failure to serve Defence (7.10 Arb)

<u>RECORDED DELIVERY</u>

IN THE MATTER OF THE ARBITRATION ACTS 1950 TO 1979

AND

IN THE MATTER OF AN ARBITRATION UNDER THE JCT ARBITRATION RULES (18 JULY 1988)

BETWEEN

RELIABLE BUILDERS LIMITED   Claimant

AND

SANCTUARY HOUSE LIMITED   Respondent

UNLESS ORDER—ORDER FOR DIRECTIONS NO 12

1.00 By my Order for Directions No 11 I gave consent to the Respondent to re-serve his Statement of Defence and Counterclaim not later than 5.00 p.m. 8 October 1993 in addition the Respondent was directed to pay the 'costs thrown away' as set out in that Order.

2.00 To date the Respondent has neither re-served his Statement, paid the 'costs thrown away' or made written application for an extension of time under Rule 6.7.1 before the expiry of the time for service.

3.00 ACCORDINGLY I HEREBY DIRECT THAT

UNLESS the Respondent, within seven days of the date of this Direction, re-serves his Statement of Defence and Counterclaim, I shall proceed on the basis that he will not be serving same.

4.00 Should the Respondent fail to re-serve his Statement within the seven-day period, and then he subsequently serves same, it shall be of no effect unless I am satisfied that there was good and proper reason why an application was not made within the time required by Rule 6.7.1 and why the Statement was not served within the seven-day period specified by this Order.

5.00 Costs of, incidental to and consequent on, this Order to be paid by the Respondent in any event.

Date: 11 October 1993   **D Emsee MSc FRICS FCIArb**
                             Registered Arbitrator

To: Jayrich Associates   Representatives for the Claimant
                             FAO Joel Redman

     Kalmsyde & Joyoff   Solicitors for the Respondent
                             FAO James Crighton

Order for Directions No 13—Re Taxation Preliminary Issue Costs (7.11 Arb)

<u>FAX & POST</u>

IN THE MATTER OF THE ARBITRATION ACTS 1950 TO 1979

AND

IN THE MATTER OF AN ARBITRATION UNDER THE JCT ARBITRATION RULES (18 JULY 1988)

BETWEEN

RELIABLE BUILDERS LIMITED   Claimant

AND

SANCTUARY HOUSE LIMITED   Respondent

ORDER FOR DIRECTIONS NO 13

WHEREAS

1.00 Further to my Order for Directions No 11—item 3.00—as the Claimant's 'costs thrown away', as defined by the said item 3.00, have not been agreed, I have been requested, by letter from the Claimant dated 13 October 1993, to tax those 'costs' on a commercial basis, as previously directed by me.

ACCORDINGLY I NOW DIRECT AS FOLLOWS:

2.00 The Claimant shall prepare an itemised bill of the relevant costs in the form that the bills have either been submitted, or are to be submitted, from consultant to client.
If there are separate fee earners involved these should be itemised separately.

3.00 This bill to be delivered to me, and to the Respondent, not later than 5.00 p.m. on Tuesday 19 October 1993.

4.00 Provided the Claimant delivers his bill, as directed in 3.00 above, the Respondent is to deliver to me and to the Claimant, not later than 5.00 p.m. 25 October 1993, a detailed response listing each and every objection with specific reasons for that objection, together with copies of any supporting authorities.

5.00 I reserve the right to call for any relevant documentation from the Claimant and to inspect the Claimant's privileged files in respect of any item included on the bill.

6.00 Although I have agreed to deal with this taxation by 'documents only' I reserve the right to orally examine any witness in cost proceedings which I may call.

7.00 I will encapsulate my determination in an Interim Award.

The parties are agreed that they will accept a lump-sum determination. However, the Respondent has requested reasons on legal issues, the extent of which she still has to define, including a question of law on which the Respondent might wish to appeal. If the Respondent fails to provide this information to me before I prepare my Award on Taxation, I shall not give reasons.

8.00 I will deal with the costs of taxation in my Award.

9.00 Liberty to Apply.

10.00 Costs in the cost reference.

Date: 15 October 1993

To: Jayrich Associates

    Kalmsyde & Joyoff

D Emsee MSc FRICS FCIArb
Registered Arbitrator

Representatives for the Claimant
FAO Joel Redman

Solicitors for the Respondent
FAO James Crighton

**7.11 Arb
227**

Order for Directions No 12A—Rejection of re-served Defence (7.12 Arb)

<u>RECORDED DELIVERY</u>

IN THE MATTER OF THE ARBITRATION ACTS 1950 TO 1979

AND

IN THE MATTER OF AN ARBITRATION UNDER THE JCT ARBITRATION RULES (18 JULY 1988)

BETWEEN

RELIABLE BUILDERS LIMITED   Claimant

AND

**7.12 Arb
228**

SANCTUARY HOUSE LIMITED   Respondent

UNLESS ORDER—ORDER FOR DIRECTIONS NO 12A

1.00 By my Order for Directions No 11 I gave consent to the Respondent to re-serve his Statement of Defence and Counterclaim not later than 5.00 p.m. 8 October 1993.

2.00 Following an UNLESS ORDER—ORDER FOR DIRECTIONS 12, 11 October 1993, the Respondent re-served his Statement of Defence and Counterclaim on 18 October 1993.
By item 5.07 of my Order for Directions No 2, I order that

> The Respondent's Statement of Counterclaim shall incorporate a Scott Schedule with full particulars of each item of alleged defective work separately listed and costed out.

The Scott Schedule included with the Respondent's Re-served Statement does not particularise the alleged defects as directed. As a result I do not accept this schedule as good service as directed.

3.00 ACCORDINGLY I HEREBY DIRECT that

UNLESS the Respondent, within seven days of the date of this Direction, re-serves his Statement of Defence and Counterclaim, with a Scott Schedule as directed by me in item 5.07 of my Order for Directions No 2, I shall proceed on the basis that he will not be serving same.

4.00 Should the Respondent fail to re-serve his Statement within the seven-day period with the Scott Schedule properly particularised and then he subsequently serves same, it shall be of no effect unless I am satisfied that there was good and proper reason why an application was not made within the time required by Rule 6.7.1 and why the Statement was not served within the seven-day period specified by this Order.

5.00 Costs of, incidental to and consequent on, this Order to be paid by the Respondent in any event.

Date: 18 October 1993   **D Emsee MSc FRICS FCIArb**
                                   Registered Arbitrator

To: Jayrich Associates   Representatives for the Claimant
                                   FAO Joel Redman

    Kalmsyde & Joyoff   Solicitors for the Respondent
                                   FAO James Crighton

**7.12 Arb
229**

Re-Re-Amended Statement of Defence and Counterclaim (7.13)

IN THE MATTER OF THE ARBITRATION ACTS 1950 TO 1979

AND

IN THE MATTER OF AN ARBITRATION UNDER THE JCT ARBITRATION RULES (18 JULY 1988)

BETWEEN

RELIABLE BUILDERS LIMITED   Claimant

AND

SANCTUARY HOUSE LIMITED   Respondent

7.13
230

³RE³-²RE²-¹AMENDED¹ STATEMENT OF DEFENCE AND COUNTERCLAIM

DEFENCE

1. Paragraphs 1 to 4 of the Statement of Case are admitted save that insofar as the Claimant has summarised or cited selectively from the Contract Conditions the Respondent will refer to those Conditions in full at the hearing hereof.
2. There were further express terms of the Contract as follows:
   (i) by Contract Condition 1.2 that the quality and quantity of the work should be that set out in the specification/schedules of work; and
   (ii) by Contract Condition 2,1 that the Claimant would begin and regularly and diligently proceed with the works and complete the same by the date of completion, being 10th December 1991;
   (iii) by Contract Condition 2.3 that the Claimant should use constantly its best endeavours to prevent delay and should do all that might be reasonably required to the satisfaction of the Architect to proceed with the works;
   (iv) by Contract Condition 2.9 that when in the opinion of the Architect/the Supervising Officer Practical Completion of the Works were complete he should forthwith issue a certificate to that effect and Practical Completion of the Works should be deemed for all the purposes of the Contract to have taken place on the day named in the Certificate;
   (v) by Contract Condition 4.11 that it was a condition of any claim by the Claimant to loss and expense that a written application be made for it within a reasonable time of it becoming reasonably apparent that it was incurred or was likely to be incurred.

3. It was an implied term of the Contract by virtue of the Supply of Goods and Services Act 1982 Section 15, alternatively an implication of law so as to give the contract business efficacy, that the Claimant would carry out the contract with reasonable skill and care.
4. Save that it is denied that a term was implied into the Contract that the Respondent would take all steps reasonably necessary to enable the Claimant to execute the works in a regular and orderly manner, paragraph 5 is admitted.
5. Save insofar as expressly admitted hereafter, paragraph 6.1 is denied.

6. Paragraphs 6.2 is admitted.

7. As to paragraph 6.3 it is admitted that the works were Practically Completed as at the 31st March 1992 but it is denied that the works were wholly complete [2]and reference is made to the Scott Schedule at Appendix A which records the defective and incomplete work.[2]

8. Paragraph 6.4 is admitted. The Respondent will set off against the said sum of £146,000 so much of its Counterclaim herein as may be necessary to extinguish the same.

9. In respect of paragraph 6.5 it is admitted and averred that the Respondent deducted £32,000 in respect of defective works. [3]Accordingly the Certificates issued respecting the Works which incorporate the defective works were for an overvalue and the Claimant was entitled to set off the said sum of £32,000 against the over certified balance.[3] [3]By reason of the said defective works the Respondent is entitled to a declaration that the true and proper value of Certificates 6, 7, and 10, net of retention was the sums of £79,800, £46,896 and £26,800 respectively thereby extinguishing the Claimant's claim to the said sum of £32,000 and the Respondent seeks such a declaration by its Counterclaim hereto. The adjustments to made to[3] Certificates are shown in Appendix B hereto.[3]

10. Paragraph 6.6 is admitted and averred. The Works are not wholly complete, no Certificate of Practical Completion has been issued and the Claimant is not entitled to the issue of a Final Certificate.

11. Delay

Save as hereinafter expressly admitted, paragraph 7 is denied and the Claimant is put to strict proof of each and every allegation of delay therein contained. [3]As to paragraph 7.2, the Defendant's response to Appendix C is set out in Appendix C hereto.[3] The Claimant left site on or about 13th April 1992 and was thereby in repudiatory breach of contract which breach is hereby accepted by the Respondent by reason whereof time is at large and the Claimant is not entitled to loss and expense in respect of any delay and the Respondent's pleading hereafter is subject thereto. Subject thereto the Respondent admits a delay of nine weeks and three days [3]as shown on the Respondent's programme at Appendix D hereto.[3] Adopting the numbering set out in the Statement of Case: (Claimants numbering in brackets)

(7.2.1) Removals/Demolitions and Form New Openings

(7.2.1) It is admitted that certain internal walls identified in TAP's drawings as non-load-bearing were in fact load-bearing. These areas were discovered by TAP shortly after the Claimant commenced on-site. In any event a reasonably competent builder would have ascertained which walls were load-bearing and which were not prior to commencing demolition. Revised drawings were issued on 7th May 1991 together with a Variation Order of the same date. The said drawings and Variation Order allowed the Claimant more than sufficient time to assimilate the variation into the Contract Programme without disruption or additional cost. In breach of contract condition 2.1 and/or 2.3 and/or 3.5 the Claimant failed forthwith to comply with the Variation Order and was itself responsible for part of the delay. The Respondent admits to a delay of three weeks and four days and the Claimant is entitled to an extension of time thereby.

(7.2.1.2) Further, in the week commencing 30th April 1991, Miss Frances Hutch of TAP, in conversations on-site with Mr John Watts, the Site Foreman (as recorded in the Site Meeting minutes dated 7th May 1991 set out TAP's intended resolution of the problem. In breach of condition 2.3 to use constantly its best endeavours to prevent delay the Claimant failed forthwith to act on that information.

(7.2.1.3) Further again, any short term delay caused by the revision to the internal walls was not critical to the completion of the Works. Alternatively, any such delay was not the dominant cause of any critical delay that occurred to the Contract Programme at that time.

(7.2.2) Works to the Lift-shaft

(7.2.2.1) It is admitted that TAP issued instruction 2a in connection with the construction of the lift-shaft, such variation being caused by the necessity to revise the brickwork and to introduce concrete ring beams.

(7.2.2.2) It is further admitted that the lift-shaft was a critical activity, but it is denied that the Architects Instruction caused delay to the Works. In breach of its obligation to use constantly its best endeavours to prevent delay as provided for by condition 2.3, the Claimant, failed to reschedule the commencement of the construction of the lift-shaft to an earlier date than that contained in the Claimant's original Contract Programme, but retained the original commencement date.

(7.2.3) Roof repairs and replacement windows

(7.2.3.1) It is admitted that certain of the the slates were laminated. The Respondent does not plead to the Claimant's contention that it had to take greater care than it anticipated in removal of the slates as the Statement of Case does not plead that any such additional work was a consequence of the Respondent's breach of its obligations and, therefore, discloses no cause of action. The Respondent denies any such breach as may be alleged and reserves the right to plead further to this allegation at such time as it may be properly particularised.

(7.2.3.2) Further or in the alternative it is not admitted that the two weeks' delay, or any delay, was caused to the Claimant by reason of the state of the slates.

(7.2.3.3) It is admitted that more repair was required to the timbers than estimated in the Specification and it is admitted that four weeks and one day delay was thereby caused. It is denied that eight weeks' delay was caused as the Claimant claims. The Respondent admits that the Claimant is entitled to an extension of time of four weeks and one day thereby.

(7.2.3.4) It is admitted that the scaffolding was removed before the roof leadwork was complete. This was a consequence of the requirement to glaze the windows as soon as they were installed so as to make the building weathertight and enable the first fixing trades to proceed. It is averred, however, that if the Claimant had carried out the roofing works regularly and diligently and in accordance with the Contract Programme as required by condition 2.1 the scaffolding would have been available for sufficient time to enable the Claimant to have completed the leadwork.

(7.2.3.5) It is admitted and averred that the scaffolding was required for six weeks longer than anticipated. This was caused by:

    (i) the Claimant's defaults as set out aforesaid;
    (ii) the Claimant's requirement to carry out remedial works to its own defective leadwork;
    (iii) late supply by the Claimant's subcontractor of flue lining detailing.

In any event these matters ran concurrently with other delays.

(7.2.3.6) The fitting of the windows was further delayed by the supply to the Claimant by its supplier of windows with defective rebates in the opening lights. It is denied that the Respondent is responsible for such delay or that the Claimant is entitled to an extension of time in respect of it.

(7.2.4) First Fix and Second Fix

(7.2.4.1) It is admitted and averred that the first fix works were not completed until 24th September 1991 but by reason of the facts and matters set out aforesaid it is denied that the delay was caused by the Respondent or that the Claimant is entitled to an extension of time in respect of it. It is admitted that some additional work was ordered in respect of the carpentry first fix operation but it is denied that entitled the Claimant to an extension of time of more than one week. It is denied that the extra works were critical to the commencement of the mechanical and electrical first fix works. It is averred that one week's delay was caused by the refusal of the Claimant's mechanical and electrical subcontractor to commence the first fix mechanical and electrical works when areas of site became available. It is admitted and averred that the mechanical and electrical first fixes commenced seven weeks late. Save as expressly admitted aforesaid it is denied that the delay was caused by the Respondent or that the Claimant is entitled to an extension of time in respect of it. The Respondent therefore admits that the Claimant is entitled to an extension of time of one week.

(7.2.4.2) In breach of the Claimant's obligation to proceed regularly and diligently with the works as provided by contract condition 2.1 and/or constantly to use its best endeavours to prevent delay as provided by contract condition 2.3 the Claimant failed to maintain or ensure that its subcontractors maintained adequate resources on-site. Specifically, in a conversation between Mr John Watts and Miss Frances Hutch on-site on or about 10th September 1991, Mr Watts confirmed that he was experiencing difficulties with a subcontractor who was avowedly dedicating resources to other sites at the expense of Sanctuary House.

(7.2.4.3) It is admitted and averred that the carpentry second fix in the old part of Sanctuary House commenced eight weeks late and that the Mechanical and Electrical second fix was similarly delayed. Save as expressly admitted aforesaid it is denied that the delay was caused by the Respondent or that the Claimant is entitled to an extension of time in respect of it.

(7.2.4.4) It is admitted that TAP, on the Respondent's behalf, varied, the specification for the mechanical and electrical second fix works by reason of which certain minor redesign had to be carried out by the mechanical and electrical subcontractor. It is further admitted, and averred, that the mechanical and electrical works to the old part of Sanctuary House were completed 10 weeks late. It is, however, denied that such revision was the proximate or dominant cause of the delay. The primary and substantive cause was incompatibility, at the first attempt at fixing, between the services and the attachment to the adjacent structures. It was the responsibility of the Claimant, whether directly or through its subcontractor, to design the mechanical and electrical services so as to comply with the Specification 12/f. By reason of the aforesaid, the subcontractor issued the installation drawings late thereby delaying TAP in the completion and issue of the construction drawings for the new extension. If the subcontractor had issued the installation drawings as reasonably required for the regular and diligent carrying out of the works, the minor amendments ordered in respect of the performance specification could have been incorporated without incurring additional delay.

(7.2.4.5) Further delay was caused to the second fix works by reason of continuing failure by the Claimant, through its subcontractors, adequately to resource the works. In support of that contention the Respondent will rely at the hearing hereof on the Claimant's labour returns. It is admitted that the works were, by the end of the second fix delayed by 11 weeks. By reason of the said underresourcing and by reason of the other facts and matters set out aforesaid, it is denied, save as expressly admitted that the delay was caused by the Respondent or that the Claimant is entitled to an extension of time in respect of it.

7.13
233

(7.2.5) Decorating and Commissioning Works

(7.2.5.1) It is admitted and averred that the decorating works (followed by commissioning and snagging) could not commence until the second fix works were complete and, therefore, were commenced 10 weeks late. Save as expressly admitted aforesaid it is denied that the delay was caused by the Respondent or that the Claimant is entitled to an extension of time in respect of it.

(7.2.5.2) It is admitted that the decorating works were delayed by three days. It is admitted that the Respondent altered the colour scheme and the architect issued an instruction to cover this item. It is admitted that the Claimant is entitled to an extension of time in respect of such delay.

12. Claim for an Extension of Time

It is admitted and averred that the Works were delayed and at the date hereof remain incomplete but save as expressly admitted aforesaid, it is denied that the delay was occasioned by the reasons in the Statement of Case. By reason of the Claimant's repudiatory breach, as hereby accepted, as referred to in paragraph 11 hereof, time at large and the Claimant is not entitled to an extension of time and the Respondent's pleading hereafter is subject thereto. Without prejudice to that contention, by reason of the facts and matters set out at paragraph 10 hereof [3]and at Appendix C hereof[3] it is admitted that the Claimant is entitled to an extension of time of nine weeks and three days from 10th December 1991 to 14th February 1992 but it is denied that the Claimant is entitled to any further extension of time as pleaded at paragraph 8 of the Statement of Case or at all. The Claimant was responsible for a delay of six weeks and four days and continuing and by reason of Clauses 2.6 and 2.7 of the Contract Conditions and the Appendix to the Conditions, and by reason thereof the Respondent was entitled to withhold £59,964.29 liquidated damages. The Respondent is entitled to set off against the balance withheld of £86,035.71 so much of its Counterclaim herein as may be necessary to extinguish that sum.

13. Loss and expense

The Claimant failed to make written application to TAP within a reasonable time of its allegedly becoming apparent that it had incurred or was likely to incur direct loss and/or expense in accordance with clause 4.11 of the Conditions of Contract and it is thereby denied that the Claimant is entitled to loss and/or expense. The remainder of the Defence is subject to that denial. Further, or in the alternative, it is not admitted that the Claimant has suffered any loss and expense and the Claimant is put to strict proof of each and every item claimed. [3]Further, or in the alternative Without prejudice to the above the Respondent admits as a figure the amounts contained herein and shown at Appendix E hereto.[3] Insofar as the Claimant has particularised its claim for loss and expense in paragraph 10 of the Statement of Case, the Respondent pleads as follows (Claimant's numbering in brackets):

(10.1.1) Prolongation

It is denied that the Claimant is entitled to a 16-week extension of time. Subject to paragraphs 11 and 12 hereof it is admitted that the Claimant is entitled to a nine-week and three-day extension of time.

(1) Staff. The ganger was included in the Claimant's rates for measured work and the Claimant is not entitled to additional recovery of the ganger's time as a preliminary item. The quantity surveyor is included in the Claimant's claim for overheads and irrecoverable under this head.

(2) Site Accommodation. The Claimant is the owner of its own site huts and temporary buildings. It is denied that the proper method of claim in respect of them is by reference to internal hire charges. The proper basis of calculation is the depreciation of the items plus an allowance for loss of use of the purchase cost, and maintenance costs.

(3) Site Expenses. The Claimant is the owner of its own small tools. It is denied that the proper method of claim in respect of thorn is by reference to internal hire charges. The proper basis of calculation is the depreciation of the items plus an allowance for loss of the purchase cost, and maintenance costs.

(4) Transport. The Claimant owned its own van. It is denied that the proper method of claim in respect of it is by reference to internal hire charges. The proper basis of calculation is the

depreciation of the van plus an allowance for loss of use of the purchase cost and maintenance costs.

[3]The Respondent admits as a figure the total sum of £12,144 in respect of prolongation costs as shown in Appendix E hereto subject to its pleading in paragraph 13 above.[3]

(10.1.2) Uneconomic Working

Save as expressly admitted it is denied that the Claimant was unable to make the best use of its labour in the manner planned or in the most economic manner. Further or in the alternative, it is denied that the Respondent was obliged to ensure that the Claimant was able to work in the manner it planned or in the most economic manner, the Respondent's obligations being limited to enabling the Claimant to complete within the contract period.

(1) Late Provision of Information. Save that it is admitted that TAP were required to provide the Claimant with information as reasonably required by the Claimant having regard to the actual progress of the works, the first sentence of 10.1.2.1 is denied. It is further denied that TAP provided information late as set out in Paragraph 7 and in Appendix C of the Statement of Case or at all [3]save as set out in Appendix C hereof.[3] Further or in the alternative it is denied that any provision of late information disrupted the Claimant's manner of working.

7.13
235

(2) Variations. It is admitted that variations were ordered by TAP on the Respondent's behalf though the accuracy of the Claimant's list of variations at Appendix F is denied save insofar as confirmed at Appendix J—hereof. The variations, were, however, ordered timeously such that it was possible for the Claimant to accommodate them without disruption. [3]The Respondent's response to Appendix C is at Appendix C hereof.[3]

(3) Interference by the Respondent's other Contractors. It is denied that the Respondent's other contractors caused disruption to the Claimant. The Claimant's own delays to the contract resulted in programme clashes and it is denied that any such disruption is the responsibility of the Respondent. [3]The Claimant's response to Appendix C is at Appendix C hereof.[3]

If, which is denied, the Claimant has suffered disruption, the basis of calculation of the figure of £50,743.24 as set out at Appendix D of the Statement of Case is not admitted [3]without prejudice to that contention the Respondent admits as a figure the sum of £13,515 as set out in Appendix F hereof.[3]

(10.1.3) Additional Staff and Equipment Due to Alleged Disruption

Save as expressly admitted aforesaid it is denied that TAP supplied information late or that any late supply of information disrupted the Plaintiff or extended programmed time periods; it is denied that the number or timing of variations disrupted the Plaintiff or extended programmed time periods; the concept of 'lateness of variations' other than as a function of 'timing' is not understood and not pleaded; it is denied that the Respondent interfered with other subcontractors.

It is not admitted that the Claimant had to retain staff on-site for extended periods to complete bricklaying and finishing operations or that equipment was hired for extended periods in order to complete the bricklaying and finishing operations. The alleged particulars of staff costs, equipment, hire costs and periods of prolongation at Appendix D are not admitted.

The figure of £15,334 is not admitted. [3]Without prejudice to that contention the Respondent admits as a figure the sum of £6956 as set out in Appendix G hereof.[3]

(10.1.4) Overheads and Profits

Save as expressly admitted aforesaid it is denied that the Claimant is entitled to an extension of time or to loss and expense. Further, or in the alternative, it is not admitted that the Claimant was involved in, or could have become involved in, other contracts in respect of which it could, in any event, have deployed its site team and head office staff. In the further alternative, it is denied that the proper method of calculation of lost overheads and profits is the Hudson formula as set out in Appendix E of the Statement of Case and it is not admitted that the Claimant has incurred lost overheads and profit of £36,666.66. [3]Without prejudice to that contention the Respondent admits as a figure the sum of £9,679.99 as set out in Appendix H hereof.[3]

(10.1.5) Inflation Costs

It is denied that the Claimant is entitled to inflation costs as claimed or at all. The Claimant would have not suffered the alleged losses if it had purchased its goods and materials in accordance with the original procurement pattern.

Further it is denied that the proper method of calculating inflation costs is on the basis of differences in the Building Cost Index relating to the original contract period and any period of delay in respect of which the Claimant may be entitled to an extension of time.

(10.2/10.3) Save as expressly admitted aforesaid, it is denied that the Claimant is entitled to loss and expense as claimed under these paragraphs or at all.

(10.4) Interest

Having regard to the Claimant's failure to make written application to TAP within a reasonable time of its becoming apparent that it had incurred or was likely to incur direct loss and/or expense in accordance with condition 4.11 of the Conditions of Contract specifically the Claimant's failure to give notice to the Defendant until the service of the Statement of Case on 12th July 1993 that interest as direct loss and/or expense was allegedly being incurred, it is denied that the Claimant is entitled to the same. Further or in the alternative it is not admitted that the Claimant has incurred such charges and the Claimant is put to strict proof thereof.

14. Variations, Provisional Sums and Contingencies

Adopting the Claimant's numbering:

(11.1) Variations
(11.1.1) It is admitted that TAP instructed variations within the meaning of clause 3.6 of the Contract.
(11.1.2) It is denied that all the purported variations contended for in Appendix F were instructed. [3]An analysis of the variations actually instructed, together with their valuations is at Appendix J hereof.[3]
(11.1.3) It is admitted that the omissions required to the Contract as a result of variations to the Contract totalled £63,351.04. It is denied that additions totalled £142,035.27. [3]The true and proper figure for additions is[3] [3]£124,590.69 as set out in Appendix J hereto.[3]

(11.2) Provisional Sums
(11.2.1) The omissions required to be made from and the additions required to be made to the Contract Sum for expenditure of provisional sums are admitted.

(11.3) Contingencies

(11.3.11) It is admitted that contingency sums totalling £13,600 require omission from the Contract Sum.

15. Remeasurable Sum

Paragraphs 12.1 and 12.2 are admitted. Save in respect of 'Guttering Change UPVC to cast aluminium', it is further admitted that the items set out in paragraph 2.3 require remeasurement. The guttering as specified in the Contract should have been cast iron with lead rainwater heads. As a concession the Architect accepted powder-coated aluminium. UPVC should not have been used. Further, or in the alternative any change in the specification falls to be valued as a variation and not to be remeasured.

Further again, the remeasurement figures for the remaining items are denied. [3]It is averred that the true figures are:[3]

[3]		
Removal of topsoil and reduced level dig		
Trench excavation and cart away	£1680.00	
Brickwork to foundations		
Landscaping cut, fill and cart away	£1870.00	
External Works	£809.00	
Main Driveway	£480.00	
Car Parking	£1240.00	

The Remeasured sum to be added to the Contract Sum is, therefore £6079. [3]

7.13
237

16. Final Account

Paragraphs 13.1 and 13.2 are admitted. As to 13.3 the total sum payable to the Claimant subject to the Respondent's rights of set-off as pleaded herein is [3]~~£633,980.51~~ as follows:

[3]	Omit	Add
Tender Sum		622,171.95
Agreed Reduction		72,171.95
Contract Sum		550,000.00
Provisional Sums	76,750.00	107,011.87
Variations	63,351.04	124,590.68
Contingencies	13,600.00	
Remeasured Items		6,079.00
	153,701.04	
		787,681.55
		153,701.04
Gross Measured Account	TOTAL	£633,980.51

3

17. Adjustments

As to Paragraph (14):

1. Paragraph 14.1.1 is admitted. The Respondent will set off against this sum so much of its Counterclaim herein as may be necessary to extinguish the same.
2. It is admitted and averred that £32,000 was withheld by the Respondent in respect of defective work. [2]A Scott Schedule identifying the said defects is set out at Appendix A hereof.[2]
3. It is admitted and averred that the second moiety of retention has been withheld. By reason of the aforesaid defects the Works are not practically complete and the Claimant is not entitled to the issue either of a Certificate of Practical Completion within the meaning of Condition 2.9 of the Contract Conditions or to a Final Certificate within the meaning of Condition 4.6 of the Contract Conditions.

18. As to paragraph 14.2 it is admitted and averred that the Respondent has not paid Certificate 12. The works valued therein were subject to defects in that the basement flooded such that the Certificate was not issued in accordance with Contract Condition 4.2 and the Respondent seeks a Declaration in its Counterclaim hereto. Should any amount be found due to the Claimant in respect thereof the Respondent will set off by way of extinction of such sum so much of its Counterclaim herein as may be necessary.

19. The amount due to the Claimant pursuant to the Contract (but not owing to the Claimant by reason of the Respondent's entitlement to set-off) net of the Claimant's alleged entitlement to loss and expense is:

Gross Measured Account	£633980.51
Certified to date	£610450.00
TOTAL DUE	£23530.51

20. Alleged Breaches of Contract

Save that subject to paragraph 12 hereof, it is admitted that the Claimant is entitled to an extension of time of nine weeks and three days paragraph 15.1.1 is denied.

21. Paragraph 15.2.1.1 is denied.

22. As to paragraph 15.2.1.2, it is denied that the Respondent failed to take all steps reasonably necessary to enable the Claimant to discharge its obligations under the Contract and/or to execute the Works in a regular and orderly manner. Further, or in the alternative, it is denied that it was an implied term of the Contract that the Respondent and/or TAP would take all steps reasonably necessary to execute the Works in a regular and orderly manner.

23. Paragraph 15.2.1.3 is denied. The Respondent refers to paragraph 11 [3]and Appendix C hereof.[3]

24. Save as expressly admitted above in respect of the Claimant's like claims for loss and expense arising under the Contract, paragraph 15.2.2 is denied and the Respondent is put to strict proof of each particular of alleged damage.

25. Alleged non-payment and late payment of interim certificates issued by TAP. As to paragraph 15.3.1 it is admitted and averred that the Respondent has not satisfied Certificate 12. By reason of the matters set out in paragraph 18 hereof it is denied that the Respondent is thereby in breach of Condition 4.2.

26. As to paragraph 15.3.2 it is admitted that the Respondent wrongfully deducted liquidated damages. If it be the Claimant's case that the Respondent is not entitled to unliquidated damages for breach of contract, that is denied. By reason of the Respondent's acceptance of the Claimant's repudiatory breach, as referred to in paragraphs 11 and 12

hereof, time became at large and the Respondent is entitled so such damages for delay as are provable at Common Law and are claimed in the Counterclaim hereto.

27. As to paragraph 15.3.3, by reason of the Claimant's defective work the Respondent is entitled to an Award for the sum of £32,634 [3]in respect of costs to remedy the defects shown in the Scott Schedule at Appendix A hereto.[3]

28. It is denied that the Claimant informed the Respondent on 8th April or at all that it might incur financing charges.

29. Paragraph 15.3.4 is admitted. Save as expressly admitted aforesaid the Particulars of Claims set out in paragraph 15.3.5 are denied and the Claimant is put to strict proof thereof.

30. As to paragraph 15.4, by reason of the Claimant's defective workmanship the Claimant is not entitled to the issue either of a Certificate of Practical Completion or a Final Certificate. By reason thereof, the sums set out in paragraphs 11 to 14 are not due. Further or in the alternative, by reason of the Respondent's rights of set-off as set out in the Counterclaim hereto the said sums are not owing.

31. It is denied that the Claimant is entitled to interest as pleaded at paragraph 16.

32. Save as hereinbefore admitted, each and every allegation of the Statement of Case is denied as if the same were set out and traversed seriatim.

33. Insofar as any sums may be found due to the Claimant in respect of its claim herein the Respondent will set off by way of extinction or diminution of that Sum so much of its Counterclaim herein as may be necessary.

7.13
239

COUNTERCLAIM

34. The Respondent repeates paragraphs 1–33 hereof.

35. Defective Work

In breach of the term of the Contract set out in Paragraph 2(i) hereof, alternative Paragraph 3, the Claimant's work as at 13th April 1992 contained or was and is subject to defects [2]as set out in the schedule at Appendix A hereto.[2]

36. [3]In the premises TAP failed properly to value or to certify the works as provided for by Contract Condition 4.2 such that Interim Certificates 6,7 and 10 should have been a true and proper value, net of retention the sums of £79,800, £46,896 and £26,800 respectively as shown at Appendix B hereto.[3]

[3]36.[3] 37. Fire Doors

By item 48 of the Specification the Claimant was required to treat all corridor doors with intumescent coverings to achieve half-hour fire resistance. By about November 1992 the glass fibre matting had split and wrinkled in an unsightly fashion by reason of which the Respondent is in breach of Contract Condition 1.2 set out in Paragraph 2(i) hereof, or alternatively the term of the Contract set out at Paragraph 3 hereof and the Respondent is entitled to the cost of remedying the same being 64 doors at £110 per door totalling £7,040 [3]in addition to the defects shown in the Scott Schedule as at Appendix A hereto.[3]

[3]37.[3] 38. Gibb's Ceiling

Preliminary issue number 5 determined herein by the Arbitrator concerned the question of whether the purported Gibb's Ceiling in the drawing-room of Sanctuary House was genuine. The Arbitrator determined that it was.

[3]38.[3] 39. There were clauses of the Specification as follows:

(i) '3/21h Carefully take up all the floorboarding to first floor and set aside for reuse. Refix on completion of fireproofing works, making up with new to match as required.'

(ii) '3/21j Carefully clear out floor void and clear and cart away all debris and prepare as necessary for fireproofing work.'

(iii) 3/23d Allow the provisional sum of £2,000 for repairs and restoration of plaster and mouldings to Gibb's Ceiling in ground-floor lounge to be carried out by a specialist subcontractor.'

(iv) '3/23e The existing Gibb's Ceiling in the lounge is to be protected with particular care. In addition to their general responsibility for protection of the existing structure, the contractor is to take whatever steps as are necessary to uphold the integrity of the existing ceiling. The Contractor's attention is drawn to the need to remove and reinstate the first-floor boarding, clear out any rubbish from the ceiling void and install fireproofing within the floor structure. These and any other works affecting the Gibb's Ceiling are to be carried out in such a way and all necessary protection taken to ensure that the integrity of the ceiling is maintained at all times and on completion.

(v) '3/23f Fireproof between timber floors, all in accordance with the requirements of the building control premises to be used for nursing home purposes, using a proprietary system to be approved by the Architect.'

[3]39.[3] 40. On 24th December 1992 the ceiling collapsed. It is averred that the collapse was caused by the Claimant's breach of Contract Condition 1.2 alternatively the term of the Contract set out as Paragraph 3 hereof in that the Claimant failed to carry out the fireproofing works with the proper skill and care and/or failed adequately to secure the ceiling when carrying out the said fireproofing.

[3]40.[3] 41. In consequence of the collapse of the ceiling 15 of Sanctuary House's units became uninhabitable and were vacated until repair works had been carried out, the total period of uninhabitability being from 24th December 1992 to 14th February 1994.

[3]41.[3] 42. By reason of the Claimant's breach of contract the Respondent has suffered loss and damage [3]as set out in Appendix K hereto.[3]

[3]42.[3] 43. Further, or in the alternative, the damage to the ceiling was caused by the Claimant's negligence in failing to carry out the fireproofing works with proper skill and care and/or failing adequately to secure the ceiling when carrying out the said fireproofing by reason of which negligence [3]the Respondent counterclaim like sums as set out in Appendix K hereto.[3]

[3]43.[3] 44. Basement Flooding

On or about 15th April 1992, the basement of Sanctuary House flooded. As Preliminary Issue number six the Arbitrator herein determined that the flooding was caused by the Claimant's breach of contract. By reason of the said breach of contract the Respondent has suffered loss and damage [3]as set out in Appendix L hereto.[3]

[3]44.[3] 45. Interest

The Respondent is entitled to interest on all sums due by way of Counterclaim pursuant to Section 19A of the Arbitration Act 1950.

[3]45.[3] 46. Costs.

AND THE RESPONDENT COUNTERCLAIMS:

i A declaration that the true and proper value of Interim Certificates 6, 7 and 10 net of retention was £79,800, £46,896 and £26,800 respectively:[3]

[3]i[3]ii £7,040 pursuant to Paragraph 37 hereof;

[3]ii[3]iii [3]£418,259 pursuant to Paragraph 42 and Appendix K alternative paragraph 43 hereof;[3]

[3]iii[3]iv [3]£29,843,25 pursuant to Paragraph 44 and Appendix L hereof;[3]

v [3]Damages;[3]

[3]iv[3]vi Interest pursuant to Statute for such period or periods as the Arbitrator may deem fit;

[3]v[3]vii Costs

Served this 17th day of August 1993 by Kalmsyde & Joyoff
Solicitors for the Respondent

[1]Amended and[1] Served 18th October 1993
[2]Re-Amended and[2] Served 21st October 1993
[3]Re-Re-Amended and[3] Served 24th February 1994

[2]APPENDIX A
SCOTT SCHEDULE SHOWING
DEFECTIVE AND INCOMPLETE WORK[2]

[2]RESPONDENT'S LIST

Item	Area	Particulars of Defect	Cost to Repair	Claimants Comments	Cost to Repair	Arbitrator's Notes
1	FF.B1	Cracks in plaster. Crack between ceiling and wall junction. Excessive shrinkage to skirtings and architraves, joints all open. Shakes in door lining. Door twisted.	751			
2	FF.B3	Cracks in plaster. Crack between ceiling and wall junction. Excessive shrinkage to skirtings and architraves, joints all open. Shakes in door lining. Door twisted.	772			
3	FF.B3	Cracks in plaster. Crack between ceiling and wall junction. Excessive shrinkage to skirtings and architraves, joints all open. Shakes in door lining. Door twisted.	681			
4	FF.B4	Cracks in plaster. Crack between ceiling and wall junction. Excessive shrinkage to skirtings and architraves, joints all open. Shakes in door lining. Door twisted.	872			
5	FF.B5	Cracks in plaster. Crack between ceiling and wall junction. Excessive shrinkage to skirtings and architraves, joints all open. Shakes in door lining. Door twisted.	855			
6	FF.B6	Cracks in plaster. Crack between ceiling and wall junction. Excessive shrinkage to skirtings and architraves, joints all open. Shakes in door lining. Door twisted.	671			
7	FF.B7	Cracks in plaster. Crack between ceiling and wall junction. Excessive shrinkage to skirtings and architraves, joints all open. Shakes in door lining. Door twisted.	680			
8	FF.B8	Cracks in plaster. Crack between ceiling and wall junction. Excessive shrinkage to skirtings and architraves, joints all open. Shakes in door lining. Door twisted.	605			
9	FF.B9	Cracks in plaster. Crack between ceiling and wall junction. Excessive shrinkage to skirtings and architraves, joints all open. Shakes in door lining. Door twisted.	677			
10	GF.B1	Cracks in plaster. Excessive shrinkage to skirtings and architraves, joints all open. Shakes in door lining. Door twisted. Fracture at lintel bearing.	501			
11	GF.B2	Cracks in plaster. Excessive shrinkage to skirtings and architraves, joints all open. Shakes in door lining. Door twisted. Fracture at lintel bearing.	655			
12	GF.B3	Cracks in plaster. Excessive shrinkage to skirtings and architraves, joints all open. Shakes in door lining. Door twisted. Fracture at lintel bearing.	972			

7.13
242

[2]

²RESPONDENT'S LIST

Item	Area	Particulars of Defect	Cost to Repair	Claimants Comments	Cost to Repair	Arbitrator's Notes
13	GF.B4	Cracks in plaster. Excessive shrinkage to skirtings and architraves, joints all open. Shakes in door lining. Door twisted. Fracture at lintel bearing.	900			
14	GF.B5	Cracks in plaster. Excessive shrinkage to skirtings and architraves, joints all open. Shakes in door lining. Door twisted. Fracture at lintel bearing.	951			
15	GF.B6	Cracks in plaster. Excessive shrinkage to skirtings and architraves, joints all open. Shakes in door lining. Door twisted. Fracture at lintel bearing.	700			
16	GF.B7	Cracks in plaster. Excessive shrinkage to skirtings and architraves, joints all open. Shakes in door lining. Door twisted. Fracture at lintel bearing.	982			
17	GF.B8	Cracks in plaster. Excessive shrinkage to skirtings and architraves, joints all open. Shakes in door lining. Door twisted. Fracture at lintel bearing.	908			
18	FF.CORR.	Plaster cracks. Excessive shrinkage to skirtings and architraves, joints all open. Shakes in door lining. Door twisted. Fracture at lintel bearing.	1171			
19	GF.CORR.	Plaster cracks. Excessive shrinkage to skirtings and architraves, joints all open. Shakes in door lining. Door twisted. Fracture at lintel bearing.	1417			
20	Bathr. B.1	Plaster cracks. Plumbing leaking at sink. Inadequate fall to bath waste. Mechanical ventilation ventilates into loft and not exterior. Wall tiles lifting off wall.	602			
21	Bathr. B.2	Plaster cracks. Plumbing leaking at sink. Inadequate fall to bath waste. Mechanical ventilation ventilates into loft and not exterior. Wall tiles lifting off wall.	415			
22	Bathr. B.3	Plaster cracks. Plumbing leaking at sink. Inadequate fall to bath waste. Mechanical ventilation ventilates into loft and not exterior. Wall tiles lifting off wall.	388			
23	Bathr. B.4	Plaster cracks. Plumbing leaking at sink. Inadequate fall to bath waste. Mechanical ventilation ventilates into loft and not exterior. Wall tiles lifting off wall.	472			
24	Bathr. B.5	Plaster cracks. Plumbing leaking at sink. Inadequate fall to bath waste. Mechanical ventilation ventilates into loft and not exterior. Wall tiles lifting off wall.	403			
25	Bathr. B.6	Plaster cracks. Plumbing leaking at sink. Inadequate fall to bath waste. Mechanical ventilation ventilates into loft and not exterior. Wall tiles lifting off wall.	517			
26	Stairc. S.1	Plaster cracks. Handrail and balustrade fixed incorrectly, undue movement.	314			

7.13
243

2

²RESPONDENT'S LIST

Item	Area	Particulars of Defect	Cost to Repair	Claimants Comments	Cost to Repair	Arbitrator's Notes
27	Stairc. S.2	Plaster cracks. Movement in handrails andbalustrade. Leaks occur into this area from roofs above.	402			
28	Stairc. S.3	Plaster cracks. Handrail and balustrade fixed incorrectly, undue movement.	388			
29	Sluice Room	Cracks in plaster. Mechanical ventilation vents into loft and not to exterior.	287			
30	Kitchen.	Kitchen units and extractor fan wrongly sited. Switches to electrical appliances not accessible. Tiles lifting. Deep scratches in floor finish.	1174			
31	Kitch. lobby	Fire doors badly fitting. Cracks to walls, ceiling joinery and decorations.	315			
32	Dining Room	Cracks in plaster. Excessive shrinkage in joinery. Fire doors badly fitting. Cracks in face.	322			
33	Quiet Room	Cracks in plaster. Excessive shrinkage in joinery. Fire door badly fitting, cracks in face.	214			
34	Staff Room	Cracks in plaster. Excessive shrinkage in joinery. Fire door badly fitting, cracks in face.	208			
35	Living Quart.	Cracks in plaster. Excessive shrinkage in joinery. Fire door badly fitting, cracks in face.	392			
36	Basem.	Fire escape door/window partially bricked up. Ventilation inadequate. Lift motor room and equipment sited in wet area.	922			
37	Lift	Lift motor room inadequately ventilated. Decorations and cleaning unfinished.	309			
38	GEN1	Door knobs and handles generally not properly fixed.	452			
39	GEN2	Nurse call alarm system. Wiring incomplete on second floor and system inaudible and not fit for purpose.	434			
40	GEN3	Bath hoists incompatible with baths or vice versa.	455			
41	GEN4	All bedrooms: 2nd wash-hand basins specified and only one provided in each.	617			
42	GEN5	Electrical services grossly inadequate in cupboard under second-floor fire escape. Installation does not comply with IEE regulations.	237			
43	Stairs Corr.	Socket outlets not provided in rear staircase area. Light switches not provided in second-floor corridors.	251			
44	GEN6	Plumbing installation. No wiring diagrams provided to boilers.	75			
45	Front	Wash-hand basin on front elevation drains to rainwater drain contrary to regulations.	108			
46	Plumb.	Plumbing leaks above Gibbs ceiling. Wash-hand basins and sluices have hot water coming out of cold taps.	222			
47	GEN7	Radiator covers: Paint flaking generally.	245			

Item	Area	Particulars of Defect	Cost to Repair	Claimants Comments	Cost to Repair	Arbitrator's Notes
48	GEN8	Sluicing sinks: Rinsing taps one missing which made them unacceptable to the health authority.	85		2	
49	GEN9	Lawns damaged during works and not properly repaired subsequently.	151			
50	GEN10	Rear ramp and side access not provided initially but required by regulations.	250			
51	GEN11	Employer's materials. Breeze blocks belonging to the employer were used by the contractors without permission and without payment.	95			
52	GEN12	Decorating generally. Paint is flaking and cracking generally around the building.	600			
53	GEN13	Driveway damaged by contractor's vehicles. No making good done.	812			
54	GEN14	Door closers fitting and adjusting incomplete. Wrong type fitted to ground-floor lift lobby preventing full opening of door.	217			
55	GEN15	Fire doors generally. Fire proof film lifting off from doors generally.	1171			
56	GEN16	Window shutters. Many window shutters painted up and not openable.	811			
57	GEN17	Bedroom furniture: Worktops swollen at edge due to moisture. Wardrobe doors twisted.	1581			
		Total	32634		2	

7.13
245

³APPENDIX B³
³SCHEDULE OF DEDUCTIONS IN RESPECT³
³OF DEFECTIVE WORK FROM CERTIFICATES³

Schedule of deductions from certificates in respect of defective work

Date	Certificate	Net after retention	Damages deducted	Amount for defects	Net adjusted certificate
16.10.91	6	91,800	Nil	12000	79800
15.11.91	7	56896	36500	10000	46896
16.12.92	8	47200	45625		47200
13.1.92	9	45700	45625		45700
11.2.92	10	36800	18250	10000	26800
12.3.92	11	27900	Nil		27900

7.13
246

³APPENDIX C³
³RESPONSE TO PARTICULARS OF³
³DELAY AND PROLONGATION³

Response to Particulars of Delays and Prolongation

[Extracts Only]

Task Name	Delayed Completion (in days)	Prolongation (in days)	Reason for Delay/Prolongation
Removals/ Demolition	75	25	The Respondent admits that certain walls were in fact load-bearing when they had been identified on the drawings as non-load-bearing. It is denied that drawn information was issued late. The information was issued as soon as the error in the survey information was discovered. It is admitted that there was additional work as a result of the necessary revisions to drawn information and the instructions issued. It is denied that these events caused any more than three weeks and four days delay to the completion date.
Form New Openings	10	Nil	It is denied that any information was issued late in respect of this operation. It is admitted that there were revisions to drawings. It is admitted that there was additional work in connection with this task. It is not admitted that the changes to this task had any effect on completion date.
Form Lift-Shaft	−4	Nil	It is admitted that there was additional work as a result of Architects instruction 2a. It is admitted that this task was critical. The claimant could have commenced this task much earlier and thereby reducing the effects on completion date and producing a time saving of four days.
Roof Repairs	49	29	It is denied that there was any delay caused to the roof repairs other than that due to the additional work in repairing structural timbers. This had an effect on completion date of four weeks and one day.
First Fixings	22	7	It is accepted that there was extra work which caused a delay to completion date of one week.
Ceilings	32	Nil	This task was delayed by preceding tasks.
Second ³Fixings	40	Nil	This task was delayed by preceding tasks.

7.13
247

Task Name	Delayed Completion (in days)	Prolongation (in days)	Reason for Delay/Prolongation
Brickwork Foundations	15	Nil	It is admitted that there was additional work in the foundations to the new extension. The delay so caused ran concurrently with other operations and therefore caused no delay to completion date.
[3] Brickwork Second Floor	10	Nil	This task was delayed by preceding tasks. [3]

7.13
248

[3]APPENDIX D[3]
[3]RESPONDENTS RETROSPECTIVE DELAY[3]
[3]ANALYSIS[3]

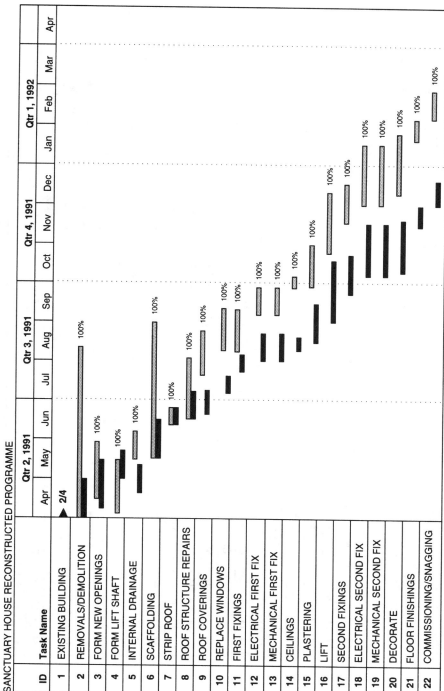

7.13
249

SANCTUARY HOUSE RECONSTRUCTED PROGRAMME

7.13
250

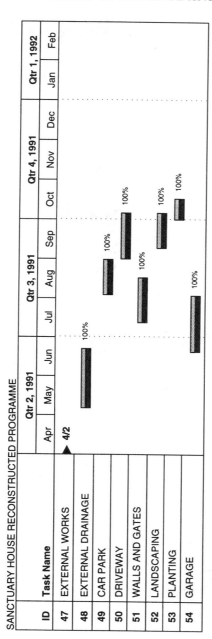

SANCTUARY HOUSE RECONSTRUCTED PROGRAMME

7.13
251

[3]APPENDIX E[3]
[3]PROLONGATION COSTS[3]

[3]**Prolongation Costs**

Site Staff

Site Agent	1 No		410.00
Foreman	1 No		360.00
Ganger	1 No		nil
Quantity Surveyor (part time)	1 No		nil
Indirect Labour (cleaning etc.)			210.00
	To Collection		980.00

Site Accommodation

Office	1 No	15.00	15.00
Store	1 No	15.00	15.00
Toilet	1 No	15.00	15.00
Mess Room	1 No	20.00	20.00
	To Collection		65.00

Transport for Operatives

Personnel Carrier	1 No	40.00	40.00
Fuel	5 Days	10.00	50.00
	To Collection		90.00

Site Expenses

(Average Weekly Expenditure)

Telephones	35.00
Electricity	30.00
Petty Cash	50.00
Small Tools	25.00
Propane	Nil
To Collection	130.00

COLLECTION

Site Staff	980.00
Site Accommodation	65.00
Transport for Operatives	90.00
Site Expenses	130.00
Total Cost Per Week	1265.00

Prolongation Costs
9 weeks 3 days @ £1,265.00 per week — 12,144.00

[3]APPENDIX F[3]
[3]UNECONOMIC WORKING[3]

	£	
[3]Contract Sum		550,000 [3]
Less:		
Preliminaries and Contingencies	76,000	
Provision Sums	76,750	
Named Subcontractors	125,000	
Domestic Subcontractors	73,500	
	351,250	351,250
		198,750

The Labour content included in the rates amounts to some 40% of the total rate.
Therefore the labour content is:

$$£198,750 \times 40\% = £79,500$$

The disturbance factor is 17% of this figure:

$$£79,500 \times 17\% = £13,515$$

7.13
253

[3]APPENDIX G[3]
[3]DISRUPTION COSTS[3]

[3] **Additional Staff and Equipment**

Additional Finishing Foreman from the 14th October 1991
to 1st November 1991

4 weeks @ £340.00	1360.00

Additional Bricklayer Foreman from the 9th April 1991
to 27th May 1991

8 weeks @ £340.00	2720.00

Plant and Equipment
Additional Hire Periods

Dumper		8 weeks @ £20.00	160.00
Forklift		15 weeks @ £40.00	600.00
5/3 mixers	2 No	8 weeks @ £17.50	280.00
Standing Scaffolding		11 weeks @ £23.00	253.00
Alterations to Scaffolding			480.00
Transformers	2 No	4 weeks @ £10.00	80.00
Extension Leads	5 No	4 weeks @ £2.50	50.00
Ladders and Trestles	Item	8 weeks @ £10.00	80.00
Sanders	2 No	4 weeks @ £10.00	80.00
Drills	2 No	4 weeks @ £7.50	60.00
Steam Stripper	1 No	3 weeks @ £6.00	36.00
Space Heaters	1 No	6 weeks @ £16.00	96.00
Dehumidifier	1 No	6 weeks @ £17.50	105.00
Skill Saws	2 No	4 weeks @ £10.00	80.00
Core Drill	1 No	8 weeks @ £4.50	36.00
Kango	1 No	8 weeks @ £20.00	160.00
Paint Strippers	3 No	8 weeks @ £15.00	120.00
Angle Grinder	2 No	8 weeks @ £15.00	120.00
			£6,956.00

7.13
254

³APPENDIX H³
³OVERHEADS AND PROFIT³

³Emden Formula   3

$$\frac{\text{Head Office Overheads and Profit}}{100} \times \frac{\text{Contract Sum}}{\text{Contract Period}} \times \text{Period of Delay}$$

b) Additional Costs   £

$$\frac{6.6\%}{100} \times \frac{550{,}000}{36} \times 9 \text{ weeks } 3 \text{ days} = 9679.99$$

3   3

7.13
255

³APPENDIX J³
³VARIATION ACCOUNT³

³ VARIATIONS

³

No	Date	Description	Omit	Add	Comment
1a	06.04.91	10 No. Building Cards	—	—	
1b	06.04.91	Drawing Issue	24,108.00	37,192.00	
1c	06.04.91	Specification Issue	—	—	
2a	14.04.91	Revisions to lift-shaft	2400.00	4271.00	
2b	14.04.91	Acceptance of G Gosling's tender			Prov Sum
2c	14.04.91	Acceptance of RT Brown's tender	—	—	Prov Sum
3a	20.04.91	Dip & strip carved brackets			C.Wks
3b	20.04.91	Label & strip moulded work			C.Wks
4a	24.04.91	Deliver sound brackets		51.00	
4b	24.04.91	Amendments to extension foundations	854.00	4,080.00	Agreed
4c	24.04.91	Omit: Rebuilding of gable wall	279.00	540.00	Agreed
4d	24.04.91	Omit: Honey comb dwarf wall	193.00		Agreed
4e	24.04.91	Joists to kitchen floor			C.Wks
4f	24.04.91	Repairs to timber frame			C.Wks
4g	24.04.91	Reissue of window details	1,413.00	16,156.00	Agreed
4h	24.04.91	Reuse existing cornice			C.Wks
4k	24.04.91	Strip door hoods & timber mouldings			C.Wks
5a	30.04.91	Repairs to timber frame: North elev.			C.Wks
5b	30.04.91	Renew tiled cill			C.Wks
5c	30.04.91	Refurb works to gable elevation			C.Wks
6a	30.04.91	Work to existing windows			C.Wks
6b	30.04.91	Replace lead apron to W/3/3		421.00	
6c	30.04.91	Additional span to garage roof		67.50	Agreed
6d	30.04.91	Extension & utility room floor levels			
6e	30.04.91	Extension floor slab			
6f	30.04.91	Remedial to soffit of lintel D/G/4			C.Wks
6g	30.04.91	Lintel to door D/G/5		110.00	Agreed
6h	30.04.91	Seal off storm water drain		3.76	Agreed
6i	30.04.91	Omit: storm water manhole No. 2	394.00		Agreed
6j	30.04.91	Seal off foul water manhole		20.00	Agreed
6k	30.04.91	Revised storm water drain	160.59	76.61	Agreed
6l	30.04.91	Modify rainwater gully; kitchen		93.24	Agreed
6m	30.04.91	Modify rainwater gully; extension		138.15	Agreed
6n	30.04.91	Construct storm water manhole No. 2		589.25	Agreed
6o	30.04.91	Construct new soakaway		726.38	Agreed
6p	30.04.91	Adjust gully for kitchen waste		96.25	
		Carried Forward	42,518.59	64,632.14	

³

No	Date	Description	Omit	Add	Comment
		Brought Forward	42,518.59	64,632.14	
7a	08.05.91	Adjust carcassing & outlet positions			Prov Sum
7b	08.05.91	Conceal cables			Prov Sum
7e	08.05.91	Relocated switches			Prov Sum
7f	08.05.91	Relocate pendant fitting			Prov Sum
7g	08.05.91	Provide pendant fitting & switch			Prov Sum
8a	17.05.91	Remove rubble inserts to fireplaces			C.Wks
9a	28.05.91	Lead soakers & apron flashing		519.00	Agreed
9b	28.05.91	Work around W/2/3			C.Wks
9c	28.05.91	New lintel & brickwork		232.21	Agreed
10a	05.06.91	Feathered lining to W/1/7		33.00	Agreed
10b	05.06.91	Work to eaves of north elevation		490.75	Agreed
10c	05.06.91	Work to fireplaces			
10e	05.06.91	Work to fireplace No. 1		44.00	Agreed
10f	05.06.91	Work to fireplace No. 3		15.00	Agreed
10g	05.06.91	Stairwell fascia		12.00	Agreed
10h	05.06.91	Work to chimney; east elevation			C.Wks
10i	05.06.91	Replace stepped weathering			C.Wks
11a	17.06.91	Needle up stone chimney breast			C.Wks
11b	17.06.91	Remove partition betw'n windows; bed 2		57.10	Agreed
11c	17.06.91	Drawing issue; tie rods		698.00	Agreed
12a	24.07.91	Omit: plasterboard; Add: hardboard			C.Wks
12b	24.07.91	50 mm wood wool slabs		60.00	Agreed
12c	24.07.91	Remove vent & patrass & make good		101.20	Agreed
12d	24.07.91	Replace stone quoin			C.Wks
12e	24.07.91	Supply & fit register plate		36.30	Agreed
13a	13.08.91	Replace lead flat, fit fascia, form drips			C.Wks
13b	13.08.91	Apron flashing to be dressed over		230.00	
13c	13.08.91	Redress ends of roof valley gutter		160.00	Agreed
13d	13.08.91	Renew apron flashing		162.00	Agreed
13e	13.08.91	Work to W/2/1 & W/2/3		580.90	Agreed
14a	13.09.91	Drawing issue (Revised)	5,161.00	7,112.00	
14b	13.09.91	Architrave & dado details	1,211.00	1,427.80	Agreed
15a	13.09.91	Drawing issue (Revised)	2,112.00	3,150.00	Agreed
15b	13.09.91	Installation of entry phone			Prov Sum
		Carried Forward	51,002.59	79,753.40	

7.13
257

3

3

³ VARIATIONS (Cont)

No	Date	Description	Omit	Add	Comment
		Brought Forward	51,002.59	88,326.33	
16a	17.10.91	Amend sink specification	225.00	357.45	Agreed
16b	17.10.91	Revised Spec. M&E			M&E
17a	17.10.91	Gas service to cooker (A G Plumbs)			Prov Sum
18a	18.10.91	Pay Reject Tiles invoice		158.63	Agreed
18b	18.10.91	Colour of tiles		41.80	Agreed
18c	18.10.91	Work to attic bedroom			C.Wks
19a	18.10.91	Renew abutments to W/3/4			C.Wks
19b	18.10.91	Remove render step		50.00	Agreed
19c	18.10.91	Replace incorrect lead covering			Agreed
19d	18.10.91	Replace door D.3.3		132.00	Agreed
19e	18.10.91	Fit new skirting in attic No. 2		25.00	Agreed
19f	18.10.91	Timber fillet to D.G.13		15.00	Agreed
20a	21.10.91	Settle Boulton & Paul invoice			Prov
21a	25.10.91	Accept John Lewis quotation			Prov
22a	28.10.91	Work by electrician			
22b	28.10.91	New architraves		60.50	Agreed
22c	28.10.91	Issue of colour schedule			
23a	30.10.91	Removal of asbestos panelling			C.Wks
23b	30.10.91	Amend bath spec		33.06	Agreed
23c	30.10.91	Insulate roof space			C.Wks
23d	30.10.91	Form access to above roof space			C.Wks
24a	11.11.91	Dimensions of gas hob			
25a	21.11.91	Renew tiled roof slopes		184.60	Agreed
25b	21.11.91	Work to garden walls		2,626.63	Agreed
25c	21.11.91	Stone dust rendering		23.00	Agreed
25d	21.11.91	Wrap soil stack with glass wool		13.00	Agreed
25e	21.11.91	Pendant fittings			Prov Sum
25f	21.11.91	Location of fluorescent fittings			Prov Sum
25g	21.11.91	Wiring of pendants			Prov Sum
26a	21.11.91	Reposition ceiling lights in kitchen			Prov Sum
26b	21.11.91	Stone strings and gable to sth elev			C.Wks
26c	21.11.91	Obscure glass		255.00	Agreed
26d	21.11.91	Glazing bars		298.00	Agreed
26e	21.11.91	Form bulkhead in first-floor bathroom		74.28	Agreed
26f	21.11.91	Case heating pipework		28.00	Agreed
26g	21.11.91	Replace architrave; D.G.1		33.00	Agreed
		Carried Forward	51,227.59	84,162.35	

7.13
258

³ VARIATIONS (Cont)   3

No	Date	Description	Omit	Add	Comment
		Brought Forward	51,227.59	84,162.35	
26h	21.11.91	Drawing issue Extension (Revised)	7,118.00	9,242.00	
26i	21.11.91	Drawing issue Extension (Revised)	2,620.00	3,114.00	
27a	22.11.91	Shelving in airing cupboard		105.30	Agreed
28a	04.12.91	Lighting schedule			Prov Sum
29a	04.12.91	Omit: sheathing & floor finishes	1,656.00		Agreed
29b	04.12.91	Variety floors quote		2,905.63	Agreed
30a	06.12.91	Lead flashings to dormers			C.Wks
30b	06.12.91	Dormer cornices			C.Wks
30c	06.12.91	Remove casing beads			C.Wks
30d	06.12.91	Gable wall, smooth finish rendered			C.Wks
31a	09.12.91	Drawing issue, joinery only		2,448.80	
31b	09.12.91	Drawing issue		2,811.00	
32a	13.12.91	Renew ceiling in lobby	24.20	84.26	Agreed
32b	13.12.91	Repair rotten dado in lobby			C.Wks
32c	13.12.91	Omit: painting to stair handrail	70.00		Agreed
32d	13.12.91	New WC at first floor			Prov Sum
32e	13.12.91	Case vertical heating pipes		35.46	Agreed
32f	13.12.91	Ceilings to basements		949.00	Agreed
33a	13.12.91	Plaster as specification			
33b	13.12.91	New abutments to gable chimneys		256.56	Agreed
33c	13.12.91	Remove rubble from fireplace			C.Wks
33d	13.12.91	Weather chimney stack		50.00	Agreed
33e	13.12.91	Increase tile eaves overhang		171.77	Agreed
33f	13.12.91	Paint chimney support metalwork		31.14	Agreed
34a	13.12.91	Dimmer switches			Prov
34b	13.12.91	Plywood panel		22.00	Agreed
34c	13.12.91	Face mounted cables			Prov Sum
35a	17.12.91	Patrass for entry phone		98.28	Agreed
35b	17.12.91	Toilet roll holders	108.90	154.99	Agreed
35c	17.12.91	Lead hood to W/1/10			C.Wks
35d	17.12.91	Lead slate to v.p			C.Wks
35e	17.12.91	Work to attic window W/3/4			C.Wks
35f	17.12.91	New lead saddle		70.71	Agreed
35g	17.12.91	Additional undercoat; bed 2		35.20	Agreed
35h	17.12.91	Remove rotten timber in basement		97.90	Prov Sum
36a	20.12.91	25×50 mm skirting in kitchen worktop		104.15	Agreed
36b	20.12.91	Reposition radiator in entrance lobby			Prov Sum
		Carried Forward	62,824.69	106,950.43	

7.13
259

³ VARIATIONS (Cont)

No	Date	Description	Omit	Add	Comment
		Brought Forward	62,824.69	106,950.43	
36d	20.12.91	Confirmation that gas valve adequate			Prov Sum
36e	20.12.91	Marble mantle shelf to living room		118.56	Agreed
36f	20.12.91	Remake back gutters; attic bed 2			C.Wks
36g	20.12.91	Work to chimneys			C.Wks
36h	20.12.91	Picture rail in bed 1		80.00	Agreed
36i	20.12.91	Gas supply to fire places			Prov Sum
36j	20.12.91	Marble hearth to bed 2		29.00	Agreed
37a	06.01.92	Reissue of colour schedule	100.80	189.00	Agreed
38a	06.01.92	Batten sect & wardrobe rail; attic b/r		130.56	Agreed
38b	06.01.92	John Try account; carved sections		84.38	Agreed
38c	06.01.92	Treat ends to cills & trim of windows		10.00	Agreed
38d	06.01.92	New rainwater pipe		84.00	Agreed
38e	06.01.92	Work to rainwater gutter outlet		46.00	Agreed
38f	06.01.92	Fixing of ceiling lighting fittings			C.Wks
39a	08.01.92	Remove loose rendering & rerender			C.Wks
39b	08.01.92	Remove paint from copings & M G		153.00	Agreed
39c	08.01.92	Work to front entrance door D.G.1			C.Wks
39d	08.01.92	Extend short worktop		70.00	C.Wks
39e	08.01.92	Repoint stonework north elevation			C.Wks
39f	08.01.92	Stain new floorboards to match existing			C.Wks
39h	08.01.92	Cut & remake external putties			
39i	08.01.92	Repoint leaded lights W.G.10,11		21.00	Agreed
39j	08.01.92	Rake out & repoint mortar; basement 2			
40a	14.01.92	Work to staircase		342.00	Agreed
41a	15.01.92	Revised redecoration		904.00	Agreed
41b	15.01.92	Take up & relay stone paving		221.00	Agreed
41c	15.01.92	Refix door & frame D.A.14		46.00	Agreed
41d	15.01.92	Remove hearth & make good; att rm		65.88	Agreed
41e	15.01.92	Work to garden steps		95.00	
41f	15.01.92	Leave clean stone on site			
41g	15.01.92	Coir matting to lobby & garden entr.		105.16	Agreed
41h	15.01.92	Adjust bottom of doors & fit th/hold		81.75	Agreed
41i	15.01.92	Fireplace installation		125.00	
42a	27.01.92	Replace consumer unit			Prov Sum
42b	27.01.92	Relocate bracket fitting			Error
		Carried Forward	62,925.49	109,951.72	

7.13
260

³ VARIATIONS (Cont)   3

No	Date	Description	Omit	Add	Comment
		Brought Forward	62,925.49	109,951.72	
42c	27.01.92	Alterations to electrical fittings			Prov Sum
43a	29.01.92	Dining-room decorations		512.00	
44a	03.02.92	Make good & point open joints		56.76	Agreed
44b	03.02.92	Complete rendering to roof space			C.Wks
44d	03.02.92	Repairs to stone string; sth elev			C.Wks
44e	03.02.92	Roof level inspection			
45a	05.02.92	Letter plate		153.48	Agreed
45b	05.02.92	Tool back stone dust rendering		109.00	
45c	05.02.92	General trim lead			
45d	05.02.92	Redress wings of lead hood			
45e	05.02.92	Redress lead apron			
45g	05.02.92	New door D/G/1 omit letter plate		430.76	
45h	05.02.92	Fit chubb mortice lock		50.00	
46a	06.02.92	Wks roof level-E VALLEY		170.00	
46b	06.02.92	Wks roof level-W VALLEY		181.50	
46d	06.02.92	Wks Dormer gable STH ELEV		192.50	
47a	13.02.92	Preparation of floors		725.00	Agreed
47c	13.02.92	Change single way switches			Prov Sum
49a	13.02.92	Smoke detectors		63.90	Agreed
49b	13.02.92	Testing electrical installation			Prov Sum
49c	13.02.92	Testing heating and HW installation			Prov Sum
50a	24.02.92	Additional security devices		648.21	Agreed
51a	24.02.92	Lay paving slabs		271.00	
53a	28.02.92	Works to bedroom 1		47.30	Agreed
53b	28.02.92	Works to airing cupboard and living room		14.30	Agreed
53c	28.02.92	Key for shutter catches		10.00	Agreed
53d	28.02.92	Mortice lock		30.08	Agreed
53e	28.02.92	Additional shelf		30.00	Agreed
54a	28.02.92	Key for shutter catches		5.00	
54b	28.02.92	Amend furniture W/3/4	41.05	13.45	Agreed
54c	28.02.92	New nosing			C.Wks
54d	28.02.92	Renew rotten stonework		62.28	
54f	28.02.92	Rake out and repoint garden wall			C.Wks
55a	28.02.92	Adjust: Provisional Sums			
		Carried Forward	62,966.54	113,702.96	

7.13
261

³ VARIATIONS (Cont)

No	Date	Description	Omit	Add	Comment
		Brought Forward	62,966.54	113,702.96	
56a	28.02.92	New moulded plinth blocks		64.90	Agreed
57a	03.03.92	Light fitting			Prov Sum
57b	03.03.92	Cable and outlet for fitting room			Prov Sum
57c	03.03.92	Paint finish for doors			
57d	03.03.92	Omit top coat, add wallpaper	16.50	56.00	Agreed
57e	03.03.92	Margins to fielded panels		1,606.00	
57f	03.03.92	Redecoration of shutter cases			C.Wks
57g	03.03.92	Change garage roof tiles		518.00	
58a	06.03.92	Omit wall unit, add lighting fitting			Prov Sum
58b	06.03.92	Install socket outlet		9.00	Agreed
58c	06.03.92	Change pelmet lighting fittings			Prov Sum
58d	06.03.92	Fit security bolts		30.80	Agreed
58e	06.03.92	Fit coat peg rail		29.02	Agreed
59a	06.03.92	Sash locks to windows	368.00	606.00	Agreed
60a	09.03.92	Revised Glazing		954.00	
60b	09.03.92	Change light fittings			Prov Sum
60c	09.03.92	Revised call system		1,208.00	
61a	13.03.92	Plinth for safe		171.00	
61b	13.03.92	TV aerial outlets			Prov Sum
61c	13.03.92	Pavings garage forecourt		1,200.00	
61d	13.03.92	Service shutter		800.00	
61e	13.03.92	Fit Preservation Trust plaque		15.00	
61f	13.03.92	Security window locks		170.00	
61g	13.03.92	Front door lock		70.00	
62a	17.03.92	North Slopes Roof repairs			C.Wks
62b	17.03.92	North Slopes Roof repairs			C.Wks
63a	20.03.92	Change colours dining room			Not Ins.
63b	20.03.92	Make good rendering/decorate			C.Wks
64a	20.03.92	Flood lighting			Prov Sum
64b	20.03.92	Room plaques		210.00	
64c	20.03.92	Revise ceiling finish		151.00	
65	23.03.92	Kitchen floor tiles		508.00	
66	28.03.92	Attendance Direct Contractors		270.00	
67	28.03.92	New servery hatch		981.00	
68	11.04.92	Attendance Direct Contractors		321.00	
69	28.04.92	Fire Officer's requirements		588.00	
70	30.04.92	Change colours bed 1		278.00	
71	06.05.92	Wallpaper dining room			Not Ins.
72	08.05.92	Fire blankets in kitchen		208.00	
		TOTAL ADDS/OMITS	63,351.04	124,590.68	

7.13
262

[3]APPENDIX K[3]
[3]GIBBS CEILING[3]

[3]**Particulars of Losses in connection with collapse of Gibbs Ceiling**   3

	£	£
Cost of repair		
Architects fees (net of VAT)	5,500.00	
Restoration works by specialist contractor (net of VAT)	38,424.00	
	43,924.00	43,924
Loss of profits		
Loss of income	330,960.00	330,960
Incremental costs incurred		
Emergency accommodation	6,480.00	
Staff overtime over Christmas period	1,495.00	
Increased promotional costs to relet rooms	2,740.00	
Financing costs	29,400.00	
	40,115.00	40,115
Incremental cost savings		
Cleaning staff salaries and Employer's National Insurance Contributions	(7,460.00)	
Heat and light	(9,280.00)	
	(16,740.00)	(16,740)
Diminution in value of Sanctuary House	20,000.00	20,000
	TOTAL	418,259

7.13
263

3   3

[3]APPENDIX L[3]
[3]BASEMENT FLOODING[3]

[3]Particulars of Losses in connection with Basement Flooding [3]

Equipment was irretrievably damaged and required replacement, linen and staff clothes were also damaged beyond remedy and as a consequence of the damage to the washing equipment additional laundry bills were incurred. Remedial tanking works had to be carried out.

	£	£
Two 35-pound industrial washing machines and two industrial dryers	14,050.00	
plus VAT	2,458.75	
	16,508.75	16,508.75
Free-standing dehumidifying equipment	750.00	
plus VAT	131.25	
	881.25	881.25
Additional laundry bills	3,348.00	
plus VAT	585.90	
	3,933.90	3,933.90
Residents clothes/Linen and staff clothes/uniforms	1,882.00	
plus VAT	329.35	
	2,211.35	2,211.35
Remedial tanking works	5,360.00	
plus VAT	938.00	
	6,298.00	6,298.00
Total		29,843.25

7.13
264

[3]

Interim Award on Taxation (7.14 Arb)

IN THE MATTER OF THE ARBITRATION ACTS 1950 TO 1979

AND

IN THE MATTER OF AN ARBITRATION UNDER THE JCT ARBITRATION RULES (18 JULY 1988)

BETWEEN

RELIABLE BUILDERS LIMITED   Claimant

AND

SANCTUARY HOUSE LIMITED   Respondent

TAXATION OF COSTS
INTERIM AWARD

1.00 The Claimant entered into a Contract, on or about 28 March 1991, with the Respondent to undertake building works and services at the Respondent's premises known as SANCTUARY HOUSE (formerly The Old Manor House) WOODBRIDGE, SUFFOLK.

2.00 The Contract was goverened by the terms and conditions of the JCT Intermediate Form of Building Contract for works of a simple content (IFC '84) 1984 Edition to and including Amendment 5.

The Contract contained an arbitation agreement in Article 5 and Clause 9.

WHEREAS

3.00 A dispute arose between the parties and the Claimant gave notice to the Respondent and the parties, having failed to agree on an arbitrator, I was subsequently appointed by the President of the Royal Institution of Chartered Surveyors (RICS), by appointment, dated 20 February 1993, all in accordance with the provisions of Clause 9 above.

I submitted my Terms and Conditions to the parties and these were returned by the Claimant on 26 February 1993 and by the Respondent 23 March 1993.

4.00 A Preliminary Meeting took place between me, the parties and their representatives on 23 March 1993 where the parties opted for Rule 6.

A timetable for the submission of the parties' Statements of case, Defence, etc was agreed to following the determination by me of some Preliminary Issues.

Subsequently the Respondent, as a result of a change of solicitor, by letter 14 September 1993, sought leave to Re-serve his Defence and Counterclaim.

Having considered the Claimant's objection to this Request I consented, by letter 16 September 1993, to the Respondent's Re-service on condition that the Respondent paid all costs thrown away as result.

5.00 By my Order for Directions No 11, in which I set out new directions as a result of granting the Respondent's request by item 3.00, I directed of that Order as follows:

'Costs Thrown away'

By the Respondent's conduct of the reference to date a number of Orders have been given by me concerning 'costs thrown away' and to be paid by the Respondent in any event.

ACCORDINGLY

the Respondent is to pay to the Claimant FORTHWITH all of his reasonable costs, reasonably incurred, which have become abortive as a result of the Respondent's conduct in this reference.

These costs include, but are not necessarily confined to, those incidental to and consequential on the following:

    (i) Any abortive 'Pleading' including Further and Better Particulars.

    (ii) Order for Directions No 7.

    (iii) Order for Directions No 8.

    (iv) Order for Directions No 11 (this Order).

    (v) Late service of Defence and Counterclaim—see my letter 10 August 1993.

    (vi) Cancellation of Inspection Meeting 16 August 1993—see my letter 12 August 1993.

    (vii) Cancellation of the Hearing Dates as scheduled at item 3.00, Order for Directions No 5—16 July 1993.

These costs to be taxed by me, on a commercial basis, if not agreed.

In addition, the Respondent is to pay FORTHWITH my costs thrown away by the same events as per the attached Fee Statement.

Should the Respondent fail to pay, within 14 days of the request for payment, the amounts ordered by me in this Direction then, on application of the Claimant, I will encapsulate this Direction into an Interim Award.'

6.00 By my Order for Directions No 2, item 21.00, I directed that:

'I will be required to tax the parties' costs in the event that they are not agreed. The basis of the taxation will be on 'reasonable amount, reasonably incurred commercial man basis'—not the standard basis as laid down in the White Book. The Form of Bill may be that prepared on a solicitor and client basis.'

7.00 The parties were unable to agree what costs should be paid by the Respondent to the Claimant under this direction.

8.00 The Respondent also failed to pay my 'costs thrown away' as specified by this direction and detailed in the Fee Statement dated 17 September 1993, which was subsequently submitted to the Respondent.

ACCORDINGLY

9.00 The Claimant, by letter, 13 October 1993, formally requested taxation of these costs, by documents only, following which I issued Order for Directions No 13, detailing what was required of the parties in connection with the taxation exercise.

10.00 In accordance with item 2.00 of Order for Directions No 13, the Claimant delivered to me, copied to the Respondent, on 19 October 1993, details of various costs some of which covered the 'costs thrown away' to be taxed as paid as part of this present exercise.

11.00 These costs were not in the form on which I could carry out this taxation exercise particularly, bearing in mind, that it was a documents only procedure. Therefore, after further faxed correspondence these costs were resubmitted to me on 20 October 1993.

The Respondent's solicitor delivered his Reply to the Claimant's submission on costs on 25 October 1993 as directed by me, by item 4.00 of my Order for Directions No 13.

7.14 Arb
266

12.00/ The Respondent's solicitor, in his Reply, *inter alia*, made the following points:
12.01

    12.01.1 Travel time should be charged at half rate—Agreed.

    12.01.2 Proportional reduction of 'costs thrown away' should be made for issues extant—Agreed.

    12.01.3 It is long established (in High Court proceedings) that the expenses of the party attending his own representative are not costs to be allowed in taxation. Mr Crighton referred me to Ord. 62 RSC and cited *Atkins* v *Johnson Matthey & Co* and submitted that I was bound by the same principles. In the alternative, to pay both the Claimant's representative for management time incurred would amount to double recovery.

12.02 I received the Claimant's Reply to Mr Crighton's submission on the above, by his letter 29 October 1993. Whilst I do not apply the same reasoning as Mr Redman I broadly come to the same conclusion and that is this.

    12.02.1 I am not bound by the White Book but I must act judicially in determining this issue.

    12.02.2 When informing the parties, at the Preliminary Meeting on 23 March 1993, that I would tax their costs if not agreed, I explained then that I should do so on a 'commercial man basis' and went on to say that this was not 'the standard basis' as defined by the White Book and that the form of Bill may be on a solicitor and own client basis. My ultimate test being a reasonable costs, reasonably incurred.

    12.02.3 In applying this test I believed that I may take into account costs incurred by management which would otherwise have increased the costs charged by the party's representative, i.e. Mr Redman. This doubly so when the management time in question is also expended by a party's principal witness.

Accordingly I have allowed a reasonable proportion of management time.

12.03 The Claimant also claimed for his clients solicitor's costs, much of which appeared to be in respect of the abortive County Court case, the costs of which are not included in this present exercise.

I had already warned the Claimant, by letter 19 October 1993, that without a breakdown of his client's solicitor's costs, I would be unable to identify whether any of their costs come under this present category of 'costs thrown away' for which their client is not being recompensed elsewhere. No breakdown was received.

Accordingly, for the purpose of this taxation only, I disallow these solicitor's costs in their entirety.

12.04 Mr Redman considered that I should include the costs of the County Court action referred to above. Mr Crighton agreed and, on the assumption that I did, asked me to give a Reasoned Award on the issues set in 13.00 below.

12.05 However, having disallowed the solicitor's costs in their entirety for the reasons given in 12.03 above I am unable to consider these costs. In any event before doing so I would need to be convinced that I had jurisdiction to deal with costs incurred in a prior court action.

13.00   Item 7.00 of my Order for Directions No 13 directed, *inter alia*, that:

    'The parties are agreed that they will accept a lump-sum determination. However, the Respondent has requested reasons on legal issues, the extent of which she still has to define, including a question of law on which the Respondent might wish to appeal. If the

Respondent fails to provide this information to me before I prepare my Award on Taxation, I shall not give reasons.'

The only issue on which the Respondent asked me to give reasons was on the matter of legal aid as set out below.

'Does Section 17 of the Legal Aid Act 1985 apply to legal costs incurred in a County Court action which subsequently, by Order of the County Court, fall to be decided by the Arbitrator.'

As I am not considering the County Court costs as part of this current exercise, for the reasons given in 12.05 above, I shall not attempt to answer that question or give further reasons for my determination.

14.00 **ACCORDINGLY I DETERMINE THAT:**

14.01 The Respondent pay **FORTHWITH** to the Claimant the sum of £4148 (Four Thousand One Hundred and Forty-eight Pounds) which sum includes £617.79 (Six Hundred and Seventeen Pounds Seventy-nine Pence) by way of Value Added Tax.

14.02 **I FURTHER DETERMINE** that the Respondent shall pay **FORTHWITH** to me the sum of £4668.47 (Four Thousand Six Hundred and Sixty-eight Pounds Forty-seven Pence) which sum includes £695.30 (Six Hundred and Ninety-five Pounds Thirty Pence) by way of Value Added Tax as set out in my Fee Statement dated 17 September 1993 to which shall be added £20.25 (Twenty Pounds Twenty-five Pence) interest, in accordance with item 6.00 (of Terms and Conditions) giving a total of £4688.72 (Four Thousand Six Hundred and Eighty-eight Pounds Seventy-two Pence).

7.14 Arb 268

15.00 Costs of the Award

The costs of this my Award, which I hereby tax and settle in the sum of £1480 (One Thousand Four Hundred and Eighty Pounds) which sum includes £220.43 (Two Hundred and Twenty Pounds Forty-three Pence) by way of Value Added Tax on my fees, shall be borne by the Respondent.

16.00 Costs Paid by Claimant

Should the Claimant have paid any of my costs in 14.02 and 15.00 above then the Respondent must reimburse the Claimant the total amount paid **FORTHWITH.**

17.00 Costs of the Taxation

17.01 **I HEREBY DIRECT** that the Claimant's costs of this taxation be paid by the Respondent **FORTHWITH.**

17.02 In the event that the costs of taxation are not agreed they will be taxed by me on a 'commercial man' basis.

17.03 Within seven days of the date of this my Award the Claimant shall submit his costs to the Respondent, in the event that the Respondent does not pay these costs within a further seven days, the Claimant may make a written submission to me to tax these costs.

17.04 The Respondent has seven days thereafter to lodge any objections with me after which I shall make my determination on the cost of this taxation by 'documents only.'

Given under my hand at Hunstanton this second day of November 1993.

In the presence of

Name ....

Address ....

Occupation ....

....

D Emsee MSc FRICS FCIArb
Registered Arbitrator

Order for Directions No 14—Re Specific Discovery (7.15 Arb)

<u>Fax & Post</u>

IN THE MATTER OF THE ARBITRATION ACTS 1950 TO 1979

AND

IN THE MATTER OF AN ARBITRATION UNDER THE JCT ARBITRATION RULES (18 JULY 1988)

BETWEEN

RELIABLE BUILDERS LIMITED   Claimant

AND

SANCTUARY HOUSE LIMITED   Respondent

ORDER FOR DIRECTIONS NO 14

WHEREAS

1.00 The Respondent applied to me by letter 1 November 1993 for discovery of documents, listed in that letter, in the power and possession of the Claimant and

WHEREAS

2.00 I invited the parties to deal with this discovery voluntarily, the Claimant responded by letter, 4 November 1993, objecting to such discovery on the grounds that it was not relevant to the issues.

3.00 Having considered the Request and the Claimant's objections

I HEREBY DIRECT THAT

4.00 The Claimant gives discovery of the said documents not later than 5.00 p.m. 10 November 1993. In the event of the Claimant failing to give discovery the Respondent may apply to me for further directions.

5.00 Costs to be costs in the reference.

Date: 4 November 1993   **D Emsee MSc FRICS FCIArb**
                                   Registered Arbitrator

To: Jayrich Associates   Representatives for the Claimant
                                    FAO Joel Redman

   Kalmsyde & Joyoff   Solicitors for the Respondent
                                    FAO James Crighton

Requests for Further & Better Particulars of Re-re-amended Defence and Counterclaim (7.16)

IN THE MATTER OF THE ARBITRATION ACTS 1950 TO 1979

AND

IN THE MATTER OF AN ARBITRATION UNDER THE JCT ARBITRATION RULES (18 JULY 1988)

BETWEEN

RELIABLE BUILDERS LIMITED   Claimant

AND

SANCTUARY HOUSE LIMITED   Respondent

REQUEST FOR FURTHER AND BETTER PARTICULARS OF THE *RE-RE-AMENDED* STATEMENT OF DEFENCE AND COUNTERCLAIM

Defence

Under paragraph 9

OF: all of this paragraph

Request

    (1) Set out with full particularity which certificates it is alleged were overvalued and what adjustments it is claimed should be made in respect of the same.

        It is averred that the true and proper value of certificate 6, 7 and 10, net of retention was the sum of £79,800.00, £46.896.00 and £26,800.00 respectively as set out in Appendix 1 hereto.

Under Paragraph 14

OF: '(11.1.2) it is denied that all the purported variations contended for in Appendix F were instructed.'

Request

    (2) State with full particularity which variations the Respondent alleges were not instructed.

OF: '(11.1.4) ... it is denied that additions totalled £142,035.27.

    Request

    (3) Of this pregnant negative state what the Respondent contends the total additions to compromise and give full particulars as to how that sum is calculated

Under paragraph 15

OF: '... the remeasurement figures for the remaining items are denied.'

Request

(4) State what it is alleged are the true remeasurement figures for the said items.

Under paragraph 16

OF: '... the total sum payable to the Claimant subject to the Respondent's rights of set-off as pleaded herein is £633,980.51.'

Request

(5) State how the figure of £633,980.51 is calculated.

Under paragraph 41

OF: '... the Respondent has suffered loss and damage.'

Request

(6) Set out with full particularity each item of alleged loss and damage and itemise the costs thereof.

7.16
271

Under paragraph 43

OF: 'By reason of the said breach of contract the Respondent has suffered loss and damage.'

Request

(7) Set out with full particularity each item of alleged loss and damage and itemise the costs thereof.

Served this 15th November 1993 by Jayrich Associates, Swansea House, 48 Queens Road, Norwich, Norfolk NR2 LO6

APPENDIX 1
SCHEDULE OF DEDUCTIONS FROM CERTIFICATES IN RESPECT OF DEFECTIVE WORK

Date	Certificate	Net after retention	Damages deducted	Amount for defects	Net adjusted certificate
16.10.91	6	91,800	NIL	12,000	79,800
15.11.91	7	56,896	36,500	10,000	46,896
16.12.92	8	47,200	45,625		47,200
13.1.92	9	45,700	45,625		45,700
11.2.92	10	36,800	18,250	10,000	26,800
12.3.92	11	27,900	NIL		27,900

7.16
272

Order for Directions No 15—Unless Order Re Further and Better Particulars (7.17 Arb)

IN THE MATTER OF THE ARBITRATION ACTS 1950 TO 1979

AND

IN THE MATTER OF AN ARBITRATION UNDER THE JCT ARBITRATION RULES (18 JULY 1988)

BETWEEN

RELIABLE BUILDERS LIMITED   Claimant

AND

SANCTUARY HOUSE LIMITED   Respondent

UNLESS ORDER—ORDER FOR DIRECTIONS NO 15

7.17 Arb
273

WHEREAS

1.00 The Claimant, by letter 15 November 1993, requested the Respondent to clarify some points of the Statement of Defence and Counterclaim served on 18 October 1993. The Respondent informed me that he considered this to be a 'fishing expedition' and did not intend to reply.

2.00 The Claimant has now requested me to order the Respondent to provide Further and Better Particulars of this Statement of Defence and Counterclaim

and

3.00 I have considered the Request in the light of the criteria which I outlined at the Preliminary Meeting with the parties, 23 March 1993, and agree that the particulars sought meet this criteria.

ACCORDINGLY I HEREBY DIRECT

4.00 That the Respondent serve a Reply to these Further and Better Particulars not later than 5.00 p.m. on 1 November 1993.

5.00 Should the Respondent fail to provide fully particularised answers to this Request he will be debarred from counterclaiming those items not properly particularised.

6.00 Liberty to Apply.

7.00 Costs of the Claimant's application in connection with this Order and the costs of this Order to be paid by the Respondent in any event.

Date: 15 November 1993

D Emsee MSc FRICS FCIArb
Registered Arbitrator

To: Jayrich Associates

Representatives of the Claimant
FAO Joel Redman

Kalmsyde & Joyoff

Solicitors for the Respondent
FAO James Crighton

Reply to Request for Further and Better Particulars of Re-re-amended Defence and Counterclaim (7.18)

IN THE MATTER OF THE ARBITRATION ACTS 1950 TO 1979

AND

IN THE MATTER OF AN ARBITRATION UNDER THE JCT ARBITRATION RULES (18 JULY 1988)

BETWEEN

RELIABLE BUILDERS LIMITED   Claimant

AND

SANCTUARY HOUSE LIMITED   Respondent

7.18
274

REPLY TO REQUEST FOR FURTHER AND BETTER PARTICULARS OF THE *RE-RE-AMENDED* STATEMENT OF DEFENCE AND COUNTERCLAIM PURSUANT TO A REQUEST DATED 15TH NOVEMBER 1993

Defence

Under paragraph 9

OF: all of this paragraph

Request

(1) Set out with full particularity which certificates it is alleged were overvalued, and what adjustments it is claimed should be made in respect of same.

It is averred that the true and proper value of certificate 6, 7 and 10, net of retention was the sum of £79,800.00, £46,896.00 and £26,800.00 respectively as set out in Appendix 1 hereto.

Under paragraph 14

OF: '(11.1.2) it is denied that all the purported variations contended for in Appendix F were instructed.'

Request

(2) State with full particularity which variations the Respondent alleges were not instructed.

Answer

An analysis of the variations actually instructed, together with their valuations is at Appendix J—7.13 of the Re-Re-Amended Statement of Defence and Counterclaim.

OF: '(11.1.4) ... it is denied that additions totalled £142,035.27.'

REPLY TO REQUEST FOR FURTHER AND BETTER PARTICULARS

Request

    (3) Of this pregnant negative state what the Respondent contends the total additions to comprise and give full particulars as to how that sum is calculated.

Answer

The true and proper figure for additions is £125,590.69 as set out in Appendix J—7.13 of the Re-Re-Amended Statement of Defence and Counterclaim.

Under paragraph 15

OF: '...the remeasurement figures for the remaining items are denied.'

Request

    (4) State what it is alleged are the true remeasurement figures for the said items.

Answer

Removal of topsoil and reduced level dig	
Trench excavation and cart away	£1,680.00
Brickwork foundations	
Landscape cut fill and cart away	£1,870.00
External works	£809.00
Main driveway	£480.00
Car parking	£1,240.00

The remeasured sum to be added to the Contract Sum is, therefore, £6,079.00.

Under paragraph 16

OF: '...the total sum payable to the Claimant subject to the Respondent's rights of set-off as pleaded herein is £633,980.51.'

    (5) State how the figure of £633,980.51 is calculated.

Answer

	Omit £	Add £
Tender sum		622,171.95
Agreed reduction		72,171.95
Contract Sum		550,000.00
Provisional Sums	76,750.00	107,011,87
Variations	63,351.04	124.590.68
Contingencies	13,600.00	
Remeasured items		6,079.00
	153,701.04	
		787,681.55
		153,701.04
Gross Measured Account	TOTAL	£633,980.51

Under paragraph 41

OF: '...the Respondent has suffered loss and damage.'

Request

    (6) Set out with full particularity each item of alleged loss and damage and itemise the costs thereof.

Answer

See Appendix 2 hereof.

Under paragraph 43

OF: 'By reason of the said breach of contract the Respondent has suffered loss and damage.'

Request

(7) Set out with full particularity each item of alleged loss and damage and itemise the costs thereof.

Answer

See Appendix 3 hereof.

Served this 22nd November 1993 by Kalmsyde & Joyoff, 48 Crown Street, Ipswich, Suffolk IP5 2QR.

7.18
276

APPENDIX 1
SCHEDULE OF DEDUCTIONS FROM CERTIFICATES IN RESPECT OF DEFECTIVE WORK

Date	Certificate	Net after retention	Damages deducted	Amount for defects	Net adjusted certificate
16.10.91	6	91,800	NIL	12,000	79,800
15.11.91	7	56,896	36,500	10,000	46,896
16.12.92	8	47,200	45,625		47,200
13.1.92	9	45,700	45,625		45,700
11.2.92	10	36,800	18,250	10,000	26,800
12.3.92	11	27,900	NIL		27,900

7.18
277

APPENDIX 2
PARTICULARS OF LOSSES IN CONNECTION WITH COLLAPSE OF GIBBS CEILING

	£	£
Cost of repair		
Architects fees (net of VAT)	5,500.00	
Restoration works by specialist contractor (net of VAT)	38,424,00	
	43,924.00	43,924
Loss of profits		
Loss of income	330,960.00	330,960
Incremental costs incurred		
Emergency accommodation	6,480.00	
Staff overtime over Christmas period	1,495.00	
Increased promotional costs to relet rooms	2,740.00	
Financing costs	29,400.00	
	40,115.00	40,115
Incremental cost savings		
Cleaning staff salaries and Employer's National Insurance Contributions	(7,460.00)	
Heat and light	(9,280.00)	
	(16,740.00)	(16,740)
Diminution in value of Sanctuary House	20,000.00	20,000
TOTAL		£418,259

7.18
278

APPENDIX 3
PARTICULARS OF LOSSES IN CONNECTION WITH BASEMENT FLOODING

Equipment was irretrievably damaged and required replacement, linen and staff clothes were also damaged beyond remedy and as a consequence of the damage to the washing equipment additional laundry bills were incurred. Remedial tanking works had to be carried out.

	£	£
Two 35-pound industrial washing machines and two industrial dryers	14,050.00	
plus VAT	2,458.75	
	16,508.75	16,508.75
Free-standing dehumidifying equipment	750.00	
plus VAT	131.25	
	881.25	881.25
Additional laundry bills	3,348.00	
plus VAT	595.90	
	3,943.90	3,943.90
Residents clothes/linen and staff clothes/uniforms	1,882.00	
plus VAT	329.35	
	2,211.35	2,211.35
Remedial tanking works	5,360.00	
plus VAT	938.00	
	6,298.00	6,298.00
TOTAL		29,843.25

7.18
279

Reply to Defence and Counterclaim (7.19)

IN THE MATTER OF THE ARBITRATION ACTS 1950 TO 1979

AND

IN THE MATTER OF AN ARBITRATION UNDER THE JCT ARBITRATION RULES (18 JULY 1988)

BETWEEN

RELIABLE BUILDERS LIMITED   Claimant

AND

SANCTUARY HOUSE LIMITED   Respondent

REPLY AND DEFENCE TO COUNTERCLAIM

REPLY

1. The Claimant joins issue with the Respondent on its Defence, save where the same consists of admissions and save as otherwise appears below. For convenience the numbering in brackets referring to the Statement of Case and as used by the Respondent is adopted where appropriate.

2. As to paragraph 3 of the Defence, in view of the express terms of the contract it is denied that any such term could be implied as alleged or at all.

3. As to paragraph 8 of the Defence it is denied that the Respondent is entitled to withhold or set off the said sum of £146,000.

4. Save as insofar as it consists of admissions paragraph 9 is denied.

5. Save as insofar as it consists of admissions paragraph 10 is denied.

6. Save as insofar as it consists of admissions paragraph 11 is denied. In the circumstances, particularly by virtue of the fact that the Respondents admit that the works were Practically Complete as at 31 March 1992, it is denied that the Claimant's actions amounted to a repudiatory breach of contract.

(7.2.1) Removals/Demolitions and Form New Openings

7. Save as insofar as they consist of admissions paragraphs ((7.2.1), (7.2.1.2) and (7.2.1.3)) are denied.

(7.2.2) Works to the Lift-shafts

8. Save as insofar as it consists of admissions paragraphs (7.2.2.1) and (7.2.2.2) are denied. The Claimant contends that as the Architect's instruction was issued on the very day works commenced on the new lift-shaft (14 April 1991) no rescheduling as alleged could have taken place.

(7.2.3) Roof Repairs and Replacement Windows

9. The Respondent's statement that the scaffolding had to be removed before the roof leadwork was complete in consequence of the requirement to glaze the windows as soon as they were installed is admitted and relied upon. In the circumstances, particularly having regard to the need to repair the timbers, the completion date was delayed by eight weeks and replacement windows caused a further delay of one week.

(7.2.3.5)

10. Save as insofar as it consists of admissions this paragraph is denied. If, which is denied, these delays were concurrent the Claimants entitlement to an extension of time, it is contended, remains valid.

(7.2.4) First Fix and Second Fix

11. (7.2.4.1) The Respondent's admission that the Claimant is entitled to an extension of one week is noted and the Claimant avers that this entitlement is cumulative and not concurrent.

12. (7.2.4.2) This paragraph is denied. With reference to the second sentence in this paragraph, it is denied that this conversation took place as alleged or at all. It is further denied that had the alleged conversation taken place, the events described would have had any causal relationship to the delay to the Works.

13. (7.2.4.5) If, which is denied, the Claimant 'underresourced' the Works Claimant contend that but for the delay and disruption caused by the Respondent and TAP the resources would have been fully adequate. The Claimant is not required to 'resource' disruption caused by the Respondent.

14. Claim for an Extension of Time

The Claimant will rely upon the Respondent's admission in paragraph 12 of its Statement of the Defence that the Claimant was entitled to extensions of time and will rely upon Contract clause 2.3 in particular the last sentence of the first paragraph thereof for its force and effect. TAP should have granted, as a minimum, the said extension of time of nine weeks and three days and the Claimant has suffered loss and damage by reason of TAP's failure in respect thereof.

15. Loss and Expense

As to paragraph 13, by virtue of their presence on-site, TAP and the Respondent had knowledge of the disturbances of regular progress. The Claimant will rely on clause 4.11 of the Conditions of Contract for its full force and effect. In the premises, submission of the particulars of loss and expense with the Claimant's draft final account on 3 June 1992 was within a reasonable time.

16. (10.1.1) Prolongation

Having regard to the provisions of clause 4.11 and the fact that it is admitted that the Claimant is entitled to a nine-week, three-day extension of time, the Claimant contend that their entitlement in principle to prolongation costs is established. However, such costs should be based on the Claimant's entitlement to a 16-week extension of time.

17. (10.1.2) Uneconomic Working

The Respondent having admitted that the Contract contained an implied term in the terms pleaded in 5.1.1 of the Amended Statement of Case and relying on clause 4.11 of the Conditions of Contract for its full force and effect, the Claimant repeats its claim.

7.19
281

DEFENCE TO COUNTERCLAIM

18. The Amended Statement of Case is repeated hereunder.

19. Save as is hereinafter expressly admitted or expressed to be not admitted, each and every allegation in the Counterclaim shall be deemed to be denied as if such allegation had been specifically set out herein and traversed seriatim.

20. Defective Work

Clause 1.2 of the Conditions of Contract state that:
'Where or to the extent that quantities are not contained in the Specification/Schedule of Work and there are no Contract Bills, the quality and quantity of the work included in the Contract Sum (stated in Article 2) shall be deemed to be that in the Contract Document taken together; provided that if works stated or shown on the Contract Drawings is inconsistent with the description, if any, of that work in the Specification/Schedules of Work than that which is stated or shown on the Contract Drawing shall prevail for the purpose of this clause.'

The Claimant will refer to clause 1.2 and the other Conditions of Contract for their full force and effect. Paragraph 35 of the Contract is not admitted and paragraph 36 is denied.

21. Fire Doors

The glass fibre matting was as specified by the Respondent. In the premises it is denied that the Claimant is in breach of Contract Condition 1.2 or at all. Further and in the alternative the splitting and wrinkling was caused by the Respondent heating the premises at too high a temperature too quickly.

22. Gibbs Ceiling

Save that the clauses of the Specification as cited do appear in the Specification, and that the ceiling collapsed on 24 December 1992, paragraphs 39, 40, 41, 42 and 43 are denied. It is admitted that from 26 December 1992 the Health Authority closed a floor of Sanctuary House comprising 15 units. The Claimant will rely on the clauses of the Specification for their full force and effect. The collapse of the ceiling was caused by inherent weaknesses, responsibility for which rests with the Respondent. Further and in the alternative the Defendants have failed properly to mitigate their losses, amongst other matters, through not commencing the restoration work until October 1993.

23. Referring to Appendix K, in particular the claim for diminution in value as a result of the collapse of the Gibbs ceiling found therein, the Respondents alleged losses are denied.

24. Basement Flooding

Save that it is admitted that on 15 April 1992 the basement of Sanctuary House flooded, it is denied that the Claimant's breach of contract caused the full extent of the loss alleged to have been suffered in clauses 44 and 45.

24. Interest

The Respondents claim for interest is denied.

AND THE CLAIMANT CLAIMS

25. A declaration that the Counterclaim be dismissed with costs.

Served the 26th day of November 1993 by Jayrich Associates on behalf of the Claimants.

Second Proof of Evidence of Harold Hocking (7.22)

IN THE MATTER OF THE ARBITRATION ACTS 1950 TO 1979

AND

IN THE MATTER OF AN ARBITRATION UNDER THE JCT ARBITRATION RULES (18 JULY 1988)

BETWEEN

RELIABLE BUILDERS LIMITED   Claimant

AND

SANCTUARY HOUSE LIMITED   Respondent

**7.22
283**

SECOND PROOF OF EVIDENCE OF HAROLD HOCKING

I, HAROLD EDWARD HOCKING Managing Director of Reliable Builders Limited of Snape Yard, Woodbridge, Suffolk

WILL SAY as follows:

1. This is my Second Proof of Evidence in relation to the above arbitration and should be read in conjunction with my earlier Proof.
2. The purposes of my Second Proof is to deal with the following specific issues.

    (i) RBL's claim for payment of the penultimate Certificate.
    (ii) Remedial works to the basement.
    (iii) Alleged defective work.
    (iv) RBL's claim for payment of the balance of the final account.
    (v) RBL's claim to an extension of time.
    (vi) RBL's claim for loss of expense.
    (vii) RBL's claim for finance charges.
    (viii) The collapsed ceiling.

3. On 27 April 1992 Mr Reeves reported to me that the Penultimate Certificate, dated 13 April 1992, had not been paid. I instructed Mr Reeves to enquire of Mr Bliss why the Certificate had not been paid. He reported to me that Mr Bliss claimed that there were many defects in the work and that until his bankers were satisfied they would not release any further money.
4. I spoke to Mr Goldstone, who was the bank's representative, who had attended the meeting on 13 April. He was evasive and said that it was up to Mr Bliss whether payment should be made.
5. I instructed Mr Reeves to speak again with Mr Bliss and informed him that if payment was not received then we would have no option but to seek our remedy in the County Court. I believe that Mr Reeves spoke to Mr Bliss on at least two occasions and he maintained that he was entirely in the hands of his bankers. I instructed Mr Reeves to confirm his telephone calls

by letter to Mr Bliss and when this did not result in payment I contacted the company's solicitors and instructed them to commence an action for the recovery of this money.

6. I have noted that in the Arbitrator's Interim Award he has concluded that the tanking, although sound, was not taken high enough up the basement walls. Since we carried out the original work I wish to clarify that my company would be willing to carry out further waterproofing work to the basement by raising the level of the tanking which seems to be a satisfactory solution to the problem.

7. I have discussed with Mr Reeves the severe shrinkage in the existing joinery in the property and, in particular, the problems of the fire doors. It was clear that before we started work on this project the property had been empty for some time and in a state of disrepair. However, given the length of job I feel that by the time the work was complete the joinery would have dried out in the normal way without damage.

8. During my subsequent visits to the property, following occupation, it did strike me that particularly during the winter months, the building was heated to an abnormally high temperature. I have noted that the design criteria for the heating system included a requirement that most of the building should be heated to a temperature of 24 degrees centigrade. It is my feeling that this unnaturally high temperature has been the cause of shrinkage in the timber.

7.22
284

9. I left the production of the final account to Mr Reeves and had not expected there to be any difficulty in agreeing this with the architect. However, to my surprise the architect seems to be disputing many items of additional work which were ordered by them or the client. The site foreman, John Watts, appears to have a good relationship with Miss Hutch despite frustration caused by late information from the architect and the disruptions caused by the Employer's own tradesmen, particularly the kitchen fitters. Mr and Mrs Bliss both took a keen interest in the work and naturally from time to time gave John Watts instructions, and I am quite sure that by and large he would have informed the architect of these. I am at a loss, therefore, to understand why the architect is now disputing payment for this additional work.

10. So far as the Extension of Time is concerned Mr Reeves and John Watts have more detailed knowledge of the disruption caused by late information and particularly, towards the end of the project, the client's own tradesmen. However, from my position I obviously became aware that the project was beginning to run late and impressed upon Mr Reeves that we must make requests for information in writing and I believe the correspondence shows that we did this. I should also say that when I attended site meetings and progress was discussed, we regularly expressed our concern at the delays being caused by late information. I cannot recall an occasion when the architect disputed this. Much of the time at site meetings was taken up with discussions about when the information would be given to us.

11. I am quite sure that the architect has known all along that the real cause of the delays was late information and they certainly would have known at the time the disruption that was caused by the client's tradesmen. We certainly expected that there would be little difficulty in obtaining an Extension of Time right up to the actual completion at the end of March 1992.

12. Our loss and expense claim, of course, is based upon the extension of time to which we believe we are entitled. Mr Reeves, John Watts and the whole site set-up had to be kept in place for much longer than we expected and we believe that as a matter of principle, we are entitled to loss and expense for the entire period. I will, of course, leave the details of the claim to Mr Reeves who put together this claim as part of the final account.

13. As far as financing charges are concerned, this company, in common with other builders, runs an overdraft with our bank. We, of course, take this into account in bidding for work but only for the original contract period. Late payment of Certificates, and late recovery of costs during the overrun period meant that our overdraft was somewhat stretched and I believe that we are entitled to recovery of the interest paid.

14. So far as the collapsed ceiling is concerned I appreciate the disruption this caused to Mr and Mrs Bliss and their business. I was myself informed late on Christmas Eve that the

ceiling had collapsed and offered to make an inspection with Mr Reeves on Christmas Morning. I am frankly at a loss to understand why this ceiling collapsed.

The clause in the original specification, sent to us with the invitation to tender, read as follows:

C1.3/23d

Allow the provisional sum of £2000 for the repairs and reinstatement of the ceiling and mouldings to the Gibbs ceiling in the ground-floor lounge. This work is to be carried out by a specialist subcontractor to be approved by the Architect. (The Georgian Restoration Group is suggested and would be approved by the Architect, but the contractor may request approval to an alternative specialist.)

Knowing the Georgian Restoration Group's reputation we were happy to use them for this work. We, of course, relied on them to carry out this work properly because they knew so much more than we did about this very specialised work.

15. In addition to the repair work to this ceiling we were required to fireproof above it to the following specification:

C1 3/21h:

Carefully take up all the floorboarding to first floor and set aside for reuse. Refix on completion of the fireproofing works, making up with new to match as required:

C1 3/21j:

Carefully clear out floor void and clear and cart away all debris and prepare as necessary for fireproofing work.

C1 3/27b:

Fireproof between timber joists in the ceiling space, all in accordance with the requirements of the Building Control Officer, for the premises to be used for nursing home purposes, using a proprietary system to be approved by the Architect.

RBL carried out this work of fireproofing with our own workforce strictly in accordance with the specification and Firesafe Limited's instructions, who were the manufacturers we selected and who were approved by the Architect. This work was entirely separate from the original ceiling itself and from what I saw after the collapse of this ceiling, I cannot see that this fireproofing work had anything to do with that collapse.

During my visit on Christmas Day, when Miss Hutch was present, Mr Reeves referred to a conversation that they had had previously when he had suggested that, because many of the plaster keys had broken off, the ceiling should be supported by the 'soft wiring'. I believe that this suggestion had originated from the Georgian Restoration Group following their observations during their work of restoration. This Group are, of course, specialists in this field and are therefore knowledgeable about such things.

I understand that Miss Hutch chose not to give an instruction for this 'soft wiring' to be carried out and it seems to me that this is where the responsibility, for this unfortunate collapse, really lies rather than with my company, who, so far as I can see carried out all the work specified.

Signed .... Dated ....
Harold Hocking

7.22
285

Second Proof of Evidence of John Watts (7.23)

IN THE MATTER OF THE ARBITRATION ACTS 1950 TO 1979

AND

IN THE MATTER OF AN ARBITRATION UNDER THE JCT ARBITRATION RULES (18 JULY 1988)

BETWEEN

RELIABLE BUILDERS LIMITED   Claimant

AND

SANCTUARY HOUSE LIMITED   Respondent

SECOND PROOF OF EVIDENCE OF JOHN WATTS

I, JOHN WATTS of 10 Edwina Villas, Norwich

WILL SAY as follows:

1. This is my Second Proof of Evidence in relation to the above arbitration and deals with my involvement with the contract for the refurbishment works and extension at Sanctuary House, Woodbridge. This Proof should be read in conjunction with my earlier Proof.

2. The purpose of this Second Proof is to outline the history of the progress of this job, of which I have personal knowledge, and specifically to deal with matters which caused delay, prolongation, disruption and uneconomic working.

3. We took possession of this site on 2 April 1991 and immediately commenced the demolition of the walls which are marked on the drawings as 'non-load-bearing'. After we had demolished some of these walls I noted movement in the upper floors and the roof structure and immediately contacted the architect.

Miss Hutch came on to the site and ascertained that their drawings were inaccurate as some of the walls which we had removed were, in fact, structural. We were instructed to jack-up the floors and roof, where the structural walls had been removed, and told that revised drawings would be sent to us shortly. These drawings were received on 7 May.

Due to the errors on the original drawings and the delay in receiving the new drawings, the demolitions were not completed until 14 June—a month later than originally planned.

4. Following completion of the demolition work, around mid-July, the next two months were spent dealing with dry rot and the injection of a DPC which was ordered by the architect as an extra. It quickly became clear, once we had exposed the timbers, that the dry rot was far more extensive than the architect had originally envisaged. We did not, in fact, complete this dry rot and damp-proof work until 12 September.

5. We programmed to start work on the lift-shaft two weeks or so after commencing on-site but the day this work was due to start we received an instruction, from the architect, revising the specification for this shaft. The architect had decided she wanted Waltons engineering bricks and a concrete ring beam at each floor.

It will be appreciated that laying engineering bricks is a much slower process than ordinary brickwork. This, and the introduction of the concrete beams, meant that the revised lift-shaft took us much longer than originally planned. It also delayed other work, in particular, the header tank could not be installed until the shaft was completed. Nor could we complete adjacent internal partitions. Overall this new lift-shaft took five weeks longer than programmed.

6. When it came to the roof we found that many of the slates had laminated. Miss Hutch, the architect, instructed us to preserve as many of these slates as possible, despite their poor condition. She told me that they had only anticipated that about 10 per cent new slates would be required. This instruction meant that we had to take great care in the removal of slates, which took at least two weeks longer than we had expected this work to take. As it happened the architect condemned most of the original slates and we were only able to use old slates on the garage.

This, together with the piecemeal replacement of timbers caused by the dry rot, held us up until early September whereas we had originally expected to finish the roof by early July.

I mentioned the replacement of timbers because although, early on, it seemed obvious to me that most of the roof timbers should be replaced, Miss Hutch confided that nothing had been allowed for this work and suggested that we replaced timbers piecemeal in the hope that we could limit the amount of work that we did. In the end we replaced the lot.

7. When the roof covering was finished we still had no details of the lead flashings. At this point we needed to start work on the replacement windows and, in any case, it would have been uneconomic to keep the scaffolding in place just for the flashings, so we struck it. When we got the details of the leadwork we had to do it from scaffold towers. Even then we did not finish the windows until six weeks later than programmed.

8. The final problem with this roof came around Christmas 1991 when it leaked. We discovered water was coming in through a junction in the leadwork in the valley between the new and the old roof.

I looked at this with Miss Hutch who agreed that we had done our work as shown on TAP's drawings.

Following our inspection together she sent us some new details and this meant that we had to strip part of the new roof in order to install this new leadwork.

9. When the replacement windows were installed we were able to start First Fix. There was much more First Fix than we had originally planned for, due to the large amount of replacement work caused by the dry rot. The late start of the carpenters' First Fix delayed the mechanical and electrical First Fix.

10. The work to the ceiling, plastering and the lift installations were all delayed by about seven weeks due to the late completion of the earlier works which I have just described.

11. This general late running had a knock-on effect on the carpenters' Second Fix which started about eight weeks later than programmed. In order to keep this work within the time originally allowed, we brought on additional labour.

12. The electrical and mechanical work was carried out by the main subcontractors, but this work was delayed by about eight weeks for the reasons I have already given and, in addition, TAP issued some late amendments to the performance specification for this work which not only caused further delay, but increased the amount of builders work in connection with this work. In some cases we had to go back and cut holes by hand which would, in the ordinary course of things, have been formed as we proceeded.

13. The way we planned this work was for our subcontractors, working with a single gang, to complete the work in the existing building and then move into the extension. Thus, the delay in carrying out the work in the existing building also delayed the commencement of operations in the new extension.

Our work on the substructure in new extension started as planned on 2 April but it took us two weeks or so longer than planned. This was due to the increase in the depth of the foundations required over and above what was shown on the original drawings. This was another example of the earthworks being all up the creek!

14. The rest of the extension was also delayed due mainly to the knock-on effect of the

delays in the main house. We lost another couple of weeks in the substructure as our brickies had to go back to the main house to sort out the lift-shaft.

We had programmed this job so that the gangs would move from the main house to the extension so this meant that all the delays on the main house followed through into the extension. For example, we couldn't finish our First and Second Fix—really the M & E—until 15 days later than originally programmed.

15. Although the whole works were carried out later than programmed the architect still hadn't produced her colour schedules by the time we came to start the decorations. The colours were specified to have been British Standard shades but these did not suit the client. Mrs Bliss was frequently on-site during this work and made us change the colour shades on some walls several times. The sitting-room wall, for example, was coated five times before Mrs Bliss was satisfied. The colours that we ended up with were not the British Standard shades that were specified.

16. When we tendered for this job we noted that the clients intended to use their own tradespeople to install the nurse call system, the burglar alarms and their own laundry and kitchen equipment.

They let these contracts and the kitchen equipment people insisted on delivering their equipment, as originally planned, in the middle of October. This meant that we had to temporarily store this equipment as the kitchen was not ready to receive it. This caused us some considerable disruption. Not only did we have to work round it, but we had to move it from time to time before it could be eventually put into its final site. The clients tradespeople installed their equipment in a piecemeal fashion, as and when areas of the building were completed. As a result we were considerably disrupted by these people.

17. Our final job was the external works. These too were delayed by the general delay in completing the building. For example, we couldn't finish the drainage system until the downpipes were in place which, themselves, were delayed.

The car park could not be done until all of the heavy materials had been delivered. The external walls and gates to the garage, were built by the bricklayers who were engaged on the main building. This work could not start until the new extension was finished.

Finally, we could not even start the landscaping and planting when we should have been able to, as the information was not available from the architect. We received this information some two months later than originally programmed.

18. To summarise, there was far more work involved in the dry rot and subsequent replacement timbers and work to the roof than originally envisaged. This, together with the general lateness throughout the contract of information from the architect—TAP seemed to wait until we were virtually ready to start the work on a particular area before they considered what was required—and the additional work required by the architect's instructions, meant that we did not finish this job until the end of March 1992 whereas we had originally aimed to finish in early December 1991.

I truly believe that, had all the information been available to us when we required it, and had the architect carried out a proper survey before deciding on the extent of works required, we could have completed our work within the 36 weeks contract period.

Signed .... Date ....
       John Watts

Second Proof of Evidence of William Reeves (7.24)

IN THE MATTER OF THE ARBITRATION ACTS 1950 TO 1979

AND

IN THE MATTER OF AN ARBITRATION UNDER THE JCT ARBITRATION RULES (18 JULY 1988)

BETWEEN

RELIABLE BUILDERS LIMITED   Claimant

AND

SANCTUARY HOUSE LIMITED   Respondent

SECOND PROOF OF EVIDENCE OF WILLIAM REEVES

I, WILLIAM REEVES of 28 Riverside Mansions, Ipswich

WILL SAY as follows:

1. This is my Second Proof of Evidence in relation to the above arbitration and in terms of my involvement with the contract for the refurbishment works at Sanctuary House, Woodbridge, this Proof should be read in conjunction with my earlier Proof.

2. The purpose of this Second Proof is to deal with the following specific issues.

    (i) The late payment of Certificates.
    (ii) RBL's Claim for payment of the Penultimate Certificate.
    (iii) RBL's Claim for payment of the balance of the Final Account.
    (iv) TAP's lateness in providing information.

3. Late Payment of Certificates

Payment of our monthly certificates was consistently late as can be seen from Appendix 1 to this proof. We were in overdraft for the entire period of this contract and were paying interest at, what works out to be, 6.245 per cent over NatWest Bank Rate, when all charges, commitment fees, etc are included.

For this reason it was imperative that Certificates were honoured in accordance with the contract terms. We were confident of prompt payment when we learned, even before we agreed final terms, that a reputable bank was behind the funding of this project, but unfortunately our faith was misplaced.

4. Payment of the Penultimate Certificate

RBL's claim, in this respect, is due to the non-payment of the Penultimate Certificate, which was dated 13 April 1992 and issued following an inspection meeting, on 8 April 1992, on-site, at which I was present together with Mr Hocking and John Watts. The Client, Mr Bliss, also attended this inspection and was accompanied by the architects Frances Hutch and Max D'Iffy together with the client's banker's representatives, Mr Paul Goldstone.

The amount of the certificate was £10,954. Fourteen days after its issue, when we still had not received payment, I telephoned Mr Bliss to ascertain why. He told me that there was so much work that needed putting right that, until he and his banker's were satisfied, his bank would not release any further money.

I pointed out that following the inspection visit, we had remedied the bulk of the defects identified during that visit. Those not picked up were all minor items and would be dealt with at the end of the Defects Liability Period. Mr Bliss retorted that he was in the hands of his bankers.

In the end, despite several more telephone calls to Mr Bliss, this certificate was never honoured. On the advice of Mr Hocking, my Managing Director, I warned Mr Bliss, at least twice by telephone and once by registered letter, that we would have no option but to seek our remedy in the County Court.

We commenced our action in the Court, for the recovery of this money, in mid-May 1992.

In September 1993, on the advice of our solicitor, we abandoned our action in the County Court and, through an Ad Hoc Arbitration Agreement, included our claim for this money in the arbitration which was then running.

7.24
290

5. Balance of the Final Account

Shortly after we commenced our action, in the County Court, for the payment of our Penultimate Certificate, I completed and submitted our Draft Final Account to TAP.

This account included a Loss & Expense claim covering the extended contract period. We had commenced work, on this job, at the beginning of April 1991, on a 36-week contract. Through reasons, totally beyond our control, specifically, but not exclusively, late information from the architect and disruptions caused by the Employer's own tradesmen, we were on-site for 12 months.

A small firm such as ours cannot run more than one project of this size at a time and thus these extra 16 weeks or so were a dead loss to us—thus the Loss & Expense claim.

The balance of the money claimed in the Final Account covered many extras which had been ordered, either by the Architect or the Client—in this case both Mr and Mrs Bliss on separate occasions. I prepared a list of these extras and they are now incorporated into Mr Redman's Expert Report.

I agree that we were a little lax in confirming all such instructions to vary the works but, until we submitted our Final Account, we had no reason to assume that we would not be paid for such variations.

We were subsequently told, by Miss Hutch, that the items disallowed in our Final Account as extras covered work which, in her opinion, formed part of our original contract.

She averred that what was required was either covered by notes on the contract drawings or in the Specification. Alternatively, where there was no specific reference in detail, what we were required to provide was obvious to any competent builder.

However, we maintain that all the items claimed were either ordered as extras or were necessary because nothing was shown, or noted on the drawings or specified to cover that particular item now in dispute.

Perhaps I should add that I assisted Mr Redman with the measurement and costing of the Final Account items and confirm the correctness of the same.

I telephoned Mr Bliss and Mr D'Iffy on several occasions between the delivery of this Draft Final Account and the 18 August 1992, when Mr Bliss informed me, by telephone, that he had deducted Liquidated damages from the money that we were claiming was owed to us and, in addition, there were still a number of defects outstanding not least the work to the basement laundry, and would therefore not be paying the balance of the Final Account which we had submitted 10 weeks or so earlier.

Subsequently, when it became clear that we were not going to be paid, we formally submitted our Final Account on 30 October 1992.

To date nothing has been paid since Certificate No 11—the one before the Penultimate Certificate.

6. TAP's Lateness in Providing Information

John Watts channelled nearly all of his requests for information through me in the office. I say nearly all because, inevitably on a job of this nature, with the architect on-site at least once a week. Some requests were made verbally.

I have listed, in Appendix 2 to this Proof, the more important requests to TAP, the dates on which these requests were made, either verbally or in writing, and the dates when the information was actually received on-site. As will be seen the gap between the request and the provision was often many weeks. I am not suggesting that we were delayed as a result in every instance but an examination of the Site Minutes will be sufficient to show how often we expressed our concern at the delay that was being caused through late information.

7.24
291

7. General

Three general points I would like to make.

The first concerns the disruption caused by the Client's own tradesmen. There were a number of these, the most important, and therefore the most disruptive was the Kitchen Equipment firm. John Watts, our site foreman, was so concerned about the chaos being caused by these people, quite close to the end of the job, that he asked me to visit the site and see for myself. This I did on Friday 28 February 1992. They had six fitters on-site that day and had not only taken over the kitchen area, in which we were still working, but a couple of the adjacent rooms and adjoining corridors. I spoke to their foremen and he told me that they expected to be on-site for at least 10 days, he also said that the client had completely changed the layout of the kitchen from that originally planned and as a result many of the electrical plumbing connections would have to be altered. When I got back to the office I wrote to the architects as I had on various occasions (see P/C9, P/C10 and P/C12) complaining about this disruption but never received a reply.

Secondly I must mention the cracking problem. RBL accept that there is a severe cracking problem on this job—particularly the fire doors. As I said earlier it was part of my job to place the orders with the various subcontractors and suppliers, this included placing an order with Shawpruff for the application of the fireproofing.

Shawpruff is a reputable firm with whom we have done business for many years. During that time we have not received a single complaint from any of our clients concerning Shawpruff's work. My own opinion is that the cracking has been caused by too rapid over-heating of the building. It was never allowed to dry out naturally. The client was anxious to let the accommodation and as a result turned on the heating in March 1992, to a very high temperature, and maintained this level of heat for a prolonged period thus causing the cracking.

The final point that I want to make concerns the collapsed ceiling.

I was called by Mr Hocking, on Christmas Day 1992, to attend with him to inspect the devastation caused by the collapse of this ceiling. The architect was there as well and I reminded her of the conversation that we had had when we came to consider commencing the repairs to this ceiling. We had inspected the plaster key by removing all of the floor-boarding in the room above. Many of these keys had broken off and I suggested that we should 'soft wire' those parts of the ceiling where the key had gone. Miss Hutch was not prepared to order us to carry out this work as an extra and maintained that it was our responsibility to ensure that the integrity of the ceiling was maintained.

Whilst I accepted that it was our responsibility to protect the ceiling against damage during our work I could not accept that we had to go as far as incurring the expense of 'soft wiring'—how could we possibly have known of this possibility when we tendered for the job? I accept the specification makes it clear that we were to provide all necessary protection to existing building, temporary support where required and carrying out all necessary works to ensure that the building was left in a sound condition on completion. In my view such a 'mopping up' clause could not reasonably include work of the nature of 'soft wiring' a valuable plaster ceiling.

We used the nominated specialist firm, the Georgian Restoration Group, to carry out this work of repair following which we installed the fireproofing in the void above using our own workmen. Again, I ensured that John Watts had fully detailed manufacturers instructions, on-site for this work.

Having reasonably complied with the contractual requirements it is totally unreasonable for RBL to be asked to compensate SHL for losses that they claim to have sustained as a result of the loss of this ceiling.

7.24
292

....

William Reeves   Date

APPENDIX 1
SCHEDULE OF CERTIFICATES

	Date of Valuation	Date Due	Date Money Rec'd	Amount £
1	06.05.91	20.05.91	28.05.91	32,800
2	10.06.91	24.06.91	04.07.91	41,200
3	15.07.91	29.07.91	15.08.91	53,800
4	12.08.91	26.08.91	11.09.91	76,800
5	09.09.91	23.09.91	07.10.91	88,600
6	16.10.91	30.10.91	14.11.91	91,800
7	15.11.91	29.11.91	12.12.91	56,896
8	16.12.91	30.12.91	12.01.92	47,200
9	13.01.92	27.01.92	01.02.92	45,700
10	11.02.92	25.02.92	15.03.92	36,800
11	12.03.92	26.03.92	18.04.92	27,900
12	13.04.92	27.04.92	—	10,954

7.24
293

APPENDIX 2
SCHEDULE OF REQUESTS FOR INFORMATION AND DETAILS OF INFORMATION RECEIVED LATE

Task Name	Information Requested/ Late Information	Date Info Received
Removals/ Demolition	(1) Erroneous survey information (2) Late provision of revised drawing nos DWG00004/B and DWG00005/B (3) Additional work arising as a result of Issue of Architects instructions nos 4f, 4g, 4h, 5a, 5c, 6b, 6c, 10b	See dates on Architect's drawings or on AI's (but note many revised drawings retain the original issue date)
Form New Openings	(1) Erroneous survey information (2) Late provision of revised drawing nos DWG00004/B and DWG00005/B (3) Additional work arising as a result of Issue of Architects instructions nos 4g, 6a, 6g	Ditto
Form Lift-Shaft	(1) Additional work arising as a result of Issue of Architects instructions no 2a.	Ditto
Plastering Screed	(1) Delay and disruption caused by Respondent's contractor Alert Alarms. It was not possible to commence this task until a wiring diagram for the nurse call alarm system was provided on 3/10/91.	Ditto

(Extracts only—the list continues)

7.24
294

APPENDIX 3
CALCULATION OF ACTUAL RATE OF INTEREST INCURRED OVER PERIOD BETWEEN APRIL 1991 AND MARCH 1992

The overall figure is made up as follows:

(i) Bank overdraft rate 3% over base*

(ii) Annual commitment fee 1.5%* of facility amount. On basis of average balances over the period as per the attached calculations this equates—2.98% average.

(iii) Quarterly service charges—based on charges actually made against balances shown on the attached sheets—0.265% average.

	Total
Interest	3
Commitment fee	2.98
Service charge	0.265
	6.245%

*See attached letter from local Bank Manager.

7.24
295

Report of Joel Redman (7.25)

IN THE MATTER OF THE ARBITRATION ACTS 1950 TO 1979

AND

IN THE MATTER OF AN ARBITRATION UNDER THE JCT ARBITRATION RULES (18 JULY 1988)

BETWEEN

RELIABLE BUILDERS LIMITED   Claimant

AND

SANCTUARY HOUSE LIMITED   Respondent

EXPERT'S REPORT OF JOEL LIONEL REDMAN

DATED: 21ST FEBRUARY 1994

SPECIALIST FIELD: QUANTITY SURVEYOR

ASSISTED BY: NO ASSISTANCE

ON BEHALF OF: RELIABLE BUILDERS LIMITED

ON THE INSTRUCTIONS OF: RELIABLE BUILDERS LIMITED

SUBJECT MATTER: QUANTUM, LOSS AND/OR EXPENSE AND FINAL ACCOUNT

SECTION 1

INTRODUCTION

1.1 My full names are JOEL LIONEL REDMAN. I am a Chartered Quantity Surveyor and Chartered Builder. I qualified in 1963 and have been in practice on my own for some 12 years. I am a Partner in the practice of Jayrich Associates of Swansea House, Queens Road, Norwich.

As well as my professional work I also work with building contractor's doing estimating and post-contract work on a variety of contracts. My office is not far from the Claimant's offices in Woodbridge and I have worked, on a number of jobs, with them over a number of years.

1.2 Mr Hocking, the managing director of the Claimants, on or about the beginning of May 1991, asked me to act for them to agree the interim valuations and also to deal with any remeasurement work on the final account.

1.3 I am instructed to give an experts report on the outstanding items on the final account and to demonstrate the amount of direct loss and/or expense incurred by the Claimant in execution of the Works.

1.4 To assist in establishing the delay to the Works, the entitlement to extension of time is dealt with in a separate section in this report. The programme comparing the planned progress of the Works and the actual progress also illustrates the tasks on which the Claimant suffered disruption.

1.5 There is also a section in this report that deals with the outstanding issues on the final account and the issues which flow from that account.

1.6 The source of the cost information used in connection with the loss and/or expense calculations are the Claimant's monthly job cost accounts. These are prepared by the Claimant's in house accounts department using a standard computerised job costing package.

SECTION 2

ENTITLEMENT TO EXTENSION OF TIME

2.1 This section of my report deals with the claimant's entitlement to extension of time which also gives the grounds for entitlement to loss and/or expense. In order to measure the critical effects of delays on the completion date for the project I have reviewed the Claimant's programme. This programme was not produced using any proprietary computer planning package. I have illustrated the delay and disruption to the project by making a comparison between planned and actual progress.

7.25
297

2.2 I have assessed the progress of the Works before and after the dates of the relevant events which the Claimant contends delayed the completion date. My assessment of the periods of delay caused to individual activities have been applied in an incremental manner. The programme has then been run to analyse whether the delay to the activity caused a delay to the contract completion date.

2.3 After each stage of the analysis and prior to the next delay assessment, the programme has been reviewed to take account of the actual completion dates of the relevant activities. No adjustment has been made to the initial programme logic unless it is demonstrated from the contemporary records that this was the Claimant's intention.

2.4 For programme information, I have relied upon the Claimant's bar chart numbered 1340/1. For progress information I have relied upon the contemporaneous weekly reports recorded by the Claimant and countersigned by the Architect as a true record of progress made.

2.5 Removals/Demolitions and Form New Openings

2.5.1 The Claimants took possession of the site on 2nd April 1991. One week after that date, as programmed, the Claimants began to demolish those internal identified on the Architects' drawings as 'non-load-bearing'. They ascertained, by observed undue movement in the floor and roof structure, that the Respondents' survey and/or the Architects' drawings were inaccurate in that some of the walls identified as non-load-bearing were in fact structural.

2.5.2 On 10th April 1991 the Claimant was forced to cease all further demolition of the internal walls. At this time 10 per cent of the programmed demolition had been carried out which was in accordance with the programme requirements at that time.

2.5.3 The Claimant was instructed to install temporary props until structural walls were rebuilt and/or amended in accordance with the Architects revised drawings. These were not issued until 7th May 1991.

2.5.4 The demolition of the internal walls and/or the construction of the new openings in the walls were due to be completed on the 12th May 1991. As a direct result of the issue of the erroneous survey information and the revised drawings and the extra work entailed therein, the outstanding 90 per cent of the demolition work and the formation of the new openings could not be completed until 14th June 1991, a delay of four weeks.

2.5.5 The completion of this activity was critical to the progress of the works as the internal partitions, both load-bearing and non-load-bearing could not be completed until after the substantial completion of the demolition works and therefore the actual completion date was also delayed by four weeks.

2.5.6 It became apparent that the Respondent or the Architect on his behalf had totally underestimated the extent to which the existing building would require repair to become a viable and useable building once again. The time spent between the 14th July 1991 and completion of the removals/demolitions work on 12th September 1991 was all in connection with additional work in removing the timber infected with dry rot and replacing brickwork infested with the dry rot spores. During this period the Architect also decided on the necessity for an injected damp-proof course system. All these works were placed in hand as soon as the instructions were received. The Claimant could not have completed these additional works any sooner than the 12th September 1991.

2.6 Works to the Lift-Shaft

2.6.1 The original lift-shaft was to be constructed in common brickwork and was programmed to be completed in four weeks. On 14th April 1991, the day on which this work was due to start, the architect issued instruction 2a which revised the brickwork specification of the lift-shaft to Waltons engineering bricks and further, introduced a reinforced concrete ring beam at each floor level as required by the Structural Engineer.

2.6.2 The use of engineering bricks reduced the maximum daily lift of brickwork from 1500 mm to 900 mm and in reality increases the period of time required for the construction of the lift-shaft by 60 per cent. This equates to an increase in the original programme period from four weeks to six weeks and two days.

2.6.3 The delay to the lift-shaft was further compounded by the introduction of the concrete ring beams. The completion of the lift pit to ground floor was delayed until the ring beam had been actually constructed and cured. On subsequent levels the shaft was delayed by the time taken to prepare the brickwork and place the ring beam. I have assessed that this additional work caused a further delay of one week.

2.6.4 The delay to the completion of the lift-shaft was critical as the head of the shaft provided support for certain key roof elements and also the water tanks. In addition none of the adjacent internal partitions could be commenced until the relevant level of the lift-shaft had been completed.

2.6.4 The issue of the instruction on the day the work was due to commence caused an initial delay of one week while the new materials necessary for the revised work were obtained. The remaining delay is caused by the revised specification and the additional work in the ring beams. The whole of this work took eight weeks instead of the planned four weeks and was not completed until the 12th June 1991, some five weeks later than planned.

2.7 Scaffolding, Strip Roof, Roof Structure Repairs, Roof Coverings, Replace windows

2.7.1 These operations are inter-linked because of the dependence on use of scaffolding to both execute the work to the roof and to replace the high level windows. Notwithstanding that problems had been encountered inside the building the Claimant commenced the scaffolding operation on time as per his original programme.

2.7.2 The whole of the roof coverings were then to be stripped and this operation commenced as per the original programme. Many of the slates, which were to be used to re-cover the roof, were found to be laminated and broke on lifting. The Architect demanded that the Claimant took more care to preserve as many slates as possible because he had not budgeted in replacing so many of the slates as was to prove to be necessary. The correspondence shows that at the time the Architect was blaming the Claimant for the level of breakage's being incurred. Had he carried out a proper survey prior to the works commencing it would have been all too apparent that the degree to which the slates had laminated meant that even if they could have been removed whole they would not have proved suitable for re-covering the roof. The additional two weeks taken to strip the roof was all consumed by the additional care to be taken, which in any event proved to no avail. Only sufficient slates were saved to cover the garage roof, the main roof was covered with new slates.

2.7.3 The problems then continued, the original intention had been to repair a proportion of the structural timbers which were in need of repair. However, the dry rot found in the interior of the building was also found to be extensive in the roof structure. However, the Architect faced with the prospect of considerable extra expense which had not been contemplated in the budget given to the Respondent sought to replace timbers on a piecemeal basis instead of taking the decision he ultimately took to replace all the timbers. This piecemeal approach is the cause of the repair works extending from the 4th July 1991 to the 26th August 1991, a delay of some eight weeks.

2.7.4 This in turn delayed the replacement of the roof coverings. Instead of completing roof coverings on 9th July 1991 as planned completion did not occur until 4th September 1991.

2.7.5 The Architect was late in issuing the appropriate instructions on the new leadwork to the existing building roof and this in turn resulted in the last of the roof coverings being executed from scaffold towers so that the main scaffolding could be struck to allow the new windows to be installed.

2.7.6 The replacement windows operation followed as early as possible having regard to the delay to roofing operations. These were completed 2nd September 1991 some six weeks late.

2.7.7 Collectively all of these operations were delayed until the 5th September 1991. The comparative bar chart shows activity on the scaffolding activity into November 1991. The reason for this is that tower scaffolding was still in place to reconstruct chimneys and to install the new flue linings. Again these matters are extra work to the contract.

2.7.8 The bar chart also shows activity on the roof coverings operation through to 13th February 1992. This covers the work involved with the chimneys and flue linings and also work in connection with the lead flashings and the junction with the roof to the new extension. During the wet weather in December 1991 and January 1992 an ingress of water was discovered which when investigated was found to be due to poor detailing by the Architect of the leadwork forming the flashings to the existing roof and the valleys at the junction with the existing and new roof. This was subsequently re-detailed by the Architect and the appropriate areas of the roof were stripped, the new lead installed and the roof coverings replaced.

Whilst the bars on the bar chart are shown as continuous they do not illustrate continuous activity. They include float time in the same way that the solid bars on the original programme include float.

2.8 First Fixings

2.8.1 First fixings could not be commenced until such time as the building was both watertight and secure. The carpenter first fix therefore commenced as soon as the replacement windows were installed. The additional work in stripping out the building in turn created additional first fixing work in reinstatement. Because the carpenter first fix was extended by additional work the point at which the first fix on the mechanical and electrical could commence was two weeks after commencement of the carpenter first fix and not one week as the original programme logic.

2.8.2 The original programme logic was that the mechanical and electrical first fix on the new extension would follow on from the services first fixes on the existing building. This would permit the work to be carried out by one gang from each of the services subcontractors.

Accordingly the subcontracts with the named subcontractors provided a logic where only one gang from each would be required to carry out the services installations for both first fix and second fix operations.

2.8.3 The actual progress bars on the attached programme show that this original logic was followed, with the services first fix on the new building following immediately on from the services first fix on the existing building. The works on the existing building thus impacted on the work to the new extension.

2.9 Ceilings, Plastering

2.9.1 The ceilings and plastering followed exactly the same logic and duration as the original programme save that the start dates were both some seven weeks later than planned due to delay to preceding trades.

2.10 Lift

2.10.1 Although the lift commencement date followed the logic of the original programme the actual commencement was some seven weeks later than planned due to delays by preceding trades.

7.25
300

2.11 Second Fixings

2.11.1 The carpenter second fixings commenced some eight weeks later than planned due to delays by preceding trades. Notwithstanding that the carpenter second fixings operation had increased in scope due to variations this operation nevertheless was completed within the original planned duration because the Claimant increased his labour force in an attempt to reduce the effects to the overall delay to the works.

2.11.2 The electrical and mechanical works were carried out by named subcontractors on the basis of the contract drawings and the performance data set out in pages 129 to 178 of the specification.

2.11.3 The design produced by both the subcontractors complied with the requirements of the Respondents Specification but late amendments to the performance data by the Architect delayed the completion of the final design and the scope of the subcontract works. The commencement of the services second fix had already been delayed by eight weeks due to delay by preceding trades.

2.11.4 The changes to the services packages also increased the amount of builders work in connection therewith and the timing of the execution of this work to the extent that the forming of holes was through finished work and was executed hand in hand with the services second fix instead of the holes being pre-formed in the normal construction process.

2.11.5 As with the first fix services operation the work in the existing building also impacted on the work to the new extension. The subcontract arrangement was that each subcontractor would provide a single gang to follow on from the installation in the existing building to carry out second fix work in the new extension. This logic is reflected in the original programme and was followed exactly in the actual sequence of the works. The increased duration of the services second fix operations reflects the increased scope of this work brought about by the changes in the performance specification.

NEW EXTENSION

2.12 Substructures

2.12.1 The works to the new extension commenced as planned on 2nd April 1991. What became immediately apparent was that the quantities produced by the Architect were not representative of the works to be carried out. The increase in the reduced level dig quantities, foundation trenches and brickwork all lead to an increase in the time required to complete substructures up to completion of oversite. Instead of completing as planned on the 3rd May 1991 with the additional work completion did not actually occur until the 21st May 1991, a delay of two weeks and three days.

2.13 Superstructure

2.13.1 The delay to the substructure caused a delay to the superstructure brickwork and the concrete first floor. Although the superstructure followed the same logic as the original programme the roof coverings were not completed until the 15th September 1991 a total delay of four weeks and three days. The additional two weeks being lost due to the gang of bricklayers having to revert back to work on the lift-shaft in the existing building and due to difficulties in forming the junction between the new roof and the incomplete existing roof.

2.14 First and Second Fixings

2.14.1 As described in paragraphs 2.8 and 2.11 above the logic of the programme for the new extension had a dependence on the completion of the first and second fixings in the existing building. The delay to the first and second fixings therefore overflowed into the programme for the new extension. The mechanical and electrical second fixings were completed some 15 weeks later than planned.

7.25
301

2.15 Decorating Both Buildings

2.15.1 The decorating operations, surprisingly only increased by a total of three days in their respective durations. The Architect was late in providing the colour schedules notwithstanding that there had already been substantial delays to all of the preceding works. What became apparent was that he had not taken sufficient trouble to explain the colour schedules to the Respondent or more particularly the lady of the house. As the decorations proceeded there were parts of the colour scheme that Mrs Bliss could 'simply not live with' not at first or with many of the other attempts. There were areas where the walls were coated some five times before the satisfactory tints and shades were achieved which were to the Respondent's satisfaction. The colours produced were not the British Standard shades which formed the basis of the original specification but the product of experiment from on-site process of mixing and coating sample areas in the correct sunlight conditions.

2.16 Direct Contracts

2.16.1 The original completion date was the 10th December 1991 and it was indicated in the contract documents that the Respondent would provide call and security systems and his own kitchen and laundry equipment through direct contracts.

2.16.2 Notwithstanding that the Respondent had notice that the works were in delay he still had his equipment delivered on the 14th October 1991 as per his original intention. Rooms were commandeered for storage and the Claimant had to work around the equipment and move it from room to room as the building contract was completed.

2.16.3 From the First of December 1991 the Respondent sought to allow the direct contractors access to install the equipment. However the installation could only proceed on an intermittent basis as the Claimant completed in the required areas. The Claimant suffered both delay and disruption from the second fixings stage of his works. He has always maintained in correspondence and subsequently that such freedom of access was not required by the contract and that he could have made up time and completed earlier than 31 March 1992 had he not suffered the interference caused by the direct contractors.

2.17 External Works

2.17.1 The external works were affected by delays to preceding trades. The external drainage was dependant on completion of the internal drainage to the existing building and the new extension. The external drainage system was to be connected to the tails leaving the buildings and to the rainwater downpipes. Until these were in place the falls from the tails to the existing drainage system could not be determined. The external drainage therefore commenced two weeks and one day later than planned due to the late completion of the internal drainage.

2.17.2 The work to the car park had to wait until such time as sufficient of the scaffolding had been removed to permit access to the parking area.

2.17.3 Work to the driveway could not be commenced until the building works were sufficiently advanced and all major deliveries made before the main access to the site was cut off.

2.17.4 The work to the walls and gates and to the garage were dependant upon the bricklaying gang. Until the brickwork was completed to the new extension on 12 August 1991 brickwork could not be commenced in connection with the external boundary walls or the garage.

2.17.5 The landscaping work and the planting were both late in commencing due to lack of information from the Architect. The additional topsoil arising from the excavations to the new extension foundations was incorporated in the landscaping scheme which was finally designed some two months later than planned.

2.18 Conclusions

2.18.1 The Claimant could not have completed the works any sooner than 31 March 1992 in all the circumstances. The Claimant suffered delay through the following primary causes:

(a) Clause 2.4.7—the Claimant not having received in due time the necessary instructions;

(b) Clause 2.4.8—the execution of work not forming part of the Contract by the Respondent himself or by persons employed or otherwise engaged by the Respondent;

(c) Clause 2.4.5—compliance with the Contract Administrators instructions and the extra work caused thereby.

2.18.2 The Architect has not granted any extensions of time and this should be remedied. The Architect has refused to carry out the review required under Clause 2.3 of the Contract to grant the full extension of time to which the Claimant is properly entitled. The Respondent has mistakenly deducted 16 weeks Liquidated and Ascertained Damages in the sum of £146,000. This sum should be paid to the Claimant.

SECTION 3

PROLONGATION COSTS

3.1 This section of my report deals with the loss and/or expense arising from the prolongation to the Contract Period. The Contract commenced on 2 April 1991 and was due for completion on 10 December 1991. The Date for Completion was exceeded by some 16 weeks and the works were not completed until 31 March 1992. For the reasons stated in

7.25
302

section 2 the Claimant is entitled to an extension of time for completion of the Works to cover the whole of the overrun period.

Although the Contract Administrator has not granted the extension of time to which the Claimant is entitled the cost in this section are calculated on the basis that the time will be awarded in the arbitration.

3.2 The primary causes of delay to the Works are:

(a) Clause 4.12.1 the Contractor not having received in due time necessary instructions.
(b) Clause 4.12.3 the execution of work not forming part of the Contract by the Employer himself or by persons employed or otherwise engaged by the Employer.
(c) Clause 4.12.7 compliance with the Contract Administrators instructions.

3.3 These causes of delay also entitle the Claimant to the direct loss and/or expense he has incurred as a result of these matters under Clause 4.11 of the Contract.

3.4 As a result of these matters the Claimant incurred losses under the headings described below. The calculations are included at the end of the section but their source and the reasons for their inclusion are stated under the appropriate headings.

3.5 Site Staff

As a result of the contract overrun the Claimant had to continue to employ his full supervisory and administrative team on the site. There was no opportunity to reduce the staffing levels as the variations and thus the intensity of the workload continued up to the date of practical completion.

The Claimant continued to employ:

John Watts—Site Agent
Fred Brown—Trade Foreman
Peter Murphy—Ganger
Graham Smith—Quantity Surveyor
and additional labour to carry out the ongoing cleaning and site service operations.

3.6 The costs in connection with these staff are calculated as follows:

John Watts is paid a salary on a weekly basis. The total costs to employ are his weekly wage, national insurance costs, pension payments and contributions towards his annual and Bank holiday pay. The costs have been extracted from the company wage rolls which are also posted to the job cost.

Fred Brown is paid on an hourly basis and is paid for overtime worked. His wages therefore vary each week depending upon the overtime worked. The total costs to employ have been averaged over the period of delay to arrive at the weekly costs shown. The source of the cost information is the wage rolls and the job costs.

Peter Murphy is also hourly paid and his costs are calculated on the same basis as those for Fred Brown.

The indirect labour is the weekly average as per the job costs.

3.7 Site Accommodation

The source of these costs is from those charges made to the job costs. They give both the duration of hire and the rates for hire. I believe the rates for hire are internal plant hire rates as all the site accommodation is owned by the Claimant.

3.8 Transport for Operatives

The source of these costs is from those charges made to the job costs. The van is charged to the contract on a weekly hire basis. The fuel costs are taken from fuel bought or from the records of the pump in the Claimants yard. The costs are based on average pump prices on garage forecourts.

3.9 Site Expenses

The telephone and electricity charges are taken from the quarterly accounts of the supply companies and averaged to give a weekly charge. Petty cash is taken from the average charge to the contract throughout the duration. Small tools is a standard charge made to all contracts. Propane is the charge for gas consumed for drying the works.

3.10. Prolongation Costs

3.10.01	Site Staff			
	Site Agent	1 No		410.00
	Foreman	1 No		360.00
	Ganger	1 No		300.00
	Quantity Surveyor (part time)	1 No		240.00
	Indirect Labour (cleaning etc.)	2 No		210.00
	To Collection			1,520.00

3.10.02	Site Accommodation			
	Office	1 No	30.00	30.00
	Store	1 No	30.00	30.00
	Toilet	1 No	30.00	30.00
	Mess Room	1 No	40.00	40.00
	To Collection			130.00

3.10.03	Transport for Operatives			
	Van	1 No	80.00	80.00
	Fuel	5 Days	10.00	50.00
	To Collection			130.00

3.10.04	Site Expenses (Average Weekly Expenditure)	
	Telephones	35.00
	Electricity	30.00
	Petty Cash	50.00
	Small Tools	50.00
	Propane	27.00
	To Collection	192.00

Collection

3.10.01	Site Staff	1,520.00
3.10.02	Site Accommodation	130.00
3.10.03	Transport for Operatives	130.00
3.10.04	Site Expenses	192.00
	Total Cost Per Week	1,972.00

7.25 304

Prolongation Costs
16 weeks @ £1,972.00 per week   31,552.00

Prolongation costs carried forward
to Summary of Costs   31,552.00

SECTION 4

ADDITIONAL STAFF AND EQUIPMENT

4.1 The Works were not only delayed beyond the original date for completion. They were also disrupted in that there was prolongation of each of the stages on the Claimant's programme and a shift in the times in which the Works were being executed.

4.2 The reasons for this change in operations are the lateness of issue of information and the number and timing of variations.

4.3 This necessitated the Claimant retaining staff on-site for longer than planned in respect of bricklaying and finishing operations. It was also necessary to retain items of plant and equipment on-site longer than planned.

4.4 The costs have been extracted from the job costs for the extra periods of duration over and above those originally planned.

7.25
305

4.5. Additional Staff and Equipment

4.5.1   Additional Finishing Foreman from the 7th September 1992 to 11th December 1992.

13 weeks @ £340.00   4,420.00

4.5.2   Additional Bricklayer Foreman from the 14th July 1991 to 6th October 1991

12 weeks @ £340.00   4,080.00

4.5.3   Plant and Equipment
Additional Hire Periods

Dumper		10 weeks @ £40.00	400.00
Forklift		20 weeks @ £80.00	1,600.00
5/3-mixers	2 No	12 weeks @ £35.00	420.00
Standing Scaffolding		18 weeks @ £46.00	828.00
Alterations to Scaffolding			480.00
Transformers	2 No	15 weeks @ £20.00	300.00
Extension Leads	5 No	15 weeks @ £5.00	75.00
Ladders and Trestles	Item	10 weeks @ £20.00	200.00
Sanders	2 No	10 weeks @ £20.00	200.00
Drills	2 No	15 weeks @ £15.00	225.00
Steam Stripper	1 No	3 weeks @ £12.00	36.00
Space Heaters	1 No	6 weeks @ £32.00	192.00
Dehumidifier	1 No	6 weeks @ £33.00	198.00
Skill Saws	2 No	12 weeks @ £20.00	240.00
Core Drill	1 No	10 weeks @ £9.00	90.00
Kango	1 No	15 weeks @ £40.00	600.00
Paint Strippers	3 No	10 weeks @ £30.00	300.00
Angle Grinder	2 No	15 weeks @ £30.00	450.00

Total Additional Stall and Equipment carried forward to summary of cost   15,334.00

SECTION 5

HEAD OFFICE COSTS AND PROFIT

5.1 Because the Claimant was retained on-site for longer than anticipated and the reasons he was retained on-site entitle him to both extension of time and direct loss and/or expense he was unable to deploy his site team and his head office staff on new or other contracts to enable him to recover profit and overheads elsewhere.

5.2 The under-recovery of profit and overheads is part of the Claimants loss and/or expense. This has been evaluated using the Hudson Formula which the Judge in *J F Finnegan* v *Sheffield City Council* 1988 stated that he preferred the Hudson Formula as a means of evaluating this head of additional cost.

5.3 The head office overhead and profit percentage has been verified from the Claimant's tender build-up files.

(a) Hudson Formula

$$\frac{\text{Head Office Overheads and Profit}}{100} \times \frac{\text{Contract Sum}}{\text{Contract Period}} \times \text{Period of Delay}$$

(b) Additional Costs   £

7.25
306

$$\frac{15.00\%}{100} \times \frac{550,000}{36 \text{ weeks}} \times 16 \text{ weeks} = 36,666.66$$

SECTION 6

DISTURBANCE OF LABOUR

6.1 Due to the late receipt of information from the Contract Administrator, the timing and magnitude of variations and the interference to the Works by others engaged direct by the respondent, the Claimant was unable to make best use of his labour either in the manner planned or in the most economic manner.

6.2 As a result of this disturbance to the planned Works the Claimant has incurred losses because his operatives could not achieve those outputs on which he priced and which he would normally anticipate his operatives to achieve without such disturbances.

6.3 The calculation below shows the total labour costs for the contract calculated on an average working hours/average cost rate. The labour costs in the tender have been calculated using 45 per cent as the proportion of labour included in the rates and prices for the Claimant's own work.

6.4 The labour recovered in the final account is calculated on the same basis at 45 per cent of the rates and prices for the Claimants own work.

6.5 The labour total cost is then set against the labour recovered in the final account and this represents the Claimant's loss due to disturbance of labour.

Average Weekly Labour Costs

Total number of operative man days	—	836 man days
Total number of weeks 36 + 16	—	52 weeks
Average rate per hour	—	7.00
Average hours worked per week	—	45 hours per week

$$\frac{\text{Total number operative man days}}{\text{No. of weeks}} \times \text{hours per week} \times \text{rate per hour}$$

$$\frac{836}{52} \times 45 \times 7.00 = £5,064.23$$

Labour included in Tender Documents:

		£
Contract Sum		550,000.00
Less Preliminaries & Contingencies	76,000.00	
Provisional Sums	76,750.00	
	152,750.00	152.750.00
		397,250.00
Labour content included within		
the rates amounts to some 45%	397,250.00 × 45%	178,762.50

Disturbance of labour = Total cost
Less labour included within the rates and recovered through variations

	£	£	£
Total Cost: 5064.23 × 52 weeks			263,339.96
Less—Labour contained within the rates		178,762.50	
Labour recovered through variations	142,035.27		
Less omits	63,351.04		
	78,684.23		
Use 43% for adjustment of labour 78,684.23 × 43%		33,834.22	
		212,596.72	212,596.72
Total Disturbance of Labour costs carried forward to Summary of Costs			£50,743.24

```
7.25
307
```

SECTION 7

INFLATION COSTS

7.1 The Claimant was retained on-site for some 16 weeks longer than anticipated through matters which entitle him to both extension of time and direct loss and/or expense.

7.2 As a result the Claimant incurred additional costs due to inflation. These are calculated using the differences in the Building Cost Index.

The Claimant has been detained on-site for a longer period than they had intended and it follows that, as a consequence of this, they have incurred losses through inflation.

Provision for Inflation in Contract Sum based on the Building Cost Index

	£	£
Contract Sum	550,000.00	
Less Provisional Sums and Contingencies	90,350.00	
	459,650.00	
$\frac{142 - 139}{139} \times £459,650.00 =$		9,920.50

Effect on Inflation on Final Account Sum

	£	£
Final Account	645,346.10	
Less Provisional Sums	107,011.87	
	538,334.23	
$\frac{143 - 139}{139} \times £538,334.23 =$		15,419.63
Less Contract provision for Inflation:		9,920.50
Total Additional Cost of Inflation		5,571.30

SECTION 8

FUNDING COSTS

8.1 Application was made to the Contract Administrator on 3 June 1992 for an ascertainment of the direct loss and/or expense. A reasonable period for ascertainment is one month at which point a sum was due and payable.

8.2 The Contract Administrator has not certified any sums in respect of direct loss and/or expense at all and the Claimant is entitled to the costs of funding that money from the time the loss was incurred until such time as he receives it.

8.3 The Claimants loss and/or expense is summarised as follows before the application of finance costs:

Item	Amount
Prolongation Costs	31,552.00
Additional Staff and Equipment	15,334.00
Head Office Costs and Profit	36,666.66
Disturbance of Labour Costs	50,743.24
Inflation Costs	5,571.30
Total	£139,867.20

7.25
308

These costs were incurred progressively during and after the original contract period as follows:

Description	Date From	Date To	Mid Point
Prolongation	10/12/91	31/3/92	3/2/92
Additional Staff	10/6/91	31/3/92	19/10/91
Head Office Costs	10/12/91	31/3/92	3/2/92
Disturbance Costs	10/6/91	31/3/92	19/10/91
Inflation Costs	29/7/91	31/3/92	28/11/91

8.4 The accumulation of costs is therefore as follows:

Date	Cost Head	Cumulative Amount
19/10/91	Additional Staff/Disturbance	£66,077.24
28/11/91	Inflation Costs	£71,648.54
3/2/92	Prolongation/Head Office	£139,867.20

8.5 The Claimant pays interest at Bank Rate plus 3 per cent on his overdraft facility compounded at quarterly rest periods. This is the basis on which the calculations are therefore made.

Base Rates	%	Days	Compound at
19.10.91	10.50	198	72 & 163
05.05.92	10.00	162	91
16.09.92	12.00	3	
18.09.92	10.00	4	
22.09.92	9.00	25	8
16.10.92	8.00	29	
13.11.92	7.00	76	48
28.01.93	6.00		

From	To	Days	Principal	Rate %	Amount
19/10/91	28/11/91	39	66,077.24	13.5	953.14
29/11/91	31/12/91	33	71,648.54	13.5	874.50
1/1/92	3/2/92	34	73,459.18	13.5	923.77
4/2/92	31/3/92	57	141,694.84	13.5	2,987.24
1/4/92	5/5/92	35	145,605.85	13.5	1,884.90
6/5/92	30/6/92	91	145,605.85	13	4,719.22
1/7/92	15/9/92	79	152,209.97	13	4,282.73
16/9/92	18/9/92	3	152,209.97	15	187.65
19/9/92	22/9/92	4	152,209.97	13	216.84
23/9/92	30/9/92	8	152,209.97	12	400.33
1/10/92	16/10/92	16	157,297.52	12	827.42
17/10/92	13/11/92	29	157,297.52	11	1,374.73
14/11/92	31/12/92	48	157,297.52	10	2,068.57
1/1/93	28/1/93	28	161,568.24	10	1,239.43
				Total	£22,940.47

and from the 28.01.93 accruing at 9 per cent compounded quarterly subject to any change in base rates.

7.25
309

SECTION 9

FINAL ACCOUNT

9.0 Final Account Summary (Agreed Items)

9.1 The schedules which follow represent the summaries of the agreed items which form the basis of computation of the adjusted Contract Sum. The term agreed means that all the dimensions and measurements are agreed but not necessarily the rates and pricing which form the value of the variations.

9.2 The final account was submitted on 3 June 1992, which was within the time required by the contract. The Claimant submitted all the supporting documentation required by the Contract to the Architect to make all the adjustments to the Contract Sum.

9.3 The works were completed on 31 March 1992. The defects liability period was six months and the period for final adjustment of the contract sum was also six months. This means that a Final Certificate should have been issued by 30 September 1992.

	Omit	Add
Tender Sum		622,171.95
Agreed Reduction		72,171.95
Contract Sum		550,000.00
Provisional Sums	76,750.00	107,011.87
Variations	63,351.04	142,035,27
Contingencies	13,600.00	—
Remeasured Items		10,939.00
	153,701.04	
		809,986.14
		153,701.04
TOTALS		656,285.10

Provisional Sums

	Omit	Add
A.I. No.2 (b)	18,200.00	27,853.77
A.I. No.2 (b)	1,200.00	1,506.98
A.I. No.2 (c)	16,000.00	18.225.26
A.I. No.2 (c)	3,600.00	4,293.54
A.I. No.20 (a)	—	1,971.78
A.I. No.21 (a)	—	2,903.72
A.I. No.55 (b)	15,750.00	18,217.72
A.I. No.55 (b)	12,000.00	19,251.54
A.I. No.55 (b)	10,000.00	12,787.56
	76,750.00	107,011.87

7.25
310

Variations

No	Date	Description	Omit	Add	Comment
1a	06.04.91	10 No. Building Cards	—	—	
1a	06.04.91	Drawing Issue	24,108.00	37,192.00	
1c	06.04.91	Specification Issue	—	—	
2a	14.04.91	Revisions to lift-shaft	2,400.00	4,271.00	
2b	14.04.91	Acceptance of G Gosling's tender			Prov Sum
2c	14.04.91	Acceptance of R T Brown's tender	—	—	Prov Sum
3a	20.04.91	Dip & strip carved brackets		156.23	
3b	20.04.91	Label & strip moulded work		371.00	
4a	24.04.91	Deliver sound brackets		51.00	
4b	24.04.91	Amendments to extension foundations	854.00	4,080.00	Agreed
4c	24.04.91	Omit: Rebuilding of gable wall	279.00	540.00	Agreed
4d	24.04.91	Omit: Honey comb dwarf wall	193.00		Agreed
4e	24.04.91	Joists to kitchen floor		664.59	
4f	24.04.91	Repairs to timber frame		190.00	
4g	24.04.91	Reissue of window details	1,413.00	16,156.00	Agreed
4h	24.04.91	Reuse existing cornice		255.00	
4k	24.04.91	Strip door hoods & timber mouldings		564.00	
5a	30.04.91	Repairs to timber frame: North elev.		1,312.67	
5b	30.04.91	Renew tiled cill		360.00	
5c	30.04.91	Refurb works to gable elevation		1,813.12	
6a	30.04.91	Work to existing windows		579.00	
6b	30.04.91	Replace lead apron to W/3/3		421.00	
6c	30.04.91	Additional span to garage roof		67.50	Agreed
6d	30.04.91	Extension & utility room floor levels			
6e	30.04.91	Extension floor slab			
6f	30.04.91	Remedial to soffit of lintel D/G/4		150.00	
6g	30.04.91	Lintel to door D/G/5		110.00	Agreed
6h	30.04.91	Seal off storm water drain		3.76	Agreed
6i	30.04.91	Omit: storm water manhold No.2	394.00		Agreed
6j	30.04.91	Seal off foul water manhole		20.00	Agreed
6k	30.04.91	Revised storm water drain	160.59	76.61	Agreed
6l	30.04.91	Modify rainwater gully; kitchen		93.24	Agreed
6m	30.04.91	Modify rainwater gully; extension		138.15	Agreed
6n	30.04.91	Construct storm water manhole No.2		589.25	Agreed
6o	30.04.91	Construct new soakaway		726.38	Agreed
6p	30.04.91	Adjust gully for kitchen waste		96.25	
		Carried Forward	42,518.59	71,047.75	

7.25
311

Variations (Cont)

No	Date	Description	Omit	Add	Comment
		Brought Forward	42,518.59	71,047.75	
7a	08.05.91	Adjust carcassing & outlet positions			Prov Sum
7b	08.05.91	Conceal cables			Prov Sum
7e	08.05.91	Relocated switches			Prov Sum
7f	08.05.91	Relocate pendant fitting			Prov Sum
7g	08.05.91	Provide pendant fitting & switch			Prov Sum
8a	17.05.91	Remove rubble inserts to fireplaces		384.00	
9a	28.05.91	Lead soakers & apron flashing		519.00	Agreed
9b	28.05.91	Work around W/2/3		224.06	
9c	28.05.91	New lintel & brickwork		232.21	Agreed
10a	05.06.91	Feathered lining to W/1/7		33.00	Agreed
10b	05.06.91	Work to eaves of north elevation		490.75	Agreed
10c	05.06.91	Work to fireplaces			
10e	05.06.91	Work to fireplace No.1		44.00	Agreed
10f	05.06.91	Work to fireplace No.3		15.00	Agreed
10g	05.06.91	Stairwell fascia		12.00	Agreed
10h	05.06.91	Work to chimney; east elevation		210.50	
10i	05.06.91	Replace stepped weathering		197.96	
11a	17.06.91	Needle up stone chimney breast		409.00	
11b	17.06.91	Remove partition betw'n windows; bed 2		57.10	Agreed
11c	17.06.91	Drawing issue; tie rods		698.00	Agreed
12a	24.07.91	Omit: plasterboard; Add: hardboard			
12b	24.07.91	50 mm wood wool slabs		60.00	Agreed
12c	24.07.91	Remove vent & patrass & make good		101.20	Agreed
12d	24.07.91	Replace stone quoin		168.00	
12e	24.07.91	Supply & fit register plate		36.30	Agreed
13a	13.08.91	Replace lead flat, fit fascia, form drips		564.00	
13b	13.08.91	Apron flashing to be dressed over		230.00	
13c	13.08.91	Redress ends of roof valley gutter		160.00	Agreed
13d	13.08.91	Renew apron flashing		162.00	Agreed
13e	13.08.91	Work to W/2/1 & W/2/3		580.90	Agreed
14a	13.09.91	Drawing issue (Revised)	5,161.00	7,112.00	
14b	13.09.91	Architrave & dado details	1,211.00	1,427.80	Agreed
15a	13.09.91	Drawing issue (Revised)	2,112.00	3,150.00	Agreed
15b	13.09.91	Installation of entry phone			Prov Sum
		Carried Forward	51,002.59	88,326.33	

7.25
312

Variations (Cont)

No	Date	Description	Omit	Add	Comment
		Brought Forward	51,002.59	88,326.33	
16a	17.10.91	Amend sink specification	225.00	357.45	Agreed
16b	17.10.91	Revised Spec. M&E			M&E
17a	17.10.91	Gas service to cooker (A G Plumbs)			Prov Sum
18a	18.10.91	Pay Reject Tiles invoice		158.63	Agreed
18b	18.10.91	Colour of tiles		41.80	Agreed
18c	18.10.91	Work to attic bedroom		499.00	
19a	18.10.91	Renew abutments to W/3/4		172.00	
19b	18.10.91	Remove render step		50.00	Agreed
19c	18.10.91	Replace incorrect lead covering			Agreed
19d	18.10.91	Replace door D.3.3		132.00	Agreed
19e	18.10.91	Fit new skirting in attic No.2		25.00	Agreed
19f	18.10.91	Timber fillet to D.G.13		15.00	Agreed
20a	21.10.91	Settle Boulton & Paul invoice			Prov
21a	25.10.91	Accept John Lewis quotation			Prov
22a	28.10.91	Work by electrician			
22b	28.10.91	New architraves		60.50	Agreed
22c	28.10.91	Issue of colour schedule			
23a	30.10.91	Removal of asbestos panelling		231.85	
23b	30.10.91	Amend bath spec		33.06	Agreed
23c	30.10.91	Insulate roof space		23.00	
23d	30.10.91	Form access to above roof space		184.16	
24a	11.11.91	Dimensions of gas hob			
25a	21.11.91	Renew tiled roof slopes		184.60	Agreed
25b	21.11.91	Work to garden walls		2,626.63	Agreed
25c	21.11.91	Stone dust rendering		23.00	Agreed
25d	21.11.91	Wrap soil stack with glass wool		13.00	Agreed
25e	21.11.91	Pendant fittings			Prov Sum
25f	21.11.91	Location of fluorescent fittings			Prov Sum
25g	21.11.91	Wiring of pendants			Prov Sum
26a	21.11.91	Reposition ceiling lights in kitchen			Prov Sum
26b	21.11.91	Stone strings and gable to sth elev		742.00	
26c	21.11.91	Obscure glass		255.00	Agreed
26d	21.11.91	Glazing bars		298.00	Agreed
26e	21.11.91	Form bulkhead in first-floor bathroom		74.28	Agreed
26f	21.11.91	Case heating pipework		28.00	Agreed
26g	21.11.91	Replace architrave; D.G.1		33.00	Agreed
		Carried Forward	51,227.59	94,587.29	

7.25
313

Variations (Cont)

No	Date	Description	Omit	Add	Comment
		Brought Forward	51,227.59	94,587.29	
26h	21.11.91	Drawing issue Extension (Revised)	7,118.00	9,242.00	
26i	21.11.91	Drawing issue Extension (Revised)	2,620.00	3,114.00	
27a	22.11.91	Shelving in airing cupboard		105.30	Agreed
28a	04.12.91	Lighting schedule			Prov Sum
29a	04.12.91	Omit: sheathing & floor finishes	1,656.00		Agreed
29b	04.12.91	Variety floors quote		2,905.63	Agreed
30a	06.12.91	Lead flashings to dormers		518.00	
30b	06.12.91	Dormer cornices		376.00	
30c	06.12.91	Remove casing beads		212.00	
30d	06.12.91	Gable wall, smooth finish rendered		257.00	
31a	09.12.91	Drawing issue, joinery only		2,448.80	
31b	09.12.91	Drawing issue		2,811.00	
32a	13.12.91	Renew ceiling in lobby	24.20	84.26	Agreed
32b	13.12.91	Repair rotten dado in lobby		35.20	
32c	13.12.91	Omit: painting to stair handrail	70.00		Agreed
32d	13.12.91	New WC at first floor			Prov Sum
32e	13.12.91	Case vertical heating pipes		35.46	Agreed
32f	13.12.91	Ceilings to basements		949.00	Agreed
33a	13.12.91	Plaster as specification			
33b	13.12.91	New abutments to gable chimneys		256.56	Agreed
33c	13.12.91	Remove rubble from fireplace		179.00	
33d	13.12.91	Weather chimney stack		50.00	Agreed
33e	13.12.91	Increase tile eaves overhang		171.77	Agreed
33f	13.12.91	Paint chimney support metalwork		31.14	Agreed
34a	13.12.91	Dimmer switches			Prov
34b	13.12.91	Plywood panel		22.00	Agreed
34c	13.12.91	Face mounted cables			Prov Sum
35a	17.12.91	Patrass for entry phone		98.28	Agreed
35b	17.12.91	Toilet roll holders	108.90	154.99	Agreed
35c	17.12.91	Lead hood to W/1/10		170.00	
35d	17.12.91	Lead slate to v.p		80.00	
35e	17.12.91	Work to attic window W/3/4		20.00	
35f	17.12.91	New lead saddle		70.71	Agreed
35g	17.12.91	Additional undercoat; bed 2		35.20	Agreed
35h	17.12.91	Remove rotten timber in basement		97.90	Prov Sum
36a	20.12.91	25×50 mm skirting in kitchen worktop		104.15	Agreed
36b	20.12.91	Reposition radiator in entrance lobby			Prov Sum
		Carried Forward	62,824.69	119,222.64	

Variations (Cont)

No	Date	Description	Omit	Add	Comment
		Brought Forward	62,824.69	119,222.64	
36d	20.12.91	Confirmation that gas valve adequate			Prov Sum
36e	20.12.91	Marble mantle shelf to living room		118.56	Agreed
36f	20.12.91	Remake back gutters; attic bed 2		412.00	
36g	20.12.91	Work to chimneys		512.00	
36h	20.12.91	Picture rail in bed 1		80.00	Agreed
36i	20.12.91	Gas supply to fire places			Prov Sum
36j	20.12.91	Marble hearth to bed 2		29.00	Agreed
37a	06.01.92	Reissue of colour schedule	100.80	189.00	Agreed
38a	06.01.92	Batten sect & wardrobe rail; attic b/r		130.56	Agreed
38b	06.01.92	John Try account; carved sections		84.38	Agreed
38c	06.01.92	Treat ends to cills & trim of windows		10.00	Agreed
38d	06.01.92	New rainwater pipe		84.00	Agreed
38e	06.01.92	Work to rainwater gutter outlet		46.00	Agreed
38f	06.01.92	Fixing of ceiling lighting fittings		175.00	
39a	08.01.92	Remove loose rendering & re-render		41.20	
39b	08.01.92	Remove paint from copings & M G		153.00	Agreed
39c	08.01.92	Work to front entrance door D.G.1		29.00	
39d	08.01.92	Extend short worktop		70.00	
39e	08.01.92	Repoint stonework north elevation		195.00	
39f	08.01.92	Stain new floorboards to match existing		209.00	
39h	08.01.92	Cut & remake external putties		904.50	
39i	08.01.92	Repoint leaded lights W.G.10, 11		21.00	Agreed
39j	08.01.92	Rake out & repoint mortar; basement 2		180.00	
40a	14.01.92	Work to staircase		342.00	Agreed
41a	15.01.92	Revised redecoration		904.00	Agreed
41b	15.01.92	Take up & relay stone paving		221.00	Agreed
41c	15.01.92	Refix door & frame D.G.14		46.00	Agreed
41d	15.01.92	Remove hearth & make good; att rm		65.88	Agreed
41e	15.01.92	Work to garden steps		95.00	
41f	15.01.92	Leave clean stone on-site			
41g	15.01.92	Coir matting to lobby & garden entrance		105.16	Agreed
41h	15.01.92	Adjust bottom of doors & fit threshold		81.75	Agreed
41i	15.01.92	Fireplace installation		125.00	
42a	27.01.92	Replace consumer unit			Prov Sum
42b	27.01.92	Relocate bracket fitting		40.00	
		Carried Forward	62,925.49	125,014.63	

7.25
315

Variations (Cont)

No	Date	Description	Omit	Add	Comment
		Brought Forward	62,925.49	125,014.63	
42c	27.01.92	Alterations to electrical fittings			Prov Sum
43a	29.01.92	Dining-room decorations		512.00	
44a	03.02.92	Make good & point open joints		56.76	Agreed
44b	03.02.92	Complete rendering to roof space		70.00	
44d	03.02.92	Repairs to stone string; sth elev		84.60	
44e	03.02.92	Roof level inspection			
45a	05.02.92	Letter plate		153.48	Agreed
45b	05.02.92	Tool back stone dust rendering		109.00	
45c	05.02.92	General trim lead			
45d	05.02.92	Redress wings of lead hood			
45e	05.02.92	Redress lead apron			
45g	05.02.92	New door D/G/1 omit letter plate		430.76	
45h	05.02.92	Fit chubb mortice lock		50.00	
46a	06.02.92	Wks roof level-E VALLEY		170.00	
46b	06.02.92	Wks roof level-W VALLEY		181.50	
46d	06.02.92	Wks Dormer gable STH ELEV		192.50	
47a	13.02.92	Preparation of floors		725.00	Agreed
47c	13.02.92	Change single way switches			Prov Sum
49a	13.02.92	Smoke detectors		63.90	Agreed
49b	13.02.92	Testing electrical installation			Prov Sum
49c	13.02.92	Testing heating and HW installation			Prov Sum
50a	24.02.92	Additional security devices		648.21	Agreed
51a	24.02.92	Lay paving slabs		271.00	
53a	28.02.92	Works to bedroom 1		47.30	Agreed
53b	28.02.92	Works to airing cupboard and living room		14.30	Agreed
53c	28.02.92	Key for shutter catches		10.00	Agreed
53d	28.02.92	Mortice lock		30.08	Agreed
53e	28.02.92	Additional shelf		30.00	Agreed
54a	28.02.92	Key for shutter catches		5.00	
54b	28.02.92	Amend furniture W/3/4	41.05	13.45	Agreed
54c	28.02.92	New nosing		37.00	
54d	28.02.92	Renew rotten stonework		62.28	
		Carried Forward	62,966.54	128,979.75	

7.25
316

Variations (Cont)

No	Date	Description	Omit	Add	Comment
		Brought Forward	62,966.54	128,979.72	
54f	28.02.92	Rake out and repoint garden wall		541.80	
55a	28.02.92	Adjust: Provisional Sums			
56a	28.02.92	New moulded plinth blocks		64.90	Agreed
57a	03.03.92	Light fitting			Prov Sum
57b	03.03.92	Cable and outlet for fitting room			Prov Sum
57c	03.03.92	Paint finish for doors			
57d	03.03.92	Omit top coat, add wallpaper	16.50	56.00	Agreed
57e	03.03.92	Margins to fielded panels		1,606.00	
57f	03.03.92	Redecoration of shutter cases		212.00	
57g	03.03.92	Change garage roof tiles		518.00	
58a	06.03.92	Omit wall unit, add lighting fitting			Prov Sum
58b	06.03.92	Install socket outlet		9.00	Agreed
58c	06.03.92	Change pelmet lighting fittings			Prov Sum
58d	06.03.92	Fit security bolts		30.80	Agreed
58e	06.03.92	Fit coat peg rail		29.02	Agreed
59a	06.03.92	Sash locks to windows	368.00	606.00	Agreed
60a	09.03.92	Revised Glazing		954.00	
60b	09.03.92	Change light fittings			Prov Sum
60c	09.03.92	Revised call system		1,208.00	
61a	13.03.92	Plinth for safe		171.00	
61b	13.03.92	TV aerial outlets			Prov Sum
61c	13.03.92	Pavings garage forecourt		1,200.00	
61d	13.03.92	Service shutter		800.00	
61e	13.03.92	Fit Preservation Trust plaque		15.00	
61f	13.03.92	Security window locks		170.00	
61g	13.03.92	Front door lock		70.00	
62a	17.03.92	North Slopes Roof repairs		158.00	
62b	17.03.92	North Slopes Roof repairs		172.00	
63a	20.03.92	Change colours dining room		322.00	
63b	20.03.92	Make good rendering/decorate		110.00	
64a	20.03.92	Flood lighting			Prov Sum
64b	20.03.92	Room plaques		210.00	
64c	20.03.92	Revise ceiling finish		151.00	
65	23.03.92	Kitchen floor tiles		508.00	
66	28.03.92	Attendance on Direct Contractors		270.00	
67	28.03.92	New servery hatch		981.00	
68	11.04.92	Attendance Direct Contractors		321.00	
69	28.04.92	Fire Officer's requirements		588.00	
70	30.04.92	Change colours bed 1		278.00	
71	06.05.92	Wallpaper dining room		351.00	
72	08.05.92	Fire blankets in kitchen		208.00	
		TOTAL OMITS/ADDS	63,351.04	142,035.27	

7.25
317

Contingencies

	Omit	*Add*
Specification Item 1.30	5,600.00	—
Specification Item 1.30	8,000.00	—
	£13,600.00	—

SECTION 10

REMEASURED ITEMS NOT AGREED

		ADD
1.00	Additional removal of topsoil and reduced level dig	1,440.00
2.00	Additional trench excavation and cart away	450.00
3.00	Brickwork to foundations	630.00
4.00	External Works	2,223.00
5.00	Main Driveway	749.00
6.00	Car Parking	1,680.00
7.00	Landscaping cut fill and topsoil	2,167.00
8.00	Rainwater goods change UPVC to cast aluminium powder coated	1,600.00
	TOTAL	£10,939.00

7.25
318

SECTION 11

SUMS DUE UNDER THE FINAL ACCOUNT AND CASH RECONCILIATION

Statement of Sums Due Under Final Account, excluding loss and/or expense claim

		£
FINAL ACCOUNT		656,285.10
Sums Certified up to and including Certificate No. 12 dated 13 April 1992		610,450.00
	Total Due	45,835.10
Cash Received (VAT ex.)	£412,296	
Liquidated Damages	£146,000	
Defects	£ 32,000	
Certificate No.12	£ 10,954	
Second Moiety Retention	£ 9,200	
	£610,450	
	Total Cash Shortfall	£243,989.10

SECTION 12

LATE PAYMENT OF CERTIFICATES

12.1 Notwithstanding that certificate number 12 dated 13 April 1992 has not been honoured, Certificates numbers 1 to 11 were not honoured in the time required by the contract. The table below represents the pattern of late payments made by the Respondent.

Certificate Number	Date	Due Date	Date Paid	Net Amount £
1	6.5.91	20.5.91	28.5.91	32,800
2	10.6.91	24.6.91	4.7.91	41,200
3	15.7.91	29.7.91	15.8.91	53,800
4	12.8.91	26.8.91	11.9.91	76,800
5	9.9.91	23.9.91	7.10.91	88,600
6	16.10.91	30.10.91	14.11.91	91,800
7	15.11.91	29.11.91	12.12.91	56,896
8	16.12.91	30.12.91	12.1.92	47,200
9	13.1.92	27.1.92	1.2.92	45,700
10	11.2.92	25.2.92	15.3.92	36,800
11	12.3.92	26.3.92	18.4.92	27,900
12	13.4.92	27.4.92	—	10,954

12.2 The table below shows the interest due on the late payments.

Amount	Days Late	Interest Rate	Total £
32,800.00	8	14.5	104.24
41,200.00	10	14.5	163.67
53,800.00	17	14.0	350.81
76,800.00	16	14.0	471.32
88,600.00	14	13.5	458.78
91,800.00	14	13.5	475.35
56,896.00	13	13.5	273.56
47,200.00	13	13.5	226.94
45,700.00	5	13.5	84.51
36,800.00	18	13.5	244.99
27,900.00	23	13.5	237.34
10,954.00	8	13.5	32.41
10,954.00	91	13.0	355.02
11,341.43	79	13.0	319.11
11,341.43	3	15.0	13.98
11,341.43	4	13.0	16.15
11,341.43	8	12.0	29.82
11,720.49	16	12.0	61.65
11,720.49	29	11.0	102.43
11,720.49	48	10.0	154.13
12,038.70	28	10.0	92.35
		TOTAL	£4,268.56

7.25
319

and from the 28.01.93 accruing at 9 per cent compounded quarterly subject to any change in base rates.

12.3 The Respondent also deducted liquidated and ascertained damages from the payments made to the Claimant. Unusually these deductions were made from certificate number 7 onwards which was paid late (two days after the original completion date). The damages deducted from that certificate were the equivalent of damages due for four weeks. The Respondent therefore deducted damages in anticipation of late completion rather than after late completion had occurred. Despite the protestations of the Claimant this practice continued by the Respondent until such time as a total of £146,000 had been deducted from certificates.

12.4 If, as is my contention, the damages are not due at all the Claimant should be entitled to interest on the damages wrongfully withheld from the time at which they were deducted, until such time as they are repaid. If any amount of the damages is awarded to the Respondent some recompense will be required in the form of interest for the fact that the damages were deducted earlier than permitted by the Contract.

12.5 The damages were deducted in the following pattern and attract interest at 3 per cent above Bank base rates:

Certificate	Date Damages Deducted	Amount of Damages
7	12.12.91	36,500
8	12.1.92	45,625
9	1.2.92	45,625
10	15.3.92	18,250
	TOTAL	£146,000

12.6 The calculation of interest on late payment of certificates takes account of any interest due on damages for the period up to payment of the certificate itself. The table below shows the interest due on damages from the dates on which the certificates were honoured and therefore the damages were withheld.

Amount	Days	Interest Rate	Total £
36,500.00	19	13.5	256.50
36,756.50	12	13.5	163.13
83,381.50	20	13.5	616.79
129,006.50	43	13.5	2,051.73
147,256.50	16	13.5	871.43
150,959.58	5	13.5	279.17
150,959.58	56	13.0	3,010.91
150,959.58	78	13.0	4,193.78
150,959.58	2	15.0	124.07
150,959.58	4	13.0	215.06
150,959.58	8	12.0	397.04
159,179.61	17	12.0	889.65
159,179.61	29	11.0	1,391.48
159,179.61	48	10.0	2,093.32
163,554.06	28	10.0	1,254.66
		TOTAL	£17,808.72

and from the 28.01.93 accruing at 9 per cent compounded quarterly subject to any change in base rates.

7.25
320

SECTION 13

RESPONDENT'S LIST OF DEFECTS

13.1 This section of my report deals with the Respondent's list of defects for which he claims the sum of £32,634. The item references are those on the Respondents Scott Schedule.

13.2 Scott Schedule Items 1 to 19 Inclusive

13.2.1 These items generally cover cracks in plaster, cracks at junction between ceiling and wall junction. Excessive shrinkage to skirtings and architraves, joints all open. Shakes in door lining and doors twisted. Fractures at lintel bearings.

13.2.2 The plaster cracks are due to the excessive use of the heating system immediately after handover of the building. The Respondent was warned by the Claimant at a meeting three days before handover that the building had not had the opportunity to dry out properly over the winter months. Plastering had only been completed prior to Christmas 1991 and what was required was a gradual heat and a through flow of ventilation to enable the building to dry naturally. When the Claimants operatives visited the house in April 1992 to carry out minor defects work it was noted that the heating system had been turned up to maximum and that condensation was visible from the outside of the building and could be seen running down the windows. There were also signs of surface dampness on the interior walls of the building. The internal joinery had already started to move and there were 'blow marks' on the plaster, a sign of rapid egress of moisture. One of the staff at the house remarked when questioned, that the residents, being elderly, were constantly complaining that they were cold. The orders were therefore to run the heating at maximum.

The Claimant therefore attributes the plaster cracks and the movement in the joinery to the excessive heat in the building at a time when the building should have been allowed to dry naturally.

13.2.3 It is my view that with regard to these particular items the Claimant has no liability and there the remedy of these defects is a matter for the Respondent and his advisers. I would therefore price the Claimant's contribution in this instance at nil.

7.25
321

13.3 Scott Schedule Items 20 to 25 Inclusive

13.3.1 These items are in connection with the bathrooms. The cracking to the plaster is caused by the exceptional use of the heating system as described above and there is no need to consider it further in this section.

13.3.2 The lifting of the wall tiles is partly due to the misuse of the heating system and partly due to the use of the wrong adhesive. The Claimant warned the Architect that the adhesive specified for the wall tiles was unsuitable for use on plaster backgrounds. The Architect nevertheless insisted on its use having received assurances from the manufacturers representative.

13.3.3 The mechanical extract system does ventilate into the loft space rather than to the exterior of the building. The Claimant executed this work as measured in the Contract Documents. There were no terminations measured to the exterior of the building and it is submitted that any further work to terminate the vents to the exterior is extra work for which the Claimant is entitled to be paid.

13.4 Scott Schedule Items 26 to 29 Inclusive

13.4.1 The plaster cracks are due to the misuse of the heating system as described above. The Claimant has acknowledged there is a problem with the fixing of the handrails and has offered to remedy that problem when the Respondent honours the outstanding certificate for payment.

I assess that the problem can be corrected with about a day's work for one man for the three staircases which is a value of £70.

13.4.2 The leaks into stair 2 area have been investigated and the ingress of water has been found to be around the lead flashings to the valleys between the junction of the existing and the new extension. I have obtained an estimate from the plumbing firm who did the original leadwork who put the value of remedying this defect at no more than £80. If the Claimant were allowed back on-site to remedy this problem the cost to him would be nil as his plumbing subcontractor has acknowledged the defect and will remedy it at his own cost.

13.4.3 The terminations of the mechanical ventilation system were not measured in the contract bills and the Claimant is therefore entitled to be paid for these as extra work.

13.5 Scott Schedule Items 30 to 31 Inclusive

13.5.1 The Claimant cited the kitchen units and extractor fan in the positions shown on the contract drawings. There were subsequent changes to those drawings on introduction of the Respondent's own kitchen equipment but no instructions were issued to change the position of the units installed. The lack of accessibility of the switches is also caused by the Respondent's equipment.

13.5.2 The deep scratching to the floor finishes was caused by the Respondent's own operatives when they installed the kitchen equipment.

13.5.3 The cracking to plaster excessive shrinkage to joinery and the tiles lifting are all due to misuse of the heating system as described above.

13.5.4 The door to the kitchen lobby was fitted correctly by the Claimant during the course of the works. It is the Claimant's view that this door was damaged by the Respondent's operatives when they installed the kitchen equipment.

13.6 Scott Schedule Items 32 to 35 Inclusive

13.6.1 All of the cracking and damage in these areas is due to the misuse of the heating system described above.

7.25
322

13.7 Scott Schedule Item 36

13.7.1 The fire escape door/window was partially bricked up in accordance with the contract drawings. The Architect issued a verbal instruction to cease work on this item and no further instructions were given so the work was left in a partially completed state.

13.7.2 The ventilation system and the lift motor room are in accordance with the Architect's details.

13.8 Scott Schedule Item 38

13.8.1 The Claimant admits that the door knobs and handles are generally not properly fixed. The Architect chose Italian door furniture and there were no instructions in English. The Claimant only discovered at a later date when the Respondent was having difficulty with the door furniture that the grub screws were missing. I agree the sum of £452 as being the cost of remedying the defect.

13.9 Scott Schedule Item 39

13.9.1 The Nurse call system was fitted by the Respondent's own operatives. The Claimant therefore has no liability in respect of this item.

13.10 Scott Schedule Item 40

13.10.1 The baths and the hoists are entirely in accordance with the Architect's specification. It is admitted that the hoists are the wrong pattern for the bath but this is a matter for the Respondent and his Architect.

13.11 Scott Schedule Item 41

13.11.1 There is a conflict between the specification and the measured items. The fix only item in pricing document includes all items of work to be covered by the contract sum and therefore only one wash hand basin per room is required.

13.12 Scott Schedule Item 42

13.12.1 It is agreed that the electrical installation in the cupboard under the stairs does not comply with the IEE regulations. However, this work was executed by a named subcontractor and it is therefore his liability and not the Claimants.

13.13 Scott Schedule Item 43

13.13.1 An investigation has revealed that the socket outlets and switch points were plastered over after the electrician had completed his first fix operations. The face plates have now been installed and the items function.

13.14 Scott Schedule Item 44

13.14.1 The wiring diagrams for the boiler have now been found and handed to the Respondent.

13.15 Scott Schedule Item 45

13.15.1 It is agreed that this was an error and the sum of £108 is also agreed.

```
7.25
323
```

13.16 Scott Schedule Item 46

13.16.1 The plumbing leaks above the 'Gibbs ceiling were corrected at the time they were first notified. The indicators on the tap heads can be changed so that they are correctly marked for hot and cold water. The costs for doing this are £40.

13.17 Scott Schedule Item 47

13.17.1 The reason the paint is flaking from the radiators is that the Architect wrongly specified that the radiators should have an undercoat. It is normal practice to treat radiators with only gloss paint. The lack of flexibility of the undercoat and the extreme use of the heating system are the cause of the paint flaking.

13.18 Scott Schedule Item 48

13.18.1 It is admitted that a tap is missing to the sluicing sink and the cost of £85 is accepted as the likely remedial cost.

13.19 Scott Schedule Item 49

13.19.1 The Claimant repaired the lawns as part of the contract works. The reason that there are dead patches is caused by the Respondent's cats urinating in the same areas.

13.20 Scott Schedule Item 50

13.20.1 It is accepted that the ramp and side access have not been provided. These were shown on an early drawing which did not form part of the contract set and the Claimant did not therefore construct them. If they remain a requirement now they are extra work and the Claimant should be paid for carrying this work out.

13.21 Scott Schedule Item 51

13.21.1 The Claimant did not use the Respondent's breeze blocks. The contract specification did not require the use of breeze blocks anywhere.

13.22 Scott Schedule Item 52

13.22.1 The flaking and cracking of the paintwork is due to the excessive use of the heating system as described above.

13.23 Scott Schedule Item 53

13.23.1 It is not accepted that the driveway was in a damaged state when the Claimant left the works. There is damage present now but it is not known who caused the damage.

13.24 Scott Schedule Item 54

13.24.1 It is accepted that the door closers may require some adjustment now. The Claimant has a contract where he is required to remedy defects, not to provide ongoing maintenance to the building.

13.24.2 It is accepted that the door closer to the lift lobby does not match the pattern of the other door closers in the building. This is because the Architect gave a verbal instruction to use a stock item from a local builders merchant when one of the door closers was stolen. That pattern of door closer does not permit full opening.

7.25
324

13.25 Scott Schedule Item 55

13.25.1 It is admitted that the fireproof film is lifting from the face of several of the doors. The Claimant was not familiar with this particular method of fireproofing and warned the Architect at the time. It is apparent that the film is lifting due to the presence of trapped moisture in the doors. There was no warning on the manufacturer's literature concerning moisture content of the base on to which the coating was to be applied and in every other respect the Claimant complied with the specification.

13.26 Scott Schedule Item 56

13.26.1 It is accepted that there are some window shutters which are painted up but not on the scale that the Respondent would suggest. The sum estimated to correct this matter is £440.

13.27 Scott Schedule Item 57

13.27.1 The bedroom furniture was provided by the Respondent's own supplier. It was inevitable that the cheap worktops which are a flaxboard base would not remain stable in the presence of the moisture from the handbasins mounted in the tops.

13.27.2 Similarly the wardrobe doors are mounted on a pair of butts instead of a piano hinge and the catches are a poor fit. It was inevitable that the doors would twist.

SECTION 14

SUMMARY

14.01 The Claimant is entitled to an extension of time of 16 weeks.

14.02 The Claimant is entitled to the following sums:

Section	Description	Amount £
2	Refund Liquidated Damages	146,000.00
3	Prolongation Costs	31,552.00
4	Additional Staff & Equipment	15,334.00
5	Head Office Costs	36,666.66
6	Disturbance of Labour	50,743.24
7	Inflation Costs	5,571.30
8	Funding Costs	22,940.47
11	Final Account	45,835.10
11	Second Moiety of Retention	9,200.00
11	Certificate No. 12	10,954.00
11	Money held for Defects	32,000.00
12	Late Payment	4,268.56
12	Interest on Damages	17,808.72
	TOTAL	428,874.05

7.25
325

APPENDIX 1

BAR CHARTS

7.25
326

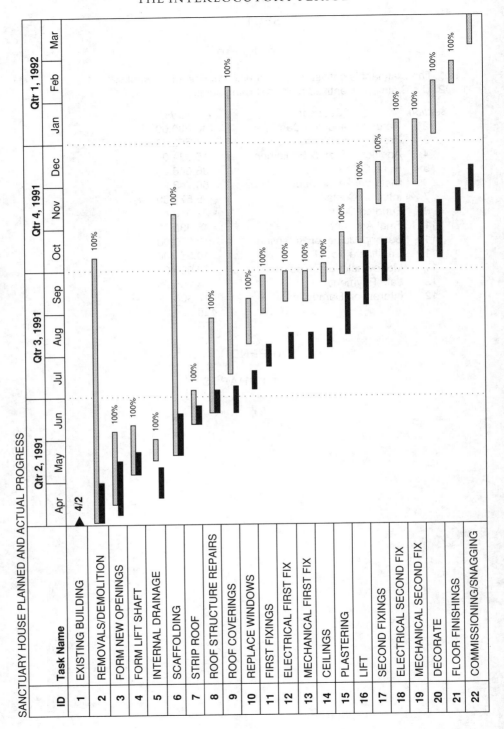

SANCTUARY HOUSE PLANNED AND ACTUAL PROGRESS

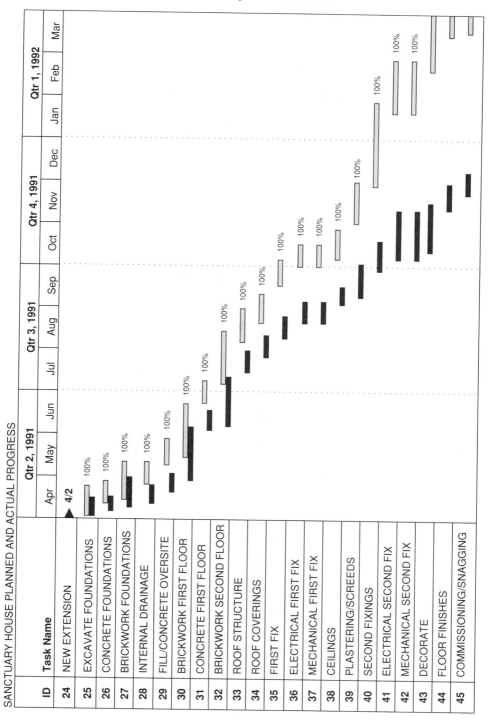

SANCTUARY HOUSE PLANNED AND ACTUAL PROGRESS

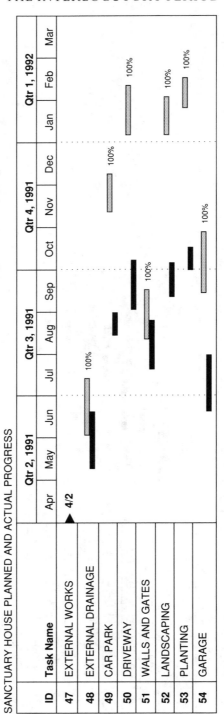

SANCTUARY HOUSE PLANNED AND ACTUAL PROGRESS

7.25
328

Second Proof of D R Sharkey (7.26)

AN ARBITRATION BETWEEN
RELIABLE BUILDERS LIMITED
AND
SANCTUARY HOUSE LIMITED

SECOND REPORT BY D R SHARKEY BSC ARICS

Ref: DRS/ATC/3477
Date: February 1994

Introduction

I am David Robert Sharkey BSc ARICS of Worthingtons, Chartered Building Surveyors of 2 John's Green, Ipswich, Suffolk. This is my second report in this arbitration. I have previously reported on the cause of the basement flooding at Sanctuary House, Woodbridge, Suffolk and this report should be read in conjunction with that earlier report dated May 1993.

7.26
329

Instruction

I have now been instructed by Jayrich Associates, Construction Claims Consultants representing Reliable Builders Limited to provide a report on the following:

1. Remedial works to basement.
2. The quantum of consequential losses resulting from the flooding of the basement.
3. The collapse of the ceiling in the lounge.
4. The remedial works to the fireproof doors.

I inspected the property on 11 January 1993 to view the collapsed ceiling and have considered the specification for refurbishment work to Sanctuary House prepared by The Architectural Partnership of Norwich, dated November 1990.

Remedial Works to Basement

In his Interim Award the Arbitrator held that the builder was in breach of contract in regard to the waterproofing of the basement. Following an agreement between the parties' respresentatives a meeting took place with the Respondent's expert Mr Longdon on 29 November 1993 under the chairmanship of the Arbitrator. At that meeting Mr Longdon proposed that the remedial works should consist of extending the tanking six inches higher than it had been constructed. It was my opinion that this was a satisfactory solution and Mr Longdon and I were able to agree a brief specification for the works which is attached as Appendix A to this report. It was also agreed that the Claimants would carry out the work as specified at the Respondent's convenience.

Consequential Losses Resulting from Basement Flooding

At the meeting with Mr Longdon and the Arbitrator on 29 November 1993 I was asked to consider information provided by Mr Longdon in respect of consequential losses. I confirmed that I agreed that the cost of replacing two washing machines and two dryers was £14,050.00 excluding VAT. I was also able to agree that the cost of replacing the dehumidifying system was £750.00 excluding VAT.

I was then asked to consider a schedule of items of resident's clothing which it was alleged had been damaged by the flooding. The Schedule had been prepared by the matron and values had been put on the items by Mr Longdon. I was unable to agree to Mr Longdon's values.

Although the schedule of items which I understand were temporarily stored in open baskets when the flooding occurred does not seem unreasonable, the lack of any proper description indicating age or condition of the items makes valuation extremely difficult. Mr Longdon's prices seem to be based on the cost of replacement of items with new but it seems to me unlikely that this was so and in my opinion the amount claimed should be discounted to represent second-hand values.

At the same meeting I was also invited to agree a value for the linen, staff clothes and uniforms belonging to Sanctuary House Limited which were also damaged beyond repair by the flooding. In the case Mr Longdon was able to provide copies of invoices for these items which were purchased just six weeks before the flood. He also produced a schedule prepared by Mrs Bliss of the items ruined in the flooding. It was my opinion that the list claimed to have been damaged appeared reasonable and I was able to agree to their value being calculated by reference to the original costs given that all the items were nearly new. The total amount agreed was £1,498.00 excluding VAT.

7.26
330

Collapsed Ceiling

Background

I understand that Reliable Builders Limited were engaged to carry out extensive refurbishment works and the construction of an extension to Sanctuary House, Woodbridge for Mr and Mrs Bliss, trading as Sanctuary House Limited under a JCT Intermediate Form of Contract. The specification includes the following clauses in connection with the work to the ceiling:

3/23d:
Allow the provisional sum of £2,000 for repairs and reinstatement of the ceiling and mouldings to the Gibbs ceiling in the ground-floor lounge. This work is to be carried out by a specialist subcontractor to be approved by the Architect. (The Georgian Restoration Group is suggested and would be approved by the Architect, but the contractor may request approval to an alternative specialist.)

3/21h:
Carefully take up all floorboarding to first floor and set aside for reuse. Refix on completion of fireproofing works, making up with new to match as required.

3/21j:
Carefully clear out floor void and clear and cart away all debris and prepare as necessary for fireproofing work.

3/27b:
Fireproof between timber joists in ceiling space all in accordance with the requirements of the Building Control for premises to be used for nursing home purposes using a proprietary system to be approved by the Architect.

I understand that Reliable Builders Limited appointed the Georgian Restoration Group as their subcontractor and that they carried out the work involved in restoring the ceiling, including the damaged mouldings. I understand that Reliable Builders Limited's own workforce took up the floorboarding and cleaned out the floor void using a vacuum machine. Reliable Builders Limited chose to use a fireproof system manufactured by Firesafe Limited with the Architect's approval. The process involves a proprietary material which is supplied in dry form, mixed on-site with water and applied in the minimum 30 mm layer to a wire mesh fixed between the joists just above the timber laths to the existing ceiling.

The works to Sanctuary House were completed on 31 March 1992. On 24 December 1992 the whole of the ceiling in the lounge collapsed.

I understand that in summary, the allegations contained in the Counterclaim are that Reliable Builders Limited failed to carry out the fireproofing works with proper care, that this resulted in damage to the existing Gibbs ceiling, which eventually collapsed. It is also alleged that Reliable Builders Limited should have taken steps by way of soft wiring to other suitable means to secure the existing ceiling to prevent its collapse.

Restoration of Gibbs ceiling

The initial works of restoration (prior to the collapse) of the Gibbs ceiling was carried out by the specialist subcontractor, the Georgian Restoration Group. They are a reputable company and one which the Architect was not only willing to approve but happy to recommend. There have at no time been any allegations that their work was anything other than satisfactory. It is likely therefore that, given their specialist knowledge, they took great care not to damage the ceiling in any way.

7.26
331

Other work

Reliable Builders Limited took up the first-floor boarding and cleaned out the void. I understand that they did this with care and used vacuum machines to clear the debris. There is no record of any complaints by the Architect about the way in which this was done and no damage was reported to the existing ceiling.

Fireproofing works

These were carried out by Reliable Builders Limited. I have examined the wire mesh which was used and I am satisfied that it meets the requirements of Firesafe Limited. Also, the material appears to be correctly laid to the required thickness. When open mesh is used with a wet material some of the material is bound to be squeezed through the wire mesh and no doubt some would have fallen onto the ceiling. However, I think it unlikely that this would have been heavy enough to cause a ceiling to collapse.

Ceiling collapse

In my view the ceiling collapse was most probably due to the poor state of the key between the plaster and the timber laths, which with thermal movement due to the high temperatures maintained within the building since completion, caused this very old ceiling to finally fail. I understand that the Georgian Restoration Group did draw the Architect's attention to the very poor state of the plaster key and suggested that it should have been wired up, but that the Architect decided that this was not necessary.

Conclusion

In my opinion the collapse of the ceiling was due to normal deterioration, particularly of the key between plaster and laths, coupled with the effects of high temperatures maintained throughout the building. I cannot therefore see that Reliable Builders Limited were in any way responsible.

Reinstatement of Ceiling

When I met with Mr Longdon, before the Arbitrator last November, we were told that the work of reinstatement of this ceiling had recently been completed.

For the purpose of the arbitration we had been asked to obtain three different quotations from a jointly agreed specialist firm for this work, and had previously been given coloured photographs of the original ceiling on which to base these quotations.

I understood that the purpose of this exercise was for us to comment on the reasonableness, or otherwise, of the actual cost incurred in doing the work.

Following consultation with Mr Longdon I obtained three alternative quotations from Charles B Carter Limited of Norwich, who specialise in this sort of work. The first quotation in the sum of £38,360 ex VAT was for a matching replica ceiling using original materials.

The second alternative was also for a matching replica but this time using modern materials and the third alternative was for a plain ceiling.

I have appended details of this quotation and specification as Appendix A to this report.

At the meeting in November we were told that the actual cost of the reinstatement was £38,424 ex VAT which we both agreed compared favourably with Carter's price of £36,360 ex VAT. As a result we had no hesitation in agreeing that the actual costs incurred were reasonable.

We also considered the architect's fee of 15 per cent of the cost of this specialised work, rounded off to £5,500 ex VAT which, again, we were prepared to accept was reasonable.

Fireproofing of Doors

Whilst I have not been asked to deal with the cause of the alleged failure of the fireproofing of the existing doors I have been asked to deal with quantum in respect of this item. As instructed I have met with Mr Longdon and discussed with him the likely cost of removing and cleaning off all the fireproofing to these doors and reinstating to provide half-hour fire protection. The work would also necessarily include the renewal of the intumescent strip to the edges of the door and the work would involve temporarily removing each door and rehanging on completion. I am able to confirm my agreement with Mr Longdon that the reasonable cost of carrying out this work is £110.00 per door excluding VAT. I am also able to confirm that the number of doors involved is 64.

....

D R Sharkey BSc ARICS

20 Feb 1994
....

Date

7.26
332

APPENDIX A

BRIEF SPECIFICATION AND BUDGET COSTS
FOR
GIBBS CEILING REPLACEMENT
LOCATION—EAST ANGLIA

February 1994

Brief Specification

Generally

Ceiling dimensions assumed to be 18' × 30' approx with a ceiling to floor height of 12 to 15 feet. It is assumed that adjacent wall surfaces and the like remain intact and no allowances are made for remedial works to these surfaces. Provide access scaffolding for the works and take down and prepare to receive replacement ceiling.

In all instances we have allowed for decorating the ceiling in one colour only and for temporarily lifting and subsequently replacing the floorboarding above.

No allowances have been made for electrical works.

7.26
333

Alternative No. One (Using traditional materials)

Provide riven oak lathing to soffit and plaster with traditional lime plaster. To perimeter of ceiling provide a dentil cornice and plain cross mouldings to give a 'Doric' effect. No further enrichments have been allowed for and no multicolour final decorations.

Alternative No. Two (Using modern materials)

Replace ceiling with stainless steel lathing with stainless steel fixings to soffit and plaster in metal bonding plaster. Provide fibrous cornice to perimeter and plain cross mouldings to give the 'Doric effect' mentioned in Alternative No. One. Again no further enrichments have been allowed for and no multicolour final decorations.

Alternative No. Three (Plain ceiling using modern materials)

Replace ceiling as in Alternative No. Two above and provide fibrous plaster cornice to perimeter. No further cross members or enrichments have been allowed for giving only a plain ceiling with ornamental cornice.

Budget Estimates

Alternatives One and Two below are based on reproducing the decoration and mouldings, as nearly as possible, to match the original, as recorded on the photographs attached.

Alternative Three is for a plain ceiling as specified.

Alternative One	£38,424 excluding VAT
Alternative Two	£24,850 excluding VAT
Alternative Three	£9,652 excluding VAT

The work will take approximately 1—1½ months from order.

All of the above prices remain open for acceptance for three months from today's date.

Report of Jamal Hussein (7.27)

REPORT IN RESPECT OF THE ARBITRATION BETWEEN
RELIABLE BUILDERS LIMITED AND SANCTUARY HOUSE LIMITED
OVER COLLAPSED CEILING AT SANCTUARY HOUSE, WOODBRIDGE

For Jayrich Associates on behalf of Reliable Builders Limited
Jamal Hussein BSc(Econ) FCA ACArb FBAE

ARBITRATION BETWEEN
RELIABLE BUILDERS LIMITED AND SANCTUARY HOUSE LIMITED
REPORT ON CLAIM FOR LOSS OF PROFITS BY MR JAMAL HUSSEIN

1. Introduction

1.1. I have been requested by the solicitors of Reliable Builders Limited ('RBL'), through their representatives Jayrich Associates, to review a claim for loss of profits brought against RBL by Sanctuary House Limited ('SHL'). My qualifications and experience are detailed in Appendix A.

1.2. SHL owns and operates a nursing home. A ceiling collapsed in the home on 24 December 1992, and the Health Authority ordered the closure of 15 rooms until the ceiling was repaired. Repair work was delayed until 4 October 1993 and the rooms were available for relet by 3 November. SHL are claiming from RBL the costs of restoring the ceiling of £43,924 and loss of profits resulting from the closure of the rooms of £354,335.

1.3. This report sets out my work and conclusions on SHL's claim for loss of profits. The report considers SHL's calculation of the lost profits and also the extent to which the loss of those profits was reasonably avoidable.

2. SHL's claim for loss of profits

2.1. SHL's claim for loss of profits is set out in a report by Mr Mark Page dated 15 February 1994. I believe this calculation to be significantly overstated for the reasons set out in paragraphs 2.2 to 2.15 below. It is accepted that these costs could not be established until all the units were relet. It is common ground that the letting of the 15 units is as set out in Appendix B hereto with the final unit relet on 14 February 1994.

Loss of fee income

2.2. I believe SHL's calculation of lost fee income is overstated for the following reasons:

SHL's calculation of lost fee income		£330,960
'Lost' fee income after repairs complete (see para 2.3)	£(47,460)	
Average weekly fee rate of £400, not £420 (see para 2.6)	(13,500)	
Average occupancy of home of 80%, not 100% (see para 2.7)	(180,000)	
		(240,960)
Actual lost fee income		£90,000

'Lost' fee income after repairs complete

2.3. SHL's calculation includes lost fee income for the period subsequent to the date that the repair of the ceiling was complete and the rooms were available for let (7 November 1993—45 weeks from date the 15 rooms were closed). The period for calculating the lost profits should cover the period over which the ability of the building to generate profits was impaired, and not any subsequent periods.

2.4. Notwithstanding the appropriate period, the average level of occupancy of the home for the period subsequent to the date the repairs were complete is 85 per cent, which I believe to be close to the average level of occupancy which would have been achieved in any event (see paragraph 2.7 below).

2.5. Consequently, I believe SHL's calculation is overstated by £47,460, calculated as follows:

15 rooms × (52.53 – 45) weeks on average × £420 per week = £47,460

Average weekly fee rate of £400, not £420

2.6. SHL's calculation assumes that the rooms would all have been let at a fee of £420 per week. This is the rate at which the rooms were relet. However, in December 1992 the rooms were let at a fee of £400 per week. In the light of low occupancy rates and the competitive pressures from other homes in the area (see paragraphs 2.7 to 2.11 below), I believe a rate of £400 per week to the end of October 1993 is more appropriate. Accordingly I believe that SHL's calculation is overstated by £13,500, calculated as follows:

15 rooms × 45 weeks × (£420 – £400) per week = £13,500

Average occupancy of home 80%, not 100%

2.7. SHL's calculation assumes that all 15 of the closed rooms would have been let throughout the period—and therefore that the home as a whole would have enjoyed a 100% occupancy rate. I believe that this assumption is incorrect for the reasons set out in paragraphs 2.8 to 2.10 below:

2.8. Details of occupancy during the relevant period were sought from other nursing homes in the area. The results of these enquiries are set out in Appendix C. They show that the level of occupancy was 79% on average and ranged from 72% to 87%.

2.9. The remaining 37 (52 less 15) rooms were not all occupied throughout the period that the 15 rooms were closed. This suggests that the 15 rooms would not all have been occupied, even if they had been available.

2.10. In the six months prior to the closure of the rooms, the average occupancy of the rooms in the home was 81%. Subsequent to the repair of the ceiling, the average occupancy of rooms has been 83%.

2.11. I believe that an average occupancy of 80% or 42 rooms (52 rooms × 80%) would be more appropriate. On the assumption that the 15 closed rooms would have been used last, this implies that, on average, only 5 of the 15 rooms would have been fully occupied. Therefore, I believe SHL's calculation is overstated by £180,000, calculated as follows:

(15 – 5) rooms × 45 weeks × £400 per week = £180,000

Newspaper and magazine advertising

2.12. SHL's calculation includes the cost of newspaper and magazine advertising from October to December 1993 of £2,740. No other advertising occurred during this period and two-thirds of the cost relates to periods after the building was repaired. The advertising makes no specific reference to the reopened rooms and would have benefited the business generally. I believe that this expenditure would have been incurred even if the rooms had not been closed and, in any event, the costs are offset by the income benefits relating to the other 37 rooms. Accordingly, I believe that SHL's calculation is overstated by £2,740.

Incremental heat and light savings

2.13. Heat and light costs are electricity charges. SHL have assumed that one-third of these costs relating to common areas, principally the kitchens and laundry room, do not depend on the number of occupants. However, it is likely that the electricity costs of the kitchens and laundry room will have a significant element that does depend on the number of occupants. I estimate this element to be 50% and therefore I believe that the cost savings would be (based on 80% occupancy):

$$\frac{£34,400 \times 5/6}{(52 - 15) \text{ rooms}} \times 5 \text{ rooms (on average)} = £3,874$$

Therefore, I believe that SHL have overstated the cost savings by £5,406 (£9,280 less £3,874). The cost savings are *over*stated because SHL have assumed 100% occupancy for the home.

7.27
336

Interest charged on additional bank overdraft

2.14. SHL claim that additional bank borrowing were required as a result of the loss of trading profits incurred as a result of the collapse of the ceiling. SHL calculates the interest on these additional borrowings to be £29,400.

2.15. As summarised in Section 4 below, I believe SHL's calculation of the loss of trading profits incurred to be significantly overstated. Accordingly, I believe SHL's calculation of the additional bank borrowings which were required also to be significantly overstated. I believe the interest on any additional borrowings to be no more than £2,350 and that SHL's calculation is overstated by £27,050. My detailed calculations are set out in Appendix D.

3. Avoidable losses

3.1. I believe that certain of SHL's costs could reasonably have been avoided by SHL and therefore should be included as incremental costs savings omitted from SHL's claim.

Temporary accommodation of residents

3.2. SHL incurred costs of £6,480 on temporary accommodation to rehouse certain residents for a short period following the closure of the rooms. However, other accommodation of a suitable standard was available which was both cheaper and closer to Sanctuary House than the accommodation actually used by SHL. Appendix E sets out details of the availability of rooms and the rates of those rooms in Whickham House, a nursing home in Wickham Market.

3.3. I believe it is reasonable to expect that SHL should have made enquiries of local nursing homes to identify the availability and rates of their rooms. I further believe SHL should have identified that Wickham House had suitable rooms available which were cheaper than those actually used to rehouse the residents. Accordingly, I believe SHL should have incurred temporary accommodation costs of only £4,220 and therefore that SHL's calculation is overstated by £2,260.

Staff costs

3.4. Prior to the closure of the rooms, SHL employed 52 staff, 20 of which were carers.

Following the closure, two cleaning staff only were made redundant, although the number of available rooms fell 29% from 52 to 37 and an entire floor of the home was closed. All other staff were kept on. It was clear by early January 1993 that the rooms would remain closed until the autumn of that year. I believe it is reasonable to expect that SHL should have let go at least five of its carers during this period, in order to save the associated staff costs.

3.5. SHL paid overtime to staff on Christmas Day and Boxing Day 1992 at 2.5 times the basic rate, amounting to £1,495. Company policy at the time was to pay wages on public holidays at 1.5 times the basic rate. I believe it is reasonable to expect that SHL should have paid overtime at this rate on the two days in question. Accordingly, I believe SHL should have incurred additional staff costs on these days of only £875.

3.6. Therefore, I believe SHL reasonably could have saved in total at least £54,720 in staff related costs, calculated as follows:

5 carers at £12,000 pa × 10m/12m	£50,000
Employers' NIC at 10.2%	5,100
	55,100
Less costs of rehiring staff in October 1993	(1,000)
Avoidable staff costs of carers (see para 3.4)	£54,100
Avoidable Christmas overtime (see para 3.5)	620
Total costs that reasonably could have been avoided	£54,720

4. Conclusions

4.1. SHL has calculated its loss of profits to be £354,335. I believe this calculation to be significantly overstated for the following reasons:

Loss of profits claimed by SHL	£354,335
Overstatement of loss of fee income (see para 2.2)	(240,960)
Overstatement of incremental promotional costs (see para 2.12)	(2,740)
Overstatement of incremental electricity cost savings (see para 2.13)	5,406
Overstatement of interest expense on incremental borrowings (see para 2.15)	(27,050)
Loss of profits as adjusted	88,991
Avoidable losses:	
Cheaper temporary accommodation not used (see para 3.3)	(2,260)
Staff cost savings not realised (see para 3.6)	(54,720)
Total damages as recalculated	£32,011

4.2. I believe the loss of profits by SHL to be no more than £88,991. I also believe that the loss of profits of at least £56,980 could have been reasonably avoided by SHL. Accordingly, I believe that the total damages of SHL in respect of loss of profits should amount to no more than £32,011.

Signed _____   15 Feb 1994
    Jamal Hussein

APPENDIX A
QUALIFICATIONS AND EXPERIENCE OF MR JAMAL HUSSEIN,
BSc (Econ), FCA, ACArb, FBAE

I am a former partner of Armstrong Hughes & Co., where I headed the healthcare industry group. I now work as a consultant in private practice. I graduated in Economics with Accounting and Finance from the London School of Economics in 1970 and qualified as a chartered accountant in 1973.

Over the last 20 years, my responsibilities have included both audit and financial consulting for a range of clients, particularly those in the healthcare industry. In the last 10 years I have specialised in claims consulting. I am a Member of the Institute of Arbitrators and the Centre for Alternative Dispute Resolution, and a Fellow of the British Academy of Experts. I have been responsible for expert reports produced and evidence adduced on over 70 cases of litigation and arbitration.

APPENDIX B
SCHEDULE OF DATES FROM WHICH CLOSED ROOMS WERE SUBSEQUENTLY RELET

7.27
338

[Not included here due to its length]

APPENDIX C
SUMMARY OF ENQUIRIES OF NURSING HOMES IN SUFFOLK REGARDING OCCUPANCY RATES

[Not included here due to its length]

APPENDIX D
ADDITIONAL BORROWING REQUIREMENTS AND ASSOCIATED INTEREST COSTS

[Not included here due to its length]

APPENDIX E
AVAILABILITY AND RATES OF ROOMS IN WICKHAM HOUSE, WICKHAM MARKET
CHRISTMAS 1992

[Not included here due to its length]

Report of Richard Rutley (7.28)

RICHARD RUTLEY, PhD, MA, FRICS

SANCTUARY HOUSE ARBITRATION

Opinion concerning the effect on value of the loss of the Gibbs ceiling.

Instruction

I, Richard Rutley of 1 Grosvenor Square London W1, am instructed by Messrs (Kalmsyde & Joyoff, Solicitors) to advise on the alteration in the value which may be ascribed to Sanctuary House, Woodbridge, Suffolk as a result of the loss of the Gibbs ceiling.

Introduction

I am a Chartered Surveyor who qualified by virtue of obtaining a degree in Land Economy from Cambridge University and subsequently completing articles with Alexander Smallpiece & Co (now after six mergers part of ONO (Japan) Realtors the leading international firm with shares quoted on the Tokyo, New York and London Stock Exchanges). I was subsequently employed by Rutley Developers.

I hold the degree of Doctor of Philosophy from Upstate University, Hudson Falls, NY, USA.

I am currently professor of the Built Environment at the University of the Level Ground and have a small specialist practice in depreciation of special architectural features in Listed Buildings.

The Dispute

The ceiling of the sitting room was lost in a fall on Christmas Eve 1992. It was a Gibbs ceiling of considerable interest and importance which is now totally fragmented and incapable of restoration. The photographs, which are presented separately, show the devastation that occurred. There are others who are far better qualified to discuss the possibilities of restoration. I am concerned with what must be described as the financial side of the dispute.

In all cases it is preferable that all reasonable steps are taken to ensure there will be no financial impact on the value of the property by virtue of the requirement to reinstate costly and often truly irreplaceable architectural features within a building.

It is a very rare occurrence that a collapse of this nature takes place without some form of outside interference but nevertheless the owners of such buildings should be mindful of such obscure possibilities. Too often, in my experience, have the truly catastrophic possibilities been ignored whilst the more mundane occurrences which take place, with some regularity, are insured against.

Insurance of such rare ceilings is so infrequent that the omission in this case is not unusual, nor in my opinion culpable. I would, however, advise that it was insured in future.

I understand that the replacement cost of a ceiling such as was lost, including fees, was around £50,000.

Following enquiries from the No-Nonsense Insurance Co I am informed that, before they would be prepared to insure such a ceiling against accidental damage, including collapse, they would require it to be supported by, the commonly recognised 'tray system', sketches of which are attached to this proof as Appendix A. I understand that the cost of installing such support is likely to be in the region of £12,000. I established this figure from the median of three that I received from firms specialising in such work, with whom I am familiar, as a result of my work in connection with Listed Buildings.

The No-Nonsense Insurance Company have quoted a premium rate of 0.35% of the replacement cost of the ceiling once the support system is in place. This equates to £210 p.a. See Appendix B.

Conclusion

Any would-be purchaser of an old property would always attempt to discount the asking price by the cost of any remedial work that requires to be carried out on that property.

Thus, in my opinion, a would-be purchaser of the property with a unique feature, such as this Gibbs ceiling, would discount the purchase price by approximately £15,500 to allow for having to install the 'tray system' and then continue to carry the additional insurance premium on this feature.

The figure is arrived at by taking the cost of the 'tray system' and adding to it the Present Value of the insurance premium of £210 in perpetuity. I calculate that the sum required to be invested to produce this annual premium would be £3,489, or say £3,500.

7.28
340

THUS, I CONCLUDE THAT THIS PROPERTY IS ACTUALLY WORTH APPROXIMATELY **£15,500** LESS WITH THE GIBBS CEILING THAN IT WOULD IF IT HAD A COMMONPLACE CEILING INSTEAD.

....
Professor R Rutley PhD MA FRICS   Date

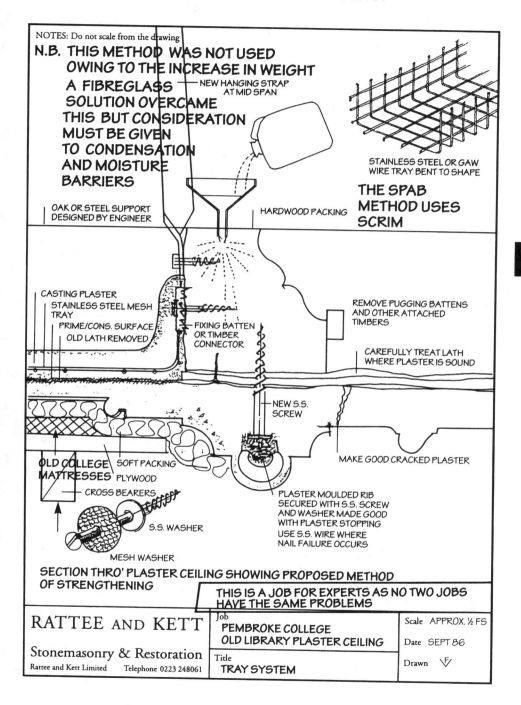

NOTES: Do not scale from the drawing

N.B. THIS METHOD WAS NOT USED
OWING TO THE INCREASE IN WEIGHT
A FIBREGLASS — NEW HANGING STRAP AT MID SPAN
SOLUTION OVERCAME
THIS BUT CONSIDERATION
MUST BE GIVEN
TO CONDENSATION
AND MOISTURE
BARRIERS

STAINLESS STEEL OR GAW
WIRE TRAY BENT TO SHAPE

THE SPAB
METHOD USES
SCRIM

OAK OR STEEL SUPPORT
DESIGNED BY ENGINEER

HARDWOOD PACKING

7.28
341

CASTING PLASTER
STAINLESS STEEL MESH
TRAY
PRIME/CONS. SURFACE
OLD LATH REMOVED

FIXING BATTEN
OR TIMBER
CONNECTOR

REMOVE PUGGING BATTENS
AND OTHER ATTACHED
TIMBERS

CAREFULLY TREAT LATH
WHERE PLASTER IS SOUND

NEW S.S.
SCREW

MAKE GOOD CRACKED PLASTER

OLD COLLEGE SOFT PACKING
MATTRESSES PLYWOOD
CROSS BEARERS

S.S. WASHER

MESH WASHER

PLASTER MOULDED RIB
SECURED WITH S.S. SCREW
AND WASHER MADE GOOD
WITH PLASTER STOPPING
USE S.S. WIRE WHERE
NAIL FAILURE OCCURS

SECTION THRO' PLASTER CEILING SHOWING PROPOSED METHOD
OF STRENGTHENING

THIS IS A JOB FOR EXPERTS AS NO TWO JOBS
HAVE THE SAME PROBLEMS

RATTEE AND KETT	Job PEMBROKE COLLEGE OLD LIBRARY PLASTER CEILING	Scale APPROX. ½ FS
Stonemasonry & Restoration		Date SEPT 86
Rattee and Kett Limited Telephone 0223 248061	Title TRAY SYSTEM	Drawn ⅌

THE 'TRAY SYSTEM'—APPENDIX A/2

TEMPORARY SUPPORT METHOD USING
WIRE SLINGS

        WIRE SLING PASSED THROUGH
        DRILLED PLASTER AND
        SECURED TO JOIST
        PLY PANELS
        FELT ROLLS

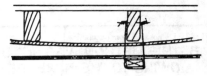

TEMPORARY SUPPORT METHOD USING
FLOOR PROPS

        FELT ROLLS
        PLY PANELS
        BEARERS AND PROPS

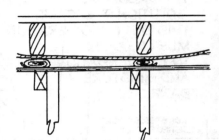

REPAIRS TO PLASTER CEILINGS

**7.28
342**

SUPPORT FOR SMALL AREAS
COMPLETED
BRASS SCREW
PLASTER OF PARIS BRIDGE
BETWEEN JOISTS
ORIGINAL PLASTER

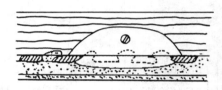

SUPPORT FOR LARGER AREAS
COMPLETED
BATTENS SCREWED TO JOISTS
6mm COPPER MESH TRAY
NEW PLASTER – SECOND BED
NEW PLASTER – FIRST BED
DECAYED LATHS REMOVED
ORIGINAL PLASTER

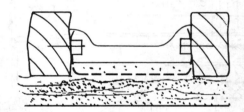

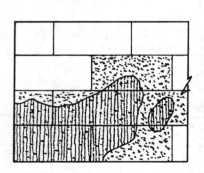

represents extent of
loss of adhesion with
backing

represents extent of
repair

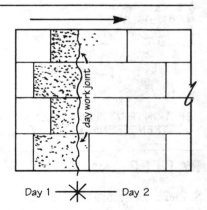

Day 1   —✳—   Day 2

represents extent of
Day 1 work to be cut off
and rendered in with
Day 2 work

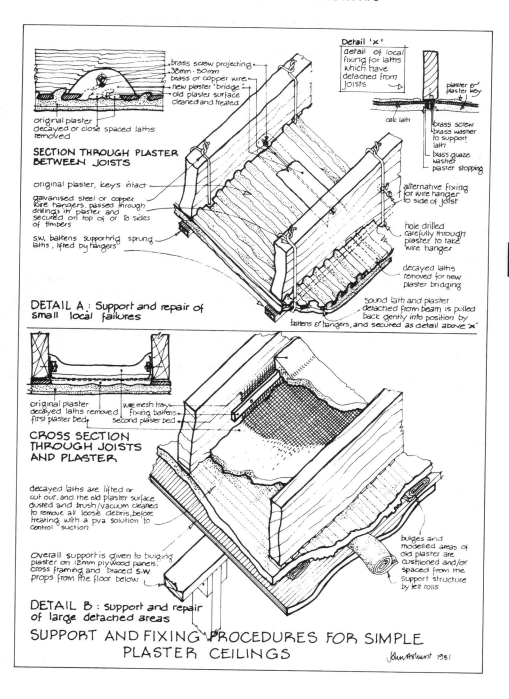

Detail 'x'
detail of local fixing for laths which have detached from joists

brass screw projecting 38mm - 50mm
brass or copper wire
new plaster 'bridge'
old plaster surface cleaned and treated

original plaster decayed or close spaced laths removed

plaster or plaster key

oak lath

brass screw
brass washer to support lath

brass guaze washer
plaster stopping

alternative fixing for wire hanger to side of joist

SECTION THROUGH PLASTER BETWEEN JOISTS

original plaster, keys intact

galvanised steel or copper wire hangers, passed through drillings in plaster and secured on top of or to sides of timbers

s.w. battens supporting sprung laths, lifted by hangers

hole drilled carefully through plaster to take wire hanger

decayed laths removed for new plaster bridging

DETAIL A : Support and repair of small local failures

sound lath and plaster detached from beam is pulled back gently into position by battens & hangers, and secured as detail above 'x'

7.28
343

original plaster
decayed laths removed
first plaster bed
wire mesh tray
fixing battens
second plaster bed

CROSS SECTION THROUGH JOISTS AND PLASTER

decayed laths are lifted or cut out, and the old plaster surface dusted and brush/vacuum cleaned to remove all loose debris, before treating with a pva solution to control suction

bulges and modelled areas of old plaster are cushioned and/or spaced from the support structure by felt rolls

Overall support is given to bulging plaster on 12mm plywood panels, cross framing and braced s.w. props from the floor below

DETAIL B : support and repair of large detached areas

SUPPORT AND FIXING PROCEDURES FOR SIMPLE PLASTER CEILINGS

John Ashurst 1981

APPENDIX B

THE NO-NONSENSE INSURANCE COMPANY

No-No House, Ipswich, Suffolk

DE/728   28 March 1994

Richard Rutley Esq
Rutley Associates
1 Grosvenor Square
London W1

Dear Mr Rutley

re: Sanctuary House,Woodbridge

7.28
344

I refer to our recent telephone conversation when we discussed the decorative ceiling in the sitting room, in this listed, Queen Anne period, building.

In a house such as this, where the ceiling is over 270 years old, we would require your client to use a reputable conservation firm to install the 'tray system', of supporting this existing ceiling, in accordance with the attached drawings and specifications, before we would consider covering this ceiling at replacement value.

Once the 'tray system' support, has been effected, we would be prepared to cover this ceiling at its replacement cost, plus fees, say £60,000, at a premium of 0.35% per annum, rising by inflation, but only against insurable perils. If the ceiling were to collapse through lack of maintenance or causes other than through an insurable peril, such risk is uninsurable.

I trust this is helpful.

Yours sincerely

J Bucks
General Manager

Proof of Evidence of Ifram Carmel (7.29)

IN THE MATTER OF THE ARBITRATION ACTS 1950 TO 1979

AND

IN THE MATTER OF AN ARBITRATION UNDER THE JCT ARBITRATION RULES (18 JULY 1988)

BETWEEN

RELIABLE BUILDERS LIMITED   Claimant

AND

SANCTUARY HOUSE LIMITED   Respondent

7.29
345

PROOF OF EVIDENCE OF IFRAM CARMEL

I, IFRAM CARMEL, of 128 Victoria Square, Hackney, London

WILL SAY as follows:

Instruction

I have been instructed by the Reliable Builders Limited, through their representatives, Messrs Jayrich Associates, to give my Expert Opinion on the present state of the fireproofing on the corridor doors at Sanctuary House, Woodbridge Suffolk.

Qualifications

Higher National Diploma in Chemistry and Surface Coating Technology through Day Release at the Thames and South Bank Polytechnic (1978).

Experience

Since leaving school, in 1976, my whole working career has been spent in the Coating Industry.

I joined Global Product Services Plc in 1976, as a laboratory assistant, initially in Quality control and later as an Assistant Chemist. In this latter role I carried out supervised development work and customer sample preparations on a range of Coatings, Adhesives and Sealants.

In 1982 I joined Boreham and Sons Ltd. as a paint chemist working on the development of Intumescent and Flame Retardant Coatings.

In 1984 I was recruited to work for Cadbury Industrial Coatings Ltd working on the development of new Intumescent Coatings and technical trouble shooting.

In 1990 I joined my present firm, Calib Protective Coatings Ltd as Assistant Technical Support Manager and was promoted to Manager of the Technical Division/Fireproofing in the summer of 1992.

My present job involves me in giving technical advice, both by telephone and on-site, including trouble shooting and providing specifications for Intumescent and Flame Retardant Coating Systems. I also serve as my company's representative on Trade Association bodies.

Site Visit

I carried out a site inspection on 18 November 1993 to investigate the splitting and wrinkling of the glass fibre matting. Inspection of the doors showed that on virtually all panels, splitting had occurred along at least one edge of the panel. Cracking of the paint film and wrinkling of the glass fibre had also occurred to varying degrees and was more severe on some doors than others. It was also noted that on some doors, wrinkling of the paint film had occurred on areas other than the panels, where no glass fibre had been applied, although, on most doors the paint film was still intact.

The property is a nursing home where a very high ambient temperature is maintained for the frail elderly residents. Undoubtedly this temperature was much lower when the doors where actually treated.

7.29
346

Original Schedule of Works

I have examined the original documentation and item 48 of the specification reads as follows:

'All corridor doors are to be treated to achieve half-hour fire resistance. Groove edges to receive intumescent strip and fit overhead closers.'

The Works

During January 1991 Shawpruff applied for CPC half-hour fire check door system to existing panelled doors at the above site. Subsequently, the glass fibre matting has split and wrinkled giving an unsightly appearance.

Specification of System Used

'One coat CPC Intumescent Emulsion to panels of doors only with CPC Fine Weave glass fibre embedded into Emulsion. One further coat of CPC Intumescent Emulsion applied to the whole of risk side and edges. Once dry, one further coat CPC Intumescent Emulsion applied to whole of risk side and edges followed by two coats of CPC Flame Retardant paint.'

Conclusion

In my opinion the failure of this coating is due to the shrinkage of the doors. These doors are said to be over 200 years old and due to what, I understand, was the derelict state of the building before the work of restoration began, were likely to have been damp at the time of application.

The subsequent heating of the building has drawn the moisture from the doors leading to shrinkage in the timber and subsequent splitting and delamination of the glass fibre.

15 February 1994

....
Ifram Carmel   Date
Manager of Technical Division/Fireproofing
Calib Protective Coatings Ltd

Second Proof of Evidence of William Hubert Bliss (7.31)

IN THE MATTER OF THE ARBITRATION ACTS 1950 TO 1979

AND

IN THE MATTER OF AN ARBITRATION UNDER THE JCT ARBITRATION RULES (18 JULY 1988)

BETWEEN

RELIABLE BUILDERS LIMITED   Claimant

AND

SANCTUARY HOUSE LIMITED   Respondent

7.31
347

SECOND PROOF OF EVIDENCE OF WILLIAM HUBERT BLISS

I, WILLIAM HUBERT BLISS of Sanctuary House, Woodbridge, Suffolk

WILL SAY as follows:

1. This is my Second Witness Statement in the above Arbitration, the First having been made in respect of the Preliminary Issues.

2. I left the National Health Service, towards the end of 1989, where I had worked for over 17 years, latterly as an Administrator.

3. My wife Constance, who was a Nursing Sister, and I, decided to invest my redundancy in an upmarket Nursing Home for the frail elderly, combining my wife's nursing skills with my administrative ones.

4. I read for a Master's Degree in Business Studies at Manchester and graduated in 1971. I was therefore able to put together a Feasibility Study on the type of home that we sought to run. I shopped this study around the City and eventually, the merchant banking arm of the London & Outer Hebrides Bank expressed an interest in principle.

5. The initial study was based on a hypothetical model but once the bank had approved this in principle we intensified our search for the right property.

6. We were very fortunate in locating a lovely Queen Anne house, in Woodbridge, almost immediately after it had come on to the market. There was a lot of interest in this property and, although we paid somewhat over the odds for it, I persuaded the bank that we would quickly recover the difference by being able to ask a slightly higher weekly rate.

7. The Old Manor House, as it was called before we eventually renamed it Sanctuary House, was in an appalling condition. I am not sure how long it had been empty but the roof was breached, in one or two places, and letting in the rain. In any case, we wanted an unimproved property because of the amount of special work we would have to do to meet all the regulations, although perhaps not as derelict as The Old Manor House. However, I rejigged my Feasibility Study, based on the actual work that would be required to the property, and the bank approved the loan necessary to pay the fees and put the building work in hand.

8. We were very impressed with the Architects we were put in touch with, TAP of Norwich. They seemed to know just what was required in a Home such as this. Apparently they had

been involved in the design of several sheltered schemes for various local Housing Associations.

9. I dealt at length, in my earlier proof, with the situation when the tenders came back in early 1991 and this proof should therefore be read in conjunction with my first one. It is, however, worth reiterating the business of the remeasurement as this touches on the final account figure. Although I did not entirely understand this point at the time, the Architect said that we would have to agree to a partial remeasurement—involving the earthworks—but he was confident that this would not involve a significant extra. Indeed, he told me that, as a quid pro quo, he had done a good deal on the drainage and might actually effect a small saving.

10. Whilst impressing upon the Architect, Mr D'Iffy, the critical need to work within budget, I reluctantly agreed to his proposal—apparently I had little choice—as I stated in my earlier proof, the builders had already started work.

11. I had stressed to TAP that we wanted to finish at least two weeks before Christmas, preferably three, in order to get as many residents installed prior to the holiday period. Any hiccough with the builder could put this timing in jeopardy.

12. I revised my budget figures once more, building in the known contract price and the contracted completion dates, still working on the assumption of a pre-Christmas finish.

7.31
348

13. I had little to do with the actual building works except to complain from time to time about the apparent lack of progress.

14. Through my previous contacts I was able to organise a number of my own tradesmen to carry out our specialist work. Through the Architect, Mr D'Iffy, I agreed the dates when these specialist tradesmen would come on-site to do their own work. It was made clear to me that if I did not wish to incur a penalty I had to have them on-site when the particular part of the work was ready to receive them. This caused a certain amount of confusion towards the end of the job as the builders should, by all accounts, have virtually finished but were, in effect, up to three months behind. I remember the biggest problem occurred over my kitchen equipment. The suppliers and installers made it clear that we either took it when planned or waited six months, which obviously we could not afford to do.

15. It became clear, in the early autumn, that we would not finish when we had planned. This meant informing all the people who had answered the advertising campaign. Some of them were quite abusive and certainly we lost over 50 per cent of those who had expressed firm interest.

16. In the event, the building was not finished until the beginning of April 1992—over three months late! In effect, we had lost three months' income. Although we had not engaged all of our staff over this period, we did have to pay the Matron and three key nursing staff whom we did not wish to lose.

17. As a result, I had a very difficult meeting with the bank, in the early part of 1992, who picked over my figures with a fine-tooth comb. In the end, they decided that we could probably trade ourselves out of trouble. However, Mr Paul Goldstone, the bank's surveyor/representative, strongly urged me not to pay the last Certificate, in April 1992, as there were too many defects. On mature consideration I agreed to withhold the money until we got what we had paid for.

18. I joined the Architect, the builders and Mr Goldstone on an inspection visit on the 8th April 1992, when the list of defects was drawn up.

19. Mr Reeves, of RBL, offered to carry out the bulk of these repairs and said that anything outstanding would be dealt with by RBL at the end of the six-months period when the builder came back to pick up final defects.

20. Although I received calls from RBL after this to the effect that they had carried out the work as promised, neither I nor my wife were satisfied and, as a result, refused to release the money. In speaking to RBL we always were quite specific as to our complaints, although I

must admit that, post-contract, we never actually formally wrote to them listing these complaints.

21. In the meantime, and only two weeks or so after we took over the building, we suffered the first of two disasters—our basement flooded ruining the washing and drying machines as well as large quantities of linen and uniforms belonging to SHL as well as a great deal of the residents' private clothing. Bearing in mind that none of them had been in residence for more than two weeks, and some only for a few days, this was an appallingly bad piece of PR for the Home and caused a great deal of bad feeling, not only amongst the residents, but also amongst their relatives who had placed them there. There was even talk from one or two to the effect that if this sort of thing was going to happen they would remove their relatives.

22. The equipment, that had been ruined, had come from abroad and we were told that the delivery time for new equipment was three months. In the meantime, we incurred some very substantial laundry bills.

23. Why the basement flooded I know not, except that we had experienced one of the wettest years on record and it seems that the water table was high. However, I recall having instructed the Architect to waterproof this cellar as part of the building work as we had planned to use it as a laundry.

24. As we were in the Defects Liability Period, the responsibility rested on the builder. They refused to pay out on the residents' private clothing as they said that each resident should carry their own insurance. This, of course, caused further difficulties with the residents and their relations and at least five cases, where the relation responsible had not actually effected insurance at that time—their excuse generally being that they really had not had time in the 10–14 days or so since their relation had moved in—we actually paid to replace the linen and clothing ourselves rather than disturb an already shaky relationship with our new residents.

25. Having overcome these problems, and only three months or so after returning the laundry to operation, the second disaster struck—the magnificent Gibbs ceiling in the sitting room collapsed, on, of all days, Christmas Eve 1992.

26. I could not believe the amount of dust that the plaster from this collapsed ceiling had generated. Apart from the fragments around the edge, every scrap of the ceiling had shattered. Dust had penetrated everywhere. We were forced, that very evening, to move three residents, located above the sitting room, and the following day the Health Authority closed the entire floor, on two grounds. They claimed firstly, that it was a health hazard; presumably the dust, potential draughts and questionable integrity of the fireproofing in the floor void and secondly, was our inability to provide the amount of amenity accommodation, required by the regulations, for the number of residents that we had.

27. We were told to move our residents as soon as possible—14 of the 15 units were let at the time and the fifteenth had already been earmarked for a resident due to take up occupation on 3 January 1993.

28. Fortunately, a number of the 14 residents in occupation were away with relatives for Christmas but, nevertheless, we still had to find 15 spaces in a home close by. The nearest one, that seemed capable of accommodating all of our residents—in a newly completed wing—was located in Aldeburgh. The problem was that this home was not quite up to our standards and the residents, and their relatives, formed themselves into an Action Group and insisted on compensation—by way of a reduced weekly charge—to cover the inconvenience caused by the additional travel, distress to the elderly relatives, etc. I had no option but to agree, otherwise we would have lost all of our 15 residents permanently. As it was, only around half of them returned to Sanctuary House, almost 45 weeks after the disaster, when the ceiling had been replaced and the Health Authority had lifted its ban.

29. The reason the restoration had taken so long was that the people responsible for Listed Buildings had got involved. They sent along an expert on the Georgian period, around mid-January, and then followed months of frustration whilst we tried to persuade these people

7.31
349

to allow us to replace the ceiling with a reproduction one. The argument raged back and forth as to whether we should use original type materials, i.e. oak lathes etc., or modern materials, such as standard metal lathing, supporting a faithful copy of the original. We were fortunate in having detailed colour photographs from an early set of Sale Particulars. The cost of replacing the ceiling with original materials was estimated at something in the region of £50,000 whereas, on the other hand, to replace a fairly plain ceiling using modern materials could be achieved for something less than 20 per cent of that figure.

30. In the end, they opted for a copy of the original ceiling using original type materials and work started at the beginning of October 1993 and was completed in early November.

31. Our losses, of course, had been horrendous over this period, something in the region of £6,000 per week. Again, I have to say how helpful were our bank but I was fearful that at any time they could decide to withdraw their support and recall their loan, in which case, of course, we would have lost everything.

32. During the period when these 15 rooms were unoccupied, we did our best to stem the loss by cutting costs wherever it was feasible.

33. At a very early stage my wife and I sat down and considered every single member of staff with a view to making some of them redundant but we had over 20 carers on our books at that time and, after very careful and mature consideration, decided that we could not afford to let any of them go. They had been hard to recruit in the first instance, it would be expensive in terms of Agency fees to recruit new staff and, in any case, some of the elderly residents had already become attached to individual carers.

34. In the event, we were only able to let go two of our cleaning staff.

35. As soon as the work on the restoration of the ceiling began we commenced an advertising campaign in newspapers and magazines with a view to filling the space as soon as it was available. We were very successful in this campaign and had several takers for the accommodation immediately after it became available again in early November. We filled up the remaining places between then and the time when the last unit was occupied on 21 February 1994.

36. I have provided all of the financial information covering our losses over the period of disclosure to an independent expert, Mr Mark Page. I have seen and read his report dated 15 February 1994 and confirm that the figures that he has used in compiling this report, provided by me, are correct.

37. On a general point, I have to say that at all times Sanctuary House was willing, and able, to pay RBL for the work that it had contracted to do. The difficulty, as I have explained, was that RBL's work was not satisfactory.

38. When we embarked on this project, using RBL, we owned a historic building containing a unique feature—the Gibbs ceiling. Today that building has lost that feature which can never be replaced. It seems only right that we should be compensated for any diminution in value as a result.

39. When we started out on this exercise, it was on a sound financial basis and one which I had proved, to the satisfaction of the bank, would work. Today, through absolutely no fault of our own, we find ourselves on the verge of financial ruin, it seems, through the incompetence of RBL.

Again, it has to be right that we at least recover money that we have lost. No amount of money could adequately compensate my wife and I for the distress and inconvenience that we have suffered over this long nightmarish period.

....

William Bliss   Dated

7.31
350

Witness Statement of Constance Bliss (7.32)

IN THE MATTER OF THE ARBITRATION ACTS 1950 TO 1979

AND

IN THE MATTER OF AN ARBITRATION UNDER THE JCT ARBITRATION RULES (18 JULY 1988)

BETWEEN

RELIABLE BUILDERS LIMITED   Claimant

AND

SANCTUARY HOUSE LIMITED   Respondent

```
7.32
351
```

WITNESS STATEMENT OF CONSTANCE BLISS

I, CONSTANCE CHARMERS-PARRIS BLISS

WILL SAY as follows:

1. When my husband, William Bliss, was made redundant in 1989, we jointly decided to invest his redundancy money in a nursing home. My nursing background—I was promoted to Ward Sister in 1986—coupled with my husband's experience as an Administrator in the National Health Service, seemed, to us, to be a perfect combination.

2. We settled on East Anglia, as a location for the home, as we both had roots there and besides it is a popular area for retirement homes.

3. We were very fortunate when an old friend of ours, an estate agent, Tony Mullocks, found a suitable property, The Old Manor House, in Woodbridge, Suffolk. It was ideal for our needs—a beautiful Queen Anne house in three acres of its own grounds.

4. The house had been unoccupied for some time and was in urgent need of repair. However, this suited us as we knew that we would have to carry out extensive alterations in order to satisfy the requirements of the Local Authority, the Health Authority, the Fire service, etc.

5. The overall cost of the purchase, refurbishment and fitting out was far beyond our means, our redundancy money barely covering 25 per cent of the total required. Mr Bliss prepared an impressive Feasibility Study and as a result we were offered a loan for the balance of money that we needed. The rate of interest that we were asked to pay seemed very high but my husband was confident that we could cope. In any case I left such matters to him and concentrated on the nursing side of the venture.

6. We were lucky enough to find a sympathetic firm of local architects, TAP, who, it seemed, were experienced in designing accommodation for the elderly.

7. When the tenders came in some months later, we were a little concerned that the cost was already above our Budget, but my husband sorted this out with the architects and the builders. I do remember him saying that we were running a very tight ship but should be alright, given a fair wind.

8. I had little to do with the building works but did visit from time to time to see how the work

of conversion was progressing. It was as well that I did for the builder, RBL, seemed to have little knowledge of the specialised nature of the end-user. There were things that would have been obvious to anyone who had anything to do with an elderly relative, let alone a builder who was experienced in building accommodation for the elderly. For example, the height and type of light switches for one and the position of the emergency Nurse Call system for another.

9. As a result I did have to tell the builder's foreman, Mr Watts, from time to time, to make some changes, however at no time did I authorise any extra work for which we were to pay.

10. The first problem arose out of the lateness of the building works. We had planned for a Christmas opening as we were aware that a number of people with elderly, infirm relatives, welcomed a break over holiday periods and we felt that our timing would be an attractive incentive for interested parties to secure a place and thus we anticipated a rapid take-up.

11. However, the building works were delayed and did not finish until the end of March/ beginning of April 1992. By then we had a large number of potential residents on our books and we let all of the units very quickly. Nevertheless we had lost three months income and the money that the contract allowed us to recover from the builder did not cover this loss.

12. Only weeks after we took over, the basement flooded and ruined our expensive washing and drying machines, as well as a substantial amount of clothing, uniforms and linen belonging to us together with a great deal of residents clothing.

7.32
352

13. It took some time to replace this equipment, as it had to come from overseas. In the meantime we ran up some very high laundry bills.

14. To date we have never received compensation for any of the costs involved from this flood which were made worse by our lack of insurance cover. We attempted to recover from the builder but he did not want to know. This added an additional financial burden to what was an already difficult situation.

15. Once we got over the basement problem things picked up and went smoothly enough until Christmas Eve 1992, when the most tragic event of all occurred—our beautiful Gibbs ceiling in the sitting room fell off and was smashed beyond repair.

16. I was upstairs at the time, with Miss Glover, our Matron, attending to one of the residents, but we heard the crash quite clearly.

I rushed downstairs to see my husband emerging from the sitting room enveloped in a cloud of dust. Frankly we were devastated by this catastrophe. This ceiling, which was unique, was one of the reasons we bought The Old Manor House in the first place. In fact, I verily believe that this feature was the reason why there was so much interest in this property during the very short time it was actually on the market and why we had to pay almost £15,000 over our original offer to secure it.

17. Immediately following this disaster, we were forced to evacuate the three bedridden residents immediately above the sitting room. Dust was already permeating through the floor, despite it being carpeted. The frail elderly are prone to bronchial problems and we could not take a chance. Fortunately there was one vacant room on the same floor awaiting the arrival of a new resident in the New Year, but the other two had to be accommodated in private rooms belonging to residents who had joined their relatives for Christmas. Of course, we had to telephone for permission to use these rooms and that meant some difficult explanations. In the event one of the people we telephoned contacted the Health Authority who sent someone round on Christmas Day to inspect the damage. This gentleman there and then closed the entire floor—dubbing it a health hazard.

18. We were at our wits' end. There were 15 units on this floor; almost one-third of our entire accommodation. Only one of these rooms was vacant, and that, as I said, to be filled shortly. We rang round and found a Home in Aldeburgh, about 15 miles away, which could accommodate all 15 in a newly completed wing.

They offered to take our residents for one month only, after which time they could either become their residents or we would have to move them elsewhere.

19. It was Hobson's choice—we accepted their terms. Although some of the original residents did return to Sanctuary House, when the whole business of the ceiling was finally resolved, some 13 months later, the whole affair proved to be very expensive for us. Precisely what the cost was, I am not certain, as I left such matters to my husband. In any case I was too distressed to concern myself with that side of things as I had enough problems with the nursing end.

20. I did, however, participate in some very difficult decisions, that we had to take, over staff redundancies. Once the Listed Building people became involved, it quickly became clear that it would be some time before we would be able to use this floor again—they were not particularly helpful about how we should proceed and were far more interested in the ceiling than the fate of our residents. They seemed totally oblivious to the fact that the longer they delayed giving a decision, the greater our losses.

21. In the meantime we were grossly overstaffed for the remaining rooms. Our dilemma was that we did not want to lose certain members of staff who would be extremely difficult, not to mention expensive in terms of fees, to replace. In the end we only got rid of two of our cleaning staff and therefore carried all 20 care staff on the remaining accommodation.

22. Our bankers appeared to be sympathetic but I understood, at the time, from my husband, that it was touch and go as to whether or not they continued to support us. It was all very worrying.

7.32
353

23. This wretched business has virtually ruined us financially—it has been an absolute nightmare. We are not looking for compensation for the distress and inconvenience we have been put to, merely the recovery of the money we have lost through no fault of our own.

....

Constance Bliss

....

Dated

Proof of Evidence of Hermione Marigold Glover (7.33)

IN THE MATTER OF THE ARBITRATION ACTS 1950 TO 1979

AND

IN THE MATTER OF AN ARBITRATION UNDER THE JCT ARBITRATION RULES (18 JULY 1988)

BETWEEN

RELIABLE BUILDERS LIMITED   Claimant

AND

SANCTUARY HOUSE LIMITED   Respondent

7.33
354

PROOF OF EVIDENCE OF HERMIONE MARIGOLD GLOVER

I, HERMIONE MARIGOLD GLOVER, of Seabreeze Cottage, Hillcrest Lane, Brancaster, Norfolk

WILL SAY as follows:

1. I was approached by Constance Bliss, in the summer of 1991, and, as a result, I was asked to assume the post of Matron of a new Home which she and her husband, Mr William Bliss were intending to open at the end of the year.

2. I had previously worked with Mrs Bliss, at a number of different nursing establishments, in the preceding eight years, or so.

3. I was happy to accept the post which, was not only a very responsible one but one that I would undoubtedly find rewarding and challenging, as I had always had a leaning towards nursing the frail elderly.

4. I actually took up my duties on 1 November 1991 although the building works, on Sanctuary House, as the Home was to be called, were not yet finished.

5. The problem was I had to give three months notice to my previous employers and they had already found a replacement for me and did not therefore require me to stay on. As it was only fair that I should not be out of pocket, the Blisses agreed that I should be paid from 1 November and assist in a general way wherever I could in preparing the Home to receive its residents.

6. Of course, one of my main duties, in any event, was to recruit our caring staff, who I was to interview, with Mrs Bliss.

7. As it appeared unlikely that the Home would be ready to receive guests until the Spring, we did not start our advertising campaign until January. Frankly, over the intervening two months or so there was very little for me to do; as a result I felt rather embarrassed at being paid. However, I have an elderly Mother who relies upon me to support her, so I had little choice.

8. After the late start, we did not manage to open until the beginning of April 1992. In the meantime a number of the prospective residents had found accommodation and, indeed sadly, some of them had passed on.

9. However, through an extensive advertising campaign and assistance from an agency, that we used, we managed to fill the Home fairly quickly.

10. No sooner than we appeared to be back on track, than the basement laundry flooded. This occurred two or three weeks after we had opened, and scarcely before we had got ourselves properly organised. The washing and drying machines were ruined; so was a lot of clothing and staff uniforms.

11. Many of the residents were very upset over the loss of their personal belongings and would not be placated by the offer of buying them new ones. This is not an unusual trait in elderly people who often become overly attached to familiar things.

12. In addition to the residents themselves, many of their relatives were scathing about the accident. They seem to think that SH itself was responsible for what was an accident entirely beyond our control.

13. This disaster caused me personally some considerable additional workload, mainly in connection with the external laundry arrangements that I had to make. Also there was an additional problem over insurance. SH apparently was not covered for resident's belongings. I know that we had considered joining The Nursing Home Association which, with their special insurance policy, would have covered us against such loss. Unfortunately, with one thing and another, at that early stage, we had not yet got around to making our application.

14. The worst event took place on Christmas Eve 1992. My brother had taken Mother for the festive season and I had offered to work, together with Mr and Mrs Bliss, over that period, to care for the 24 or so residents who were not going elsewhere, and thus give the majority of the carers a well-earned rest.

7.33
355

15. When the ceiling in the Gibbs room collapsed early that evening, fortunately all of the residents were in bed, but the noise and dust disturbed the three occupants above this room and it was necessary to move them immediately into other rooms. This we had to do initially without permission from the absent occupants of these rooms—it was a real emergency. However, after settling them down, we tried to locate either the residents of these rooms themselves, or their relatives to seek consent. Two of them vehemently objected—so much for 'goodwill to all men'—and we had to move these two yet again once we had found two more accommodating residents.

16. The Blisses and I, with our skeleton staff, managed to cope on Christmas Eve; however, it was clear that we might have problems on Christmas Day. Mr Bliss gave me the unenviable task of ringing round to see if there were any of our other carers who had not gone away and who would be prepared to come in.

17. It is not surprising that most of those that I spoke to were reluctant to give up their family Christmas but with the inducement of double time and a half and an appeal to their loyalty, I persuaded five of them to make the sacrifice.

18. Clearly we needed to make more permanent plans as the temporary occupation of the rooms, let to other residents, would have to cease shortly after Christmas. As we were all but fully let we were forced to seek accommodation elsewhere, but decided to wait until 27 December, before making enquiries, when the worst of the Christmas disruption would be over.

19. One of the resident's relatives informed the Health Authority about the collapse, and on Christmas Day morning an inspector paid us a visit. After a thorough inspection he told us to close the entire floor above the sitting room. Apart from the dust, it seems that with the loss of this large room we were unable to meet the requirements for amenity space.

20. Thus when we started our search for alternative accommodation we were asking for 15 bed spaces for, what might be, as we then thought, a month or two.

21. We were fortunate enough to find a suitable home—MacMillan House—not too far away in Aldeburgh, which had just completed building on a new wing and was in the throes of letting. They offered to help us out with all 15 residents but for one month only. After that any of them still there would have to become their residents if they wanted to stay on. We had little

choice but to accept these terms as there was only one other alternative which, frankly, was not acceptable to us.

22. This other alternative was accommodation in Wickham Hall, Wickham Market. Although this was much closer to Woodbridge than Aldeburgh—5–6 miles as against 15—without putting too fine a point on it, this Home caters for a different class of resident to those in SH. I know that it was considerably cheaper than MacMillan House, but, after discussing it with the Blisses, we all agreed that it would not do.

23. A fleet of cars and three ambulances were required to move the eight residents, on December 28, many of whom were in tears at the rude disturbance to their routine and the possible loss of companions and friends. Some of them were so bewildered they did not understand what had happened. It was all very distressing, both for staff and residents.

24. When the dust had settled, so to speak, Mr and Mrs Bliss asked me to join them and discuss possible staff redundancies. I made my position clear. All 20 of my carers had been hand-picked by me and were all experienced nursing staff specialising in the frail elderly and would be difficult to replace. In any event, Mr Bliss told me that he hoped to be up and running again some time in February. So it seemed pointless to lose good staff only to try to appoint new ones in February. This was particularly so as we would have to start advertising in January to have them in place say 6/8 weeks later. It just did not make sense to get rid of any of our carers under these circumstances.

25. When advertising costs and possible agency fees were taken into account we decided that we would probably lose more than we would gain.

26. Later Mr Bliss told me that his bankers were putting pressure on him to effect some savings in order to compensate for the loss of income. I suggested that he looked at the part-time staff—cleaning and kitchen staff and the like.

27. February came and went and we seemed no nearer reopening the lost floor. The Gibbs room ceiling seemed to have caused quite a lot of excitement among some important bodies.

28. Previously I had scarcely been aware who was this architect, James Gibbs, but it transpired that he had been quite important and various historical people got involved as well as the local planners. Unfortunately it appeared that the different interested bodies could not agree on the way forward.

29. I know that, for quite a long time, one group were insisting that we consider restoring the ceiling using the original plasterwork. I am not a builder but anyone with common sense would have realised that this was a virtual impossibility—it would have taken years to glue all of the tiny bits together, that is if you could ever find how the pieces fitted, which I very much doubt.

30. Anyway, this delayed matters until the summer and beyond. Every time that we discussed possible staff redundancies Mr Bliss assured me that he expected consent to repair the ceiling any day. In the end we only actually got rid of two cleaners.

31. I know that this whole affair imposed a severe strain on the Blisses finances, as Mr Bliss confided in me on more than one occasion. However, I do not believe that they could have acted any differently from the way that they did given the circumstances.

32. When we did eventually reopen the floor—over a year after the accident—only six of the original residents returned, dear Mrs P having passed on meantime and the others decided to stay at MacMillan House.

33. I recall, that during the period that our residents were in temporary accommodation in MacMillan House, some of their relatives organised a committee to complain about the quality of the accommodation and service there. SH offered the best and our residents had been spoilt by us. No other local Home could match the quality of our service.

34. I know, for a fact, that we had to compensate some of the residents as I dealt with their relatives myself.

35. Frankly, Christmas 1992, and the year that followed, I wish to forget. Not only was the collapsed ceiling and the immediate aftermath very distressing for me but the poor Blisses were very worried as to whether they could survive financially throughout the period that the 15 rooms were closed.

36. Although I was not always privy to their concern, Mr Bliss always gave the appearance of remaining cheerful and told the staff not to worry as he thought everything would be alright.

37. Mr and Mrs Bliss were martyrs over this whole sorry business and somebody should pay—certainly not them.

....

Hermione Glover

....

Date

7.33
357

Second Witness Statement of Frances Hutch (7.34)

IN THE MATTER OF THE ARBITRATION ACTS 1950 TO 1979

AND

IN THE MATTER OF AN ARBITRATION UNDER THE JCT ARBITRATION RULES (18 JULY 1988)

BETWEEN

RELIABLE BUILDERS LIMITED   Claimant

AND

SANCTUARY HOUSE LIMITED   Respondent

SECOND PROOF OF EVIDENCE OF FRANCES HUTCH

I, FRANCES KIMBER HUTCH of the Look-Out, Hollesley Bay, Suffolk,

WILL SAY as follows:

I have been asked specifically to deal with the following issues.

(1) RBL's general performance.
(2) Late information.
(3) The Client's own tradesmen.
(4) Late payment of certificates.
(5) The final account.
(6) The Gibbs ceiling.
(7) Defective works.

I was responsible for the day-to-day supervision of this project. I visited the site at least once a week during the currency of the works—sometimes two or three times—other than one holiday period which my principal Mr D'Iffy, visited in my stead.

At all other times I was available either through my office or through my mobile telephone.

1. RBL's general performance

My relationship with the site foreman, Mr John Watts, was very good. I have to say, however, that I do not feel that he always got the support from Mr Reeves, RBL's contract administrator, that he needed or indeed deserved. For example, materials often did not arrive when required and there were often shortages of labour.

The quality of RBL's work was generally acceptable but there were abnormally high levels of defects at the final inspection meeting, 8 April 1992. I was accompanied on this visit by the client, Mr William Bliss, my principal, Mr D'Iffy and the client's banker representative, Mr Paul Goldstone. We met with Messrs Hocking, Reeves and Watts from RBL.

I had nothing to do with advising the client concerning the deduction of liquidated and ascertained damages—this was dealt with by my principal. However, I understand that the client did not pay the penultimate certificate, which I issued following this inspection visit on 8 April 1992. I have learnt, subsequently, that this was on the advice of his banker, Mr Goldstone, and, as a result, I can say that many of the defects listed on 8 April inspection visit were never remedied.

2. Late information

Most of the information that RBL required was covered in specification notes or in the detailed notes on the drawings. At the first site meeting, 8 April 1991, I asked Mr Hocking to ensure that requests for information were relayed sufficiently in advance of requirement to allow TAP reasonable time to produce it. This did not always happen. Frequently I would receive a telephone call from John Watts asking what I wanted in a particular detail, at the same time telling me that his workmen had literally come to a standstill on that particular piece of work, or they had stopped working on it and had moved to a different part of the site. This occurred several times during the works. Unfortunately I neither recorded the dates of these telephone calls or the specific information which was requested.

I can say, however, that TAP generally provided information requested of it within 7–10 days, which I consider reasonable. Of course, where there was a degree of urgency we did our best to provide the information much quicker, say, within 2–3 days. As many of the requests were made verbally we did not keep a comprehensive record of them.

Also, being a small job, we did not record precisely when we provided certain information although, if it was contained on a drawing, the date of that drawing would give a general indication. Having said that, the date was not always changed when a revision to a particular drawing was made which was minimal.

7.34
359

3. The client's own tradesmen

I understand that RBL are claiming that the client's own tradespeople caused considerable disruption. I accept that the site foreman, John Watts, complained to me, on two or three occasions, about these tradespeople but I took these complaints to be more of a general grouse than a serious matter to be noted and dealt with.

There were three main areas of work undertaken by specialist contractors engaged directly by the client.

(i) Kitchen equipment.
(ii) Motorised bath.
(iii) Nurse call alarm system.

I agree that the kitchen equipment arrived on-site early and proved to be a nuisance in as much that it had to be stored and protected. It also had to be moved from one storage area to another on at least one occasion.

I recall there being a problem with both plumbing and electrical connections once the specialist tradespeople came on-site to install this equipment. However, none of the foregoing was, to my mind, more disruptive than one would expect on work of this nature.

I cannot accept that the motorised bath caused any substantial disruption to RBL. Admittedly the equipment arrived late but as it only had to be placed in position, there being no permanent fixing, this should not have caused a problem for RBL.

Finally, the nurse call alarm system did cause a little bother. Again, the client changed her mind several times as to which system she would have and once, having settled on 'Emcall' left it too late to get the tradespeople on-site before most of the finishings were completed.

There were also, quite understandably, a few relocations by our client once they got the feel of the layout of the Home.

In my view the disruption caused to RBL was minimal as this system is surface mounted and the work of making good finishes was adequately compensated for in the Final Account.

4. Late payment of certificates

RBL have complained of late payment of Certificates. First of all, on a number of occasions, the initial delay was caused by Mr Reeves being unable to attend site on days appointed for the monthly valuation. This caused the valuation and subsequently the Certificate, to be issued late. On top of that the Certificate had to be processed by SHL's bankers which took, on balance, about 3/4 weeks following the issue of that Certificate. RBL were certainly made aware of the banks involvement, at the site meeting, on 8 April 1991 and thus the potential for delay.

5. Final account

I have seen what my principal, Mr D'Iffy, says in his Proof of Evidence about RBL's claim for extras and I entirely agree with his comments. I have been through RBL's list of alleged extras and, with a few exceptions, for which payment has been included in the Final Account, all the items which RBL were claiming as extras should, in my opinion, form part of the original Lump-Sum Contract and therefore be included in RBL's tender price. A number of these so-called extras were the result of instructions from me requesting RBL to comply with the requirement to provide replacement materials as far as possible, to match existing. The example I cite is the rainwater goods, which RBL initially provided in cheap plastic rather than cast iron with lead hoppers, as existing. As a concession in this instance I authorised RBL to use powder coated cast aluminium but made it clear, at the time that there would be no price adjustment for this variation.

6. Gibbs ceiling

Evidence on the reason for the collapse of the Gibbs ceiling I leave to the Experts. However, as Job architect I have first-hand knowledge of what occurred on the site.

RBL employed a specialist firm, as indeed they were required to do under the terms of the specification. In the event they used the Georgian Restoration Group (GRG), a firm whom we were happy to approve.

The work involved replacing an area of ceiling approximately two metres square which had fallen off and in addition repairing a substantial amount of the fine mouldings and scroll work which characterised these superb ceilings.

The lead foreman of GRG, Fred Pilcher, remarked to me at the time that the plaster had dried out and some of the keying, between the wooden lathes were suspect; however, his view was that with careful handling it would probably be OK. He told me that if we were at all worried about this ceiling we could have it wired up. The technique they use is to use a very fine drill through the wooden lathes and then insert soft wires tied to the joists. A painstaking and expensive process for which our client had not budgeted, so I was pleased to learn, from Mr Pilcher, that he did not consider this work was essential.

GRG were able to inspect the keying of the entire ceiling as the flooring in the room above had been removed in order to facilitate the installation of the fireproofing required by the Building Control people.

Sadly Mr Pilcher died last year when he fell off the roof of a mansion that his firm was restoring in Berkshire. The only other specialist who worked on this ceiling now works for Euro Disneyland in France.

This fireproofing followed the work of restoration on the ceiling below. It was carried out by RBL's own workforce ostensibly following the manufacturers instruction.

Our specification for this fireproofing was as follows:

'Fireproof between timber floors all in accordance with the requirements of the Building Control for premises to be used for nursing home purposes, using a proprietary system to be approved by the Architect.'

The system selected by RBL was that manufactured by Firesafe Ltd. I had no hesitation in approving the Firesafe system as TAP had used it before without mishap. The process involves a wet application supported by chicken wire nailed between the joists.

RBL's workmen were very sloppy when carrying out this work and I had, on more than one occasion, to speak to John Watts, the site foreman, about the amount of water to be used so that the consistency of the fireproofing material is right for handling and packing between the joists. I did not see RBL's men using proper calibrated measuring vessels when they were adding the water and I believe that they made the mixture too wet.

The result was that some of the fireproofing appeared to fall through the chicken wire and rest on the ceiling below adding weight and straining the, already suspect, keyed plaster.

7. Defective works

I have already referred to the abnormally high level of defects identified by Mr D'Iffy and me when we carried out our inspection prior to the issuing of the penultimate Certificate.

The predominant problem concerned was that of cracking, not only in the new plasterwork and finishings but also in joinery. Frames and joints generally shrunk and opened up unsightly gaps. The worst problem involved the fireproofing to the corridor doors. The specialist coating was not only cracking but was also lifting off the surface and delaminating.

On a visit with the fire officer, shortly after this inspection meeting, he expressed grave concern as to the efficacy of the fireproofing. He was not prepared to condemn the doors completely but said he would return for a further visit once the new work had settled down, in order to ensure that the disintegration of the fireproofing did not worsen. In any event, from my viewpoint, this coating was unacceptable aesthetically and I asked for the work to be executed again.

On the question of dry rot the specification specifically identified areas to treat as follows:

'The contractor is to replace all timber affected by dry rot and to treat adjacent brickwork/plastering etc, in the approved manner, in order to ensure that all traces of dry rot are eradicated.'

For wet rot the specification required that:

'The contractor shall inspect all existing exposed timbers for wet rot, including cutting out and replacing where necessary.'

In both instances I consider that RBL only carried out what they were contracted to do. They were clearly prepared to take the risk of the extent of this work when they tendered. After all they are experienced builders and were advised to inspect the building before submitting their price for the work.

Signed ....   Date ....
      Frances Hutch

7.34
361

Second Proof of Evidence of Maximilian D'Courcy D'Iffy (7.35)

IN THE MATTER OF THE ARBITRATION ACTS 1950 TO 1979

AND

IN THE MATTER OF AN ARBITRATION UNDER THE JCT ARBITRATION RULES (18 JULY 1988)

BETWEEN

RELIABLE BUILDERS LIMITED   Claimant

AND

SANCTUARY HOUSE LIMITED   Respondent

7.35
362

SECOND PROOF OF EVIDENCE OF MAXIMILIAN D'COURCY D'IFFY

This the SECOND WITNESS STATEMENT of, Maximilian D'Courcy D'Iffy of The Old Water Mill, Brightlingsea, Essex, who

WILL SAY as follows:

I previously gave a Proof of Evidence, in this arbitration, on the Preliminary Issues.
   This current Proof should be read in conjunction with the earlier one.
   I have been asked specifically to deal with the following substantive issues.

   (1) Liquidated and Ascertained Damages.
   (2) Defective Work.
   (3) Variations.
   (4) The Contractor's Claim for Loss and Expense.

   In giving this evidence I am to make it clear that the day-to-day supervision of this project was left to my assistant, Frances Hutch, who reported to me, from time to time, on the progress of the works.
   Once the initial negotiations with the client and the managing director of RBL had been completed, I had little more to do with the project other than, from time to time, being kept up-to-date with the progress of the works and paying the occasional site visit.
   From my records I made three, or possibly four, site visits during the currency of this contract.

1. Liquidated and Ascertained Damages (LADs)

In discussions which I had with Miss Hutch, from time to time, on the progress of the works, I recall her constant complaints about RBL being short of labour and as a result they appeared always to be behind programme. After being on-site for three or four months, and following my second site visit, it was clear to me that they had no hope of finishing on time.
   I asked Miss Hutch to write to Mr Hocking, the managing director of RBL and ask what steps they intended to take to ensure completion on time. I understand that no satisfactory answer was received.
   When the original contract completion date, 9 December 1991, passed, I advised the client, in accordance with the provisions of the Contract, to deduct LAD.

2. Defective Works

On my site visits I observed, for myself, that the quality of the work was, in some instances, poor. When I accompanied Miss Hutch, the client and his banker, Paul Goldstone, on site visits with RBL on 8 April 1992, we compiled a substantial list of defects which required remedying. Shortly after that visit the basement flooded. I believe it was due to that, and the extensive list of defects, the penultimate certificate was never paid.

My assistant and I were particularly concerned about the fireproofing on the corridor doors which, even at that early stage, exhibited signs of cracking.

During the Defects Liability Period, this cracking worsened. Also, other large cracks appeared in the plastering and wall finishings, once the heating was turned on.

3. Variations

When my assistant, Miss Hutch, brought RBL's Final Account for me to look at, we discovered that they had claimed many extras. A number of these were, what we considered, clearly RBL's responsibility to provide under the Lump-Sum Contract and were, therefore, not claimable as extras.

There were variations on this Contract but the number of them was, in my opinion, normal for a contract of this nature. For those variations with which I was personally involved, I am not aware of any of them which caused disturbance to the normal progress of the works either through prolonging the works or through causing disruption.

7.35
363

4. Loss and Expense

RBL have claimed that late information was the reason for their delayed completion. However, TAP provided all the information, requested of them, sufficiently early, in my opinion, in relation to RBL's progress on-site, to avoid RBL being disrupted or alternatively delayed.

I again reiterate the point that RBL were always running late and therefore any alleged late information from TAP must be viewed in the light of RBL's progress on-site.

Signed ....   Date ....
        Maximilian D'Courcy D'Iffy

Report of Miles Maclean (7.36)

IN THE MATTER OF THE ARBITRATION ACTS 1950 TO 1979

AND

IN THE MATTER OF AN ARBITRATION UNDER THE JCT ARBITRATION RULES (18 JULY 1988)

BETWEEN

RELIABLE BUILDERS LIMITED   Claimant

AND

SANCTUARY HOUSE LIMITED   Respondent

EXPERT'S REPORT OF MILES MACLEAN

DATED: 21 FEBRUARY 1994

SPECIALIST FIELD: QUANTITY SURVEYOR

ASSISTED BY: JAMES BROWN

ON BEHALF OF SANCTUARY HOUSE LIMITED

ON THE INSTRUCTIONS OF MR BLISS

SUBJECT MATTER: QUANTUM, LOSS AND/OR EXPENSE AND FINAL ACCOUNT

SECTION 1

INTRODUCTION

1.1 My full names are MILES HENRY MACLEAN. I am a Chartered Quantity Surveyor. I qualified in 1961 and have been in practice on my own for some 15 years. I am a partner in the practice of Hunter Maclean of Sudbury, Suffolk. I was Chairman of the local branch of the RICS Quantity Surveying Division in 1991. I am also a keen and active member of the local branch of the Round Table.

1.2 It was through my activities in Round Table I met Mr Bliss. I also met his wife on social occasions. They are a delightful couple.

On or about the 15 September 1991 I met Mr. Bliss at a Round Table meeting. Mr Bliss told me of a problem he had in connection with a building contract he had let for the conversion and extension to Sanctuary House. He and his wife were to use the converted building as a nursing home for the elderly.

1.3 At that time the building project was already in delay and there were indications that the costs were escalating. He appointed my practice to advise him in connection with the building project. It was critical to Mr Bliss that the project was completed on time and within cost as he had invested a large part of his own savings in the project and had borrowed the balance from the Bank.

1.4 The time for completion was critical as Mr Bliss had arranged through several of his business associates that he would take their aged parents as residents of the home. He had taken deposits in respect of fees which totalled £18,000 which he would have to return if he did not take the residents.

1.5 He had also committed himself to the Bank on the basis that the project was on a fixed price and that the cost of the building project plus the amount of professional fees would not be exceeded. He therefore had a fixed sum in terms of his savings, deposits and the bank loan which made the total sum which could not be exceeded.

1.6 We checked the monthly valuations until the project finished on 31 March 1992. We also advised the Architect on the extension of time applications which were made by the Claimant.

1.7 I have been instructed to prepare an expert's report on the following matters:

(a) entitlement to extension of time
(b) entitlement to direct loss and/or expense
(c) the final account
(d) defects.

1.8 I have met with the Claimant's expert, Joel Redman and found him to be most co-operative in that he provided the Claimant's records in connection with this project. I have also had the facility of the Architect's file to assist me in preparing my report.

7.36
365

SECTION 2

EXTENSION OF TIME

2.1 The building contract consisted of the rehabilitation and conversion of Sanctuary House into a private nursing home. The contract included a large extension to the rear of the building and considerable works to the grounds.

2.2 The date for possession of the site was 1 April 1991, the contract duration was 36 weeks giving a completion date of 10 December 1991.

2.3 The Architect has not granted any extensions of time. The Claimant has issued four notices of delay seeking extensions of time through to the actual completion date of 31 March 1992.

2.4 The nature and scope of the works was shown on the Claimant's programme issued on 25 March 1991. The actual start and end dates for all key activities have been extracted from contemporaneous records and one recorded on the base programme which shows planned and actual periods of construction. Whilst I agree the bar charts produced by the Claimant showing planning and actual durations and completion of activities, I do not agree that the bars shown on the chart denote continuous activity.

2.5 The key exercise which I have completed is the identification of what was the actual critical path as opposed to the projected critical path. Had the Claimant introduced additional labour (used his best endeavours) he could have avoided or reduced the effects of delay and completed the project at a much earlier date.

2.6 The conclusions reached in the following sections give my view on what a fair and reasonable extension of time would be had the Claimant acted in a manner to avoid or reduce the effects of delay using his best endeavours. The view so formed should coincide with the extension of time due to the Claimant based on the actions of the Architect acting in a reasonable manner during the final review of delay related matters as required under Clause 2.3 of the Building Contract. It attempts to reflect the process carried out by the Architect during the assessment of extensions of time that were on should have been issued.

2.7 Following the identification of the actual critical path, based on real events, it is possible to concentrate only on the actual causes of delays to those activities which fall on the actual critical path. Other elements of the construction which do not lie on the critical path can be ignored in respect of assessments concerning extensions of contract completion date although individual assessments of these activities may be made at some point in order to defend disruption claims.

Existing Building

2.8 Removals/Demolition and Form New Openings

2.8.1 The Claimant contends that the delay to the demolition of those internal walls which were to be removed to form longer common areas delayed the completion date by four weeks. Whilst it is clear that the revisions to the internal walls delayed the completion of the demolition works, other more dominant events effected the progress of the works.

It is accepted that the Architect did not issue his formal drawings to the Claimant until 7 May 1991. However, there were discussions on-site a week prior to that date where the Architect made clear his intentions to surmount the problems. Any reasonable contractor could have proceeded on the basis of those discussions and completed the works to the internal walls one week earlier by 7 June 1991 making the delay to the demolition works only three weeks.

2.8.2 It is not accepted that the Claimant could not complete the work in connection with dry rot infestation and the injected damp-proof course system any sooner than 12 September 1991. From the Claimant's own records the average labour force on this work was four operatives. Had he increased the number of operatives to six he would have completed this work by 13 August 1991. The actual effect on completion date of this operation is three weeks and four days; the remaining period to 13 August 1991 runs concurrently with other operations.

2.8.3 The Claimant's activity Form New Openings was programmed to be carried out partly concurrently with the demolition works. This activity was prolonged because the steelwork required to trim the openings was not procured by the Claimant sufficiently in advance of site requirements. The delay caused was increased as 50% of the trimming beams were incorrectly manufactured and needed to be replaced. This halted the formation of the floor opening and disrupted adjacent activities due to the prolonged necessity for propping.

2.9 Works to the Lift-Shaft

2.9.1 The Claimant was aware that the specification of the brickwork for the lift-shaft construction was dependent on the specific structural requirements of the selected lift. The original design for the lift-shaft was for construction in common brickwork. After consultation with the structural engineer the Architect issued an instruction to construct the shaft in engineering brickwork with concrete ring beams to support the lift guide tracks at each opening in the floor.

2.9.2 The Claimant has contended that the construction of the lift-shaft was a critical activity. In relation to the original programme sequence and logic I would agree. However, the construction of the lift-shaft could have been commenced earlier as it was a structurally independent activity once the shaft openings had been formed through the ground and first-floor levels. The delays caused by earlier activities, in effect, introduced a period of float into the programme in respect of the lift-shaft construction.

2.9.3 The Claimant could therefore have commenced construction of the shaft on 9 April 1991 but he delayed this activity until 6 May 1991, i.e. he retained the original programme logic even though there was no necessity to do so. A request for information was only issued one week before this later date. If the Claimant had started this activity on 9 April 1991 the lift-shaft activity could have been completed by 16 May 1991 and there would have been no delay to the works at all.

2.9.4 The Claimants decision to maintain the original start date for the lift-shaft was at his risk. Within days of commencing on-site he had realised that there were problems with the preceding operations and he should have reprogrammed, used his best endeavours, to avoid a delay. The Claimant therefore has no valid grounds for an extension of time under this heading.

2.10 Scaffolding, Strip Roof, Roof Structure Repairs, Roof Coverings, Replace Windows

2.10.1 Extensive works had to be carried out to the existing roof. This can hardly come as a surprise to anybody who has experience of restoration work especially with a building of this type and age.

Accordingly provision was made in the specification by way of the items describing these works and provisional sums to cover the risk factor of what might be discovered when the roof was opened up. There was also extensive notes on the drawings in connection with works to the roof.

2.10.2 The Architect maintained throughout the currency of these works that the claimant took insufficient care in removing the slates and this increased the level of breakages. The claimant was advised in the specification, 'Remove slates carefully and preserve for reuse', that the slates were to be reused. So few slates were actually saved that the whole of the main roof area had to be covered with new slates. The Claimant refused to provide new slates until the Architect agreed to both the issue of an instruction and payment for the materials. I am aware of the Claimant's argument that it took an additional two weeks throughout the exercise of more care to strip the slates. I do not agree with this argument. Whatever care as was necessary to strip the slates for reuse is the risk the Claimant contracted for and that risk in terms of time is what should be allowed for in the Claimant's programme. Accordingly, I would allow no extra time for additional care in stripping slates. In any event too few slates were preserved and this is indicative of lack of care, not more care. I can also find no reason that the Respondent should pay for new slates. The Claimant contracted to preserve slates and failed to do so, the replacement is therefore at his risk.

2.10.3 It is agreed that there were more structural timbers in need of repair than those originally specified. A provisional sum catered for the need to replace additional timbers. The Claimant argues that the Architect sought to replace timbers on a piecemeal basis. The Architect could only make a decision on what to replace as the Claimant proceeded. Had the Claimant proceeded more quickly this would have enabled the Architect to make his decisions earlier.

2.10.4 It was inevitable that if the claimant was late in carrying out the strip and repair operations that the roof coverings would be late in completion. It is agreed that actual completion of roof coverings did not occur until 4 September 1991. However two weeks could have been saved on stripping the roof slates and had the whole of the roof been stripped more expeditiously the decision to replace the structural timbers was part of the contract works. The Claimant should therefore have made due allowance in his programme items for work in connection with the provisional sum. Notwithstanding this, it is acknowledged that there is three weeks extra work in connection with repairs to the roof and the Claimant would be entitled to an extension of time of three weeks in connection with this work.

2.10.5 The Architect could not decide what method of lead flashing to adopt until such time as the Claimant was sufficiently advanced with the roof coverings so the Architect could see where and how flashings would be required. The Architect may therefore have been late having regard to the Claimants planned operations but he was not late having regard to the actual progress that the Claimant was making.

There were some extra flashings required and having regard to this the Claimant would be entitled to a further one week and one day extension of time.

2.10.6 It is acknowledged that as soon as the works to the roof were complete the Claimant proceeded to strike the scaffolding and install the replacement windows. It was important that the windows were glazed as soon as they were installed as without the glass the building would not be weather-tight or secure to enable the first fixing trades to proceed. This activity was delayed and disrupted because the first batch of windows supplied did not have a rebate in the opening lights of sufficient depth to take the double glazed units and the glazing board. A week was lost while the Claimant altered the opening lights at his joinery shop.

2.10.7 My conclusions on these programme items are that the Claimant has justification for some extension of time but not to the extent that he claims. An extension of time of a total of four weeks and one day should be granted to cover the additional works in connection with the roof structure and leadwork.

2.10.8 It is acknowledged that the Claimant was involved with further works through to 13 February 1992. Further works in connection with the ingress of water into the building were not due to the poor detailing of the leadwork by the Architect but due to the poor workmanship by the Claimant. The installation of the flue linings was executed late but this was through no fault of the Architect. The flue lining detailing and the materials were to be supplied by the named subcontractor for mechanical works. It was he who was late in providing detailed drawings for approval by the Architect and then he had difficulty in obtaining the pattern flue lining specified. Any claims in connection with the failure of the lead flashings and the flue linings are a matter between the Claimant and his subcontractors.

7.36
368

2.11 First Fixings

2.11.1 It is accepted that first fix operations ought to have commenced three weeks later than planned due to the additional works in connection with the roof. This would have given a start date of 14 August 1991 and not the Claimants actual start date of 24 September 1991. The Claimant had therefore lost six weeks through matters which do not entitle him to extensions of time.

2.11.2 It is also accepted that there was additional work required in the carpenter first fix operation. This additional work would entitle the Claimant to an extension of time of a further one week.

2.11.3 However, it is not accepted that the additional work to the carpenter first fix gave any grounds for the mechanical and electrical first fix to start two weeks after commencement of the carpenter first fix instead of the one week as per the original programme logic. The Claimant's files show that there were in fact areas available and they had written to both the mechanical and electrical subcontractors with the view to a start date in accordance with the original programme logic. Both the subcontractors had written back stating that Sanctuary House was not the only contract they were working on and due to previous delays they were working on other contracts and could not commence before 2 September 1991.

2.11.4 The Claimant's daily labour returns also show that the subcontractors did not maintain their full labour strength on-site everyday. Upon investigating this matter it was found that both subcontractors were servicing other contract commitments they had with the labour which should have been working on Sanctuary House.

Had they maintained full labour strength throughout they would have completed their work by 23 September 1991 and this would have enabled a start on the new extension on 24 September 1991 thus giving the continuity of working that the Claimant had planned.

2.11.5 In view of the fact that this project was in serious delay it is not unreasonable to expect these subcontractors to give the job their full attention by providing a full labour force, and absorbing the float time which was in their original programme.

2.12 Ceilings, Plastering, Lift

2.12.1 I have no comment to make on these operations save that they were delayed by the preceding operations.

2.13 Second Fixings

2.13.1 It is accepted that the Claimant increased his labour force to complete carpenter second fixings within the planned duration, albeit eight weeks later than planned. This is an example of what the Claimant should have done earlier in the project, use his best endeavours by increasing his labour force to avoid the effects of delay.

2.13.2 It is accepted that the Architect did make changes to the performance specifications for the mechanical and electrical works. However these changes are not the primary cause of delay in respect of these works.

2.13.3 The named subcontractors were required to provide full layout and detailed design of their respective services. Although no mention was made in the Contract Documents, it must be incumbent upon the subcontracts and the Claimant to co-ordinate the services design with each service and the other structural and finishing work. Neither the Claimant nor the subcontractors took cognisance of the need to co-ordinate services design, therefore the first attempt produced several clashes between the services themselves and their location to the adjacent structures. They made no provision for the services that the Respondent was to install using direct contractors, although the fact that there would be direct contractors was mentioned in the specification.

2.13.4 In order to assist the named subcontractors so that they could rectify the clashes, the Architect issued further sections and details showing the designated services zones and the ducts and casings required.

As a result of their design defects the named subcontractors issued their installation drawings late. This in turn delayed the Architect in the completion and issue of the construction drawings for the new extension.

Had the subcontractors issued their original drawings on time there is no reason that they could not have made the minor amendments required by the performance specification changes without causing further delay to the works.

2.13.5 It is not accepted that the additional durations to the services installations was caused by the changes made to the performance specification for the services installations.

Again examination of the Claimant's labour returns shows that full labour strength was not maintained by the subcontractors throughout the duration of their installation works. Had they have done so the float in their programmed durations could have been used to save a further week on overall project duration.

New Extension

2.14 Substructures

2.14.1 It is accepted that there was an increase in the quantities for reduced level dig, foundation excavation and brickwork. However, the Architect did not warrant these quantities to be correct from the outset. The agreement was only to remeasure quantities that were listed in TAP's letter to the Claimant dated 15 April 1991. This has been confirmed in the Arbitrator's Interim Declaratory Award.

It is accepted that there is an actual delay of two weeks and three days due to the additional work to the substructures. Whilst this delay does have some effect on the progress of the new extension, in any event this delay runs concurrent with the delays to demolitions and form openings. The Claimant would therefore be not entitled to an extension of time in respect of this item.

2.15 Superstructure

2.15.1 It is accepted that a delay to the substructure would affect commencement and completion to the superstructure. The delay I have acknowledged above is two weeks and three days. The Claimant actually commenced superstructure on the 10 May 1991.

Had the Claimant commenced the work to the lift-shaft on 9 April 1991 as proposed in paragraph 2.9 above and had he not caused some of the delay to the existing roof himself the further delay to the superstructure would have been wholly avoided.

2.16 Decorating Both Buildings

2.16.1 It is agreed that an Architect's Instruction was issued concerning the colour schemes. The Claimant is therefore entitled to a further three days extension of time for this item.

2.17 Direct Contracts

2.17.1 It was indicated in the Contract Documents that the Respondent would have certain works carried out by his own specialists directly employed by him. If the Claimant had notice that such direct contracts would be carried out I fail to see that he has any cause to complain. He should have made due allowance in his programme for the direct works to be carried out. It should be noted that the Claimants original bar chart 1340/1 made no provision for the direct contract works to take place.

It is accepted that the Respondent had the equipment delivered on 14 October 1991 as per his original intentions. However, he had no choice in this matter, he was committed to contracts with his suppliers where he would suffer penalties if he did not take the equipment.

The Respondent has suffered additional cost which he has not sought to recover from the Claimant through the direct contractors having to work around and in a sequence to suit the Claimants progress.

2.18 External Works

2.18.1 I accept the Claimant's Bar Chart showing actual progress and have examined the arguments put forward by Joel Redman the Claimant's expert. Whilst I accept the matters put forward as fact, the whole of the external works are in my view non-critical and do not warrant consideration for extension of time.

2.19 Practical Completion

2.19.1 It is accepted that Practical Completion, in effect, took place on 31 March 1992. At a final inspection which took place on 8 April 1992 a list noting 254 items which were defective was established. Although the building had been accepted as being Practically Completed the magnitude of the list indicates the Claimant had failed to produce the standards required in the specification.

2.19.2 The Respondent had commenced installing monitoring and emergency call equipment two weeks before Practical Completion. These items had originally been programmed to be installed after Practical Completion.

2.19.3 The additional elements were installed during a period when the Claimant was doing his own snagging bringing the work of the finishing trades to what he thought was an acceptable standard. This did not prove to be the case as evidenced by the substantial defects list. The Claimant's own snagging was the dominant cause of delays during the three-week period prior to the issue of the Practical Completion Certificate.

2.19.4 In my opinion the Claimant was not entitled to any extension of time under this heading.

2.20 Provisional Sums

2.20.1 The contract contained £183,761.87 in provisional sums and contingencies and these form part of the contract sum of £550,000. They in fact represent 16.42727% of the contract sum and should be taken to also represent that percentage of the 36-week contract period. This equates to 5.91 weeks which in my submission the Claimant has or should have included such an allowance within his programme. This may account for the shortfall between the time I would be prepared to recommend and the actual time taken by the Claimant.

2.21 Conclusions

In Appendix 1 my reconstructed programme based on all of my observations above show that the completion date should be extended to 17 February 1992. This equates to an extension of time of nine weeks and three days. The Respondent is therefore entitled to retain £59,964.29 in respect of liquidated and ascertained damages.

SECTION 3

PROLONGATION COSTS

3.10 This section of my report deals with the Claimant's claim for direct loss and/or expense. I have some reservations as to whether there is an entitlement at all because the Claimant in my view issued his applications late having regard to the time at which the loss and/or expense was actually incurred. This is a matter for the Arbitrator.

It is agreed that the Date for completion was 31 March 1992 which exceeded the original Date for completion by some 16 weeks.

However, it is not agreed that the Claimant is entitled to an extension of time or for the cost for that full period.

Section 2 indicates that the Claimant would be entitled to an extension of time until 17 February 1992.

3.20 The primary cause of delay to the works is clause 4.12.7 compliance with the Contract Administrators Instructions.

This cause of delay would also entitle the Claimant to direct loss and/or expense under Clause 4.11 of the Contract.

3.30 I have examined the cost information supplied by the Claimant and can agree on a figures as figures basis the weekly rates for all the items in the claim. However, this is not to say that I agree to the admissibility of these costs. My particular observations are given below.

3.40 Site Staff

I have examined the Claimant's pricing of his preliminary items from his tender build-up file and find that he only priced for a Site Agent and Trades Foreman in his supervision costs.

It is my view that the provision for Peter Murphy the Ganger was in the Claimant's rates for work items. Where work items have been varied and the quantities increased part of the cost of Peter Murphy has been recovered in those work items. I would therefore abate the costs claimed for Peter Murphy to nil.

It is my view that the provision for Graham Smith the quantity surveyor is in the Claimant's provision for overheads. This will therefore have been adjusted in the claim for overheads and should not be duplicated here. In any event I cannot see how indirect overheads can be viewed as a time-related cost.

3.50 Site Accommodation

The Claimant owns his site huts and temporary buildings and they are charged to each contract under system of internal hire charges. The rates that the Claimant sets for internal hire charges are equivalent to the hire rates found commercially in the market place. This may be suitable as a basis for job costing but it is not appropriate to use these rates as the basis for calculating loss and/or expense. It is my view that the correct basis for the consideration of such costs is the depreciation on such items plus an allowance for loss of use of the capital to purchase new buildings, plus maintenance costs.

I therefore feel that it is appropriate to abate the costs claimed by 50 per cent.

3.60 Transport for Operatives

I have viewed these costs from the Claimant's records and I find that the personnel carrier is a vehicle owned by the Claimant. The rates charged to the contract are internal hire rates and again I feel that the correct way to deal with this item is on the basis of costs of depreciation plus an allowance for loss of use of capital plus running and maintenance costs. I would therefore abate the costs claimed for this item by 50 per cent.

7.36
372

3.70 Site Expenses

The telephone and electricity charges are based on invoiced costs and are correct. I would therefore include those costs without further comment.

The small tools are charged on internal hire rates and again I would query this and include only an amount to cover depreciation plus loss of use of capital plus maintenance costs. I would therefore abate these charges by 50 per cent.

The costs of propane for drying the works are a one-off cost. The works only have to be dried once and this should be included in the contract sum. I would therefore not allow the costs of the propane gas at all in any claim.

3.10 Prolongation Costs

3.10.01 Site Staff

Site Agent	1 No	410.00
Foreman	1 No	360.00
Ganger	1 No	nil
Quantity Surveyor (part time)	1 No	nil
Indirect Labour (cleaning etc.)		210.00
	To Collection	980.00

3.10.02 Site Accommodation

Office	1 No	15.00	15.00
Store	1 No	15.00	15.00
Toilet	1 No	15.00	15.00
Mess Room	1 No	20.00	20.00
	To Collection		65.00

3.10.03 Transport for Operatives

Personnel Carrier	1 No	40.00	40.00
Fuel	5 Days	10.00	50.00
	To Collection		90.00

3.10.04 Site Expenses

(Average Weekly Expenditure)

Telephones	35.00
Electricity	30.00
Petty Cash	50.00
Small Tools	25.00
Propane	Nil
To Collection	130.00

Collection

3.10.01	Site Staff	980.00
3.10.02	Site Accommodation	65.00
3.10.03	Transport for Operatives	90.00
3.10.04	Site Expenses	130.00
	Total Cost Per Week	1,265.00

7.36
373

Prolongation Costs

9 weeks 3 days @ £1,265.00 per week = £12,144.00

Prolongation costs carried forward to Summary of Costs = £12,144.00

SECTION 4

ADDITIONAL STAFF AND EQUIPMENT

4.1 The costs the Claimant is seeking under this heading are disruption costs rather than prolongation costs. It is accepted that there was a shift in the Claimant's programme but it is not accepted that this is all the Respondent's liability. As expounded in section 2 of this report there are areas of delay and disruption to the works which are the Claimant's responsibility.

4.2 I do not therefore accept that the durations claimed are correct having regard to the proper liability of the Respondent. Nor do I accept all of the weekly charges as tabled by the Claimant.

4.3 The wages charged for the additional staff are taken from the Claimant's cost records and I have verified these to be the correct weekly costs. However, I do not accept the durations for these charges.

4.4 The plant and equipment has all been charged at the Claimant's internal weekly hire charge rates. Although I have verified the figures to be correct I do not accept that these costs represent the Claimant's loss. The correct rates are in my view those which reflect an amount to cover depreciation plus loss of use of capital plus maintenance charges. I would therefore abate these charges by 50 per cent. I do not agree that the periods for which the charges are made represent the Respondent's liability.

4.5 The following schedule shows the charges I would be willing to accept.

Additional Staff and Equipment

Additional Finishing Foreman from 14 October 1991
to 1 November 1991

4 weeks @ £340.00   1,360.00

Additional Bricklayer Foreman from 9 April 1991
to 27 May 1991

8 weeks @ £340.00   2,720.00

Plant and Equipment
Additional Hire Periods

Dumper		8 weeks @ £20.00	160.00
Forklift		15 weeks @ £40.00	600.00
5/3-mixers	2 No	8 weeks @ £17.50	280.00
Standing Scaffolding		11 weeks @ £23.00	253.00
Alterations to Scaffolding			480.00
Transformers	2 No	4 weeks @ £10.00	80.00
Extension Leads	5 No	4 weeks @ £2.50	50.00
Ladders and Trestles	Item	8 weeks @ £10.00	80.00
Sanders	2 No	4 weeks @ £10.00	80.00
Drills	2 No	4 weeks @ £7.50	60.00
Steam Stripper	1 No	3 weeks @ £6.00	36.00
Space Heaters	1 No	6 weeks @ £16.00	96.00
Dehumidifier	1 No	6 weeks @ £17.50	105.00
Skill Saws	2 No	4 weeks @ £10.00	80.00
Core Drill	1 No	8 weeks @ £4.50	36.00
Kango	1 No	8 weeks @ £20.00	160.00
Paint Strippers	3 No	8 weeks @ £15.00	120.00
Angle Grinder	2 No	8 weeks @ £15.00	120.00
			£6,956.00

7.36
374

SECTION 5

HEAD OFFICE COSTS AND PROFIT

5.1 The Claimant has sought to justify the head office costs and profit through being retained on-site by use of the Hudson Formula. I do not agree that this formula reflects the Claimant's actual costs in this situation.

5.2 I have examined the Claimant's audited accounts for the past three years and find that his recovery of profit and overheads averages 11.2 per cent over that period. Further, it is likely in the period over which Sanctuary House was executed that the Claimant will show a loss. I think this is further exacerbated by the fact that the Claimant gave a discount of 11.6 per cent on the contract price.

5.3 The Emden Formula is similar in application to the Hudson Formula save that it recognises that the percentage allowance on the contract price will not necessarily represent what the contractor will recover. The actual recovery rate forms the percentage rather than the contract allowance. I would not make any allowance for profit in my calculation as the Claimant is in a loss-making situation and he has not demonstrated that he can make the profit elsewhere. This would diminish the percentage used in any calculation to 6.6 per cent.

5.4 The basis of my calculation is therefore as follows:

(a) Emden Formula

$$\frac{\text{Head Office Overheads and Profit}}{100} \times \frac{\text{Contract Sum}}{\text{Contract Period}} \times \text{Period of Delay}$$

(b) Additional Costs   £

$$\frac{6.6\%}{100} \times \frac{550,000}{36} \times 9 \text{ weeks 3 days} = \text{£9,679.99}$$

SECTION 6

DISTURBANCE OF LABOUR

6.1 This section of my report deals with the Claimant's disturbance of labour claim. The basis of the claim is that due to the late receipt of information from the Architect, the timing and magnitude of variations and the interference to the Works by others engaged direct by the Respondent, the Claimant was unable to make best use of his labour either in the manner planned or in the most economic manner.

6.2 Whilst I can accept that there has been some disturbance to the Works I cannot agree entirely with the extent of the disruption alleged by the Claimant nor with the methodology adopted by the Claimant to calculate the losses which arise as a result of that disturbance.

6.3 I do not accept that late information was a cause of any disturbance to the Claimant's actual method of working. The Claimant has sought to obtain a full extension of time for the whole of the period he was on-site. To justify this he has analysed his programme and the delaying events to show both extended bars on the programme (the disturbed operations) and the overall effect (the extended date). My analysis of the situation is that the Claimant is entitled to some consideration of the overall delay which would entitle him to an extension of time but not for the whole period he was on-site and that there is some extension in respect of particular operations (disturbance factor) but not anywhere near to the extent that the Claimant seeks.

6.4 The timing of supply of information and the timing and magnitude of the variations are both matters which warrant consideration but not to the extent that the Claimant claims. My analysis of the delay indicates there were areas where the Claimant was in culpable delay (delay of his own making) and that having regard to this, although all information was not issued timeously having regard to the Claimant's original programme it was issued timeously having regard to the actual progress the Claimant was making.

6.5 Variations are an inevitability in building contracts and particularly a contract of this nature where there are extensive refurbishment works to be carried out. I cannot help but think the Claimant could and should have made some allowance in his pricing and planning of these works for the inevitability of variations in this project. This is a factor that I take into account in my calculations. Further there are areas (particularly the stripping out works and stripping the roof) where if the Claimant had progressed in a more expeditious manner this would have enabled the Architect to have issued the variations at a much earlier date. The Architect cannot be expected to know everything; a competent builder should get on with it to allow the Architect to make the appropriate design decisions.

6.6 I now consider the method by which the disturbance costs should be calculated. My consideration of time gives an overall entitlement to an extension of nine weeks three days on the 36-week contract. I therefore consider that the maximum disturbance factor can be no more than 9.6/36ths of the whole or 25.17%. Further, this figure assumes that the Claimant achieved perfection in all things, that his original price was correct, that he habitually achieves the outputs on which he bases his price, that none of his subcontractors or suppliers ever lets him down and that his management and programming is perfect. This I believe is unlikely and

7.36
375

I would therefore abate the disturbance factor by one-third or reduce it to 17% to take account of these factors.

6.7 The Claimant's expert has shown me figures based on the total number of operatives on-site and I have checked the Claimant's daily site diaries and time sheets and found the overall numbers and their working hours to be correct. However, these records include everybody who was on-site, including the domestic and named subcontractors who have not actually made any claims against the Claimant and therefore he cannot have suffered any loss on this proportion of the Works.

6.8 I also do not accept that the Claimant's labour content of the Works is 45% it is nearer to 40% of the element which excludes all the domestic and named subcontractors.

6.9 My calculation is therefore on a much simpler basis than that of the Claimant and is as follows:

	£	£
Contract Sum		550,000
Less:	£	
Preliminaries and Contingencies	76,000	
Provisional Sums	76,750	
Named Subcontractors	125,000	
Domestic Subcontractors	73,500	
	351,250	351,250
		£198,750

The Labour content included in the rates amounts to some 40% of the total rate. Therefore the labour content is:

£198,750 × 40% = £79,500

The disturbance factor is 17% of this figure:

£79,500 × 17% = £13,515.

This is the allowance I would make to cover the Claimant's losses.

SECTION 7

INFLATION COSTS

7.1 The Claimant has sought to make a claim for the costs of inflation in connection with the prolongation of the Works. I do not agree with the Claimant's method of calculation or entitlement under this head.

7.2 The sum is calculated on the basis of the differences in the Building Cost Index relative to the original contract period and the actual contract period to which the Claimant claims full entitlement to extension of time. The Building Cost Index does not represent the cost to which the Claimant has been put as a result of the prolongation to the contract period. The only method by which such costs can be calculated is to examine in detail the actual increases in cost of all the materials and labour employed on the contract compared with the base rate costs of the same items. The difference so calculated represents the cost of the prolongation to the Works. This would assume that the Claimant had procured his materials and goods in the same logic as originally intended.

7.3 However this would also assume that there was a liability for these costs. The Claimant is in my view under a duty to mitigate his losses where he is put to loss through delay and disruption to the Works. What the Claimant should have done, therefore was to purchase all the materials and goods to the original procurement pattern and thus avoided any losses whatsoever. On this basis I would not allow the Claimant any costs whatsoever.

SECTION 8

FUNDING COSTS

8.1 The Claimant seeks funding costs which consist of a calculation for interest due on the sums allegedly outstanding since 3 June 1992. It is the Claimant's responsibility to make his claims timeously to enable the Architect to consider their validity and to ascertain the amount due. The claim was late in that it was not presented until after the contract completion date.

8.2 Had the claim been presented during the currency of the Works the Architect could have ascertained the amount due and it would have been certified and paid to the Claimant. At the time the claim had been presented it was apparent that a dispute had arisen under the Contract and it was therefore inappropriate for the Architect to certify any further sums.

8.3 Thus if the Claimant had issued his claim timeously the costs of funding would have been wholly avoided. The Claimant has therefore failed to mitigate his loss and should therefore not be entitled to any sum whatsoever.

8.4 Notwithstanding the view I have formed on liability I have checked the Claimant's bank charges and can confirm on a figures as figures basis that I agree the interest rates, the periods between rate changes and the dates on which the interest should be compounded.

7.36
377

SECTION 9

FINAL ACCOUNT

9.1 I have taken considerable trouble to be fair and reasonable in examining the final account prepared by the Claimant. I can confirm that against all the items comprising the final account I have been able to agree on a figures as figures basis the dimensions and therefore the billed quantities which form those items. I cannot agree that all the items which form the Claimant's final account schedules are admissible in the account as variations.

9.2 This contract was not a bill of quantities or remeasurement type contract. This is a lump-sum contract based on a priced specification and drawings and was deemed to include works which were necessary whether or not they were specifically mentioned in the documents or not. Also included are items which are to match the construction of the existing building. There are general notes on the drawings to this effect.

9.3 It is agreed that the Claimant submitted the final account on 3 June 1992, which was within the timescale required by the contract. It is also agreed that the Claimant submitted all the supporting documentation required by the contract necessary for the adjustments to be made to the Contract Sum.

9.4 The Architect only issued written instructions where he thought there were valid variations. There was a misunderstanding as to the extent of the works to be covered by the lump sum and the Claimant did not make it clear to the Architect which items he really required instructions for and why he required those instructions.

9.5 This matter became all the more confusing to the Architect because the Claimant's staff issued duplicate copies of the notes made in the site book stating that instructions had been given verbally. Many of the instructions were not given verbally; the Contract does not make any provision for verbal instructions. The Architect, with my assistance therefore had to conduct an extensive exercise to decide which items were variations and which were not. An explanation also had to be given to Mr Bliss and his wife, at final account stage, so that they understood what the variations were and what their liability might be.

9.6 This exercise took a considerable time and it had become apparent that there was to be a dispute that would be taken to Arbitration. I believe the Architect took some advice and accordingly decided that it was inappropriate to issue any further certificates.

9.7 My summary of the position is as follows:

	£ Omit	£ Add
Tender Sum		622,171.95
Agreed Reduction		72,171.95
Contract Sum		550,000.00
Provisional Sums	76,750.00	107,011.87
Variations	63,351.04	124,590.68
Contingencies	13,600.00	—
Remeasured items		6,079.00
	153,701.04	
		787,681.55
		153,701.04
Gross Measured Account	**TOTAL**	£633,980.51

Provisional Sums

	£ Omit	£ Add
A.I. No.2 (b)	18,200.00	27,853.77
A.I. No.2 (b)	1,200.00	1,506.98
A.I. No.2 (c)	16,000.00	18,225.26
A.I. No.2 (c)	3,600.00	4,293.54
A.I. No.20 (a)	—	1,971.78
A.I. No.21 (a)	—	2,903.72
A.I. No.55 (b)	15,750.00	18,217.72
A.I. No.55 (b)	12,000.00	19,251.54
A.I. No.55 (b)	10,000.00	12,787.56
	£76,750.00	£107,011.87

7.36
378

Variations

No	Date	Description	Omit	Add	Comment
1a	06.04.91	10 No. Building Cards	—	—	
1b	06.04.91	Drawing Issue	24,108.00	37.192.00	
1c	06.04.91	Specification Issue	—	—	
2a	14.04.91	Revisions to lift-shaft	2,400.00	4,271.00	
2b	14.04.91	Acceptance of G Gosling's tender			Prov Sum
2c	14.04.91	Acceptance of R T Brown's tender	—	—	Prov Sum
3a	20.04.91	Dip & strip carved brackets			C.Wks
3b	20.04.91	Label & strip moulded work			C.Wks
4a	24.04.91	Deliver sound brackets		51.00	
4b	24.04.91	Amendments to extension foundations	854.00	4,080.00	Agreed
4c	24.04.91	Omit: Rebuilding of gable wall	279.00	540.00	Agreed
4d	24.04.91	Omit: Honey comb dwarf wall	193.00		Agreed
4e	24.04.91	Joists to kitchen floor			C.Wks
4f	24.04.91	Repairs to timber frame			C.Wks
4g	24.04.91	Reissue of window details	1,413.00	16,156.00	Agreed
4h	24.04.91	Reuse existing cornice			C.Wks
4k	24.04.91	Strip door hoods & timber mouldings			C.Wks
5a	30.04.91	Repairs to timber frame: North elev.			C.Wks
5b	30.04.91	Renew tiled cill			C.Wks
5c	30.04.91	Refurb works to gable elevation			C.Wks
6a	30.04.91	Work to existing windows			C.Wks
6b	30.04.91	Replace lead apron to W/3/3		421.00	
6c	30.04.91	Additional span to garage roof		67.50	Agreed
6d	30.04.91	Extension & utility room floor levels			
6e	30.04.91	Extension floor slab			
6f	30.04.91	Remedial to soffit of lintel D/G/4			C.Wks
6g	30.04.91	Lintel to door D/G/5		110.00	Agreed
6h	30.04.91	Seal off storm water drain		3.76	Agreed
6i	30.04.91	Omit: storm water manhole No.2	394.00		Agreed
6j	30.04.91	Seal off foul water manhole		20.00	Agreed
6k	30.04.91	Revised storm water drain	160.59	76.61	Agreed
6l	30.04.91	Modify rainwater gully; kitchen		93.24	Agreed
6m	30.04.91	Modify rainwater gully; extension		138.15	Agreed
6n	30.04.91	Construct storm water manhole No.2		589.25	Agreed
6o	30.04.91	Construct new soakaway		726.38	Agreed
6p	30.04.91	Adjust gully for kitchen waste		96.25	
		Carried Forward	42,518.59	64,632.14	

7.36
379

Variations (Cont)

No	Date	Description	Omit	Add	Comment
		Brought Forward	42,518.59	64,632.14	
7a	08.05.91	Adjust carcassing & outlet positions			Prov Sum
7b	08.05.91	Conceal cables			Prov Sum
7e	08.05.91	Relocated switches			Prov Sum
7f	08.05.91	Relocate pendant fitting			Prov Sum
7g	08.05.91	Provide pendant fitting & switch			Prov Sum
8a	17.05.91	Remove rubble inserts to fireplaces			C.Wks
9a	28.05.91	Lead soakers & apron flashing		519.00	Agreed
9b	28.05.91	Work around W/2/3			C.Wks
9c	28.05.91	New lintel & brickwork		232.21	Agreed
10a	05.06.91	Feathered lining to W/1/7		33.00	Agreed
10b	05.06.91	Work to eaves of north elevation		490.75	Agreed
10c	05.06.91	Work to fireplaces			
10e	05.06.91	Work to fireplace No.1		44.00	Agreed
10f	05.06.91	Work to fireplace No.3		15.00	Agreed
10g	05.06.91	Stairwell fascia		12.00	Agreed
10h	05.06.91	Work to chimney; east elevation			C.Wks
10i	05.06.91	Replace stepped weathering			C.Wks
11a	17.06.91	Needle up stone chimney breast			C.Wks
11b	17.06.91	Remove partition betw'n windows; bed 2		57.10	Agreed
11c	17.06.91	Drawing issue; tie rods		698.00	Agreed
12a	24.07.91	Omit: plasterboard; Add: hardboard			C.Wks
12b	24.07.91	50 mm wood wool slabs		60.00	Agreed
12c	24.07.91	Remove vent & patrass & make good		101.20	Agreed
12d	24.07.91	Replace stone quoin			C.Wks
12e	24.07.91	Supply & fit register plate		36.30	Agreed
13a	13.08.91	Replace lead flat, fit fascia, form drips			C.Wks
13b	13.08.91	Apron flashing to be dressed over		230.00	
13c	13.08.91	Redress ends of roof valley gutter		160.00	Agreed
13d	13.08.91	Renew apron flashing		162.00	Agreed
13e	13.08.91	Work to W/2/1 & W/2/3		580.90	Agreed
14a	13.09.91	Drawing issue (Revised)	5,161.00	7,112.00	
14b	13.09.91	Architrave & dado details	1,211.00	1,427.80	Agreed
15a	13.09.91	Drawing issue (Revised)	2,112.00	3,150.00	Agreed
15b	13.09.91	Installation of entry phone			Prov Sum
		Carried Forward	51,002.59	79,753.40	

7.36
380

Variations (Cont)

No	Date	Description	Omit	Add	Comment
		Brought Forward	51,002.59	79,753.40	
16a	17.10.91	Amend sink specification	225.00	357.45	Agreed
16b	17.10.91	Revised Spec. M&E			M&E
17a	17.10.91	Gas service to cooker (A G Plumbs)			Prov Sum
18a	18.10.91	Pay Reject Tiles invoice		158.63	Agreed
18b	18.10.91	Colour of tiles		41.80	Agreed
18c	18.10.91	Work to attic bedroom			C.Wks
19a	18.10.91	Renew abutments to W/3/4			C.Wks
19b	18.10.91	Remove render step		50.00	Agreed
19c	18.10.91	Replace incorrect lead covering			Agreed
19d	18.10.91	Replace door D.3.3		132.00	Agreed
19e	18.10.91	Fit new skirting in attic No.2		25.00	Agreed
19f	18.10.91	Timber fillet to D.G.13		15.00	Agreed
20a	21.10.91	Settle Boulton & Paul invoice			Prov
21a	25.10.91	Accept John Lewis quotation			Prov
22a	28.10.91	Work by electrician			
22b	28.10.91	New architraves		60.50	Agreed
22c	28.10.91	Issue of colour schedule			
23a	30.10.91	Removal of asbestos panelling			C.Wks
23b	30.10.91	Amend bath spec		33.06	Agreed
23c	30.10.91	Insulate roof space			C.Wks
23d	30.10.91	Form access to above roof space			C.Wks
24a	11.11.91	Dimensions of gas hob			
25a	21.11.91	Renew tiled roof slopes		184.60	Agreed
25b	21.11.91	Work to garden walls		2,626.63	Agreed
25c	21.11.91	Stone dust rendering		23.00	Agreed
25d	21.11.91	Wrap soil stack with glass wool		13.00	Agreed
25e	21.11.91	Pendant fittings			Prov Sum
25f	21.11.91	Location of fluorescent fittings			Prov Sum
25g	21.11.91	Wiring of pendants			Prov Sum
26a	21.11.91	Reposition ceiling lights in kitchen			Prov Sum
26b	21.11.91	Stone strings and gable to sth elev			C.Wks
26c	21.11.91	Obscure glass		255.00	Agreed
26d	21.11.91	Glazing bars		298.00	Agreed
26e	21.11.91	Form bulkhead in first-floor bathroom		74.28	Agreed
26f	21.11.91	Case heating pipework		28.00	Agreed
26g	21.11.91	Replace architrave; D.G.1		33.00	Agreed
		Carried Forward	51,227.59	84,162.35	

7.36
381

Variations (Cont)

No	Date	Description	Omit	Add	Comment
		Brought Forward	51,227.59	84,162.35	
26h	21.11.91	Drawing issue Extension (Revised)	7,118.00	9,242.00	
26i	21.11.91	Drawing issue Extension (Revised)	2,620.00	3,114.00	
27a	22.11.91	Shelving in airing cupboard		105.30	Agreed
28a	04.12.91	Lighting schedule			Prov Sum
29a	04.12.91	Omit: sheathing and floor finishes	1,656.00		Agreed
29b	04.12.91	Variety floors quote		2,905.63	Agreed
30a	06.12.91	Lead flashings to dormers			C.Wks
30b	06.12.91	Dormer cornices			C.Wks
30c	06.12.91	Remove casing beads			C.Wks
30d	06.12.91	Gable wall, smooth finish rendered			C.Wks
31a	09.12.91	Drawing issue, joinery only		2,448.80	
31b	09.12.91	Drawing issue		2,811.00	
32a	13.12.91	Renew ceiling in lobby	24.20	84.26	Agreed
32b	13.12.91	Repair rotten dado in lobby			C.Wks
32c	13.12.91	Omit: painting to stair handrail	70.00		Agreed
32d	13.12.91	New WC at first floor			Prov Sum
32e	13.12.91	Case vertical heating pipes		35.46	Agreed
32f	13.12.91	Ceilings to basements		949.00	Agreed
33a	13.12.91	Plaster as specification			
33b	13.12.91	New abutments to gable chimneys		256.56	Agreed
33c	13.12.91	Remove rubble from fireplace			C.Wks
33d	13.12.91	Weather chimney stack		50.00	Agreed
33e	13.12.91	Increase tile eaves overhang		171.77	Agreed
33f	13.12.91	Paint chimney support metalwork		31.14	Agreed
34a	13.12.91	Dimmer switches			Prov
34b	13.12.91	Plywood panel		22.00	Agreed
34c	13.12.91	Face mounted cables			Prov Sum
35a	17.12.91	Patrass for entry phone		98.28	Agreed
35b	17.12.91	Toilet roll holders	108.90	154.99	Agreed
35c	17.12.91	Lead hood to W/1/10			C.Wks
35d	17.12.91	Lead slate to v.p.			C.Wks
35e	17.12.91	Work to attic window W/3/4			C.Wks
35f	17.12.91	New lead saddle		70.71	Agreed
35g	17.12.91	Additional undercoat; bed 2		35.20	Agreed
35h	17.12.91	Remove rotten timber in basement		97.90	Prov Sum
36a	20.12.91	25×50 mm skirting in kitchen worktop		104.15	Agreed
36b	20.12.91	Reposition radiator in entrance lobby			Prov Sum
		Carried Forward	62,824.69	106,950.43	

7.36
382

Variations (Cont)

No	Date	Description	Omit	Add	Comment
		Brought Forward	62,824.69	106,950.43	
36d	20.12.91	Confirmation that gas valve adequate			Prov Sum
36e	20.12.91	Marble mantle shelf to living room		118.56	Agreed
36f	20.12.91	Remake back gutters; attic bed 2			C.Wks
36g	20.12.91	Work to chimneys			C.Wks
36h	20.12.91	Picture rail in bed 1		80.00	Agreed
36i	20.12.91	Gas supply to fire places			Prov Sum
36j	20.12.91	Marble hearth to bed 2		29.00	Agreed
37a	06.01.92	Reissue of colour schedule	100.80	189.00	Agreed
38a	06.01.92	Batten sect & wardrobe rail; attic b/r		130.56	Agreed
38b	06.01.92	John Try account; carved sections		84.38	Agreed
38c	06.01.92	Treat ends to cills & trim of windows		10.00	Agreed
38d	06.01.92	New rainwater pipe		84.00	Agreed
38e	06.01.92	Work to rainwater gutter outlet		46.00	Agreed
38f	06.01.92	Fixing of ceiling lighting fittings			C.Wks
39a	08.01.92	Remove loose rendering & rerender			C.Wks
39b	08.01.92	Remove paint from copings & M G		153.00	Agreed
39c	08.01.92	Work to front entrance door D.G.1			C.Wks
39d	08.01.92	Extend short worktop		70.00	C.Wks
39e	08.01.92	Repoint stonework north elevation			C.Wks
39f	08.01.92	Stain new floorboards to match existing			C.Wks
39h	08.01.92	Cut & remake external putties			
39i	08.01.92	Repoint leaded lights W.G.10, 11		21.00	Agreed
39j	08.01.92	Rake out & repoint mortar; basement 2			C.Wks
40a	14.01.92	Work to staircase		342.00	Agreed
41a	15.01.92	Revised redecoration		904.00	Agreed
41b	15.01.92	Take up & relay stone paving		221.00	Agreed
41c	15.01.92	Refix door & frame D.G.14		46.00	Agreed
41d	15.01.92	Remove hearth & make good; att rm		65.88	Agreed
41e	15.01.92	Work to garden steps		95.00	
41f	15.01.92	Leave clean stone on-site			
41g	15.01.92	Coir matting to lobby & garden entr.		105.16	Agreed
41h	15.01.92	Adjust bottom of doors & fit th/hold		81.75	Agreed
41i	15.01.92	Fireplace installation		125.00	
42a	27.01.92	Replace consumer unit			Prov Sum
42b	27.01.92	Relocate bracket fitting			Error
		Carried Forward	62,925.49	109,951.72	

7.36
383

Variations (Cont)

No	Date	Description	Omit	Add	Comment
		Brought Forward	62,925.49	109,951.72	
42c	27.01.92	Alterations to electrical fittings			Prov Sum
43a	29.01.92	Dining-room decorations		512.00	
44a	03.02.92	Make good & point open joints		56.76	Agreed
44b	03.02.92	Complete rendering to roof space			C.Wks
44d	03.02.92	Repairs to stone string; sth elev			C.Wks
44e	03.02.92	Roof level inspection			
45a	05.02.92	Letter plate		153.48	Agreed
45b	05.02.92	Tool back stone dust rendering		109.00	
45c	05.02.92	General trim lead			
45d	05.02.92	Redress wings of lead hood			
45e	05.02.92	Redress lead apron			
45g	05.02.92	New door D/G/1 omit letter plate		430.76	
45h	05.02.92	Fit chubb mortice lock		50.00	
46a	06.02.92	Wks roof level-E VALLEY		170.00	
46b	06.02.92	Wks roof level-W VALLEY		181.50	
46d	06.02.92	Wks Dormer gable STH ELEV		192.50	
47a	13.02.92	Preparation of floors		725.00	Agreed
47c	13.02.92	Change single way switches			Prov Sum
49a	13.02.92	Smoke detectors		63.90	Agreed
49b	13.02.92	Testing electrical installation			Prov Sum
49c	13.02.92	Testing heating and HW installation			Prov Sum
50a	24.02.92	Additional security devices		648.21	Agreed
51a	24.02.92	Lay paving slabs		271.00	
53a	28.02.92	Works to bedroom 1		47.30	Agreed
53b	28.02.92	Works to airing cupboard and living room		14.30	Agreed
53c	28.02.92	Key for shutter catches		10.00	Agreed
53d	28.02.92	Mortice lock		30.08	Agreed
53e	28.02.92	Additional shelf		30.00	Agreed
54a	28.02.92	Key for shutter catches		5.00	
54b	28.02.92	Amend furniture W/3/4	41.05	13.45	Agreed
54c	28.02.92	New nosing			C.Wks
54d	28.02.92	Renew rotten stonework		62.28	
54f	28.02.92	Rake out and repoint garden wall			C.Wks
55a	28.02.92	Adjust: Provisional Sums			
		Carried Forward	62,966.54	113,702.96	

7.36
384

Variations (Cont)

No	Date	Description	Omit	Add	Comment
		Brought Forward	62,966.54	113,702.96	
56a	28.02.92	New moulded plinth blocks		64.90	Agreed
57a	03.03.92	Light fitting			Prov Sum
57b	03.03.92	Cable and outlet for fitting room			Prov Sum
57c	03.03.92	Paint finish for doors			
57d	03.03.92	Omit top coat, add wallpaper	16.50	56.00	Agreed
57e	03.03.92	Margins to fielded panels		1,606.00	
57f	03.03.92	Redecoration of shutter cases			C.Wks
57g	03.03.92	Change garage roof tiles		518.00	
58a	06.03.92	Omit wall unit, add lighting fitting			Prov Sum
58b	06.03.92	Install socket outlet		9.00	Agreed
58c	06.03.92	Change pelmet lighting fittings			Prov Sum
58d	06.03.92	Fit security bolts		30.80	Agreed
58e	06.03.92	Fit coat peg rail		29.02	Agreed
59a	06.03.92	Sash locks to windows	368.00	606.00	Agreed
60a	09.03.92	Revised Glazing		954.00	
60b	09.03.92	Change light fittings			Prov Sum
60c	09.03.92	Revised call system		1,208.00	
61a	13.03.92	Plinth for safe		171.00	
61b	13.03.92	TV aerial outlets			Prov Sum
61c	13.03.92	Pavings garage forecourt		1,200.00	
61d	13.03.92	Service shutter		800.00	
61e	13.03.92	Fit Preservation Trust plaque		15.00	
61f	13.03.92	Security window locks		170.00	
61g	13.03.92	Front door lock		70.00	
62a	17.03.92	North Slopes Roof repairs			C.Wks
62b	17.03.92	North Slopes Roof repairs			C.Wks
63a	20.03.92	Change colours dining room			Not Ins.
63b	20.03.92	Make good rendering/decorate			C.Wks
64a	20.03.92	Flood lighting			Prov Sum
64b	20.03.92	Room plaques		210.00	
64c	20.03.92	Revise ceiling finish		151.00	
65	23.03.92	Kitchen floor tiles		508.00	
66	28.03.92	Attendance on Direct Contractors		270.00	
67	28.03.92	New servery hatch		981.00	
68	11.04.92	Attendance Direct Contractors		321.00	
69	28.04.92	Fire Officer's requirements		588.00	
70	30.04.92	Change colours bed 1		278.00	
71	06.05.92	Wallpaper dining room			Not Ins.
72	08.05.92	Fire blankets in kitchen		208.00	
		TOTAL OMITS/ADDS	63,351.04	124,590.68	

7.36
385

SECTION 10

REMEASURED ITEMS NOT AGREED

10.1 The Claimant seeks payment for eight items under this heading. The contract was a lump-sum contract which was to include for all works necessary to complete the project. Unusually the documents included a specification which had quantities against the items. Neither the Respondent nor his professional advisers warranted the accuracy of the quantities; the actual quantities required were to be established by the tenderers.

10.2 In the subsequent negotiations leading to making the building contract it was agreed that there would be certain remeasurement of parts of the works, i.e. those quantities on TAP's list in their letter dated the 15 April 1991.

10.3 I have checked the Claimant's quantities for the items and found them to be in order and would therefore agree them on a figures as figures basis. However, I would not agree to their inclusion in the final account *per se*.

10.4 I do not agree the Claimant's rates and prices included against these items.

10.5 Accordingly items 1 to 3 inclusive have been repriced at my own rates. These total £2,520 in the Claimant's submission but should in my view be adjusted to the sum of £1,680.

10.6 Item 4 concerns the external works. This item includes not only the works below ground level but also the works above ground which were clearly shown upon the drawings. The Claimant was in a position to have made his own assessment as to the accuracy of the quantities for this part of the works and accordingly these parts of this item should not be adjusted. Making appropriate adjustment for these items the Claimant's figure of £2,223 reduces to £809.

10.7 Item 5 concerns the main driveway. Again this consists of works that were above ground level and therefore determinable by the Claimant and works below ground level at which there was some risk in that the depths of reduced level dig could vary due to the unknown nature of the ground. It is accepted that this area included some soft spots. Again, I would reduce the Claimant's figures to take account of the surface area works which were determinable from the outset. The effect of these adjustments is to reduce the figures from £749 to £480.

10.8 Item 6 concerns the car parking area. This should follow the pattern of the previous adjustments I have made in the preceding paragraphs. It is accepted that in this particular area there were soft spots and the remains of an old air raid shelter were found which had to be excavated and refilled. The effect of the adjustments is to reduce the Claimant's figures from £1,680 to £1,240.

10.9 Item 7 concerns the landscaping cut and fill and topsoiling. I have again adjusted the rates to suit my own levels of pricing. The effect of this is to reduce the Claimant's figures from £2,167 to £1,870.

10.10 Item 8 concerns a change of rainwater goods from UPVC to cast aluminium. I do not know why the Claimant has sought to include this as an item of remeasurement, it is more appropriately dealt with in the variation account. However, I doubt whether this item should be included in the account at all. Consistently on the Architects drawings there is a note requiring the Claimant to match the existing construction and detailing. The existing building has cast iron gutters with cast iron downpipes and lead hoppers with a crest of one of the former owners. It is this construction the Claimant was supposed to match. The Claimant was insistent at site meetings he had priced on UPVC rainwater goods of matching sections and this was all he was obliged to provide. The Architect has granted a concession on his original specification by allowing the Claimant to provide powder coated aluminium and not the cast iron and lead construction originally required. There ought to be a saving which recognises this concession, however such a saving is not being sought by the Respondent.

Summary

Paragraph	Amount
10.5	1,680
10.6	809
10.7	480
10.8	1,240
10.9	1,870
10.10	Nil
Total	6,079

SECTION 11

SUMS DUE UNDER THE FINAL ACCOUNT

Statement of Sums Due Under Final Account, excluding loss and/or expense claim.

	£
Gross Final Account	633,980.51
Certificate No. 12 dated 13th April 1992 (gross)	610,450.00
Amount Due Measured Final Account	£23,530.51

Cash Reconciliation

Cash Paid (VAT ex)	412,296.00
Liquidated Damages (now adjusted in final summary)	146,000.00
Cost to Remedy Defects (now adjusted in final summary)	32,000.00
Certificate No. 12 (not honoured)	10,954.00
Second Moiety Retention	9,200.00
	£610,450.00

7.36
387

SECTION 12

LATE PAYMENT OF CERTIFICATES

12.1 Although no changes were made to the contract itself the Claimant knew that the Respondent's banking arrangements were such that he would not be able to meet the contractual timetable for payment of certificates. The Claimant was told this when he complained about the late payment of the first certificate. I would not consider it appropriate therefore to consider any sums as due for late payment of certificates.

12.2 The Claimant is not entitled to any sum in respect of interest charges on deductions made for liquidated and ascertained damages. These were deducted in good faith on the advice of the Respondent's Architect.

SECTION 13

RESPONDENT'S LIST OF DEFECTS

13.1 I do not intend to give a detailed report on the Respondent's list of defects. I was involved in the preparation of the Respondent's Scott Schedule for these items and was responsible for obtaining the prices to remedy the defects.

13.2 The prices were obtained from Widemark Builders Limited and I have included an appropriate allowance for moving furniture, equipment and resident's possessions from room to room while the work is being done.

13.3 My comments are restricted to the reasoning as to why the Claimant is liable for the defects rather than my costings. I have not followed this on a room by room basis but have dealt with each defect in turn. The Scott Schedule deals with what is to be found in each room.

13.4 *Plaster Cracks.* These are a major problem. The Claimant states that the cause is excessive use of the heating system. The Claimant knew that the heating system would be run at higher than normal temperatures to ensure that the aged residents remained warm. His obligation was to dry the works to a sufficient extent that the cracking problem would not occur.

13.5 *Cracking and Shrinkage in Joinery.* The same principle applies here as in the preceding paragraph.

13.6 *Plumbing.* The leaks and inadequate falls to waste pipes are simply matters of poor workmanship.

13.7 *Mechanical Ventilation.* This is simply a matter of failure to complete the works.

13.8 *Remaining Items.* These are all examples of poor workmanship or failure to complete the works.

7.36
388

SECTION 14

SUMMARY

14.1 The Claimant is entitled to an extension of nine weeks and three days.

14.2 The Respondent is therefore entitled to retain £59,951.25 in respect of liquidated and ascertained damages.

14.3 The summary of my view of the Claimant's entitlement arising from each of the sections in my report are tabulated below:

Section	Description	Amount £
2	Refund Damages Deducted	146,000.00
2	Retain Damages Entitlement	(59,964.29)
3	Prolongation Costs	12,144.00
4	Additional Staff and Equipment	6,956.00
5	Head Office Costs	9,679.99
6	Disturbance Costs	13,515.00
7	Inflation Costs	Nil
8	Funding Costs	Nil
11	Sums due under Final Account	23,530.51
11	Refund Deductions for Defects	32,000.00
11	Certificate No. 12	10,954.00
11	Second Moiety Retention	9,200.00
12	Interest on Late Payment	Nil
12	Interest on Damages	Nil
13	Costs in Connection with Defects	(32,634.00)
	Total Due to Claimant	£171,381.21

APPENDIX

BAR CHARTS

SANCTUARY HOUSE RECONSTRUCTED PROGRAMME

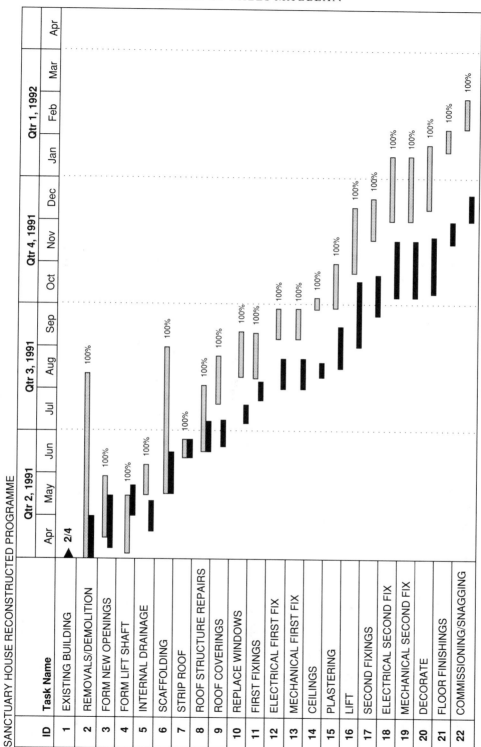

ID	Task Name
1	EXISTING BUILDING
2	REMOVALS/DEMOLITION
3	FORM NEW OPENINGS
4	FORM LIFT SHAFT
5	INTERNAL DRAINAGE
6	SCAFFOLDING
7	STRIP ROOF
8	ROOF STRUCTURE REPAIRS
9	ROOF COVERINGS
10	REPLACE WINDOWS
11	FIRST FIXINGS
12	ELECTRICAL FIRST FIX
13	MECHANICAL FIRST FIX
14	CEILINGS
15	PLASTERING
16	LIFT
17	SECOND FIXINGS
18	ELECTRICAL SECOND FIX
19	MECHANICAL SECOND FIX
20	DECORATE
21	FLOOR FINISHINGS
22	COMMISSIONING/SNAGGING

SANCTUARY HOUSE RECONSTRUCTED PROGRAMME

7.36
390

ID	Task Name	Qtr 2, 1991			Qtr 3, 1991			Qtr 4, 1991			Qtr 1, 1992			
		Apr	May	Jun	Jul	Aug	Sep	Oct	Nov	Dec	Jan	Feb	Mar	Apr
24	NEW EXTENSION	4/2												
25	EXCAVATE FOUNDATIONS		100%											
26	CONCRETE FOUNDATIONS		100%											
27	BRICKWORK FOUNDATIONS		100%											
28	INTERNAL DRAINAGE		100%											
29	FILL/CONCRETE OVERSITE			100%										
30	BRICKWORK FIRST FLOOR			100%										
31	CONCRETE FIRST FLOOR				100%									
32	BRICKWORK SECOND FLOOR					100%								
33	ROOF STRUCTURE					100%								
34	ROOF COVERINGS						100%							
35	FIRST FIX						100%							
36	ELECTRICAL FIRST FIX							100%						
37	MECHANICAL FIRST FIX							100%						
38	CEILINGS								100%					
39	PLASTERING/SCREEDS								100%					
40	SECOND FIXINGS									100%				
41	ELECTRICAL SECOND FIX										100%			
42	MECHANICAL SECOND FIX										100%			
43	DECORATE											100%		
44	FLOOR FINISHES											100%		
45	COMMISSIONING/SNAGGING											100%		

SANCTUARY HOUSE RECONSTRUCTED PROGRAMME

ID	Task Name	Qtr 2, 1991			Qtr 3, 1991			Qtr 4, 1991			Qtr 1, 1992	
		Apr	May	Jun	Jul	Aug	Sep	Oct	Nov	Dec	Jan	Feb
47	EXTERNAL WORKS	▲ 4/2										
48	EXTERNAL DRAINAGE			100%								
49	CAR PARK					100%						
50	DRIVEWAY						100%					
51	WALLS AND GATES					100%						
52	LANDSCAPING							100%				
53	PLANTING							100%				
54	GARAGE					100%						

7.36
391

391

Second Report of S A Longdon (7.37)

SANCTUARY HOUSE, WOODBRIDGE, SUFFOLK

THE SECOND REPORT OF MR S A LONGDON, FRICS, ACIARB

I am Stanley Arthur Longdon FRICS ACIArb Chartered Building Surveyor of The Meads, Green Lane, Stowmarket, Suffolk. My CV remains as set out in my first report.

I have already given my opinion on the cause of the basement flooding at Sanctuary House, Woodbridge, Suffolk and the learned Arbitrator in his Interim Award accepted my opinion that the builder, Reliable Builders Limited, was responsible. I have now been commissioned to give my opinion as to the proper specification for the remedial works and to deal with the consequential losses by the flooding. I have also been asked to report on the second disaster to strike this particular property, the collapse of the magnificent Gibbs ceiling in the residents' lounge on the ground floor. Lastly, I have been asked to give my opinion on the failure of the fire resistant coating applied to the original fine panel doors in the corridors.

Basement Flooding

Following the Arbitrator's Interim Award and my expert opinion given in my first report that the tanking should have been six inches higher than originally constructed by the builder, my further opinion has been sought as to the suitable specification for the medial works. In my opinion the lower six inches of the waterproof rendering should be removed and the tanking extended upwards by the same amount.

On the instructions of Kalmsyde and Joyoff Solicitors of 48 Crown Street, Ipswich, I attended at the offices of the Claimant's representative Mr Joel Redman, on 29 November 1993 and met Mr Sharkey the Claimant's building surveyor under the chairmanship of the learned Arbitrator Mr D Emsee. Mr Sharkey accepted my opinion and we agreed a detailed specification for the remedial works which is appended to this report as Appendix A.

I was also instructed to give my expert opinion on the Respondent's claim for the loss of laundry equipment and dehumidifying equipment ruined by the disastrous flooding of the basement and also the ruined laundry. I obtained from Mr Bliss his original invoices from CFA Supplies Limited for the two 35 lb industrial washing machines and the two 50 lb industrial dryers purchased by him on 17 April 1992 at a total outlay cost of £14,050.00 plus £2,458.75 VAT. In my opinion this figure is the best estimate of the value of this equipment that can be obtained and is the amount by which Mr Bliss should be compensated for their loss. Mr Bliss has also purchased from the same supplier free-standing dehumidifying equipment at a cost of £750.00 plus VAT. This is vital equipment in a laundry area and in my opinion will cost the same amount to replace.

In respect of the laundry and linen, staff clothes and uniforms owned by Mr Bliss's company and which were ruined in the flood, I have been supplied with a list of the residents' laundry which was being dealt with at the time. This was prepared by the matron shortly after the flood when she realised that the builder might be responsible for their loss. Putting an average price against each item for its replacement I am of the opinion that the loss is £384.00. Unfortunately Mr Sharkey was unable to agree my figure for this item. The list and prices are shown at the end of this report as Appendix B. This deals with the laundry owned by the residents which was lost in the flood. There was also linen and staff clothes and uniforms owned by Sanctuary House Limited. The items ruined by the flood waters were listed by Mrs Bliss a few days after the flood. All of this staff clothing etc is almost new having been purchased only six weeks or thereabouts before the catastrophic flood. I have seen the invoices for the documents to cost out the list of spoiled clothing. The list attached to this report as Appendix C totals £1,498.00 the value of which is agreed with Mr Sharkey to which VAT should be applied at the standard rate.

Gibbs Ceiling

In respect of the ceiling, I attended the subject property on 9 January 1993 at the invitation of Mr D'Iffy and found that the debris was still as it was when the ceiling collapsed. I have also perused the specification for the work.

As is my normal custom I am obliged to state that I have not inspected woodwork or any parts of the property which are hidden, unexposed or inaccessible and therefore cannot be commented on with any degree of intimacy. So I am therefore unable to confirm or deny that any such parts are free from defect. This paragraph should be noted and borne in mind throughout this report.

From various clauses in Section 3 of the specification I deduced that the builder was supposed to have repaired the Glbbs ceiling using a specialist and then installed fireproof insulation between the joists from above which necessitated the deboarding of the first floor.

I have carried out a careful examination of the debris which comprised of the plaster and ornate cornices of most of the ceiling and most of the lathing except at the east end of the room. There was also a large amount of fireproofing material some of which was adhered to the back of the plaster and the laths. I also noticed that the nails used to fix the laths were generally rusty.

My attention has been drawn to the architectural expert's report on the ceiling prepared by Mr Rector in which he identified the laths of being of oak and the fixing nails as being of ferrous cut nails. I know from experience that oak can have a very detrimental effect on iron and this is mentioned in an important textbook on the subject 'The Repair and Maintenance of Houses' by Ian A Melville and I A Gordon at page 671 where tannic action is explained.

7.37
393

Mr Rector stated in his report that the deterioration of the nails largely contributed to the ceiling failure. In my professional opinion this was only a partial cause of the collapse. From the amount of fireproof material amongst the debris it is quite clear to me that the builder allowed large quantities of the fireproof material to fall onto the ceiling probably as a result of too much water in the mix. Mr D'Iffy tells me that his assistant Miss Hutch had occasion to complain more than once to the builders that the mix was too wet and that they should take great care to prevent fireproofing material from falling from the ceiling. The weight of this material on the delicate ceiling in my opinion was also a contributory cause of its collapse.

A clause in the preambles to the specification has been brought to my attention. It reads:

> The existing Gibbs ceiling in the lounge is to be protected with particular care. In addition to their general responsibility for protection of the existing structure the contractor is to take whatever steps as are necessary to uphold the integrity of the existing ceiling. The contractor's attention is drawn to the need to remove and reinstate the first-floor boarding, clear out any rubbish from the ceiling void and install fireproofing within the floor structure. These and any other works affecting the Gibbs ceiling are to be carried out in such a way and all necessary precautions taken to ensure that the integrity of the ceiling is maintained at all times and on completion.

The meaning of this requirement in my professional opinion is that the builder should have done whatever he considered necessary to the ceiling in order that it was in sound condition at the end of the job. Miss Hutch says that she had a conversation with the foreman of the specialist company who restored the ceiling and that he said that the ceiling could be wired up. He was obviously just saying that to get Miss Hutch to give an instruction for this work to be undertaken so that he could be paid extra for it. The foreman must have known that the ceiling needed to be secured and the builder should have carried out this work at no extra cost, because that is what the clause in the preamble made him liable to do.

However, there was in my opinion a more likely cause of the collapse of the ceiling. On May 20 1993 I made a further inspection of the first-floor structure over the area where the ceiling had collapsed. The carpets to the floors in the three rooms above the resident's lounge had been removed and some floorboards lifted. The wire mesh to the fireproofing was examined and it was discovered that although below the centre room and the one at the east end the mesh had been fixed with screws, the mesh below the room at the west end was fixed with nails. I also noticed that although all the floorboarding had been fixed with screws there were many instances where the screw heads were deformed and flattened clearly indicating to me that the screws had been driven home by hammer rather than by screwdriver.

It is my opinion that the builders should have fixed both the wire and mesh for the fire proofing and refixed the floorboards above the ceiling with screws and not nails which cause vibration to the floor joists when hammered home. He should also have fixed any screws properly with a screwdriver and not used a hammer. I am satisfied in my own mind that the vibration caused by hammering would have severely weakened both the plaster key and fixings to the laths and eventually caused the ceiling to collapse. (See detail showing plaster key in Appendix D.)

Messrs Melville and Gordon in their well-known book mentioned many instances where ceilings have been weakened due to various causes but have collapsed much later without any warning at all. References are given on pages 672 and 673 of their book. It is therefore not necessarily surprising that the ceiling did not collapse at the time when the builder was carrying out the work but at a later date.

In my professional opinion although the magnificent ceiling was old and the plaster key and nails were weakened these were not the particular cause of its collapse. In my opinion the builder carried out the fireproofing in a sloppy manner by allowing material to fall onto the ceiling. He also failed to secure the ceiling by wiring it up, but more importantly he caused undue vibration by nailing some of the wire mesh and by hammering rather than screwing the screws fixing the floorboards which in my opinion was the primary cause of the ceiling collapse.

The ceiling having been found, by the Arbitrator, to be a genuine Gibbs ceiling, it was agreed that if it was decided to replace it with a matching replica, this work would have to be carried out by a very specialist firm to a very high standard. I had liaised with Mr Sharkey prior to my meeting on 29 November 1993, under the chairmanship of the Arbitrator and we had agreed that the best firm to obtain a check price from, for this work, which we understood had recently been completed, was Charles B Carter Limited of Norwich. We asked this firm to give us three alternative quotations, the first two being for a matching replica ceiling—one using original materials and the other using modern ones. The third alternative was for a plain ceiling. We obtained these three quotations as we realised that the Arbitrator may well decide that the ceiling should have been replaced with something other than a matching replica, using original materials.

The copy of these quotations is attached as an Appendix E to my report. From this it will be seen that alternative 1—the replica with original materials—is quoted at £38,360 ex VAT. This compares very favourably with the actual cost of this work at £38,424 plus VAT. Therefore, Mr Sharkey and I have no hesitation in saying that should the Arbitrator decide that a matching replica ceiling was the correct form of reinstatement, the figure of £38,424 plus VAT for this work, is acceptable. We also agreed at our meeting in November that the fee charged by the architect of £5,500 ex VAT, although representing a high percentage cost of this work due to its very specialist nature, we decided that this too was reasonable.

Fireproofing Doors

The last issue which I have been commissioned to deal with concerns the failure of the fireproofing of a large number of fine panelled doors in the property. Item 48 in the specification requires the builder to treat a total of 64 doors to achieve half-hour fire resistance. In addition, the edges of the doors were to be grooved to receive intumescent strips to complete the treatment. I understand that Mr D'Iffy when preparing his specification had discussed this type of treatment with one of the well-known suppliers of this treatment Calib Protective Coatings Limited and had obtained a quotation from one of the approved

7.37
394

specialist companies who carry out this work, Shawpruff. In order to assist the builder Mr D'Iffy provided a copy of this quotation to them during the tender period. I understand that the builder in fact chose to use Shawpruff who carried out the treatment to the doors in accordance with their own suggested specification. The system comprises three coats of intumescent emulsion in which a fine weave glass fibre material is embedded. Once this is dry the doors are painted with two coats of flame retardant paint. As far as the intumescent strip is concerned the door edges are simply grooved out and the intumescent strip fitted.

I attended at the subject property and carried out an inspection on 10 December 1993 at the invitation of Mr D'Iffy. I noted cracking and wrinkling of the coating on almost all the doors which had been treated and in some cases this was quite severe. In the worst cases the whole of the intumescent covering including the fibreglass matting, had pulled away from the timber surface in some cases in quite large patches.

I am informed that these defects were not noticeable at the end of the defects liability period under the contract but began to appear subsequently and that the intumescent application became progressively worse quite rapidly. I also noted splits and cracks in the doors themselves. This suggests to me that the timberwork has shrunk and this will have been due to the timberwork having been damp and then drying out following completion of the work. I understand that before the work began the property was in something of a derelict state and no doubt at the time all the joinery was damp. In my opinion the most likely cause of the failure of the intumescent treatment of the doors was due to the fact that it was applied to damp woodwork which has since shrunk as it has dried out. In my opinion both the builder and their subcontractor should have known that any type of painting treatment should not be applied to damp timber. I hold the view that this was a case of poor workmanship and that the builder is liable for the remedial work.

7.37
395

Although the Claimant's building surveyor Mr Sharkey is as I understand it not dealing with the cause of the failure of the fireproofing he and I have discussed the cost of renewing the treatment of these doors, a number of quotations have been obtained and as a result Mr Sharkey and I have agreed that the reasonable cost of remedial work to the doors is £110.00 per door excluding VAT.

....   Date ....

Stanley Arthur Longdon, FRICS, ACIArb

APPENDIX A

SANCTUARY HOUSE, WOODBRIDGE, SUFFOLK

AGREED OUTLINE SPECIFICATION FOR REMEDIAL WORKS TO BASEMENT TANKING

1. Carefully remove timber capping to top of blockwork lining and set aside for re-use.

2. Carefully hack off waterproof rendering approximately 250 mm above existing blockwork and make good brickwork as necessary to receive Bituthene.

3. Carefully remove top course of existing blockwork and make good as necessary.

4. Provide and fix Bituthene in accordance with manufacturer's instructions overlapping minimum 150 mm to existing Bituthene and at corner laps.

5. Build up 2 courses of blockwork to match existing in cement and sand mortar.

6. Make good waterproof rendering to match existing.

7. Render and set to new blockwork and make good to existing plaster as necessary all to match existing.

8. Refix timber capping making up with new to match existing as necessary.

9. Make good all decorations as necessary to match existing.

7.37
396

APPENDIX B

LIST OF RESIDENTS' LAUNDRY RUINED IN THE BASEMENT FLOOD

[List not included due to length]

Conclusion
My assessment of this loss is £384.

APPENDIX C

LIST OF STAFF CLOTHING AND UNIFORMS RUINED IN THE BASEMENT FLOOD

[List not included due to length]

Conclusion
My assessment of this loss, which is agreed with the Claimants' Expert, Mr Sharkey, is £1,498.

39mm   10mm   ⅛" (3mm) or ½" (13mm)
1½"   ⅜"   SPLIT OR RIVEN OAK
                OR HAZEL LATH
        plaster keys   ↓

1
2
3

Full size section of typical
three coat work on lath

Ref: DESCRIPTION AND THICKNESS		MIX PROPORTIONS				
		TYPE i LIME PLASTER		TYPE ii LIME GAUGED WITH GYPSUM		
		LIME PUTTY	SAND	GYPSUM A,B or C	LIME PUTTY	SAND
1 Render Coat.	⅜" (9mm)	1	3 *	1	1	6
2 Floating Coat	¼" (6mm)	1	3 *	1	1	6
						"Backing coat"
3 Setting Coat	⅛" (3mm)	3	2 **	1	1	—
						"Finishing coat"

NOTES:

Render coat: "Coarse stuff *" is reinforced with hair or synthetic alkali resistant fibres well beaten in. Quantity: 15kg/m³. This coat is cross-keyed with a lath scratcher
Floating coat: "Coarse stuff *" reinforced as render coat. This coat is keyed with a devil float
Setting coat: "Setting ** stuff". This thin coat is applied in three operations:-
ⓐ trowel on with laying-on trowel ⓑ trowel and float ⓒ compact by scouring with a cross-grained wood float lubricated with water to avoid shrink-crazing.

lath scratcher   devil float   nails

TYPICAL "RENDER, FLOAT AND SET" DETAILS
FOR LATH AND PLASTER CEILING

John Ashurst 1981

7.37
397

APPENDIX E

BRIEF SPECIFICATION AND BUDGET COSTS
FOR
GIBBS CEILING REPLACEMENT
LOCATION—EAST ANGLIA

February 1994

Brief Specification

Generally

Ceiling dimensions assumed to be 18′ × 30′ approx with a ceiling to floor height of 12 to 15 feet. It is assumed that adjacent wall surfaces and the like remain intact and no allowances are made for remedial works to these surfaces. Provide access scaffolding for the works and take down and prepare to receive replacement ceiling.

In all instances we have allowed for decorating the ceiling in one colour only and for temporarily lifting and subsequently replacing the floorboarding above.

No allowances have been made for electrical works.

7.37
398

Alternative No. One (Using traditional materials)

Provide riven oak lathing to soffit and plaster with traditional lime plaster. To perimeter of ceiling provide a dentil cornice and plain cross mouldings to give a 'Doric' effect. No further enrichments have been allowed for and no multicolour final decorations.

Alternative No. Two (Using modern materials)

Replace ceiling with stainless steel lathing with stainless steel fixings to soffit and plaster in metal bonding plaster. Provide fibrous cornice to perimeter and plain cross mouldings to give the 'Doric effect' mentioned in Alternative No. One. Again no further enrichments have been allowed for and no multicolour final decorations.

Alternative No. Three (Plain ceiling using modern materials)

Replace ceiling as in Alternative No. Two above and provide fibrous plaster cornice to perimeter. No further cross members or enrichments have been allowed for giving only a plain ceiling with ornamental cornice.

Budget Estimates

Alternatives One and Two below are based on reproducing the decoration and mouldings, as nearly as possible, to match the original, as recorded on the photographs attached.

Alternative Three is for a plain ceiling as specified.

Alternative One	£38,360 excluding VAT
Alternative Two	£24,850 excluding VAT
Alternative Three	£9,652 excluding VAT

The work will take approximately 1—1½ months from order.
All of the above prices remain open for acceptance for three months from today's date.

Report of Mark Page (7.38)

REPORT ON DAMAGES IN THE MATTER OF THE ARBITRATION BETWEEN RELIABLE BUILDERS LIMITED AND SANCTUARY HOUSE LIMITED

1. INTRODUCTION AND SUMMARY

Introduction

1.1. We have been requested by Mr James Crighton of Kalmsyde & Joyoff, the Respondent's solicitors, to review the counterclaim by the Respondent, Sanctuary House Limited ('SHL'), against the Claimant, Reliable Builders Limited ('RBL').

1.2. This report sets out the work we have performed in relation to this dispute and our conclusions. The report has been prepared under the supervision of Mr Mark Page whose qualifications and experience are set out in Appendix I.

Background

1.3. SHL owns and operates a Grade 1 listed Queen Anne house as a nursing home at Woodbridge, Suffolk. We understand that between April 1991 and March 1992 RBL remodelled the interior of the building, including repairs to the Gibbs ceiling.

1.4. On 24 December 1992 the Gibbs ceiling collapsed. Subsequently, 15 of the home's 52 accommodation units were closed until the ceiling was repaired, in order to comply with Health Authority regulations. Due to the Home's listed status, consent for repair works was sought from English Heritage. This was obtained in late September 1993. Restoration began on 4 October 1993 and was completed on 3 November. The 15 units were finally all relet by 14 February 1994.

1.5. RBL are claiming for monies they aver are due to them under the building contract. SHL are counterclaiming for the cost of repairing the ceiling and loss of profits, directly related to the collapse, totalling £398,259.

1.6. We understand that SHL are also claiming for the diminution in the value of the property resulting from the loss of the Gibbs ceiling. That claim is not considered here.

Conclusions

1.7 We believe that SHL incurred costs of £43,924 in restoring the Gibbs ceiling and suffered a loss of profits of £354,335, giving total damages of £398,259. These figures have been calculated without any reference to the impact of taxation.

1.8. We believe that our calculations result in a reasonable and prudent estimate of the loss suffered by the Respondent, for the reasons set out in the body of this report.

2. SCOPE OF WORK AND APPROACH

2.1. In the course of our work we have had access to the accounting and other records of SHL. We have not performed an audit of these records. However, nothing has come to our attention in the course of our work to cause us to question the records we have relied upon.

2.2. We have also held discussions with the following employees of SHL: Mr William Bliss (managing director), Mrs Constance Bliss (director), Mrs Laura Buzzard (finance director).

2.3. We have calculated the costs incurred in restoring the Gibbs ceiling separately from the loss of profits. The loss of profits represents lost income plus incremental costs incurred less incremental cost savings. The lost income represents the fee income from letting accommodation units which would have been earned but for the collapse of the ceiling. The incremental costs incurred are those which would not have been incurred but for the collapse and the incremental cost savings are those costs which would have been incurred but for the collapse.

3. CALCULATION OF DAMAGES

3.1. Our calculation of the damage suffered by SHL as a result of the collapse of the 'Gibbs ceiling is summarised below, and detailed in the paragraphs in brackets after each caption:

	£	£	£
Costs incurred in restoring the ceiling			
Architect's fees (ex VAT)		5,500	
Restoration work by specialist contractor (ex VAT)		38,424	
			43,924
Loss of profits			
Loss of income			
Fees relating to unlet accommodation units [3.3]		330,960	
Incremental costs incurred			
Emergency accommodation of residents [3.4]	6,480		
Staff overtime over Christmas period [3.5]	1,495		
Increased promotional costs to relet rooms [3.6]	2,740		
Financing costs [3.7]	29,400		
		40,115	
Incremental cost savings			
Cleaning staff salaries & employers' NIC [3.8]	(7,460)		
Heat & light [3.9]	(9,280)		
		(16,740)	
			354,335
TOTAL DAMAGES CLAIMED			£398,259

Loss of income

3.2. The lost income has been calculated on the assumption that, but for the collapse of the ceiling, the 15 accommodation units which were closed would have earned fees of £420 per week from the date they were closed to the date they were relet. Following an advertising campaign to announce the interior remodelling, the demand for the home was high. Throughout the period the 15 units were closed, the remaining 37 units were mostly fully let, apart from isolated units for relative short periods. The 15 units were all relet at £420 per week by 14 February 1994.

3.3. On average the 15 accommodation units were unoccupied for 52.53 weeks each. The loss of fee income is calculated as follows:

15 units × 52.53 weeks on average × £420 per week = £330,960

Costs of emergency accommodation of residents

3.4. Alternative accommodation had to be found at short notice to rehouse temporarily those residents affected by the closure of the units. The costs of this accommodation amounted to £6,480—see schedule in Appendix II.

Staff overtime over Christmas period

3.5. The collapse of the ceiling on Christmas Eve required staff to work unplanned overtime on Christmas Day and Boxing Day. This overtime was paid at 2.5 times the basic rate due to the short notice and the season and amounted to £1,495—see details in Appendix III.

Promotional costs to relet rooms

3.6. This represents actual expenditure on newspaper and magazine advertising in the winter of 1993. The expenditure was necessary to ensure that the 15 accommodation units would be relet. But for the collapse of the ceiling, this expenditure would not have been required—see details in Appendix IV.

Financing charges

3.7. SHL has had to increase its bank overdraft as a result of the losses incurred due to the collapse of the ceiling. The interest charges on these additional borrowings up to 14 February 1994 amount to £29,400—see details in Appendix V.

Reduction in cleaning staff

3.8. Following the closure of the floor on which the 15 accommodation units were situated, certain staff were made redundant on 29 December 1992. The staff were rehired on 8 November 1993. Salary and associated cost savings amount to £7,460—see details in Appendix III.

Heat and light cost savings

3.9 As a result of the closure of the floor on which the 15 accommodation units were situated, heating and lighting costs were saved. The saving has been calculated on the basis of the actual heating and lighting costs for the period from 25 December 1992 to 6 November 1993 of £34,400. Management estimate that two-thirds of this cost, or £22,900 relates directly to accommodation units and that one-third relates to common areas, such as day areas, administrative areas, kitchens and laundry rooms. The saving is estimated as:

$$\frac{£22,900}{(52-15) \text{ accommodation units}} \times 15 \text{ accommodation units} = £9,280$$

Signed .... Date ....
        Mark Page

APPENDIX I
QUALIFICATIONS AND EXPERIENCE OF MR MARK PAGE
BA(Hons) (Oxon), ACA, MBAE

Mr Page is a partner in the Forensic Service Group of Arthur Price, with specific responsibility for work in the healthcare industry. He qualified as an accountant in 1984 and has been a partner since 1990.

Mr Page performs a range of financial and business consulting assignments, although he has increasingly specialised in commercial litigation and company valuations. He has given evidence in the High Court, the Crown Court and before an independent Tribunal. He is a member of the British Academy of Experts and has acted as an independent expert appointed by the President of the ICAEW.

APPENDIX II
COSTS OF EMERGENCY ACCOMMODATION OF RESIDENTS

[*Not included here due to its length*]

7.38
402

Summary
We assess the total cost of temporary accommodation at £6,480.

APPENDIX III
DETAILS OF STAFF AND ASSOCIATED COSTS DURING CLOSURE
24 DECEMBER 1992 TO 8 NOVEMBER 1993

[*Not included here due to its length*]

Summary
(1) The total cost of staff overtime (Christmas 1992) was £1,495.
(2) The total staff salaries and associated cost savings due to redundancies were £7,460.

APPENDIX IV
DETAILS OF PROMOTIONAL COSTS ASSOCIATED WITH RELETTING

[*Not included here due to its length*]

Summary
Total increased promotional costs were £2,740.

APPENDIX V
DETAILS OF ADDITIONAL FINANCING CHARGES

[*Not included here due to its length*]

Summary
Thus interest charges on additional borrowings up to and including 14 February 1994 were £29,400.

Report of Clifford Knight (7.39)

CLIFFORD KNIGHT BSc (Estate Management) FRICS FSVA ACIArb

SANCTUARY HOUSE ARBITRATION

Opinion concerning Diminution in Value of House through loss of Gibbs ceiling.

Instruction

I, Clifford Knight, of 79 Mount Place, London W2, am instructed by Messrs Kalmsyde & Joyoff, solicitors, to advise on the diminution in value which has resulted from the total loss of the Gibbs ceiling at Sanctuary House, Woodbridge, Suffolk.

Introduction

I read Estate Management at Reading University and, following graduation, in 1956, I joined a firm of Chartered Surveyors in the City of London, completed my professional examinations and training and became an Associate of the Royal Institution of Chartered Surveyors in 1959. Fellowship was achieved in 1973.

7.39
403

I am currently a partner in Janes, Harring & Oddmans (JHO), Chartered Surveyors and became head of the valuation department in 1985.

Before I joined JHO. I worked in the Cambridge office of Chuffer, Link and Paine (CLP), Chartered Surveyors, as a negotiator in the country house department. CLP have a wide and varied practice which covers, *inter alia*, East Anglia.

When I joined my present firm, in 1975, I also specialised in the upper end of the country house market and although I now manage the entire valuations department, I am still involved, day to day, with that particular area of our work.

The Dispute

I visited Sanctuary House on 12 January 1994 specifically to inspect the sitting room and assess what, if any, diminution in value had occurred as a result of the loss of the Gibbs ceiling.

This ceiling had collapsed completely and all that remained of the original feature was the oak laths and approximately five per cent, in area, of the plasterwork and this in ragged fragments around the perimeter.

I was familiar with Sanctuary House, or the Old Manor House as it used to be called, as I had negotiated its sale, whilst at CLP, sometime in September 1974.

The key feature, of this beautiful Queen Anne house, was the Gibbs ceiling, in what is now known as the sitting room but was originally the drawing room.

The ceiling was one of Gibbs's finest works; highly decorative, multicoloured, with many superb embellishments including a distinctive sculpture of swans.

Fortunately we had engaged a professional photographer to take a detailed picture of the ceiling, which we included in our Sales Particulars in 1974. We certainly considered then, and I still hold that view, that this unique feature was an important selling point in the sale of this property.

I did not witness the devastation which occurred, I am told, on Christmas Eve 1992, but I have been shown details, and close-up photographs, professionally taken of the exposed timber laths and the plaster debris, shortly after the tragedy occurred. Copies of these photographs are attached, as well as a copy of the coloured photograph taken in 1974. My colleague, for the Claimant, Professor Richard Rutley, provided the recent photographs and, as such, I therefore take them to be common ground.

It is clear to me, from these photographs, that the plaster is so fragmented as to be unrecognisable as the Gibbs ceiling it was. There did not appear to be any undamaged section of the original ceiling worth attempting to replace.

I am informed that one of the issues in dispute between the parties concerns the possible diminution in value in this property as a result of the loss of this unique feature.

Valuation

I make this valuation on the basis that the lost ceiling was genuinely one designed by, and constructed under the direction of, James Gibbs, *circa* 1682–1754. Having had the benefit of inspecting this house in some detail in 1974 I can say that, in my opinion, this was a genuine Gibbs ceiling having seen a number of such, both Gibbs and Adams ceilings, in various properties in my 37 years in this business.

If I were selling this house today I would be able to draw potential purchasers' attention to many other fine features but, alas, no longer to the Gibbs ceiling. Even if the ceiling, in the drawing room, were replaced with what was, to all intents and purposes, a ceiling identical to that that was lost, it could never be anything other than a modern reproduction and thus less attractive as a selling point.

I am aware that the replacement costs of such a ceiling, with fees and VAT, exceeds £40,000 but I believe that this is irrelevant in assessing it's potential enhancement value as a sales feature.

I make no secret of the fact that, despite almost 40 years' experience in this specialised market, to attempt to assess the value of an individual feature, such as this ceiling, is a difficult task and certainly one that cannot be achieved with any great precision.

I approach this valuation from the viewpoint of a negotiatotor, the role I know best, in this market.

I asked myself, apart from promoting such a feature in the sales literature, could I honestly expect to attract a higher price because of it? After mature and detailed consideration of past transactions of properties with outstanding features, I came to the conclusion that there was no question that a ceiling such as it was, would attract a higher price than a house without such a feature.

I then addressed the question of how much such a feature would be likely to attract, bearing in mind that valuation itself is no science and the value of anything is what someone is prepared to pay, or more exactly what a willing buyer would pay a willing seller, I concluded that in terms of added value I would expect to achieve at least £10,000 more for a house of quality with a genuine Gibbs ceiling than one without such a unique feature.

Equally, using the same criteria, I would be surprised if I was able to persuade a purchaser to spend say, £20,000 more, for such a ceiling, despite being able to show him that a reproduction ceiling would cost in excess of £40,000.

7.39
404

Conclusion

In my opinion Sanctuary House has suffered a diminution in value, as a result of the loss of the Gibbs ceiling, of between £10,000 and £20,000.

Signed ....   Date 18 February 1994
          Clifford Knight BSc
          (Estate Management)
          FRICS FSVA ACIArb

7.39
405

CHAPTER 8

Pre-Hearing Review

Sample Sheet—Summary of Arbitration Cases (8.1 Arb)

SUMMARY OF ARBITRATION CASES/13 AS AT 17 DECEMBER 1993

Date of Appt Nom'd by	Claimant Respondent Ref No	Subject Matter	Amount in Dispute C£ C/C£ Approx Rounded Figures	Stage Settled Date	Comments
20/2/93 RICS	RELIABLE BUILDING LTD SANCTUARY HOUSE LTD 4884	Claim for RBL for monies outstanding from unpaid Certificate and balance of Final Account. Counter-claim defective works and consequential losses of closure of floor say	C£430,000 C/C £460,000	 —	All o/s directions complied with? Arrange Pre-Hearing Review say mid-Jan.

8.1 Arb 407

Order for Directions No 16 Calling Pre-Hearing Review Meeting (8.2 Arb)

IN THE MATTER OF THE ARBITRATION ACTS 1950 TO 1979

AND

IN THE MATTER OF AN ARBITRATION UNDER THE JCT ARBITRATION RULES (18 JULY 1988)

BETWEEN

RELIABLE BUILDERS LIMITED   Claimant

AND

SANCTUARY HOUSE LIMITED   Respondent

8.2 Arb 408

ORDER FOR DIRECTIONS NO 16—BY CONSENT

1.00 There shall be a Pre-Hearing Review Meeting to be held at the offices of Kalmsyde & Joyoff, 48 Crown Street, Ipswich, Suffolk at 10.00 a.m. on Monday 10 January 1994.

2.00 The conduct of the meeting will follow the attached Agenda (8.3 Arb).

3.00 Liberty to Apply.

4.00 Costs to be costs in the reference.

Date: 19 December 1993   **D Emsee, MSc FRICS, FCIArb**
                               Arbitrator

To: Jayrich Associates   Representatives for the Claimant
                               FAO Joel Redman

    Kalmsyde & Joyoff   Solicitors for the Respondent
                               FAO James Crighton

Agenda for Pre-Hearing Review Meeting (8.3 Arb)

IN THE MATTER OF THE ARBITRATION ACTS 1950 TO 1979

AND

IN THE MATTER OF AN ARBITRATION UNDER THE JCT ARBITRATION RULES (18 JULY 1988)

BETWEEN

RELIABLE BUILDERS LIMITED   Claimant

AND

SANCTUARY HOUSE LIMITED   Respondent

PRE-HEARING REVIEW MEETING

8.3 Arb
409

at 10.00 a.m. on 10 January 1994 at the offices of Kalmsyde & Joyoff, 48 Crown Street, Ipswich, Suffolk.

AGENDA

1.00 Introductions

1.01 Confirmation of identity and status of those present.

2.00 Review of issues still in dispute.

3.00 Current position regarding

3.01 Any outstanding Directions.

3.02 Agreement of plans, photographers and other documents.

3.03 Legal representation at the Hearing?

3.04 Identification of Witnesses.

3.05 Hearing bundle.

    3.05.1 Will it be 'Agreed'?

    3.05.2 Properly paginated and annotated (if Claimant's and Respondent's bundles—ensure both the same pagination).

    3.05.3 Core bundle of principal documents?

    3.05.4 What do parties want me to read?
    Three-day delay to remove material objected to.

    3.05.5 Nothing in bundles will become evidence read until adduced as such at the Hearing.

3.06 Law Reports and authorities—copy to Arbitrator seven days before Hearing, with passages (highlighted) on which they wish to rely.

3.07 Sealed offers—how to deal with.

4.00 Determine arrangements for the Hearing

4.01 Estimated duration.

4.02 Claimant will arrange.
Accommodation—retiring rooms?
Set up—witnesses table. (See Arbitrator's preferred layout attached).

4.03 Commencing date. Four-day sitting week. Each sitting day will run from 10.00 a.m. to 5.00 p.m. with one hour recess for luncheon.

4.04 Date for exchange of Witnesses proofs.
Witnesses proofs—to be exchanged simultaneously.
Exchanged proofs to be admitted as evidence-in-chief.

4.05 Date for exchange of Rebuttals to Witnesses proofs—if option adopted.

4.06 Date for delivery of Hearing bundle.

4.07 Date for delivery of advocates opening submissions.

5.00 To Ascertain whether any Further Directions are sought

8.3 Arb 410

6.00 Questions requiring research

When preparing for Hearing take note of any questions which require research to answer, i.e. give your Witnesses notice.

7.00 Security for the Arbitrator's costs

8.00 To deal with any other outstanding matter

D Emsee, MSc, FRICS, FCIArb
Registered Arbitrator
19 December 1993

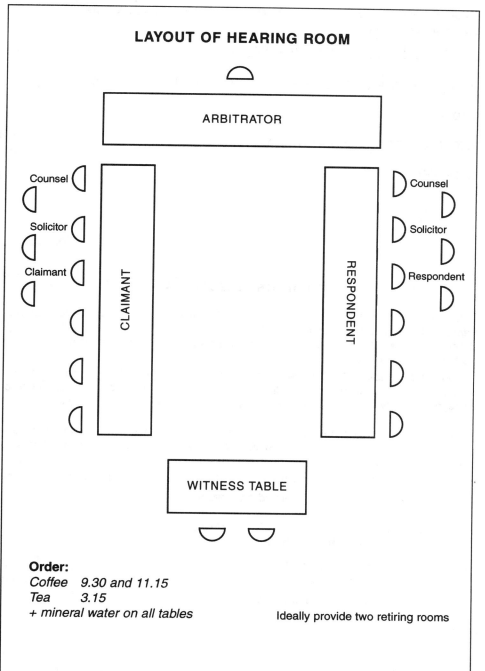

LAYOUT OF HEARING ROOM

ARBITRATOR

Counsel

Solicitor

Claimant

CLAIMANT

RESPONDENT

Counsel

Solicitor

Respondent

8.3 Arb
411

WITNESS TABLE

Order:
Coffee   9.30 and 11.15
Tea   3.15
+ mineral water on all tables   Ideally provide two retiring rooms

Typical Order for Directions 'A' re failure to exchange Witness Statements (8.4/1 Arb)

Urgent Fax & Letter (Recorded Delivery)

IN THE MATTER OF THE ARBITRATION ACTS 1950 TO 1979

AND

IN THE MATTER OF AN ARBITRATION

BETWEEN

Claimant

AND

Respondent

ORDER FOR DIRECTIONS 'A'

**8.4/1 Arb
412**

1.00 The venue for the hearing referred to in 8.00 of my Order for Directions No 7 dated 12 February 1991, shall be at the offices of Messrs
   The hearing shall commence at 10.30 a.m. on April 11 and is scheduled to take four working days, April 11, 12, 15 and 17.

2.00 After considering the Claimant's application dated 5 April 1991, concerning the lack of response from the Respondent to the Claimant's request for exchange of witnesses' proofs of evidence, which were directed to be exchanged not later than 5.00 p.m. today 5 April.

I HEREBY DIRECT that the Respondent shall be debarred from calling any witness whose signed statement has not been exchanged, and a copy delivered to me, not later than 4.00 p.m. on 9 April 1991.

3.00 The costs of, and incidental to, this Order, to be paid by the Respondent in any event.

4.00 Please confirm receipt of this Order by return of fax.

Date: 5 April 1991 **D Emsee MSc, FRICS, FCIArb**
Registered Arbitrator

To: Solicitors for the Claimant
   FAO

   Solicitors for the Respondent
   FAO

Typical Order for Directions 'B' re changed Hearing dates and exchange of Witness Statements (8.4/2 Arb)

<u>Urgent Fax & Letter (Recorded Delivery)</u>

IN THE MATTER OF THE ARBITRATION ACTS 1950 TO 1979

AND

IN THE MATTER OF AN ARBITRATION

BETWEEN

Claimant

AND

Respondent

ORDER FOR DIRECTIONS 'B'

1.00 Following receipt and consideration of the exchange of correspondence between the parties and between the parties and me dated 9 April, as detailed in my letter to the parties dated 11 April I HEREBY DIRECT as follows:

2.00 My Order for Directions 'A' be revoked.

3.00 UNLESS within seven days hereof the Respondent agrees new hearing dates with the Claimant, I shall fix dates myself without further reference to the parties. My available dates are given in the attached letter.

4.00 The Respondent shall have until 5.00 p.m. on 16 April 1991 to exchange witnesses' statements. The Respondent is debarred from calling any witness whose signed statement have not been so exchanged and a copy delivered to me.

5.00 The costs of this Order, and of this adjournment, which include my cancellation charges in accordance with my Terms for four working days, to be paid by the Respondent in any event.

6.00 Please confirm receipt of this Order.

Date: 11 April 1991   **D Emsee, MSc, FRICS, FCIArb**
Registered Arbitrator

To: Solicitors for the Claimant
FAO

Solicitors for the Respondent
FAO

8.4/2 Arb 413

Order for Directions No 17 following Review Meeting (8.5 Arb)

IN THE MATTER OF THE ARBITRATION ACTS 1950 TO 1979

AND

IN THE MATTER OF AN ARBITRATION UNDER THE JCT ARBITRATION RULES (18 JULY 1988)

BETWEEN

RELIABLE BUILDERS LIMITED   Claimant

AND

SANCTUARY HOUSE LIMITED   Respondent

ORDER FOR DIRECTIONS NO 17

Upon hearing Counsel for both Parties, the following Directions are given by CONSENT (unless otherwise noted) and it is HEREBY DIRECTED that:

1.00 Review of Issues

Each party will produce a statement of the issues as they see them. Such statement to be delivered to me, copied to the other side, with the hearing bundle and other documents, not later than midday 28 February 1994.

2.00 Current Position Generally

2.01 There were no matters outstanding arising from my Directions.

2.02 The parties will attempt to agree a schedule of common ground but, at this stage, no Direction will be given regarding this matter.

2.03 Both parties will be represented at the Hearing by Counsel.

2.04 The witnesses that each party intends to call are as follows:

For the Claimant
Witnesses of Fact
Harold Hocking — Managing Director RBL
William Reeves — Contract Administrator RBL
John Watts — Site Foreman RBL

Expert Witnesses
Joel Redman — Claims Consultant
David Sharkey — Building Surveyor
Richard Rutley — Valuation Surveyor
Jamal Hussein — Accountant
Ifram Carmel — Fireproof Coating Specialist

For the Respondent
   Witnesses of Fact
   William Bliss   —   M/D SHL
   Constance Bliss —   Dir SHL
   Hermione Glover —   Matron SHL
   Max D'Iffy   —   Architect, Senior Partner TAP
   Frances Hutch   —   Job Architect TAP

   Expert Witnesses
   Stanley Longdon —   Building Surveyor
   Miles Maclean   —   Quantity Surveyor
   Clifford Knight   —   Valuation Surveyor
   Mark Page   —   Accountant

It is understood that no witnesses of fact may be called who have not exchanged proofs of evidence, as directed by order for Directions No 2, item 13.00. Similarly no expert may be called who has not exchanged reports, as directed by Order for Directions item 9.02.

2.05 An 'agreed' Hearing bundle will be prepared and a core bundle of principal documents. This latter bundle will be delivered to me not later than 1 March 1994 and it should be read by me prior to the commencement of the Hearing.

All bundles remain the primary responsibility of the Claimant, who is also responsible for ensuring that they are properly paginated and annotated.

On receipt of the core bundle I will await three days before reading it, in order to give each party the opportunity of checking through it and asking me to have removed any document for which that party claims privilege. On receipt of this request such document will be removed by my secretary or pupil and returned to the applying party.

Should the other party object to the document's removal I will hear both parties at the commencement of the Hearing and then determine whether that document is to be admitted or not.

2.06 Should either party wish to refer to authorities or Law Reports not previously included with their statements, then copies of such, with the relevant passages suitably highlighted, should be delivered to me, copied to the other side, not later than 1 March 1994.

2.07 I shall be handed a sealed envelope, by Claimant's Counsel, at the commencement of the Hearing which will contain either details of any 'without prejudice' offer to settle the Claim and/or the Counterclaim, or it may contain either a blank sheet of paper or a note to the effect that no such offers have been made.

This envelope will not be opened by me until I have determined the substantive issues and completed the draft of that part of my Award. It will then be opened in front of a witness who will attest to the fact by signing the envelope.

3.00 Hearing Arrangements

3.01 Both parties will attempt to agree a venue which meets my minimum requirements. In the event of agreement the Claimant will let me have details of such agreed location, not later than 5.00 p.m. 25 January 1994.

3.02 All pre-hearing documents, including Counsels' opening submissions, as directed, will be delivered to me not later than midday 28 February 1994.

3.03 Counsel to give notice, not later than midday 28 February 1994, to the other side of any questions that they are likely to put in cross-examination which may require research to answer.

3.04 The strict rules of evidence may be waived, particularly in respect to Leading

8.5 Arb 415

Questions and Hearsay, subject to a sensible application of this relaxation and an acceptance, by me, of reasonable objection by either Counsel.

Both parties reserve the right to apply to me, during the Hearing, to restore adherence to the strict rules and recognised procedures if they consider that the agreed relaxation is not working.

3.05 Immediately following Claimant's Counsel's Opening, the Respondent's Counsel will outline her Defence.

AND IT IS FURTHER DIRECTED THAT

4.00 Security for Costs

I have given notice to the parties that I intend to exercise my rights both under Rule 12.1.3 and clause 8) of my Terms and Conditions to seek security from the parties for my fees and expenses.

In view of the cross applications for security, received today from each party, I will defer my application and deal with it at the same time as I deal with that of the parties.

5.00 Costs in the reference.

6.00 Liberty to apply.

Date: 11 January 1994   **D Emsee, MSc FRICS, FCIArb**
                          Registered Arbitrator

To: Jayrich Associates   Representative for the Claimant
                           FAO Joel Redman

    Kalmsyde & Joyoff   Solicitors for the Respondent
                           FAO James Crighton

8.5 Arb
416

Typical Order for Directions 'C' re Notice under Civil Evidence Act (8.6 Arb)

IN THE MATTER OF THE ARBITRATION ACTS 1950 TO 1979

AND

IN THE MATTER OF AN ARBITRATION UNDER THE JCT ARBITRATION RULES (18 JULY 1988)

BETWEEN

RELIABLE BUILDERS LIMITED   Claimant

AND

SANCTUARY HOUSE LIMITED   Respondent

ORDER FOR DIRECTIONS NO 'C'

8.6 Arb 417

WHEREAS on 11 January 1994

1.00 The Claimant served notice on the Respondent under s.2 of the Civil Evidence Act 1968 requesting agreement to admit the written evidence of Mr   and Mr   attached as Appendices A & B, Mr Richard Rutley's expert report, without having to call that witness

AND

2.00 On 19 January 1994, the Respondent serve a counter notice, as required by this Act, requesting that both witnesses be called.

3.00 Having considered this notice and counterclaim and the content of the statements referred to in the said notice and counter notice

I HEREBY DIRECT that

3.01 The first witness, Mr   , need not be called and I will admit the said statement in evidence.

3.02 The second witness, Mr   , should be called in order for me to admit his statement in evidence.

4.00 Costs in the reference.

5.00 Liberty to apply.

Date: 21 January 1994   **D Emsee, MSc FRICS, FCIArb**
                               Registered Arbitrator

To: Jayrich Associates   Representative for the Claimant
                               FAO Joel Redman

    Kalmsyde & Joyoff   Solicitors for the Respondent
                               FAO James Crighton

Typical Order for Directions 'D' following *typical* Pre-Hearing Review (8.7 Arb)

<u>Fax & Post</u>

IN THE MATTER OF THE ARBITRATION ACTS 1950 TO 1979

AND

IN THE MATTER OF AN ARBITRATION UNDER THE JCT ARBITRATION RULES (18 JULY 1988)

BETWEEN

Y LIMITED   Claimant

AND

Z LIMITED   Respondent

AND

X PLC   Third Party

ORDER FOR DIRECTIONS NO 'D'

Following the Pre-Hearing Review held at   s' offices, 17 April 1993, the following Directions are given

BY CONSENT unless otherwise noted.

(Note: All deadline dates, given below, shall be 1993 and shall mean 5.00 p.m. on the date stated, unless otherwise noted.)

1.00 Further and Better Particulars

The following Requests are still outstanding and will be answered by the dates given below:
  1.01 By X   to Y   (re   &   s' letter 12 March 1993) by 24 April
       1993.
  1.02 By Y   to Z   . Request 14 January 1993—items, 12, 18 and 22–27 inclusive
       (re   s' letter 16 April) by 2 May.
  1.03 By Z   to Y   re plant hire costs (re   s' letter 16 April) will be dealt
with in Witness Statements but a copy of this part of the Reply by 9.00 a.m. 21 April.

2.00 Documents

The parties will be limited to relying on those documents disclosed up to and including 2 May with the delivery of the Reply to 1.02 above.

If any party wishes to refer to any documents not disclosed by 2 May, consent to do so will only be at my absolute discretion.

3.00 Pleadings

3.01 Pleadings will close with the delivery of the Reply to 1.02 above.

3.02 Item 2.00 of my Order for Directions No 10 is hereby cancelled. It is now agreed that XYZ will prepare a comprehensive cross-reference of each discrete issue pleaded including claim, defence, reply and any Requests for Further and Better Particulars and Replies (whether formal or informal) including, where appropriate, reference to Schedules.

3.03 All pleadings, together with Schedules, Requests and Replies, as above, will be filed separately as part of the Hearing Bundle with the index, as set out above.

3.04 The index alone will be delivered to me not later than 7 May.

4.00 Further Inspection Visit

4.01 Z   intends to carry out more tests on the   in order to more particularise defects (if any).

4.02 They will inform X   and Y   when these tests will be carried out to give them the opportunity of having representatives present to observe these tests.

4.03 I will also be invited to attend and observe these tests.

4.04 X   , Y   and I will be informed, as soon as possible, when these tests are scheduled to be carried out.

8.7 Arb 419

5.00 Meeting with Experts—9 February 1993

5.01 Y   will prepare and deliver, by 21 April, a note of their understanding of what was agreed at the meeting of experts, chaired by me, 9 February 1993. In particular, this note will answer points 18 (1) and (2) of Miss   's List of Issues sent out under cover of   's letter 16 April 1993.

5.02 Z   to confirm to Y   , by 23 April, copied to X, if finish date for Activity 700 was agreed, as averred by Y, as 20 October 1991?

5.03 At this meeting Z's representative agreed to produce an Activity Bar Chart illustrating how Z alleges that Y caused disruption to the works. Any response to the note in 5.01 above will include this Bar Chart and will be delivered not later than 29 April.

5.04 Counsel for Y   noted that, at a meeting in early November 1992, Y   asked for Critical Path Analyses (CPAs) for other Works Contractors where their work overlapped with Y's. Such CPAs were never provided.

Counsel for Z has no recollection of such CPAs being requested. However, Z will consider the possibility of providing these voluntarily between now and the commencement of the Hearing.

This being so, Counsel for Y   will make no formal application, at this stage, for such CPAs.

6.00 Order for Directions No 11

6.01 Item 8.02 is still outstanding. Y   will provide to Z   , copied to X   and me, not later than 21 April.

6.02 Items 8.03 and 8.04. Z   will provide to Y, copied to X and me, not later than 29 April.

6.03 Item 8.06. Items 8.06.1 and 8.06.2 have already been provided. Items 8.06.3 and 8.06.4 are dealt with by way of assessment/reconstruction. The original worksheets having been lost/destroyed in the recent move.

Item 8.06.5. Two 'typical' months selected are November and January. These months will be used in respect of workshop fabrication time *only* and Z/X reserve the right to request that other months are also looked at following the outcome of looking at these two 'typical' months.

7.00 Common Ground

List of broad issues only to be provided after meetings with Experts and to be delivered to me, not later than 13 May. Y   responsible for the preparation of a consolidated schedule of common ground.

8.00 Issues

The date for item 18.00, Order for Directions No 9, shall now be 14 May, at which time each party is to deliver to me, and to the other parties, a list of outstanding issues of dispute between them and the other parties.

9.00 Law Reports/Authorities

Copies of all authorities and/or Law Reports, on which the parties wish to rely, with relevant passages suitably highlighted, will be delivered to me and the other parties, not later than 14 May.

10.00 Counsel's Submissions

10.01 Written opening submissions, to be delivered to me, copied to the other parties, not later than 14 May. Each Counsel will be allotted up to two hours to orally introduce their case and outline their Defence to the other parties' case.

10.02 Closing submissions will be delivered to me, copied to the other parties, not later than seven days following the last Hearing day and thereafter Counsel will make an oral submission on this written submission again, limited to two hours each, on a date to be determined at the close of the Hearing.

11.00 Reasoned Award

11.01 Counsel will incorporate, in their written opening and closing submissions, formulation of any point of law, on which they require me to give reasons in my Award—such formulation to be identified under a discreet heading, not merely embodied within the general submission.

11.02 Given that the submissions identify the points of law, it is accepted that such will satisfy the requirement of Rule 11.1.

11.03 A 'Final Award, save as to Costs' is required with arrangements for a separate Costs Hearing to be made at the close of the Hearing.

11.04 I am required to incorporate my determination of the issues in dispute between all three parties into one Award.

12.00 Security for Costs

12.01 For Z's Costs

Y/Z are confident that a satisfactory Guarantee will be entered into if not, this application for Security will be the subject of a further application.

12.02 For My Costs/Expenses

All three parties will bear one-third of the Security for my costs/expenses, details of which I shall submit shortly, together with a further Interim Fee Statement, which will also be met in equal proportions by all three parties.

13.00 Experts

13.01 Item 8.01 of Order for Directions No 9 is changed to 'three Experts of different disciplines'. It is also accepted that some witnesses may be witnesses of fact and opinion which, in turn, may mean that more than three individuals give opinion evidence.

13.02 The Experts from each party will meet, on Tuesday 22 April at 10.00 a.m. to attempt to agree on variations currently scheduled as in dispute. This meeting will take place at 's offices at and, if necessary, and at the joint convenience of the Experts, further meetings, on the days following 22 April, will be arranged, if there is scope for further progress.

13.03 Experts from each party will meet, on Thursday 30 April at 10.00 a.m. to attempt to agree on elements of *quantum only* on both Y's and Z's Loss and Expense Claims. This meeting will take place at 's offices at Street, and, if necessary, and at the joint convenience of the Experts, further meetings, on the days following 30 April, will be held if there is further scope for progress.

13.04 No separate meetings will take place between me and the Experts before the dates scheduled for the Hearing.

13.05 Experts' reports will be exchanged on 7 May.

14.00 Witnesses of Fact

8.7 Arb
421

14.01 The parties intend to call the following witnesses:

14.01.1—Y
Joe Bloggs	—	Contracts Manager
Francis Hutch	—	Project Architect
Tom Kitchen	—	Assistant Architect
John Sidley	—	Independent QS
Alan Plover	—	Y's Job QS
Kevin Bodger	—	Godsgift
	—	Consultant
Charles Notts	—	Y's Finance Director

14.01.2—Z
Peter Farmer	—	Construction Manager
Tim Grey	—	Contract Administrator

14.03.3—X
William Whilder	—	Project Manager
Simon Black	—	Assistant
Mervyn Peyton	—	Admin.

14.02 The date in item 12.03 of Order for Directions No 9 shall be altered to 28 April. In addition, the parties will exchange Rebuttals to these proofs on 7 May.

15.00 Hearing Bundle

15.01 The preparation of the Hearing Bundle shall be the responsibility of Y who should ensure that it is properly paginated and annotated.

15.02 Bundles to be exchanged not later than 8 May.

15.03 My bundle will be delivered direct to the Hearing location.

15.04 Not later than 12 May, each party will inform me, copied to the other parties, what documents, of those in my possession, they wish me to read/study in preparation for the Hearing.

15.05 The Claimant will provide me with a revolving stand sufficiently large to accommodate my entire Hearing Bundle.

16.00 *Modus Operandi* for Hearing

16.01 The sequence of examination of issues will be discussed at the commencement of the Hearing, at which time it will be decided what matters, if any, with which I am to deal with the Experts alone—such meetings, if any, to be held on the days allocated to the Hearing.

16.02 While Counsel were not unanimous on the practicality of prior notification of cross-examination questions, it was agreed that they would meet, prior to the Hearing, to attempt to agree on the division of time allocated to each within the maximum of the 40 days allocated for the Hearing. If, during the hearing, it seems to Counsel that this voluntary arrangement is not working, or it is having the effect of prejudicing one or other parties' case then Counsel have Liberty to Apply to review this arrangement.

I will be notified, at the commencement of the Hearing, of whatever agreement is reached on this issue between Counsel.

In any event, although prior notification of cross-examination questions is not agreed, I ask Counsel to take note of item 8.00 of the Pre-Hearing Review Agenda.

16.03 In determining the order of events for the Hearing the Extension of Time Claim will be dealt with at an early stage.

16.04 I may photograph each witness subject to objection from that witness.

I may tape-record the proceedings—such recording to be solely for my own use.

17.00 Offers to Settle

17.01 Should any party wish to make a Calderbank offer to settle—that is 'without prejudice' save as to costs—the parties have agreed that such should be made not later than 2 May with acceptance thereof not later than 9 May.

17.02 On the day on which I hear costs submissions I shall be handed a sealed envelope in which there shall be details of any offer to settle. I will open this envelope, in the presence of the parties, having heard their cost submissions.

18.00 Costs to be costs in the reference.

19.00 Fit for Counsel.

20.00 Liberty to Apply.

Date: 18 April 1993   **D Emsee, MSc, FRICS, FCIArb**
Arbitrator

Messrs   Solicitors for Y
FAO Miss

Messrs   Solicitors for Z
FAO Miss

Messrs   Solicitors for X
FAO Mr

8.7 Arb
422

Typical Unless Order for Directions 'L' where party fails to comply with Directions for Specific Discovery (8.8 Arb)

IN THE MATTER OF THE ARBITRATION ACTS 1950 TO 1979

AND

IN THE MATTER OF AN ARBITRATION UNDER THE JCT ARBITRATION RULES (18 JULY 1988)

BETWEEN

RELIABLE BUILDERS LIMITED   Claimant

AND

SANCTUARY HOUSE LIMITED   Respondent

UNLESS ORDER—ORDER FOR DIRECTIONS NO 'L'

**8.8 Arb
423**

1.00 WHEREAS the Claimant requested inspection of various additional documentation by letter 10 June 1993 ref   and following an exchange of correspondence between the Claimant's solicitor and the Respondent's solicitor 10–13 June inclusive

I HEREBY DIRECT

that UNLESS the Respondent make such documents available for discovery not later than 5.00 p.m. on Monday   June 1993 the Respondent's counterclaim for loss of production shall be struck out with associated costs to the Claimant.

2.00 The costs of and incidental to this Direction to be paid by the Respondent in any event.

Date: 1993   **D Emsee, MSc, FRICS, FCIArb
                        Registered Arbitrator**

To: Jayrich Associates   Representatives for the Claimant
                          FAO Joel Redman

    Kalmsyde & Joyoff   Solicitors for the Respondent
                          FAO James Crighton

CHAPTER 9

Security for Costs

Ad Hoc Arbitration Agreement empowering Arbitrator to deal with Security for Costs (9.1 Arb)

IN THE MATTER OF THE ARBITRATION ACTS 1950 TO 1979

AND

IN THE MATTER OF AN ARBITRATION UNDER THE JCT ARBITRATION RULES (18 JULY 1988)

BETWEEN

XYZ BUILDERS LIMITED   Claimant

AND

BLEAK HOUSE LIMITED   Respondent

**9.1 Arb
425**

ARBITRATION AGREEMENT

We, **XYZ BUILDERS LTD** and **BLEAK HOUSE LTD** hereby agree that D Emsee, Arbitrator in this reference, shall have power to order that the Claimant, and the Counter-Claimant (if appropriate), give security for the costs of the arbitration, or any part thereof, in such form or in such amount as the Arbitrator, in his absolute discretion, shall determine.

The Arbitrator's determination of security of costs applications shall be by 'documents only' unless otherwise agreed.

Should the Arbitrator decide that it is necessary for him to take independent financial advice once he has received all the necessary documentation the parties agree to his consulting an independent expert and hereby agree to reimburse the Arbitrator the reasonable cost thereby incurred.

Signed ....   For Claimant
                                     XYZ Builders Ltd

Signed ....   For Respondent
                                     Bleak House Ltd
                                     Date ....

Order for Directions No 18 re Security for Costs (9.2 Arb)

IN THE MATTER OF THE ARBITRATION ACTS 1950 TO 1979

AND

IN THE MATTER OF AN ARBITRATION UNDER THE JCT ARBITRATION RULES (18 JULY 1988)

BETWEEN

RELIABLE BUILDERS LIMITED   Claimant

AND

SANCTUARY HOUSE LIMITED   Respondent

ORDER FOR DIRECTIONS NO 18

Further to the Claimant's Application, 11 January 1994, and the Counter-Claimant's Application of the same date, for Security for their Costs, I exercise the power I have by virtue of Rules 12.1.3, 12.1.6 and my own Terms and Conditions cl. 8, signed by the Claimant 26 February 1993 and by the Respondent on 23 March 1993.

ACCORDINGLY I HEREBY DIRECT as follows:

1.00 The Claimant is to provide credible evidence to me by Affidavit, copied to the Respondent, showing why he believes that the Respondent will not be able to pay the Claimant's costs if the Claimant is successful in defending the Respondent's Counterclaim in this reference. This Affidavit to be served not later than 5.00 p.m. 20 January 1994.

2.00 The Respondent is to provide credible evidence to me by Affidavit, copied to the Claimant, showing why he believes that the Claimant will not be able to pay the Respondent's costs if the Respondent is successful in defending the Claim in this reference. This Affidavit to be served not later than 5.00 p.m. 20 January 1994.

3.00 Both Affidavits 1.00 and 2.00 above to state the amount of security required and to be accompanied by a skeleton make-up of costs showing the amount of the applying party's costs incurred to date and an estimate of their future costs.

4.00 Following receipt of these Affidavits the Claimant and the Respondent will serve on me, copied to the other side, not later than 5.00 p.m. 27 January 1994, an Affidavit in reply. Such Affidavits will be accompanied by copies of all documents necessary to support the contentions in that Affidavit, i.e. annual accounts, bank statements, etc.

5.00 If, on receipt of the Affidavits reply and supporting documentation, the financial position of either party is not absolutely clear to me from these documents then, on my request, that party will arrange for a separate Affidavit from an independent financial adviser, interpreting these financial statements.

6.00 In addition, or alternatively, on receipt of all Affidavits and supporting documents, I may then decide that I need independent assistance to interpret these documents prior to determining this issue. If I decide on this step I will inform the parties of the name of the person from whom I intend to take advice and give them 24 hours to agree or object. The reasonable costs incurred of consulting an independent expert will be reimbursed to me as part of my fees and expenses.

7.00 I shall hear the parties, or their representatives, on these respective applications, on 14 February 1994, at Jayrich Associates' offices at Swansea House, 48 Queens Road, Norwich, Norfolk. The Hearing will commence at 10.00 a.m. and continue, if necessary, until 5.30 p.m. with one hour recess for luncheon.

BY CONSENT the parties agree to divide the time available equally between them and to restrict the hearing of this matter to one day.

8.00 I shall embody my determination on this issue in an Order for Directions. In the same Order I shall include security for my own fees and expenses in accordance with cl. 8 of my Terms and Conditions.

9.00 Should either party fail to provide such security as I may direct, either for my own fees and expenses or those of another party, then I may stay the proceedings until such Direction is complied with costs 'thrown away' to be paid by the defaulting party in any event.

10.00 Liberty to Apply.

11.00 Costs in the reference.

3 January 1994	**D Emsee, MSc, FRICS, FCIArb** **Arbitrator**
To: Jayrich Associates	Representatives for the Claimant FAO Joel Redman
Kalmsyde & Joyoff	Solicitors for the Respondent FAO James Crighton

9.2 Arb 427

427

Order for Directions No 19, Award of Security for Costs (9.3 Arb)

IN THE MATTER OF THE ARBITRATION ACTS 1950 TO 1979

AND

IN THE MATTER OF AN ARBITRATION UNDER THE JCT ARBITRATION RULES (18 JULY 1988)

BETWEEN

RELIABLE BUILDERS LIMITED   Claimant

AND

SANCTUARY HOUSE LIMITED   Respondent

ORDER FOR DIRECTIONS NO 19—SECURITY FOR COSTS

9.3 Arb 428

In accordance with the jurisdiction conferred upon me by Rules 12.1.3, 12.1.6 and my Terms and Conditions cl.8) and following the hearing on the parties' cross applications to provide security for the other's costs in this arbitration, held at Jayrich Associates' offices, Swansea House, 48 Queens Road, Norwich, Norfolk, on 14 February 1994, at which I heard Mr Redman for the Claimant and Miss O'Brien, of Counsel, for the Respondent,

IT IS ORDERED THAT

1.00 The Claimant shall provide security for the Respondent's costs in this arbitration in the sum of £80,000 (Eighty Thousand Pounds).

2.00 Security shall be provided by means of a legal charge over the parcel of land, offered and owned by the Claimant company's managing director, situated at 18 Marshland Road, Colchester, as detailed in HEH '3' of Mr Harold Edwin Hocking's Affidavit sworn on 19 January 1994.

3.00 The Respondent shall provide security for the Claimant's costs of defending the counterclaim in this arbitration in the sum of £85,000 (Eighty-Five Thousand Pounds).

This security shall be in cash or in such other form as shall be satisfactory to the Claimant.

In the event of failure to agree on the form of security the question shall be referred to me for determination and my decision shall be final.

4.00 The Claimant shall provide security for my fees and expenses in this arbitration in the sum of £5000 (Five Thousand Pounds) and in view of the Respondent's counterclaim, the Respondent shall also provide security for my fees and expenses in the sum of £5000 (Five Thousand Pounds), all in accordance with the powers conferred on me by the parties' signature to my Terms (cl. 8).

This security is not client's money but represents fees to which I would be entitled, by virtue of my Terms, should this case settle or the Hearing be postponed for some reason. The money will not therefore be kept in a separate account.

5.00 The parties have until 5.00 p.m. on Friday 25 February 1994 to comply with this Order for Directions after which, on application of either party, at my absolute discretion, I may order that all further proceedings in this arbitration shall be stayed until the security directed, has been provided.

    6.00 The costs to be Costs in the Reference.

    7.00 Fit for Counsel.

GIVEN UNDER MY HAND IN LONDON THIS 21ST DAY OF FEBRUARY 1994

D Emsee MSc FRICS FCIArb
Arbitrator

To: Jayrich Associates	Respondents for the Claimant FAO Joel Redman
Kalmsyde & Joyoff	Solicitors for the Respondent FAO James Crighton

9.3 Arb
429

429

CHAPTER 10

The Hearing

1. Checklist for Hearing (10.1 Arb)

CHECKLIST FOR HEARING

Bibles
Pens including coloured markers (plus refill cartridges)
Ruler
Counsel's Notebook—ready marked up
Glasses
Tape Recorder/Tapes/Batteries
Polaroid Camera/Film/Flash and spares
Pocket Watch
Bundles previously sent including:
    Pleadings
    Witness Proofs
    Opening Submissions
    Legal Authorities

Textbooks

Mustill & Boyd
Merkin
Neil F Jones
Cato
Form of Contract and appropriate Textbook on Form
Notes for Hearing
DE's written summary of current situation

At Commencement of Hearing

(i) Hear both sides of summary of outstanding issues—has dispute narrowed?

(ii) Discuss order of witnesses.
    If Scott Schedule—both experts sworn together?

(iii) Strict Rules of Evidence
    If, and to what extent should they be relaxed particularly in connection with hearsay?

(iv) Is there a sealed envelope?

D Emsee, MSc, FRICS, FCIArb
21 September 1994

2. Notes for Hearing (10.2 Arb)

NOTES FOR HEARING

Start by inviting introductions of those present then invite Claimant to start.

Ask questions after re-examination in explanation of answers given. Rarely intervene in cross-examination.

If Hearing adjourned before Witness has concluded all three stages of examination remind Witness that he is still under oath and must not discuss the matters in dispute until he has concluded his Evidence.

Arguments on points of law best left until Evidence is complete.

When Arbitrator is convinced on a point he can indicate that he is prepared to accept something as fact without further evidence being given on that point.

If, in Evidence-in-Chief matters are introduced which the Arbitrator considers cannot possibly assist him to decide the issues before him he should ask the advocate whether this section of evidence can possibly be relevant.

If a question is put in re-examination that did not arise out of cross-examination allow it and then invite the opposing advocate to cross-examine on that point.

End hearing by inviting each party, in turn, Respondent first then Claimant, to address you on Interest (if pleaded) then on Costs.

10.2 Arb
432

3. List of Issues (10.3)

RELIABLE BUILDERS LIMITED V SANCTUARY HOUSE LIMITED— ARBITRATION

List of Issues agreed between Counsel

(Handed to Arbitrator at commencement of Hearing)

1. To how much, if any, extension of time is the Claimant entitled?

2. To how much, if any, is the Claimant entitled by way of repayment of liquidated damages?

Subsidiary question: Is the Respondent entitled to a certificate of non-completion and, if yes, what are the terms of that certificate?

3. To what is the Claimant entitled under the final account, excluding claims to loss and expense and excluding any set-offs for defects?

Subsidiary question: Is the Claimant entitled to payment of certificate 12?

4. To how much, if any, is the Claimant entitled by way of loss and expense?

5. To how much, if any, is the Claimant entitled by way of damages for breach of contract arising out of hindrance of its progress by the Respondent?

6. To how much, if any, is the Claimant entitled by way of damages for breach of contract arising out of non-payment of certificates?

7. To how much, if any, by way of interest is the Claimant entitled?

8. Were there breaches of contract which resulted in defects in the works executed by the Claimant? If so, what is the value of those defects which the Respondent was entitled to set off against Architect Certificates?

9. To what damages (including consequential losses) is the Respondent entitled?

10. To how much, if any, by way of interest is the Respondent entitled?

Dated: 4 March 1994

Toby Belcher
Counsel for the Claimant

Bernadette O'Brien
Counsel for the Respondent

10.3
433

4. Typical Oath or Affirmation (10.4 Arb)

FORM OF OATH

I swear by Almighty God that the evidence I shall give touching the matters in dispute in this Reference shall be the truth, the whole truth and nothing but the truth.

FORM OF AFFIRMATION

I solemnly, sincerely and truly declare and affirm that I will true answers make to all such questions as shall be asked of me touching the matters in this Reference.

10.4 Arb
434

5. Respondent's Closing Submissions (10.5)

IN THE MATTER OF THE ARBITRATION ACTS 1950 TO 1979

AND

IN THE MATTER OF AN ARBITRATION UNDER THE JCT ARBITRATION RULES (18 JULY 1988)

BETWEEN

RELIABLE BUILDERS LIMITED   Claimant

AND

SANCTUARY HOUSE LIMITED   Respondent

RESPONDENT'S CLOSING SUBMISSIONS

1.00 *General*

1.1 The Arbitrator has directed that final submissions be made in writing. This submission deals both with the Respondent's defence to the claim and its own counterclaim.

1.2 In accordance with the principle that the Claimant, in any particular claim, should have the last word, the Respondent reserves the right to make further submissions in response to RBL's case on the Counterclaim.

2.00 *The Delay Claim*

2.1 This delay claim reduces itself, in the Respondent's submission to some 13 headings. These have been broadly agreed with the Claimant and amount to the following:

   (1) Removals, demolitions and form openings
   (2) Form lift-shafts
   (3) Roof repairs—strip roof
   (4) Roof repairs—timber
   (5) Window replacements
   (6) Carpentry first fix
   (7) M & E first fix to existing building
   (8) M & E first fix to extension
   (9) Carpentry second fix
 (10) M & E second fix to existing building
 (11) M & E second fix to new extension
 (12) Roof repairs—leadwork
 (13) Decorations

2.1.1 These submissions deal with each of these items in turn.

2.2 Removals, demolition and form openings

2.2.1 The Claimant's case amounted to three items: that there was inaccurate survey information; that drawings 04/B and 05/B were provided late and caused delay and that there was additional work in AI's 4f, 4g, 4h, 5a, 5c, 6a, 6b, 6c and 10b—which led to delay.

2.2.2 In evidence the Respondents accepted—as they do now—that there was inaccurate survey information issued initially. But it is the Respondent's case, supported by the evidence, that the required amendments were reissued in accordance with the requirements of the programme. There was no delay.

2.2.3 It is not accepted that the evidence supported the Claimant's case that drawings 04/B and 05/B were issued late. Even if they were late, no delay was caused.

2.2.4 The fact of additional work on the AI's is accepted. But, again, there has been no evidence of delay.

2.2.5 In the event the evidence did not support a case that this item was on the critical path. The relevant critical activity was the lift-shaft.

2.2.6 Even this was a critical item or might have been, the dominant delay at the time was in the area of the lift-shaft—the incorrect fabrication of the trimmer beams. This was a matter for the contractor.

2.2.7 No award of extension of time should be made under this heading.

2.3 Form Lift-shaft

2.3.1 The Claimant claims delay caused by additional work as set out in AI 2a. Essentially the claim is for one week's critical delay.

2.3.2 The Respondent accepts that the construction of the lift-shaft was amended by AI 2a.

2.3.3 In any event it was clear from the evidence that the Claimant had failed to reprogramme the works when it could have done so, and so avoided the delay. Insofar as it suffered delay, it was its own fault.

2.3.4 Further this item was arguably not on the critical path.

2.3.5 Examination of the evidence does not support the Claimant's contention that critical delay resulted to elements of the roof.

2.3.6 Any assessment of extension of time for this item should be made in the light of concurrent delay caused by the use of engineering bricks.

[*Counsel's submissions continued in this vein covering all 13 items.*]

10.5
436

2.14 Conclusion on Extension of Time

2.14.1 As will be seen from the above the Respondent accepts critical delay of nine weeks three days. See also Maclean report at 2.21.

2.14.2 The admitted delay all carried loss and expense.

2.14.3 The following part of the submission will consider the financial consequences of this concession, and the evidence on quantum generally.

3.00 Loss and Expense

3.1 General

3.1.1 It is an overriding factor that application for loss and expense was made late. The claim should not be permitted at all.

3.1.2 Subject to this, and without prejudice to this point, the Respondent makes its submissions on the various head of loss below.

3.1.3 It should be noted (see Maclean para 3.30) that the Respondent accepts the Claimant's figures as weekly rates.

3.2 Site Staff

3.2.1 The evidence suggested by Mr Maclean's contentions, viz:

(a) That the Claimant only paid for a site agent and a trades' foreman in his supervision costs;

(b) That the provision for Peter Murphy, the Ganger, was in the Claimant's rates for work items. Where work items have been varied and the quantities increased, part of the cost of Peter Murphy has been recovered.

(c) That the provision for Graham Smith, the quantity surveyor, is in the Claimant's provision for overheads and should not be duplicated.

3.3 Site Accommodation

3.3.1 The evidence support Mr Maclean's contentions, viz:

(a) It is not appropriate to use internal hire charges to calculate loss and expense;

(b) The correct basis for the consideration of such costs is the depreciation of such items plus an allowance for loss of the use of capital;

(c) The Claimant's claim should be reduced by 50 per cent.

[Counsel's submission continued by going through each item of loss and expense in a similar fashion.]

3.14 Conclusion on Loss and Expense

3.14.1 The evidence has supported Mr Maclean's conclusions and figures.

3.14.2 These conclusions are as follows:

Prolongation costs	12,144
Additional staff and equipment	6,956
Head Office costs	9,680
Disturbance of labour	13,515
Inflation	Nil
	£42,295

4.00 *A Sum Claimed under the Contract*

4.1 The amount claimed under the contract is £45,835.10. The calculation of this sum is set out at paragraph 14.3 of the Amended Statement of Claim.

4.2 There is the further sum of £10,954 not paid under certificate 12. It is set out at paragraph 14.2.

4.3 It is accepted that subject to the counterclaim, the sum of £10,954 is payable to the Claimant. The Respondent's calculation of the final account exceeds the gross value of certificate 12. It will be necessary for the Arbitrator, in making his Award, to take into account deductions in respect of defects, liquidated sums and retention, as may be appropriate.

4.4 The Respondent contends that the gross value of the final account is £633,981. This compares with the Claimant's calculation at £656,285.

4.5 Although the difference is relatively small it will be necessary for the Arbitrator to examine and reach conclusions upon the differences between the parties.

4.6 As a general contention, the Respondent submits that the Arbitrator should prefer their figures, i.e. those of Mr Maclean. The latter was unshaken in cross-examination and a very credible witness all-round.

4.7 The Arbitrator has no need to concern himself with omissions. These are agreed at £63,351. Differences do, however, arise over additions. These are as follows:

Item 3a	Dip & strip carved brackets	£156.23
Item 3b	Label and strip moulded work	£371.00
	(Etc)	

10.5
437

4.8 In his oral evidence Mr Maclean explained, in each instance, why he declined to allow the Claimant for each item. Broadly his case was that the item in question was not a variation. It is submitted that those explanations were cogent and convincing and should be adopted wholesale by the Arbitrator.

4.9 There appears to be no continuing dispute (if ever there was one) over provisional sums and contingencies

4.10 There is, however, a dispute over remeasurement. The dispute is over some £10,939 and relates to the following items:

	Amount Claimed
(1) Additional removal of topsoil and reduced level dig	1,440.00
(2) Additional trench excavation and cart away	450.00
(3) Brickwork to foundations	630.00
(4) External works	2,223.00
(5) Main driveway	749.00
(6) Car parking	1,680.00
(7) Landscaping cut fill and topsoil	2,167.00
(8) Rainwater goods change UPVC to cast aluminium powder coated	1,600.00
	£10,939.00

4.11 Mr Maclean has dealt with these items in section 10 of his report. In cross-examination he was questioned at length but was unshaken in his views. The Respondent submits that the Arbitrator should adopt his evidence and find for the Respondent on these items.

4.12 Accordingly the sum due under the final account is for £633,981 calculated as set out in Maclean's report.

5.00 Repudiatory Breach and Liquidated Damages

5.1 As is clear from the Statement of Defence, the Respondent's primary case (see paragraph 11) is that the Claimant was in repudiatory breach of contract, after leaving the site on 12 April 1992. It is submitted that the evidence bears out this pleading and that the Arbitrator should find a repudiatory breach to have occurred.

5.2 If a repudiatory breach has occurred, time is at large and the Respondent accepts it is unable to levy liquidated damages. It is, however, entitled to unliquidated damages.

5.3 In such an event the Arbitrator is invited to assess an appropriate period for completion, and make an award of unliquidated damages.

5.4 If this first argument does not commend itself to the Arbitrator, the Respondent accepts that the Claimant is entitled to an extension of time of nine weeks and three days.

5.5 In this event the Respondent is entitled to retain some £59,964 in respect of liquidated damages.

5.6 It is unnecessary that there be a certificate of non-completion. Such a certificate is not a condition precedent. The wording is very loose. One only has to read Brent v Rowlinson [1990] 6 Construction LJ 292 (a copy of which is attached) to reach this conclusion.

6.00 Breach of Contract Claim

6.1 The Claimant makes various claims in respect of breach of contract.

6.2 The first of these is at paragraph 15.1 of the Statement of Case. It is alleged that TAP failed to respond to the Claimant's applications for extension of time and failed to grant an appropriate extension of time.

6.3 It is submitted that the known facts do not amount to such a breach. The Architect dealt with the matter properly throughout. He did not simply ignore the applications which, in any event, were not submitted in enough detail for him to deal with them. Even if he was in breach it is all irrelevant. The Claimant will, through these proceedings, achieve the extension he seeks together with interest. There is no point in this plea or claim.

6.4 The same is true of the alternative claim to loss and expense pleaded at paragraph 15.2.1 of the Amended Statement of Case. Again, the Claimant simply repeats the claim it makes through the contractual mechanism. This route should be rejected.

6.5 The claim to the certified sum set out as breach of contract at paragraph 15.3.1 of the Amended Statement of Case, is a debt claim and cannot be pleaded in this way. In any event it is admitted to the extent set out above at paragraph 4.3 hereof.

6.6 The same is true of the claim in respect of liquidated damages set out at paragraph 15.3.2 of the Statement of Case. In any event, subject to the claim for unliquidated damages set out in section 5.0 above, the Respondent concedes that credit should be given for all liquidated damages wrongly deducted (as found by the Arbitrator on the alternative bases set out above). If appropriate, which will be discussed below, credit will (it is accepted) fall to be given for interest.

6.7 As for the claim made in paragraph 15.3.3 of the Statement of Claim it is accepted that £32,000 was withheld. The money was withheld, as the evidence has clearly shown, because the works were defective and the Claimant was, therefore, not entitled to the benefit of the money. Under ordinary principles of law the Respondent was entitled to set off his expenses, and that he has sought to do.

6.8 The calculations of interest made at paragraph 15.3.5 of the Statement of Claim and in Appendices I Parts A and B are not accepted. Insofar as interest may need to be calculated, the Arbitrator is invited to accept the rates and rests prepared by Mr Maclean in his evidence and carry out such calculations as may be necessary.

6.9 As to paragraph 15.4 of the Statement of Claim, the evidence has shown the work carried out to be defective. It follows that it has never been appropriate to issue a Final Certificate, and this claim must fail.

7.00 *Counterclaim for Defective Work*

7.1 The Respondent seeks to set off its counterclaim against any sums which may be found due to the Claimant.

7.2 The first such counterclaim is set out at paragraph 35 of the Defence and in Appendix C thereof and also in the Scott Schedule.

Mr Maclean has dealt briefly with them in his report at section 13, but for the most part the evidence was oral. The Arbitrator may also have acquired an understanding of them from his site visit.

7.3 Detailed comment has been set out in an additional column to the Schedule and is appended hereto.

An example is as follows:

   Item 1 Evidence proves that there were defects as alleged. Evidence also supports the proposition that the specification required the finish not to contain such defects. It is accepted that the cost to repair is only a proportionate part of a larger quotation, but this is the best analysis of remedial cost that the Respondent can make.

7.4 If the Arbitrator accepts (as he is urged to do) each of the items in the Scott Schedule, and the costs attached thereto, the effect is that the Interim Certificates numbered 6, 7 and 10 should have been issued respectively, in the following sums of £79,800, £46,896 and £26,800.

7.5 Should it be, after the Arbitrator has made all relevant findings, that Interim Certificate

12 should have been issued in a sum other than that on its face, the Arbitrator is asked to revise the Certificate appropriately in his Award.

8.00 *Fire Doors*

8.1 By item 48 of the Specification, the Claimant was required to treat all corridor doors with intumescent coverings to achieve half-hour fire resistance. This was not disputed at the hearing.

8.2 The Respondent submits that the evidence showed that by about November 1993 the glass fibre matting had split and wrinkled in an unsightly fashion.

8.3 In consequence there was a breach of contract, whether the breach be of Condition 1.2, or the implied terms.

8.4 It is not thought that the Claimant seriously contends that the defect does not exist. The argument is over the cause. The Claimant contends that the cause is excessive use of the heating system; the Respondent says that the Claimant knew that the heating system would be run at a higher temperature than normal to ensure that the aged residents remained warm.

8.5 It follows, the Respondent submits, that if the Claimant knew of the higher-than-normal temperatures, the Claimant should have taken steps to dry the works to a sufficient extent that the cracking problem would not occur.

8.6 The evidence, it is submitted, has demonstrated that the Claimant did know.

8.7 The cost of correction has been shown to be 64 doors at £110 per door totalling £7,040.

9.00 *Gibbs Ceiling*

9.1 There is no dispute that the Claimant was required to carry out fireproofing works in the ceiling space above the Gibbs ceiling, using a system and a specialist firm, both of which were to be approved by the Architect.

9.2 The Respondent did not assert any fault by the Claimant in its choice of system and did approve the choice of specialist subcontractor.

9.3 It is vitally important to bear in mind the specification requirement as to the protection of the ceiling. The installation of the fireproofing would inevitably put the ceiling at risk. The essential words are these:

'In addition to their general responsibility for protection of the existing structure, the contractor is to take whatever steps are necessary to uphold the integrity of the ceiling.'

'These and any other works affecting the Gibbs ceiling are to be carried out in such a way and all necessary protection taken to ensure that the integrity of the ceiling is maintained at all times and on completion.'

9.4 It is quite clear, on the evidence that the Contractor failed to take essential steps to protect the integrity of the ceiling. In particular he must have allowed some fireproofing to fall onto the top side of the ceiling. Inadequate precautions were taken.

9.5 It is said that the Architect was warned of the fragile nature of the plaster keys in this ceiling. This a defence that says (or seems to say) that the collapse was waiting to happen.

9.6 The Respondent maintains that there was little evidence which supports the absence of proper plaster keys. If the Claimant is right, then the issue is one of causation. If the actions of the Contractor (or his inactions) were the dominant cause of the collapse (and it is submitted that they were), then the Contractor is liable.

9.7 There was no dispute that 15 of the rooms became uninhabitable. The evidence supported the Respondent's case that the relevant vacancy period was from 24 December 1992 to 14 February 1994.

9.8 Generally, the Respondent claims the losses were supported by the evidence. The Respondent relies, in particular, on the evidence given by its accountant and its evidence of loss of value.

10.00 *Diminution in Value of Property*

10.1 The Respondent maintains that evidence showed that there was a diminution in the value of the property, due to the loss of the Gibbs ceiling.

10.2 Expert evidence put this figure at between £10,000 and £20,000 which was supported by the Respondent's own evidence.

10.3 It is submitted that a figure of £15,000, which the Respondent avers was the additional amount they paid for this property due to the presence of the Gibbs ceiling, up to £20,000, as suggested by the Respondent's expert Mr Knight, is the correct figure to award for this loss.

10.4 The Claimant's proposition that value increased following the loss of this unique feature was demonstrably absurd.

11.00 *Basement Flooding*

11.1 The last item is the basement flooding. It occurred on 15 April 1992. The Arbitrator has already determined that the flooding was caused by the Claimant's breach of contract.

11.2 The only matters in issue were therefore, the loss and damage suffered.

11.3 We heard in evidence that the parties' respective experts had agreed that the Claimant could carry out this remedial work. It is settled law that specific performance should not be ordered where damages are an adequate remedy.

11.4 As a figure for this work has been agreed between the experts, and was supported by evidence, it is submitted that this is the figure which the Arbitrator should award.

12.00 *General*

12.1 The Respondent claims, and is entitled to, statutory interest on its counterclaim.

12.2 The quantum and period of interest is in the discretion of the Arbitrator. The quantum should, in the submission of the Claimant, be not less than two per cent over base rate.

12.3 Despite an apparent agreement between Messrs Sharkey and Longdon that the Contractors should be given the opportunity to carry out the agreed remedial works to the basement, the Respondent maintains that the correct remedy is damages (at the figure agreed by the experts) not least because the Respondent has lost confidence in the Contractor and would not wish the Contractor to execute these works.

10.5
441

13.00 *Summary*

13.1 By way of counterclaim the Respondent primarily seeks the various sums of damages it has set out in the prayer in the Counterclaim, together with interest.

13.2 Additionally it claims

(i) a declaration that Interim Certificate 12 should have been issued in the sum of £21,680 (negative);

(ii) the form of the declaration sought in respect of the Interim Certificate will be affected by the actual sum by which the Certificate was inaccurate. Further, it may, in fact, be more appropriate for the Arbitrator simply to 'reverse' the certificate, and this prayer should be read in the alternative.

....
Miss O'Brien
Counsel for the Respondent
25 April 1994

6. Claimant's Closing Submissions (10.6)

IN THE MATTER OF THE ARBITRATION ACTS 1950 TO 1979

AND

IN THE MATTER OF AN ARBITRATION UNDER THE JCT ARBITRATION RULES (18 JULY 1988)

BETWEEN

RELIABLE BUILDERS LIMITED   Claimant

AND

SANCTUARY HOUSE LIMITED   Respondent

CLAIMANT'S CLOSING SUBMISSIONS

1.00 *General*

1.1 The Claimant has been shown a copy of the Respondent's final submission and uses herein the same paragraph numbering for convenience and follows the same order.

1.2 This submission covers both the claim and the counterclaim.

2.00 *The Delay Claim*

2.1 General

2.1.1 The Claimant accepts that the delay claim can be conveniently set out under 13 headings. They are set out in the Respondent's submission.

2.1.2 These submissions deal with each of these in turn.

2.2 Removals, Demolition and Form Openings

2.2.1 The Claimant maintains that there were three items which caused delay: inaccurate survey information; the late provision of revised drawings 04/B and 05/B and additional works as set out in AI's 4f, 4g, 4h, 5a, 5c, 6a, 6b, 6c, 6g and 10b.

2.2.2 The Respondent accepts that there was inaccurate survey information. Although they now contend that there was no delay because amendments were issued in time to prevent it, the evidence (it is submitted) suggested quite the opposite.

2.2.3 Again, the Respondent's case in respect of drawings 04/B and 05/B was barely credible. It was clear that these drawings were issued far too late to avoid disruption to progress.

2.2.4 The Respondent can hardly deny that the AI's covered extra work. The delay, it is submitted, was self-evident.

2.2.5 The item was on the critical path. That this was the case would be obvious to the Arbitrator, given his expertise and experience.

2.2.6 In its evidence the Respondent sought to suggest that the dominant delay at the time was in the area of the lift-shaft. The Claimant does not accept this. What was dominant is obviously difficult to assess, but in the Claimants' submission, the delays it sets out in this complaint had the necessary qualities. Unfortunately, authority does not provide a particularly good guide.

2.2.7 An extension of time of four weeks should be granted for the delay under this head.

2.3 Form Lift-shaft

2.3.1 A further extension of time of one week is claimed for additional work as set out in AI 2a.

2.3.2 So far as the Claimant knows, it is not disputed that the construction of the lift-shaft was amended by AI 2a.

2.3.3 The amendments were:

(a) revision of the brickwork specification to Waltons engineering bricks;
(b) the introduction of a reinforced concrete beam at each floor.

2.3.4 The evidence (it is submitted) showed that the use of engineering bricks reduced the maximum daily lift, so that the period required for construction of the lift-shaft rose by 60 per cent.

2.3.5 The evidence too (it is submitted) showed a delay to the shaft consequent upon placing of the ring beam. Mr Redman suggested, in his evidence, a period of 1 week 3 days.

2.3.6 The additional critical delay was, however, only one week. See the evidence of Mr Redman.

2.3.7 If, however, item 1 above fails, the Claimant relies on this item as constituting five-weeks critical delay.

2.3.8 It is submitted that Mr Redman's evidence that this item was on the critical path should be accepted.

'This delay to the completion of the lift-shaft was critical as the head of the shaft provided support for certain key roof elements and also the water tanks.'

See his report in 2.6.4.

[*Counsel's submissions continued in this vein covering all 13 items.*]

2.14 Conclusion on Extension of Time

2.14.1 The Claimant could not have completed the works any sooner than 31 March 1992.

2.14.2 It is, therefore, entitled to an extension of time of 16 weeks.

2.14.3 It is to be noted that even the Respondent accepts critical delay of nine weeks three days.

2.14.4 The next part of this submission will consider quantum.

3.00 Loss and Expense

3.1 Weekly Rates

3.1.1 It is worth noting that the Respondent accepts the Claimant's figures as the weekly rates (see Maclean para 3.30) though he does not accept the admissibility of the items.

3.2 Site Staff

3.2.1 The evidence suggested the Claimant's case that it had to continue to employ its full supervising and administrative team on-site. There was no opportunity to reduce the staffing levels as the variations (and thus the intensity of the workload) continued up to the date of practical completion.

10.6
443

3.2.2 Those who were employed were, John Watts, the site agent; Fred Brown, a trade foreman; Peter Murphy, a ganger; Graham Smith, a quantity surveyor; and an additional general site service labour gang.

3.2.3 Although suggested in cross-examination that the contrary was the case, it is clear that no costs for Peter Murphy have been recovered in the rates.

3.2.4 It was also suggested that there was duplication of charging for Graham Smith, the quantity surveyor, being carried in the overheads. Again, this was clearly not the case.

3.3 Site Accommodation

3.3.1 The Claimant maintains its claim for £130 per week in this respect.

3.3.2 It is accepted that these rates were internal plant hire rates.

3.3.3 The expert evidence was to the effect that such charges were normal in the industry. They would be accepted by the Arbitrator.

[*Counsel's submissions continued by going through each item of loss and expense in a similar fashion.*]

3.4 Conclusion on Loss and Expense

3.4.1 The evidence tended to support Mr Redman's conclusions and was not shaken in cross-examination.

3.4.2 Thus, the following figures are urged upon the Arbitrator:

Prolongation	31,552
Additional Staff and Equipment	15,334
Head Office Costs	36,667
Disturbance of Labour as agreed during the Hearing by the Experts	28,480
Inflation	5,571
	£117,604

10.6
444

4.00 *Sum Claimed under the Contract*

4.1 The Claimant contends that the final account value is £656,285.10. See paragraph 14.3 of the Amended Statement of Claim. The sum certified is £610,450. There is a balance of £45,835.10.

4.2 It is accepted, it is believed, by the Respondent that the sum of £10,954 is now due under Interim Certificate 12. Whilst the Defence foreshadowed an argument that this certificate was overvalued, it is now clear that this was not the case, the Respondent apparently conceding a final account value well above this figure.

4.3 In examining the final account the Claimant contends that the Arbitrator should accept the figures of Mr Redman. He was a good witness. He had clearly done substantially more background work than Mr Maclean.

4.4 The differences between the parties are over additions rather than omissions. Appended hereto is a list of the differences.

4.5 There is no written evidence in respect of any of these items, although the Arbitrator was addressed on each and there was substantial supporting information by way of invoices and other paperwork. It is not intended to make any detailed submissions here as to do so would be lengthy and unnecessary. The views and evidence of Mr Redman are urged upon the Arbitrator. The Arbitrator is equally invited to apply his own experience, subject to the usual caveat that he must have put any such experience (or his views) to the parties before reaching his decision.

4.6 There is no dispute in respect of provisional sums and contingencies.

4.7 There are disputes over remeasured items, certain of which are not agreed. These are as follows:

(1) Additional removal of topsoil and reduced level dig	£1,440
(2) Additional trench excavations and cart away	£450
(3) Brickwork to foundations	£630
(4) External works	£2,223
(5) Main driveway	£749
(6) Car parking	£1,680
(7) Landscaping cut fill and topsoil	£2,167
(8) Rainwater goods	£1,600

4.8 The Respondent allows £1,680 for the first three items against the Claimant's total of £2,520; £809 for item 4; £480 for item 5; £1,240 for item 6; £1,870 for item 7 and nothing for item 8.

4.9 Mr Redman did not deal with these items in his report but in evidence he did deal with the points made by Mr Maclean. It is unnecessary to rehearse the detailed arguments here since they are matters of technical detail which may well be in the mind of the Arbitrator.

The views of Mr Redman are urged upon the Arbitrator—who will, in any event, apply his own experience in these matters.

4.10 As stated above, if Mr Redman's views are adopted in total, the value of the Final Account is £656,285.10.

5.00 *Repudiatory Breach and Liquidated Damages*

5.1 The Arbitrator is invited to reject the Respondent's case that the Claimant was in repudiatory breach of contract in leaving the site in April 1992. The works were practically complete. To leave site could not in any circumstances be a breach of contract, let alone a repudiatory breach.

5.2 Time is, accordingly, not at large, and no questions of unliquidated damages arise.

5.3 There is, therefore, a straightforward and conventional case of the award of an extension of time and the repayment of liquidated damages wrongfully deducted.

5.4 Out of its secondary case the Respondent has accepted an extension of time of nine weeks and three days.

5.5 It follows that, even on the case put forward by the Respondent, the sums retained by the Respondent at present are excessive, by the order of £86,000.

5.6 Were the Arbitrator to award the full extension of time claimed, the Claimant would be entitled to the repayment of £146,000 (plus interest).

5.7 Obviously the Arbitrator will need to make appropriate adjustments to the liquidated damages if he awards less than the full extension of time.

5.8 In any event the Claimant maintains that it is essential that, before any liquidated damages are deducted, there be a certificate of non-completion. Contrary to the Respondent's submission such a certificate is a condition precedent. The Arbitrator's attention is drawn to *Bell* v *CBF* (1989) 46 Build LR 102 (see copy attached).

6.00 *Breach of Contract Claims*

6.1 The Claimant makes various of its claims on the basis of breach of contract.

6.2 At paragraph 15.1.1 of the Statement of Claim the Claimant pleads that, in breach of Clause 2.3 of the contract, TAP failed to respond to the Claimant's applications for an extension of time, and failed to grant an extension of time.

6.3 Clause 2.3 is self-explanatory. In certain circumstances the Architect must make an extension of time.

6.4 The relevant circumstances existed in 1992. The Contractor, it is submitted, had given

10.6
445

proper written notice of delay for a reason set out within the contract. The Claimant was entitled to an extension. But the Architect failed to deal with his claims, or deal with it properly. The Architect (and so his client) was in breach.

6.5 The consequences of the breach are obvious:

(i)   Liquidated damages have been wrongfully deducted. The Claimant is entitled to the sums wrongfully deducted and interest (as damages);

(ii) The claim to loss and expense has not been assessed. The Claimant is entitled to the sums he should have been paid by way of loss and expense as damages, together with interest.

6.6 At paragraph 15.2.1 of the Statement of Claim the Claimant claims its loss and expense as damages for these reasons.

6.7 First, it is said that the Respondent, or TAP, have hindered the Claimant from performing the works under the contract. The implied term is well established. See *Keating on Building Contracts*, 5th ed., p. 45 *et seq.*; 6th ed., p. 48 *et seq.*, and others. No further facts can be relied upon other than those which go to make up the contractual claim for loss and expense, but it is submitted that the facts and evidence support a breach of this term and, in the circumstances, the Claimant is entitled to an award under this head, albeit that it will overlap with any award for loss and expense.

6.8 Secondly, it is alleged that the Respondent, or TAP, did not take all steps reasonably necessary to enable the Claimant to discharge the obligations under this contract and/or execute the works in a regular and orderly manner. Again, it is submitted, that this term is well established; see *Keating*. Again no further facts are relied upon and the submission at paragraph 6.7 above is repeated.

6.9 Thirdly, it is alleged that the Respondent, or TAP, failed to issue such further drawings or details as were necessary to enable the Claimant to complete the works in accordance with the conditions of the contract. This implied term, it is submitted, is only a development of the previous two, is fully supported by the textbooks and, in any event, obvious. As with the previous two, no further facts are relied upon and the submission at paragraph 6.7 above is repeated again.

10.6
446

6.10 The damage resulting from each of the above (three) breaches is set out at paragraph 15.2.2 of the Statement of Claim, and no further comment is required here.

6.11 At paragraph 15.3.1 of the Statement of Claim the Claimant seeks payment of the sum due under Certificate 12, as damages, for breach of contract. Little explanation is needed.

Clause 4.2 requires that the Respondent pay sums due under the contract. This is a sum which has not been paid within 14 days from the Certificate.

6.12 At paragraph 15.3.2 of the Statement of Claim, the Claimant contends that the deduction of liquidated damages was also a breach of the payment provision. Again, this is self-explanatory. The deduction should not have been made if the Claimant was entitled to an extension of time.

6.13 At paragraph 15.3.3 of the Statement of Claim, the Claimant alleges that the deduction of £32,000, by the Respondent, in respect of defects was in breach of the contract. There was no provision for such a deduction; the contract permits only the arrangement in respect of retention. Given the contractual mechanism there is no additional room for unilateral set-off.

6.14 Nothing need be said about paragraph 15.3.4 of the Statement of Claim.

6.15 The losses are set out in paragraph 15.3.5 of the Statement of Claim. Insofar as interest is concerned, the costs set out by the Claimant are costs or rates actually incurred and no difficulty with them should be experienced.

The Respondent has agreed figures as figures for the Claimant's bank charges, rates and periods, as set out by the Claimant.

The Arbitrator is invited to adopt the Claimant's rates and rests.

6.16 Little more need be said in respect of paragraph 15.4 of the Statement of Claim. The evidence (it is submitted) showed quite clearly that the Architect failed to comply with its obligations in respect of the Final Certificate.

In consequence, the Claimant has not been paid sums due to it under the contract, which it claims under this head as damages.

This claim is obviously put in the alternative.

7.00 *Counterclaim for Defective Work*

7.1 Save for the point made at paragraph 6.13 above, the Claimant accepts that, for the purposes of the arbitration, the Arbitrator may set off against any sums which he finds due to the Claimant, any other sums which he finds due to the Respondent in respect of defects.

7.2 The first of the counterclaims is that set out at paragraph 35 of the Defence and in Appendix A thereto. The claim is for £32,634. Mr Redman has dealt with these items at Section 13 of his report, but there was considerable additional oral evidence and discussion.

The Claimant also realises that the Arbitrator visited the site and will have some knowledge of these defects gleaned from that visit.

7.3 The Scott Schedule, with comments from both the Respondent and the Claimant is attached as Appendix A to the Respondent's Statement of Defence and should be read in conjunction with the evidence given by the various witnesses. In addition to the evidence heard by the Arbitrator at the full hearing the Arbitrator had the benefit of a site inspection of these defects and met with the experts alone prior to and during the Hearing to discuss these defects. Accordingly, it is submitted, the Arbitrator has ample evidence upon which to base his determination of this issue.

7.4 The plea at paragraph 36 of the Defence is denied. Even if there was work which was defective it would not follow that the Interim Certificate should have been reduced. Interim Certificates are, in any event, only approximate valuations.

8.00 *Fire Doors*

10.6
447

8.1 By item 48 of the specification the Claimant was required to treat all corridor doors to achieve half-hour fire resistance. This was, of course, carried out.

8.2 The Claimant does not dispute that some time later (it makes no admission as to when) the covering had acquired a wrinkled appearance. It accepts it was unsatisfactory.

8.3 The Claimant does not, however, accept it was thereby in breach of contract.

8.4 As the evidence emerged it became clear that the real issue between the parties was whether or not the Claimant knew or, perhaps, should have known that the building would be heated to temperatures considerably higher than what might be termed 'normal' and in particular whether such abnormally high heat would be applied as rapidly as it was.

8.5 In any event, had the Claimant been aware of the Respondent's intention to run the heating at full bore from day one he would have advised him to introduce the heating gradually. It is submitted that it was this rapid build-up of heat drying out the excessive moisture absorbed by these doors whilst the building was derelict, which caused the wrinkling of the coating. See the Report and evidence of Mr Carmel.

8.6 The Claimant concedes that he knew that the eventual end use of the property was for an elderly persons home but did not know that it was for the frail elderly and, as such, would require a constant abnormally high temperature to be maintained. Had he known that this would be the case it would have carried out (or required the subcontractor) to carry out the works in a way which would have minimised the risk to the fire coatings.

8.7 In any event, had the Claimant been aware of the abnormally high temperature to be used, he would have advised the Respondent to introduce the heating gradually, to build up to the required optimum environmental heat for this home for the frail elderly.

It was the rapid build-up of heat, drying out the excessive moisture absorbed by these doors whilst the building was derelict, which (it is submitted) caused the wrinkling.

8.8 The evidence, however, did not show that the Claimant had the requisite knowledge about either the eventual level of heat or the rapid build-up. An attempt was made in cross-examination to demonstrate that the contractor should have had the knowledge from his own experience but, it is submitted, that this showed nothing at all.

In any event what may be true of one facility is not necessary true of another.

Nor was there very much in the documentation from which the contractor could have gleaned the situation; although clause 48 of the Specification indicated that the heating system would be run at a relatively high temperature, there was certainly no direct statement informing him of this day-to-day running internal temperature or indeed, more importantly, how quickly it was intended that the unspecified optimum temperature would be achieved.

8.9 It is submitted, therefore, that the case fails.

8.10 It is accepted that if the Respondent is entitled to the costs of correcting the defect, the sum claimed of £7,040 is reasonable.

9.00 *Gibbs Ceiling*

9.1 As it emerged, this dispute came down to three matters:

(i) What level of protection was the Contractor bound to provide?
(ii) Whether or not the Contractor had taken adequate steps to protect the ceiling?
(iii) Whether or not the Architect had been warned that the plaster key was inadequate?

9.2 As for the first point, the relevant part of the specification reads as follows:

'In addition to their general responsibility for protection of the existing structure, the Contractor is to take whatever steps are necessary to uphold the integrity of the ceiling.'

'These and any other works affecting the Gibbs ceiling are to be carried out in such a way and all necessary protection taken to ensure that the integrity of the ceiling is maintained at all times and on completion.'

10.6
448

9.3 It is submitted that this means nothing more than that the Contractor is bound to take whatever steps would be necessary to maintain the integrity of a ceiling in a proper condition. The Contractor cannot be obliged by this clause to make a ceiling which is unstable into one which is stable; in other words, if a ceiling has an inherent defect which affects its integrity, the Contractor cannot, by this clause, be required actually to improve its integrity.

9.4 Thus, it is submitted that, in this case, and in answer to the second point that the evidence showed that the Contractor *did* in fact take steps to protect the ceiling and *did* in fact take steps which would have been adequate had the ceiling itself possessed the level of integrity which the Contractor was entitled to assume that it did.

9.5 It is accepted that some fireproofing material probably fell on to the top of the ceiling. It is not accepted that the extent of this was as much as suggested by the Respondent, nor is it accepted that this was the cause of the collapse.

9.6 The cause of the collapse, it is submitted, was the lack of a proper plaster key. In its submission the Respondent suggests that there was little evidence of such an inadequacy. But the Claimant's case is that the evidence overwhelmingly supported its position that this was the case. It was equally clear that the Architect had been told of this by the Contractor. In the circumstances it is evident that the Claimant had discharged any duty it might have owed to the Respondent.

9.7 The Claimant makes no comment on the damages (see paragraphs 9.7 and 9.8 of the Respondent's submission).

448

10.00 *Diminution in the Value of the Property*

10.1 The Claimant accepts that the proposition that the value of the building increased as a result of the collapse of the ceiling was a surprising one.

10.2 It was not, however, absurd (as suggested by the Respondent). There would be bound to be costs associated with the ceiling which, to some buyers at the very least, would detract from the value of the building.

10.3 The assessment by the Respondent himself that he paid some £15,000 more on account of this feature was highly subjective, and should not be taken into account.

10.4 The Claimant submits that it would be appropriate to treat this head of claim as neutral and make no award.

11.00 *Basement Flooding*

11.1 As the Respondent states the last item is the basement flooding, and it occurred on 15 April 1992. The Arbitrator, it is accepted, has already decided that the flooding was caused by the Claimant's breach of contract.

11.2 The Claimant has agreed to carry out the relevant remedial work. At paragraph 12.3 of its submission the Respondent asserts that the correct remedy is in damages.

It is, it is submitted, too late so to contend for damages in the light of the agreement made. The Arbitrator should order in terms that the Claimant execute these works.

11.3 The Respondent claims £384 for the losses incurred by the residents for which the Respondent was liable. As this figure is based on a replacement cost it is submitted that it should be discounted to reflect second-hand value. The Claimant concedes that the Arbitrator should use his discretion to determine the correct figure for this item in which case the proposed indemnity is unnecessary and, in any event is unsatisfactory; *inter alia*, it will leave the dispute open. The Arbitrator is requested therefore to refuse to grant the indemnity.

12.00 *Interest*

12.1 The Claimant is entitled to interest on its claims. This interest takes three forms.

12.2 First the Claimant is entitled to financing charges on its loss and expense. Such entitlement is derived from *Minter* v *WHTSO* (1980) 31 BLR 1. Although, in that case, the finance charges were confined to the period between the loss and expense being incurred and the making of a written application for the loss and expense, it is submitted that in the wording of this contract, such finance charges are recoverable to the date of the award.

[*Counsel then continued with a discussion of the* Minter *case.*]

12.3 The claim for financing charges is a claim to compound interest. It is not thought that this is controversial.

12.4 It is common ground between the parties that the claim to financing charges must be a real claim in the sense that the charges must have actually been incurred. It is submitted that the evidence supported the Claimant's case that it actually incurred these charges.

12.5 Parallel with the claim for financing charges is the claim for statutory interest, which arises under s.19A of the Arbitration Act 1950. This is a claim to simple interest. It is submitted that the appropriate period is from when the monies should have been certified to the date of the award. The period and rate is in the discretion of the Arbitrator. The Arbitrator will recall that the Statement of Case (7.8) originally pleaded interest at a rate of 3 per cent over bank base rate.

However, the Arbitrator will recall that Mr Reeves, in his second proof of evidence, showed that the actual rate of interest incurred by RBL was 6.245 per cent over NatWest bank rate.

As a result I sought leave to amend the Claimant's Statement of Case, during my oral closing, to reflect this actual proved rate of interest and leave was granted.

Whilst it is appreciated that the Arbitrator has absolute discretion as to the rate that he

10.6
449

awards, which does not necessarily have to equate to the actual incurred rate, it is hoped that the Arbitrator will exercise his discretion as close to that rate as he feels is reasonable.

12.6 Thirdly, in respect of the damages claim, it is submitted that the Claimant is entitled to interest as damages. It is important that it was known (and this was not in dispute) that the Claimant would suffer overdraft charges if held out of its money. The relevant authorities (which are well known to the Arbitrator) are *Wadsworth* v *Lydall* [1981] 2 All ER 401 and *Holbeach Plant Hire Ltd and Anor.* v *Anglian Water Authority* 14 Con LR 101.

13.00 *Summary*

13.1 Accordingly, the Claimant maintains its claims herein, as set out in the Amended Statement of Claim.

13.2 The counterclaim is generally denied, save that the Claimant admits the claim in respect of the basement flooding to the extent set out.

Date: 2 May 1994 ....
Toby Belcher
Counsel for the Claimant

APPENDIX I

List of Differences between the parties over sums due under contract.

[Details not included due to length.]

10.6
450

7. Typical Rent Review Award (10.7 Arb)

Dated this   day of   19

In the matter of the Arbitration Acts 1950 to 1979

and in the matter of an arbitration between

(the Claimant)

and

(the Respondent)

re: *[address]*

FIRST INTERIM RENT REVIEW AWARD

(final on all matters except costs)

WHEREAS:

1. By a lease dated *[date]* (the Lease) made between *[name]* (1) and *[name]* (2), *[address of property]* (the Property) was let for a term of *[No.]* years from *[date]*.

2. As successor in title to *[name]* the present landlord and the Claimant is *[name]*.

3. As successor in title to *[name]* the present tenant and the Respondent is *[name]*.

4. A dispute (the Dispute) has arisen as to the amount of the Open Market Rental Value (the Rent) of the Property as at *[date]* (the Date) pursuant to the rent review in *[clause/schedule No.]* of the Lease.

5. Clause *[No.]* of the Lease contains an arbitration agreement to submit the Dispute to arbitration.

6. I, *[full name]* of *[address]* having given my advance consent by letter dated *[date]* to the arbitration office of the Royal Institution of Chartered Surveyors was appointed arbitrator to determine the Dispute by the President of the R.I.C.S. by letter dated *[date]*.

7. By consent it was agreed that the arbitration be conducted on documents only with written representation procedure without a preliminary meeting. By an agreed timetable and by consent that procedure has been completed.

8. I have read the copy, confirmed by the parties' representatives as a true copy, of the completed stamped counterpart Lease supplied to me and I have read and considered all representations delivered to me on behalf of the parties hereto.

9. I have inspected the Property and looked at the comparable premises cited by the parties' representatives.

10. On the application of the parties I am requested to publish an interim award, final on all matters except costs.

11. The parties have requested a reasoned award.

I HEREBY PUBLISH THIS MY FIRST INTERIM AWARD, FINAL AS TO ALL MATTERS EXCEPT COSTS

12. The Claimant is represented by Mr C *[name]* of *[name of firm]*, Chartered Surveyors of *[town]*. The Respondent is represented by Mr R *[name]* of *[name of firm]*, Chartered Surveyors of *[town]*. I thank the parties' representatives for their careful attention and assistance given to me in this matter.

13. The property is a ground-floor shop unit within a purpose-built shop and office development (the Complex). Clause *[No.]* of the Lease contains the rent review

provisions as to the amount of the Rent. The Lease is deemed to be incorporated on the face of this award.

14. The Claimant (represented by Mr. C   ) contends the amount of the Rent on the Date was £   p.a.; the Respondent (represented by Mr. R   ) £   p.a. It is common ground that the accepted method of zoning and the adoption of 20ft zones should be applied to the Property and the comparables whereby the front part of the shop, to a depth of 20ft is worth, say, £x p.f.s., the next 20ft back is worth £x/2, the next portion back £x/4 and so on. To reflect this agreement the floor area is adjusted in terms of zone A. They have agreed the floor area of the Property in terms of zone A (ITZA) for valuation purposes.

More specifically:

Mr. C   's Rental Valuation:

Ground Floor ITZA f.s × £ p.f.s.	£_____	p.a.
Plus benefit of return frontage %	£_____	p.a.
	£_____	p.a.

Mr. R   's Rental Valuation:

Ground Floor ITZA f.s × £ p.f.s.	£	p.a.

15. From the representations I identify the issues within the Dispute as follows:

A. The admissibility of an arbitrator's rent review award on a comparable property.
B. Whether or not any inducement in a comparable letting shall be taken into account in the analysis of that comparable.
C. The relevance of one of the comparables introduced by the parties.
D. The weight I should attach to each of the comparables.
E. The adjustments to the comparables to derive the zone A rent for the Property.
F. Whether or not an addition should be made to reflect the return frontage and, if so, the amount of the addition.

16. All the comparables introduced are within the Complex.

The facts of the comparables are not disputed; the relevance and analyses are.

For ease of reference I refer to the comparables (the Comparables) by the comparable number as set out below.

17. Comparables introduced by both representatives:

17.1 Comp. 1—   [occupant]   [address]

Transaction—open market letting;   year lease from   [date]; rent £   p.a. exclusive subject to five yearly rent reviews.
Floor area—sales   f.s plus   f.s. storage and loading bay areas.
(sales ITZA   f.s.).
Claimant's zone A contests analysis—£   p.f.s.p.a.
Respondent's zone A contested analysis £   p.f.s.p.a.

18. Comparables introduced by the Claimant:

18.1 Comp. 2—   [occupant]   [address]

Transaction—open market letting;   year lease from   [date]; rent £   p.a. exclusive subject to five yearly rent reviews.
Area—sales   f.s.
(sales ITZA   f.s.).
Claimant's uncontested zone A analysis—£   p.f.s.p.a. subject to Respondent's contentions on analysis difficulties.

18.2 Comp. 3—   [occupant]   [address]

10.7 Arb
452

Transaction—rent review effective from　　　　　[*date*] agreed at £　　　p.a. exclusive;　　year lease from　　　　　　[*date*] subject to five yearly rent reviews.
　　Area—sales　　f.s. plus　　　f.s. storage area.
　　(sales ITZA　　f.s.).
Claimant's and Respondent's agreed zone A analysis £　　　p.f.s.p.a.

19. Comparables introduced by the Respondent.
19.1 Comp. 4—　　　　　[*occupant*]　　　[*address*]

Transaction—rent review effective from　　　　　[*date*] agreed at £　　　p.a. exclusive;　　year lease from　　　　　　[*date*] subject to five yearly rent reviews.
　　Area—sales　　f.s. plus　　　f.s. storage areas.
　　(sales ITZA　　f.s.).
Respondent's contested Zone A analysis—£　　　p.f.s.p.a.
Claimant contends comparable not relevant.

20. The meaning of 'Open Rental Value' is contained in clause　　　[*No.*] of the Lease.
21. As to A. (the admissibility of a rent review award): This relates to a rent review award on　　　[*address*]. Mr. C　　　introduces it as evidence of the general level of rents in the Complex. Mr. R　　　says I should treat the award as inadmissible citing *Land Securities* v *Westminster City Council* (1992). I hold that the award is inadmissible as evidence; accordingly I have shut it out of my mind.
22. As to B. (whether or not any inducement in a comparable letting shall be taken into account in the analysis of that comparable): This issue arises to enable like to be compared with like. The question is an issue as to the true construction of clause　　　of the Lease. My decision on the issue will determine whether, on an analysis of the rent of a comparable letting, that rent should be adjusted downwards to reflect the effect of any inducement granted.
　　Clause　　　in the Lease relevant to this issue reads:
　　'. . .'.

I am referred to the following two cases on this issue:
'　　　　v.　　　　'
'　　　　v.　　　　'

Mr. C　　　submits that on a true construction of clause　　　of the Lease the Rent should be a headline rent to the effect that any inducement granted to an ingoing tenant on a comparable letting shall not be taken into account in the analysis; accordingly the rent on analysis should not be reduced to reflect any inducement. Mr. R　　　disagrees, submitting the rent on analysis should be reduced to reflect such inducement.
　　I find the reasoning in '. . .' more powerful than '. . .' related to this issue and find Mr. R　　　's submission more persuasive. Accordingly I hold that, in the analysis of the comparables, an allowance by way of deduction shall be made to reflect any such inducement.
23. As to C. (the relevance of one of the Comparables): The relevance of comp. 4 is contested. Mr. C　　　contends this rent review is not relevant to the Dispute because the shop is considerably larger than the Property and in any event the analysis is not agreed. Mr. R　　　contends the evidence is relevant, especially as the date of the rent review is the same date as the Date, and is, therefore, admissible; further, that non-agreement on the analysis does not negate admissibility. Comp. 4 is close to the Property and must, in my judgment, be relevant; the fact that it is significantly larger than the Property is not grounds for negating relevance. Accordingly I decide the comp. 4 rent review transaction is relevant and admissible. The weight I attach to the evidence is another matter which is within my discretion as my judgment.

24. As to D. (the weight I should give to each of the Comparables): Generally, the less closely analogous a comparable is as to the date of the transaction, the location of a comparable relative to the Property, the characteristics of a comparable in comparison with the Property the less weight I attach to it. I decide that evidence of open market lettings is preferable to evidence of negotiated rent reviews. Mr. R   contents that a negotiated rent review settlement is good evidence of market rents as it is unlikely to have been agreed without the full knowledge of the facts of other open market lettings. Further, that where parties, as in comp. 3 and 4 are professionally represented in rent reviews I should attach significant weight to rent review evidence. Mr. R   's contentions are not disputed. I have no evidence that parties were not represented in the rent review transactions; accordingly I attach significant weight to them.

Dealing with each of the Comparables in turn I find as follows:

24.1 As to Comp. 1—This open market letting on   [date] is some   [No.] years before the Date. The unit is close to the Property. Mr. C   contends the location is inferior to the Property; Mr. R   contends it is superior. The analysis is disputed. I find the location is superior but marginal only. Neither party disputes that I should attach weight to this transaction accordingly I do so but I accept Mr. C   's uncontested contention that I should exercise some caution as the transaction is   [No.] years before the Date.

24.2 As to Comp. 2—This open market letting is a post-dated transaction ([date]) Mr. C   contends this shop is situated in an arguable inferior trading position; Mr. R   contends for a superior location. The analysis is disputed. I find the location is marginally inferior. I attach limited weight to this letting because it is a post-dated transaction in excess of   [months].

24.3 As to Comp. 3—Neither party contends I should attach significant weight to this rent review in adducing the zone a rent for the Property. Their contentions centre on disputed analyses relevant to an end allowance addition in the Rent for the return frontage to the Property. Accordingly I attach little weight to the amount of the rent agreed at the rent review but note the disputed analyses in my consideration in the exercise of my judgment on the return frontage allowance I address in para. 26, 26.1.

24.4 As to Comp. 4—This rent review is on the same date as the Date but this shop is over six times the size of the Property and the representatives do not agree the analysis. I find the rent review helpful but not persuasive.

24.5 In summary: I attach the greatest weight to   which is/are in close proximity to the Property. I derive assistance from   . I derive very limited assistance from   .

25. As to D. (the analysis of the comparables and adjustments to derive the zone A rent): Disputed analyses centre on the effect of inducements on comparable lettings to compare like with like. I have already decided this issue at para. 22. Accordingly I prefer the analyses contended for by Mr. R

25.1 Having considered the analysis of the comparables I then make adjustments to the comparables on the factual evidence and opinion evidence to derive the zone A rent of the Property. I find that no incontrovertible evidence of the Rent of the Property has been adduced. Accordingly, to arrive at the zone A rent I bear in mind all the factors given in evidence, bearing in mind the figures that have been put to me and the helpful assistance of Mr. C   and Mr. R   . On weighing all those factors together as a matter of judgment, not as a matter of calculation and upon that basis, on taking all these matters into account I prefer the zone A rent contended for by Mr. R

[*Note that if the decision follows inevitably from incontrovertible evidence of the Rent or from facts found married to the law correctly ascertained, this paragraph will not be appropriate; the decision will be a matter of calculation as there will be no element of judgment.*]

10.7 Arb
454

25.2 I decide that the zone A rent that should be applied to the Property in assessing the Rent is £   ([*words*]) p.f.s.p.a.

26. As to E. (whether or not an addition should be made to reflect the return frontage and, if so, the amount of the addition): Mr. C   contends that a   % addition should be made to the zone A rent to reflect the considerable benefit of the return frontage, supported by his opinion evidence that it is reasonable to expect an uplift of not less than   % in a modern purpose-built development; further supported by his analysis of Comp. 3. Mr. R   contends the Property suffers from lack of storage and a restricted width of   ft. (narrower than any of the other shops within the Complex) restricting perimeter displays to the return frontage; all of which I refer to as 'disabilities'. Mr. R   says that any benefit from the increased prominence afforded by the return frontage is offset by the 'disabilities', accordingly no addition should be made for the return frontage.

26.1 On the evidence I find that an addition should be made to reflect the return frontage but that there is some merit in Mr. R   's contentions as to 'disabilities'. I reflect this by deciding that the amount of the addition shall be   %.

27. Having made my decisions on the issues within the Dispute the arithmetic of my award of the amount of the Rent is as follows:

Floor area in terms of zone A— f.s. × £ p.f.s.p.a.	=	£	p.a.
Plus % to reflect the return frontage	=	£	p.a.
Total		£	p.a.

[*Note that if the Arbitrator is not setting out all the evidence it may be prudent to say so by an appropriate paragraph, e.g. 'I have not set out all the evidence but I have considered it and for the reasons I have given I find and hold that the amount of the rent is £   ([words]).'*]

28. I have reached my conclusion on the evidence of the parties' representatives.

ACCORDINGLY I AWARD AND DETERMINE THAT

29. The amount of the Rack Rental Value of the Property was, on   [*date*], £   ([*words*]) per year.

30. **I FURTHER AWARD AND DIRECT THAT** I tax and settle my total costs of this my first interim award at £   (including VAT in the sum of £   ).

31. **I FURTHER AWARD AND DIRECT THAT** I reserve to my further interim or final award my award as to the costs of the reference and the apportionment of the total costs of this my first interim award if not agreed. As to all other matters this is my final award.

MADE AND PUBLISHED THIS   DAY OF   19 .
Signed: .... [*signature*]
            .... [*full name*]
In the presence of:
[*witness*]
[*Note that if this had been a final award, to include a direction for fractional costs (without any other unusual or special circumstances), appropriate amendments would be made to include reasons if departing from the usual practice that costs follow the event. An example of reasons might be:*

'The Rent contended for by the Claimant was £   ; the Respondent £   . As I have found substantially in favour of the   [*Claimant/Respondent*] I decide, in the exercise of my discretion, to direct a fractional award as to costs.'

Paras. 30 and 31 would be substituted with the following:
'30. I further award and direct that the Claimant shall pay a part of the total costs of this my

final award, which part I tax and settle at £   ([*words*]) including VAT in the sum of £   and that the Respondent shall pay a part of my total costs of this my final award, which part I tax and settle at £   ([*words*]) including VAT in the sum of £   and that if either party shall, in the first instance, have paid to me more than the amount for which it is liable herein the other party shall reimburse that party the amount of the excess forthwith on the taking up of this award.

31. I further award and direct that the [*Claimant/Respondent*] shall pay to the (Respondent/Claimant)   [*fraction/percentage*] of the (Respondent's/Claimant's) costs of the reference to be taxed [by me on a commercial basis] if not agreed.

32. This is my final award [except as to taxation of the [*Respondent's/Claimant's*] costs of the reference if not agreed].']

10.7 Arb
456

CHAPTER 11

The Award

1. Claimant's Particulars of Delay—Arbitrator's Analysis (11.1 Arb)

CLAIMANT'S PARTICULARS OF DELAY—ARBITRATOR'S ANALYSIS

Task Name	Delay to start date of the Task	Increase to the duration of the Task	Delay to completion date of the Task	Delay to the contract Completion Date	Comment (generally from experts report)	Reasons for Delay (generally from pleadings)
01: Removals, demolitions, form openings	0	19	23	4	(1) See under reasons for delay.	(1) Inaccurate survey information (2) Late provision of revised drawings 04/B and 05/B (3) Additional work as set out in AI's 4f, 4g, 4h, 5a, 5c, 6a, 6b, 6c & 10b
02: Form lift-shaft	1	3	3	1 [5w]	(1) See under reasons for delay.	(1) Additional work as set out in AI 2a
03: Roof repairs—strip roof	0	2	2	2 [7w]	(1) No additional delay to Completion date as this Task can be carried out concurrently with Tasks 01 & 02. (2) The late completion of this task delayed the start date of Task: 04 by 2 weeks.	(1) Inaccurate survey information (2) Delaminated existing roof slates
04: Roof repairs—timbers	2	7	7	8 [15w]	(1) Additional delay to Completion Date due to the effect on the progression of the internal works. (2) The late completion of this task delayed the start date of Task: 06 by 6 weeks.	(1) Inaccurate survey information (2) Dry rot to roof timbers (3) Piecemeal instructions to replace roof timbers
05: Window replacement	4	1	6	inc above	(1) The late completion of this task delayed the start date of Task: 06 by 6 weeks.	(1) Delay to roof timber replacement caused scaffolding to be in position for an extra 6 weeks (2) Replacement windows could not be installed until scaffold was removed
06: Carpentry First Fix	6	1	6	1 [16]	(1) The task duration increased due to an increase in the scope of the Carpentry first fix works.	(1) Carpentry first fix could not start until building was watertight, i.e. windows installed (2) Increase in scope of work due to Task No. 01

**11.1 Arb
457**

457

Task Name	Delay to start date of the Task	Increase to the duration of the Task	Delay to completion date of the Task	Delay to the contract Completion Date	Comment (generally from experts report)	Reasons for Delay (generally from pleadings)
07: M&E first fix to existing building	6	1	6	inc above	(1) The start date of this Task was further delayed by an increase of 1 week in the duration of the Carpentry first fix task.	
08: M&E first fix to new extension	6	0	6	inc above	(1) The start date of this Task was delayed by the late completion date of Task: 06.	(1) M&E first fix to the Extension could not commence until the M&E first fix to the Existing building was completed
09: Carp second fix	8	0	13	inc above	(1) The Task start date was delayed by 7 weeks due to the late completion date of Task: 07 & 08. (2) The Task start date delayed by a further 1.5 weeks due to ongoing delays to Tasks: 01, 02, 03 & 04?	(1) Previous delay to ceilings and plaster (2) Previous delays to lift and adjacent elements
10: M&E second fix to existing building	8	2	10	inc above	(1) The Task start date was delayed by 8.5 weeks due to the late commencement of Task: 09. (2) The duration was increased due to the amended M&E performance spec.	(1) Change to M&E performance specification (2) This introduced a redesigned and additional works
11: M&E second fix to new extension	15	0	15	inc above	(1) The Task start date was delayed by the late completion of Task: 10. (2) The duration was increased due to the amended M&E performance specification and additional or varied work.	(1) M&E second fix to the Extension could not commence until the M&E second fix to the Existing building was completed
12: Substructure to new extension	9	2w 3d	2w 3d	2w 3d	The task commenced on time but the duration increased due to extra work.	The task was late on completion due to increases in the quantity of work to be done
13: Decorations	12	1	16	[16]	(1) The duration was increased due to the late issue of the final colour schedule.	(1) Late issue of colour schedule (2) Delay due to work of employers' 'direct' contract work

11.1 Arb 458

2. Respondent's Comments on the Particulars of Delay—Arbitrator's Analysis (11.2 Arb)

RESPONDENTS' COMMENTS ON THE PARTICULARS OF DELAY— ARBITRATOR'S ANALYSIS

Task Name	Delay to start date of the Task	Increase to the duration of the Task	Delay to completion date of the Task	Delay to the contract Completion Date	Comment (generally from experts' report)	Reasons for Delay (generally from pleadings)
01: Removals, demol. & form openings	0	15	15	3w 4d	(1) Delay to a Task which was not all on the Critical path and/or the Contractor failed to reprogramme the Task.	(1) It is admitted that inaccurate survey information was initially issued but that the required amendments were reissued in accordance with the requirements of the programme. (2) In any event any delay caused was not a dominant event.
02: Form lift-shaft	−19	3	−1	0	(1) Delay to a Task which was not on the Critical path and/or the Contractor failed to reprogramme the Task.	(1) It is admitted that the construction of the lift-shaft was amended due to the necessity to revise the brickwork and introduce concrete ring beams. (2) The contractor failed to reprogramme the Works to mitigate the delay.
03: Roof repairs—strip roof	0	0	0	0	(1) Any delay caused was the Claimant's risk.	(1) It is admitted that certain slates were delaminated but that the replacement of these slates did not cause any delay.
04: Roof repairs—timbers	0	4	6	4w 1d [8]	(1) See under reasons for delay.	(1) It is admitted that the duration of this Task was increased by 4 weeks 1 day only (not 8 weeks as contended in the P of C).
05: Window replacement	6	1	7	0	(1) See under reasons for delay.	(1) It is admitted that the start of this Task was delayed by 6 weeks. (2) This delay was due to the defaults of the Claimant and/or the remedial works required to defective window rebates.
06: Carpentry first Fix	3	1	4	1 [9]	(1) Task duration increased due to additional work to Carpentry first fix Task. (2) Carpentry first fix could not start until building was watertight, i.e. windows installed.	(1) It is admitted that the Claimant is due an extension of time of 1 week (P of D para 7.2.4.1)

**11.2 Arb
459**

Task Name	Delay to start date of the Task	Increase to the duration of the Task	Delay to completion date of the Task	Delay to the contract Completion Date	Comment (generally from experts' report)	Reasons for Delay (generally from pleadings)
07: M&E first fix to existing building	5	0	5	0	(1) The task start date was delayed by additional Carp first fix works (+1 week) this is accepted as a relevant event. (2) The Task start date was further delayed by 6 weeks due to a lack of regular and diligent work by the Claimant's M&E subcontractor.	(1) No delay to the Completion date.
08: M&E first fix to new extension	5	0	5	0	(1) The Task start date was delayed by additional Carp first fix works (+1 week) this is accepted as a relevant event. (2) The Task start date was further delayed by 6 weeks due to a lack of regular and diligent work by the Claimant's M&E subcontractor.	(1) No delay to the Completion date.
09: Carp second fix	8	0	8	0	(1) The start date of this Task was delayed by 8 weeks due to the late completion date of Tasks: 07 & 08.	(1) No delay to the Completion date.
10: M&E second fix to existing building	8	2	10	0	(1) The delay to the start date of this Task was due to the late completion date of Task: 09. (2) The duration increased due to the Claimant's failure to issue the M&E design drawings and thereby delaying the issue of construction drawings.	(1) No delay to the Completion date.
11: M&E second fix to new extension	9	2	11	0	(1) The delay to the start date of this Task was due to the late completion date of Task: 09. (2) The Task completion date was further delayed by 5 weeks due to a lack of regular and diligent work by the Claimant's M&E subcontractor.	(1) No delay to the Completion date.
12: Substructures to new extension	0	2w 3d	2w 3d	0	It is accepted that there is an increase in the quantity of the work but the delay is concurrent with other events.	The increase in the task duration did not affect completion date.

Task Name	Delay to start date of the Task	Increase to the duration of the Task	Delay to completion date of the Task	Delay to the contract Completion Date	Comment (generally from experts' report)	Reasons for Delay (generally from pleadings)
13: Decorations	10	1	11	3d [9w 3d]	(1) The delay to the start date of this Task was due to the late completion date of Task: 11, i.e. Claimant's responsibility. (2) The Task completion date was further delayed by 1 week due to a lack of regular and diligent work by the Claimant and/or poor workmanship.	(1) No delay to the Completion date.

11.2 Arb
461

461

3. Outline of Award relating to Extensions of Time—Weighing the Evidence—Arbitrator's Analysis (11.3 Arb)

OUTLINE OF AWARD RELATING TO EXTENSIONS OF TIME—WEIGHING THE EVIDENCE—[ARBITRATOR'S ANALYSIS]

Task Name	Extension of time required by Claimant (cumulative total in [ ] brackets)	Extension of time as assessed by Respondent (cumulative total in [ ] brackets)	Extension of time awarded (cumulative total in [ ] brackets)	Building Contract clause reference	Outline reasons for delay
01: Removals, Demolitions and Form Openings	4 [4]	3w 4d [3w 4d]	3w 4d [3w 4d]	cl 2.4.7	It is common ground that the survey information issued by TAP was inaccurate. It showed non-load-bearing walls where they were in fact load-bearing. Revised drawings were issued on 7 May 1991. Additional work was instructed as set out in Ai's 4f, 4g, 5a, 5c, 6a, 6c & 10b. The Respondent admits to a delay of 3w 4d. The Claimant seeks an extension of 4w. The Respondent denies that this was a dominant cause of delay. On balance I prefer the evidence of Maclean that the Claimant could have taken steps to incorporate this work into his programme so as to minimise the effects of the delay.
02: Form lift-shaft	1 [5]	0 [3w 4d]	1 [4w 4d]	cl 2.4.5 (3.6)	Some of the delay to the lift-shaft could have been avoided. It could have been commenced earlier. There was an error by the Claimant in constructing the trimmer beams. There was a variation to the design to the lift-shaft, AI 2a. This caused a critical delay to key structural roof elements. The main purlins and the water tank were supported off the head of the lift-shaft. The delay claimed by the Claimant is valid. Notwithstanding the error on the trimmer beams the main cause of the delay was the change to use of engineering bricks. The error on the trimmer beams ran concurrently with the main delay.
03: Roof repairs—strip roof	2 [7]	0 [3w 4d]	0 [4w 4d]	na	It is admitted that certain of the slates to the roof were delaminated. The roof stripping and associated work was delayed: however, in the event this was not critical. The Works were already being delayed by the construction of the lift-shaft.
04: Roof repairs—timbers	8 [15]	4w 1d [8]	4w 1d [9]	cl 2.4.7	The argument that instructions about the replacement of the roof timbers relied on the progress of the Contractor is not accepted. It was possible to inspect the timbers at any time. The Contractor was under no obligation to provide temporary waterproofing to cater for the possibility of this delay. This includes the delay caused by the leadwork.
05: Window replacement	6 inc above [15]	0 [8]	0 [9]	na	This element could have been removed from the Critical Path by installing temporary waterproofing—a much more straightforward task than that of protecting the roof. The risk of damaging water ingress is also less in the event of any failure of the waterproofing.
06: Carpentry first Fix	1 [16]	1 [9]	1 [10]	cl 2.4.5 (3.6)	The commencement of this activity was delayed by the preceding critical elements but it was further delayed by the introduction of variations which substantially increased the scope of the works. The extension of time of 1w is admitted.

Task Name	Extension of time required by Claimant (cumulative total in [ ] brackets)	Extension of time as assessed by Respondent (cumulative total in [ ] brackets)	Extension of time awarded (cumulative total in [ ] brackets)	Building Contract clause reference	Outline reasons for delay
07: M&E first fix to existing building	6 inc above [16]	0 [9]	0 [10]	na	There is no valid reason as to why the M&E first fix activities should have been delayed by a period greater than the cumulative delay already incurred.
08: M&E first Fix to new extension	6 inc above [16]	0 [9]	0 [10]	na	See item 07. It is also not accepted that the M&E first fix work to the new extension could not have been carried out concurrently with that in the existing building. The risk of any delay caused by the decision to continue to employ only one gang of operatives is the contractors in any event.
09: Carp second Fix	13 inc above [16]	0 [9]	0 [10]	na	There is no valid reason as to why the Carpentry second fix activities should have been delayed by a period greater than the cumulative delay already incurred.
10: M&E second fix to existing building	10 inc above [16]	0 [9]	2 [12]	cl 2.4.7	The architect attempted to 'off-load' elements of design which were his responsibility by introducing an amended and enhanced performance specification. The subcontractors' 'shop' drawings were issued late but this was primarily due to the increased nature and scope of design drawings they were forced to produce in order to meet the requirements of the new specification and also because of basic co-ordination input which should have been supplied by the Architect.
11: M&E second fix to new extension	15 inc above [16]	0 [9]	0 [12]	na	By this stage it should have been obvious that there was a potential to better the original programme by progressing the M&E works in the new extension concurrently with those works in the existing building. A one-week delay occurred to the new extension due to the change in the performance specification but if reprogrammed it would have been concurrent with that caused in the existing building (the 5 weeks claimed due to the 'sequential' addition of the original activity duration is totally unsupportable).
12: Substructures to new extension	2w 3d inc above [16]	0 [9]	0	na	No evidence was given by Redman to support his contention that this actually caused a delay to completion.
13: Decorations	16 inc above [16]	3d [9w 3d]	5 [12.5]	cl 2.4.7	Delay and disruption was caused by the late variations to the decorations.

11.3 Arb 463

4. Agreed Minutes of Meeting between HM Customs & Excise (VAT Office) and Law Society—23 October 1991 (11.4)

APPENDIX J

(referred to in paragraph 9.2)

SETTLEMENT OF DISPUTES: AGREED MINUTES OF A MEETING WITH THE LAW SOCIETY ON 23 OCTOBER, 1991.

Introduction

The Law Society said that the Tribunal decision in *Cooper Chasney Ltd* v *CCE* (LON/89/1409Z) had generated comment and correspondence within the VAT Sub-Committee of the Law Society's Revenue Law Committee on the basis that it might be understood as throwing doubt on the guidance contained in Customs' Press Notice of 19 November 1987. An approach was therefore made to Customs, who had replied that they did not consider the decision to be in conflict with the Press Notice. The Law Society, however, felt that there were several aspects of the settlement of disputes where VAT treatment is not straightforward and that further clarification was necessary. It was important that solicitors should be applying the correct principles and assurance from Customs with a view to giving agreed guidance to the profession would be welcome.

Customs' original approach

Customs & Excise's original approach had been that giving up a right to sue somebody in return for payment was a taxable supply and it satisfied s.3(2)(b) of the VAT Act 1983, which provides that anything which is not a supply of goods but is done for a consideration (including, if so done, the granting, assignment *or surrender of any right*) is a supply of services (if done in the course or furtherance of a business).

There had never been any question that if a payment by way of compensation was made pursuant to a Court Order, this was outside the scope. However, given that basic principle, and the uncertainty surrounding out of court settlements prior to the issue of the Press Notice, it had seemed that customs were forcing taxpayers to go all the way through the courts and not to enter any settlement by way of compromise, in order to guarantee that any payment would not attract VAT. Customs had reviewed their policy in the light of the decision in the case of *Whites Metal Company* v *CCE* (LON/86/686Z, NO. 2400) where the VAT Tribunal had held that services were not supplied by a plaintiff to a defendant in reaching a settlement of an action in tort.

Press Notice 82/87

The Press Notice had been issued, with the object of restricting its application to genuine disputes only. If a settlement agreement was worded in terms that the plaintiff was giving up rights to sue the defendant in exchange for a sum of money, this was not a supply. If the agreement not to sue and to settle out of court confirmed a previously agreed price, or confirmed a reduction to a previously agreed price, VAT would be adjusted, using the credit note mechanism, by reference to the price finally agreed. The situation when payment was made subject to a Court Order remained unchanged.

Since the Press Notice had been issued, very few cases had been brought to VAT headquarters. Cooper Chasney and Edenroc were notable exceptions. Customs believed that both these decisions were in accordance with the Press Notice. Local offices had been dealing with queries. However, it was the Law Society's view that the lack of cases which had been brought could indicate unawareness of the potential traps where elements of a settlement could attract a VAT liability.

Customs had considered, when drafting the Press Notice, the particular example of royalties when there had been an inadvertent breach of copyright. If payment was partly to compensate for a past breach, and partly for permission to use in the future the material subject to copyright, there should be a reasonable apportionment. A distinction needed to be drawn. Payment by way of compensation in respect of a past transgression was outside the scope, but payment in consideration of allowing the future use of the copyright material was in respect of a taxable supply.

Cooper Chasney Limited v CCE (LON/89/1409Z)

In the Law Society's view the facts of *Cooper Chasney* were perhaps more straightforward than difficulties which could be experienced in practice. In that case, the plaintiff had expressly allowed the defendant to use the name 'Infolink' in the future, (a name which the plaintiff had previously used in his business), but the terms of the settlement were that in return for payment to the plaintiff by the defendant of an agreed sum, the plaintiff reverted to his own name (Cooper Chasney Ltd) and agreed to discontinue proceeding against the defendant. It was clear that the elements of the agreement went beyond breaches which had occurred in the past and giving up a right to sue.

Customs said that in deciding what the payment in the settlement of a dispute was for, they look carefully at the words used by the parties (as in *Cooper Chasney*, where an agreement had been entered into which had been set out in the decision) and tax the parties accordingly.

Practical Consequences

The Law Society asked if Customs were happy that Press Notice 82/87 was correct, and they confirmed that they were satisfied with the general approach, and did not think it should be extended, for example, on the basis of the decisions in *Neville Russell* v *Customs & Excise* (1987 VAT TR 194) and *Gleneagles Hotel plc* v *Customs and Excise* (1986 VAT TR 196), to indicate that anything done in exchange for consideration is a supply.

Customs did not consider that a person had an intrinsic right to sue so that by not suing, a person was not necessarily giving up any right. Customs thought the position could be analysed by saying that a person was really exercising an option not to enforce an alleged wrong, rather than giving up any right. The acceptance of an offer not to sue is taken because the reason for wanting to sue in the first place is settled on receipt of payment.

11.4
465

Customs agreed that if VAT was never mentioned in negotiating a settlement, the plaintiff could suddenly find that the amount of cash he received in his settlement was reduced by VAT. There was a suggestion that this could be avoided by adding to the agreement for settlements the words 'VAT will be added [to the agreed sum] if applicable'. However, it would obviously be preferable to issue clear guidance to avoid the necessity of requiring such terms automatically to be added to settlement wordings.

The Law Society asked if Customs agreed that liquidated damages paid under contracts were also outside the scope, and Customs confirmed this. Such cases would not involve litigation, but were within the spirit of the Press Notice. If a contract contained provisions for damages in respect of a breach, this would generally be within the Press Notice, but if a plaintiff was giving up a separate right, for example, the right to receive notice, this could be a taxable supply.

Customs have agreed a 'Joint Statement of Practice' (JSP) with the principal leasing association in order to avoid contractual arguments and any ambiguity over the correct VAT treatment of termination payments and rebates/refunds of rentals arising under equipment leases. The object of the JSP is to establish a common treatment which provides that:

(1) all lease termination payments may be treated as being in respect of taxable supplies, i.e. of the right to terminate. Here the termination payment is usually calculated by references to the amount of rental payments outstanding under the primary lease period and;

(2) where on expiry or termination of an equipment lease, the lessee receives from the lessor a rebate or refund of rentals, no adjustment for VAT previously charged need be made. However, credit notes should be endorsed 'This is not a credit note for VAT purposes'.

Importantly, the JSP does not override any contractual arrangements in force. If the lessors wish to revert to the terms of their original agreements, they may do so. For example, lease termination payments may arise on default by a lessee which are by way of liquidated damages and therefore outside the scope of VAT.

Taxpayers who were not within the major leasing associations could rely on this agreement, but they would not necessarily be aware of it. It was confirmed that local VAT offices had knowledge of it.

Specific Examples

The Law Society's letter to the Solicitor's Office at Customs of 18 June had listed examples of where we had sought Customs' guidance on specific issues. There were raised for discussion, and the following answers given:

1. Customs confirmed that Press Notice 82/87 covered only payments made *after* proceedings had commenced. If it was clear that payments had been made before proceedings had been commenced, but such payments would not be within s.3(2)(b), Customs would extend outside the scope treatment to such payments.

2. In the area of involuntary supplies (e.g. a dispute concerning right of light for which damages are awarded) Customs confirmed that only damages in respect of past infringements would be outside the scope. Where a settlement covered past infringements, and also permission to continue in the future the conduct which gave rise to those infringements, Customs would accept a reasonable apportionment. The Law Society asked about the case where the court required a party to give up a right (e.g. a right of light or an intellectual property right) in exchange for a payment from the other party. Customs said that this was a difficult point which they would need to consider further. Article 6(1) of the Sixth Directive was relevant where it referred to 'tolerating an act or situation' as a possible supply for VAT purposes. Questions concerning rights of light can cause problems. Much depends on whether a payment is made in return for the right to take someone else's light or whether it is compensation for the loss of light subsequent to an adjacent building being constructed. It could be argued in exceptional circumstances that the court is deciding what level of consideration is due in return for the granting of the right. However, it is thought that in the majority of cases the payment will be damages imposed upon the payer by the court and therefore outside the scope of VAT. For example, in cases where the court decides that light may be taken and that compensation is payable this will be seen as outside the scope of VAT—there is no consensual element.

3. Where litigation has involved a supply on which VAT had already been accounted for (but the price was not paid) and the result is a reduction in the price paid for the supply, it may be necessary for a supplier to issue a credit note in order to recover part of the VAT which he had previously accounted for and which he had not received. Customs confirmed that in such a case, the credit note could be accepted as valid and it would prima facie be necessary for the recipient of the supply to repay to Customs the tax which he had already claimed back.

4. By way of clarification as to when damages were considered to be compensatory and when such payments would constitute consideration for taxable supplies, Customs offered

the example of a local authority digging up a pavement in front of a parade of shops. Compensation for loss of trade suffered as a result of their action paid by the local authority to a shopkeeper would not be regarded as a taxable supply. However, if a shopkeeper was paid by the local authority to allow them to work on his land, the payment would be consideration for a taxable supply.

Customs said that they would want to consider in greater detail the question of warranty claims. For example, in a standard rated property transaction, where a warranty had understated the rent and the contract provided for a reduction in the purchase price in such a situation, the procedure set out in 3 above would apply, and the vendor would have to issue a credit note to recover that part of the VAT previously accounted for. The example of net assets of a business having been overstated in warranties given on sale was not so relevant since if it was a question of shares, it would be in the realm of exempt supplies anyway. Compensation in these circumstances would be regarded as outside the scope unless the agreement provided for a reduction in price.

5. Where the settlement involved cross supplies (other than the mere surrender of the right of action) tax would be payable by each party, without netting off, according to the nature of the supply. The situation may arise that there may be a consideration paid in return for a party agreeing to enter into an agreement. For example, in the property industry, reverse premiums may be paid to a potential tenant in consideration of the tenant agreeing to enter into a property lease or for agreeing to carry out building, refurbishment or demolition works, viz. Neville Russell and Battersea Leisure.

If the supply under the agreement was e.g. free services, VAT would not be due.

6. Customs confirmed that interest on damages is outside the scope of VAT. It has been confirmed in the European decision in *BAZ Bausystem AG* v *Finanzant Munchen fur Korperschaften* [1982] ECR 2527 that interest would not increase consideration for a supply.

If an international breach had occurred, the same basic principles should be followed. For example, Schedule 3 to the VAT Act 1983 should not apply to a cross-border giving up of rights. Apparently, the Dutch and the Germans had had bilateral discussions and had confirmed that they would apply outside the scope treatment on the same basis as in the UK.

11.4
467

5. Final Award—Save as to Costs (11.5 Arb)

IN THE MATTER OF THE ARBITRATION ACTS 1950 TO 1979

AND

IN THE MATTER OF AN ARBITRATION UNDER THE JCT ARBITRATION RULES (18 JULY 1988)

BETWEEN

RELIABLE BUILDERS LIMITED   Claimant

AND

SANCTUARY HOUSE LIMITED   Respondent

FINAL AWARD—SAVE AS TO COSTS

1.00 Background to the dispute

1.01 When William Bliss was made redundant in late 1989, from his post as an administrator in the National Health Service, he and his wife Constance, decided to invest his redundancy money in a Nursing Home for the Frail Elderly.

1.02 William's administrative skills and Constance's experience as a Nursing Sister, seemed to them to be an ideal combination for running such a home.

1.03 Having completed a Feasibility Study which, had received tacit approval from his bankers, the Blisses, purchased The Old Manor House, in Woodbridge, Suffolk—a fine Queen Anne house—which, they considered, once converted and extended, would be ideal for their purpose.

1.04 Maximilian D'Courcy D'Iffy is the principal of The Architectural Practice of Norwich (TAP), a firm specialising in works of conversion in listed buildings as well as being experienced in projects involving the housing of the elderly.

1.05 Mr D'Iffy was also a long-time friend of the Blisses, so what more natural, on acquiring a listed building to be converted to a nursing home, than to invite his practice to provide the architectural services for this project.

1.06 Although Mr D'Iffy was the Architect 'named' in the Contract—the day-to-day work was carried out by his assistant, an Associate Partner, Frances Hutch.

1.07 TAP invited the Reliable Builders Limited (RBL)—a long-established construction company, founded in 1924—amongst others, to tender for this project. RBL submitted a tender for the refurbishment and extension of Sanctuary House (as it was to become known) on 31 January 1991.

1.08 TAP had sufficient experience of this sort of job in the past to know that the small local builder who was likely to put in a genuine tender would probably only do so if some sort of Bill of Quantities was provided. TAP did not consider that the size or complexity of the project warranted the full-blown services of a professional quantity surveyor but they did engage one to prepare, what was described on its cover, as follows:

Tender Budget—Nov '90.
Draft Bill of Quantities—For Guidance Only

Sanctuary House Limited are not liable for any
inaccuracies in quantities or dimensions.

1.09 In addition to the note of warning on the Draft Bill that it was 'For Guidance Only', the Specification—also sent to Tenderers—emphasised the 'Lump Sum' nature of the contract and

'reminded the contractors that under no circumstances will ... any work ... be remeasured'

Additionally, the tenderers were asked to submit their own '... priced Bill of Quantities' which RBL failed to do as they said they were given insufficient time to prepare them.

1.10 Mr Hocking, the managing director of RBL, dealt with all tender enquiries although not with the detailed preparation of their tender.

1.11 RBL submitted their Tender, dated 31 January 1991, in the sum of £617,148.24 ex VAT.

No reservation was made, in this letter, about the lack of time to check the quantities or the reservation of the right to remeasure works on completion.

Only subsequent to submitting their tender did Mr Hocking complain to TAP about the lack of information concerning ground levels, although all tenderers were supplied with a 'Site Level Drawing'. His complaint was more to do with their not being given sufficient time to check these levels or the draft quantities.

1.12 Mr D'Iffy had been hoping for a price within his client's budget figure of £540,000 and as a result, following receipt of RBL's tender, various telephone conversations took place between Mr D'Iffy and Mr Hocking. The end result of these telephone negotiations was an agreed contract sum of £550,000, a reduction of 11.6 per cent from a corrected tender figure of £622,171.95.

RBL confirmed this revised contract sum, by letter to TAP, 28 March 1991, and for the first time in writing, reiterated their concern about the approximate nature of the quantities and the effect on unknowns, particularly the earthworks.

1.13 TAP telephoned RBL, in reply to this letter and suggested that this whole question of the fixed-price, lump-sum nature of the contract (and thus the approximate quantities) would best be resolved at the site meeting scheduled 8 April.

The outcome of this 8 April meeting was agreement on a limited list of items which would be the subject of remeasurement. The details of which were subsequently confirmed by letter 15 April 1991 from Mr D'Iffy to RBL. After the list was agreed at the 8 April meeting the parties signed the IFC '84 Form, which had been previously prepared, and therefore made no reference to the list just agreed.

**11.5 Arb
469**

1.14 Work had started on-site on 2 April 1991 and was due for completion on 10 December 1991 but in the event was not finished until 31 March 1992.

1.15 Following completion RBL compiled their Final Account and submitted it to TAP. There followed an exchange of correspondence in November and December 1992 over the Final Account from which it became clear that RBL and TAP had a different view of the items which were to be remeasured as agreed at the site meeting 8 April 1991.

Full details of the exchange of the correspondence between the parties in connection with the pre-contract negotiations and the subsequent exchange over the Final Account are given in my Interim Declaratory Award, referred to in 4.03 below.

1.16 Three weeks or so after the completion of this project, the basement laundry, which had been tanked as part of the building contract, flooded, damaging equipment and clothing.

1.17 On Christmas Eve 1992, the Gibbs ceiling, in the sitting room of Sanctuary House, collapsed and as a result the Health Authority closed the entire floor above, comprising 15 rooms.

This closure meant temporarily accommodating the displaced residents in a nearby Home whilst the restoration of the ceiling was under discussion.

1.18 As Sanctuary House was a Grade 1 listed building, in addition to the local planners, the Historic Building people became involved in the discussion concerning restoration. The outcome was that restoration work did not begin until late October 1993 and was completed on 3 November 1993. Reletting of the 15 rooms commenced immediately following this work and the last unit was reoccupied on 21 February 1994.

In the intervening period between the ceiling collapse and the final reletting following restoration, SHL had sustained losses amounting to approximately £6000 per week.

In addition, they had been put to additional expense through having to send out their laundry following the flooding of the basement and through having to transport and temporally rehouse their displaced tenants.

1.19 In April 1992 SHL had failed to honour the Penultimate Certificate and in May 1992 RBL commenced proceedings in the County Court for payment of this certificate.

1.20 Following the exchange of correspondence, concerning the Final Account, referred to earlier, the parties were unable to agree and, after sending SHL a Notice of a Dispute, RBL applied, on 1 February 1993, to the Royal Institution of Chartered Surveyors for the appointment of an arbitrator, in accordance with Article 5 of IFC '84.

2.00 Appointment

2.01 Disputes having arisen I, DAVID EMSEE of Toad Hall, Hunstanton Water, Norfolk, was appointed by the President of the Royal Institution of Chartered Surveyors, by appointment dated 20 February 1993.

2.02 The reference being governed by the JCT Arbitration Rules (1988), I informed the parties that the Notification Date, under these Rules, was 24 February 1993.

3.00 The Contract

3.01 The Form of Contract is the JCT intermediate Form of Building Contract (IFC '84) 1990 Edition, signed by both parties on 8 April 1991.

3.02 Article 5 of IFC '84 is an Arbitration Clause.

11.5 Arb 470

4.00 Interlocutories and Hearing

4.01 A Preliminary Meeting took place, between me, the parties and their representatives, on 23 March 1993 at the Claimant's surveyors offices in Norwich, Norfolk.

The Claimant had not opted for Rule 7 to apply, by informing me, in accordance with Rule 4.2.2, seven days before the Preliminary Meeting.

The Respondent informed me, by letter 28 February 1993, that he would only attend the Preliminary meeting 'without prejudice'. It subsequently transpired that the reason for this reservation was a jurisdictional point.

Agreement was reached, at the preliminary meeting that Rule 6—Full Procedure with Hearing—should apply.

4.02 It was also agreed that I should determine some Preliminary Issues in advance of the substantive issues and although a timetable was agreed for service of the Statements on the substantive issues, this timetable was not to be activated until 28 days after the publication of the Award on the Preliminary Issues. In addition to the timetable, the entire conduct of the reference was discussed and, where agreed, was recorded in my subsequent Order for Directions.

4.03 The matters to be determined as Preliminary Issues were also set out in that Order, No 2, dated 25 March 1993.

Full details of the interlocutory proceedings and the subsequent Hearing, which lead to my determination of these Preliminary Issues, are set out in my INTERIM DECLARATORY AWARD (5.18 Arb) which I published on 10 June 1993.

4.04 Following publication of this Interim Award, as the parties were unable to agree on the Costs that I awarded, I was invited to hear submissions on the costs of the Preliminary Issues. Having received and considered submissions and heard counsel for both sides, on 31 August 1993 I published my determination on these costs in my Order for Directions No. 10 (7.7 Arb), dated 1 September 1993.

4.05 The parties' Statements on the substantive issues were served in accordance with the agreed timetable, or within extended times that I directed.

4.06 As requested by the parties, I carried out an inspection visit of the subject property, on 23 August 1993.

4.07 On 1 September 1993 I was informed, by the Respondent, that he had instructed a new solicitor, Mr Crighton. Subsequently, Mr Crighton, sought my consent to Re-Serve the Defence and Counterclaim, which consent was given and the Respondent was ordered to pay all resultant 'costs thrown away'; these costs to be taxed by me if not agreed.

In the event, these costs were not agreed and following submissions from the parties, in compliance with my Directions, I published an INTERIM AWARD on TAXATION on 2 November 1993 (7.14 Arb). The Respondent paid the costs that I awarded, on 11 November 1993. Full details of the interlocutory proceedings covering this taxation exercise can be found in this Interim Award on Taxation.

4.08 On 6 September 1993 the Claimant abandoned the County Court action over payment of the Penultimate Certificate in favour of consolidating the action with this present arbitration. An 'Ad Hoc Arbitration Agreement', extending my jurisdiction to deal with this issue, was subsequently signed by both parties (4.4 Arb).

4.09 By letter 1 October 1993 I suggested that I meet with the parties various Experts with a view to narrowing the issues. The parties agreed to this suggestion and meetings took place, between me and the various experts, at the end of November and early December 1993. Full details of these meetings and what was agreed are to be found in the Hearing Bundle (PC/35, PC/36, PC/37 and PC/38).

4.10 At the Preliminary Meeting both parties had indicated that they would require a Reasoned Award and neither were prepared to enter into an Exclusion agreement under Section 3 of the Arbitration Act 1979. Subsequently, on 15 June 1993, the Claimant did sign an Exclusion Agreement.

11.5 Arb 471

4.11 On 10 January 1994 I held a Pre-Hearing Review meeting following which I issued my Order for Directions No. 17 (8.5 Arb) confirming what had been agreed.

4.12 On 11 January 1994 cross applications were made to me for Security of Costs. A Hearing was held on this issue on 14 February 1994. Full details of the interlocutory proceedings and my determination can be found in my Order for Directions No. 19, dated 21 February 1994 (9.3 Arb).

4.13 A Hearing was held on the substantive issues, which commenced on 7 March 1994 and concluded on 18 April 1994—18 sitting days in all, interrupted for one week due to a car accident which I had on 22 March.

4.14 At the Hearing the parties were both represented by Counsel—the Claimant by Mr Belcher and the Respondent by Miss O'Brien. Throughout the reference the Claimant has been represented by Mr Redman, Claims Consultant and, since 2 September 1993, the Respondent has been represented by Mr Crighton, solicitor.

4.15 At the close of the hearing I reminded Mr Belcher that he was to give me a note of the questions on which he required Reasons. He referred me to the List of Issues agreed with Miss O'Brien (10.3). I subsequently reconsidered this list and accepted that he had complied with the requirements of Rule 11.1.

5.00 Preliminary Issues

5.01 The Preliminary Issues which I determined were:

5.01.1 How and when was the contract formed?

5.01.2 What are the Terms and Conditions of the contract?

5.01.3 What items are subject to remeasurement?

5.01.4 What rates are to be applied to the contract work in general and the status of the discount?

5.01.5 The Gibbs Ceiling—is it genuine?

5.01.6 Is the builder in breach of contract over the waterproofing of the basement?

5.02 First Issue

How and when was the Contract formed?

5.02.1 Mr Belcher, in his Opening Submissions, posed three sub-issues to Miss O'Brien's First Issue for me to consider.

5.02.2 Sub-Issue 1 Whether the Contract is to be found

5.02.2.1 solely in the IFC '84 Form or

5.02.2.2 whether it is also to be found in the letters to which the Claimant refers in sub-paragraph 2.11 of the Statement of Case.

5.02.3 Sub-Issue 2

5.02.3.1 If (5.02.2.2), whether all the contract documents when read together will have the effect for which the Claimant contends.

Claimant contends:

5.02.3.2 That a true construction of the contract is contained in all the documents which are pleaded and not exclusively in IFC '84 contract.

5.02.4 Sub-Issue 3 If (5.02.2.1) whether the written contract should be rectified.

5.02.5 On the First Issue I found

THAT THE CONTRACT WAS FORMED AT THE **8** APRIL **1991** MEETING WHEN THE PARTIES AGREED THAT IT WOULD BE SUBJECT TO REMEASUREMENT LIMITED TO THOSE ITEMS LISTED IN THE APPENDIX TO TAP'S LETTER TO RBL DATED **15** APRIL **1991**.

And I held on this first issue

THAT THE CONTRACT IS TO BE FOUND IN THE IFC '**84** FORM AND IN THE **15** APRIL **1991** LETTER REFERRED TO ABOVE.

And I further held on Sub-Issue 3 that

THE AGREEMENT BETWEEN THE CLAIMANT AND THE RESPONDENT ON THE IFC '**84** FORM **8** APRIL **1991** IS RECTIFIED TO INCLUDE, AS A CONTRACT CONDITION, THE LIST OF ITEMS SUBJECT TO REMEASUREMENT AS SET OUT IN THE LETTER DATED **15** APRIL **1991**, FROM THE RESPONDENT'S ARCHITECT, MR D'IFFY, ADDRESSED TO THE CLAIMANT.

5.03 Second Issue

What are the Terms and Conditions of the Contract?

On the Second issue I found

THAT THE CONTRACT DOCUMENTS COMPRISE, OR ARE EVIDENCED BY, THE FOLLOWING:

5.03.1 Letter RBL to TAP 31 January 1991.

5.03.2 Letter TAP to RBL dated 20 March 1991 including the contract referred to therein as follows:

The JCT Intermediate Form of Building Contract (IFC '84) 1990 Edition.

5.03.3 Letter TAP to RBL dated 15 April 1991 together with 'Agreed list of Items Subject to Remeasurement' attached thereto—2 pages.

5.03.4 The 'Tender Budget' dated November 1990 as a Schedule of Rates only as amended by letter TAP to RBL dated 20 March 1991.

5.03.5 The Invitation to Tender, 7 January 1991, together with the documents referred to therein, as set out in para. 7.01 above.

5.04 Third Issue

What items are subject to remeasurement?

On the Third Issue I found

THAT THE ITEMS SUBJECT TO REMEASUREMENT, EXCLUDING MATTERS COVERED BY ARCHITECTS INSTRUCTIONS AND/OR DEFINED AS VARIATIONS, IS LIMITED TO THE AGREED LIST ATTACHED TO TAP'S LETTER 15 APRIL 1991.

5.05 Fourth Issue

What Rates are to be applied to the Contract Work in General and what is the Status of the Discount?

On the Fourth Issue I found

THAT THE RATES TO BE APPLIED TO THE CONTRACT WORK GENERALLY WILL BE THE RATES AS SCHEDULED IN THE TENDER BUDGET DATED NOVEMBER 1990 ADJUSTED BY THE AGREEMENT, 7 MARCH 1991, IN EFFECT A DISCOUNT OF 11.6 PER CENT.

THE STATUS OF THE DISCOUNT THEN IS SUCH AS TO REDUCE EACH OF THE INDIVIDUAL RATES MAKING UP RBL'S PRICED TENDER AS AMENDED.

5.06 Fifth Issue

The Gibbs Ceiling—is it genuine?

I found on the Fifth Issue

THAT THE CEILING IN THE SITTING ROOM OF SANCTUARY HOUSE, WHICH COLLAPSED ON CHRISTMAS EVE 1992 WAS ERECTED IN THE EARLY EIGHTEENTH CENTURY AND WAS DESIGNED BY THE ARCHITECT JAMES GIBBS, OR UNDER HIS SUPERVISION. IN ADDITION THE DECORATIVE PLASTERWORK WAS EXECUTED BY MASTER CRAFTSMEN SUCH AS BAGUTTI, VASALLI AND SERENA.

11.5 Arb
473

5.07 Sixth Issue

Is the builder in breach of contract over the waterproofing of the basement?

I found on the Sixth Issue that

THE BUILDER IS IN BREACH OF CONTRACT CONCERNING THE WATERPROOFING OF THIS BASEMENT; SPECIFICALLY IN BREACH OF CLAUSE 3/15A OF THE SPECIFICATION.

5.08 Costs

As stated in 4.04 above

I FURTHER DIRECTED THAT THE COSTS OF THE HEARING ON THE PRELIMINARY ISSUES, AND THE COSTS INCIDENTAL BE PAID BY THE CLAIMANT IN ANY EVENT. (Order for Directions No. 10—7.7 Arb)

6.00 Substantive Issues

I now deal with the substantive issues.

AND NOW

I, the said, D EMSEE, having considered the evidence adduced in the submissions made by and on behalf of both parties

HEREBY MAKE AND PUBLISH THIS MY FINAL AWARD SAVE AS TO COSTS

6.01 And the Claimant Claims:

6.01.1 A declaration that the Claimant is entitled to an extension of time of 16 weeks to 31 March 1992.

6.01.2 A declaration that the Claimant is entitled to a refund of the sum of £146,000 wrongfully deducted by way of liquidated damages or alternatively damages (including interest as special damages).

6.01.3 A declaration that the Claimant is entitled to a refund in respect of sums wrongfully withheld in respect of alleged defects or alternatively damages.

6.01.4 The amount due under the contract totalling £45,835.10 or alternatively damages.

6.01.5 The release of the second moiety of the retention fund.

6.01.6 Loss and expense totalling £139,867.20 together with £22,940.47 interest thereon which (subject to any change in base rates) continues to accrue at 9% per annum from 28 January 1993 and compounded at quarterly intervals or alternatively damages.

6.01.7 The sum of £10,954 in respect of Interim Certificate 12 either pursuant to the contract or alternatively as damages for breach of contract together with interest as special damages for non-payment of Interim Certificate 12 and late payment of either Interim Certificates.

6.01.8 Interest in addition to that claimed as special damages, as damages for breach of contract or alternatively 19A Interest.

6.01.9 Costs.

6.01.10 Further or other relief.

6.02 And the Respondent Counterclaims

6.02.1 A declaration that the true and proper value of Interim Certificates 6, 7 and 10 net of retention was £79,800 and £48,896 and £26,800 respectively.

6.02.2 £7,040 in respect of the defect fire doors.

6.02.3 £418,259 in respect of losses in connection with the collapse of the Gibbs ceiling.

6.02.4 £29,833.25 in respect of losses in connection with the basement flooding.

6.02.5 Damages.

6.02.6 Interest pursuant to Statute for such period or periods as the Arbitrator may deem fit.

6.02.7 Costs.

I now deal with each of the issues in turn following the numbering on the Lists of Issues handed to me by Counsel at the commencement of the Hearing.

7.00 Issue 1—Extension of Time Claim

7.01 To how much, if any, extension of time, is the Claimant entitled?

It is common ground between the Parties that there is an entitlement to extension of time under the Contract.

At paragraph 7. of The Amended Statement of Case (7.8), the Claimant claims an entitlement to have the Contract completion date extended to the 31st March 1992, an additional period of 16 weeks.

At paragraph 11. of the Re-Re-amended Statement of Defence and Counterclaim (7.13) the Respondent admits an entitlement to an extension of time of nine weeks and three days, which would give an extended completion date to the 17th February 1992.

The issues concerning extension of time arise under specific tasks on the Claimants programme for the Works.

The tasks under which the issues arise are as follows:

01. Removals and Demolitions.
02. Form Lift-shaft.
03. Roof repairs—strip roof.
04. Roof repairs—timbers.
05. Window replacement.
06. Carpentry first fix.
07. Mechanical and Electrical First Fix to existing building.
08. Mechanical and Electrical First Fix to new extension.
09. Carpenter Second Fix.
10. Mechanical and Electrical Second Fix to existing building.
11. Mechanical and Electrical Second Fix to new extension.
12. Substructure to new extension.
13. Decorations.

7.02 Removals and Demolitions

It is common ground that the survey drawings issued by TAP were inaccurate. Some walls which were designated non-load-bearing, in fact, proved to be load-bearing. Removals and demolition work ceased until the revised drawings 04/B and 05/B were produced and issued on the 7th May 1991. These revised drawings contained additional work. This additional work was covered by Architects Instructions 4f, 4g, 4h, 5a, 5c, 6a, 6b, 6c and 10b.

11.5 Arb
475

The Claimant seeks an extension of time of four weeks for this additional work.

The Respondent concedes that the Claimant is entitled to an extension of time under this head but only of three weeks as he avers that the Claimant failed to proceed with this varied work, on the oral instructions given at the time this matter was brought to the Architect's attention.

With a conceded delay in connection with the dry rot infestation and the injection of a damp-proof course, the Respondent accepts that the Claimant is entitled to an extension of time of three weeks and four days for this work.

I find that the four-week delay, contended for by the Claimant, could have been reduced by commencing the lift-shaft activity earlier. In the event the argument for further delay is defeated due to the more dominant impact of the incorrect fabrication of the trimmer beams to the lift-shaft floor openings.

ACCORDINGLY ON THE REMOVALS AND DEMOLITION OPERATION I FIND THAT THE CLAIMANT IS ENTITLED TO AN EXTENSION OF TIME OF THREE WEEKS AND FOUR DAYS UNDER CLAUSE 2.4.7 OF THE CONTRACT.

7.03 Form Lift-shaft

It is common ground that there was delay to the lift-shaft operation which ran concurrently with the removals and demolitions operation.

It is also common ground that Architect's Instruction 2a introduced a change in specification to the construction of the lift-shaft. It was to be constructed with engineering bricks and with concrete ring beams.

The Claimant seeks an extension of time of one week for the delay caused by executing the changed and extra work.

The Respondent denies that this change of specification was the cause of any delay. He avers that the Claimant could have commenced work to the lift-shaft at an earlier date than he did and thus mitigated the delay.

The Respondent averred that the Claimant made an error in constructing the trimmer beams but offered no evidence in support of this contention.

The Claimant accepts that the work to the lift-shaft could have commenced earlier but suggests that the delay would still not have been avoided due to the failure of the Architect to resolve the nature and size of the lift at a sufficiently early date to allow the Claimant to reprogramme his works.

I am satisfied that the delays to the lift-shaft caused by the late resolution of the nature and size of the lift was the dominant cause of the delay and this was a critical event in that the head of the shaft supported main purlins and the water tanks.

ACCORDINGLY ON THE LIFT-SHAFT OPERATION I FIND THAT THE CLAIMANT IS ENTITLED TO AN EXTENSION OF TIME OF ONE WEEK UNDER CLAUSE 2.4.5 OF THE CONTRACT.

7.04 Roof Repairs—Strip Roof

The Claimant seeks an extension of time of two weeks for the extra work required in stripping the roof slates. He claims that had the survey been carried out properly he would have had a better idea of the extent that the existing slates had delaminated.

The Respondent accepts that few slates were able to be reused but puts this down to the lack of care by the Claimant. He concedes that certain of the slates were delaminated, however, he does not admit that this was the cause of any delay to completion of the Works.

I am satisfied that the delay in stripping the slates was concurrent with the other delays being caused by the lift-shaft for which I have already awarded an extension.

11.5 Arb 476

ACCORDINGLY ON THE ROOF REPAIRS—STRIP ROOF OPERATION I FIND THAT THE CLAIMANT IS NOT ENTITLED TO AN EXTENSION OF TIME.

7.05 Roof Repairs—Timbers

The Claimant seeks an eight-week extension of time on this task. Extensive dry rot was discovered to the roof timbers. The extent of which had not been foreseen by the Architect who instructed that the timbers be replaced on a piecemeal basis. This approach proved to be unworkable. It had to be abandoned, in the event all of the roof timbers were replaced.

The Respondent admits that more timbers were replaced than was allowed for in the Specification and accepts that this, plus a late amendment to the lead flashings, caused an overall delay of four weeks and one day.

I was satisfied, from the evidence I heard that it was not reasonable to have expected the Claimant to have provided extensive temporary weather protection of the roof area to allow the operation to have commenced earlier.

On the other hand I believe that it would have been possible for the Architect to have made an inspection earlier and thereby made a decision on the extent of the roof timbers to be replaced.

The Claimant offered no evidence in support of the eight weeks claimed, I therefore accept the period for the delay, caused by the replacement of roof timbers and lead flashings is as admitted by the Respondent.

ACCORDINGLY ON THE ROOF REPAIRS—TIMBERS OPERATION I FIND THAT THE CLAIM-ANT IS ENTITLED TO AN EXTENSION OF TIME OF FOUR WEEKS AND ONE DAY UNDER CLAUSE 2.4.7 OF THE CONTRACT.

7.06 Window Replacement

The Claimant avers that the scaffolding remained in place for six weeks longer than planned due to the extra work in connection with the roof timbers. He also contended that the windows could not be installed until the scaffolding was removed and that, as a result, the replacement of these became a critical activity.

Whilst the Respondent admits that the scaffolding remained in place six weeks longer than planned he claims this was due to unjustifiably long periods taken by the Claimant to strip the roof. The Respondent also claims that a further delay was caused in replacing the windows due to the Claimant having to remedy defective rebates.

Under cross-examination the Claimant's expert admitted that it would have been possible to have provided temporary weather-proofing to almost all of the window openings, at relatively little cost and by so doing have removed this task from the critical path.

ACCORDINGLY ON THE WINDOW REPLACEMENT OPERATION I FIND THAT THE CLAIMANT IS NOT ENTITLED TO AN EXTENSION OF TIME.

7.07 Carpentry First Fix

The Claimant seeks an extension of time of one week for the additional work executed in this operation. This, he claimed, was caused by the replacement of internal timber work found necessary due to the presence of dry rot.

As the Respondent also admits a delay of one week due to this cause, I accept that period.

ACCORDINGLY ON THE CARPENTRY FIRST FIX OPERATION I FIND THAT THE CLAIMANT IS ENTITLED TO AN EXTENSION OF TIME OF ONE WEEK UNDER CLAUSE 2.4.5 OF THE CONTRACT.

7.08 Mechanical and Electrical First Fix to Existing Building

11.5 Arb 477

The Claimant claims that this operation commenced six weeks late.

The Respondent denies that this caused any greater delay to the completion of the Works than had already been incurred by this stage.

I heard no evidence to persuade me that the Respondent's view of this delay was other than the correct one.

ACCORDINGLY ON THE MECHANICAL AND ELECTRICAL FIRST FIX TO EXISTING BUILDING I FIND THAT THE CLAIMANT IS NOT ENTITLED TO AN EXTENSION OF TIME.

7.09 Mechanical and Electrical First Fix to New Extension

The Claimant claims that the commencement of this operation was delayed through earlier causes of delay and that the subcontractor could only provide one gang to carry out this work. This resulted in the works to the new extension proceeding sequentially, with the work on the existing building, and not concurrently.

The Respondent rejected this argument as he believed that additional local labour could have been engaged without undue difficulty. Under cross-examination Redman agreed.

ACCORDINGLY ON THE MECHANICAL AND ELECTRICAL FIRST FIX TO NEW EXTENSION I FIND THAT THE CLAIMANT IS NOT ENTITLED TO AN EXTENSION OF TIME.

7.10 Carpenter Second Fix

Both sides agreed that this operation had only been delayed by the cumulative effect of delays to previous operations.

The Claimant increased the number of operatives employed on this task and thus avoided any critical delay.

ACCORDINGLY ON THE CARPENTER SECOND FIX I FIND THAT THE CLAIMANT IS NOT ENTITLED TO AN EXTENSION OF TIME.

7.11 Mechanical and Electrical Second Fix to Existing Building

The Claimant seeks an extension of time, of two weeks, because a change to the specification was issued by TAP after this task had commenced. The enhancement to the performance specification to this work required that the subcontractor carry out some redesign which in turn created additional work. Consequently there was a delay in the issue of the subcontractor 'shop' drawings.

The Respondent denies that this was the proximate or dominant cause of any delay. Their case is that it was the late issue of the subcontract drawings caused TAP to issue their co-ordination drawings late.

Under cross-examination the Respondent's expert, Mr Maclean admitted a two-week delay to this task caused by the design problem.

ACCORDINGLY ON THE MECHANICAL AND ELECTRICAL SECOND FIX TO EXISTING BUILDING I FIND THAT THE CLAIMANT IS ENTITLED TO AN EXTENSION OF TIME OF TWO WEEKS UNDER CLAUSE 2.4.5 OF THE CONTRACT.

7.12 Mechanical and Electrical Second Fix to New Extension

The Claimant claims that changes in the specification created additional work. This coupled with the need to work sequentially because of the availability of only one gang to work on the services caused delay.

I have already found that the Claimant could have engaged more labour and thus carried out this work concurrent with the work on the existing building.

11.5 Arb 478

ACCORDINGLY ON THE MECHANICAL AND ELECTRICAL SECOND FIX TO NEW EXTENSION I FIND THAT THE CLAIMANT IS NOT ENTITLED TO AN EXTENSION OF TIME.

7.13 Substructure to New Extension

No evidence was given to support the Claimant's contention that this task caused delay to completion.

Mr Maclean gave evidence that the delay ran concurrently with other events. In this instance I accept Mr Maclean's evidence.

ACCORDINGLY ON THE SUBSTRUCTURE TO NEW EXTENSION I FIND THAT THE CLAIMANT IS NOT ENTITLED TO AN EXTENSION OF TIME.

7.14 Decorations

The Claimant claims a three-day extension of time for additional work brought about by the Respondent changing the colour scheme during the course of the decoration work.

The Respondent admits the delay of three days and that an instruction effecting this change was issued.

ACCORDINGLY ON THE DECORATIONS I FIND THAT THE CLAIMANT IS ENTITLED TO AN EXTENSION OF TIME OF THREE DAYS UNDER CLAUSE 2.4.5 OF THE CONTRACT.

7.15 Summary of Findings on Extension of Time

My findings on the issues concerning extension of time are summarised as follows:

Task	Time Awarded	Contract Clause
7.01. Removals and Demolitions	3w 4d	2.4.7
7.02. Form Lift-shaft	1w	2.4.5
7.03. Roof Repairs—Strip Roof	Nil	
7.04. Roof Repairs—Timbers	4w 1d	2.4.7
7.05. Window Replacement	Nil	
7.06. Carpentry First Fix	1w	2.4.5
7.07. Mechanical and Electrical First Fix to Existing Building	Nil	
7.08. Mechanical and Electrical First Fix to New Extension	Nil	
7.09. Carpenter Second Fix	Nil	
7.10. Mechanical and Electrical Second Fix to Existing Building	Nil	
7.11. Mechanical and Electrical Second Fix to New Extension	2w	2.4.5
7.12. Substructure to New Extension	Nil	
7.13. Decorations	3d	2.4.5
TOTAL	12w 3d	

ACCORDINGLY ON EXTENSIONS OF TIME I FIND THAT THE CLAIMANT IS ENTITLED TO AN EXTENSION OF TIME OF 12 WEEKS AND THREE DAYS MADE UP AS FOLLOWS:

Four weeks and three days under clause 2.4.5 of the Contract—'Compliance with Architects instructions under clause 3.6—Variations'.

Three weeks under clause 2.4.7—'The Contractor not having received in due time the necessary instructions, drawings, details or levels from the Architect'.

7.16 **ACCORDINGLY I FIND THAT THE NEW COMPLETION DATE FOR THE CONTRACT IS 6 MARCH 1992.**

8.00 Issue 2—Liquidated and Ascertained Damages

To how much, if any, is the Claimant entitled by way of repayment of liquidated and ascertained damages?

11.5 Arb
479

Subsidiary Question. Is the Respondent entitled to a Certificate of Non-Completion and, if yes, what are the terms of that Certificate?

8.01 The Respondent has retained the sum of £146,000 in respect of liquidated and ascertained damages. This has been calculated at the Contract rate of £9125, per week, for the period of 16 weeks.

The Claimant seeks repayment of the whole of £146,000 on the premise that it is entitled to an Extension of Time for the full period of 16 weeks that the Contract overran.

The Respondent seeks to retain the sum of £59,964.29 in respect of liquidated and ascertained damages on the premise that the Claimant is entitled only to an Extension of Time of nine weeks and three days.

The Claimant submits that the Respondent wrongfully deducted these damages as a Certificate of Non-completion is a necessary condition precedent to such deduction.

Mr Belcher invites me to reject the Respondent's submission that the Claimant was in repudiatory breach by leaving the site on 8 April 1992 and as a result the Respondent avers that 'time is at large'.

This argument is rejected by the Claimant who suggests that this is a conventional case of an award of an extension of time and a repayment of liquidated and ascertained damages. In justification of this argument, Mr Belcher points out that it is common ground that the works were practically complete, at that date, and as such the Claimant could not be in breach of contract.

Mr Belcher continues to maintain that before such damages can be deducted a Certificate of Non-completion is a necessary pre-condition. He refers me to *Bell* v *CBF* (1989) 46 Build LR 102, in support.

On the other hand, Miss O'Brien accepts that liquidated and ascertained damages were wrongfully deducted but with 'time at large' the Respondent was still entitled to unliquidated damages and further a Certificate of Non-completion is not a necessary condition precedent to such deduction. In the alternative, she says, that if that argument does not commend itself to me, the Respondent is entitled to deduct such liquidated damages, and cites *Brent* v *Rowlinson* (1990) 6 Const LJ 292, as authority in support, in which case the Respondent concedes that credit should be given for the damages wrongfully deducted.

Notwithstanding the effects of the failure of the Architect to issue a Non-completion Certificate I believe that I have authority under the Arbitration clause in the Contract to substitute the lack of such certificate with my own decision based on the evidence I had heard and the authorities referred to me.

The provision in the Contract is:

> Clause 9.3 'and to determine all matters in dispute which shall be submitted to him in the same manner as if no such certificate, opinion, decision, requirement or notice had been given.'

I have awarded an extension of time of 12.5 weeks and the entitlement to liquidated and ascertained damages must follow the provisions in the Contract under clause 2.7:

> 'the Contractor shall pay or allow the Employer liquidated damages at the rate stated in the Appendix for the period which the Works shall remain or have remained incomplete'.

The period for which the works have remained incomplete is the period beyond the Date for Completion stated in the Appendix to the Contract or any extended time fixed under clause 2.3 of the Contract by the Architect.

The extended time to be fixed by the Architect has now been substituted in this my award.

The Works were therefore completed 3.5 weeks late and the Claimant is liable to pay the Respondent liquidated and ascertained damages at the rate stated in the Appendix to the Contract for that period. The rate stated in the Appendix is £9,125 per week. As the rate is per week the Respondent is entitled to nothing for the part of the week the Works remained incomplete.

11.5 Arb 480

Having considered the submissions and the authorities,

I FIND AND HOLD

(i) That the Claimant was not in repudiatory breach and that at no time evinced an intention of no longer regarding himself bound by the contract and accordingly the contract subsists.

(ii) That 'time was not at large'.

(iii) That a Certificate of Non-completion is not a condition precedent to the deduction of Liquidated and Ascertained damages.

ACCORDINGLY I FIND AND HOLD that the Claimant is liable to allow the Respondent the sum of £27,375 (Twenty-Seven Thousand Three Hundred and Seventy-five pounds) in respect of Liquidated and Ascertained Damages.

The Respondent has already deducted £146,000 in respect of liquidated and ascertained damages and should therefore refund the balance.

ACCORDINGLY I FIND THAT THE RESPONDENT IS LIABLE TO PAY TO THE CLAIMANT THE SUM OF £118,625 (ONE HUNDRED AND EIGHTEEN THOUSAND SIX HUNDRED AND TWENTY-FIVE POUNDS) IN RESPECT OF LIQUIDATED & ASCERTAINED DAMAGES WRONGFULLY DEDUCTED.

9.00 Issue 3—Final Account

To what is the Claimant entitled under the Final Account, excluding claims to loss and expense and excluding any set-offs for defects?

Subsidiary Question: Is the Claimant entitled to payment of Certificate No. 12?

I shall deal with this issue under four heads:

- (i) Variations.
- (ii) Remeasured Items.
- (iii) Certificate No. 12.
- (iv) General and Summary.

9.01 Variations

9.01.1 The parties agreed that I should meet with their respective Experts with a view to narrowing the issues. A detailed note of this agreement is to be found in the letter to me from the Respondent's solicitor, dated 11 October 1993.

Subsequently meetings took place between me and Messrs Redman and Maclean on 29 and 30 November 1993 and a note of what was agreed at these meetings was prepared and signed by these two Experts and is to be found in the Hearing Bundle (PC/37).

At the Hearing, on 11 April 1994, I heard evidence on those items of work, classified as category b), which it is denied are variations at all, because it is alleged that they were either not instructed, or form part of the Lump-Sum Contract.

9.01.2 On 7 March 1994, the first day of the Hearing, Miss O'Brien handed to me an updated Schedule of these variations, dated 6 March 1994, showing the amounts agreed or contended for by the respective parties where they had been unable to agree.

9.01.3 Following this full Hearing, by agreement with the parties I meet alone with these two Experts, during the Hearing, on 11 and 12 April 1994 where I heard these Experts on the matters of quantum on which they had been unable to agree.

9.01.4 The parties had previously indicated that they did not require me to deal variation by variation in this Award but would accept a lump-sum assessment by me if liability under this head of claim.

ACCORDINGLY having considered the submissions made by, and on behalf of, the parties together with the evidence adduced before me by the Experts, in respect of the Claimant's head of Claim, specifically as set out on pages 36 & 37 of the Claimant's Expert's Report, I find that the total amount of the Additions is £134,076.48.

There was no dispute concerning the amount of the omissions at £63,351.04. Therefore:

I FIND THAT THE RESPONDENT IS LIABLE TO PAY THE CLAIMANT THE SUM OF £70,725.44 (SEVENTY THOUSAND, SEVEN HUNDRED AND TWENTY-FIVE POUNDS 44p) IN RESPECT OF VARIATIONS.

9.02 Remeasurement Items—Not Agreed

9.02.1 It was agreed that I should deal with the items under this head in the same way as I dealt with the Variations above. The letter 11 October 1993, referred to above, applies and this matter was covered at the meetings of 29 & 30 November 1993 and the outcome recorded in the Expert's Report (PC/37).

11.5 Arb
481

9.02.2 A similar agreement was made concerning treatment of a lump-sum award for this head of claim.

ACCORDINGLY having considered the submissions made by, and on behalf of, the parties together with evidence adduced before me by the parties' respective Experts, in respect of the Claimant's head of claim specifically as set out on page 45 of the Claimant's Expert's Report.

> I FIND THAT THE RESPONDENT IS LIABLE TO PAY THE CLAIMANT THE SUM OF **£8405** (EIGHT THOUSAND FOUR HUNDRED AND FIVE POUNDS) IN RESPECT OF REMEASUREMENT ITEMS NOT AGREED.

9.03 Certificate No. 12

9.03.1 It is common ground that this Penultimate Certificate was issued on 13 April 1992 in the sum of £10,954, was never paid.

9.03.2 I heard conflicting evidence as to why this Certificate was not honoured. However, nothing that I heard convinced me that this money was not otherwise than wrongfully withheld.

> I FIND AND HOLD THAT THE RESPONDENT IS LIABLE TO PAY THE CLAIMANT THE SUM OF **£10,954** (TEN THOUSAND NINE HUNDRED AND FIFTY-FOUR POUNDS) IN RESPECT OF CERTIFICATE NO. **12.**

9.04 Final Account

9.04.1 There were sums which form part of the Computation of the Adjusted Contract Sum (Final Account) in accordance with clause 4.5 of the Contract which were never in issue but they nevertheless need to be summarised as part of my Award to arrive at total sums due.

9.04.2 This summary of the Adjusted Contract Sum is as follows:

Item	Omit £	Add £	
Contract Sum		550,000.00	Not In Issue
Provisional Sums	76,750.00	107,011.87	Not In Issue
Variations	63,351.04	134,076.48	As Para. 9.01
Contingencies	13,600.00	Nil	Not In Issue
Remeasurement Items		8,405	As Para 9.02
Sub-Total	153,701.04	799,493.35	
		153,701.04	
Adjusted Contract Sum		645,792.31	
Less. Amount Certified to Date		610,450.00	
AMOUNT DUE UNDER FINAL A/C		£35,342.31	

9.04.3 As the amount of Certificate No 12 is included in the Amount Certified to Date above, the total amount due to the Claimant under this head of Final Account—excluding Liquidated & Ascertained Damages and money withheld against Defects, both of which are dealt with as separate issues—is as follows:

Under Final A/C as above	£35,342.31
Certificate No 12	£10,954.00
Total Due	£46,296.31

ACCORDINGLY I FIND THAT THE RESPONDENT IS LIABLE TO PAY THE CLAIMANT A TOTAL SUM OF **£46,296.31** (FORTY-SIX THOUSAND, TWO HUNDRED AND NINETY-SIX POUNDS **31p**) UNDER THE FINAL ACCOUNT—ISSUE THREE.

11.5 Arb 482

10.00 Issue 4—Loss and Expense

To how much, if any, is the Claimant entitled by way of Loss & Expense?

In para. 13 of the defence, the Respondent avers that the Claimant failed to make application within a reasonable time in accordance with cl 4.11 of the Conditions of Contract. The Claimant submits, that by virtue of the particulars of loss and expense included with the Claimant's Draft Final Account, on 3 June 1992, the application was made in accordance with cl. 4.11.

I accept the Claimant's submission that application for loss and expense was made in accordance with the Conditions of Contract.

I shall deal with this issue under the following heads:

    (i) Prolongation Costs
    (ii) Additional Staff and Equipment
    (iii) Head Office Overheads
    (iv) Disturbance of Labour
    (v) Inflation

10.01 Prolongation Costs

It is common ground that, in this particular case, the loss and/or expense under this heading is linked to the extension of time granted by me.

All the sums claimed were agreed between experts on a figures as figures basis.

10.01.1 Staffing

It was Mr Maclean, the Respondent's expert's contention that:

    (i) the Claimant was only put to cost in respect of a site agent and a trades foreman
    (ii) the provision for Peter Murphy, the Ganger was in the Claimant's rates for work items. Thus, where work items have been varied and the quantities increased, part of the cost of Peter Murphy has been recovered;
    (iii) the provision for Graham Smith, the quantity surveyor, is already in the Claimant's provision for overheads and should not be duplicated.

In response to Mr Maclean, Mr Redman, the Claimant's expert contends that:

    (i) that the Claimant had to continue to employ its full supervising and administrative team on-site throughout the duration of the project. There was no opportunity to reduce the staffing levels as the variations (and thus the intensity of the workload) continued up to the date of practical completion;
    (ii) those who were employed were, John Watts, the site agent; Fred Brown, a trade foreman; Peter Murphy, a ganger; Graham Smith, a quantity surveyor; and an additional general site service labour gang;
    (iii) that no costs for Peter Murphy have been recovered in the rates;
    (iv) the costs of Graham Smith, the quantity surveyor, were not being carried in the overheads.

11.5 Arb 483

10.01.2 Site Accommodation and Personnel Carrier

On this element of cost Mr Maclean contended:

    (i) it is not appropriate to use internal hire rates to calculate loss and expense;
    (ii) the correct basis is the cost of depreciation of such plus an allowance for loss of use of capital;
    (iii) the Claimant's claim should be reduced by 50 per cent.

Mr Redman's response to these points was:

(i) it is accepted that these rates were internal plant hire rates.

(ii) such charges are normal in the industry.

Mr Maclean provided no evidence in support of his contentions on the recovery of staffing costs or the site accommodation and personnel carrier.

Mr Redman satisfied me that the staffing costs had been priced as a preliminary type item and could therefore be justifiably claimed under this head.

I accept Mr Redman's evidence that the weekly cost under this head is £1972. Thus applying this figure to the 12.5 weeks' extension of time which I have awarded, gives a total of £24,650.

ACCORDINGLY I FIND THAT THE RESPONDENT IS LIABLE TO PAY THE CLAIMANT THE SUM OF £24,650 (TWENTY-FOUR THOUSAND SIX HUNDRED AND FIFTY POUNDS) FOR SITE STAFF, SITE ACCOMMODATION & PERSONNEL CARRIER.

10.01.3 Additional Staff and Equipment

It is common ground that this is a claim for disruption costs and is not dependent on any extension of time awarded.

All the sums claimed were agreed between experts on a figures as figures basis. The additional staff costs were agreed but not the periods they were required to be on-site.

On the rates to be applied to the equipment, both experts put up the same argument as they put forward in respect of the staff accommodation (see 10.02.1 above).

Mr Maclean provided evidence on the periods to which these costs should relate which Mr Redman was unable to rebut to my satisfaction. I therefore accept Mr Maclean's evidence on the periods to which these costs should apply.

Based on Mr Maclean's periods of time and Mr Redman's rates the sum due is as follows:

	No.	Period Weeks	Rate Per Week £	Total £
Staff				
Finishing Foreman	1	4	340	1360
Bricklayer Foreman	1	8	340	2720
Plant and Equipment				
Dumper	1	8	40	320
Forklift	1	15	80	1200
5/3 1/2 MIXER	2	8	35	280
Standing Scaffolding	1	11	46	506
Alterations to Scaffolding	1	1	480	480
Transformers	2	1	20	20
Extension Leads	5	4	5	20
Ladders & Trestles	1	8	20	160
Sanders	2	4	20	80
Drills	2	4	15	60
Steam Stripper	1	3	36	108
Space Heaters	1	6	32	192
Dehumidifier	1	6	33	198
Skill Saws	2	4	20	80
Core Drill	1	8	9	72
Kango	1	8	40	320
Paint Strippers	3	8	30	240
Angle Grinders	2	8	30	240
			TOTAL	£8656

11.5 Arb
484

ACCORDINGLY I FIND THAT THE RESPONDENT IS LIABLE TO PAY THE CLAIMANT THE SUM OF £8656 (EIGHT THOUSAND SIX HUNDRED AND FIFTY-SIX POUNDS) IN RESPECT OF ADDITIONAL STAFF AND EQUIPMENT.

10.01.4 Head Office Overheads

It is common ground that in this particular case that the loss and/or expense under this heading is linked to the extension of time which I have granted.

Each expert adopted a recognised formula method of calculating the sum due under this head of claim.

Mr Redman adopted the Hudson formula for his calculation and Mr Maclean used the Emden formula.

Mr Redman considered the caveats, that the Claimant could have obtained work and earned money elsewhere had he not been retained on this project and gave evidence of a project that the Claimant had to turn away.

From Mr Maclean's evidence it was clear to me that he had taken an accounting period into consideration which distorted the figures he had used.

I am therefore satisfied that the figures and the formula used by Mr Redman are the more appropriate, save that the period to be adopted is not the 16 weeks he used but the 12.5 weeks, as awarded by me for the extension of time, as follows:

$$\frac{12.5}{16} \times £36{,}666.66 = £28{,}645.83$$

ACCORDINGLY I FIND THAT THE RESPONDENT IS LIABLE TO PAY THE CLAIMANT THE SUM OF £28,645.83 (TWENTY-EIGHT THOUSAND SIX HUNDRED AND FORTY-FIVE POUNDS 83p) IN RESPECT OF HEAD OFFICE OVERHEADS

10.01.5 Disturbance of Labour

It is common ground that this is a claim for disruption costs and is not dependent on any extension of time awarded.

During cross-examination Mr Redman admitted that there were some factors, for which the Claimant would be liable that he had not taken into account in his calculations.

On day 15 of the Hearing I was given a figure which had been agreed between the experts the previous evening, for this item of claim. Counsel agreed that I should adopt that figure in my Award.

ACCORDINGLY I FIND THAT THE RESPONDENT IS LIABLE TO PAY THE CLAIMANT THE SUM OF £28,480 (TWENTY-EIGHT THOUSAND FOUR HUNDRED AND EIGHTY POUNDS), IN RESPECT OF THE CLAIM FOR DISTURBANCE OF LABOUR.

10.01.6 Inflation costs

There is no common ground on this issue.

Mr Redman had adopted a formula-based calculation using the published Building Cost Index to arrive at his figure for inflation. He admitted that this calculation was hypothetical but as the sum in contention was small in terms of the overall claim, he maintained that, the ends justified the means.

11.5 Arb
485

I accept the proposition that, on the balance of probabilities, any building contract which overruns by a period of 12.5 weeks is likely to involve the builder in some increases in cost.

Mr Maclean's evidence, on this matter, was inconsistent with the evidence he gave on other issues. Whilst acknowledging the overrun of nine weeks and three days and also some disruption element, he failed to investigate the probability of the increases in cost.

On balance I prefer Mr Redman's evidence on this issue. I accept that his approach was a reasonable one, bearing in mind the small amount in issue.

ACCORDINGLY I FIND THAT THE RESPONDENT IS LIABLE TO PAY THE CLAIMANT THE SUM OF £5571.30 (FIVE THOUSAND FIVE HUNDRED AND SEVENTY-ONE POUNDS AND 30p) IN RESPECT OF THE CLAIM FOR INFLATION COSTS.

10.01.7 Summary of Findings on Loss and/or Expense

My findings on the loss and/or Expense issues are summarised as follows:

Issue	Amount Awarded to the Claimant £
Prolongation	24,650.00
Additional Staff and Equipment	8,656.00
Head Office Overheads	28,645.83
Disturbance of Labour	28,480.00
Inflation	5,571.30
TOTAL	£96,003.13

ACCORDINGLY I FIND THAT THE RESPONDENT IS LIABLE TO PAY THE CLAIMANT THE TOTAL SUM OF £96,003.13 (NINETY-SIX THOUSAND AND THREE POUNDS 13p) IN RESPECT OF ALL HEADS OF CLAIM UNDER LOSS AND/OR EXPENSE—ISSUE 4.

11.00 Issue 5—Disturbance

To how much, if any, is the Claimant entitled by way of damages for breach of contract arising out of the hindrance of its progress by the Respondent?

11.0.1 This issue has been covered in the assessment of the Extension of Time (Issue 1) and in the Disturbance of Labour as part of Issue 4 above.

11.5 Arb 486

ACCORDINGLY I MAKE NO SEPARATE AWARD FOR THIS ISSUE.

12.00 Issue 6—Certificates

To how much, if any, is the Claimant entitled by way of damages for breach of contract arising from non-payment of certificates?

12.01 It is common ground that Certificate No. 12 was not paid at all and that Certificates numbered 1–11 were paid late.

12.02 In order to bring a claim under this head it is necessary to show that the Respondent was aware that late payment would cause the Claimant loss.

12.03 The Respondent contends that the Claimant was aware that the Respondent's banking arrangements were such that he would not be able to meet the contractual timetable for the payment of these Certificates.

12.04 The Claimant avers that he made the Respondent aware, prior to his signing the contract, on 8 April 1992, that he was working on an overdraft and as such any failure to pay certificates within the 14 days provided for in the contract would incur finance charges.

12.05 I heard evidence from both parties on this issue and I am satisfied that the Claimant's version of events is the correct one and, in particular, I am not convinced that he was told that the Respondent's banking arrangements would mean that he could not meet the contractual dates for payment of these Certificates.

12.06 As a result I am satisfied that the Claimant is entitled to special damages for this breach.

12.07 I have checked and agreed the rates of interest claimed against those for which the Claimant adduced evidence of actual interest incurred. I have also checked and agreed the number of days which these Certificates were paid late.

ACCORDINGLY I AWARD DAMAGES AS CLAIMED IN PART B OF APPENDIX 1 OF THE AMENDED STATEMENT OF CASE AS CLAIMED BUT EXTENDED UP TO THE DATE OF THIS AWARD.

I FIND THAT THE RESPONDENT IS LIABLE TO PAY THE CLAIMANT, AS SPECIAL DAMAGES, THE SUM OF £10,338.80 (TEN THOUSAND THREE HUNDRED AND THIRTY-EIGHT POUNDS 80p) IN RESPECT OF THIS LATE PAYMENT—ISSUE 6.

13.00 Issue 7—Interest

To how much, if any, by way of interest is the Claimant entitled?

13.01 The Claimant claims interest under the following heads of claim.

(i) On the amount awarded for loss and expense.
(ii) On monies wrongfully withheld against defects. (See Issue 8.)
(iii) As 'special damages' for monies wrongfully deducted for Liquidated and Ascertained Damages.
(iv) On monies found to be due under the Final Account.

13.02 By virtue of the reasons given in Issue 6 above, viz. that the Respondent was aware that the Claimant would be incurring finance charges through operating on an overdraft for this project:

I FIND AND HOLD THAT THE RESPONDENT IS LIABLE FOR THE FOLLOWING AMOUNTS OF INTEREST:

		£
13.03	(i) On the amount I awarded for Loss & Expense	37,016.00
	(ii) On the amount wrongfully deducted for defects	6,197.22
	(iii) On the monies wrongfully deducted for LADs	28,484.63
	(iv) On the monies due under the Final Account	9,516.61
	Total Awarded	£81,214.46

ACCORDINGLY I FIND THAT THE RESPONDENT IS LIABLE TO PAY TO THE CLAIMANT THE SUM OF £81,214.46 (EIGHTY-ONE THOUSAND TWO HUNDRED AND FOURTEEN POUNDS 46p) AS SPECIAL DAMAGES OR INTEREST UNDER ISSUE 7.

Counterclaim

I now deal with those issues concerning the Respondent's Counterclaim.

14.00 Issue 8—Defects

What defects were there in the works executed by the Claimant (which constituted breaches of contract)?

14.01 I consider this issue under three heads:

    (i) General defects as detailed on the Scott Schedule—Appendix A of the Re-re-Amended Statement of Defence and Counterclaim.
    (ii) The Gibbs Ceiling.
    (iii) The Basement laundry.

14.02 Scott Schedule defects

Where the experts had been unable to agree liability on defects listed in the Scott Schedule, I heard evidence at the hearing on these specific items.

Counsel had agreed that I could make a lump-sum award for defects and as such need not deal with each individual item listed on that schedule, however, I will comment briefly on two items which comprise the substantial claim for defects:

    (i) The general cracking.
    (ii) The fire doors.

14.02.1 General cracking

I heard much evidence concerning the running of the heating system. On the one hand the Respondent maintains that the Claimant was aware, or ought to have been aware, of the high temperature that this home would be run at once it was occupied by the frail elderly residents.

The Claimant's case is, that although he was aware, from the specification, of the high temperature at which the heating system would be run, he would have expected this high level of heat to have been applied gradually, in which case there would probably not have been the excessive amount of cracking that there was.

On this point I was convinced by the Claimant's evidence and took this into account when deciding on the quantum element for the items on the Scott Schedule.

ACCORDINGLY I DO NOT FIND THE CLAIMANT LIABLE FOR THE SHRINKAGE CRACKS CAUSED BY THE TOO RAPID INTRODUCTION OF THE HEATING.

14.02.2 Fire Doors

In addition to the witnesses of fact I heard evidence from Mr Ifram Carmel—an expert in fire proofing coatings.

It was Mr Ifram's company that actually coated the doors on behalf of the Claimant in accordance with the requirements of the Specification.

Whilst accepting that Mr Ifram's evidence is not entirely independent, I found it convincing and I accept that the cracking of the fire door which was responsible for the wrinkling and unsightly appearance of the glass fibre coating was the fault of the Respondent.

As with the other cracking I believe that these fire doors were affected by the rapid build-up of heat, exacerbated in this instance by the excess moisture which these doors had absorbed during the period that the property had been unoccupied.

I accept from the evidence that I heard, that had the building been allowed to dry out at a normal gradual rate this particular problem was unlikely to have occurred.

I took this into account when assessing quantum for the Scott Schedule items.

ACCORDINGLY I DISALLOW THE RESPONDENT'S CLAIM IN RESPECT OF THE FIRE DOORS

14.03 Gibbs ceiling

I now consider the Respondent's claim in respect of liability for the loss of the Gibbs ceiling which I had determined, as a Preliminary Issue, was genuine.

The contractual requirements in connection with the repair of this ceiling were set out in the Specification which I had determined, as a Preliminary Issue, was part of the contract documents.

Clause 3/23d of this Specification provided for the expenditure of the Provisional Sum of £2000 by a specialist firm to be approved by the Architect. The Claimant engaged The Georgian Restoration Group to undertake this work; which firm was first approved by the Architect.

In evidence it was accepted that, at no time, was there any complaint about the actual work of restoration carried out by this company. No evidence was adduced that any act or omission by this Group, in executing their work, caused, or contributed to, the collapse. For this reason I shall concentrate on the work carried out directly by the Claimant company, viz. the installation of the fireproofing in the void above the subject ceiling.

The Claimant assumed an overall responsibility to protect this ceiling against damage, through Clause 3/23e of the Specification, which states:

> 'The existing Gibbs ceiling in the lounge is to be protected with particular care ... the contractor is to take whatever steps are necessary to uphold the integrity of the existing ceiling. The contractor's attention is drawn to the need to remove and reinstate the first-floor boarding, clear out any rubbish from the ceiling void and install fireproofing within the floor structure. These and other works affecting the Gibbs ceiling are to be carried out in such a way and all necessary precautions taken to ensure that the integrity of the ceiling is maintained at all times and on completion.'

Specification clauses 3/21h–j and 3/23e–f set out in detail the preparatory work to be carried out prior to this fireproofing being installed.

No evidence was adduced to show that the Claimant did not comply with the requirements of these clauses.

We heard evidence from Mr Reeves that, having exposed the floor void, they noticed that many of the plaster keys of the ceiling had broken off and as a result he had suggested to the Architect, Miss Hutch, that they should 'soft wire' those parts of the ceiling where these keys were missing.

Mr Reeves's evidence is that Miss Hutch was not prepared to instruct RBL to carry out this work of 'soft wiring', maintaining that it was their responsibility to ensure that the integrity of the ceiling was maintained.

Miss Hutch's evidence was that it was the Georgian Restoration Group's lead foreman, Fred Pilcher, who had first drawn her attention to the broken keys. Mr Pilcher had told her that with careful handling the ceiling would probably be all right but if she was worried about it then she could have the ceiling wired. Despite Mr Reeves's evidence, Miss Hutch was quite clear, in cross-examination that Mr Reeves had not, at any time, discussed with her the possibility of 'soft wiring' this ceiling.

11.5 Arb 489

Mr Reeves accepted that had the ceiling been 'soft wired' it would probably not have collapsed but considered an expensive operation such as 'soft wiring' was beyond the scope of the general protection clause 3/23e.

Different witnesses gave various explanations as to why they thought the ceiling had collapsed.

Mr Sharkey, an Expert Witness for the Claimant, expressed the opinion that thermal movement, accelerated by the high temperature maintained within the building, once it was occupied, was the primary cause for the eventual collapse. No evidence was adduced in support of this opinion and therefore I give this little weight.

Mr Longdon suggested two other contributory causes.

(i) The added weight of fireproofing material which was allowed to fall onto the upper surface of the ceiling, the key of which, it is accepted, was already weakened.

(ii) The vibration caused through nailing the wire mesh, designed to contain the fireproofing in the floor void, as well as that vibration caused when the floorboards, above this fireproofing, were replaced and fixed with nails rather than screws.

In support of this opinion Mr Longdon produced a textbook from a leading authority; *The Restoration of Listed Buildings* by Melville & Gordon. I was referred to a passage in this book which cited examples of ceilings, with a similar construction to that of Sanctuary House, collapsing some considerable time after work, similar in nature to that carried out on this project had been completed.

This passage gave a number of reasons for such delayed collapse which included the two possibilities suggested by Mr Longdon.

Mr Longdon had observed a considerable quantity of fireproofing material amongst the plaster debris on the floor of the sitting room. When I had inspected the property I noted that the fireproofing was very largely intact despite the collapse of the ceiling below it. This suggested to me that this fireproofing material had been allowed to escape through the wire mesh and to lie on the already fragile ceiling. I put this to both Mr Reeves and to Mr Sharkey at the end of their re-examination but both maintained that the correct amount of water, as recommended by the manufacturers, had been used in mixing this fireproofing material.

My view was supported by Miss Hutch's evidence when she told us that she had mentioned, on a number of occasions during this operation, that the fireproofing material appeared to be too wet and it was dropping through the mesh. She also gave evidence that the manufacturers instructions were quite specific about the amount of water to be used in conjunction with this fireproofing but that at no time had she seen any calibrated measuring vessels used to gauge this mix.

Mr Rector thought that the deterioration of the ferrous nails may have also contributed to the eventual collapse. Although I could not entirely discount this possibility I consider that it would be too much of a coincidence that something which had been quietly rusting for 250 years should fail a relatively short while after the work, carried out by the Claimant, had been completed.

Having reconsidered all the Expert evidence on this issue together with the factual evidence given by the various witnesses I find that the primary cause of the collapse was the Claimant's failure to take care in installing the fireproofing material, in particular causing vibration through nailing and in allowing wet material to drop through the mesh onto the upper surface of this ceiling.

ACCORDINGLY I HOLD THAT THE CLAIMANT IS IN BREACH OF CONTRACT AND THEREFORE LIABLE FOR THE COLLAPSE OF THIS CEILING.

11.5 Arb 490

14.04 Basement Laundry

Having determined, as a Preliminary Issue, that the Claimant was in breach of contract over the waterproofing of the basement, I have no need to make any further award, as to liability, under this Issue 8.

15.00 Issue 9—damages

To what damages (including consequential losses) is the Respondent entitled?
I deal with this issue under the following heads:

(i) General defects.
(ii) Gibbs ceiling.
(iii) Basement laundry.

15.01 General defects

The parties agreed that I should meet with their respective Experts with a view to agreeing quantum only on these alleged defects. A detailed note of this agreement is to be found in the letter to me from the Respondent's solicitor, dated 11 October 1993 (PC/35).

Subsequently, meetings took place between me and Messrs Redman and Maclean on 29 and 30 November 1993 and a note of what was agreed at these meetings was prepared and signed by these two Experts and is to be found in the Hearing bundle B at p.174 (PC/37).

On 7 March 1994, the first day of the Hearing, Miss O'Brien handed to me an updated Scott Schedule of these alleged defects, dated 6 March 1994, showing the amounts agreed or contended for by the respective parties where they had been unable to agree.

Following the full Hearing, by agreement with the parties, I meet alone with these two Experts, during the Hearing, on 11 and 12 April 1994 where I heard these Experts on the matters of quantum on which they had been unable to agree.

The Respondent, in his Re-re-amended Statement of Defence and Counterclaim, sought a Declaration as to the true and proper values of Certificates 6, 7 and 10, net of retention.

I DECLARE the value of these Certificates to be as follows:

Certificate No.	£
6	84,101
7	56,896
10	36,800

ACCORDINGLY having considered the submissions made by, and on behalf of, the parties together with evidence adduced before me by the parties respective Experts, in respect of the Respondent's head of counterclaim, specifically as set out on page 45 of the Scott Schedule, forming part of the Re-re-amended Statement of Defence and Counterclaim:

I MAKE A LUMP-SUM AWARD, AS AGREED (SEE 14.02 ABOVE) AND FIND THAT THE RESPONDENT IS LIABLE TO PAY THE CLAIMANT THE SUM OF £24,301 (TWENTY-FOUR THOUSAND THREE HUNDRED AND ONE POUNDS) IN RESPECT OF DEFECTIVE WORKS (ISSUE 8).

15.02 Gibbs ceiling

Under this head there are three discrete claims:
(i) The cost of restoration.
(ii) The diminution in value of the property due to the loss of this unique feature.
(iii) The claim for consequential losses flowing from the collapse and the subsequent closure of the 15 units of accommodation.

11.5 Arb
491

15.02.1 Cost of Restoration

The two Experts, Messrs. Sharkey and Longdon, following my direction, had obtained various quotations for the restoration of this ceiling, in advance of my determining liability on this issue.

The most appropriate price obtained to reconstruct this ceiling using materials similar to those used originally roughly equated to the actual cost incurred by SHL in restoring this ceiling.

These Experts were also agreed that the Architect's fee incurred in connection with this work of restoration was reasonable.

ACCORDINGLY I FIND THE CLAIMANT IS LIABLE TO PAY THE RESPONDENT THE SUM OF £43,924 (FORTY-THREE THOUSAND NINE HUNDRED AND TWENTY-FOUR POUNDS) IN RESPECT OF THE COST OF THE RESTORATION OF THE GIBBS CEILING.

15.02.2 Claim for Diminution in the Value of the Property due to the loss of the Gibbs ceiling

On this issue we heard two experts, Professor Richard Rutley for the Claimant and Clifford Knight for the Respondent. In addition, I heard the evidence of the Respondents, William and Constance Bliss.

Professor Rutley attempted to persuade me, by some ingenious method of valuation, that a property such as Sanctuary House was actually worth £15,500 more without a Gibbs ceiling such as the one which was destroyed than one with it.

I find this evidence totally unconvincing and therefore reject it.

Clifford Knight satisfied me that he is experienced in the sale of residential properties with unusual features and he suggested that a feature such as the Gibbs ceiling would be likely to add between £10,000 and £20,000 to the value. I accept that this is a realistic range.

The Blisses both gave evidence, to the effect, that they paid more for this property because of the presence of this ceiling. I accept this and their evidence that there was possibly more interest from other potential purchasers as a result of this feature. Both Respondents contended that they had paid £15,000 more for the property with this ceiling than they would have done had it not been there.

I am not totally convinced on this point and therefore, in the absence of any better evidence, I opt for the lower of the ranges of the values put forward by the Respondent's expert, Mr Knight, and I assess the diminution in value at £10,000.

> ACCORDINGLY I FIND THE CLAIMANT LIABLE TO PAY TO THE RESPONDENT THE SUM OF **£10,000** (TEN THOUSAND POUNDS) IN RESPECT OF THEIR CLAIM FOR DIMINUTION IN THE VALUE OF THE PROPERTY DUE TO THE LOSS OF THE GIBBS CEILING.

15.02.3 Loss of Profits arising from the collapse of the Gibbs ceiling

This counterclaim is made under the following heads:

		£
Loss of Income—fees relating to unlet accommodation		330,960
Incremental costs incurred		
Emergency accommodation of residents	6,480	
Staff overtime over the Christmas period	1,495	
Increased promotional costs to relet rooms	2,740	
Financing costs	29,400	40,115
Incremental cost savings		
Cleaning staff salaries and Employers' NIC	(7,460)	
Heat and light	(9,280)	(16,740)
Total Damages Claimed		£354,335

15.02.3.1 **Loss of Income.** This claim amounted to £330,960 calculated as follows:

$$15 \text{ units} \times 52.53 \text{ weeks} \times £420 = £330,960.$$

The 52.53 weeks represents the 45 weeks that the 15 units were vacant following the ceiling collapse up to the date when the repair was completed, plus an average of 7.53 weeks taken over all the 15 units during the three-month period which these rooms were being relet. These periods are common ground and not disputed by the Claimant.

I have considered the Reports of the two expert accountants, Mr Hussein for the Claimant and Mr Page for the Respondent, and the evidence that they gave to the tribunal.

Having determined that RBL are liable for the direct losses attributable to their ceiling collapse it falls to me to determine the quantum of that loss.

Mr Hussein assesses the loss of income at £90,000. In doing so he makes a number of assumptions which vary from those made by Mr Page.

In his calculation of losses Mr Page has assumed 100 per cent occupancy of all the rooms for the whole of the 52.53 week period. This is clearly unsustainable in the light of both Mr Hussein's evidence, on average occupancy and, indeed, Mr Page's own evidence that some vacancies would have occurred but, for which, he makes no allowance.

After carefully considering the arguments I find that a reasonable average level of occupancy to allow would be 83 per cent.

Mr Page has assumed that the 15 rooms would have been let at £420 per week, per unit, over the entire period. However, the income from each of these rooms, immediately prior to the collapse in December 1992, was £400 per week. It is common ground that they were eventually relet at £420 per week. It seems reasonable, therefore, to take the average loss over the period as £410 per week per room.

Reverting, once more, to the average occupancy level if 83 per cent is taken as the average, then on average, over the period of the 52.53 weeks, nine rooms throughout the Home would have been vacant—say three vacancies amongst the 15 rooms and the balance amongst the other 37.

Having said that, I accept that the closure of the 15 rooms, and their subsequent reletting, affected this overall level of occupancy adversely. It took three months to relet all 15 rooms whereas, from the evidence, I believe that this reletting could have been achieved in half the time which it took.

This view is further reinforced by Mr Bliss's evidence that 'around half of them (the residents) returned' when the repairs were complete. This then, in effect, became seven instant relets.

THUS, TAKING ALL OF THESE FACTORS INTO ACCOUNT I FIND THAT THE LOSS OF INCOME IS OVERSTATED BY £91,016 AND THUS REDUCE MR PAGE'S FIGURE FROM £330,960 TO £239,944.

15.02.3.2 Incremental Costs Incurred

15.02.3.2.1 *Emergency Accommodation of Residents.* I accept SHL's evidence that the alternative accommodation into which they moved their displaced residents, MacMillan House in Aldeburgh, was an acceptable alternative to Sanctuary House.

ACCORDINGLY I ALLOW THE AMOUNT CLAIMED OF £6,480.

11.5 Arb
493

15.02.3.2.2 *Staff Overtime over the Christmas Period.* I accept SHL's reasons for offering their staff a higher than normal level of overtime to sacrifice their Christmas holiday to assist with the emergency which followed the collapsed ceiling.

ACCORDINGLY I ALLOW THE AMOUNT CLAIMED OF £1,495.

15.02.3.2.3 *Increase Promotional Costs to Relet Rooms.* I accept that some exceptional measures were justified in attempting to relet the 15 vacated rooms when they became available once more for occupation.

ACCORDINGLY I ALLOW 15/22NDS OF THE £2,740 CLAIMED = £1,868.

15.02.3.2.4 *Financing Costs.* It is common ground that RBL were aware, before they entered into this contract that SHL would borrow heavily to finance this venture.

I accept Mr Hussein's contention that SHL's trading losses are overstated in this calculation attributable to their additional borrowing resulting from the ceiling collapse.

I therefore reduce the amount I will allow under this head, by the same percentages as the loss of income has been reduced.

ACCORDINGLY, I ALLOW **72.5%** OF THE **£29,400** CLAIMED = **£21,315.**

15.02.3.3 Incremental Cost Savings

15.02.3.3.1 *Staff Salaries and Employers NIC.* It is accepted that SHL have a duty to mitigate their losses and in this regard the only head under which savings were sensibly achievable, lay in the number of staff that they retained, following the evacuation of the 15 rooms which, thus, reduced the number of rooms occupied, and needing to be served by carers, by 29 per cent.

It was accepted by Mr & Mrs Bliss, and the matron, Miss Glover, that in retrospect they should have taken more drastic steps to reduce their staff levels than they did in the event in only letting go two of their cleaning staff.

In my view SHL should have dispensed with at least five of their temporary (agency) staff within a month or so of the reduction of resident numbers.

I accept Mr Hussein's estimate of the additional savings which could have been effected for a period of 10–12 months following the collapse.

ACCORDINGLY, I FIND THE SAVING UNDER THIS HEAD, WHICH SHOULD HAVE BEEN MADE TO BE **£61,560 (£54,100 + £7,460).**

15.02.3.3.2 *Heat and Light.* I prefer Mr Hussein's estimate of the potential saving under this head. He has, in my view, a sounder accounting basis for arriving at his estimate than that adopted by Mr Page.

ACCORDINGLY, I FIND THE SAVING UNDER THIS HEAD SHOULD BE ALLOWED IN THE SUM OF **£3,874.**

Summary of Counterclaim for Loss of Profits

			£
15.02.3.1	Lost Income		239,944
15.02.3.2	Incremental costs incurred		
15.02.3.2.1	Emergency accommodation of residents	6,480	
15.02.3.2.2	Staff overtime over Christmas period	1,495	
15.02.3.2.3	Increased promotional costs to relet rooms	1,868	
15.02.3.2.4	Financing Costs	21,315	31,158
			271,102
15.02.3.3	Incremental cost savings		
15.02.3.3.1	Carers/Cleaner salaries and Employers NIC	(61,560)	
15.02.3.3.2	Heat and Light	(3,874)	(65,434)
	Total Damages Awarded		£205,668

11.5 Arb 494

15.02.4 ACCORDINGLY I AWARD TO THE RESPONDENT THE SUM OF **£205,668** (TWO HUNDRED AND FIVE THOUSAND SIX HUNDRED AND EIGHTY-EIGHT POUNDS) AS DAMAGES, IN RESPECT OF LOSS OF PROFITS CONSEQUENTIAL UPON THE CLAIMANT'S BREACH OF CONTRACT WHICH CAUSED THE LOSS OF THE GIBBS CEILING.

15.03 Consequential Losses arising from the Flooding of the Basement

Having determined, as a Preliminary Issue, that the Claimant was in breach of contract over the waterproofing of the basement laundry (5.18 Arb—item 12.13), I considered the losses which flowed from this breach.

There were no submissions that such losses were unforeseeable and I am satisfied that the Claimant is liable for the losses claimed.

Although the parties' respective experts had agreed that it was reasonable that the Claimant should carry out the remedial works to the tanking of this basement, Miss O'Brien, in closing, made it clear that the Respondent had lost confidence in the Claimant and did not wish them to execute this remedial work. Mr Belcher submitted that it was too late to renege on this agreement but I reject that submission.

It is settled law that specific performance will not be ordered if damages are an adequate remedy for the breach and, therefore, I award damages for this item.

THE SUM AGREED BY THE PARTIES' EXPERTS FOR THIS WORK WAS **£5,360** AND, ACCORDINGLY, I ADOPT THIS FIGURE.

15.03.2 The same experts agreed the **following sums which I also adopt**:

(i) Replacement of the washing machines, driers and dehumidifier—£14,800.
(ii) Linen, staff clothing and uniforms—£1,498

15.03.3 The only remaining issue is that of the residents' clothing which was damaged by the flooding. Mr Longdon contended that the value of this clothing, at half-replacement case, was £384 but, in arriving at this figure, he admitted that he had no idea of the age or condition of any of this clothing. In the absence of any evidence to the contrary,

I AWARD TWO-THIRDS OF THE AMOUNT CLAIMED I.E. **£256.**

Summary of Counterclaim of Losses flowing from the Flooding of the Basement

	£
(i) Remedial works to the waterproofing	5,360
(ii) Replacement of washing machines, driers and dehumidifier	14,800
(iii) Replacement of linen, staff clothing and uniforms	1,498
(iv) Replacement of residents' clothing	256
Total Damages Awarded	£21,914

11.5 Arb 495

ACCORDINGLY, I FIND THAT THE CLAIMANT IS TO PAY TO THE RESPONDENT THE SUM OF **£21,914** (TWENTY-ONE THOUSAND NINE HUNDRED AND FOURTEEN POUNDS) IN RESPECT OF LOSSES CONSEQUENTIAL ON THE CLAIMANT'S BREACH OF CONTRACT WHICH CAUSED THE FLOODING OF THE BASEMENT.

15.04 Summary of Damages Awarded under Issue 9

			£	£
15.01	Defective Work			(24,301)
15.02	Gibbs Ceiling			
	15.02.1	Cost of Restoration	43,924	
	15.02.2	Diminution in Value of Property	10,000	
	15.02.3	Loss of Profits	205,668	
				259,592
15.03	Flooded Basement			21,914
		Total Damages Awarded under Issue 9		£257,205

ACCORDINGLY, I FIND THAT THE CLAIMANT IS LIABLE TO PAY TO THE RESPONDENT THE SUM OF £257,205 (TWO HUNDRED AND FIFTY-SEVEN THOUSAND TWO HUNDRED AND FIVE POUNDS) IN RESPECT OF DAMAGES FOR BREACH OF CONTRACT—ISSUE 9.

16.00 Issue 10—Interest

To how much, if any, by way of interest, is the Respondent entitled?

16.01 The Respondent has claimed interest, pursuant to statute (19A interest) for such period or periods as I may deem fit.

16.02 Accordingly, I award interest on the sums awarded to the Respondent as follows:

		£
16.02.1	On the cost of the Restoration of the Gibbs ceiling	1,619.17
	On the diminution in the value of the property	Nil
	On the Loss of Profits	3,997.85
	On the losses resulting from the flooding of the basement	3,508.28
	Total Interest Awarded	**£9,125.30**

ACCORDINGLY I FIND THAT THE CLAIMANT IS TO PAY TO THE RESPONDENT THE SUM OF £9,125.30 (NINE THOUSAND ONE HUNDRED AND TWENTY-FIVE POUNDS 30p) IN RESPECT OF INTEREST—ISSUE 10.

17.00 Value Added Tax

As I have been informed that both parties are registered for Value Added Tax, and I have been given to understand that each can fully recover any VAT paid, all sums awarded are exclusive of VAT.

It is for each party to claim whatever VAT is due on these sums from the other parties.

If, for whatever reason, my understanding is incorrect and either party is unable to recover any VAT paid by them, then that party should make a written submission to me setting out the reasons for this inability to recover VAT and details of the amounts involved.

In the event of receiving such submissions I will deal with any further sums to be paid from either party, to the other, in respect of such non-recoverable VAT paid, when I publish my Award on Costs.

18.00 Grand Summary of Sums Awarded

18.01 To the Claimant

		£
18.01.1	Repayment of LAD's—para 8.01	118,625.00
18.01.2	Under the Final Account—para 9.04.2	46,296.31
18.01.3	As Loss and Expense—para 10.01.8	96,003.13
18.01.4	Due to Disturbance of Labour—para 11.01	Inc'd in 18.01.3
18.01.5	As damages for late payment of Certificates—para 12.07	10,338.80
18.01.6	As Interest para 13.03	81,214.46
	Total Awarded to the Claimant	**£352,477.77**

18.02 To the Respondent

		£
18.02.1	As Damages for Breach of Contract—para 15.04	257,205.00
18.02.2	As Interest—para 16.02.1	9,125.30
	Total Awarded to the Respondent	**£266,330,30**

18.03 Net Difference

		£
18.01	Total Awarded to Claimant	352,477.77
18.02	Total Awarded to Respondent	266,330.30
	Net Award to Claimant	£ 86,147.47

19.00 Costs

19.01 Costs of the Reference

Both Counsel made a brief oral submission on Costs at the conclusion of the hearing but requested me to publish a Final Award—Save as to Costs.

Counsel agreed to make separate written submissions on Costs and a timetable for these submissions was also agreed.

Following receipt of these written submissions, Counsel requested that I publish a Final Award—On Costs—Save as to the Settlement of Costs, on 'documents only' and to be a Reasoned Award.

For the avoidance of doubt concerning any costs orders given during the reference, such orders are confirmed herewith and deemed to be incorporated in this Award.

19.02 Costs of the Award

The Costs of the Award I tax and settle at £33,329.83 (thirty-three thousand, three hundred and twenty-nine pounds 83p), which sum includes £5,832.72 (five thousand, eight hundred and thirty-two pounds 72p) by way of Value Added Tax and £20.90 (twenty pounds 90p) by way of interest, on the joint and several liability of both parties.

The ultimate liability for paying these costs will be determined in my Final Award—On Costs, referred to above. If either party shall have paid, in respect of these costs, a sum greater than that which I direct in the said Final Award—On Costs, it will be ordered to reimburse the other party forthwith.

20.00 I Hereby Make and Publish this my Final Award—Save as to Costs and Award and Direct that:

20.01 THE RESPONDENT SHALL, WITHIN 14 DAYS OF THIS AWARD, PAY TO THE CLAIMANT THE SUM OF **£86,147.77** (EIGHTY-SIX THOUSAND ONE HUNDRED AND FORTY-SEVEN POUNDS 77p) IN FULL AND FINAL SETTLEMENT—EXCLUDING COSTS—OF ALL CLAIMS AND COUNTERCLAIMS HEREIN.

21.00 Fit for Counsel

I thank both Counsel for their courtesy and kind assistance.

Given under my hand at Hunstanton this 11 May 1994

In the presence of
Name ....
Address ....   **Mr D Emsee, MSc, FRICS, FCIArb**
....   **Arbitrator**
....
Occupation ....

Model Corrective Notice—re Errors in Final Award (11.6 Arb)

IN THE MATTER OF THE ARBITRATION ACTS 1950 TO 1979

AND

IN THE MATTER OF AN ARBITRATION UNDER THE JCT ARBITRATION RULES (18 JULY 1988)

BETWEEN

RELIABLE BUILDERS LIMITED

Claimant

AND

SANCTUARY HOUSE LIMITED

Respondent

ARBITRATOR'S FINAL AWARD—SAVE AS TO COSTS—CORRECTIVE NOTICE

WHEREAS I find in paragraph 15.01.1 of my Final Award, Save as to Costs, dated 11 May 1994, that I erroneously referred to the Claimant when I meant the Respondent and in paragraph 16.02 I made a clerical error in transposing figures (whereas the words in brackets were correct)

NOW I am desirous of exercising the powers given to me by Section 17 of the Arbitration Act 1950 to correct such accidental slip.

I HEREBY GIVE NOTICE that I am correcting my Award, as detailed above, and that the amount shown in item 20.01 of my Award is correct and that the remainder of my Award remains unaffected and unaltered.

Given under my hand this 26 May 1994.
In the presence of

In the presence of
Name ....
Address ....   **D Emsee, MSc, FRICS, FCIArb**
....   **Arbitrator**

....
Occupation ....

Claimant's Submission on Costs (11.7)

IN THE MATTER OF THE ARBITRATION ACTS 1950 TO 1979

AND

IN THE MATTER OF AN ARBITRATION UNDER THE JCT ARBITRATION RULES (18 JULY 1988)

BETWEEN

RELIABLE BUILDERS LIMITED   Claimant

AND

SANCTUARY HOUSE LIMITED   Respondent

CLAIMANT'S SUBMISSIONS ON COSTS

The general principles

1. The starting point for the award of costs in an arbitration, just as in litigation, is that costs follow the event. In *Lewis* v *Haverfordwest Rural District Council* [1953] 1 WLR 1486, Lord Goddard C.J. stated the general rule as follows:

> 'It is a curious circumstance—and one experiences it time and time again—that lay arbitrators always seem to think that parties should pay their own costs. Perhaps the present case and *Smeaton Co Ltd* v *Sassoon I. Setty Son & Co (No. 2)* [1953] 1 WLR 1481 before Devlin J. may be of some use as emphasizing to lay arbitrators that it has been laid down by the House of Lords in *Donald Campbell & Co* v *Pollak* reaffirming the Court of Appeal in *Ritter* v *Godfrey* [1920] 2 KB 47, that there is a settled practice in the courts that in the absence of special circumstances a successful litigant should receive his costs and that it is necessary to show some grounds for exercising the discretion of refusing an order which would give them to him, and the discretion must be judicially exercised. Those words 'judicially exercised' are always somewhat difficult to apply, but they mean the arbitrator must not act capriciously and must, if he is going to exercise his discretion, show a reason connected with the case and one which the court can see is a proper reason.'

11.7
499

The law where the Claimant is partially successful

2. 'The event' which costs should follow is, in case, the agreed award of money from one party to another. The Claimant has recovered a substantial amount of what it claimed, and in doing so defeated the Respondent's counterclaim. In the light of that the Claimant should be awarded all of its costs. This submission is supported by the following two Court of Appeal authorities.

3. In *Hanak* v *Green* [1958] 2 QB 9, the plaintiff employer sued the defendant builder for £266 for breach of contract in failing to complete certain items of work. The defendant counter-claimed for a *quantum meruit* for extra work outside the contract, and for damages and trespass, totalling £116 18s 9d (see the first paragraph of p. 12). The Judge found that the plaintiff was entitled to £74 17s 6d on the claim and the defendant was entitled to £84 19s 3d on the counterclaim.

He awarded the plaintiff the costs of her claim and the defendant the costs of the counterclaim.

4. On appeal, the defendant successfully argued that his defence amounted not only to a counterclaim but also to a set-off. As a set-off is a defence to a claim, he had defeated the claim and was consequently entitled to his costs. Morris L.J. considered the authorities at some length and stated at p. 26 that (with the exception of the £3 claim for trespass to goods) neither the plaintiffs claim nor that of the defendant could be insisted upon unless the other were taken into account. Consequently 'the defendant had an equitable set-off which defeated the plantiff's claim'.

5. Morris L.J. then went on to consider what should be the fair order for costs and decided that there should be judgment for the defendant on the claim with costs on scale 4 (being the appropriate County Court Scale for the sum claimed by the plaintiff) and judgment for the defendant on the counterclaim for £10 1s 9d with costs on scale 2. Hodson L.J. fully concurred with Morris L.J.'s judgment (see p. 16), and Sellers L.J. came to the same conclusion for the same reasons (see p. 31).

It should be noted that the defendant recovered a net figure of only 8.62 per cent of his original claim (£10 1s 9d compared with £116 18s 9d claimed), and lost on an important issue.

6. In *Nicholson v Little* [1956] 1 WLR 829, the defendant surveyor received monies for the plaintiff, but kept £84 of them, claiming that the plaintiff owed him £105 in fees. The plaintiff sued for the £84.

The judge found that the defendant was owed £61 in fees rather than £105, so that there was a balance of £22 payable to the plaintiff. The Judge awarded the plaintiff her costs, and the Court of Appeal upheld his decision on the basis that the proceedings were occasioned by the defendant's retention of her money, and the plaintiff would be out of pocket if she was not awarded her costs (see particularly Lord Denning MR at p. 832). (Similar reasoning is hinted at in *Re Elgindata Ltd (No 2)* [1992] 1 WLR 1207.)

The plaintiff, in *Nicholson*, recovered only 26 per cent of her original claim (£22 compared with £84 claimed), and substantially lost on the only issue in the case of whether she owed fees to the defendant and if so how much.

Reasons for this Rule

7. The general rule that a partially successful party should recover all of its costs is a just one for three main reasons.

The first is indicated in *Nicholson v Little*. The successful party has had to come to the court or to arbitration to recover monies that were owed to it. It would be unjust if it was out of pocket because of the costs it had to bear as a result of doing so.

8. Secondly, the rule is even-handed. If (in the present case) the Respondent had made a net recovery of any money, whether after judgment or by settlement, then it would be entitled to its costs. Perhaps more realistically in the present case, if the Respondent had made an effective sealed offer which was for more than the sum that the Claimant recovered, then the Respondent would be entitled to be paid its costs.

The Respondent has failed to do this.

9. Thirdly, the rule encourages settlement. The parties know that if they misjudge the strength of the claims of both parties, the consequences are severe because they will have to pay the costs of the other side. This encourages both parties to be cautious, which is necessary given that in most cases both parties overestimate the strength of their own case. It is in the interests of justice and in the interests of the parties that pressure is applied to them by the rules to persuade them to settle.

Application of the law to the present case

10. The Claimant in this present case is in a much stronger position than the successful

parties in *Hanak* v *Green* and *Nicholson* v *Little* for the following three reasons. Even more than them, it should recover all of its costs.

(i) The Claimant's measure of success

In this present case the measure of success enjoyed by the Claimant is comparable with that of the successful party in the two cases cited above.

The Claimant has, in round figures, recovered £352,500 net compared with an initial claim of £528,500 (after a notional adjustment for interest), see bundle A p. 8, which is a 67% recovery.

This compares very favourably with the percentages of the original claim recovered by the successful parties in *Hanak* v *Green* (8.62%) and *Nicholson* v *Little* (26%). If the Respondent's counterclaim is taken into account, which was for £505,000 after the notional interest adjustment—i.e. adding the equivalent percentage of interest to the amount claimed as was given on the sums awarded, there was little difference between the claim and counterclaim (see bundle B, p. 128). Yet the Claimant was sufficiently successful to be awarded over £86,000 after taking this very substantial counterclaim into account.

(ii) The Claimant has not lost on any of its issues

In the cases, cited above, the successful party substantially lost on an important issue. In *Nicholson* v *Little* the judge determined that the (unsuccessful) defendant was owed £61 in fees rather than £105. In *Hanak* v *Green* the Judge found that the (unsuccessful) plaintiff was entitled to £74 17s 6d for breach of contract in failing to complete certain items of work, compared with £266 claimed.

In the present case, it cannot be said that the Claimant has lost on any of its substantial issues. The issues on which the Respondent was most successful, the Basement, the Ceiling and the Diminution in the value of the property represent no more than around 10% of the amount counterclaimed.

(iii) The Claimant has had to come to arbitration

The Claimant has had to come to arbitration to recover monies that were owed to it, and it would be unjust if it were to be out of pocket because of the costs it had to bear. The present case is more extreme than *Nicholson* v *Little*.

11.7
501

11. The Claimant is a small building company which is suffering badly in the middle of a very deep recession, not least as a result of the Respondent's actions. In these unfavourable circumstances it has had to invest substantial sums of monies and a considerable amount of time of its two principal directors in pursuing its claim. Contrast the Respondent, which is a highly successful and prosperous business that has not been greatly affected by the recession—provision for caring for the elderly is increasingly in demand as the average age of the population increases, despite the state of the economy. Even recognising the comparative strengths of the parties' economic positions, the Claimant had the courage of its convictions to pursue its claim.

12. Furthermore, the determination to pursue a justified claim was in the face of a counterclaim which, if wholly successful, meant that the Claimant owed the Respondent £490,000 plus interest. The Respondent would also be entitled to its costs, which could only increase and would be very substantial indeed if the case went to arbitration.

If the Claimant had been unable to continue to pursue its claim at any stage, then it would have faced the prospect of making a very large payment to the Respondent. Such a position would have deterred many claimants from pursuing their claim at all. The Claimant's determination to obtain the monies it was owed has meant that it has defeated the Respondent's claim and made a substantial recovery.

13. It might be considered that the main issues between the parties of the Claimant's loss and expense/extension of time claim and the Respondent's loss of profit claim were difficult to resolve, and it would be understandable for a party to take a view of the case which was very different from that reached by the parties or the arbitrator at the end of the day. Thus there may be a temptation to have some sympathy for the Respondent's position.

However, the dispute starts from a basis that the Claimant was *prima facie* entitled to recover money on the unpaid certificate and on the Final Account. In addition, it was always clear that the Respondent had wrongfully deducted LADs to a far greater extent that he was entitled (as was demonstrated by the recovery, by the Claimant, of £118,625 or 81¼% of the £146,000 withheld). It was also clear that the Respondent had wrongfully withheld a substantial sum against defects of which 76% was returned to the Claimant as a result of the Arbitrator's Award.

14. The costs of claims concerning extension of time and loss and expense are generally large, and it must always have been obvious to both parties that costs were going to be a critical part of the present dispute. The Claimant has attempted to keep its costs down. In particular, by engaging a Claims Consultant and by not instructing a Solicitor. (No criticism is implied thereby of the Respondent's decision to have a solicitor present at all times.) Nevertheless, the Claimant's costs after a 20-days hearing amount to almost 50% of the amount of the claim, as was widely predicted at an early stage.

15. If the Respondent does not pay all of the Claimant's costs, whether as a result of taxation or as a result of the Claimant not obtaining 100% of its taxed costs, then the Claimant will be seriously out of pocket. In the circumstances outlined in paragraphs 11 to 14 above, this would be unjust.

16. It is submitted that the above considerations should lead to the Claimant recovering all of its taxed costs. The following matters may also be of some relevance.

(a) The Claimant agreed, in the interests of the parties costs, to consolidate the County Court action for the unpaid certificate although he had an unanswerable case for payment of this certificate.

(b) The Claimant's costs were increased by the Respondent's change of solicitor, at a critical stage of this arbitration, which resulted in an unnecessary increase in exchange of correspondence between the Claimant's representative and the Respondent's new solicitor, to bring that new solicitor 'up to speed' on this case.

In particular these costs were increased by the new solicitor requesting, and being granted, consent to Re-serve the Respondent's Defence and Counterclaim, after admitted that the original Defence and Counterclaim was so defective as to be unusable such that only a new Defence and Counterclaim would suffice. Even after this, the new Defence and Counterclaim was Amended and subsequently Re-Amended after the Claimant found it necessary to raise Requests for substantial Further and Better Particulars. Although the Claimant was awarded 'costs thrown away' to cover this Re-service, they did not adequately compensate him for the additional costs incurred.

(c) Hearing time had been needlessly wasted by having to examine both accountants' reports in such detail due to the Respondent's grossly inflated claim.

(d) In a similar vein, time spent by the Arbitrator alone with the experts and much hearing time had been wasted by Mr Maclean's unreasonable approach on the Claimant's extension of time claim, the loss and expense claim and the lengthy list of variations.

Toby Belcher
Counsel for the Claimant
26 May 1994.

11.7
502

Respondent's Submission on Costs (11.8)

IN THE MATTER OF THE ARBITRATION ACTS 1950 TO 1979

AND

IN THE MATTER OF AN ARBITRATION UNDER THE JCT ARBITRATION RULES (18 JULY 1988)

BETWEEN

RELIABLE BUILDERS LIMITED   Claimant

AND

SANCTUARY HOUSE LIMITED   Respondent

RESPONDENT'S SUBMISSIONS ON COSTS

Costs are discretionary

1. As the Judge in a trial has complete discretion in the matter of costs, so does an arbitrator. The power is given by virtue of section 18(1) of the Arbitration Act 1950:

> '... the costs of the reference and award shall be in the discretion of the arbitrator or umpire, who may direct to and by whom and in what manner those costs or any part thereof shall be paid ...'

2. The usual order is that 'Costs follow the event'. 'The event' is the outcome favourable to one side or the other in a fully argued and contested hearing. There were two 'events' in the accepted sense in this case—the claim and the counterclaim. Both cases cited, and relied upon, by the Claimants *Hanak* v *Green* and *Nicholson* v *Little* are cases where judgments were given on claims and counterclaims.

Costs where there are cross-claims

3. Where there are cross-claims, the court has a very wide discretion (*Childs* v *Blacker* [1954] 2 All ER 243, per Lord Goddard at 245, copy attached). Even when there is an 'event' for costs to follow, there is always a difficulty when there is a claim and a counterclaim.

> 'the starting point is always the rule that costs follow the event. This at once gives rise to a difficulty when there is a claim and counterclaim, the one being set off against the other. On some occasions it is then appropriate to consider each separately and, for example, to give the claimants the costs of the claim and the respondents the costs of the counterclaim. This leaves it to the parties to agree, or to the taxing authority to determine, what proportion of the costs of each party is attributable to the claim and what to the counterclaim. On other occasions it may be clear to the judge or arbitrator that the claim and counterclaim have no independent existence, the counterclaim being really a defence to the claim or vice versa. In such a case it is usually inappropriate to make cross orders for costs. One or other or neither party should be awarded all or some proportion of the costs of both claim or counterclaim.'

(Per Donaldson J (as he then was) in *Tramountana* v *Atlantic Shipping* [1978] 2 All ER 870 at 879f–h, copy attached.)

11.8
503

4. In *Hanak* v *Green* on which the Claimant relies Morris LJ said that

'neither the plaintiff's claim nor that of the defendant could be insisted upon unless the other were taken into account'.

That cannot be said to be the case in this action. There were a number of issues forming part of the respondents cross-claim that had an existence independent of the claim. Apart from the loss of profits claim there were the claims for the Basement, the Gibbs ceiling and the Diminution in the value of the property on all of which the Arbitrator found for the Respondent.

5. Despite the resulting Arbitrator's award in a net award to the Claimant the proper order in relation to this action is that each side should be awarded the costs of proving the issues on which they have succeeded *Adamson* v *Birkenhead Corpn* [1937] 2 All ER 221.

6. The main issues were those relating to the Claimant's extension of time/loss and expense claim, claim over the Gibbs ceiling and its loss of profits. Clearly there were matters which should have been susceptible of settlement before the arbitration began—for instance the proper valuation of the works and contract instructions and the cost of the defects.

7. (a) It is accepted the Claimant agreed to consolidate the County Court action over the unpaid certificate but it is denied that the Claimant had an unanswerable case for payment of this certificate.

(b) Although it is accepted that the Claimant's costs may have been increased as a result of the Respondent's change of solicitor, it is submitted that the Claimant was adequately compensated for any extra costs involved by the Arbitrator's award of 'costs thrown away'—see Arbitrator's Order for Directions No 8—16 September 1993—item 3.00.

(c) The Respondent made a genuine attempt to settle the dispute in June 1993 at which time, had the Claimant accepted the Respondent's terms, very considerable savings in the parties' costs would have resulted. However, it was due to the Claimant that these settlement talks failed and when costs are taken into account, the Claimant is now considerably more out-of-pocket than he would have been had he accepted the Respondent's terms then offered.

(d) It is denied that hearing time was needlessly wasted by the examination of the individual accountants' claims dealing with the Respondent's loss of profits. In the event, although the amount awarded was less than that claimed, the detailed examination was more than justified by the amount awarded, almost 60% of the amount claimed.

(e) It was also denied that Mr Maclean adopted an unreasonable approach to the Claimant's claims for extension of time, loss and expense and variations. Quite the reverse. On the extension of time, Mr Maclean conceded nine weeks and three days of a total of 16 weeks claimed. Mr Maclean's approach on the other two issues was the normal difference of opinion that one would expect from two surveyors holding different views when examining such claims.

**11.8
504**

Conclusions

8. The award in this arbitration embraces a payment by the Respondent to the Claimant of a sum only just over 20% of the sum originally claimed.

9. The 'costs follow the event' rule is, it is submitted, a difficult principle to apply where there are cross-claims that are independent of the claim, as has been shown in the case here.

10. In the circumstances of this arbitration it would be unjust for the Claimants to obtain 100% of their costs of the reference. It is submitted that the arbitrator should follow one of three routes in exercising his discretion:

(a) To order that each side should bear its own costs of certain of the issues: namely (i) those items of the Respondent's claim that are independent of the claim (see paragraphs 4 and 5 above); (ii) those items in the Claimant's claim which are independent of the Respondent's counterclaim, viz. the claim for extension of time and loss and expense. It would then be for the parties to agree, or failing agreement for the arbitrator on taxation to apportion, the costs falling to each of the above (see per Donaldson J in *Tramountana*, cited above).

(b) To order that the Claimant recovers his costs, or a proportion of his costs, where he has succeeded on his claim and the Respondent recovers his costs, or a proportion of his costs, where he has succeeded on his counterclaim.

(c) To take a global view of the matter and to award the Claimants a proportion of their costs. It is clear that, on any view, the sum which the Respondents have to pay to the Claimants is considerably less than that which was claimed at the start of, and throughout, the arbitration. The Respondent submits that, in the circumstances, it is appropriate that it should be ordered to pay only a proportion of the Claimants costs of the reference, such proportion to be determined by the percentage that the recovered sum bears to the sum claimed.

Bernadette O'Brien
Counsel for the Respondent
1 June 1994

11.8
505

THE AWARD

Claimant's Reply to Respondent's Submission on Costs (11.9)

IN THE MATTER OF THE ARBITRATION ACTS 1950 TO 1979

AND

IN THE MATTER OF AN ARBITRATION UNDER THE JCT ARBITRATION RULES (18 JULY 1988)

BETWEEN

RELIABLE BUILDERS LIMITED   Claimant

AND

SANCTUARY HOUSE LIMITED   Respondent

CLAIMANT'S REPLY ON COSTS

Costs should follow the event

1. The Claimant has submitted that costs should follow the event, and 'the event', in the present case is the award of money from one party to another. This submission is supported by two Court of Appeal cases, *Hanak* v *Green* and *Nicholson* v *Little*. In those cases the Court of Appeal might have decided (although they rejected this approach) that, as the successful party had lost on an important issue, he or she should be responsible for some of the costs. In the present case, such an argument is not available to the Respondent or to the Arbitrator for the additional reason that it cannot be said that either side lost on any important issue.

The Respondent's authorities

2. The Respondent relies on two cases. First, it is said (Respondent's submission paragraph 3) that the court has a wide discretion where there are cross claims, relying on *Childs* v *Blacker* [1954] 2 All ER 243 at p. 245. It is submitted that there is no general statement of principle in *Childs'* case, and the facts of the case are of no relevance whatsoever to the present case.

3. Secondly, reliance is placed by the Respondent on *Tramountana* v *Atlantic Shipping* [1978] 2 All ER 870 at 879f–h (Respondent's submissions paragraph 3). That case can be distinguished from the present one on a number of grounds:

    (a) The cited observations of Donaldson J., which are *obiter dicta*, must be read in the light of the Court of Appeal decisions in *Hanak* v *Green* [1958] and *Nicholson* v *Little* [1956] (see in particular paragraph 4 of the Claimant's Submissions). To be reconciled with what Morris L.J. decided in *Hanak* v *Green*, Donaldson J. should be taken as meaning by the expression 'independent' counterclaim that the counterclaim is not a set-off to the claim.

    (b) It is submitted that the claims for the Basement, the Gibbs ceiling, the loss of Profits and the Defects are patently set-offs of the Claimant's claims. Furthermore, they cannot be said to be 'independent' counterclaims in any sense of the word. Those counterclaims are intimately linked with the claims because they concern what happened during the course of the works, and are part of the evidence of how the Claimant executed the works.

(c) The counterclaims were very much minor issues in the arbitration, in terms of time. The principal issues which incurred most costs, both in preparation for and at the hearing were the Claimant's claim for an extension of time, and the loss and expense.

The Respondent's arguments

4. The Respondent submits that the Arbitrator should award costs in one of three ways (see Respondent's submissions paragraph 10).

It is submitted that there is neither reason nor authority in support of these contentions. Nor do they answer the fundamental points that the Claimant raised in its submissions.

The arbitrator is respectfully directed to those submissions; they are, in summary as follows:

(a) The Claimant has been very much more successful than in two Court of Appeal cases, where the partially successful party recovered all the costs. In *Hanak* v *Green* only 8.62% of the original claim was recovered, and in *Nicholson* v *Little* only 26%. In our case, after making the notional allowance for interest on the amounts claimed equivalent to that awarded, the Claimant recovered 67% of its claim. The 20% figure quoted in paragraph 8 of the Respondent's submissions (11.8) is incorrect and totally misleading as it takes no account of the counterclaim. I therefore repeat paragraph 10(i) of my submission (11.7).

(b) Unlike the two cited cases, it cannot be said that the Claimant has lost on any of its issues.

(c) The Claimant has had to come to arbitration to recover monies that were owed to it, and has had the courage to do so despite its weak financial position compared with the Respondent, and the fact that the Respondent was claiming that the Claimant should pay it money. It would be unjust if the Claimant were to be out of pocket because of the costs it had to bear; the costs were always going to be of critical importance in the present dispute.

5. Further, neither alternative suggested by the Respondent satisfies the conditions laid down by the Court of Appeal in *Re Elgindata Ltd.* To be deprived of its costs, the successful party must fail on certain of its issues, which the Claimant has not done. Furthermore, they must cause a significant increase in the length of the proceedings, which none of the issues raised by the Claimant did.

It is further submitted that the conditions laid down in *Re Elgindata Ltd* are necessary and not sufficient conditions for a successful party to be deprived of any of its costs, and must be read subject to *Hanak* v *Green* and *Nicholson* v *Little*.

6. *First alternative.* In the first alternative, it is suggested that each side should bear its own costs on two issues or groups of issues. There is a further general objection to such an approach: it would be almost impossible to apportion costs to an issue or group of issues on any sensible or accurate basis, and it would make taxation very difficult.

7. The first issue is in relation to items of the Respondent's claim which are independent of the Claimant's claim. The Claimant's reply is at paragraph 3 above.

The Times, 18th June 1992. Copy sent with earlier submissions where referred to in paragraph 6.

8. The Respondent makes a further point under paragraph 7 of his submission—that of the failure of the settlement negotiations.

This proposed settlement failed not due to the Claimant but because the Respondent did not make a realistic offer to settle what has subsequently been proved by the Arbitrator's Award to be well-founded claims.

11.9
507

9. *Second alternative.* The Respondent submits that the Arbitrator should order that the Claimant recovers his costs, or a proportion of them, where he has succeeded in his Claim and that the Respondent recovers his costs, or a proportion of them, where he has succeeded in his Counterclaim.

This proposition runs counter to the general rule in relation to the costs of a claim or a counterclaim which is where both actions succeed or fail . . . there should be no apportionment of general costs. (Butterworth's on Costs B 21 [41].)

10. *Third alternative.* The Respondent submits that it should only pay say 20% of the Claimant's costs (see Respondent's submissions (11.8) paragraph 10(c)).

11. The submission that the Claimant should pay the costs proportionate to its overall percentage success rate is totally unrealistic, and the Respondent gives neither reason nor authority to suggest why this measure should be adopted. It may be suggested that this is a rough approximation to whether the Claimant has won or lost on the issues. In addition to the general arguments raised in paragraph 4 above, there are the following more specific objections.

(a) The Claimant has not lost on any of its issues.

(b) The overall success of 20% would not be a sensible measure of the extent to which the Claimant has won and lost on the issues cited in paragraph 8 of the Respondents submissions is totally misleading and largely irrelevant. Firstly because some issues took very much more time to litigate than others, and the time spent on each issue did not bear any sensible comparison with the amount claimed. Secondly any comparison should take account of the elimination of the counterclaim and the significantly higher recovery of interest by the Claimant i.e. over £81,000.

(c) The issues were very closely related, making it wholly artificial to split the costs between them. In particular, the two main issues, that of the extension of time and the consequent recovery of loss and expense by the Claimant including liquidated damages wrongfully deducted by the Respondent, on the one hand and the Respondent's claim for loss of profits, the Gibbs ceiling and the alleged diminution in the value of the property, on the other.

Both issues depended, to large measure, on the Respondent's conduct which kept the Claimant on the site 16 weeks beyond the contract completion date.

Toby Belcher
Counsel for the Claimant
8 June 1994

**11.9
508**

Final Award on Costs—save as to Settlement of Costs (11.10 Arb)

IN THE MATTER OF THE ARBITRATION ACTS 1950 TO 1979

AND

IN THE MATTER OF AN ARBITRATION UNDER THE JCT ARBITRATION RULES (18 JULY 1988)

BETWEEN

RELIABLE BUILDERS LIMITED   Claimant

AND

SANCTUARY HOUSE LIMITED   Respondent

FINAL AWARD—ON COSTS—SAVE AS TO SETTLEMENT OF COSTS

1.00 WHEREAS
On 11 May 1994 I published an Award in the above reference, FINAL—SAVE AS TO COSTS, and this present FINAL AWARD—ON COSTS—SAVE AS TO SETTLEMENT OF COSTS is complementary to and is to be read in conjunction with the Award published on 11 May 1994.

2.00 AND WHEREAS
Clause 19.00 of the award read as follows:

'Costs of the Reference
Both Counsel made a brief oral submission on Costs at the conclusion of the Hearing but requested me to publish a Final Award—Save as to Costs.
  Counsel agreed to make separate written submissions on Costs and a timetable for these submissions was also agreed.
  Following receipt of these written submissions Counsel requested that I publish a Final Award—on Costs—Save as to Settlement of Costs, on "documents only" and to be a Reasoned Award.'

3.00 AND WHEREAS
On 26 May 1994 I received Claimant's Counsel's submissions on Costs and on 2 June 1994 the Respondent's Counsel's submissions and Response and on 9 June 1994 the Claimant's Counsel's Reply.
  Both Counsel accept that it is settled practice that 'costs follow the event'. However, they differ as to what is 'the event' in this case.

4.00 Counsel for the Claimant submits that the Claimant has recovered a substantial amount of what is claimed and in doing so defeated the Respondent's counterclaim, such that a net amount was awarded to the Claimant and in the light of this the Claimant should be awarded all of its costs.
  In support of this contention, Mr Belcher cited *Hanak* v *Green* [1958] 2 QB 9 and *Nicholson* v *Little* [1956] 1 WLR 829. He said that the Claimant had come to court to recover the money owed to it and it would be unjust if he were to be out-of-pocket as a result of doing so. He conceded that had the Respondent made a net recovery of money then it would be entitled to its costs.

11.10 Arb
509

Relying on the authorities he cited, Mr Belcher contended that the Claimant, in this case, is in a much stronger position than the successful parties in those cases. Firstly, because the Claimant has been more successful, in this present case, than the Respondent. Secondly, whereas the successful party, in each of the citing cases, lost on an important issue, that is not the position in this present case where the Claimant did not lose on any of its issues.

5.00 On specific matters effecting costs and, in particular, on the parties conduct of this reference, Mr Belcher made the following points in support of his contention that the Claimant should be awarded all its costs.

(a) The Claimant agreed, in the interests of the parties' costs, to consolidate the County Court action for the unpaid certificate although he had an unanswerable case for payment of this certificate.

(b) The Claimant's costs were increased by the Respondent's change of solicitor, at a critical stage of this arbitration, which resulted in an unnecessary increase in exchange of correspondence between the Claimant's representative and the Respondent's new solicitor, to bring that new solicitor 'up to speed' on this case.

In particular these costs were increased by the new solicitor requesting, and being granted, consent to Re-serve the Respondent's Defence and Counterclaim, after admitted that the original Defence and Counterclaim was so defective as to be unusable such that only a new Defence and Counterclaim would suffice. Even after this, the new Defence and Counterclaim was Amended and subsequently Re-Amended after the Claimant found it necessary to raise Requests for substantial Further and Better Particulars. Although the Claimant was awarded 'costs thrown away' to cover this Re-service, they did not adequately compensate him for the additional costs incurred.

(c) Hearing time had been needlessly wasted by having to examine both accountants' reports in such detail due to the Respondent's grossly inflated claim.

(d) In a similar vein, time spent by the Arbitrator alone with the experts and much hearing time had been wasted by Mr Maclean's unreasonable approach on the Claimant's extension of time claim, the loss and expense claim and the lengthy list of variations.

6.00 Miss O'Brien, on the other hand, for the Respondent, made the following submissions.

In this case there were two 'events'—the claim and the counterclaim. She said that where there are such cross-claims a Court has a very wide discretion and even where there is an 'event' for costs to follow, there is always a difficulty when there is a claim and a counterclaim. She cited Lord Goddard from *Childs* v *Blacker* [1954] 2 All ER 243 in support of this:

'. . . the starting point is always the rule that costs follow the event. This at once gives rise to a difficulty when there is a claim and a counterclaim, the one being set off against the other. On some occasions it is then appropriate to consider each separately and, for example, to give the Claimants the costs of the claim and the Respondents the costs of the counterclaim. This leaves it to the parties to agree, or to the taxing authority to determine what proportion of the costs of each party is attributable to the claim and what to the counterclaim. On other occasions it may be clear to the judge or Arbitrator that the claim and counterclaim have no independent existence, the counterclaim being really a defence to the claim or vice versa. In such a case it is usually inappropriate to make cross orders for costs. One or other or neither party should be awarded all or some proportion of the costs of both claim and counterclaim.'

She also cited Donaldson J (as he was then) in *Tramountana* v *Atlantic Shipping* [1978] 2 All ER 870 at 879f–h.

7.00 She contended that there were a number of issues forming part of the Respondent's cross-claim that had an existence independent of the claim. Apart from the loss of profits claim there were the claims for the Basement, the Gibbs ceiling and the Diminution in the value of the property on all of which the Arbitrator found for the Respondent.

8.00 In *Hanak* v *Green*, on which the Claimant relies, she said that Morris LJ said:

'. . . neither the Plaintiff's claim nor that of the Defendant could be insisted on unless the other were taken into account'.

But that cannot be said to the position in this action. Despite my Award resulting in a net payment to the Claimant the proper order, she contends, is that each side should bear its own costs inasmuch as each side has substantially succeeded in its claim against the other.

She further clarifies this by concluding that each side should bear its own costs of certain of the issues in the claim and in the counterclaim, which were independent of the other party's claim. It would then be for the parties to agree, or failing agreement, for the Arbitrator on taxation, to apportion the costs falling to each of the above. (Again she refers me to Donaldson J in *Tramountana* in support of this.)

Alternatively, Miss O'Brien submitted that I could take a global view of the matter and award the Claimant a proportion of its costs. In support of this approach she said that, it is clear that, on any view, the sum which the Respondents have to pay to the Claimants is considerably less than that which was claimed at the start of, and throughout, the arbitration. She further submitted that, in the circumstances, it is appropriate that the Respondent should be ordered to pay only a proportion of the Claimant's costs of the reference, such proportion to be determined by the percentage that the recovered sum bears to the sum claimed, namely 25%.

9.00 On the conduct point made by Mr Belcher, in his submission, Miss O'Brien had this to say:

(a) It is accepted the Claimant agreed to consolidate the County Court action over the unpaid certificate but it is denied that the Claimant had an unanswerable case for payment of this certificate.

(b) Although it is accepted that the Claimant's costs may have been increased as a result of the Respondent's change of solicitor, it is submitted that the Claimant was adequately compensated for any extra costs involved by the Arbitrator's award of 'costs thrown away'—see Arbitrator's Order for Directions No 8—16 September 1993—item 3.00.

(c) The Respondent made a genuine attempt to settle the dispute in June 1993 at which time, had the Claimant accepted the Respondent's terms, very considerable savings in the parties' costs would have resulted. However, it was due to the Claimant that these settlement talks failed and when costs are taken into account, the Claimant is now considerably more out-of-pocket than he would have been had he accepted the Respondent's terms then offered

(d) It is denied that hearing time was needlessly wasted by the examination of the individual accountants' claims dealing with the Respondent's loss of profits. In the event, although the amount awarded was less than that claimed, the detailed examination was more than justified by the amount awarded, almost 60% of the amount claimed.

(e) It was also denied that Mr Maclean adopted an unreasonable approach to the Claimant's claims for extension of time, loss and expense and variations. Quite the reverse. On the extension of time, Mr Maclean conceded nine weeks and three days of a total of 16 weeks claimed. Mr Maclean's approach on the other two issues was the normal difference of opinion that one would expect from two surveyors holding different views when examining such claims.

10.00 In his Reply to Miss O'Brien, Mr Belcher, reiterated that the 'event' in this case was

11.10 Arb 511

my award of money from one party to the other and again referred me to *Hanak* v *Green* and *Nicholson* v *Little*, Mr Belcher said:

> 'In those cases the Court of Appeal might have decided (although they rejected the approach) that, as the successful party had lost on an important issue, he or she should be responsible for some of the costs. In this case, such argument is not available to the Respondent . . . it cannot be said that either side lost on any important issue.'

11.00 Mr Belcher rejected the authority of *Childs* v *Blacker* as of no relevance to this case. Also, in rejecting reliance on *Tramountana*, Mr Belcher said, that the Respondent's counterclaim is potentially set off to the Claimant's claim and not 'independent' in any sense of the word. He reasons that they are intimately linked because they concern what happened during the course of the works.

12.00 Of Miss O'Brien's three suggested options of awarding costs, Mr Belcher said that in both *Hanak* v *Green* and *Nicholson* v *Little* the partially successful party recovered all of its costs. Yet, in this case, the Claimant has been far more successful in percentage terms than either of the successful parties in those two cases.

Mr Belcher further cites *Re Elgindata Limited (No. 2)* [1992] 1 WLR 1207 where the Court of Appeal held that to be deprived of its costs the successful party must fail on certain issues which the Claimant has not done, in this case, and further, these lost issues must cause a significant increase in the length of the proceedings. Again, this did not occur in this case.

13.00 Miss O'Brien's first alternative, Mr Belcher suggested that it was almost impossible to apportion costs to an issue or group of issues on any sensible or accurate basis.

The second alternative, suggested by Miss O'Brien; that each party receives its costs, or a proportion of them, to the extent to which they have succeed on their Claim (or Counterclaim) is rejected by Mr Belcher on the grounds that it goes against the general rule, in such case, and he cites Butterworth's on Costs in support of this.

The third alternative, whereby the Respondent should pay a proportion of the Claimant's costs is unrealistic Mr Belcher contends and points out that Miss O'Brien gives no reasonable authority why this measure should be adopted.

14.00 On the conduct points Mr Belcher said it was always clear that the Respondent had wrongfully deducted liquidated and ascertained damages to a far greater extent than he was entitled (as was demonstrated by the recovery, of over £118,000 or around 80% of the £146,000 withheld). It was also clear that the Respondent has wrongfully withheld a substantial sum against defects of which, again almost 80%, was returned to the Claimant as a result of my Award.

15.00 Finally, Mr Belcher refers to Miss O'Brien's point concerning the failure of the settlement terms and contends that the settlement talks failed, not due to the Claimant but, because the Respondent did not make a realistic offer to settle what has subsequently been proved by the Arbitrator's Award, to be well-founded claims.

16.00 **AND HAVING CONSIDERED** these submissions and the cases cited therein

AND FURTHER

in the judicial exercise of the absolute discretion invested in me over costs and that

HAVING CONSIDERED

the conduct of the parties, or their representatives, throughout the interlocutory and hearing stages of this reference

I FIND AND HOLD as follows:

17.00 I accept Miss O'Brien's contention that, in this case, there were two 'events', the claim and the counterclaim.

18.00 The counterclaim, to a significant extent has an independent existence from the claim. Had the final account been settled in the normal way, at the conclusion of the contract, and this settlement had included some form of accommodation over the LADs, there probably would have been no claim.

On the other hand the events of the flooded basement and the collapsed Gibbs ceiling would have provided a cause of action for the Respondent against the Claimant. In this regard I accept Miss O'Brien's submission of the relevance of *Childs* v *Blacker*.

19.00 I reject Mr Belcher's point that it is almost impossible to apportion costs to an issue or group of issues, on any sensible or accurate basis. I estimate that the hearing costs were approximately 50% of the total costs incurred by both parties and this hearing time is capable of very accurate apportionment. Similarly, the costs of the individual experts, who were engaged for discreet issues of claim and counterclaim, are equally capable of accurate attribution. The same would apply, to some extent, to conferences with Counsel. This would leave a relatively small proportion of costs to be reasonably apportioned to these two events.

20.00 Both parties substantially succeeded in their claims. Each was put to the expense and time and money in pursing their respective claims and as such it would not be just for either to be substantially out-of-pocket to the extent that they succeeded.

I rely on the authority of *Tramountana* to which both parties referred me, where it was said:

> 'This at once gives rise to a difficulty when there is a claim and counterclaim, the one being set off against the other. On some occasions it is then appropriate to consider each separately and, for example, to give the Claimants the costs of the claim and the Respondents the costs of the counterclaim. This leaves it to the parties to agree, or to the taxing authority to determine, what proportion of the costs of each party is attributable to the claim and what to the counterclaim.'

Whilst holding that the counterclaim largely had an independent existence from the claim, there were clearly some items of this counterclaim which can, and should, be regarded as set off items, or a defence to the claim. They were the claim for defects and the flooded basement.

21.00 ACCORDINGLY I FIND AND HOLD

21.01 THAT THE CLAIMANT SHOULD BE AWARDED THE COSTS OF THE CLAIM AND THE RESPONDENT SHOULD BE AWARDED **85%** OF ITS COSTS OF THE COUNTERCLAIM.

11.10 Arb
513

21.02 FOR THE AVOIDANCE OF DOUBT THESE APPORTIONMENTS OF COST ARE MADE AFTER DUE ALLOWANCE HAS BEEN MADE FOR ANY COSTS ORDERS ALREADY GIVEN DURING THE REFERENCE.

22.00 With their written submissions on Costs, Counsel said that they would be unable to agree any such costs awarded by me and requested me to settle these costs. Accordingly I agreed to make an Order for Directions concerning the procedure to be followed for this settlement.

23.00 For the sake of completeness I deal with the matters to which both Counsel drew my attention as being relevant to the question of costs, i.e. the conduct of the parties, or their representatives, during the reference.

(i) The Claimant *did* act in the parties' best interests concerning costs when he agreed to consolidate the County Court action into the Arbitration. Whether his case was unanswerable or not I did not consider further. Either way, running one action rather than two, was probably as much in his interests as the Respondents when it came to cost savings.

(ii) I agree that all of our costs were increased as a result of the Respondent's relative late change of solicitor. However, it is a party's prerogative to have whomsoever they choose to represent them and the change *per se* only had a marginal effect on costs. What cost in time and money was then involved in scrapping the original Defence and Counterclaim and re-serving a new one, was, in my view, even in retrospect, reasonably, if not adequately, compensated for at the time when I ordered the Respondent to pay 'costs thrown away in any event', which he did without further demur.

(iii) I did not consider that an inordinate amount of hearing time was wasted going through the accountants' reports in great detail, nor do I consider that the Respondent's claim for loss of profits was grossly exaggerated.
It could equally be argued that the Claimant's expert's assessment, at less than 10% of the amount claimed, was 'grossly exaggerated' and, had he been more reasonable, time could have been saved. In the event I awarded around 60% of the amount claimed which I believe showed that the claim for that issue was not grossly exaggerated.

(iv) Mr Belcher's complaint that Mr Maclean's approach was unreasonable is rejected. I personally did not find Mr Maclean unhelpful. I consider the very fact that he conceded nine and a half weeks' extension of time against the 16 weeks that RBL claimed, to be evidence of a reasonable attitude.

(v) On the failure of the settlement talks, I say this. Had the parties been able to come to terms then, undoubtedly, significant costs should have been avoided. However, I consider that such 'without prejudice' negotiations have no bearing on my award as to costs, whoever may have been responsible for their failure. All parties have a duty to attempt to mitigate costs of an action and may attempt to settle their differences is to be encouraged and neither side should not be dissuaded from trying and failing to settle the issues at an early stage.

24.00 Finally I deal with the 'offer to settle' contained in the sealed envelope, handed to me at the end of the hearing. This envelope was opened by my secretary in my presence once I had determined the general principles, on costs, to be applied in this case. The envelope contained one sheet of paper on which there was a Calderbank offer from the Claimant to settle the counterclaim for £250,000, inclusive of any interest awarded. Clearly, this sum fell short of the amount that I eventually found for the Respondent on the counterclaim and, as such, this offer is of no effect on my order for costs being less than the amount awarded. It is perhaps significant that neither Counsel sought to bring my attention to this offer in their submissions.

11.10 Arb 514

25.00 *Costs of the Award*

I DETERMINE that the Costs of this Award shall be borne roughly in the same proportion as the parties have succeeded in recovering their costs

AND ACCORDINGLY I DETERMINE THAT **25%** OF THESE COSTS SHALL BE BORNE BY THE CLAIMANT AND **75%** BY THE RESPONDENT.

THUS of the costs of this Award, which I hereby settle at £808.74, the Claimant shall pay forthwith £202.19 (Two Hundred and Two Pounds 19p) which sum included £30.12 (Thirty

Pounds 12p) by way of Value Added Tax and the Respondent shall pay forthwith £606.55 (Six Hundred and Six Pounds 55p) which sum includes £90.33 (Ninety Pounds 33p) by way of Value Added Tax.

If either party has paid to me more than the amount now directed that party shall reimburse the other party for the excess amount paid.

For the avoidance of doubt, all interlocutory directions, concerning costs, are incorporated in this Award.

26.00 Fit for Counsel

Given under my hand at Hunstanton this 10th day of June 1994.

In the presence of
Name ....
Address ....   **Mr D Emsee, MSc, FRICS, FCIArb**
....   **Arbitrator**
....
Occupation ....

11.10 Arb
515

CHAPTER 12

Fees

First Interim Fee Statement (12.1 Arb)

D EMSEE MSC (CONSTRUCTION LAW), FRICS, FCIARB

REGISTERED ARBITRATOR

Toad Hall, Hunstanton Water, NORFOLK

Telephone: 0999 590124; Facsimile: 0999 590690

Jayrich Associates	Weller Baines & Bishton
Construction Claims Consultant	Solicitors
Swansea House	42 South Square
48 Queens Road	Gray's Inn
Norwich	London WC1
Norfolk NR2 LO6	
	FAO Jayrich Catchpole Esq
FAO Joel Redman Esq	

Inv. 1001

Sanctuary House, Woodbridge, Suffolk

In the matter of an Arbitration between Reliable Builders Ltd and Sanctuary House Ltd

First Interim Fee Statement

To Dealing with appointment 20 February 1993.

Setting up files, dealing with Terms, Conditions, studying documentation.

Preparing for and attendance at Preliminary Meeting 23 March 1993.

Preparation for hearing of Preliminary Issues.

Receipt and consideration of Statements of Case 8 April and 6 May 1993.

Receipt and consideration of Closing Submissions 1 and 7 June 1993.

Attendance at hearing 24 and 25 May 1993 and publication of Interim Declaratory Award dated 10 June 1993.

FEES

Including all interlocutory work, consideration of correspondence, acknowledgement and replies thereto.

Fee in accordance with Terms signed by Claimant 26 February 1993 and Respondent 23 March 1993, based on time expended.

		£
36 hours 48 mins @ £80 per hour		2944.00

Disbursements	£	
Typing	55.00	
Photocopies	6.60	
Faxes/telephone	8.20	
Postage	5.40	75.20
		3019.20
Less Deposit cheque received from Claimant 26 February 1993		400.00
		2619.20
	£	
Plus VAT @ 17.5% on £3019.20	528.36	
Less VAT @ 17.5% on 3400.00	70.00	458.36
Amount Due	TOTAL	£3077.56

D Emsee, MSc, FRICS, FCIArb
Registered Arbitrator

**12.1 Arb
518**

Second Interim Fee Statement (12.2 Arb)

D EMSEE MSC (CONSTRUCTION LAW), FRICS, FCIARB

REGISTERED ARBITRATOR

Toad Hall, Hunstanton Water, NORFOLK

Telephone: 0999 590124; Facsimile: 0999 590690

Jeremy Associates
Construction Claims Consultant
Swansea House
48 Queens Road
Norwich
Norfolk NR2 LO6

FAO Joel Redman

Kalmsyde & Joyoff
48 Crown Street
Ipswich
Suffolk IP5 2QR

FAO James Crichton

Inv. 1014

Sanctuary House, Woodbridge, Suffolk

In the matter of an arbitration between Reliable Builders Ltd and Sanctuary House Ltd under the JCT Arbitration Rules (30 July 1988)

Interim Fee Claim No 2

To 'Costs thrown away' to be paid by the Respondent in any event, as per my Order for Directions 8 dated 16 September 1993.

As per time extracted from my time sheets as follows:

	Hrs	Mins
9–10 August 1993—Order for Directions No 6 and time incidental thereto	1	13
15 August 1993—Cancellation of Inspection visit scheduled for 16 August 1993	8	00
26–27 August 1993—Order for Directions No 7 and time incidental thereto		55
2–16 September 1993—Order for Directions No 8 and time incidental thereto	1	42
18 September 1993—Consideration of Defence and Counterclaim		35
8–10 November 1993—Receipt and consideration of Defence and Counterclaim and supporting documentation—now abortive. Long telephone calls from and to Mr Crighton following his appointment reviewing conduct of reference to date		40
c/f	13	05

12.2 Arb
519

FEES

	Hrs	Mins
b/f	13	05

Hearing days set aside, as per Order for Directions No 5—16 July 1993

20 Hearing days from 7 March–12 April as scheduled in Order, 7, 8, 9, 10, 14, 15 & 16 March. All between 3 and 6 months— therefore

	Hrs	Mins
$7 \times 8 = 56 \times 25\% = 14$	14	00
	27	05

Fee based on time expended as per Terms signed by Claimant 26 Feb 1993 and Respondent 23 March 1993

	£
27 hrs 5 mins @ £80 per hour	2166.67

Disbursements
Total time charged to date 68 hrs 25 mins

Total disbursements to costs to date say £180

$$\frac{27 \text{ hrs } 5 \text{ mins}}{68 \times 25} \times 180$$

	£
	71.25
	2237.92
Plus VAT @ 17.5%	391.64
TOTAL	£2629.56

D Emsee, MSc, FRICS, FCIArb
17 September 1993

12.2 Arb
520

Third Interim Fee Statement (12.3/1 Arb)

D EMSEE MSC (CONSTRUCTION LAW), FRICS, FCIARB

REGISTERED ARBITRATOR

Toad Hall, Hunstanton Water, NORFOLK

Telephone: 0999 590124; Facsimile: 0999 590690

Jayrich Associates
Construction Claims Consultant
Swansea House
48 Queens Road
Norwich
Norfolk NR2 LO6

FAO Joel Redman Esq

Kalmsyde & Joyoff
48 Crown Street
Ipswich
Suffolk IP5 2QR

FAO James Crighton Esq

Inv. 1028

Sanctuary House, Woodbridge, Suffolk

In the matter of an arbitration between Reliable Builders Ltd and Sanctuary House Ltd

Third Interim Fee Statement

To Dealing with appointment 20 February 1993.

Setting up files, dealing with Terms Conditions, studying documentation.

Preparing for and attendance at Preliminary Meeting 23 March 1993.

Preparation for hearing of Preliminary Issues.

Receipt and consideration of Statements of Case 8 April and 6 May 1993.

Receipt and consideration of Closing Submissions 1 and 7 June 1993.

Attendance at hearing 24 and 25 May 1993 and publication of Award dated 10 June 1993.

Receipt and consideration of Statement of Case 12 July 1993 in respect of substantive issues.

Receipt and consideration of Defence and Counterclaim 17 August 1993, in respect of substantive issues.

Amended Statement of Defence and Counterclaim 18 October 1993.

12.3/1 Arb
521

FEES

Re-amended Statement of Defence and Counterclaim 21 October 1993.

Dealing with Request for Further and Better Particulars 26 August 1993 and 15 November 1993 and Reply 22 November 1993.

Dealing with 'Ad Hoc' Arbitration Agreement.

Receipt and consideration of reserved Defence and Counterclaim, 18 and 21 October 1993.

Preparation and publication of Interim Award on Taxation of 'costs thrown away' 2 November 1993.

Receipt and consideration of Defence to the Counterclaim, 19 November 1993.

Meetings with Experts November/December 1993 and Interim Award 17 December 1993, covering issues determined thereby.

Preparation for and attendance at Pre-Hearing Review Meeting, 10 January 1994.

Dealing with cross-applications for Security of Costs including the Arbitrator's costs and hearing parties, 14 Febuary 1994, and Order directing payment of security, 21 February 1994.

Including all interlocutory work, Orders for Directions, consideration of correspondence, acknowledgement and replies thereto.

Fee in accordance with Terms signed by Claimant 26 February 1993 and Respondent 23 March 1993, based on time expended.

	£
132 hours 48 mins @ £80 per hour	10624.00
32 hours 24 mins @ £85 per hour	2754.00
	13378.00

Disbursements	£		
Typing	253.00		
Photocopies	30.36		
Faxes/telephone	37.72		
Travelling	149.00		
Postage	24.84		494.92
		c/f	13872.92

THIRD INTERIM FEE STATEMENT

		£
	b/f	13872.92

	£	
Less Fees received		
Claimant deposit cheque 26/2/93	400.00	
First Interim Fee received from		
Claimant 11/6/93	2619.20	
Second Interim Fee received 11/11/93	2258.82*	5278.02*
		8594.90
Plus VAT @ 17.5% on 13872.92	2427.76	
Less VAT @ 17.5% on 5257.12	920.00	1507.76
Amount Due		£10102.66

*Includes £20.90 by way of interest

D Emsee, MSc, FRICS, FCIArb
Registered Arbitrator
21 February 1994

FEES

Fee Statement in respect of Costs of Security for my Costs and Expenses (12.3/2 Arb)

D EMSEE MSC (CONSTRUCTION LAW), FRICS, FCIARB

REGISTERED ARBITRATOR

Toad Hall, Hunstanton Water, NORFOLK

Telephone: 0999 590124; Facsimile: 0999 590690

Jayrich Associates
Construction Claims Consultant
Swansea House
48 Queens Road
Norwich
Norfolk NR2 LO6

FAO Joel Redman Esq

Kalmsyde & Joyoff
48 Crown Street
Ipswich
Suffolk IP5 2QR

FAO James Crighton Esq

Sanctuary House, Woodbridge, Suffolk

In the matter of an arbitration between Reliable Builders Ltd and Sanctuary House Ltd

Fee Statement—In Respect of Costs of Security for my Costs and Expenses

To the provision of Security for my Costs and Expenses as empowered
by Rule 12.1.3 and in accordance with my Terms clause 7) signed by
the Claimant 26 February 1993 and the Respondent 23 March 1993.

As directed by my Order for Directions No 19—21 February 1993

In the sum of 10,000.00

Each party to provide a moiety of this Security

Note: VAT will be accounted for when a detailed Fee Statement is
submitted

**12.3/2 Arb
524**

Accordingly this is NOT A VAT INVOICE
   Total Amount Due

£10,000.00

D Emsee, MSc, FRICS, FCIArb
Registered Arbitrator
21 February 1994

Fourth Interim Fee Statement (12.4 Arb)

D EMSEE MSC (CONSTRUCTION LAW), FRICS, FCIARB

REGISTERED ARBITRATOR

Toad Hall, Hunstanton Water, NORFOLK

Telephone: 0999 590124; Facsimile: 0999 590690

Jayrich Associates
Construction Claims Consultant
Swansea House
48 Queens Road
Norwich
Norfolk NR2 LO6

FAO Joel Redman Esq

Kalmsyde & Joyoff
48 Crown Street
Ipswich
Suffolk IP5 2QR

FAO James Crighton Esq

Inv. 1032

Sanctuary House, Woodbridge, Suffolk

In the matter of an arbitration between Reliable Builders Ltd and Sanctuary House Ltd

Fourth Interim Fee Statement

To Dealing with appointment 20 February 1993.

Setting up files, dealing with Terms Conditions, studying documentation.

Preparing for and attendance at Preliminary Meeting 23 March 1993.

Preparation for hearing of Preliminary Issues.

Receipt and consideration of Statements of Case 8 April and 6 May 1993.

Receipt and consideration of Closing Submissions 1 and 7 June 1993.

12.4 Arb
525

Attendance at hearing 24 and 25 May 1993 and publication of Award dated 10 June 1993.

Receipt and consideration of Statement of Case 12 July 1993 in respect of substantive issues.

Receipt and consideration of Defence and Counterclaim 17 August 1993, in respect of substantive issues.

Amended Statement of Defence and Counterclaim 18 October 1993.

Re-amended Statement of Defence and Counterclaim 21 October 1993.

Dealing with Request for Further and Better Particulars 26 August 1993 and 15 November 1993 and Reply 22 November 1993.

Dealing with 'Ad Hoc' Arbitration Agreement.

Receipt and consideration of reserved Defence and Counterclaim, 18 and 21 October 1993.

Preparation and publication of Interim Award on Taxation of 'costs thrown away' 2 November 1993.

Receipt and consideration of Defence to the Counterclaim, 19 November 1993.

Meetings with Experts November/December 1993 and Interim Award 17 December 1993, covering issues determined thereby.

Preparation for and attendance at Pre-Hearing Review Meeting, 10 January 1994.

Dealing with cross-applications for Security of Costs including the Arbitrator's costs and hearing parties, 14 February 1994, and Order directing payment of security, 21 February 1994.

Receipt and consideration of Hearing Bundle, review of Pleadings, Witness Statements, etc and generally preparing for and attendance at Hearing on March 7, 8, 9, 10, 14, 15, 16, 17, 21, 29, 30, 31, April 6, 7, 8, 11, 12, 13, 14 and 18

Including all interlocutory work, Orders for Directions, consideration of correspondence, acknowledgement and replies thereto.

12.4 Arb 526

Fee in accordance with Terms signed by Claimant 26 February 1993 and Respondent 23 March 1993, based on time expended.

	£
132 hours 48 mins @ £80 per hour	10624.00
261 hours 40 mins @ £85 per hour	22241.67
	32865.67
Less Credit for one day's hearing 29 March due to my accident 8 hrs @ £85	680.00
c/f	32185.67

FOURTH INTERIM FEE STATEMENT

		£		£
			b/f	32185.67
Disbursements		£		
Typing		358.00		
Photocopies		50.38		
Faxes/telephone		39.94		
Travelling & Subsistence		669.00		
Postage		26.84		1144.16
Less Fees received			£	
Claimant deposit cheque 26/2/93			400.00	
First Interim Fee received from Claimant 11/6/93			2619.20	
Second Interim Fee received 11/11/93			2258.82*	
Third Interim Fee received 25/2/94			8594.90	
Security for my fees received from Claimant 25/2/94 and Respondent 3/3/94			10000.00†	23872.92
				9456.91
Plus VAT @ 17.5% on 33329.83		5832.72		
Less VAT @ 17.5% on 13852.02		2424.10		3408.62
Amount Due				£12865.53

* Includes £20.90 by way of interest
† No VAT included originally

D Emsee, MSc, FRICS, FCIArb,
Registered Arbitrator
11 May 1994

12.4 Arb
527

Fee Statement—re Award of Costs (12.5 Arb)

D EMSEE MSC (CONSTRUCTION LAW), FRICS, FCIARB

REGISTERED ARBITRATOR

Toad Hall, Hunstanton Water, NORFOLK

Telephone: 0999 590124; Facsimile: 0999 590690

Jayrich Associates
Construction Claims Consultant
Swansea House
48 Queens Road
Norwich
Norfolk NR2 LO6

Kalmsyde & Joyoff
48 Crown Street
Ipswich
Suffolk IP5 2QR

FAO James Crighton Esq

FAO Joel Redman Esq

Inv. 1044

Sanctuary House, Woodbridge, Suffolk

In the matter of an arbitration between Reliable Builders Ltd and Sanctuary House Ltd

Fee Statement—Re Award of Costs

To Receipt and consideration of Claimant's Counsel's
submission on Costs 25 May 1994; Respondent's
Counsel's Response 2 June 1994 and Claimant's
Counsel's Reply 9 June 1994

Drafting Final Award

Based on time involved:

		£
7 hrs 48 mins @ £85 per hour		663.00
Disbursements	£	
Typing	19.79	
Photocopies	2.90	
Postage	2.60	25.29
Plus VAT @ 17.5%		120.45
Total Amount Due		£808.74

**12.5 Arb
528**

D Emsee, MSc, FRICS, FCIArb
Registered Arbitrator
10 June 1994

Fee Statement—in respect of Settlement of Costs (12.6 Arb)

D EMSEE MSC (CONSTRUCTION LAW), FRICS, FCIARB

REGISTERED ARBITRATOR

Toad Hall, Hunstanton Water, NORFOLK

Telephone: 0999 590124; Facsimile: 0999 590690

Jayrich Associates
Construction Claims Consultant
Swansea House
48 Queens Road
Norwich
Norfolk NR2 LO6

FAO Joel Redman Esq

Kalmsyde & Joyoff
48 Crown Street
Ipswich
Suffolk IP5 2QR

FAO James Crighton Esq

Inv. 1048

Sanctuary House, Woodbridge, Suffolk

In the matter of an arbitration between Reliable Builders Ltd and Sanctuary House Ltd

Fee Statement—in respect of Settlement of Costs

To Preparation of Orders for Directions Nos 20 and 21

To Attendance at Hearing on Form of Claimant's Bill of Costs 1 July 1994

To Receipt and consideration of the following:

The Claimant's submission 20 June 1994 on the Costs of the Settlement of Costs

The Respondent's objections 27 June 1994 on the Costs of the Settlement of Costs

The Claimant's second Bill of Costs 11 July 1994

Responses to Bills of Costs listing objections 18 July 1994

To Visits to parties representatives' offices 18 July 1994 to inspect files

To Conference with Costs Draftsman in his Romford office 22 July 1994

To Preparation for and attendance at Hearing on Taxation of Costs 23 July 1994

To Consideration of evidence and preparation of Award on Settlement of Costs

All interlocutory work from 11 June 1994—25 July 1994

**12.6 Arb
529**

FEES

		£
Based on time involved		
27 hrs 54 mins @ £85 per hour		2371.50

Disbursements	£	
Travel	77.69	
Typing	97.62	
Photocopies	22.95	
Binders	2.00	
Postage	11.67	
Facsimiles	29.00	
J & J Berry's a/c attached	1100.00	1340.93
		3712.43
Plus VAT @ 17.5%		649.67
Total Amount Due		£4362.10

D Emsee, MSc, FRICS, FCIArb
Registered Arbitrator
25 July 1994

Fee Statement—in respect of Costs of the Settlement of Costs (12.7 Arb)

D EMSEE MSC (CONSTRUCTION LAW), FRICS, FCIARB

REGISTERED ARBITRATOR

Toad Hall, Hunstanton Water, NORFOLK

Telephone: 0999 590124; Facsimile: 0999 590690

Jayrich Associates
Construction Claims Consultant
Swansea House
48 Queens Road
Norwich
Norfolk NR2 LO6

FAO Joel Redman Esq

Kalmsyde & Joyoff
48 Crown Street
Ipswich
Suffolk IP5 2QR

FAO James Crighton Esq

Inv. 1052

Sanctuary House, Woodbridge, Suffolk

In the matter of an arbitration between Reliable Builders Ltd and Sanctuary House Ltd

Fee Statement—In respect of Costs of the Settlement of Costs

To Submission on the Costs of the Settlement of Costs.

To Receipt and consideration of the following:

Receipt of Respondent's submission on Costs of
Settlement—1 August 1994

Receipt of Claimant's submission on Costs of
Settlement and Claimant's Bill of Costs of Settlement—8
August 1994

Receipt of Respondent's Reply to Claimant's
submission on Costs of Settlement and objections to
Claimant's Bill of Costs—15 August 1994

All interlocutory correspondence relating thereto
Consideration of all submissions and preparation of
Award

**12.7 Arb
531**

		£
Fee based on time involved 14 hrs 35 mins @ £85 per hour		1239.58

Disbursements	£	
Typing	38.04	
Photocopies	7.20	
Binders	2.00	
Postage	4.08	
Facsimiles	11.70	63.02
	c/f	1302.60

	£
b/f	1302.96
Plus VAT @ 17.5%	227.96
Total Amount Due	£1503.56

D Emsee, MSc, FRICS, FCIArb
Registered Arbitrator
19 August 1994

CHAPTER 13

The Appeal

Summons for Extension of Time for Leave to Appeal under s.1, Arbitration Act 1979 (13.1)

IN THE HIGH COURT OF JUSTICE
QUEEN'S BENCH DIVISION
COMMERCIAL COURT

IN THE MATTER OF THE ARBITRATION ACTS 1950 TO 1979

AND

IN THE MATTER OF AN ARBITRATION UNDER THE JCT ARBITRATION RULES (18 JULY 1988)

BETWEEN

SANCTUARY HOUSE LIMITED   Plaintiff

AND

RELIABLE BUILDERS LIMITED   Defendant

SUMMONS

LET ALL PARTIES attend the Judge in the Commercial Court, Royal Courts of Justice, Strand, London, on the   day of   1994 at   o'clock in the   noon, on the hearing of an application by the above named Plaintiff.

FOR AN ORDER that the period of time within which to serve an application pursuant to Section 1 of the Arbitration Act 1979 for leave to appeal to the High Court in respect of an Award dated 11 May 1994 made by David Emsee as the said Arbitrator in an Arbitration between the Plaintiff and the Defendant be extended to Friday 1 July 1994.

AND FOR AN ORDER that the costs of an incidental to this application be paid by the Defendant.

DATED the 30 day of June 1994

To: Messrs Jayrich Associates of   Defendant's solicitors.

This Summons was taken out by Messrs Kalmsyde & Joyoff of   Solicitors for the Plaintiff.

**13.1
533**

THE APPEAL

Summons for Extension of Time to Serve Application under s.1(5), Arbitration Act 1979 (13.2)

IN THE HIGH COURT OF JUSTICE
QUEEN'S BENCH DIVISION
COMMERCIAL COURT

IN THE MATTER OF THE ARBITRATION ACTS 1950 TO 1979

AND

IN THE MATTER OF AN ARBITRATION UNDER THE JCT ARBITRATION
RULES (18 JULY 1988)

BETWEEN

SANCTUARY HOUSE LIMITED   Plaintiff

AND

RELIABLE BUILDERS LIMITED   First Defendant

AND

DAVID EMSEE   Second Defendant

SUMMONS

LET ALL PARTIES attend the Judge in the Commercial Court, Royal Courts of Justice, Strand, London, on the   day of   199 , at   o'clock in the   noon, on the hearing of an application by the above named Plaintiff.

FOR AN ORDER that the period of time within which to serve an application pursuant to Section 1(5) of the Arbitration Act 1979 for an Order directing the Arbitrator, David Emsee, to state further reasons for his Award dated 11 May 1994 made in an Arbitration between the Plaintiff and the First Defendant in which the said David Emsee was sole Arbitrator, be extended until Friday 1 July 1994.

AND FOR AN ORDER that the costs of and incidental to this application be paid by the First Defendant.

13.2
534

DATED the 30 day of June 1994

To: Messrs Jayrich Associates of Swansea House, 48 Queens Road, Norwich, Norfolk—
     First Defendant's Solicitors

and: David Emsee of Toad Hall, Hunstanton, Norfolk.

This Summons was taken out by Messrs Kalmsyde & Joyoff of 48 Crown Street, Ipswich, Suffolk, Solicitors for the Plaintiff.

Affidavit of James Crighton in support of Application for Extension of Time for Leave to Appeal (13.3)

IN THE HIGH COURT OF JUSTICE
QUEEN'S BENCH DIVISION
COMMERCIAL COURT

IN THE MATTER OF THE ARBITRATION ACTS 1950 TO 1979

AND

IN THE MATTER OF AN ARBITRATION UNDER THE JCT ARBITRATION RULES (18 JULY 1988)

BETWEEN

SANCTUARY HOUSE LIMITED   Applicant

AND

RELIABLE BUILDERS LIMITED   Respondent

AFFIDAVIT OF JAMES CRIGHTON IN SUPPORT OF APPLICATION FOR EXTENSION OF TIME

I, JAMES CRIGHTON of 48 Crown Street, Ipswich, Suffolk, Solicitor MAKE OATH and say as follows:

1. I am a solicitor in the firm of Messrs Kalmsyde & Joyoff, solicitors to the Applicant and, subject to the supervision of my principal I have the conduct of this matter and make this Affidavit from facts and matters made known to me whilst carrying out my duties as aforesaid.
2. I make this Affidavit in support of an application for an extension of time

   (a) within which to seek leave to appeal the Award given by the Arbitrator, Mr David Emsee, following an Arbitration conducted under the JCT Arbitration Rules (1988) between Reliable Builders Limited (RBL) and Sanctuary House Limited (SHL) and
   (b) within which to make an application under Section 1(5) of the Arbitration Act 1979 to direct the Arbitrator to make further reasons for his Award.

3. There is now produced and shown to me marked 'JC 1' a paginated bundle of correspondence which I shall refer to by way of page numbers throughout this Affidavit.
4. A dispute arose between RBL and SHL following building works carried out in accordance with an IFC 1984 form of Building Contract at Sanctuary House, Woodbridge, Suffolk, and the matter was referred to Arbitration. Mr David Emsee was appointed as Arbitrator in the dispute by the President of the Royal Institute of Chartered Surveyors on 20 February 1993.
5. The Arbitration hearing extended over 20 days commencing on 7 March 1994 and terminating on 18 April 1994.
6. On 11 May 1994, the Arbitrator stated that his Award was ready for collection on

13.3
535

payment of his fee account (pages 1–4). On 15 May 1994, on behalf of SHL I acknowledged receipt of the Arbitrator's aforementioned letter (page 5). Messrs Kalmsyde & Joyoff who were instructed on behalf of RBL acknowledged the same letter on 16 May 1994.

7. On 18 May 1994 I wrote to the Arbitrator (page 7) pointing out two errors in the Award. The Arbitrator acknowledged receipt of this letter on 19 May 1994 (page 8) giving the parties seven days to comment on these errors, following which, the Arbitrator issued a Corrective Notice on 26 May 1994. This Corrective Notice was sent to the offices of my client SHL. Unfortunately my client was on holiday at the time and did not return until 17 June 1994. The same day he sent the Corrective Notice to their office and after consultation with me instructed me to appeal the Award.

8. I immediately contacted Miss Bernadette O'Brien, of Counsel who had appeared on behalf of SHL in connection with the Arbitration hearing. Miss O'Brien was not in Chambers, having left for a week's holiday. I then contacted Miss O'Brien at her home address whereupon she informed me she would not be able to deal with the appeal until her return from holiday on 27 June 1994.

9. The Corrective Notice was received by this office on 17 June 1994 and thereafter Counsels' vacation intervened. Once the Corrective Notice had been received at this office and SHL's instructions taken, steps were taken with all due expedition to appeal the Award. Having regard to the matters aforesaid I would respectfully ask that the application for an extension of time within which to seek leave to appeal the Award and to apply to the Court under Section 1(5) of the Arbitration Act 1979 for the Arbitrator to make further reasons for his Award be granted.

SWORN at 20A Baker Street
      London
in Greater London this
30 day of June 1994

Before me,

A Solicitor

13.3
536

Summons for Leave to Appeal under s.1, Arbitration Act 1979 (13.4)

IN THE HIGH COURT OF JUSTICE
QUEEN'S BENCH DIVISION
COMMERCIAL COURT

IN THE MATTER OF THE ARBITRATION ACTS 1950 TO 1979

AND

IN THE MATTER OF AN ARBITRATION UNDER THE JCT ARBITRATION
RULES (18 JULY 1988)

BETWEEN

SANCTUARY HOUSE LIMITED   Plaintiff

AND

RELIABLE BUILDERS LIMITED   Defendant

SUMMONS

LET Reliable Builders Limited of Snape Yard, Woodbridge, Suffolk, attend before the Judge in the Commercial Court, Royal Courts of Justice, Strand, London WC2A 2LL on   the
          day of   199 at   o'clock in the   noon on the hearing of an application by the above named Plaintiff pursuant to Section 1 of the Arbitration Act 1979.

FOR AN ORDER that the Plaintiff has leave to appeal to the High Court on the questions of law arising out of an Award dated 11 May 1994 made by David Emsee as a sole Arbitrator in an Arbitration between the Plaintiff and the Defendant, namely whether on the facts found by the Arbitrator and/or the evidence before him the Defendant

on the grounds set out in the Notice of Motion herein (and in the Affidavit of James Crighton served herewith)

AND FOR AN ORDER that the costs of and incidental to this application be paid by the Defendant.

DATED the 30th day of June 1994

To: Messrs Jayrich Associates
    Swansea House
    48 Queens Road
    Norwich
    Norfolk
    Solicitors for the Defendant

13.4
537

This Summons was taken out by Messrs Kalmsyde & Joyoff of 48 Crown Street, Ipswich, Suffolk. Solicitors for the Plaintiff.

Notice of Originating Motion in Support of Summons for Leave to Appeal (13.5)

IN THE HIGH COURT OF JUSTICE
QUEEN'S BENCH DIVISION
COMMERCIAL COURT

IN THE MATTER OF THE ARBITRATION ACTS 1950 TO 1979

AND

IN THE MATTER OF AN ARBITRATION UNDER THE JCT ARBITRATION RULES (18 JULY 1988)

BETWEEN

SANCTUARY HOUSE LIMITED   Applicant

AND

RELIABLE BUILDERS LIMITED   Respondent

NOTICE OF ORIGINATING MOTION

TAKE NOTICE that the High Court of Justice, Queen's Bench Division, Commercial Court at the Royal Courts of Justice, Strand, London WC2A 2LL, will be moved on the expiration of clear days after the service of this Notice or as soon thereafter as Counsel can be heard, by Counsel on behalf of the above named Applicant for an order that the Arbitration Award dated 11 May 1994 made by David Emsee as sole Arbitrator in an Arbitration between the Applicant and the Respondent be varied to the effect that

when there was no, alternatively no convincing evidence before the Arbitrator on which he could reach that conclusion

should not have made consequential awards to the Respondent of additional sums and interest thereon.

Dated the   day of   199

To: The Respondents
    c/o Jayrich Associates
    Swansea House
    48 Queens Road
    Norwich
    Norfolk

13.5
538

This Notice was issued by Messrs Kalmsyde & Joyoff of 48 Crown Street, Ipswich, Suffolk—Solicitors for the Applicant

Summons pursuant to s.1(5), Arbitration Act 1979 to State Further Reasons (13.6)

IN THE HIGH COURT OF JUSTICE
QUEEN'S BENCH DIVISION
COMMERCIAL COURT

IN THE MATTER OF THE ARBITRATION ACTS 1950 TO 1979

AND

IN THE MATTER OF AN ARBITRATION UNDER THE JCT ARBITRATION RULES (18 JULY 1988)

BETWEEN

SANCTUARY HOUSE LIMITED   Plaintiff

AND

RELIABLE BUILDERS LIMITED   First Defendant

AND

DAVID EMSEE   Second Defendant

SUMMONS

LET all parties attend the Judge in the Commercial Court, Royal Courts of Justice, Strand, London on   day the   day of   199 , at   o'clock in the   noon, on the hearing of an application by the above named Plaintiff pursuant to Section 1(5) of the Arbitration Act 1979 that the Arbitrator should state further reasons for his holding that the First Defendant is entitled to

and that such further reasons should include:

(1) His reasons for holding

indicating on what specific part or parts of the evidence (including that recorded in the transcript already obtained) the Arbitrator relies in making those findings.

(2) His reasons for holding

indicating on what specific part or parts of the evidence (including that recorded in the transcript already obtained) he relies in making that finding.

AND let the Defendant within   days after service of this Summons on his counting the day of service, return the accompanying Acknowledgement of Service to the appropriate Court Office.

**13.6
539**

DATED the 30 day of June 1994

To: Messrs Jayrich Associates of Swansea House, 48 Queens Road, Norwich, Norfolk—
First Defendant's Solicitors

and: David Emsee of Toad Hall, Hunstanton, Norfolk.

This Summons is issued by Messrs Kalmsyde & Joyoff, 48 Crown Street, Ipswich, Suffolk. Solicitors for the Plaintiff.

Affidavit of James Crighton in Support of Two Summonses—for Leave to Appeal and for Further Reasons (13.7)

IN THE HIGH COURT OF JUSTICE
QUEEN'S BENCH DIVISION
COMMERCIAL COURT

IN THE MATTER OF THE ARBITRATION ACTS 1950 TO 1979

AND

IN THE MATTER OF AN ARBITRATION UNDER THE JCT ARBITRATION
RULES (18 JULY 1988)

BETWEEN

SANCTUARY HOUSE LIMITED	Plaintiff
AND	
RELIABLE BUILDERS LIMITED	First Defendant
AND	
DAVID EMSEE	Second Defendant

AFFIDAVIT OF JAMES CRIGHTON

I, JAMES CRIGHTON of 48 Crown Street, Ipswich, Suffolk, Solicitor MAKE OATH and say as follows:

1. I am a solicitor in the firm of Kalmsyde & Joyoff of the above address and had the day-to-day conduct of this matter on behalf of the Plaintiff throughout the Arbitration and throughout the hearing. The matters that I depose to herein are within my own knowledge.

2. I swear this Affidavit in support of the Plaintiff's application

    (i) for leave to appeal pursuant to Section 1 of the Arbitration Act 1979

    (ii) alternatively, for an Order that the Arbitrator be directed to provide further

SHL contend strongly that it is clear that the Arbitrator made no findings which could justify that conclusion. But in case that contention is not accepted by the Court SHL respectfully seeks an order in the terms set out in the Application under Section 1(5) of the 1979 Arbitration Act herein.

SHL equally contends that it is clear that the Arbitrator had no basis for concluding that

13.7
540

However, if that contention is not accepted then SHL respectfully seek, in the alternative, further reasons from the Arbitrator in the terms set out in the application herein.

Sworn by the said James Crighton ⎫
at 48 Crown Street, Ipswich, Suffolk ⎬
this 30 day of June 1994 ⎭

Before me

A Solicitor

Model Exclusion Agreements from *The Law and Practice relating to Appeals from Arbitration Awards* **by Professor D Rhidian Thomas (13.8)**

EXCLUSION CLAUSE IN SHORT FORM FOR FUTURE DISPUTES TO TAKE EFFECT BEFORE THE COMMENCEMENT OF THE ARBITRATION

Exclusion clause in short form for inclusion in a contract or arbitration clause for the purposes of the Arbitration Act 1979 relating to future disputes and to take effect before the commencement of the arbitration.

> The parties agree to exclude any right of application under section 2 or appeal to the High Court under section 1(2) of the Arbitration Act 1979 with respect to any question of law arising in the course of the reference or out of any award.

EXCLUSION AGREEMENT FOR FUTURE DISPUTES TO TAKE EFFECT BEFORE THE COMMENCEMENT OF THE ARBITRATION

Exclusion agreement for the purposes of the Arbitration Act 1979 relating to future disputes and to take effect before the commencement of the arbitration.

THIS EXCLUSION AGREEMENT is made the   day of   BETWEEN   [*names and addresses etc of the parties*]

WHEREAS

(1) The parties entered into an agreement dated   (*date*) [*character of the agreement for example, for the sale of certain goods*]
(2) The agreement contains an arbitration clause under which all disputes and differences arising between the parties should be determined by arbitration
(3) The parties wish that any such future disputes shall be determined finally by the Arbitrator

IT IS AGREED in accordance with the Arbitration Act 1979 Section 3 that the right of appeal by either party to the High Court under section 1 of that Act shall be excluded in relation to the award of the Arbitrator and that neither party shall have the right to apply to the High Court under Section 2(1)(a) of that Act for the determination of any question of law arising in the course of the reference to arbitration.

AS WITNESS etc

[*signatures of the parties*]

EXCLUSION AGREEMENT FOR EXISTING DISPUTES ENTERED INTO AFTER THE COMMENCEMENT OF THE ARBITRATION

13.8
541

Exclusion agreement for the purposes of the Arbitration Act 1979 relating to existing disputes and entered into after the commencement of the arbitration

I

THIS EXCLUSION AGREEMENT is made the   day of   BETWEEN   [*names and addresses etc of parties*]

WHEREAS

(1) The parties are the parties to a contract dated   [*date*]
(2) A dispute has arisen between them as to   [*nature of dispute*]
(3) In accordance with clause   of the contract   [*arbitrator(s)*] ('the Arbitrator[s]') [has *or* have] been appointed arbitrator[s] to determine that dispute
(4) The parties desire that the dispute shall be determined finally by the Arbitrator[s]

NOW IT IS AGREED in accordance with the Arbitration Act 1979 Section 3 that the right of appeal by either party to the High Court under Section 1 of that Act shall be excluded in relation to the award of the Arbitrator[s] on the above-recited dispute and that neither party shall have the right to apply to the High Court under Section 2(1)(a) of that Act for the determination of any question of law arising in the course of the reference to arbitration.

AS WITNESS etc

[*signatures of all parties*]

II

IN THE MATTER OF THE ARBITRATION ACTS 1950–1979
AND
IN THE MATTER OF AN ARBITRATION BETWEEN

Claimant

and

Respondent

EXCLUSION AGREEMENT

We the undersigned having referred to arbitration the dispute that has arisen under the contract between us dated the   day of   and having appointed   to be Arbitrator in the reference HEREBY AGREE pursuant to Section 3 of the Arbitration Act 1979 that the jurisdiction of the High Court under Sections 1 and 2 of the said Act in respect of this arbitration shall be excluded.

Signed by or on behalf of the Claimant by:
Dated this   day of   19

13.8
542

Signed by or on behalf of the Respondent by:
Dated this   day of   19

Typical Unless Order—Order for Directions 'K' (13.9 Arb)

IN THE MATTER OF THE ARBITRATION ACTS 1950 TO 1979

AND

IN THE MATTER OF AN ARBITRATION UNDER THE JCT ARBITRATION RULES (18 JULY 1988)

BETWEEN

RELIABLE BUILDERS LIMITED   Claimant

AND

SANCTUARY HOUSE LIMITED   Respondent

TYPICAL UNLESS ORDER—ORDER FOR DIRECTIONS 'K'

WHEREAS

1.00 By Order for Directions No   , dated 8 January 1995, I directed that the hearing in this Arbitration be held at a venue to be arranged by the Claimant, commencing at 10.00 a.m. on 20 February 1994.

AND WHEREAS

2.00 The Claimant's solicitor informed me and the Respondent, by faxed letter 10 January that he has booked accommodation for the hearing for Monday 20 February to Thursday 23 February 1995 inclusive.

AND WHEREAS

3.00 The Respondent has failed to acknowledge or properly comply with my last three Orders for Directions, viz. Orders numbered X, Y and Z, respectively dated

I HEREBY DIRECT that UNLESS

4.00 Not later than 5.00 p.m. on Monday 23 January 1995, the Respondent acknowledges this Order and provides good and sufficient reason why he has failed properly to comply with my previous Orders, or provides good and proper reason why I should not proceed with this reference in his absence; in compliance with the power vested in me by clause 12 of my Terms and Conditions, signed by the Claimant on   and by the Respondent on

**13.9 Arb
543**

THEN

5.00 I shall proceed with the hearing *ex parte*. This hearing shall take place at the accommodation booked, by the Claimant, at the Fleet Arbitration Centre Limited, 6th Floor, Hulton House, 161–166 Fleet Street, London EC4A 2DY commencing at 10.00 a.m. on Monday 20 February and continuing, if necessary, for the four days scheduled above.

THE APPEAL

6.00 In the event that the Respondent decides to continue with the reference and so informs me and the Claimant not later than 5.00 p.m. on Monday 23 January 1995, I refer him to clause 4) of the said Terms and Conditions concerning 'costs thrown away' by cancellation of the hearing days set aside.

7.00 Costs of and incidental to this Order to be paid by the Respondent in any event.

Date: 16 January 1995   D Emsee MSc FRICS FCIArb
                         Registered Arbitrator
To: Representative of the Claimant
    Mr XXX   Solicitors for the Respondent

RECORDED DELIVERY to both parties.

CHAPTER 14

Taxation of Costs

Order for Directions No 20 re Procedure for Settlement of Costs (14.1 Arb)

IN THE MATTER OF THE ARBITRATION ACTS 1950 TO 1979

AND

IN THE MATTER OF AN ARBITRATION UNDER THE JCT ARBITRATION RULES (18 JULY 1988)

BETWEEN

RELIABLE BUILDERS LIMITED   Claimant

AND

SANCTUARY HOUSE LIMITED   Respondent

ORDER FOR DIRECTIONS NO 20

Further to the Hearing on Costs held on 10 June 1994 the parties informed me, at the close of that Hearing, that they would not be able to agree the costs awarded by me in that Award.

In accordance with item 22.00 of my FINAL AWARD—ON COSTS—SAVE AS TO SETTLEMENT OF COSTS, and further to my powers under s.18(1) of the Arbitration Act 1950 and also my power under Rule 12.1.5 of the JCT Arbitration Rules, I agree to 'settle' these costs on a 'reasonable costs, reasonably incurred' basis by the following procedure.

ACCORDINGLY IN HEREBY DIRECT AS FOLLOWS:

As I am settling the Claimant's costs in respect of the Claim and the Respondent's costs in respect of the Counterclaim, the following references to the parties relates to these respective parties and their respective costs.

1.00 Each party shall prepare a detailed itemised narrative complete with statement of time spent by each fee earner, for each significant event, in respect of each invoice which that party has rendered to his client for this reference; such statement to clearly identify any double banking.

In addition, with these bills, I require the following information:

   (i) Details of the Respondent's solicitor's breakdown of their hourly rates with specific details of what is included in the overhead element of this hourly rate.

14.1 Arb 545

(ii) The bills to be classified as to what the Respondent's solicitors' considers is routine and non-routine work and show the status of each fee earner.

(iii) The bills should clearly show what is being claimed for:

Interlocutory attendances
Conferences with Counsel
Attendances at Hearings
Preparatory work
Settlement/Taxation

(iv) Confirmation that the Claimant's representative and the Respondent's solicitors are prepared to give me access to their time records which should also be available at the 'settlement' hearing.

(v) Copies of the experts' bills broken down, where applicable, as (iii) above.

(vi) Copies of all receipted disbursements.

Where there are separate fee earners involved these should be itemised separately.

Following consideration of the documentation and vouchers presented to me, should I not then be satisfied I reserve the right to call on either party to prepare a standard Bill, in accordance with RSC Order 62.

The narrative, summary Bill and vouchers shall be delivered to me, with a copy to the other side not later than 5.00 p.m. on 17 June 1994.

2.00 Each party shall prepare a detailed Response to the other party's Bill listing each and every objection with specific reasons for that objection, together with copies of any supporting authorities.

The Responses to be delivered to me with a copy to the other side not later than 5.00 p.m. 24 June 1994.

3.00 Each party may prepare a Reply to the Response and deliver it to me and the other party not later than 5.00 p.m. 30 June 1994.

4.00 I reserve the right to call for any relevant documentation from either party and to inspect any privileged files in respect of any items of cost to which a party makes objection.

5.00 I reserve the right to examine any witness in the cost proceedings.

6.00 There shall be a Hearing for me to hear both sides on contentious items.

This Hearing will take place at the Fleet Arbitration Centre, 6th Floor, Hulton House, 161–166 Fleet Street, London EC4Y 2DY on 4 July 1994 commencing at 10.00 a.m.

7.00 The parties have agreed that I may consult Costs Draftsman John Berry of J J Berry and Co Ltd. of Romford either before and/or after the hearing.

The fees incurred by me in consulting Mr Berry will be recovered by me as a disbursement.

8.00 The parties are agreed that I am not required to prepare a reasoned award and they will accept my lump-sum assessment.

9.00 I will deal with the Costs of Settlement in my Award.

10.00 Costs in the cost reference.

Date: 11 June 1994   **D Emsee MSc FRICS FCIArb**
                         Arbitrator

To: Jayrich Associates   Representatives for the Claimant
                          FAO Joel Redman

**14.1 Arb
546**

Kalmsyde & Joyoff   Solicitors for the Respondent
                          FAO James Crighton

Order for Directions No 21 re Forms of Bills of Costs (14.2 Arb)

IN THE MATTER OF THE ARBITRATION ACTS 1950 TO 1979

AND

IN THE MATTER OF AN ARBITRATION UNDER THE JCT ARBITRATION RULES (18 JULY 1988)

BETWEEN

RELIABLE BUILDERS LIMITED   Claimant

AND

SANCTUARY HOUSE LIMITED   Respondent

ORDER FOR DIRECTIONS NO 21—BY CONSENT

WHEREAS

1.00 The parties having informed me at the close of the hearing on 10 June, that they will not be able to agree the costs awarded by my FINAL AWARD—ON COSTS—SAVE AS TO SETTLEMENT OF COSTS, dated 10 June 1994, requested me to settle these costs as provided for in that Award AND

WHEREAS

2.00 Following that Request I made my Order for Directions No 20 as to the Form of the Bills of Costs and the timetable for that settlement and following delivery of these Bills I was informed that the Respondent was unhappy with the form of the Claimant's Bill, I agreed to hear both sides on this issue.

AND WHEREAS

3.00 Having heard both sides on 1 July 1994 on the form of the Claimant's Bill of Costs

I NOW DIRECT AS FOLLOWS:

4.00 That this Order shall supersede my Order for Directions No 20 (unless otherwise directed) and the Claimant shall prepare an itemised Bill in the form agreed at today's Hearing.

5.00 These Bills to include a detailed make-up of the parties' 'expense rate' and overall average uplift for each fee earner. These Bills to be delivered to me, and to the other party, not later than 5.00 p.m. on 23 June 1994.

In addition, with these bills, I require the information listed in item 1.00 (i)–(vi) in my Order For Directions No. 20

6.00 Provided this Second Bill is delivered not later than 11 July 1994, the Respondent is to deliver to me, and to the Claimant, not later than 18 July 1994, a detailed Response listing each and every objection with specific reasons for that objection.

7.00 No Replies to these Responses will be delivered.

8.00 I will not rigidly adhere to Order 62 but will take note of the principles generally applied to taxation under that Order, and, I will consider each party's objections in determining what is a reasonable amount, reasonably incurred, using my knowledge of the conduct of this reference.

9.00 I reserve the right to call for any relevant documentation from either party and to inspect any privileged files in respect of any item included in these Bills.

10.00 I reserve the right to examine any witness in the cost proceedings.

11.00 There shall be a one-day Hearing for me to hear both sides on contentious items.
This Hearing will take place at the Fleet Arbitration Centre Limited, 6th Floor, Hulton House, 161–166 Fleet Street, London EC4A 2DY, on 13 July 1994 commencing at 10.00 a.m.

12.00 The parties have agreed that I may consult Costs Draftsman John Berry of J J Berry and Co Ltd. of Romford either before and/or after the Hearing.
The fees incurred by me in consulting Mr Berry will be recovered by me as a disbursement.

13.00 The parties are agreed that I am not required to prepare a reasoned award on this settlement and they will accept my lump-sum assessment.

14.00 I will give directions as to the procedure for dealing with the Costs of Settlement in my Award.

15.00 Costs in the cost reference.

Date: 1 July 1994   D Emsee MSc FRICS FCIArb
                           Arbitrator

To: Jayrich Associates   Representatives for the Claimant
                           FAO Joel Redman

    Kalmsyde & Joyoff   Solicitors for the Respondent
                           FAO James Crighton

Final Award—Settlement of Costs—Save as to Costs of Settlement (14.3 Arb)

IN THE MATTER OF THE ARBITRATION ACTS 1950 TO 1979

AND

IN THE MATTER OF AN ARBITRATION UNDER THE JCT ARBITRATION RULES (18 JULY 1988)

BETWEEN

RELIABLE BUILDERS LIMITED	Claimant
AND	
SANCTUARY HOUSE LIMITED	Respondent

FINAL AWARD—SETTLEMENT OF COSTS—SAVE AS TO COSTS OF SETTLEMENT

1.00 WHEREAS

1.01 Following the publication of my Final Award 11 May 1994, I was informed that the parties were unable to agree on the costs that I had awarded and I was requested to settle these costs.

1.02 By my Order for Directions No 21 I directed 'By Consent' the form that the respective parties Bills of Costs should take and I set a timetable for the delivery of these Bills and any objections thereto.

1.03 Bills of Costs, in line with those ordered by me by my Order for Directions No 21, were delivered to me, and to the other party, on 23 June 1994 and objections to these Bills were delivered to me, and to the other party, on 30 June 1994.

2.00 AND

2.01 By way of clarification of the procedure that I intended to adopt in that Order I said:

'I will not rigidly adhere to Order 62 but will take note of the principles generally applied to taxation under that Order and, I will consider each party's objections in determining what is a reasonable amount, reasonably incurred, using my knowledge of the conduct of this reference.'

2.02 Item 12.00 of that Order reads as follows:

'The parties are agreed that I am not required to prepare a reasoned award on this settlement and they will accept a lump-sum assessment.'

3.00 Having considered the parties Bills of Costs dated 23 June 1994 and the parties' respective objections to those Bills dated 30 June 1994, and having, By Consent, consulted costs draftsman J Berry of J J Berry and Co Ltd.

AND FURTHER

having examined the parties' files, and having heard representatives from both sides and considered their submissions at the hearing on 13 July 1994

**14.3 Arb
549**

4.00 I FIND AND HOLD as follows, dealing with each of the parties' objections in their Responses dated 30 June 1994

(1) The Hourly Rates

(i) The Claimant claimed the following hourly rates:

J Redman—£125 per hour

P Fisher (Mr Redman's assistant)—£70 per hour

Both Mr Redman and Mr Fisher charged their time in 15-minute minimum increments. These hourly rates were charged irrespective of the nature of the work being undertaken—whether travelling or waiting or attending a hearing. No uplift as such was sought beyond the above rates.

The Respondent contended that these rates were out of line with those charged by other similar practitioners and proposed

J Redman—£75 per hour

P Fisher—£45 per hour

In addition they objected to the minimal 15-minute increments.

I ALLOW **the following rates:**

J REDMAN—£90 per hour

P FISHER—£50 per hour

(ii) The Respondent claimed the following hourly rates:

Partner: Messrs Catchpole and Crighton—£130 per hour.
Letters/facsimile sent @ £13 each.
Routine telephone attendance @ £13 each.
Assistants: Messrs Oliver and Pomphret (Associate Partners)—£77.50 per hour.
Letters/fascimile sent @ £7.75 each.
Routine telephone attendance @ £7.75 per hour.

With minimal assistance as appropriate and necessary from:

Assistant solicitor—(Mr Woolridge) £77.50 per hour
Trainee solicitor—£40 per hour
Paralegal—£22.50 per hour
Costs Draftsman—£67.50 per hour

The Claimant contended that the following hourly rates, subject to uplift, should apply:

Partner—£90 per hour
Assistant solicitor—£70 per hour
Trainee solicitor—£40 per hour
Paralegal—£22.50 per hour

I ALLOW **the following rates:**

PARTNER—£110 per hour
ASSISTANT SOLICITOR—£75 per hour
TRAINEE SOLICITOR—£40 per hour
PARALEGAL—£22.50 per hour

14.3 Arb 550

The fees for the Costs Draftsmen are disallowed but I have agreed reasonable fee earners time examining and presenting the Bills of Costs.

(2) Pre-Reference Costs

The Respondent submitted that the reference commenced on the Notification Date under the

Rules i.e. 24 February 1993 and that any costs incurred prior to that date should be disallowed.

I accept Mr Redman's contention that the reference commenced when he gave Notice of Dispute and I therefore accept that the time spent by Mr Redman from 18 December 1992, represented costs reasonably incurred familiarising himself with the issues and advising his client on them.

I HAVE ACCORDINGLY ALLOWED THESE COSTS.

(3) Letters and Telephone Calls

The Claimant submitted that a third of all of the Respondent's solicitor's telephone calls and letters be disallowed.

Having examined both elements I consider that many telephone calls were unduly lengthy and the time taken to deal with correspondence in some cases appears to be excessive.

ACCORDINGLY I HAVE REDUCED MOST OF BOTH ELEMENTS BY 20% OF THE COSTS CLAIMED (AFTER ADJUSTING THE HOURLY RATE AS ABOVE).

(4) Personal Attendances on the Parties

(i) The Claimant contends that a number of personal attendances by both Mr Catchpole and Mr Crighton on their client at his place of business, Sanctuary House, were unnecessarily lengthy and could have more economically been conducted in the solicitors' respective offices.

The dates and times claimed for the specific meetings are listed on p. 3 of the Claimant's objections.

The Respondent submits that, due to the nature of their client's business, their clients Mr and Mrs Bliss, found it difficult to both leave the nursing home for any length of time on the same occasion. Therefore, in order to keep them both informed about this reference, it was more economical to attend on them rather than to see each individually in their respective offices.

I accept the Respondent's submission in general but find that certain of these visits, when considered against the background of the events occurring at the time, were excessive.

I HAVE ACCORDINGLY REDUCED THE TIME CHARGES CLAIMED BY 20%.

(ii) The Respondent contends that Mr Redman's personal attendance during the hearing dates between 7 March 1994 and 18 April 1994 were unreasonably incurred.

In view of the fact that the Claimant did not use a solicitor to instruct Counsel nor to support him during the hearing, I find these time charges reasonable.

ACCORDINGLY THESE COSTS ARE ALLOWED AS CLAIMED.

(5) Sections vi(a)–(h) and (vii) p. 8 of the Claimant's Bill

The Respondent contends that all the above—excluding (d) and (g) should be disallowed.
The Claimant concedes that (f) and (d) should be withdrawn

vi(a) 50% Allowed
vi(b) Allowed
vi(c) Allowed
vi(d) Withdrawn
vi(e) Allowed
vi(f) Withdrawn

**14.3 Arb
551**

vi(g) Allowed (conceded by Respondent)
vi(h) Allowed
vii   (page 8) 30% Allowed

(6) Time Spent on Discovery, on Preparation and Consideration of Case

The Claimant claims five fee earners were not warranted and time charged was excessive. In particular the Claimant submits that Mr Crighton spent an unreasonable time familiarising himself with this case on his appointment following removal of instructions from Mr Catchpole.
  The Claimants submits that a reasonable time charge would be:

> Partner—38 hours
> Assistant (including trainee, paralegal and assistant solicitor)—120 hours
> Costs draftsman—Nil

The Respondent claims:

> Partner—60 hours: **Allowed 2/3rds**
> Assistant—190 hours: **Allowed 2/3rds**
> Assistant solicitor—**12 hours: Allowed**
> Trainee solicitor—**16 hours: Disallowed**
> Paralegal—28 hours: **Allowed 2/3rds**
> Costs Draftsman—**21 hours 36 mins: Disallowed**

(7) & (8) Uplift on Respondent's Solicitors

The Claimant contends no more than 66.6% uplift and 35% for interlocutory work and 66.6% on time with Counsel.
  The Respondent claims 70% and 35% and 70% on interlocutory work with Counsel.

> **Claimant's submission for uplift allowed.**
> **All assistants' time at hearing allowed.**
> **All time spent travelling and waiting by fee earners allowed.**

(9) Conferences with Counsel during Hearing

The Claimant contends should be no more than three or four conferences.

> **All conferences allowed.**

(10) Respondent's Counsel's Charge for Submissions and Reply on Costs

The Claimant contends these charges should not be allowed.

> **These two costs are allowed.**

(11) Disbursements

**14.3 Arb
552**

The Claimant contends that photocopying, stationery, facsimile charges and courier charges are all part of solicitors' overheads, therefore should not be allowed.

> **Counsel fees allowed in full.**
> **RICS fee allowed.**
> **Photocopying, stationery, facsimile charges—disallowed.**

Courier charges—Allowed 2/3rds
Travel expenses allowed

(12) Experts' Costs

(i) The Claimant contends that Mr Maclean's fee reflects duplicated work and also questions the necessity for daily attendance of Mr Maclean at the Hearing. The Claimant also contends that it was unreasonable for this expert to spend time taking notes and supporting Counsel.

In view of the full-time attendance by Mr Crighton for the Respondent it was unnecessary for Mr Maclean also to be in attendance full time.

Accordingly I reduce the time spent by this expert at the hearing by 50%.

(ii) The Respondent contends that Mr Redman's fee duplicated some of the work carried out by other experts. He also contends that Mr Redman's incremental charge of a minimum of 15-minute bites is unreasonable. I agree.

Accordingly, Mr Redman's charge is reduced by 15% to cover duplicated work and to make allowance for his unreasonable quarter-hourly unit charge.

5.00 In working through the Bill of Costs due allowance was made for 'costs to be paid in any event' where directed by me during the reference.

6.00 Summary of Costs Following Settlement

(i) Claimant's Costs of Claim

Total Redman's Costs allowed (including his expert's fee)		62,050.00
Disbursements allowed		
Counsel fees	46,600.00	
RICS fee	100.00	
Courier charges	138.35	
Travelling expenses	294.46	
Experts' fees (excluding Redman)	4,000.00	
		51,132.81
Total allowed		£113,182.81

(ii) Respondent's Costs of Counterclaim

Total solicitors fee allowed		20,095.00
Disbursements allowed		
Counsel's fees	13,000.00	
Courier charges	96.44	
Travelling expenses	28.63	
Experts' fees	38,000.00	
Architects' fees	5,000.00	
		56,125.07
Total allowed		£76,220.07

14.3 Arb 553

Awarded, as directed by my Final Award on Costs—Save as to Settlement of Costs, dated 10 June 1994

85% of the Respondent's Costs of Counterclaim

THUS the net payment is
Claimant's   costs   113,182.81
   Less 85% Respondent's costs
            85% × £76,220.07   64,787.06
                                                       £48,395.75

In addition, by clause 21.03 of that Final Award, I directed that costs awarded would bear interest from a date 14 days after the date of that Award.

7.00 ACCORDINGLY

7.01 I DETERMINE that the Respondent pay to the Claimant, within 14 days of the date of this my Award, the sum of £48,775.95 (Forty-Eight Thousand Seven Hundred and Seventy-Five Pounds 95p), which sum includes £380.20 (Three Hundred and Eighty Pounds 20p) by way of interest.

8.00 *Costs of the Award*

8.01 The Costs of this my Award, which I hereby settle in the sum of £4,362.10 (Four Thousand Three Hundred and Sixty Two Pounds 10p) which sum includes £1,100.00 (One Thousand One Hundred Pounds) payable to J & J Berry and Co Ltd. and includes £955.87 (Nine Hundred and Fifty Five Pounds 87p) by way of Value Added Tax on my fees and Mr Berry's account shall be borne by the Respondent and be paid forthwith.

8.02 Should the Claimant have paid these fees then the Respondent is to reimburse the Claimant the total amount paid forthwith.

9.00 *Costs of the Settlement*

9.01 The parties have requested that I settle the costs of the taxation.

9.02 The procedure agreed by the parties for this settlement is as follows:

9.02.1 It will be a 'documents only' procedure with both sides waiving any rights they might have to an oral hearing.

9.02.2 Within seven days of the date of this Award the Respondent to make a written submission on costs of the settlement of costs to me and copied to the Claimant.

9.02.3 Within seven days of the receipt by the Claimant of the Respondent's submission, the Claimant is to make his own submission with which he will include his own Bill of Costs in the form agreed at the hearing on 13 July 1994.

9.02.4 Within seven days of the receipt of the Claimant's submission, referred to in 9.02.3 above the Respondent shall serve a Response to the Claimant's submission which shall include any specific objections he may wish to make on the Claimant's Bill.

9.02.5 I am not required to give a Reasoned Award on this issue and may give a lump-sum determination.

Given under my hand at Hunstanton this 25th day of July 1994

14.3 Arb 554

In the presence of
Name ....
Address ....
....
....
Occupation ....

....
D Emsee MSc FRICS FCIArb
Arbitrator

Respondent's Submission on Costs of Settlement (14.4)

IN THE MATTER OF THE ARBITRATION ACTS 1950 TO 1979

AND

IN THE MATTER OF AN ARBITRATION UNDER THE JCT ARBITRATION RULES (18 JULY 1988)

BETWEEN

RELIABLE BUILDERS LIMITED   Claimant

AND

SANCTUARY HOUSE LIMITED   Respondent

SUBMISSION ON BEHALF OF THE RESPONDENT ON THE COSTS OF SETTLEMENT PURSUANT TO A DIRECTION IN THE FINAL AWARD ON SETTLEMENT OF COSTS DATED 25 JULY 1994

INDEX

PART 1

SUBMISSION ON COSTS OF SETTLEMENT FOR THE PERIOD TO 1 JULY 1994

14.4
555

1. Following correspondence as to the form of bill to be produced by Redman, Kalmsyde &

Joyoff conceded by letter 10 June 1994 (pp. 1–3) the form suggested by Redman. These are set out on page 2 of the said letter. Kalmsyde also complained that the form of bill proposed fell short of an itemised bill.

2. Redman objected to the conditions in Kalmsyde's letter by their letter 10 June 1994 (pp 4–5).

3. On 11 June 1994 you issued Order No 20 (pp. 9–11) which was sent under cover of a letter (pp. 6–8) in which you stated:

    (a) the conditions Kalmsyde sought to impose would be dealt with at the end of the hearing; and
    (b) if you are not satisfied as to the form of bill, then you would require an itemised bill as per Order 62 'with the penalties of costs that that infers'.

The wording in the Order echoed the wording in the letter.

4. Despite the directions given in your Order for Directions No 20, a Bill was produced by the Claimant similar to a 'solicitor and own client' bill.

5. Kalmsyde's Response to the Bill, produced pursuant to your Order, specified the reasons why they were unable to give a detailed response to that Bill in its present form. There followed further correspondence (pp. 12–15). In their letter of 13 June 1994 Kalmsyde reminded you that you had left it open to require a more itemised Bill, from either party, should the Bill they submitted not be sufficiently detailed.

6. Following Redman's letter to you 13 June 1994 (pp. 16–17) you wrote on 15 June 1994 (pp. 18–20) requiring Redman to give greater particularity. You also said that if you were in doubt about the reasonableness of any item of cost, on either party's Bill, that doubt would be resolved in favour of the paying party.

7. Redman took issue with you by their letter of 6 June 1994 (p. 21). Kalmsyde wrote on the 20 June expressing the view that Redman was creating difficulties where there were none (p. 22). This correspondence led to the Hearing on 1 July 1994. Following submissions made to you, you found the form of Bill prepared by Redman unsatisfactory and you issued a Direction ordering Redman to prepare an itemised bill (pp. 23–25).

8. Thus, in accordance with the normal rule that costs follow the event (the 'event' here being Kalmsyde's request for a more detailed Bill) and, in accordance with the warning you gave in the last paragraph, first page of your letter 11 June 1994, Kalmsyde maintain that the costs of settlement up to and including the Hearing on 1 July 1994 should be the Respondent's in any event, with the Claimant also paying the costs of yourself and Mr Berry for the same period.

PART 2
SUBMISSION ON COSTS OF SETTLEMENT FOR THE PERIOD COMMENCING 2 JULY 1994

1. The costs of settlement remain payable on the standard basis only.

2. Costs for any work duplicated by two or more fee earners should be allowed as one fee earner only and at the rate appropriate to the person with the minimum experience and knowledge able to perform the work in question. Duplicated work includes the giving of instructions by one fee earner to another.

3. The costs of the costs draftsman should not be allowed, particularly for the time spent at the Hearing. This is, what would normally be considered to be a 'solicitor and own client' item.

4. Should you allow the costs of the costs draftsman, there should be no mark-up on his basic hourly rate.

5. Ordinary disbursements, copying, etc should not be allowed.

14.4
556

6. The Claimant's costs should be made subject to a maximum fixed by you.

PART 3
SUBMISSION ON COSTS OF TAXATION AS AFFECTED BY AN OFFER MADE ON 9 JULY 1994 'WITHOUT PREJUDICE SAVE AS TO COSTS'

1. On 9 July 1994, Kalmsyde made an offer 'without prejudice save as to costs' pursuant to RSC Order 62 Rule 27 and the decision in *Tramountana Armadora SA* v *Atlantic Shipping Co SA* [1978] 2 All ER 870 within the stipulated time limit (pp. 26–39).

2. By Order 62 Rule 27(3) and (4) the fact that such an offer has been made shall be communicated to the Taxing Officer when the question of the costs of the taxation proceedings falls to be decided. The Taxing Officer may take into account any offer made which has been brought to his attention. It is appropriate to refer to this offer in this submission.

3. The offer made was £50,000 inclusive of interest, and the Claimant's costs of the taxation.

4. In the event the total of the costs awarded by you to the Claimant including interest, if any, of both the arbitration and of the taxation (after due allowance is made for any costs awarded to the Respondent) if £50,000 or less, then Kalmsyde submit that the Respondent should be awarded its costs of settlement from 9 July 1994.

DATED this eighteenth day of July 1994.

....
Kalmsyde & Joyoff
Solicitors for the Respondent

14.4
557

Claimant's Submission on Costs of Taxation and Claimant's Bill on Costs of Settlement (14.5)

IN THE MATTER OF THE ARBITRATION ACTS 1950 TO 1979

AND

IN THE MATTER OF AN ARBITRATION UNDER THE JCT ARBITRATION RULES (18 JULY 1988)

BETWEEN

RELIABLE BUILDERS LIMITED   Claimant

AND

SANCTUARY HOUSE LIMITED   Respondent

CLAIMANT'S SUBMISSION ON THE COSTS OF TAXATION

The Claimant's submission on the costs of taxation is that these should follow the event in accordance with that principle established in *Lewis* v *Haverfordwest Rural District Council* and in accordance with RSC Order 62, r 27 which states, *inter alia*, that:

'. . . the party whose bill is being taxed shall be entitled to his costs of the taxation proceedings.'

The event in this case is, of course, your Award in the Claimant's favour of its taxed costs. We enclose our client's Claim for costs of the taxation pursuant to your Award dated 25 July 1994.

Jayrich Associates
Dated this 8th day of August 1994   Claimant's representative

RELIABLE BUILDERS LIMITED V SANCTUARY HOUSE LIMITED

DAILY BREAKDOWN OF TIME SPENT DURING THE PERIOD OF 10 JUNE TO 7 AUGUST 1994 FROM TIME SHEETS CHARGED TO THE NEAREST MINUTE

Date	Activity	Partner (Mr J Redman) Hrs – Mins	Associated Partner (Mr P Fisher) Hrs – Mins	Costs Draftsman (Mr A Ginger) Hrs – Mins	Trainee Surveyor (Mr J Ritchy) Hrs – Mins
10.06.94	Considering the Arbitrator's Award and the costs submissions. General consideration re costs issues.		3 – 30		

14.5
558

CLAIMANT'S SUBMISSION ON COSTS OF TAXATION

Date	Activity	Partner (Mr J Redman) Hrs – Mins	Associated Partner (Mr P Fisher) Hrs – Mins	Costs Draftsman (Mr A Ginger) Hrs – Mins	Trainee Surveyor (Mr J Ritchy) Hrs – Mins
13.06.94	Considering costs breakdown analysis and bill of costs.	0 – 46			
14.06.94	Dealing with analysis of costs.		2 – 42		
15.06.94	Drafting correspondence to Kalmsyde & Joyoff.	0 – 38			
17.06.94	Considering correspondence with Kalmsyde & Joyoff, correspondence and liaising with W Bliss thereon.		3 – 36		
20.06.94	Telephone attendance upon Mr Emsee the Arbitrator and forwarding costs breakdown to Mr Ginger.	0 – 28			
22.06.94	Considering correspondence.	0 – 34			
23.06.94	Correspondence with Kalmsyde & Joyoff re the Arbitrator's fees.		0 – 22		
	c/f	2 – 26	10 – 20		

SUMMARY OF TOTAL TIME SPENT BY EACH FEE EARNER

Partner					
J Redman	49 hrs 27 mins	@	125.00 per hour		6,222.92
Associate Partner					
P Fisher	28 hrs 46 mins	@	70.00 per hour		2,013.66
Trainee Surveyor					
J Ritchy	38 hrs 25 mins	@	30.00 per hour		1,152.50
					9,389.08
Costs Draftsman					
Mr A Ginger	40 hrs 36 mins	@	75.00 per hour	3045.00	
	Care and Conduct @ 70%			2131.50	5,176.50
					14,565.58
			TOTAL CLAIM FOR COSTS SAY		£14,000.00

14.5
559

559

Respondent's Reply to Claimant's Submission on Costs of Settlement and Objections to Claimant's Bill on Costs of Settlement (14.6)

IN THE MATTER OF THE ARBITRATION ACTS 1950 TO 1979

AND

IN THE MATTER OF AN ARBITRATION UNDER THE JCT ARBITRATION RULES (18 JULY 1988)

BETWEEN

RELIABLE BUILDERS LIMITED   Claimant

AND

SANCTUARY HOUSE LIMITED   Respondent

REPLY ON BEHALF OF THE RESPONDENT TO THE CLAIMANT'S SUBMISSION ON THE COSTS OF SETTLEMENT AND TO THE CLAIMANT'S BILL FOR THE COSTS OF SETTLEMENT

A Reply to the Claimant's Submission on the Costs of Taxation

1. The Award of costs was on the standard basis, not solicitor and own client basis. The first bill submitted by Mr Redman was prepared on the latter basis and further, was not the bill settled. It could not, therefore be in 'the event' as defined by the Claimant.

2. We repeat Part 1, paragraph 8, of our submission on the Costs of Taxation.

B Reply to the Claimant's Solicitors Bill for the Costs of Taxation

1. The costs of the settlement are payable on the same basis as of the Arbitration, i.e. on the standard basis, not on a solicitor and own client basis.

2. The Claimant's bill has been prepared on a solicitor and own client basis.

3. Under the standard basis, the Claimant is entitled to the reasonable costs of drawing up the bill and attending on the settlement. There should be no necessity for taking instructions, research, telephone or correspondence. The bill in question is the bill which was settled.

4. We have already dealt with the costs of settlement up to and including 1 July 1994 (see Part 1 of our Submission).

5. We submit it is reasonable to allow an assistant solicitor 6 hours to prepare the bill at £75 per hour and a partner 2 hours for checking it at £110 per hour. A further 8 hours should be allowed as assistant solicitor at £75 per hour for attending the taxation. Notwithstanding our submission in Part 2, paragraph 4 of our Submission we consider an uplift of 35 per cent appropriate on the cost of attendance only.

To summarise:

14.6
560

Assistant Solicitor	6 hours		450.00
	8 hours	600.00	
	35%	210.00	810.00
			1,260.00
Partner	2 hours		220.00
			£1,480.00

6. The settlement of a bill is an administrative process and it is neither unusual nor appropriate to allow the costs of a costs draftsman. Further, save on the attendance, the costs of settlement should fall within the basic hourly charge.

7. All costs subsequent to the settlement hearing on 13 July 1994 are outside the costs of the settlement and recoverable only on a solicitor and own client basis.

8. It is particularly inappropriate for the Respondent to pay Mr Redman's costs of liaising with its client on their own bill; or of research when the matter was nothing out of the ordinary and well within Mr Redman's experience particularly bearing in mind the assistance of a costs draftsman; or of duplication of effort; or of correspondence.

9. We repeat here, save as varied above, Part 2 of our Submission on the Costs of Settlement.

10. Save as specifically agreed above we take issue with each and every item of cost included in the Claimant's Bill of Costs of the Settlement as being either wrongly included or wholly excessive in both time and amount.

Dated this 15th day of August 1994.

Signed   J Crighton
         Kalmsyde & Joyoff
Solicitors for the Respondent

14.6
561

Claimant's Reply to the Respondent's Submission on Costs of Settlement pursuant to a Final Award on Settlement of Costs dated 25 July 1994 (14.7)

IN THE MATTER OF THE ARBITRATION ACTS 1950 TO 1979

AND

IN THE MATTER OF AN ARBITRATION UNDER THE JCT ARBITRATION RULES (18 JULY 1988)

BETWEEN

RELIABLE BUILDERS LIMITED   Claimant

AND

SANCTUARY HOUSE LIMITED   Respondent

CLAIMANT'S REPLY TO THE RESPONDENT'S SUBMISSION ON THE COSTS OF SETTLEMENT PURSUANT TO A FINAL AWARD ON SETTLEMENT OF COSTS DATED 25 JULY 1994

The Claimant submits that the Arbitrator's Award on the Settlement of Costs and the Respondent's Submission on the same contain nothing which contradicts the Submission made on behalf of the Claimant, namely that the costs of the settlement 'should follow the event in accordance with that principle established in *Lewis* v *Haverfordwest Rural District Council*' and in accordance with Rules of the Supreme Court Order 62 Rule 27 which states, *inter alia*, that

> '... the party whose bill's being taxed should be entitled to his costs of the taxation proceedings.'

The event in this case is, of course, your Award in the Claimants favour of its costs, as settled by you.

With reference to the miscellaneous matters raised in the Respondent's Submission, and adopting its notation, the Claimant responds as follows:

Part 1 and Part 2—generally

The Claimant does not accept the appropriateness or validity of the Respondent's division of the costs of the settlement into the periods pre and post 15 June 1994. Given the much-publicised financial difficulties experienced by a small Contractor in the current economic climate in pursuing its claims, it is, and has always been, inevitable that considerations on costs would be critical. This being so, it was inevitable and correct that there should be full and proper consideration given to determining the principles governing your conduct of the settlement and the format of the Bill of Costs.

Your Order for Directions No. 20 was made by consent, and in accordance with this, the Claimant produced its first Bill of costs. Insofar as that contained some element of non-allowable costs, this matter was rectified in the supplementary Bill of Costs produced following the hearing on 15 June 1994. In the event and almost to the exclusion of the Second Bill, it was the first Bill which proved the most useful to all in assessing the Claimants costs,

14.7
562

since it contained far greater particulars than would ordinarily have been contained within a standard Order 62 Bill.

The first Bill enabled you and the Respondent to consider the time recorded against any given item in the Bill on any given day and, in your own case to cross-reference this with the Claimant's files. A significant part of the hearing on 15 June 1994 was spent considering such specific items and hearing evidence and/or Submissions upon them. With the level of detail available to the Respondent in the Claimant's first Bill, the Respondent had every opportunity to request that you direct your attention to specific areas of the Claimant's Bill and to the relevant correspondence files. It did not do so. Indeed, it chose not to adopt that course even following the Claimants production of its supplementary Bill of Costs. On any view, even given the wealth of information over and above that which it would ordinarily have been entitled to, the Respondent failed to make detailed and accurate Submissions on costs prior to, or indeed at the settlement hearing itself. Its use of either bill was, at best limited.

We do not accept the suggestion that the first Bill of Costs was not on the standard basis. It was not in standard format but in a form that had been agreed with the Respondent, as confirmed by their letter to the arbitrator, 12 June 1994. This Bill in its agreed form proved valuable. It was a Bill claiming costs on the standard basis and was the Claimant's attempt to demonstrate that the costs incurred were reasonable. It is misleading to describe it as having been in a 'solicitor and own client' format.

There can, of course, be no suggestion that the Respondent should have its costs up to and including the hearing on 15 June 1994, given the extent of the use made of the first Bill of Costs in the settlement hearing and given the failure of the Respondent at any stage to fully particularise contentious elements in either Bill.

Part 2

1/2. The Claimant is, of course, entitled to its costs reasonably incurred in connection with the settlement of its costs, itemised in its claim document now before you. Those principles applicable in respect of the costs of the settlement are no different to those applied by you in respect of the costs of the arbitration proper.

3. Concerning the use of costs draftsmen and their attendance at the hearing, we refer to Messrs Kalmsyde's letter dated 29 June 1994, the Arbitrator's letter dated 4 July 1994 and Mr Redman's letter 6 July 1994. As is apparent from that correspondence, the Respondent's stance made the use of draftsmen, and their attendance at the hearing, inevitable.

Given the above, the Claimant submits that the value of the attendance of the Claimant's own draftsmen, not least in time and cost saving was self-evident from the fact that it was possible to conclude the hearing within one day.

4. The Respondent offers no support for the proposition that there should be no mark-up. The Claimant submits that there is no justification in treating the Claimant's costs of settlement any differently to those incurred in its conduct of the Arbitration. In that respect it was found that there should be a mark-up, namely 70 per cent.

5. As will be apparent from the Claimant's Bill, no disbursements etc. are claimed.

6. It will, of course, be the case that you will, in your Award, direct the sum payable by the Respondent to the Claimant in respect of the costs of the settlement. That follows the well-established rule that the Claimant is entitled to its costs reasonably incurred in connection with the settlement of its costs—as itemised in its claim document.

Any suggestion, if such is made, that some arbitrary limit be imposed upon such recovery is entirely without support in the Rules of the Supreme Court or the authorities.

14.7
563

Conclusion and Summary

1. The settlement of the settlement costs should be carried out in the same principles as the settlement of arbitration costs.

2. The sums at stake, in costs, and thus the importance of the settlement of costs, were around one third of the total sum at stake in the arbitration proper, and therefore £14,000, spent on this exercise, was reasonable in all the circumstances.

Part 3

You will by now have received our letter dated 7 August 1994 concerning Kalmsyde's inclusion in its submission of its letter dated 9 July 1994 and related submissions. In accordance with that letter, the Claimant's primary submission is that, in the light of correspondence passing between the parties, it is wholly inappropriate that that letter should have been placed before you.

The balance of this section is therefore relevant only if you decide to consider the letter of 9 July 1994 and the Respondent's related submissions.

In response to Kalmsyde's letter 9 July, Mr Redman wrote on 11 July 1994 and a copy of that response is annexed hereto. Clearly, the Claimant was as anxious as any party to draw the settlement of these costs to an early close if an appropriate offer were to be made. Not least for the reasons set out in Mr Redman's response to Kalmsyde's 9 July letter, it was not possible for the Claimant to give proper consideration to the 'offer' made, let alone to accept the same. The Respondent chose not to put this offer into a meaningful form capable of protecting its costs position.

In Mr Redman's letter dated 11 July 1994 they noted the following:

1. The offer

'is not in terms such as would be directed by the arbitrator in his award at the conclusion of the settlement and is not comparable to the principal and on costs'.

Kalmsyde's were referred to the *Tramountana* case which deals with this very issue, namely that the arbitrator must be in a position to compare like with like. At paragraph (D) of the head note to the case (page 871), it is stated

'the arbitrator was not in a position to compare an offer in the form of a lump sum inclusive of costs with the amount awarded because he could not know or ascertain the amount of the Claimant's costs up to the date of the offer (which was in the middle of the arbitration) and therefore was not in a position to compare like with like (see p. 878 C to H post)'.

2. One of the terms of the 'offer' was that payment be by way of a number of instalments with some sums not to be received until as late as 1 December 1994. An award for payment by instalments is not an award to be made by an arbitrator, not least for the reason that it would be quite wrong that the successful Claimant should be required to bear the extended risk of the unsuccessful Respondent's insolvency in the present economic climate.

The further effect of this would be to deny the Claimant interest on the considerable sums due in the interim.

3. The inclusion of the costs of settlement is incorrect. The cost of settlement and the costs of the arbitration proper must of course, and can only be considered separately. The terms of the 'offer' prevent one from comparing the sum offered with that figure determined to be the costs recoverable on the arbitration proper.

On any view, we reject the suggestion that Kalmsyde's letter has any relevance to your award on the settlement of costs and, in particular, reject any suggestion that it provides any protection for the Respondent. There has not been any further 'offer' for the Claimant to consider and the Respondent's case must therefore stand or fall on the terms of its offer set out in its letter 11 July 1994.

The crucial question that you must ask yourself is that posed by Donaldson J in the *Tramountana* case (see p. 877 paras (g) and (h)), namely:

'Has the Claimant achieved any more by rejecting the offer and going on with the arbitration than he would have achieved if he had accepted the offer?'

14.7
564

The answer, in this present case to that question is clearly yes. Consider the following:

1. The Claimant has received an award in its favour of its costs of the Claim and was to pay 85% of the Respondent's costs of its Counterclaim—within 14 days of the settlement of these costs by you—not by instalments. In addition, the Claimant was ordered to pay 25% of your costs—including the fee for your costs draftsman—and the Respondent was ordered to pay the balance of 75% of these costs. These Costs of the Award to be paid forthwith, not by instalments.

The significance of the payment forthwith must not be underestimated in the context of substantial monies owing to a small contractor by a small company in the present economic climate, both in terms of the risk of the Respondent's insolvency and in terms of the interest lost/bank charges incurred.

It still remains impossible to 'compare like with like' in the context of comparing this 'offer' with your Award. However, to the limited extent that the figures may now be applied to the terms of the Respondent's 'offer' it is right to say that the Claimant's recovery is greater than the sum offered.

EVALUATION OF RESPONDENTS 'OFFER' DATED 9 JULY 1994

	'Offer'	Award	
Costs: Interest; Disbursements; Counsel Costs of Taxation Interest		48,395.75	Costs Disbursements
	50,000.00	380.20	Interest
Add 3/4 Arbitrator/Costs Draftsman	3,271.50	4,362.10	Add Full Amount Arb/Costs Draftsman
	53,271.50	53,138.05	
Less Interest lost by two instalment payments to 1/12/94	1,430.14		
		1,480.00 to 14,000.00	Add Settlement Costs—claimed £14,000 (admitted min due of £1,480)
	£51,841.36	54,618.05 to 67,138.05	

NB The above evaluation of the Respondent's 'offer' is, by necessity, based upon the assumption of its continued solvency to 1 December 1994.

Conclusion and Summary

There is admittedly no sealed offer. If the letter of 9 July is considered it will be found to be incapable of meaningful comparison and deficient by *Tramountana* standards and in its terms. In any event, the Claimant has done better by the Award than by accepting the 'offer'.

14.7
565

Toby Belcher
Counsel for the Claimant

Dated this 18 day of August 1994

ANNEXURE TO CLAIMANT'S SUBMISSION OF COSTS OF SETTLEMENT

Copy letter from Jayrich Associates

Messrs Kalmsyde & Joyoff   11 July 1994
48 Crown Street
Ipswich   WITHOUT PREJUDICE
Suffolk 1PS 2QR   SAVE AS TO COSTS
FAO J. Crighton Esq.

Dear Sirs

Re: Reliable Builders Limited v *Sanctuary House Limited*

We are responding to your letter dated 9th July 1994 marked 'without prejudice save as to costs'.
   Your letter does not conform to the appropriate format for communication of a sealed offer and as such can provide no cost protection for your clients.

   The 'offer' set out in the letter is one which is incapable of consideration and acceptance by our client in that it is not in terms such as would be directed by the Arbitrator in his Award at the conclusion of this settlement and is not comparable to the principal award on costs. We refer you to the *Tramountana* case which, you will be aware, is the leading authority on sealed offers.
   In particular, two deficiencies are noted, namely:

1. The Arbitrator is not likely to, nor, indeed, is he entitled to, direct payment of your client's liability by instalments. The Arbitrator cannot require our client to shoulder the risk of your client's insolvency, not least in the present economic climate.

2. Your inclusion of the costs of settlement is incorrect. The costs of the settlement and the costs of the Arbitration must be, and can only be, considered separately. The terms of your 'offer' are such that it is impossible for the Arbitrator to make a true comparison between the sum offered and our client's costs recoverable on the arbitration proper.

   Accordingly, we reserve the right to draw the Arbitrator's attention to this letter in connection with the issue of costs.

Yours faithfully

Jayrich Associates

14.7
566

Final Award on Costs of Settlement (14.8)

IN THE MATTER OF THE ARBITRATION ACTS 1950 TO 1979

AND

IN THE MATTER OF AN ARBITRATION UNDER THE JCT ARBITRATION RULES (18 JULY 1988)

BETWEEN

RELIABLE BUILDERS LIMITED   Claimant

AND

SANCTUARY HOUSE LIMITED   Respondent

FINAL AWARD—SETTLEMENT OF COSTS OF SETTLEMENT

1.00 WHEREAS

On 25 July 1994 I published a FINAL AWARD—SETTLEMENT OF COSTS—SAVE AS TO COSTS OF SETTLEMENT, in the above reference, pursuant to the parties' request that I settle the parties' costs if not agreed, and this FINAL AWARD is complementary to and is to be read in conjunction with the Award published on 25 July 1994.

2.00 AND WHEREAS

At close of the Hearing on Costs held on 13 July I was asked to settle the parties' Costs of Settlement, accordingly in my Award 25 July 1994 I included the following clauses:
'9.00   *Costs of the Settlement*
9.01   The parties have requested that I settle the costs of the taxation.
9.02   The procedure agreed by the parties for this settlement is as follows:
9.02.1   It will be a 'documents only' procedure with both sides waiving any rights they might have to an oral hearing.
9.02.2   Within seven days of the date of this Award the Respondent to make a written submission on costs of the settlement of costs to me and copied to the Claimant.
9.02.3   Within seven days of the receipt by the Claimant of the Respondent's submission, the Claimant is to make his own submission with which he will include his own Bill of Costs in the form agreed at the hearing on 13 July 1994.
9.02.4   Within seven days of the receipt of the Claimant's submission, referred to in 9.02.3 above the Respondent shall serve a Response to the Claimant's submission which shall include any specific objections he may wish to make on the Claimant's Bill.
9.02.5   I am not required to give a Reasoned Award on this issue and may give a lump-sum determination.'

3.00 AND WHEREAS

I received:
3.01 The Respondent's Submission dated 1 August 1994.

14.8
567

3.02 The Claimant's Bill of Costs and Reply to the Respondent's Submission dated 8 August 1994.

3.03 The Respondent's Reply to the Claimant's Submission dated 16 August 1994. (Or sent)

3.04 The following correspondence in connection with the 'Without Prejudice' offer:
Redman's to me 10 August 1994.
Messrs Kalmsyde's to me 11 August 1994.
Messrs Kalmsyde's to me 11 August 1994.
Redman's three letters to me 11 August 1994.
My letter to both sides 11 August 1994.
Redman's to me 12 August 1994.
My letter to both sides 12 August 1994.
Redman's to me 15 August 1994.
Redman's to me 17 August 1994.
My letter to both sides 18 August 1994.
Messrs Kalmsyde's to me 18 August 1994.

4.00 AND HAVING CONSIDERED

All of the above I deal firstly with two points of general principle before considering the individual items affecting the amount of my Award.

5.00 Costs Follow the Event

5.01 Both parties accept that the normal rule of costs following the event should apply but differ as to what is the 'event'.

5.02 The Respondent maintains that the 'event' should be from when Messrs Kalmsyde's requested an itemised Bill of Costs to be prepared on a standard basis—that is, in effect, from the close of the Hearing held on 1 July 1994 on the form that such a Bill should take.

5.03 The Claimant, referred me to the principle established in *Lewis v Haverfordwest Rural District Council* and the Rules of the Supreme Court Order 62, Rule 27, which states, *inter alia* ... that the party whose Bill is being taxed should be 'entitled to his costs of the taxation proceedings.'

5.04 Further the Claimant avers that the 'event', in this case, occurred on the publication of my Award—27 July 1994—in the Claimant's favour for its taxed costs.

5.05 I have reviewed the correspondence and my Directions concerning the preparation of the Bill of Costs following my Award 10 June 1994. Fundamentally, if I were to accede to the Respondent's request, I would have to agree that all the costs incurred in the preparation of the First Bill of Costs, including the Hearing on 1 July 1994, were all thrown away and, in effect, the settlement process commenced following my order for Directions No 21 resulting from that Hearing.

5.06 In order to determine this issue it is necessary to review the reasons why two separate Bills of Cost were produced.

5.07 Following the publication of my 10 June 1994 Award I was informed that the parties would not be able to agree on costs and I was asked to settle the Claimant's costs.

5.08 By way of clarification of the procedure I intended to adopt in this settlement in my letter 11 June 1994 I said:

'I am not bound by the White Book, but of course, I must act judicially. This, in effect, means that I should bear in mind the Rules laid down in the White Book in dealing with this matter.'

'I will not rigidly adhere to Order 62 but will take note of the principles generally applied to

14.8
568

taxation under order 62 ... and ... I will consider (the Respondent's) objections ... in determining the amount to be paid on 'a reasonable amount, reasonably incurred' basis, using my knowledge of the conduct of the reference.'

5.09 By my Order for Directions No 20—By Consent dated 11 June 1994 I directed that the Claimant prepare a detailed narrative Bill of Costs, as detailed in that order and this form of Bill was agreed to by the Respondent's solicitors in their letter to me 12 June 1994.

5.10 Bills of Costs, in line with those Ordered by me were delivered to me, and to the other party, as agreed on 17 June 1994 and the parties Replies on these Bills were delivered to me and to the other side on 24 June 1994.

5.11 On 27 June 1994 the Respondent raised objection to the form of Bill as presented by the Claimant and I subsequently agreed to hear both sides on the form of this Bill and this meeting took place at the offices of the Claimant's representative on 1 July 1994.

5.12 Following the Hearing on the form of the Claimant's Bill I issued Order for Directions No 21—By Consent—on 1 July 1994 detailing the agreed form of the new Bill to be prepared by the Claimant and this Revised Bill was delivered to me and to the Respondent, on 11 July 1994 and the Respondent's Response to this revised Bill was sent to me, and to the Claimant on 18 July 1994.

5.13 The Respondent now submits that all costs up to and including the 1 July 1994 on this matter be the 'Respondent's in any event'. He maintains that the first Bill of Costs prepared by the Claimant falls short of an itemised Bill.

However, this Bill was prepared in a form agreed to by the Respondent as confirmed by his letter to me dated 11 June 1994.

5.14 By Consent, the Claimant prepared a second Bill, as ordered by me in my Order for Directions No 21 and in the event this second Bill, contained little, if any, information additional to that contained in the first Bill and no further objection was taken by the Respondent to this second Bill.

5.15 The Claimant avers that the very considerable detail contained in the first Bill enabled me to undertake a more detailed examination of the Claimant's costs than would otherwise have been possible had only the second Bill been available to me.

In this respect I must agree with the Claimant. As the result of the detailed first Bill I was able to disallow a substantial element of costs, where doubt existed, in favour of the paying party. I found the first Bill of inestimable assistance.

5.16 ACCORDINGLY I REJECT the Respondent's proposal to disallow all costs up to and including 1 July 1994.

5.17 I FIND AND HOLD that COSTS SHALL FOLLOW THE EVENT; the 'event', for this purpose, occurred on the publication of my Award, dated 10 June 1994, when I determined the costs in the reference to be borne by each party.

6.00 The 'Without Prejudice' Offer

6.01 The second point of principle I deal with is the matter of the 'without prejudice' offer.

6.02 At the close of the Hearing on Costs I asked the Respondent if there was an offer to be told that there was not but there was some 'without prejudice' correspondence. I indicated that such correspondence was not relevant to my award on costs and therefore should not form part of any submission to me.

6.03 Subsequently this correspondence *was* included by the Respondents with their submission and, at the request of the Claimant, was removed and, returned (unread by me) to the Respondent, for the reasons given in my letter. In responding to Mr Redman's request to

14.8
569

have such correspondence removed, Messrs Kalmsyde's, in their letter 11 August 1994 still persisted in referring to this as 'without prejudice' correspondence (and not an offer).

6.04 In a further exchange of correspondence, between me and the parties, it became clear that there had been an offer, by letter 16 August, the Claimant's representative withdrew his objection and I was asked to take it into consideration in my Award on the costs of the settlement. The correspondence, previously removed, was returned to me.

6.05 My Award as to costs, 25 July 1994, I determined that the Respondent pay to the Claimant the sum of £48,775.95 (which sum includes interest).

6.06 In addition to this sum I ordered the Costs of the Award amounting to £4362.10 (inclusive of £1100.00 for a Costs Draftsman and £995.87 for Value Added Tax) be borne by the Respondent.

6.07 Thus the amount to be paid by the Respondent as a result of my 25 July 1994 Award was £53,138.05, the substantive award to be paid within 14 days and the amount in respect of my costs, to be paid forthwith.

6.08 The Respondent's offer, 9 October, marked 'Without Prejudice, save as to costs', was in the following terms £50,000 inclusive of interest, all disbursements, Counsel's fees, experts' costs and the like and your costs of taxation, payable as to £20,000.00 now, and the balance by instalments of £10,000 each on 1 October, 1 November, and 1 December 1994. In addition our client will pay three-quarters of the cost of the Arbitrator and of his expert, leaving your client to pay one quarter.

6.09 I have been referred, by both parties, to *Tramountana* v *Atlantic Shipping* [1978] 2 All ER 870. The Judge in this case deals with a number of principles to be considered in dealing with offers.

6.10 Where an offer is made to settle the costs of an action, not the action itself, and the Claimant has already been successful in that action, the only question remaining is whether the Claimant becomes entitled to more by continuing the action, for recovery of costs, following receipt of the offer, than he would have done had he accepted the offer. If the amount awarded is more he should, under normal circumstances, be entitled to his costs.

6.11 In this case it is not a question of costs 'following the event'. The event had already occurred before the 'offer' was made. The Claimant had succeeded in the action as documented by the Final Award on Settlement of Costs—Save as to Settlement of Costs—25 July 1994, where I had determined that the Respondent was to pay to the Claimant costs of its Claim and the Claimant was to pay to the Respondent 85% of the Respondent's costs of the Counterclaim.

6.12 I now consider the Respondent's offer in the light of the amount awarded. As at 9 July, both my costs and those of my expert were considerably less than the eventual sum of £4362.10 but, in any event, the offer was to pay three-quarters of these costs whatever they were calculated to be.

6.13 Therefore, for the purpose of comparing like with like I ignore, *pro tem*, my costs and those of my Cost Draftsman but keep in mind that the Claimant would recover a lesser amount of whatever they turned out to be than he would by continuing with the action. This leaves a comparison of the offer of £50,000.00, inclusive of Interest and the Claimant's Costs of Settlement, with the amount eventually awarded by me, of £48,395.75 plus interest of £380.20—a total of £48,775.95. However, the unknown element in the offer is the amount of the Claimant's costs.

6.14 Of the amount herein awarded by me for settlement of costs, £1,707.16 was incurred prior to 9 July 1994. This has the effect of reducing the £50,000.00 offered to £48,292.84. In order to compare like with like this amount stands to be further reduced by interest on the amount outstanding following payment of the £20,000.00 offered, and paid 1 September 1994 to the date of the final payment of £10,000.00 on 1 December 1994. In addition the Respondents offered to pay only three-quarters of my costs of £4,362.10.

6.15 I accept the Claimant's evaluation of the Respondent's offer set out in the Claimant's submission which shows that the Claimant is already better off, leaving rejected a sum equivalent to £51,841.36 against a sum equivalently awarded, after taking into account the minimum amount admitted by the Respondent in respect of the settlement of costs of £1,480 of £54,618.05 and receiving this sum not later than 8 August 1994 compared with receiving the sum offered, instalments, over a period expiring 1 December 1994.

6.16 In any event, I accept the Claimant's submission that payment by instalments cannot be compared with an award of a single sum to be paid by an earlier specified date. On this count alone therefore I find that the offer, made by the Respondent on 9 July 1994, was not analogous to a payment into court.

6.17 Finally I consider the Respondent's offer from another angle. It was marked 'Without Prejudice, save as to costs' yet, the offer itself was made inclusive of the costs of the settlement. Lord Donaldson in *Tramountana* was quite clear on this point when he said

> 'An offer to pay a lump sum to include costs is not, and should never be, the equivalent of a payment into court. If a party wishes to make a sealed offer and to have it considered in the context of an order for costs, he must offer to settle the action for £X plus costs'.

6.18 The Respondent avers that his offer was not a sealed offer but a 'Without Prejudice' offer which he now invites me to consider. However, I believe that the offer made was, to all intents and purposes, a sealed offer. If it was indeed a 'Without Prejudice' offer, as maintained by the Respondent, the judgment in *Tramountana* is quite clear that a 'Without Prejudice' offer can never be referred to by either party at any stage of the proceedings.

6.19 Accordingly I FIND, HOLD and DECLARE that the Respondent's offer of 9 July 1994, was not analogous to a payment into court by virtue of the instalments proviso and, in the event, the amount of the offer was less than the Claimant was awarded by way of costs, in my Award dated 25 July 1994, and as such the Respondent's offer has no effect on the amount of the Claimant's costs of settlement determined by this Award.

7.00 Duplicated Fee Earners' Work

The Respondent averred that work duplicated by two or more fee earners should be allowed as for one fee earner only.

Although I identified little apparent duplication, where it occurred it is DISALLOWED.

8.00 Costs Draftsman

8.01 The Respondent avers that the costs of the Costs Draftsman should be disallowed, particularly for time spent at the Hearing.

8.02 The Claimant maintains that the attendance at the Hearing was inevitable, caused as it was by the Respondent's own stance made over their insistence of their own Costs Draftsman at the Hearing.

8.03 I made it clear, at the close of the Hearing on Costs that, subject to submissions made by the parties, I was minded to disallow the costs of the Costs Draftsmen's time spent in preparation of the Bill of Costs. Nothing in the submission from the Claimant has caused me to change my mind.

ACCORDINGLY such costs are DISALLOWED

8.04 I offered, by letter to the parties 13 July 1994, to dispense with Costs Draftsmen altogether at the Hearing. This offer was rejected by the Respondent, by letter 14 July 1994 and as such, both the Claimant and I were obliged to seek the attendance of our own Costs Draftsmen. In the event they were little used and we could well have managed without them.

ACCORDINGLY I ALLOW the cost of ATTENDANCE

9.00 Mark-up

9.01 The Respondent avers that there should be no mark-up on the basic hourly rate of any fee earner.

9.02 The Claimant maintains that mark-up should be allowed no differently from that for the main arbitration. Further he points out that the Respondent offers no support for his proposition of no mark-up and accordingly claims 70%.

9.03 In my Award on Costs, dated 25 July 1994 I allowed 35% mark-up for interlocutory work and 70% for attendance at the Hearing without Counsel.

I ALLOW THE SAME PERCENTAGE attendance for the settlement of costs.

10.00 Taking Instructions from Client, Research, etc

10.01 The Respondent avers that it is inappropriate for the Respondent to pay the Claimant's costs of liaising with his client over its own Bill; and all research when the matter was nothing out of the ordinary and well within Mr Redman's experience with assistance from a qualified Costs Draftsman.

10.02 I agree with the Respondent. Liaising with their client is a 'solicitor and own client' cost. Equally, it should have been unnecessary for Mr Redman to research matters in connection with, what was, I accept, a straightforward matter bearing in mind that he was assisted by a qualified Costs Draftsman. Mr Redman has also included correspondence costs and telephone attendance on a number of matters clearly outside the scope of this settlement, i.e. in connection with room hire charges, interim awards as to costs, consideration of 'without prejudice' offers, etc.

ACCORDINGLY a substantial element of the above are DISALLOWED

11.00 Hourly Rates

11.01 The Respondent submits that the hourly rates be as follows:

Partner £110 per hour
Assistant Solicitor £75 per hour.

11.02 The Claimant submits that the following rates should apply:

Partner £130 per hour
Assistant Solicitor £77.50 per hour.
Costs Draftsman £67.50 per hour.

11.03 I award the same rates as I allowed in the Award dated 25 July 1994.

ACCORDINGLY I ALLOW

Partner £110 per hour
Assistant Solicitor £75 per hour
and in addition
Costs Draftsman £50 per hour.

**14.8
572**

12.00 Costs Subsequent to Settlement Hearing

The Respondent maintains that the costs subsequent to the Settlement Hearing on 25 July 1994 are outside the costs of taxation.

FINAL AWARD ON COSTS OF SETTLEMENT

I AGREE AND HAVE DISALLOWED ALL SUCH COSTS.

13.00 The Claimant's Costs to be Subject to a Maximum

13.01 The Respondent requests that I impose a maximum amount of costs that the Claimant can recover. However, I can see no justification for such a proposal nor, indeed, did the Respondent give me any authority in support of his proposition.

13.02 The Claimant avers that any suggestion that some arbitrary limit be imposed upon recovery of their Costs is entirely without support in the Rules of the Supreme Court or the authorities.

I AGREE AND THEREFORE REJECT THE RESPONDENT'S REQUEST.

14.00 Summary

14.01 In publishing this my FINAL AWARD I wish to express my thanks to the Claimant's representative Mr Redman and the Respondent's solicitors, Messrs Catchpole and Crighton for the assistance they gave me and for the courteous way in which they conducted themselves throughout this long and occasionally difficult reference.

14.02 The Claimant's solicitors have claimed £14,000.00 for their costs of taxation.

14.03 The Respondent submits that a figure of £1,480.00 is more reasonable.

14.04 ACCORDINGLY

14.04.1 Having considered the submissions made to me and reflecting my detailed comments above I DETERMINE that the Respondent pay to the Claimant the sum of £4,824.12 (Four Thousand Eight Hundred and Twenty-Four Pounds 12p) within 14 days of the date of this my Award.

14.04.2 For the avoidance of doubt the above sum does not include interest as I award none. Nor, as requested by the Parties, does it include Value Added Tax.

15.00 Costs of the Award

15.01 The Costs of this my Award which I hereby tax and settle in the sum of £1503.56 (One Thousand Five Hundred and Three Pounds 56p) which sum includes £227.96 (Two Hundred and Twenty-Seven Pounds 96p) by way of Value Added Tax, shall be borne by the Claimant.

15.02 Should the Respondent have paid these fees then the Claimant is to reimburse the Respondent the total amount paid forthwith.

15.03 I make this Unusual Award as to Costs in view of the very substantial element of the Claimant's costs disallowed from which it is clear that the Respondent was justified in seeking to have these costs settled by me.

Given under my hand at Hunstanton this 19th day of August 1994

In the presence of
Name ....
Address ....
....
.... D Emsee MSc FRICS FCIArb

14.8
573

The JCT Arbitration Rules (18 July 1988)★

Rule 1. Arbitration Agreements

1. These Rules are the 'JCT Arbitration Rules' referred to in the Arbitration Agreements in:

1. The Standard Form of Building Contract 1980 Edition, as amended	Article 5 and clause 41
2. The Standard Forms of Employer/Nominated Sub-Contractor Agreement (NSC/2 and NSC/2a) 1980 Edition as amended	Clause 10 (NSC/2) Clause 8 (NSC/2a)
3. The JCT Standard Forms of Nominated Sub-Contract NSC/4 and NSC/4a, 1980 Edition, as amended	Article 3 and clause 38
4. The JCT Warranty by a Nominated Supplier (TNS/2: Schedule 3 of the JCT Standard Form of Tender by Nominated Supplier), as amended	Clause 4
5. The Standard Form of Building Contract with Contractor's Design 1981 Edition, as amended	Article 5 and clause 39
6. The Intermediate Form of Building Contract for Works of simple content 1984 Edition, as amended	Article 5 and section 9
7. The Standard Form of Sub-Contract Conditions for Sub-Contractors named under the Intermediate Form of Building Contract (NAM/SC) 1984 Edition, as amended	Article 4 and clause 35
8. The Standard Form of Management Contract 1987 Edition, as amended	Article 8 and section 9
9. The Standard Form of Works Contract (Works Contract/1 and Works Contract/2) 1987 Edition for use with the Standard Form of Management Contract, as amended	Works Contract/1, Section 3 Article 3 and Works Contract/2 section 9
10. The Standard Form of Employer/Works Contractor Agreement (Works Contract/1) 1987 Edition, as amended	Clause 7
11. The Agreement for Minor Building Works 1980 Edition, as amended	Article 4 and clause 9

Rule 2. Interpretation and provisions as to time

2.1 The party who has required a dispute to be referred to arbitration is referred to as 'the Claimant'; the other party is referred to as 'the Respondent'. Where the Arbitrator has been appointed on a joint application the Arbitrator shall decide who will be the Claimant and who will be the Respondent.

2.2 The Claimant and Respondent are referred to as 'the parties' and this expression where the context so admits includes the Claimant and Respondent in any arbitration who have been joined in the proceedings under the relevant joinder provisions in the contract or subcontract or other agreement referred to in Rule 1.

2.3 'Days' means calendar days but in computing any period of days referred to in these Rules all public holidays, the four days following Easter Monday, December 24, 27, 28, 29, 30 and 31 shall be excluded.

★ © RIBA Publications Ltd. Guidance on the application of these rules is given in the JCT publication *Arbitration Rules* available from RIBA Publications Ltd.

2.4 'Arbitration Agreement' means the relevant provisions of a contract, subcontract or agreement under one of the contracts, subcontracts or agreements referred to in Rule 1.

2.5 'Notification Date' means the date of notification by the Arbitrator to the parties of his acceptance of the appointment to proceed with the reference in accordance with the Arbitration Agreement and these Rules.

2.6 Where the context so admits 'award' includes as interim award.

2.7 No time required by these Rules, or by any direction of the Arbitrator, may be extended by agreement of the parties without the express written concurrence of the Arbitrator.

Rule 3. Service of statements, documents and notices—content of statements

3.1 Each party shall notify the other party and the Arbitrator of the address for service upon him of statements, documents or notices referred to in the Rules.

3.2 The service of any statements, documents or notices referred to in these Rules shall be

by actual delivery to the other party or

by first-class post or

where a FAX number has previously been given to the sending party, by FAX (facsimile transmission) to that number.

Where service is by FAX, for record purposes the statement, document or notice served by FAX must forthwith be sent by first-class post or actually delivered.

3.3 Subject to proof of the contrary service shall be deemed to have been effected for the purpose of these Rules upon actual delivery or two days, excluding Saturdays and Sundays, after the date of posting or upon the facsimile transmission having been effected.

3.4 Any statement referred to in these Rules shall:

be in writing

set out the factual and legal basis relied upon and

be served upon the other party and a copy sent to the Arbitrator.

3.5 Without prejudice to any award in respect of general damages any statement of case or of counterclaim shall so far as practicable specify the remedy which the party seeks and where a monetary sum is being sought the amount sought in respect of each and every head of claim.

Rule 4. Conduct of the arbitration—application of Rule 5, Rule 6 or Rule 7—preliminary meeting

4.1 Not later than 21 days from the Notification Date the Arbitrator shall, unless he and the parties otherwise agree, hold a preliminary meeting with the parties at such place and on such day and at such time as the Arbitrator directs.

4.2 (1) At the preliminary meeting, or if the Arbitrator and the parties have agreed that no preliminary meeting be held then not later than 21 days from the Notification Date, the parties shall jointly decide whether Rule 5 (procedure without hearing), Rule 6 (full procedure with hearing) or, subject to Rule 4.2.2, Rule 7 (short procedure with hearing) shall apply to the conduct of the arbitration.

(2) If the Claimant wishes Rule 7 to apply to the conduct of the arbitration he shall, within a reasonable time after the commencement of the arbitration and at least 7 days before a decision under Rule 4.2.1 is required, formulate his case in writing in sufficient detail to identify the matters in dispute and submit that written case to the Respondent with a copy to the Arbitrator and state that at the preliminary meeting he will request the Respondent to agree that Rule 7 shall apply to the conduct of the arbitration. A preliminary meeting shall be held and if at that meeting the parties so agree the provisions of Rule 7 shall thereafter apply and the Arbitrator shall issue any necessary directions thereunder; if at that meeting the parties do not so agree the Arbitrator shall use a direction under Rule 4.3.1 as to whether Rule 5 or Rule 6 shall apply to the conduct of the arbitration.

4.3 (1) If the parties have not jointly decided under Rule 4.2 which Rule shall apply to the arbitration the Arbitrator shall direct that Rule 5 shall apply unless the Arbitrator having regard to any information supplied by, and/or any representations made by, the parties directs that Rule 6 shall apply.

(2) A direction under Rule 4.3.1 shall be issued within 28 days of the Notification Date or, if a preliminary meeting has been held, not later than 7 days after the date of the preliminary meeting.

4.4 Whichever of the Rules 5, 6 or 7 applies to the conduct of the arbitration all the other Rules so far as relevant and applicable shall apply.

Rule 5. Procedure without hearing

5.1 Rule 5 applies to the conduct of the arbitration where:

  1 the parties have so decided under Rule 4.2.1; or

  2 the provisions of Rule 4.3.1 have come into effect and the Arbitrator has not directed that Rule 6 shall apply.

5.2 The times for service required by Rule 5.3 shall apply unless, at a preliminary meeting, or, if no preliminary meeting has been held, then within 28 days of the Notification Date, the Arbitrator, after considering any representations made by the parties, has directed any times for service different from those required by Rule 5.3 in which case the times stated in such direction shall be substituted for the times required by Rule 5.3.

5.3 (1) The Claimant shall, within 14 days after the date when Rule 5 becomes applicable, serve a statement of case.

(2) If the Claimant serves a statement of case within the time or times allowed by these Rules the Respondent shall, within 14 days after service of the Claimant's statement of case, serve

  a statement of defence to the Claimant's statement of case; and

  a statement of any counterclaim.

(3) If the Respondent serves a statement of defence within the time or times allowed by these Rules the Claimant may, within 14 days after such service, serve a statement of reply to the defence.

(4) If the Respondent serves a statement of counterclaim within the time or times allowed by these Rules the claimant shall, within 14 days after such service, serve a statement of defence to the Respondent's counterclaim.

(5) If the Claimant serves a statement of defence to the Respondent's statement of counterclaim within the time or times allowed by these Rules the Respondent may, within 14 days after such service, serve a statement of reply to the defence.

(6) The Claimant with

  his statement of case and

  any statement setting out a reply to the Respondent's statement of defence and his statement of defence to any statement of counterclaim by the Respondent

and the Respondent with

  his statement of defence and

  any statement of counterclaim and

  any statement setting out a reply to the Claimant's statement of defence to any counterclaim

shall include a list of any documents the Claimant or Respondent as the case may be considers necessary to support any part of the relevant statement and a copy of those documents identifying clearly in each document that part or parts on which reliance is or is being placed.

5.4 If a party does not serve a statement of

  case, defence, reply to the defence, counterclaim, defence to the counterclaim or reply to the defence to the counterclaim

within the relevant time required by Rule 5.3 or directed under Rule 5.2 the Arbitrator shall notify the parties that he proposes to proceed on the basis that the party will not be serving the same unless within 7 days of the date of service of that notification the relevant statement is served. If within 7 days of the date of service of that notification the relevant statement is not received the Arbitrator shall proceed on the basis that that party will not be serving the same. If the relevant statement is subsequently served it shall be of no effect unless the Arbitrator is satisfied that there was a good and proper reason both why an application was not made within the time required by Rule 5.7.1 and why a statement was not served within 7 days of the service of his notice given under Rule 5.4.

5.5 If the Claimant either does not serve his statement of case within the time or times allowed by these Rules or if served it is of no effect by reason of Rule 5.4 the Arbitrator shall make an award dismissing the claim and ordering the Claimant to pay the Arbitrator's fees and expenses and any costs hitherto incurred by the Respondent.

5.6 Provided that where either party has, or the parties have, previously delivered to the Arbitrator a statement or statements setting out the matter or matters in dispute including the factual and legal basis relied upon together with the information where relevant required by Rule 3.5 and a list of any documents and a copy of those documents are required by Rule 5.3.6, the Arbitrator may direct that such statement or statements shall stand in place of all or any of the statements or documents to be delivered in compliance with the requirements of Rule 5.3.

5.7 (1) Subject to a written application by the Claimant or Respondent for an extension of the times for service required by Rule 5.3 or directed under Rule 5.2 being served upon the Arbitrator before the expiry of the relevant time for service, the Arbitrator may in his discretion extend by direction in writing to the Claimant and the Respondent the times for service required by Rule 5.3 or directed under Rule 5.2 provided he is satisfied that the reason for the application was in respect of matters which could reasonably be considered to be outside the control of the applicant.

(2) A copy of any written application under Rule 5.7.1 shall be served upon the other party who may, within 5 days of such service, serve written comments thereon upon the Arbitrator and serve a copy thereof upon the applicant. In exercising his discretion under rule 5.7.1 the Arbitrator shall take such written comments into account.

5.8 Where the Arbitrator considers that any document listed in any of the statements referred to in Rule 5.3 or in any statement to which Rule 5.6 refers requires further clarification by an interview with the parties or otherwise, or that some further document is essential for him properly to decide on the matters in dispute the Arbitrator may require such clarification or further document by notice in writing to the Claimant or the Respondent as appropriate and shall serve a copy of that notice upon the party not required to provide such clarification or further document. Such clarification by an interview with the parties or otherwise shall be obtained in accordance with the directions of the Arbitrator and such further document shall be supplied to the Arbitrator with a copy to the other party by the Claimant or Respondent forthwith upon receipt of the notice in writing from the Arbitrator.

5.9 (1) The Arbitrator shall publish his award within 28 days
    after receipt of the last of the statements and documents referred to in Rule 5.3 or
    after the expiry of the last of the times allowed by these Rules for their service
whichever is the earlier.

(2) The Arbitrator may decide to publish his award later than the expiry of the aforementioned 28 days period and if so he shall, prior to the expiry thereof, immediately notify the parties in writing when his award will be published.

Rule 6. Full procedure with hearing

6.1 Rule 6 applies to the conduct of the arbitration where:
    1 the parties have so decided under Rule 4.2.1; or
    2 the provisions of Rule 4.3.1 have come into effect and the Arbitrator has directed that Rule 6 shall apply.

6.2 Rule 6.2 shall apply except to the extent that the Arbitrator otherwise directs or, subject to Rule 2.7, the parties otherwise agree.

6.3 (1) The Claimant shall, within 28 days after the date when Rule 6 becomes applicable, serve a statement of case.

(2) If the Claimant serves a statement of case within the time or times allowed by these Rules the Respondent shall, within 28 days after service of the Claimant's statement of case, serve
    a statement of defence to the Claimant's statement of case; and
    a statement of any counterclaim.

(3) If the Respondent serves a statement of defence within the time or times allowed by these Rules the Claimant may, within 14 days after such service, serve a statement of reply to the defence.

(4) If the Respondent serves a statement of counterclaim within the time or times allowed by these Rules the Claimant shall, within 28 days after such service, serve a statement of defence to the Respondent's counterclaim.

(5) If the Claimant serves a statement of defence to the Respondent's statement of counterclaim within the time or times allowed by these Rules the Respondent may, within 14 days after such service, serve a statement of reply to the defence.

(6) The Claimant with
    his statement of case and
    any statement setting out a reply to the Respondent's statement of defence and
    his statement of defence to any statement of counterclaim by the Respondent
and the Respondent with
    his statement of defence and
    any statement of counterclaim and
    any statement setting out a reply to the claimant's statement of defence to any counterclaim
shall include a list of any documents the Claimant or Respondent as the case may be considers necessary to support any part of the relevant statement and a copy of the principal documents on which reliance

will be placed identifying clearly in each document the relevant part or parts on which reliance will be placed.

6.4 If a party does not serve a statement of

case, defence, reply to the defence, counterclaim, defence to the counterclaim or reply to the defence to the counterclaim

within the relevant time required by Rule 6.3 or directed or agreed under Rule 6.2 the Arbitrator shall notify the parties that he proposes to proceed on the basis that the party will not be serving the same unless within 7 days of the date of service of that notification the relevant statement is served. If within 7 days of the date of service of that notification the relevant statement is not received the Arbitrator shall proceed on the basis that the party will not be serving the same. If the relevant statement is subsequently served it shall be of no effect unless the Arbitrator is satisfied that there was a good and proper reason both why an application was not made within the time required by Rule 6.7.1 and why a statement was not served within 7 days of his notice given under Rule 6.4.

6.5 If the Claimant either does not serve his statement of case within the time or times allowed by these Rules or if served it is of no effect by reason of Rule 6.4 the Arbitrator shall make an award dismissing the claim and ordering the Claimant to pay the Arbitrator's fees and expenses and any costs hitherto incurred by the Respondent.

6.6 Provided that where either party has, or the parties have, previously delivered to the Arbitrator a statement or statements setting out the matter or matters in dispute including the factual and legal basis relied upon together with the information where relevant required by Rule 3.5 and a list of any documents and a copy of the principal documents as required by Rule 6.3.6, the Arbitrator may direct that such statement or statements shall stand in place of all or any of the statements or documents to be delivered in compliance with Rule 6.3.

6.7 (1) Subject to a written application by the Claimant or Respondent for an extension of the times for service required by Rule 6.3 or directed or agreed under Rule 6.2 being served upon the Arbitrator before the expiry of the relevant time for service, the Arbitrator may in his discretion extend by direction in writing to the Claimant and the Respondent the times for service required by Rule 6.3 or directed or agreed under Rule 6.2.

(2) A copy of any written application under Rule 6.7.1 shall be served upon the other party who may, within 5 days of such service, serve written comments thereon upon the Arbitrator and serve a copy thereof upon the applicant. In exercising his discretion under Rule 6.7.1 the Arbitrator shall take such written comments into account.

6.8 The Arbitrator shall, after receipt of the last of the statements and documents referred to in Rule 6.3 or after the expiry of the last of the times allowed by these Rules for their service, whichever is the earlier, after consultation with the parties, notify the parties in writing of the date(s) when and the place where the oral hearing will be held. The Arbitrator shall immediately notify the parties in writing of any change in such date(s) or place.

6.9 (1) The Arbitrator shall publish his award within 28 days of the close of the hearing.

(2) The Arbitrator may decide to publish his award later than the expiry of the aforementioned 28 day period and if so he shall, prior to the expiry thereof, immediately notify the parties in writing when his award will be published.

Rule 7. Short procedure with hearing

7.1 (1) Rule 7 applies to the conduct of the arbitration where the parties have so decided under Rule 4.2.2.

(2) Each party shall bear his own costs unless for special reasons the Arbitrator at his discretion otherwise directs.

7.2 Within 21 days of the date when Rule 7 has become applicable the hearing shall be held at such place and on such day and at such time as the Arbitrator shall direct. No evidence except the documents referred to in Rule 7.3 may be adduced at the hearing except as the Arbitrator may otherwise direct or allow.

7.3 (1) Not later than 7 days before the hearing documents necessary to support the oral submissions and the relevant part or parts thereof shall be identified to the other party and a copy of any such document not in the possession of the other party shall be served upon that party.

(2) A copy of the documents referred to in Rule 7.3.1 shall be served upon the Arbitrator 7 days before the hearing and shall be available at the hearing.

7.4 The Arbitrator may direct that such procedures shall be followed at the hearing and such

579

documents made available as he considers necessary for the just and expeditious determination of the dispute.

7.5 At the end of the hearing the Arbitrator shall

either   thereupon make this award and if made orally shall forthwith confirm his award in writing

or   publish his award within 7 days of the hearing.

The Arbitrator may decide to publish his award later than the expiry of the aforementioned 7 day period and if so, he shall, prior to the expiry thereof, immediately notify the parties in writing when his award will be published.

Rule 8. Inspection by Arbitrator

8.1 The Arbitrator may inspect any relevant work, goods or materials whether on the site or elsewhere. Such inspection shall not be treated as a hearing of the dispute.

8.2 Where under Rule 8.1 the Arbitrator has decided that he will inspect:

where Rule 5 applies, as soon as the parties have served all their written statements or the last of the times for such service allowed by these Rules has expired the Arbitrator shall fix a date not more than 10 days in advance for his inspection and shall inform the parties of the date and time selected;

where Rule 6 or Rule 7 applies, the Arbitrator shall fix a date for his inspection and shall inform the parties of the date and time selected.

8.3 (1) The Arbitrator may require the Claimant or the Respondent, or a person appointed on behalf of either of them, to attend the inspection solely for the purpose of identifying relevant work, goods or materials.

(2) No other person may attend the Arbitrator's inspection unless the Arbitrator shall otherwise direct.

Rule 9. Arbitrator's fees and expenses—costs

9.1 From the Notification Date the parties shall be jointly and severally liable to the Arbitrator for the payment of his fees and expenses.

9.2 In an arbitration which continues for more than 3 months after the Notification Date the Arbitrator shall be entitled to render fee notes at no less than 3-monthly intervals and the same shall be payable 14 days after delivery.

9.3 The Arbitrator shall, unless the parties inform him that they have otherwise agreed, include in his award his decision on the liability of the parties as between themselves for the payment of his fees and expenses and, subject to Rule 7.1.2, on the payment by one party of any costs of the other party.

9.4 The Claimant shall, unless the Respondent has previously done so, take up an award of the Arbitrator and pay his fees and expenses (or any balance thereof if Rule 9.2 has applied) within 10 days of the notification given by the Arbitrator to the parties of publication of the award as provided in Rule 11.3.

Rule 10. Payment to trustee-stakeholder

10.1 If the Arbitrator publishes an award in favour of the Claimant before he has published his award on all matters in a counterclaim by the Respondent, the Arbitrator upon application by the Claimant or the Respondent and after considering any representations by the parties may direct that the whole or a part of the amount so awarded shall be deposited by the Respondent with a deposit-taking bank to hold as a trustee-stakeholder (as described in Rule 10.3) pending a direction of the Arbitrator under Rule 10.2.1 or of the parties under Rule 10.2.2 or of the court under Rule 10.2.3.

10.2 The trustee-stakeholder shall hold any amount deposited as a result of a direction of the Arbitrator under Rule 10.1 in trust for the parties until such time as either

1 the Arbitrator shall direct the trustee-stakeholder (whether as a result of his award or as a result of an agreement between the parties reported to the Arbitrator or otherwise) to whom the amount deposited, including any interest accrued thereon, should be paid by the trustee-stakeholder; or

2 if the Arbitrator is deceased or otherwise unable to issue any direction to the trustee-stakeholder under Rule 10.2.1 and the Arbitrator has not been replaced, the parties in a joint letter signed by or on behalf of each of them direct the trustee-stakeholder to whom the amount deposited, including any interest accrued thereon, should be paid by the trustee-stakeholder; or

3 a court of competent jurisdiction gives directions.

10.3 An amount so deposited may, notwithstanding the trust imposed, be held by the trustee-stakeholder as an ordinary bank deposit to the credit of the bank as a trustee-stakeholder in respect of the party making the deposit pursuant to a direction of the Arbitrator under Rule 10.1 and in respect of such deposit the trustee-stakeholder shall pay such usual interest which shall accrue to and form part of the deposit subject to the right of the trustee-stakeholder to deduct its reasonable and proper charges and, if deductible, any tax in respect of such interest from the amount deposited.

Rule 11. The award

11.1 The Arbitrator shall only give reasons for his award where and to the extent required by either party by notice in writing to the Arbitrator with a copy to the other party.

11.2 (1) The Arbitrator may from time to time publish an interim award.

(2) If in any interim award the parties are directed to seek agreement on an amount or amounts due but such agreement is not reached by the parties within 28 days of receipt of that award (or within such other lesser or greater period as the Arbitrator may direct) the Arbitrator shall, on the basis of such further appropriate evidence or submissions as he may require, publish a further award on the amount due in respect of any liability or liabilities set out in the interim award.

11.3 On publishing an award the Arbitrator shall simultaneously send to the parties by first-class post, a notification that his award is published of the amount of his fees and expenses (or any balance thereof if Rule 9.2 has applied).

11.4 An Arbitrator's award can be taken up by either party on payment to the Arbitrator of his fees and expenses. The Arbitrator shall forthwith deliver the original award to the party who paid his fees and expenses and shall simultaneously send a certified copy of the award to the other party.

11.5 If, before an award is published, the parties agree on a settlement of the dispute the parties shall so notify the Arbitrator. The Arbitrator shall issue an order for the termination of the arbitration or, if requested by both parties and accepted by the Arbitrator, record the settlement in the form of a consent award. The Arbitrator's fees and expenses shall be paid upon notification that such order or consent award is ready for taking up and on payment thereof the Arbitrator shall be discharged and the reference to arbitration concluded.

Rule 12. Powers of Arbitrator

12.1 In addition to any other powers conferred by law, the Arbitrator shall have the following powers:

1 after consultation with the parties to take legal or technical advice on any matter arising out of or in connection with the arbitration;
2 to give directions for protecting, storing, securing or disposing of property the subject of the dispute, at the expense of the parties or of either of them;
3 to order that the Claimant or Counterclaimant give security for the costs of the arbitration or any part thereof, and/or for the fees and expenses of the Arbitrator, in such form and of such amount as the Arbitrator may determine;
4 to proceed in the absence of a party or his representative provided that reasonable notice of the Arbitrator's intention to proceed has been given to that party in accordance with the provisions of these Rules, including if there is to be a hearing, notice of the date and place thereof;
5 at his discretion to direct that the costs, if not agreed, shall be taxed by the Arbitrator;
6 to direct the giving of evidence by affidavit;
7 to order any party to produce to the Arbitrator, and to the other party for inspection, and to supply copies of, any documents or classes of documents in the possession power or custody of the party which the Arbitrator determines to be relevant.

12.2 Subject to the Arbitration Acts 1950 to 1979 any non-compliance by the Arbitrator with these Rules, including those relating to time, shall not of itself affect the validity of an award.

12.3 If during the arbitration it appears to the Arbitrator to be necessary for the just and expeditious determination of the dispute that a Rule for the conduct of the arbitration other than that previously applicable shall apply, the Arbitrator, after considering any representations made by the parties, may so direct and shall give such further directions as he may deem appropriate.

581

APPENDIX 2

Chartered Institute of Arbitrators
Arbitration Rules
(effective from 1 January 1988)★

Arbitration Rules (1988)

These Rules are published by the Chartered Institute of Arbitrators, to help parties and arbitrators take maximum advantage of the flexible procedures available in arbitration for the resolution of disputes quickly and economically. The Rules provide that the wishes of the parties regarding procedure will be respected so far as possible, but they also seek to ensure that the Arbitrator will have sufficient powers to direct the proceedings if the parties cannot agree on procedure or will not co-operate. The Rules may be used without reference to the Institute (unless the Institute is required to act as Appointing Authority in accordance with Article 2.1).

The Arbitration Rules of the Chartered Institute of Arbitrators are not intended for use in arbitrations relating to international contracts or disputes (i.e. where the parties come from different countries). In such cases, reference should be made to the Rules of the London Court of International Arbitration.

The Chartered Institute of Arbitrators was founded in 1915 and granted a Royal Charter in 1979. The aims of the Institute are to establish and maintain professional standards for arbitrators, and to promote the wider use of arbitration in the resolution of disputes. Its members come from a wide range of professional disciplines, both in the UK and internationally. Training programmes, leading to professional qualification as an arbitrator, are an important aspect of the Institute's activities. The Institute acts as an appointing authority, appointing arbitrators when authorised to do so by parties in dispute. It also provides a wide range of additional arbitration services. For further information please contact: Chartered Institute of Arbitrators, International Arbitration Centre, 24 Angel Gate, City Road, London EC1V 2RS. Telephone: 071-837 4483, Facsimile: 071-837 4185.

SUGGESTED CLAUSES

1. Parties to a contract who wish to have any *future* disputes referred to arbitration under the Rules of the Chartered Institute of Arbitrators may insert in the contract an arbitration clause in the following form:

'Any dispute arising out of or in connection with this contract shall be referred to and finally resolved by arbitration under the Rules of the Chartered Institute of Arbitrators, which Rules are deemed to be incorporated by reference into this clause.'

2. Parties to an *existing* dispute who wish to refer it to arbitration under the Rules of the Chartered Institute of Arbitrators may agree to do so in the following terms:

'We, the undersigned, agree to refer to arbitration under the Rules of the Chartered Institute of Arbitrators the following dispute which has arisen between us:
(Brief description of matters to be referred to arbitration)
Signed —————— (Claimant)
Signed —————— (Respondent)
Date ——————'

3. Where the Rules of the Chartered Institute of Arbitrators apply:
   (a) The parties may if they wish specify an Appointing Authority to appoint the arbitrator (or arbitrators) if the parties fail to do so or cannot agree. If no Appointing Authority is specified,

583

★ © The Chartered Institute of Arbitrators.

then the Rules provide the President or a Vice-President for the time being of the Chartered Institute of the Arbitrators will act as Appointing Authority. The following provision may be suitable if some other appointing Authority is required.

'The Appointing Authority shall be (name of institution or person).'

(b) The Rules provide a sole arbitrator will be appointed unless the parties agree otherwise. If the parties wish to specify a three-man tribunal, the following provision may be suitable:

'The arbitral tribunal shall consist of three arbitrators one of whom shall be appointed by each party and the third by the Appointing Authority.''

CHARTERED INSTITUTE OF ARBITRATORS ARBITRATION RULES
(adopted to take effect from 1 January 1988)

Where any agreement, submission or reference provides for arbitration under the Rules of the Chartered Institute of Arbitrators, the parties shall be taken to have agreed that the arbitration shall be conducted in accordance with the following Rules, or such amended Rules as the Chartered Institute of Arbitrators may have adopted to take effect before the commencement of the arbitration.

Article 1. Commencement of arbitration

1.1 Any party wishing to commence an arbitration under these Rules ('the Claimant') shall send to the other party ('the Respondent') a written request for arbitration ('the Request') which shall include, or be accompanied by:
(a) the names and addresses of the parties to the arbitration;
(b) copies of the contractual documents in which the arbitration clause is contained or under which the arbitration arises;
(c) a brief statement describing the nature and circumstances of the dispute, and specifying the relief claimed;
(d) a statement of any matters (such as the Appointing Authority, the number of arbitrators, or their qualifications or identities) with respect to which the requesting party wishes to make a proposal;
(e) if the arbitration agreement calls for each party to appoint an arbitrator, the name and address (and telephone, telex and fax numbers, if known) of the arbitrator appointed by the Claimant.
The arbitration shall be deemed to commence on the date of receipt by the Respondent of the Request for Arbitration.

1.2 For the purpose of facilitating the choice of arbitrators, within 30 days of receipt of the Request for Arbitration, the Respondent may send to the Claimant a Response containing:
(a) confirmation or denial of all or part of the claims;
(b) a brief statement of the nature and circumstances of any envisaged counterclaims;
(c) comment (including confirmation of agreement) in response to any proposals contained in the Request, as called for under Article 1.1(d), on matters relating to the conduct of the arbitration;
(d) if the arbitration agreement calls for each party to appoint an arbitrator, the name and address (and telephone, telex and fax numbers if known) of the arbitrator appointed by the Respondent.

1.3 Failure to send a Response shall not preclude the Respondent from denying the claim nor from setting out a counterclaim in its Statement of Defence. However, if the arbitration agreement calls for each party to appoint an arbitrator, failure to send a Response or to name an appointed arbitrator in it within the time specified in Article 1.2 shall constitute a waiver of the right to appoint an arbitrator.

Article 2. Appointing Authority

2.1 The parties may agree to nominate an Appointing Authority. Failing such nomination the Appointing Authority shall be the President or a Vice-President for the time being of the Chartered Institute of Arbitrators.

2.2 Any application to the Appointing Authority to act in accordance with these Rules shall be accompanied by:

584

(a) Copies of the Request and Response and any other related correspondence;
(b) Confirmation that a copy of the application has been received by the other party;
(c) Particulars of any method or criteria of selection of arbitrators agreed by the parties.

The Appointing Authority may require payment of a fee for its services.

Article 3. Appointment of arbitrator

3.1 Provided that the final number is uneven, the parties may agree on the number of arbitrators in the Tribunal. Failing such agreement there shall be a sole arbitrator. In these Rules, the expression 'the Arbitrator' includes a sole arbitrator or all the arbitrators where more than one is appointed.

3.2 The Arbitrator shall be and remain at all times wholly independent and impartial, and shall not act as advocate for any party. Before appointment if so requested by either party or the Appointing Authority any proposed arbitrator shall furnish a resume of his past and present professional activities (which will be communicated to the parties). In any event any arbitrator if so requested by either party or the Appointing Authority shall sign a declaration to the effect that there are no circumstances likely to give rise to any justified doubts as to his impartiality or independence, and that he will forthwith disclose any such circumstances to the parties if they should arise after that time and before the arbitration is concluded.

3.3 The Arbitrator may be appointed by agreement of the parties. Failing such agreement within 30 days of the commencement of the arbitration in accordance with Article 1, the Arbitrator shall upon the application of either party be appointed by the Appointing Authority.

3.4 Where the parties have agreed there shall be three arbitrators, they may also agree that each party shall appoint an arbitrator. If either party fails to make and notify the other party of such appointment within 30 days of the commencement of the arbitration under Article 1, that appointment shall be made by the Appointing Authority.

3.5 Where the parties have agreed that each shall appoint an arbitrator then, unless otherwise agreed by the parties, a third arbitrator shall be appointed by the Appointing Authority.

3.6 Where there are three or more arbitrators, they may agree who shall act as Chairman of the arbitral tribunal. Failing such agreement the Chairman shall be designated by the Appointing Authority.

3.7 If any arbitrator, after appointment, dies, is unable to act, or refuses to act, the Appointing Authority will, upon request by a party or by the remaining arbitrators, appoint another arbitrator.

Article 4. Communications between parties and the Arbitrator

4.1 Where the Arbitrator sends any communication to one party, he shall send a copy to the other party.

4.2 Where a party sends any communication (including Statements under Article 6) to the Arbitrator, it shall be copied to the other party and be shown to the Arbitrator to have been so copied.

4.3 The addresses of the parties for the purpose of all communications during the proceedings shall be those set out in the Request, or as either party may at any time notify to the Arbitrator and to the other party. Any communication by post shall be deemed to be received in the ordinary course of mail unless the contrary is proved.

4.4 With the agreement of the parties, the Arbitrator may appoint the Registrar of the Chartered Institute of Arbitrators to act as arbitration administrator (whether or not the Chartered Institute of Arbitrators is acting as Appointing Authority). Where the Registrar is so appointed, all communications and notices between a party and the Arbitrator in the course of the arbitration (except at meetings and hearings) will be addressed through the Registrar, and in the case of communications to the Arbitrator will be deemed received by him when received by the Registrar.

Article 5. Conduct of the proceedings

5.1 In the absence of procedural rules agreed by the parties or contained herein, the Arbitrator shall have the widest discretion allowed by law to ensure the just, expeditious, economical, and final determination of the dispute.

5.2 Any party wishing the Arbitrator to adopt a simplified or expedited procedure should apply to the Arbitrator for this within 15 days of notification of the Arbitrator's acceptance of his appointment.

585

5.3 In the case of a three-member tribunal the Chairman may, after consulting the other arbitrators, make procedural rulings alone.

Article 6. Submission of written statements and documents

6.1 Subject to any procedural rules agreed by the parties or determined by or requested from the Arbitrator under Article 5, the written stage of the proceedings shall be as set out in this Article (and in accordance with Article 4).

6.2 Within 30 days of receipt by the Claimant of notification of the Arbitrator's acceptance of the appointment, the Claimant shall send to the Arbitrator a Statement of Case setting out in sufficient detail the facts and any contentions of law on which it relies and the relief claimed.

6.3 Within 30 days of receipt of the Statement of Case, the Respondent shall send to the Arbitrator a Statement of Defence stating in sufficient detail which of the facts and contentions of law in the Statement of Case it admits or denies, on what grounds, and on what other facts and contentions of law it relies. Any Counterclaims shall be submitted with the Statement of Defence in the same manner as claims are set out in the Statement of Case.

6.4 Within 30 days of receipt of the Statement of Defence, the Claimant may send to the Arbitrator a Statement of Reply which, where there are Counterclaims, shall include a Defence to Counterclaims.

6.5 If the Statement of Reply contains a Defence to Counterclaims, the Respondent may within a further 30 days send to the Arbitrator a Statement of Reply regarding Counterclaims.

6.6 All Statements referred to in this Article shall be accompanied by copies (or, if they are especially voluminous, lists) of all essential documents on which the party concerned relies and which have not previously been submitted by any party, and (where appropriate) by any relevant samples.

6.7 As soon as practicable following completion of the submission of the Statements specified in this Article, the Arbitrator shall proceed in such manner as has been agreed by the parties, or pursuant to his authority under these Rules.

Article 7. Party representatives

Any party may be represented by persons of their choice, subject to such proof of authority as the Arbitrator may require. The names and addresses of such representatives must be notified to the other party.

Article 8. Hearings

8.1 Subject to Article 12, each party has the right to be heard before the Arbitrator, unless the parties have agreed to documents-only arbitration.

8.2 The Arbitrator shall fix the date, time and place of any meetings and hearings in the arbitration, and shall give the parties reasonable notice thereof.

8.3 The Arbitrator may in advance of hearings provide the parties with a list of matters or questions to which he wishes them to give special consideration.

8.4 All meetings and hearings shall be in private unless the parties agree otherwise.

Article 9. Witnesses

9.1 The Arbitrator may require each party to give notice of the identity of witnesses it intends to call. The Arbitrator may also require before a hearing the exchange of witnesses' statements and of expert reports.

9.2 The Arbitrator has discretion to allow, limit, or (subject to Article 10.2) refuse to allow the appearance of witnesses, whether witnesses of fact or expert witnesses.

9.3 Any witness who gives oral evidence may be questioned by each party or its representative, under the control of the Arbitrator, and may be required by the Arbitrator to testify under oath or affirmation in accordance with the Arbitrator Act 1950. The Arbitrator may put questions at any stage of the examination of the witnesses.

9.4 The testimony of witnesses may be presented in written form, either as signed statements or by duly sworn affidavits. Subject to Article 9.2 any party may request that such a witness should attend for oral examination at a hearing. If the witness fails to attend, the Arbitrator may place such weight on the written testimony as he thinks fit, or may exclude it altogether.

586

CHARTERED INSTITUTE OF ARBITRATORS ARBITRATION RULES

Article 10. Experts appointed by the Arbitrator

10.1 Unless otherwise agreed by the parties, the Arbitrator:
(a) may appoint one or more experts to report to the Arbitrator on specific issues;
(b) may require a party to give any such expert any relevant information or to produce, or to provide access to, any relevant documents, goods or property for inspection by the expert.

10.2 Unless otherwise agreed by the parties, if a party so requests or if the Arbitrator considers it necessary, the expert shall, after delivery of his written or oral report, participate in a hearing, at which the parties shall have the opportunity to question him and to present expert witnesses in order to testify on the points at issue.

10.3 The provisions of Article 10.2 shall not apply to an assessor appointed by agreement of the parties, nor to an expert appointed by the Arbitrator to advise him solely in relation to procedural matters.

Article 11. Additional powers of the Arbitrator

11.1 Unless the parties at any time agree otherwise, the Arbitrator shall have the power to:
(a) allow any party, upon such terms (as to costs and otherwise) as he shall determine, to amend claims or counterclaims;
(b) extend or abbreviate any time limits provided by the Rules or by his directions;
(c) conduct such enquiries as may appear to the Arbitrator to be necessary or expedient;
(d) order the parties to make any property or thing available for inspection, in their presence, by the Arbitrator or any expert;
(e) order any party to produce to the Arbitrator, and to the other parties for inspection, and to supply copies of any documents or classes of documents in their possession, custody or power which the Arbitrator determines to be relevant.

11.2 If the parties so agree the Arbitrator shall also have the power to:
(a) order the rectification in any contract or arbitration agreement of any mistake which he determines to be common to the parties;
(b) rule on the existence, validity or determination of the contract;
(c) rule on his own jurisdiction, including any objections with respect to the existence or validity of the arbitration agreement or to his terms of reference.

Article 12. Jurisdiction of the Arbitrator

12.1 In addition to the jurisdiction to exercise the powers defined elsewhere in these Rules, the Arbitrator shall have jurisdiction to:
(a) determine any question of law arising in the arbitration;
(b) receive and take into account such written or oral evidence as he shall determine to be relevant, whether or not strictly admissible in law;
(c) proceed in the arbitration and make an award notwithstanding the failure or refusal of any party to comply with these Rules or with the Arbitrator's written orders or written directions, or to exercise its right to present its case, but only after giving that party written notice that he intends to do so.

12.2 If the Claimant fails to attend any hearing of which due notice has been given, the Arbitrator may make an award on the substantive issue and an award as to costs, with or without a hearing, but such an award must be an Interim Award with the provision that it shall become a Final Award after 42 days if no application for a hearing is made by the Claimant during that period. If the Respondent fails to submit a Statement of Defence or to attend any hearing after due notice has been given, the Arbitrator may conduct the hearing in the absence of the Respondent and make an Award.

Article 13. Deposits and security

13.1 The Arbitrator may direct the parties, in such proportions as he deems just, to make one or more deposits to secure the Arbitrator's fees and expenses. Such deposits shall be made to and held by the Arbitrator, or the Chartered Institute of Arbitrators or some other person or body to the order of the Arbitrator, as the Arbitrator may direct, and may be drawn from as required by the Arbitrator. Interest on sums deposited, if any, shall be accumulated to the deposits.

13.2 The Arbitrator shall have the power to order any party to provide security for the legal or other costs of any other party by way of deposit or bank guarantee or in any other manner the Arbitrator thinks fit.

13.3 The Arbitrator shall also have the power to order any party to provide security for all or part of any amount in dispute in the arbitration.

Article 14. The award

14.1 The Arbitrator shall make his award in writing and, unless all the parties agree otherwise, shall state the reasons upon which his award is based. The award shall state its date and shall be signed by the Arbitrator.

14.2 Where there is more than one arbitrator and they fail to agree on any issue, they shall decide by a majority. Failing a majority decision on any issue, the Chairman of the tribunal shall make the award alone as if he were sole arbitrator. If an arbitrator refuses or fails to sign the award, the signatures of the majority shall be sufficient, provided that the reason for the omitted signature is stated.

14.3 The Arbitrator shall be responsible for delivering the award or certified copies thereof to the parties, provided that he has been paid his fees and expenses.

14.4 The Arbitrator may make interim awards or separate awards on different issues at different times.

14.5 If, before the award is made, the parties agree on a settlement of the dispute, the Arbitrator shall either issue an order for termination of the reference to arbitration or, if requested by both parties and accepted by the Arbitrator, record the settlement in the form of a consent award. The Arbitrator shall then be discharged and the reference to arbitration concluded, subject to payment by the parties of any outstanding fees and expenses of the Arbitrator.

Article 15. Correction of awards and additional awards

15.1 Within 14 days of receiving an award, unless another period of time has been agreed by the parties, a party may by notice to the Arbitrator request the Arbitrator to correct in the award any errors in computation, any clerical or typographical errors or any errors of similar nature. If the Arbitrator considers the request to be justified, he shall make the corrections within 14 days of receiving the request. Any correction shall be notified in writing to the parties and shall become part of the award.

15.2 The Arbitrator may correct any error of the type referred to in Article 15.1 on his own initiative within 14 days of the date of the award.

15.3 Unless otherwise agreed by the parties, a party may request the Arbitrator, within 10 days of the date of the award, and with notice to the other party, to make an additional award as to claims presented in the reference to arbitration but not dealt with in the award. If the Arbitrator considers the request to be justified, he shall notify the parties within 7 days and shall make the additional award within 30 days.

15.4 The provisions of Article 14 shall apply to any correction of the award and to any additional award.

Article 16. Costs

16.1 The Arbitrator shall specify in the award the total amount of his fees and expenses, including the charges of the arbitration administrator (if any). Unless the parties shall agree otherwise after the dispute has arisen, the Arbitrator shall determine the proportions in which the parties shall pay such fees and expenses, provided that the parties will be jointly and severally liable to the Arbitrator for payment of all such fees and expenses until they have been paid in full. If the Arbitrator has determined that all or any of his fees and expenses shall be paid by any party other than a party which has already paid them to the Arbitrator, the latter party shall have the right to recover the appropriate amount from the former.

16.2 The Arbitrator has power to order in his award that all or a part of the legal or other costs of one party shall be paid by the other party. The Arbitrator also has power to tax these costs and may do so if requested by the parties.

16.3 If the Arbitrator is abandoned, suspended or concluded, by agreement or otherwise, before the final award is made, the parties shall be jointly and severally liable to pay to the Arbitrator his fees and expenses as determined by him together with the charges of the arbitration administrator (if any).

588

Article 17. Exclusion of liability

17.1 The Arbitrator, the Appointing Authority (and the arbitration administrator if any) shall not be liable to any party for any act or omission in connection with any arbitration conducted under these Rules, save for the consequences of conscious and deliberate wrongdoing.

17.2 After the award has been made the possibilities of correction and additional awards referred to in Article 15 have lapsed or been exhausted, the Arbitrator, the Appointing Authority (and the arbitration administrator if any) shall not be under any obligation to make any statement to any person about any matter concerning the arbitration, and no party shall seek to make any arbitrator or the Appointing Authority or the arbitration administrator a witness in any legal proceedings arising out of the arbitration.

Article 18. Waiver

A party which is aware of the non-compliance with these Rules and yet proceeds with the arbitration without promptly stating its objection to such non-compliance, shall be deemed to have waived its right to object.

Arbitration Act 1950

An Act to consolidate the Arbitration Acts 1889 to 1934.

PART I. GENERAL PROVISIONS AS TO ARBITRATION

Effect of arbitration agreement, &c.

Authority of arbitrators and umpires to be irrevocable

1. The authority of an arbitrator or umpire appointed by or by virtue of an arbitration agreement shall, unless a contrary intention is expressed in the agreement, be irrevocable except by leave of the High Court or a judge thereof.

Death of party

2.—(1) An arbitration agreement shall not be discharged by the death of any party thereto, either as respects the deceased or any other party, but shall in such an event be enforceable by or against the personal representative of the deceased.

(2) The authority of an arbitrator shall not be revoked by the death of any party by whom he was appointed.

(3) Nothing in this section shall be taken to affect the operation of any enactment or rule of law by virtue of which any right of action is extinguished by the death of a person.

Bankruptcy

3.—(1) Where it is provided by a term in a contract to which a bankrupt is a party that any differences arising thereout or in connection therewith shall be referred to arbitration, the said term shall, if the trustee in bankruptcy adopts the contract, be enforceable by or against him so far as related to any such differences.

(2) Where a person who has been adjudged bankrupt had, before the commencement of the bankruptcy, become a party to an arbitration agreement, and any matter to which the agreement applies requires to be determined in connection with or for the purposes of the bankruptcy proceedings, then, if the case is one to which subsection (1) of this section does not apply, any other party to the agreement or, with the consent of the committee of inspection, the trustee in bankruptcy, may apply to the court having jurisdiction in the bankruptcy proceedings for an order directing that the matter in question shall be referred to arbitration in accordance with the agreement, and that court may, if it is of opinion that, having regard to all the circumstances of the case, the matter ought to be determined by arbitration, make an order accordingly.

Staying court proceedings where there is submission to arbitration

4.—(1) If any party to an arbitration agreement, or any person claiming through or under him, commences any legal proceedings in any court against any other party to the agreement, or any person claiming through or under him, in respect of any matter agreed to be referred, any party to those legal proceedings may at any time after appearance, and before delivering any pleadings or taking any other steps in the proceedings, apply to that court to stay the proceedings, and that court or a judge thereof, is

591

satisfied that there is no sufficient reason why the matter should not be referred in accordance with the agreement, and that the applicant was, at the time when the proceedings were commenced, and still remains, ready and willing to do all things necessary to the proper conduct of the arbitration, may make an order staying the proceedings.

[(2) Notwithstanding anything in this Part of this Act, if any party to a submission to arbitration made in pursuance of an agreement to which the protocol set out in the First Schedule of this Act applies, or any person claiming through or under him, commences any legal proceedings in any court against any other party to the submission, or any person claiming through or under him, in respect of any matter agreed to be referred, any party to those legal proceedings may at any time after appearance, and before delivering any pleadings or taking any other steps in the proceedings, apply to that court to stay the proceedings, and that court or a judge thereof, unless satisfied that the agreement or arbitration has become inoperative or cannot proceed or that there is not in fact any dispute between the parties with regard to the matter agreed to be referred, shall make an order staying the proceedings.]

Note: The words in square brackets were repealed by s. 8(2)(a) of the Arbitration Act 1975.

Reference of interpleader issues to arbitration

5. Where relief by way of interpleader is granted and it appears to the High Court that the claims in question are matters to which an arbitration agreement, to which the claimants are parties, applies, the High Court may direct the issue between the claimants to be determined in accordance with the agreement.

Arbitrators and umpires

When reference is to a single arbitrator

6. Unless a contrary intention is expressed therein, every arbitration agreement shall, if no other mode of reference is provided, be deemed to include a provision that the reference shall be to a single arbitrator.

Power parties in certain cases to supply vacancy

7. Where an arbitration agreement provides that the reference shall be to two arbitrators, one to be appointed by each party then, unless a contrary intention is expressed therein—

    (a) if either of the appointed arbitrators refuses to act, or is incapable of acting, or dies, the party who appointed him may appoint a new arbitrator in his place;

    (b) if, on such a reference, one party fails to appoint an arbitrator, either originally, or by way of substitution as aforesaid, for seven clear days after the other party having appointed his arbitrator, has served the party making default with notice to make the appointment, the party who has appointed an arbitrator may appoint that arbitrator to act as sole arbitrator in the reference and his award shall be binding on both parties as if he had been appointed by consent:

Provided that the High Court or a judge thereof may set aside any appointment made in pursuance of this section.

Umpires

8.—(1) Unless a contrary intention is expressed therein, every arbitration agreement shall, where the reference is to two arbitrators, be deemed to include a provision that the two arbitrators may appoint an umpire at any time after they are themselves appointed, and shall do so forthwith if they cannot agree.

(2) Unless a contrary intention is expressed therein, every arbitration agreement shall, where such a provision is applicable to the reference, be deemed to include a provision that if the arbitrators have delivered to any party to the arbitration agreement, or to the umpire, a notice in writing stating that they cannot agree, the umpire may forthwith enter on the reference in lieu of the arbitrators.

(3) At any time after the appointment of an umpire, however appointed, the High Court may, on the application of any party to the reference and notwithstanding anything to the contrary in the arbitration

agreement, order that the umpire shall enter upon the reference in lieu of the arbitrators and as if he were a sole arbitrator.

Note: Sub-s. (1) is printed as amended by s. 6(1) of the Arbitration Act 1979. In relation to arbitrations to which the Arbitration Act 1979 does not apply, sub-s. (1) applies in its unamended form, as follows—'Unless a contrary intention is expressed therein, every arbitration agreement shall, where the reference is to two arbitrators be deemed to include a provision that the two arbitrators shall appoint an umpire at any time after they are themselves appointed.'

Majority award of three arbitrators

9. Unless the contrary intention is expressed in the arbitration agreement, in any case where there is a reference to three arbitrators, the award of any two of the arbitrators shall be binding.

Note: This section is printed as amended by s. 6(2) of the Arbitration Act 1979. In relation to arbitrations to which the Arbitration Act 1979 does not apply, the section applies in its unamended form which reads as follows:

'**9**—(1) Where an arbitration agreement provides that the reference shall be to three arbitrators, one to be appointed by each party and the third to be appointed by the two appointed by the parties, the agreement shall have effect as if it provided for the appointment of an umpire, and not for the appointment of a third arbitrator, by the two arbitrators appointed by the parties.

(2) Where an arbitration agreement provides that the reference shall be to three arbitrators to be appointed otherwise than as mentioned in subsection (1) of this section, the award of any two of the arbitrators shall be binding.'

Power of court in certain cases to appoint an arbitrator or umpire

10.—(1) In any of the following cases—
  (a) where an arbitration agreement provides that the reference shall be to a single arbitrator, and all the parties do not, after differences have arisen, concur in the appointment of an arbitrator;
  (b) if an appointed arbitrator refuses to act, or is incapable of acting, or dies, and the arbitration agreement does not show that it was intended that the vacancy should not be supplied and the parties do not supply the vacancy;
  (c) where the parties or two arbitrators are required or are at liberty to appoint an umpire or third arbitrator and do not appoint him;
  (d) where an appointed umpire or third arbitrator refuses to act, or is incapable of acting, or dies, and the arbitration agreement does not show that it was intended that the vacancy should not be supplied, and the parties or arbitrators do not supply the vacancy;
any party may serve the other parties or the arbitrators, as the case may be, with a written notice to appoint or, as the case may be, concur in appointing, an arbitrator, umpire or third arbitrator, and if the appointment is not made within seven clear days after the service of the notice, the High Court or a judge thereof may, on application by the party who gave the notice, appoint an arbitrator, umpire or third arbitrator who shall have the like powers to act in the reference and make an award as if he had been appointed by consent of all parties.
  (2) In any case where—
  (a) an arbitration agreement provides for the appointment of an arbitrator or umpire by a person who is neither one of the parties nor an existing arbitrator (whether the provision applies directly or in default of agreement by the parties or otherwise), and
  (b) that person refuses to make the appointment or does not make it within the time specified in the agreement or, if no time is so specified, within a reasonable time
any party to the agreement may serve the person in question with a written notice to appoint an arbitrator or umpire and, if the appointment is not made within seven clear days after the service of the notice, the High Court or a judge thereof may, on the application of the party who gave the notice, appoint an arbitrator or umpire who shall have the like powers to act in the reference and make an award as if he had been appointed in accordance with the terms of the agreement.
  (3) In any case where—
  (a) an arbitration agreement provides that the reference shall be to three arbitrators, one to be appointed by each party and the third to be appointed by the two appointed by the parties or in some other manner specified in the agreement; and
  (b) one of the parties ('the party in default') refuses to appoint an arbitrator or does not do so within the time specified in the agreement or, if no time is specified, within a reasonable time,

593

the other party to the agreement, having appointed his arbitrator, may serve the party in default with a written notice to appoint an arbitrator.

[(3A) A notice under subsection (3) must indicate whether it is served for the purposes of subsection (3B) or for the purposes of subsection (3C).

(3B) Where a notice is served for the purposes of this subsection, then unless a contrary intention is expressed in the agreement, if the appointment is not made within seven clear days after the service of the notice—

    (a) the party who gave the notice may appoint his arbitrator to act as sole arbitrator in the reference; and

    (b) his award shall be binding on both parties as if he had been appointed by consent.

(3C) Where a notice is served for the purposes of this subsection, then if the required appointment is not made within seven clear days after the service of the notice, the High Court or a judge thereof may, on the application of the party who gave the notice, appoint an arbitrator on behalf of the party in default who shall have the like powers to act in the reference and make an award (and, if the case so requires, the like duty in relation to the appointment of a third arbitrator) as if he had been appointed in accordance with the terms of the agreement.

(3D) The High Court or a judge thereof may set aside any appointment made by virtue of subsection (3B).]

(4) Except in a case where the arbitration agreement shows that it was intended that the vacancy should not be supplied, paragraph (b) of each of subsections (2) and (3) shall be construed as extending to any such refusal or failure by a person as is there mentioned arising in connection with the replacement of an arbitrator who was appointed by that person (or, in default of being so appointed, was appointed under that subsection) but who refuses to act, or is incapable of acting or has died.

Note: This section is printed as amended in sub-s. (1) by s. 6(3) of the Arbitration Act 1979, the addition of sub-s. (2) by s. 6(4) of the Arbitration Act 1979 and the addition of sub-s. (3) by s. 58 of the Administration of Justice Act 1985. In relation to arbitrations to which the Arbitration Act 1979 does not apply the section reads as if the words 'required or are' were omitted from para. (c) of sub-s. (1), and sub-s. (2) were omitted altogether. Sub-s. (3) has been prospectively replaced and new sub-ss. (3A)–(3D) prospectively inserted by s. 101 of the Courts and Legal Services Act 1990, see below. S. 101(2)(3) of the Courts and Legal Services Act 1990 also prospectively apply to s. 10.

Power of official referee to take arbitrations

[**11.**—(1) An official referee may, if in all the circumstances he thinks fit, accept appointment as sole arbitrator, or as umpire, by or by virtue of an arbitration agreement.

(2) An official referee shall not accept appointment as arbitrator or umpire unless the Lord Chief Justice has informed him that, having regard to the state of official referees' business, he can be made available to do so.

(3) The fees payable for the services of an official referee as arbitrator or umpire shall be taken in the High Court.

(4) Schedule 3 of the Administration of Justice Act 1970 (which modifies this Act in relation to arbitration by judges, in particular by substituting the Court of Appeal for the High Court in provisions whereby arbitrators and umpires, their proceedings and awards are subject to control and review by the court) shall have effect in relation to official referees appointed as arbitrators or umpires as it has effect in relation to judge-arbitrators and judge-umpires (within the meaning of that Schedule).

(5) Any jurisdiction which is exercisable by the High Court in relation to arbitrators and umpires otherwise than under this Act shall, in relation to an official referee appointed as arbitrator or umpire, be exercisable instead by the Court of Appeal.

(6) In this section 'official referee' means any person nominated under section 68(1)(a) of the Supreme Court Act 1981 to deal with official referees' business.

(7) Rules of the Supreme Court may make provision for—

    (a) cases in which it is necessary to allocate references made under or by virtue of arbitration agreements to official referees;

    (b) the transfer of references from one official referee to another.]

Note: This section has been prospectively replaced by a new section 11 contained in s. 99 of the Courts and Legal Services Act 1990, see below.

Conduct of proceedings, witnesses, &c.

12.—(1) Unless a contrary intention is expressed therein, every arbitration agreement shall, where such a provision is applicable to the reference, be deemed to contain a provision that the parties to the reference, and all persons claiming through them respectively, shall, subject to any legal objection, submit to be examined by the arbitrator or umpire, on oath or affirmation, in relation to the matters in dispute, and shall, subject as aforesaid, produce before the arbitrator or umpire all documents within their possession or power respectively which may be required or called for, and do all other things which during the proceedings on the reference the arbitrator or umpire may require.

(2) Unless a contrary intention is expressed therein, every arbitration agreement shall, where such a provision is applicable to the reference, be deemed to contain a provision that the witnesses on the reference shall, if the arbitrator or umpire thinks fit, be examined on oath or affirmation.

(3) An arbitrator or umpire shall, unless a contrary intention is expressed in the arbitration agreement, have power to administer oaths to, or take the affirmations of, the parties to and witnesses on a reference under the agreement.

(4) Any party to a reference under an arbitration agreement may sue out a writ of subpoena and testificandum or a writ of subpoena duces tecum, but no person shall be compelled under any such writ to produce any document which he could not be compelled to produce on the trial of an action, and the High Court or a judge thereof may order that a writ of subpoena ad testificandum or of subpoena duces tecum shall issue to compel the attendance before an arbitrator or umpire of a witness wherever he may be within the United Kingdom.

(5) The High Court or a judge thereof may also order that a writ of habeas corpus ad testificandum shall issue to bring up a prisoner for examination before an arbitrator or umpire.

(6) The High Court shall have, for the purpose of and in relation to a referee, the same power of making orders in respect of—

    (a) security for costs;

    (b) . . .

    (c) the giving of evidence by affidavit;

    (d) examination on oath of any witness before an officer of the High Court or any other person, and the issue of a commission or request for the examination of a witness out of the jurisdiction;

    (e) the preservation, interim custody or sale of any goods which are the subject matter of the reference;

    (f) securing the amount in dispute in the reference;

    (g) the detention, preservation or inspection of any property or thing which is the subject of the reference or as to which any question may arise therein, and authorising for any of the purposes aforesaid any persons to enter upon or into any land or building in the possession of any party to the reference, or authorising any samples to be taken or any observation to be made or experiment to be tried which may be necessary or expedient for the purpose of obtaining full information or evidence; and

    (h) interim injunctions or the appointment of a receiver;

as it has for the purpose of and in relation to an action or matter in the High Court:

Provided that nothing in this subsection shall be taken to prejudice any power which may be vested in an arbitrator or umpire of making orders with respect to any of the matters aforesaid.

Note: Sub-s. (6)(b) has been prospectively repealed by the Courts and Legal Services Act 1990, s. 103, see below.

Provisions as to awards

Time for making award

13.—(1) Subject to the provisions of subsection (2) of section twenty-two of this Act, and anything to the contrary in the arbitration agreement, an arbitrator or umpire shall have power to make an award at any time.

(2) The time, if any, limited for making an award, whether under this Act or otherwise, may from time to time be enlarged by order of the High Court or a judge thereof, whether that time has expired or not.

(3) The High Court may, on the application of any party to a reference, remove an arbitrator or umpire who fails to use all reasonable dispatch in entering on and proceeding with the reference and making an award, and an arbitrator or umpire who is removed by the High Court under this subsection shall not be entitled to receive any remuneration in respect of his services.

For the purposes of this subjection, the expression 'proceeding with a reference' includes, in a case where two arbitrators are unable to agree, giving notice of that fact to the parties and to the umpire.

Note: A new s. 13A has been prospectively inserted by s. 102 of the Courts and Legal Services Act 1990, see below.

Want of prosecution

[**13A.**—(1) Unless a contrary intention is expressed in the arbitration agreement, the arbitrator or umpire shall have power to make an award dismissing any claim in a dispute referred to him if it appears to him that the conditions mentioned in subsection (2) are satisfied.

(2) The conditions are—
  (a) that there has been inordinate and inexcusable delay on the part of the claimant in pursuing the claim; and
  (b) that the delay—
    (i) will give rise to a substantial risk that it is not possible to have a fair resolution of the issues in that claim; or
    (ii) has caused, or is likely to cause or to have caused, serious prejudice to the respondent.

(3) For the purpose of keeping the provision made by this section and the corresponding provision which applies in relation to proceedings in the High Court in step, the Secretary of State may by order made by statutory instrument amend subsection (2) above.

(4) Before making any such order the Secretary of State shall consult the Lord Chancellor and such other persons as he considers appropriate.

(5) No such order shall be made unless a draft of the order has been laid before, and approved by resolution of, each House of Parliament.]

Note: This section was inserted by the Courts and Legal Services Act 1990, section 102.

Interim awards

14. Unless a contrary intention is expressed therein, every arbitration agreement shall, where such a provision is applicable to the reference, be deemed to contain a provision that the arbitrator or umpire may, if he thinks fit, make an interim award, and any reference in this Part of this Act to an award includes a reference to an interim award.

Specific performance

15. Unless a contrary intention is expressed therein, every arbitration agreement shall, where such a provision is applicable to the reference, be deemed to contain a provision that the arbitrator or umpire shall have the same power as the High Court to order specific performance of any contract other than a contract relating to land or any interest in land.

Awards to be final

16. Unless a contrary intention is expressed therein, every arbitration agreement shall, where such a provision is applicable to the reference, be deemed to contain a provision that the award to be made by the arbitrator or umpire shall be final and binding on the parties and the persons claiming under them respectively.

Power to correct slips

17. Unless a contrary intention is expressed in the arbitration agreement, the arbitrator or umpire shall have power to correct in an award any clerical mistake or error arising from any accidental slip or omission.

Costs, fees and interest

Costs

18.—(1) Unless a contrary intention is expressed therein, every arbitration agreement shall be deemed to include a provision that the costs of the reference and award shall be in the discretion of the arbitrator or umpire, who may direct to and by whom and in what manner those costs or any part thereof shall be paid, and may tax or settle the amount of costs to be sold or any part thereof, and may award costs to be paid as between solicitor and client.

(2) Any costs directed by an award to be paid shall, unless the award otherwise directs, be taxable in the High Court.

(3) Any provision in an arbitration agreement to the effect that the parties or any party thereto shall in any event pay their or his own costs of the reference or award or any part thereof shall be void, and this Part of this Act shall, in the case of an arbitration agreement containing any such provision, have effect as if that provision were not contained therein:

Provided that nothing in this subsection shall invalidate such a provision when it is a part of an agreement to submit to arbitration a dispute which has arisen before the making of that agreement.

(4) If no provision is made by an award with respect to the costs of the reference, any party to the reference may, within fourteen days of the publication of the award or such further time as the High Court or a judge thereof may direct, apply to the arbitrator for an order directing by and to whom those costs shall be paid, and thereupon the arbitrator shall, after hearing any party who may desire to be heard, amend his award by adding thereto such directions as he may think proper with respect to the payment of the costs of the reference.

(5) Section sixty-nine of the Solicitors Act 1932 (which empowers a court before which any proceeding is being heard or is pending to charge property recovered or preserved in the proceeding with the payment of solicitors' costs) shall apply as if an arbitration were a proceeding in the High Court, and the High Court may make declarations and orders accordingly.

Taxation of arbitrator's umpire's fees

19.—(1) If in any case an arbitrator or umpire refuses to deliver his award except on payment of the fees demanded by him, the High Court may, on an application for the purpose, order that the arbitrator or umpire shall deliver the award to the applicant on payment into court by the applicant of the fees demanded, and further that the fees demanded shall be taxed by the taxing officer and that out of the money paid into court there shall be paid out to the arbitrator or umpire by way of fees such sum as may be found reasonable on taxation and that the balance of the money, if any, shall be paid out to the applicant.

(2) An application for the purposes of this section may be made by any party to the reference unless the fees demanded have been fixed by a written agreement between him and the arbitrator or umpire.

(3) A taxation of fees under this section may be reviewed in the same manner as a taxation of costs.

(4) The arbitrator or umpire shall be entitled to appear and be heard on any taxation or review of taxation under this section.

Power of arbitrator to award interest

[19A.—(1) Unless a contrary intention is expressed therein, every arbitration agreement shall, where such a provision is applicable to the reference, be deemed to contain a provision that the arbitrator or umpire may, if he thinks fit, award simple interest at such rate as he thinks fit:
- (a) on any sum which is the subject of the reference but which is paid before the award, for such period ending not later than the date of the payment as he thinks fit; and
- (b) on any sum which he awards, for such period ending no later than the date of the award as he thinks fit.

(2) The power to award interest conferred on an arbitrator or umpire by subsection (1) above is without prejudice to any other power of an arbitrator or umpire to awards interest.]

597

Note: This section was added by the Administration of Justice Act 1982, section 15(6) and Part IV of Schedule 1. It came into force on 1 April 1983 by virtue of the Administration of Justice Act 1982 (Commencement No 1) order 1983, SI 1983 No 236.

Interest on awards

20. A sum directed to be paid by an award shall, unless the award otherwise directs, carry interest as from the date of the award and at the same rate as a judgment debt.

Special cases, remission and setting aside of awards, &c.

Statement of case

21. [Repealed.]

Note: The repeal of this section was affected by s. 8(3)(b) of the Arbitration Act 1979. In relation to arbitrations to which the Arbitration Act 1979 does not apply, the section applies in its unrepealed form, as follows:

'(1) An arbitrator or umpire may, and shall if so directed by the High Court, state—
  (a) any question of law arising in the course of the reference; or
  (b) an award or any part of an award,
in the form of a special case for the decision of the High Court.
(2) A special case with respect to an interim award or with respect to a question of law arising in the course of a reference may be stated, or may be directed by the High Court to be stated, notwithstanding that proceedings under the reference are still pending.
(3) A decision of the High Court under this section shall be deemed to be a judgment of the Court within the meaning of section twenty-seven of the Supreme Court of Judicature (Consolidation) Act 1925 (which relates to the jurisdiction of the Court of Appeal to hear and determine appeals from any judgment of the High Court), but no appeal shall lie from the decision of the High Court on any case stated under paragraph (a) of subsection (1) of this section without the leave of the High Court or of the Court of Appeal.'

Power to remit award

22.—(1) In all cases of reference to arbitration the High Court or a judge thereof may from time to time remit the matters referred, or any of them, to the reconsideration of the arbitrator or umpire.

(2) Where an award is remitted, the arbitrator or umpire shall, unless the order otherwise directs, make his award within three months after the date of the order.

Removal of arbitrator and setting aside of award

23.—(1) Where an arbitrator or umpire has misconducted himself or the proceedings, the High Court may remove him.

(2) Where an arbitrator or umpire has misconducted himself or the proceedings, or an arbitration or award has been improperly procured, the High Court may set the award aside.

(3) Where an application is made to set aside an award, the High Court may order that any money made payable by the award shall be brought into court or otherwise secured pending the determination of the application.

Power of court to give relief where arbitrator is not impartial or the dispute involves question of fraud

24.—(1) Where an agreement between any parties provides that disputes which may arise in the future between them shall be referred to an arbitrator named or designated in the agreement, and after a dispute has arisen any party applies, on the ground that the arbitrator so named or designated is not or may not be impartial, for leave to revoke the authority of the arbitrator or for an injunction to restrain any other party or the arbitrator from proceeding with the arbitration, it shall not be a ground for refusing the application that the said party at the time when he made the agreement knew, or ought to have known, that the arbitrator, by reason of his relation towards any other party to the agreement or of his connection with the subject referred, might not be capable of impartiality.

(2) Where an agreement between any parties provides that disputes which may arise in the future between them shall be referred to arbitration, and a dispute which so arises involves the question whether any such party has been guilty of fraud, the High Court shall, so far as may be necessary to enable that question to be determined by the High Court, have power to order that the agreement shall cease to have effect and power to give leave to revoke the authority of any arbitrator or umpire appointed by or by virtue of the agreement.

(3) In any case where by virtue of this section the High Court has power to order that an arbitration agreement shall cease to have effect or to give leave to revoke the authority of an arbitrator or umpire, the High Court may refuse to stay any action brought in breach of the agreement.

Power of court where arbitrator is removed or authority of arbitrator is revoked

25.—(1) Where an arbitrator (not being a sole arbitrator), or two or more arbitrators (not being all the arbitrators) or an umpire who has not entered on the reference is or are removed by the High Court or the Court of Appeal, the High Court may, on the application of any party to the arbitration agreement, appoint a person or persons to act as arbitrator or arbitrators or umpire in place of the person or persons so removed.

(2) Where the authority of an arbitrator or arbitrators or umpire is revoked by leave of the High Court or the Court of Appeal, or a sole arbitrator or all the arbitrators or an umpire who has entered on the reference is or are removed by the High Court or the Court of Appeal, the High Court may, on the application of any party to the arbitration agreement, either—

(a) appoint a person to act as a sole arbitrator in place of the person or persons removed; or
(b) order that the arbitration agreement shall cease to have effect with respect to the dispute referred.

(3) A person appointed under this section by the High Court or the Court of Appeal, as an arbitrator or umpire, shall have the like power to act in the reference and to make an award as if he had been appointed in accordance with the terms of the arbitration agreement.

(4) Where it is provided (whether by means of a provision in the arbitration agreement or otherwise) that an award under an arbitration agreement shall be a condition precedent to the bringing of an action with respect to any matter to which the agreement applies, the High Court or the Court of Appeal, if it orders (whether under this section or under any other enactment) that the agreement shall cease to have effect as regards any particular dispute, may further order that the provision making an award a condition precedent to the bringing of an action shall also cease to have effect as regards that dispute.

Enforcement of award

Enforcement of award

26.—(1) An award on an arbitration agreement may, by leave of the High Court or a judge thereof, be enforced in the same manner as a judgment or order to the same effect, and where leave is so given, judgment may be entered in terms of the award.

(2) If—

(a) the amount sought to be recovered does not exceed the current limit on jurisdiction in s. 40 of the County Courts Act 1959, and
(b) a county court so orders,

it shall be recoverable (by execution issued from the county court or otherwise) as if payable under an order of that court and shall not be enforceable under subsection (1) above.

(3) An application to the High Court under this section shall preclude an application to a county court, and an application to a county court under this section shall preclude an application to the High Court.

Miscellaneous

Power of court to extend time for commencing arbitration proceedings

27. Where the terms of an agreement to refer future disputes to arbitration provide that any claims to which the agreement applies shall be barred unless notice to appoint an arbitrator is given or an arbitrator is appointed or some other step to commence arbitration proceedings is taken within a time fixed by the

599

agreement, and a dispute arises to which the agreement applies, the High Court, if it is of opinion that in the circumstances of the case undue hardship would otherwise be caused, and notwithstanding that the time so fixed has expired, may, on such terms, if any, as the justice of the case may require, but without prejudice to the provisions of any enactment limiting the time for the commencement of arbitration proceedings, extend the time for such period as it thinks proper.

Terms as to costs, &c.

28. Any order made under this Part of this Act may be made on such terms as to costs or otherwise as the authority making the order thinks just:

[Provided that this section shall not apply to any order made under subsection (2) of section four of this Act.]

Note: The words in square brackets were repealed by section 8(2)(b) of the Arbitration Act 1975.

Extension of s. 496 of the Merchant Shipping Act 1894

29.—(1) In subsection (3) of section four hundred and ninety-six of the Merchant Shipping Act 1894 (which requires a sum deposited with a wharfinger by an owner of goods to be repaid unless legal proceedings are instituted by the shipowner), the expression 'legal proceedings' shall be deemed to include arbitration.

(2) For the purposes of the said section four hundred and ninety-six, as amended by this section, an arbitration shall be deemed to be commenced when one party to the arbitration agreement serves on the other party or parties a notice requiring him or them to appoint or concur in appointing an arbitrator, or, where the arbitration agreement provides that the reference shall be to a person named or designated in the agreement, requiring him or them to submit the dispute to the person so named or designated.

(3) Any such notice as is mentioned in subsection (2) of this section may be served either—

(a) by delivering it to the person on whom it is to be served; or

(b) by leaving it at the usual or last known place of abode in England of that person; or

(c) by sending it by post in a registered letter addressed to that person at his usual or last known place of abode in England;

as well as in any other manner provided in the arbitration agreement; where a notice is sent by post in manner prescribed by paragraph (c) of this subsection, service thereof shall, unless the contrary is proved, be deemed to have been effected at the time at which the letter would have been delivered in the ordinary course of post.

Crown to be bound

30. This Part of this Act [(except the provisions of subsection (2) of section four thereof)] shall apply to any arbitration to which His Majesty, either in right of the Crown or of the Duchy of Lancaster or otherwise, or the Duke of Cornwall, is a party.

Note: The words in square brackets were repealed by s. 8(2)(c) of the Arbitration Act 1975.

Application of Part I to statutory arbitrations

31.—(1) Subject to the provisions of section thirty-three of this Act, this part of this Act, except the provisions thereof specified in subsection (2) of this section, shall apply to every arbitration under any other Act (whether passed before or after the commencement of this Act) as if the arbitration were pursuant to an arbitration agreement and as if that other Act were an arbitration agreement, except in so far as this Act is inconsistent with that other Act or with any rules or procedure authorised or recognised thereby.

(2) The provisions referred to in subsection (1) of this section are subsection (1) of section two, section three, [subsection (2) of section four,] section five, subsection (3) of section eighteen and sections twenty-four, twenty-five, twenty-seven and twenty-nine.

Note: The words in square brackets were repealed by s. 8(2)(d) of the Arbitration Act 1975.

Meaning of 'arbitration agreement'

32. In this Part of this Act, unless the context otherwise requires, the expression 'arbitration agreement' means a written agreement to submit present or future differences to arbitration, whether an arbitrator is named therein or not.

Operation of Part I

33. This Part of this Act shall not affect any arbitration commenced (within the meaning of subsection (2) of section twenty-nine of this Act) before the commencement of this Act, but shall apply to an arbitration so commenced after the commencement of this Act under an agreement made before the commencement of this Act.

Extent of Part I

34. [Subsection (2) of section four of this Act shall—
    (a) extend to Scotland, with the omission of the words 'Notwithstanding anything in this Part of this Act' and with the substitution, for references to staying proceedings, of references to sisting proceedings; and
    (b) extend to Northern Ireland, with the omission of the words 'Notwithstanding anything in this Part of this Act';
but,] save as aforesaid, none of the provisions of this Part of this Act shall extend to Scotland or Northern Ireland.

Note: The words in square brackets were repealed by s. 8(2)(e) of the Arbitration Act 1975.

PART II. ENFORCEMENT OF CERTAIN FOREIGN AWARDS

Note: Part II re-enacts Part I of the Arbitration (Foreign Awards) Act 1930.

Awards to which Part II applies

35.—(1) This Part of this Act applies to any award made after the twenty-eighth day of July, nineteen hundred and twenty-four—
    (a) in pursuance of an agreement for arbitration to which the protocol set out in the First Schedule to this Act applies; and
    (b) between persons of whom one is subject to the jurisdiction of some one of such Powers as His Majesty, being satisfied that reciprocal provisions have been made, may by Order in Council declare to be parties to the convention set out in the Second Schedule to this Act, and of whom the other is subject to the jurisdiction of some other of the Powers aforesaid; and
    (c) in one of such territories as His Majesty, being satisfied that reciprocal provisions have been made, may by Order in Council declare to be territories to which the said convention applies;
and an award to which this Part of this Act applies is in this Part of this Act referred to as 'a foreign award'.

(2) His Majesty may by a subsequent Order in Council vary or revoke any Order previously made under this section.

(3) Any Order in Council under section one of the Arbitration (Foreign Awards) Act 1930, which is in force at the commencement of this Act shall have effect as if it had been made under this section.

Note: The following states became Contracting States for the purposes of the protocol in the First Schedule:

Albania (T.S. 56/1925 Cmd. 2577).
Austria (T.S. 29/1928 Cmd. 3266).
Bahamas (T.S. 43/1931 Cmd. 4015).
Belgium (T.S. 56/1925 Cmd. 2577).
Brazil (T.S. 38/1932 Cmd. 4249).
British Guiana (T.S. 32/1926 Cmd. 2804).
British Honduras (T.S. 32/1926 Cmd. 2804).
Burma (excluding Karenni States) (T.S. 75/1938 Cmd. 5930).

601

Ceylon (T.S. 75/1926 Cmd. 2804).
Czechoslovakia (T.S. 43/1931 Cmd. 4015).
Danzig (T.S. 75/1938 Cmd. 5930).
Denmark (T.S. 56/1925 Cmd. 2577).
Estonia (T.S. 33/1929 Cmd. 3491).
Falkland Islands and Dependencies (T.S. 32/1926 Cmd. 2804 & T.S. 39/1934 Cmd. 4809).
Finland (T.S. 56/1925 Cmd. 2577).
France (T.S. 29/1928 Cmd. 3266).
Gambia (Colony and Protectorate) (T.S. 32/1926 Cmd. 2804 & T.S. 39/1934 Cmd. 809).
Germany (T.S. 56/1925 Cmd. 2577).
Gibraltar (T.S. 32/1926 Cmd. 2804).
Gold Coast (including Ashanti, Northern Territories and Togoland under British Mandate) (T.S. 32/1926 Cmd. 2804 & T.S. 43/1931 Cmd. 4015).
Greece (T.S. 32/1926 Cmd. 2804).
India (T.S. 56/1937 Cmd. 5654).
Iraq (T.S. 32/1926 Cmd. 2804).
Italy (T.S. 56/1925 Cmd. 2577).
Jamaica (including Turks and Caicos Islands and the Cayman Islands) (T.S. 32/1926 Cmd. 2804 & T.S. 43/1931 Cmd. 4015).
Japan (including Chosen, Taiwan, Karafuto, leased territory of Kwangtung and Japanese Mandated Territories) (T.S. 28/1928 Cmd. 3266 & T.S. 33/1929 Cmd. 3491).
Kenya (Colony & Protectorate) (T.S. 32/1926 Cmd. 2804 & T.S. 39/1934 Cmd. 4809).
Leeward Islands (T.S. 32/1926 Cmd. 2804).
Luxemburg (T.S. 52/1930 Cmd. 3816).
Malta (T.S. 32/1926 Cmd. 2804).
Mauritius (T.S. 32/1926 Cmd. 2804).
Monaco (T.S. 29/1927 Cmd. 3022).
Netherlands (including Netherlands Indies, Surinam and Curaçao) (T.S. 56/1925 Cmd. 2577; T.S. 75/1938 Cmd. 5930 & T.S. 31/1940 Cmd. 6253).
Newfoundland (T.S. 56/1925 Cmd. 2577).
New Zealand (T.S. 32/1926 Cmd. 2804).
Northern Rhodesia (T.S. 32/1926 Cmd. 2804).
Norway (T.S. 29/1927 Cmd. 3022).
Palestine (excluding Trans-Jordan) (T.S. 32/1926 Cmd. 2804 & T.S. 39/1934 Cmd. 4809).
Poland (T.S. 43/1931Cmd. 4015).
Portugal (T.S. 52/1930 Cmd. 3816).
Roumania (T.S. 56/1925 Cmd. 2577).
St. Helena (T.S. 32/1926 Cmd. 2804).
Siam (T.S. 52/1930 Cmd. 3816).
Southern Rhodesia (T.S. 56/1925 Cmd. 2577).
Spain (T.S. 32/1926 Cmd. 2804).
Sweden (T.S. 33/1929 Cmd. 3491).
Switzerland (T.S. 29/1928 Cmd. 3266).
Tanganyika Territory (T.S. 32/1926 Cmd. 2804).
Trans-Jordan (T.S. 39/1934 Cmd. 4809).
Uganda (T.S. 33/1929 Cmd. 3491).
United Kingdom of Great Britain and Northern Ireland (T.S. 4/1925 Cmd. 2312).
Windward Islands (Grenada, St. Lucia, St. Vincent) (T.S. 32/1926 Cmd. 2804).
Zanzibar (T.S. 32/1926 Cmd. 2804).

Orders in Council made under the Act of 1930 are still in force for the following territories whose sovereigns are parties to the convention in the Second Schedule:

Antigua (S.R. & O. 1933 No. 42).
Bahamas (S.R. & O. 1931 No. 669).
Belgium (S.R. & O. 1930 No. 674), with Congo and Ruanda-Urundi (S.R. & O. 1930 No. 1096).
British Guiana (S.R. & O. 1931 No. 669).
British Honduras (S.R. & O. 1931 No. 669).
Burma (S.R. & O. 1939 No. 152).
Danzig (S.R. & O. 1938 No. 1360).
Denmark (S.R. & O. 1930 No. 674).
Dominica (S.R. & O. 1933 No. 42).
Estonia (S.R. & O. 1930 No. 674).
Falkland Is. (S.R. & O. 1931 No. 669).

602

France (S.R. & O. 1931 No. 669).
Germany (S.R. & O. 1930 No. 1096).
Gibraltar (S.R. & O. 1931 No. 669).
Gold Coast ((a) Colony; (b) Ashanti; (c) Northern Territories; (d) Togoland under British Mandate) (S.R. & O. 1931 No. 669).
Italy (S.R. & O. 1931 No. 166).
Jamaica (including Turks and Caicos Islands and Cayman Islands) (S.R. & O. 1931 No. 669).
Kenya (S.R. & O. 1931 No. 669).
Leeward Islands (S.R. & O. 1933 No. 42).
Luxemburg (S.R. & O. 1930 No. 1096).
Malta (S.R. & O. 1935 No. 133).
Mauritius (S.R. & O. 1931 No. 898).
Newfoundland (S.R. & O. 1931 No. 166).
New Zealand (with Western Samoa) (S.R. & O. 1930 No. 674).
Northern Rhodesia (S.R. & O. 1931 No. 898).
Palestine (excluding Trans-Jordan) (S.R. & O. 1931 No. 669).
Portugal (S.R. & O. 1931 No. 166).
Roumania (S.R. & O. 1931 No. 898).
Siam (S.R. & O. 1931 No. 898).
Spain (S.R. & O. 1930 No. 674).
Sweden (S.R. & O. 1930 No. 674).
Switzerland (S.R. & O. 1930 No. 1096).
Tanganyika Territory (S.R. & O. 1931 No. 669).
Uganda Protectorate (S.R. & O. 1931 No. 669).
United Kingdom (S.R. & O. 1930 No. 674).
Windward Islands (S.R. & O. 1931 No. 669).
Zanzibar (S.R. & O. 1939 No. 669).

Orders in Council under the 1950 Act have been made in respect of the following territories whose sovereigns are parties to the convention in the Second Schedule (see S.I. 1978 No. 186, and (for Grenada) S.I. 1979 No. 304):

The United Kingdom of Great Britain and Northern Ireland	Greece
Belize	Grenada
British Virgin Islands	India
Cayman Islands	The Republic of Ireland
Falkland Islands and Dependencies	Israel
Gibraltar	Italy
Hong Kong	Japan
Montserrat	Kenya
Turks and Caicos Islands	Luxembourg
West Indies, Associated States (Antigua, Dominica,	Mauritius
St. Lucia, St. Vincent, St. Christopher, Nevis and	Netherlands (including the Netherland Antilles)
Anguilla)	New Zealand
Austria	Pakistan
Belgium	Portugal
Czechoslovakia	Romania
Denmark	Spain
Finland	Sweden
France	Switzerland
Federal Republic of Germany	United Republic of Tanzania
German Democratic Republic	Thailand
	Yugoslavia

Effect of foreign awards

36.—(1) A foreign award shall, subject to the provisions of this part of this Act, be enforceable in England either by action or in the same manner as the award of an arbitrator is enforceable by virtue of section twenty-six of this Act.

(2) Any foreign award which would be enforceable under this Part of this Act shall be treated as binding for all purposes on the persons as between whom it was made, and may accordingly be relied on by any of those persons by way of defence, set off or otherwise in any legal proceedings in England, and any references in this Part of this Act to enforcing a foreign award shall be construed as including references to relying on an award.

603

Conditions for enforcement of foreign awards

37.—(1) In order that a foreign award may be enforceable under this Part of this Act it must have—

(a) been made in pursuance of an agreement for arbitration which was valid under the law by which it was governed;

(b) been made by the tribunal provided for in the agreement or constituted in manner agreed upon by the parties;

(c) been made in conformity with the law governing the arbitration procedure;

(d) become final in the country in which it was made;

(e) been in respect of a matter which may lawfully be referred to arbitration under the law of England;

and the enforcement thereof must not be contrary to the public policy or the law of England.

(2) Subject to the provisions of this subsection, a foreign award shall not be enforceable under this Part of this Act if the court dealing with the case is satisfied that—

(a) the award has been annulled in the country in which it was made; or

(b) the party against whom it is sought to enforce the award was not given notice of the arbitration proceedings in sufficient time to enable him to present his case, or was under some legal incapacity and was not properly represented; or

(c) the award does not deal with all the questions referred or contains decisions on matters beyond the scope of the agreement for arbitration.

Provided that, if the award does not deal with all the questions referred, the court may, if it thinks fit, either postpone the enforcement of the award or order its enforcement subject to the giving of such security by the person seeking to enforce it as the court may think fit.

(3) If a party seeking to resist the enforcement of a foreign award proves that there is any ground other than the non-existence of the conditions specified in paragraphs (a), (b) and (c) of subsection (1) of this section, or the existence of the conditions specified in paragraphs (b) and (c) of subsection (2) of this section, entitling him to contest the validity of the award, the court may, if it thinks fit, either refuse to enforce the award or adjourn the hearing until after the expiration of such period as appears to the court to be reasonably sufficient to enable that party to take the necessary steps to have the award annulled by the competent tribunal.

Evidence

38.—(1) The party seeking to enforce a foreign award must produce—

(a) the original award or a copy thereof duly authenticated in manner required by the law of the country in which it was made; and

(b) evidence proving that the award has become final; and

(c) such evidence as may be necessary to prove that the award is a foreign award and that the conditions mentioned in paragraphs (a), (b) and (c) of subsection (1) of the last foregoing section are satisfied.

(2) In any case where any document required to be produced under subsection (1) of this section is in a foreign language, it shall be the duty of the party seeking to enforce the award to produce a translation certified as correct by a diplomatic or consular agent of the country to which that party belongs, or certified as correct in such other manner as may be sufficient according to the law of England.

(3) Subject to the provisions of this section, rules of court may be made under section [84 of the Supreme Court Act 1981], with respect to the evidence which must be furnished by a party seeking to enforce an award under this Part of this Act.

Note: The words in square brackets were substituted by the Supreme Court Act 1981, Sch. 5.

Meaning of 'final award'

39. For the purposes of this Part of this Act, an award shall not be deemed final if any proceedings for the purpose of contesting the validity of the award are pending in the country in which it was made.

Saving for other rights, &c.

40. Nothing in this Part of this Act shall—

(a) prejudice any rights which any person would have had of enforcing in England any award or of availing himself in England of any award if neither this Part of this Act nor Part I of the Arbitration (Foreign Awards) Act 1930, had been enacted; or

(b) apply to any award made on an arbitration agreement governed by the law of England.

Application of Part II to Scotland

41.—(1) The following provisions of this section shall have effect for the purpose of the application of this Part of this Act to Scotland.

(2) For the references to England there shall be substituted references to Scotland.

(3) For subsection (1) of section thirty-six there shall be substituted the following subsection:

'(1) A foreign award shall, subject to the provisions of this Part of this Act, be enforceable by action, or, if the agreement for arbitration contains consent to the registration of the award in the Books of Council and Session for execution and the award is so registered, it shall, subject as aforesaid, be enforceable by summary diligence.'

(4) For subsection (3) of section thirty-eight there shall be substituted the following subsection:

'(3) The Court of Session shall, subject to the provision of this section, have power, exercisable by statutory instrument, to make provision by Act of Sederunt with respect to the evidence which must be furnished by a party seeking to enforce in Scotland an award under this Part of this Act.'

Note: This section is printed as amended by the Statutory Instruments Act 1946 and the Law Reform (Miscellaneous Provisions) (Scotland) Act 1966.

Application of Part II to Northern Ireland

42.—(1) The following provisions of this section shall have effect for the purpose of the application of this Part of this Act to Northern Ireland.

(3) For subsection (1) of section thirty-six there shall be substituted the following subsection:

'(1) A foreign award shall, subject to the provisions of this Part of this Act, be enforceable either by action or in the same manner as the award of an arbitrator under the provisions of the Common Law Procedure Amendment Act (Ireland) 1856 was enforceable at the date of the passing of the Arbitration (Foreign Awards) Act 1930.'

[(4) For the reference, in subsection (3) of section thirty-eight, to section ninety-nine of the Supreme Court of Judicature (Consolidation) Act 1925, there shall be substituted a reference to section sixty-one of the Supreme Court of Judicature (Ireland) Act 1877, as amended by any subsequent enactment.]

Note: The words in square brackets, as amended by Sch. 1 to the Northern Ireland Act 1962, were repealed by s. 122(2) of and Sch. 7 to the Judicature (Northern Ireland) Act 1978.

[Saving for pending proceedings

43. Any proceedings instituted under Part I of the Arbitration (Foreign Awards) Act 1930 which are uncompleted at the commencement of this Act may be carried on and completed under this Part of this Act as if they had been instituted thereunder.]

Note: This section was repealed by the Statute Law (Revision) Act 1978.

PART III. GENERAL

Short title, commencement and repeal

44.—(1) This Act may be cited as the Arbitration Act 1950.

(2) This Act shall come into operation on the first day of September, nineteen hundred and fifty.

(3) The Arbitration Act 1889, the Arbitration Clauses (Protocol) Act 1924, and the Arbitration Act 1934 are hereby repealed except in relation to arbitrations commenced (within the meaning of

605

subsection (2) of section twenty-nine of this Act) before the commencement of this Act, and the Arbitration (Foreign Awards) Act 1930 is hereby repealed; and any reference in any Act or other document to any enactment hereby repealed shall be construed as including a reference to the corresponding provision of this Act.

FIRST SCHEDULE. PROTOCOL ON ARBITRATION CLAUSES SIGNED ON BEHALF OF HIS MAJESTY AT A MEETING OF THE ASSEMBLY OF THE LEAGUE OF NATIONS HELD ON THE TWENTY-FOURTH DAY OF SEPTEMBER, NINETEEN HUNDRED AND TWENTY-THREE

The undersigned, being duly authorised, declare that they accept, on behalf of the countries which they represent, the following provisions:

1. Each of the Contracting States recognises the validity of an agreement whether relating to existing or future differences between parties, subject respectively to the jurisdiction of different Contracting States by which the parties to a contract agree to submit to arbitration all or any differences that may arise in connection with such contract relating to commercial matters or to any other matter capable of settlement by arbitration, whether or not the arbitration is to take place in a country to whose jurisdiction none of the parties is subject.

Each Contracting State reserves the right to limit the obligation mentioned above to contracts which are considered as commercial under its national law. Any Contracting State which avails itself of this right will notify the Secretary-General of the League of Nations, in order that the other Contracting States may be so informed.

2. The arbitral procedure, including the constitution of the arbitral tribunal, shall be governed by the will of the parties and by the law of the country in whose territory the arbitration takes place.

The Contracting States agree to facilitate all steps in the procedure which require to be taken in their own territories, in accordance with the provisions of their law governing arbitral procedure applicable to existing differences.

3. Each Contracting State undertakes to ensure the execution by its authorities and in accordance with the provisions of its national laws of arbitral awards made in its own territory under the preceding articles.

4. The tribunals of the Contracting Parties, on being seized of a dispute regarding a contract made between persons to whom Article 1 applies and including an arbitration agreement whether referring to present or future differences which is valid in virtue of the said article and capable of being carried into effect, shall refer the parties on the application of either of them to the decision of the arbitrators.

Such reference shall not prejudice the competence of the judicial tribunals in case the agreement or the arbitration cannot proceed or becomes inoperative.

5. The present Protocol, which shall remain open for signature by all States, shall be ratified. The ratifications shall be deposited as soon as possible with the Secretary-General of the League of Nations, who shall notify such deposit to all the signatory States.

6. The present Protocol shall come into force as soon as two ratifications have been deposited. Thereafter it will take effect, in the case of each Contracting State, one month after the notification by the Secretary-General of the deposit of its ratification.

7. The present Protocol may be denounced by any Contracting State on giving one year's notice. Denunciation shall be effected by a notification addressed to the Secretary-General of the League, who will immediately transmit copies of such notification to all the other signatory States and inform them of the date on which it was received. The denunciation shall take effect one year after on which it was notified to the Secretary-General, and shall operate only in respect of the notifying State.

8. The Contracting States may declare that their acceptance of the present Protocol does not include any or all of the under-mentioned territories: that is to say, their colonies, overseas possessions or territories, protectorates or the territories over which they exercise a mandate.

The said States may subsequently adhere separately on behalf of any territory thus excluded. The Secretary-General of the League of Nations shall be informed as soon as possible of such adhesions. He shall notify such adhesions to all signatory States. They will take effect one month after the notification by the Secretary-General to all signatory States.

The Contracting States may also denounce the Protocol separately on behalf of any of the territories referred to above. Article 7 applies to such denunciation.

SECOND SCHEDULE.
CONVENTION ON THE EXECUTION OF FOREIGN ARBITRAL AWARDS
SIGNED AT GENEVA ON BEHALF OF HIS MAJESTY ON THE TWENTY-
SIXTH DAY OF SEPTEMBER, NINETEEN HUNDRED AND TWENTY-
SEVEN

Article 1

In the territories of any High Contracting Party to which the present Convention applies, an arbitral award made in pursuance of an agreement, whether relating to existing or future differences (herein-after called 'a submission to arbitration') covered by the Protocol on Arbitration Clauses, opened at Geneva on September 24th 1923, shall be recognised as binding and shall be enforced in accordance with the rules of the procedure of the territory where the award is relied upon, provided that the said award has been made in a territory of one of the High Contracting Parties to which the present Convention applies and between persons who are subject to the jurisdiction of one of the High Contracting Parties.

To obtain such recognition or enforcement, it shall, further, be necessary:

(a) That the award has been made in pursuance of a submission to arbitration which is valid under the law applicable thereto;

(b) That the subject-matter of the award is capable of settlement by arbitration under the law of the country in which the award is sought to be relied upon;

(c) That the award has been made by the Arbitral Tribunal provided for in the submission to arbitration or constituted in the manner agreed upon by the parties and in conformity with the law governing the arbitration procedure;

(d) That the award has become final in the country in which it has been made, in the sense that it will not be considered as such if it is open to *opposition, appel* or *pourvoi en cassation* (in the countries where such forms of procedure exist) or if it is proved that any proceedings for the purpose of contesting the validity of the award are pending;

(e) That the recognition or enforcement of the award is not contrary to the public policy or to the principles of the law of the country in which it is sought to be relied upon.

Article 2

Even if the conditions laid down in Article 1 hereof are fulfilled, recognition and enforcement of the award shall be refused if the Court is satisfied:

(a) That the award has been annulled in the country in which it was made;

(b) That the party against whom it is sought to use the award was not given notice of the arbitration proceedings in sufficient time to enable him to present his case; or that being under a legal incapacity, he was not properly represented;

(c) That the award does not deal with the differences contemplated by or falling within the terms of the submission to arbitration or that it contains decisions on matters beyond the scope of the submission to arbitration.

If the award has not covered all the questions submitted to the arbitral tribunal, the competent authority of the country where recognition or enforcement of the award is sought can, if it thinks fit, postpone such recognition or enforcement or grant it subject to such guarantee as that authority may decide.

Article 3

If the party against whom the award has been made proves that under the law governing the arbitration procedure, there is a ground, other than the grounds referred to in Article 1(a) and (c), and Article 2(b) and (c), entitling him to contest the validity of the award in a Court of Law, the Court may, if it thinks fit, either refuse recognition or enforcement of the award or adjourn the consideration thereof, giving such party a reasonable time within which to have the award annulled by the competent tribunal.

Article 4

The party relying upon an award or claiming its enforcement must supply, in particular:

607

(1) The original award or a copy thereof duly authenticated, according to the requirements of the law of the country in which it was made;

(2) Documentary or other evidence to prove that the award has become final, in the sense defined in Article 1(d), in the country in which it was made;

(3) When necessary, documentary or other evidence to prove that the conditions laid down in Article 1, paragraph 1 and paragraph 2(a) and (c), have been fulfilled.

A translation of the award and of the other documents mentioned in this Article into the official language of the country where the award is sought to be relied upon may be demanded. Such translation must be certified correct by a diplomatic or consular agent of the country to which the party who seeks to rely upon the award belongs or by a sworn translator of the country where the award is sought to be relied upon.

Article 5

The provisions of the above Articles shall not deprive any interested party of the right of availing himself of an arbitral award in the manner and to the extent allowed by the law or the treaties of the country where such award is sought to be relied upon.

Article 6

The present Convention applies only to arbitral awards made after the coming into force of the protocol on Arbitral Clauses, opened at Geneva on September 24th 1923.

Article 7

The present Convention, which will remain open to the signature of all the signatories of the Protocol of 1923 on Arbitration Clauses, shall be ratified.

It may be ratified only on behalf of those Members of the League of Nations and non-Member States on whose behalf the Protocol of 1923 shall have been ratified.

Ratifications shall be deposited as soon as possible with the Secretary-General of the League of Nations, who will notify such deposit to all the signatories.

Article 8

The present Convention shall come into force three months after it shall have been ratified on behalf of two High Contracting Parties. Thereafter, it shall take effect, in the case of each High Contracting Party, three months after the deposit of the ratification on its behalf with the Secretary-General of the League of Nations.

Article 9

The present Convention may be denounced on behalf of any Member of the League or non-Member State. Denunciation shall be notified in writing to the Secretary-General of the League of Nations, who will immediately send a copy thereof, certified to be in conformity with the notification, to all the other Contracting Parties, at the same time informing them of the date on which he received it.

The denunciation shall come into force only in respect of the High Contracting Party which shall have notified it and one year after such notification shall have reached the Secretary-General of the League of Nations.

The denunciation of the Protocol on Arbitration Clauses shall entail, ipso facto, the denunciation of the present Convention.

Article 10

The present Convention does not apply to the Colonies, Protectorates or territories under suzerainty or mandate of any High Contracting Party unless they are specially mentioned.

The application of this Convention to one or more of such Colonies, Protectorates or territories to which the Protocol on Arbitration Clauses, opened at Geneva at September 24th 1923, applies, can be effected at any time by means of a declaration addressed to the Secretary-General of the League of Nations by one of the High Contracting Parties.

Such declaration shall take effect three months after the deposit thereof.

The High Contracting Parties can at any time denounce the Convention for all or any of the Colonies, Protectorates or territories referred to above. Article 9 hereof applies to such denunciation.

Article 11

A certified copy of the present Convention shall be transmitted by the Secretary-General of the League of Nations to every Member of the League of Nations and to every non-Member State which signs the same.

Arbitration Act 1979

Judicial review of arbitration awards

1.—(1) In the Arbitration Act 1950 (in this Act referred to as 'the principal Act') section 21 (statement of case for a decision of the High Court) shall cease to have effect and, without prejudice to the right of appeal conferred by subsection (2) below, the High Court shall not have jurisdiction to set aside or remit an award on an arbitration agreement on the ground of errors of fact or law on the face of the award.

(2) Subject to subsection (3) below, an appeal shall lie to the High Court on any question of law arising out of an award made on an arbitration agreement; and on the determination of such an appeal the High Court may by order—

    (a) confirm, vary or set aside the award; or

    (b) remit the award to the reconsideration of the arbitrator or umpire together with the court's opinion on the question of law which was the subject of the appeal;

and where the award is remitted under paragraph (b) above the arbitrator or umpire shall, unless the order otherwise directs, make his award within three months after the date of the order.

(3) An appeal under this section may be brought by any of the parties to the reference—

    (a) with the consent of all the other parties to the reference; or

    (b) subject to section 3 below, with the leave of the court.

(4) The High Court shall not grant leave under subsection (3)(b) above unless it considers that, having regard to all the circumstances, the determination of the question of law concerned could substantially affect the rights of one or more of the parties to the arbitration agreement; and the court may make any leave which it gives conditional upon the applicant complying with such conditions as it considers appropriate.

(5) Subject to subsection (6) below, if an award is made and, on an application made by any of the parties to the reference—

    (a) with the consent of all the other parties to the reference, or

    (b) subject to section 3 below, with the leave of the court,

it appears to the High Court that the award does not or does not sufficiently set out the reasons for the award, the court may order the arbitrator or umpire concerned to state the reasons for his award in sufficient detail to enable the court, should an appeal be brought under this section, to consider any question of law arising out of the award.

(6) In any case where an award is made without any reason being given, the High Court shall not make an order under subsection (5) above unless it is satisfied—

    (a) that before the award was made one of the parties to the reference gave notice to the arbitrator or umpire concerned that a reasoned award would be required; or

    (b) that there is some special reason why such a notice was not given.

(6A) Unless the High Court gives leave, no appeal shall lie to the Court of Appeal from a decision of the High Court—

    (a) to grant or refuse leave under subsection 3(b) or 5(b) above; or

    (b) to make or not to make an order under subsection (5) above.

(7) No appeal shall lie to the Court of Appeal from a decision of the High Court on an appeal under this section unless—

    (a) the High Court or the Court of Appeal gives leave; and

    (b) it is certified by the High Court that the question of law to which its decision relates either is one of general public importance or is one which for some other special reason should be considered by the Court of Appeal.

611

(8) Where the award of an arbitrator or umpire is varied on appeal, the award as varied shall have effect (except for the purposes of this section) as if it were the award of the arbitrator or umpire.

Note: Sub-s. (6A) was added by s. 148(2) of the Supreme Court Act 1981.

Determination of preliminary point of law by court

2.—(1) Subject to subsection (2) and section 3 below, on an application to the High Court made by any of the parties to a reference—
  (a) with the consent of an arbitrator who has entered on the reference or, if an umpire has entered on the reference, with his consent, or
  (b) with the consent of all the other parties,
the High Court shall have jurisdiction to determine any question of law arising in the course of the reference.
  (2) The High Court shall not entertain an application under subsection (1)(a) above with respect to any question of law unless it is satisfied that—
  (a) the determination of the application might produce substantial savings in costs to the parties; and
  (b) the question of law is one in respect of which leave to appeal would be likely to be given under section 1(3)(b) above.
  (2A) Unless the High Court gives leave, no appeal shall lie to the Court of Appeal from a decision of the High Court to entertain or not to entertain an application under subsection 1(a) above.
  (3) A decision of the High Court under [sub-section (1) above] shall be deemed to be a judgment of the court within the meaning of section [16 of the Supreme Courts Act 1981] (appeals to the Court of Appeal), but no appeal shall lie from such a decision unless—
  (a) the High Court or the Court of Appeal gives leave; and
  (b) it is certified by the High Court that the question of law to which its decision relates either is one of general public importance or is one which for some other special reason should be considered by the Court of Appeal.

Note: The words in square brackets were substituted by the Supreme Court Act 1981, s. 148(3) and Sch. 5. S. 148 of that Act added sub-s. (2A).

Exclusion agreements affecting rights under sections 1 and 2

3.—(1) Subject to the following provisions of this section and section 4 below—
  (a) the High Court shall not, under section 1(3)(b) above, grant leave to appeal with respect to a question of law arising out of an award, and
  (b) the High Court shall not, under section 1(5)(b) above, grant leave to make an application with respect to an award, and
  (c) no application may be made under section 2(1)(a) above with respect to a question of law,
if the parties to the reference in question have entered into an agreement in writing (in this section referred to as an 'exclusion agreement') which excludes the right of appeal under section 1 above in relation to that award or, in a case falling within paragraph (c) above, in relation to an award to which the determination of the question of law is material.
  (2) An exclusion agreement may be expressed so as to relate to a particular award, to awards under a particular reference or to any other description of awards, whether arising out of the same reference or not; and an agreement may be an exclusion agreement for the purposes of this section whether it is entered into before or after the passing of this Act and whether or not it forms part of an arbitration agreement.
  (3) In any case where—
  (a) an arbitration agreement, other than a domestic arbitration agreement, provides for disputes between the parties to be referred to arbitration, and
  (b) a dispute to which the agreement relates involves the question whether a party has been guilty of fraud, and
  (c) the parties have entered into an exclusion agreement which is applicable to any award made on the reference to that dispute,
then, except in so far as the exclusion agreement otherwise provides, the High Court shall not exercise its

powers under section 24(2) of the principal Act (to take steps necessary to enable the question to be determined by the High Court) in relation to that dispute.

(4) Except as provided by subsection (1) above, sections 1 and 2 shall have effect notwithstanding anything in any agreement purporting—

(a) to prohibit or restrict access to the High Court; or

(b) to restrict the jurisdiction of that court; or

(c) to prohibit or restrict the making of a reasoned award.

(5) An exclusion agreement shall be of no effect in relation to an award made on, or a question of law arising in the course of a reference under, a statutory arbitration, that is to say, such an arbitration as is referred to in subsection (1) of section 31 of the principal Act.

(6) An exclusion agreement shall be of no effect in relation to an award made on, or a question of law arising in the course of a reference under, an arbitration agreement which is a domestic arbitration agreement unless the exclusion agreement is entered into after the commencement of the arbitration in which the award is made or, as the case may be, in which the question of law arises.

(7) In this section 'domestic arbitration agreement' means an arbitration agreement which does not provide, expressly or by implication, for arbitration in a State other than the United Kingdom and to which neither—

(a) an individual who is a national of, or habitually resident in, any State other than the United Kingdom, nor

(b) a body corporate which is incorporated in, or whose central management and control is exercised in, any State other than the United Kingdom,

is a party at the time the arbitration agreement is entered into.

Exclusion agreements not to apply in certain cases

4.—(1) Subject to subsection (3) below, if an arbitration award or a question of law arising in the course of a reference relates, in whole or in part, to—

(a) a question or claim falling within the Admiralty jurisdiction of the High Court, or

(b) a dispute arising out of a contract of insurance, or

(c) a dispute arising out of a commodity contract,

an exclusion agreement shall have no effect in relation to the award or question unless either—

(i) the exclusion agreement is entered into after the commencement of the arbitration in which the award is made or, as the case may be, in which the question of law arises, or

(ii) the award or question relates to a contract which is expressed to be governed by law other than the law of England and Wales.

(2) In subsection (1)(c) above 'commodity contract' means a contract—

(a) for the sale of goods regularly dealt with on a commodity market or exchange in England or Wales which is specified for the purposes of this section by an order made by the Secretary of State; and

(b) of a description so specified.

(3) The Secretary of State may by order provide that subsection (1) above—

(a) shall cease to have effect; or

(b) subject to such conditions as may be specified in the order, shall not apply to any exclusion agreement made in relation to an arbitration award of a description so specified;

and an order under this subsection may contain such supplementary, incidental ·and transitional provisions as appear to the Secretary of State to be necessary or expedient.

(4) The power to make an order under subsection (2) or subsection (3) above shall be exercisable by statutory instrument which shall be subject to annulment in pursuance of a resolution of either House of Parliament.

(5) In this section 'exclusion agreement' has the same meaning as in section 3 above.

Interlocutory orders

5.—(1) If any party to a reference under an arbitration agreement fails within the time specified in the order or, if no time is so specified, within a reasonable time to comply with an order made by the arbitrator or umpire in the course of the reference, then, on the application of the arbitrator or umpire or of any party to the reference, the High Court may make an order extending the powers of the arbitrator or umpire as mentioned in subsection (2) below.

(2) If an order is made by the High Court under this section, the arbitrator or umpire shall have power, to the extent and subject to any conditions specified in that order, to continue with the reference in default of appearance or of any other act by one of the parties in like manner as a judge of the High Court might continue with proceedings in that court where a party fails to comply with an order of that court or a requirement of rules of court.

(3) Section 4(5) of the Administration of Justice Act 1970 (jurisdiction of the High Court to be exercisable by the Court of Appeal in relation to judge-arbitrators and judge-umpires) shall not apply in relation to the power of the High Court to make an order under this section, but in the case of a reference to a judge-arbitrator or judge-umpire that power shall be exercisable as in the case of any other reference to arbitration and also by the judge-arbitrator or judge-umpire himself.

(4) Anything done by a judge-arbitrator or judge-umpire in the exercise of the power conferred by subsection (3) above shall be done by him in his capacity as judge of the High Court and have effect as if done by that court.

(5) The preceding provisions of this section have effect notwithstanding anything in any agreement but do not derogate from any powers conferred on an arbitrator or umpire, whether by an arbitration agreement or otherwise.

(6) In this section 'judge-arbitrator' and 'judge-umpire' have the same meaning as in Schedule 3 to the Administration of Justice Act 1970.

Minor amendments relating to awards and appointments of arbitrators and umpires

6.—(1) In subsection (1) of section 8 of the principal Act (agreements where reference is to two arbitrators deemed to include provision that the arbitrators shall appoint an umpire immediately after their own appointment)—

  (a) for the words 'shall appoint an umpire immediately' there shall be substituted the words 'may appoint an umpire at any time'; and
  (b) at the end there shall be added the words 'and shall do so forthwith if they cannot agree'.

(2) For section 9 of the principal Act (agreements for reference to three arbitrators) there shall be substituted the following section:

'Majority award of three arbitrators

9. Unless the contrary intention is expressed in the arbitration agreement, in any case where there is a reference to three arbitrators, the award of any two of the arbitrators shall be binding.'

(3) In section 10 of the principal Act (power of court in certain cases to appoint an arbitrator or umpire) in paragraph (c) after the word 'are', in the first place where it occurs, there shall be inserted the words 'required or are' in the words from 'or where' to the end of the paragraph shall be omitted.

(4) At the end of section 10 of the principal Act there shall be added the following subsection—

  '(2) In any case where—
    (a) an arbitration agreement provides for the appointment of an arbitration or umpire by a person who is neither one of the parties nor an existing arbitrator (whether the provision applies directly or in default of agreement by the parties or otherwise), and
    (b) that person refuses to make the appointment or does not make it within the time specified in the agreement or, if no time is so specified, within a reasonable time,
  any party to the agreement may serve the person in question with a written notice to appoint an arbitrator or umpire and, if the appointment is not made within seven clear days after the service of the notice, the High Court or a judge thereof may, on the application of the party who gave the notice, appoint an arbitrator or umpire who shall have the like powers to act in the reference and make an award as if he had been appointed in accordance with the terms of the agreement.'

Application and interpretation of certain provisions of Part I of principal Act

7.—(1) References in the following provisions of Part I of the principal Act to that Part of that Act shall have effect as if the preceding provisions of this Act were included in that Part, namely,—

  (a) section 14 (interim awards);
  (b) section 28 (terms as to costs of orders);
  (c) section 30 (Crown to be bound);
  (d) section 31 (application to statutory arbitration); and
  (e) section 32 (meaning of 'arbitration agreement').

614

(2) Subsections (2) and (3) of section 29 of the principal Act shall apply to determine when an arbitration is deemed to be commenced for the purposes of this Act.

(3) For the avoidance of doubts, it is hereby declared that the reference in subsection (1) of section 31 of the principal Act (statutory arbitrations) to arbitration under any other Act does not extend to arbitration under section 92 of the County Courts Act 1959 (cases in which proceedings are to be or may be referred to arbitration) and accordingly nothing in this Act or in Part I of the principal Act applies to arbitration under the said section 92.

Short title, commencement, repeals and extent

8.—(1) This Act may be cited as the Arbitration Act 1979.

(2) This Act shall come into operation on such day as the Secretary of State may appoint by order made by statutory instrument; and such an order—

    (a) may appoint different days for different provisions of this Act and for the purposes of the operation of the same provision in relation to different descriptions of arbitration agreement; and

    (b) may contain such supplementary, incidental and transitional provisions as appear to the Secretary of State to be necessary or expedient.

(3) In consequence of the preceding provisions of this Act, the following provisions are hereby repealed, namely—

    (a) in paragraph (c) of section 10 of the principal Act the words from 'or where' to the end of the paragraph;

    (b) section 21 of the principal Act;

    (c) in paragraph 9 of Schedule 3 to the Administration of Justice Act 1970, in subparagraph (1) the words '21(1) and (2)' and subparagraph (2).

(4) This Act forms part of the law of England and Wales only.

Arbitration Bill 1996—A Commentary

(The text of the Bill, and a Table of Destinations and Derivations, follows this Commentary)

INTRODUCTION

Recent moves toward codifying and amending English arbitration law date back to 1989, when the Departmental Advisory Committee on Arbitration Law, chaired by Lord Mustill, recommended the adoption of a new Arbitration Act incorporating many of the existing features of existing law but expressed in a more user-friendly fashion and resolving uncertainties. The impetus for these recommendations had been the adoption by UNCITRAL of a Model Law, which many countries had either implemented or had stated their intention to implement. The 1989 DAC report came out against the wholesale adoption of the Model Law, as the DAC regarded English law as superior in a number of respects (in addition to being too well established to justify gratuitous modification), but nevertheless recognised that, wherever possible, English law should be brought into line with the Model Law. The Goverment, despite having accepted the report, took no action to proceed matters, and it was left to the private initiative of a group of arbitrators and practising lawyers headed by Arthur Marriott to produce a draft bill, which was circulated for comment in 1992. The Bill did not make dramatic alterations to the law, but had the overriding benefit of clarity, and the DAC, by this time chaired by Lord Steyn, recommended that the Government should take up the initiative and produce its own Bill based upon the work done by Marriott.

In February 1994 the DTI published its own Bill, which was circulated for consultation. The 1994 Bill was rather bolder than the Marriott Bill in emphasising the rights of the parties to an arbitration agreement to fix their own procedures, and demonstrated a clear intention to move closer to the Model Law than the 1989 DAC had thought appropriate. The general view on consultation was, however, that the Bill did not go far enough in "deregulating" arbitration proceedings, and number of important points of principle (e.g. of the enforceability "equity clauses") were left unresolved. In the wake of these comments, the 1994 Bill was shelved, but the reform process was not allowed to fade away. In July 1995 the DAC, now under the chairmanship of Lord Justice Saville, published a new Arbitration Bill with commentary on its various clauses. A short consultation period was allowed, with the Government making it clear that it would legislate provided that there was substantial agreement amongst consultees on the proposed wording. The July 1995 Bill had three objectives:

(a) to restate the law in a clear and accessible way, making it readily understandable to all actual and potential users;

(b) to introduce measures which speed up and reduce the costs of the arbitration process, in particular by limiting recourse to the courts both during and after the proceedings;

(c) to increase the scope of party autonomy, allowing the parties, and in default, the arbitrators, to determine the course of the arbitration.

The July 1995 Bill witnessed an even closer move towards the Model Law, but did not go as far as wholesale adoption.

The consultation process saw evidence from a wide range of interested parties, including government departments who had not previously been involved in the process. It was clear that a wholesale redrafting of the July 1995 Bill was required before draft legislation could be presented to Parliament. Fears that the Government might not be prepared to devote the necessary resources to this enterprise proved to be unfounded, and in December 1995 the official wording of Arbitration Bill was published and received its first reading in the House of Lords. The December 1995 Bill embodied the majority of the principles originally proposed in the July 1995 Bill, but substantial drafting changes were made and some important policy changes were introduced. The most important was the December 1995 Bill's move away from the autonomy of the parties and towards the autonomy of the arbitrators in determining the procedure to be adopted. Doubtless many changes, largely technical but some substantive, will be made to the Bill as it undergoes its Parliamentary journey, and it is anticipated at the time of writing, in February 1996, that there will be an Arbitration Act 1996 by the summer of 1996. The following commentary is on the version of the Bill published in February 1996, and closely follows the published ordering of sections, which is, fortunately, logical.

SCOPE OF THE BILL

Unusually for an Act of Parliament, cl 1 of the Bill sets out its stated principles, and confers upon them an overriding importance in that the Bill is to be construed by the courts with these principles in mind. They are:

(a) the object of arbitration is to obtain the fair resolution of disputes by an impartial tribunal without unnecessary delay or expense;

(b) the parties should be free to agree how their disputes are resolved, subject only to such safeguards as are necessary in the public interest;

(c) in matters governed by the Bill, the court should not intervene unless empowered to do so.

The courts do not, therefore, have any residual powers of intervention, and in the case of doubt arbitrators may resolve any procedural difficulty as they think fit without fear of being challenged unless their conduct amounts to "serious irregularity". Where a matter has to be referred to court, the Bill restricts delays by appeals from the court's ruling, by requiring the leave of the judge for any appeal to be made.

The Bill applies to an arbitration agreement if a number of conditions are met. First, the agreement must be in writing (cl 5), and it may incorporate standard arbitration terms. The law is unchanged on this point from s 32 of the 1950 Act, although it is now made clear that mere written evidence of an agreement is enough, and that an exchange of written submissions in arbitral or legal proceedings in which the existence of an agreement is alleged by one party and not denied by the other may constitute an arbitration agreement. Arbitrators are thus free to hold the arbitration in accordance with the terms of the Bill once the existence of an agreement has been acknowledged by both sides in their exchanges. As is the case under the 1950 Act, an oral arbitration agreement, assuming that its existence can be proved, is binding as a result of the saving provision in cl 81, but the Bill does not govern it, which means that the rights and duties of the parties and the arbitrators depend upon the uncertain rules of the common law: an arbitrator would be well advised to obtain an agreement in writing from the parties where no other record exists. Secondly, there must be sufficient connection with England, Wales or Northern Ireland (Scotland has its own legislation based on the Model Law) under English conflict of laws rules (cl 2). In practical terms, this means that the Bill will apply where English law has been chosen or is otherwise the law governing the arbitration agreement (which will be the case where the matter is a purely domestic one), or where the seat of the arbitration is in England, Wales or Northern Ireland. The seat of an arbitration is a new concept in legislation, although it had been afforded earlier judicial recognition, and the definition in cl 3 makes it clear that the seat is not necessarily the place in which the arbitrators actually hold their hearings, but is the focal point of the arbitration: arbitrators who decide to travel to another jurisdiction to inspect property or to hear evidence do not thereby take the arbitration outside the Bill. The seat is of particular significance, in that the seat is the place which determines where the award is made under cl 53, a provision discussed below. Thirdly, the Bill is, under cl 4, primarily a default provision. Some parts of the Bill, listed in Sched 1, apply irrespective of the wishes of the parties, on wider public policy grounds (e.g. the power of the court to remove arbitrators, the immunity of arbitrators and enforcement of arbitration awards), while the remainder of the Bill applies only where the parties have themselves failed to reach any agreement on the point in question. In conducting the arbitration, the arbitrators must, therefore, having satisfied themselves that the issue is not one governed by the mandatory provisions of the Bill, look in the first instance to what the parties have actually agreed, provided that the agreement is in writing (as oral agreements on any issue are to be disregarded under cl 5), and only then to the default provisions of the Bill.

PARALLEL JUDICIAL PROCEEDINGS

Clause 6 of the Bill makes a major change to the law. Under the Arbitration Acts 1950, s 4, and 1975, s 1, where a party to an arbitration agreement commenced judicial proceedings on an issue falling within the arbitration agreement, and the other sought a stay of the judicial proceedings so that the matter could proceed to arbitration, a distinction was drawn between domestic (UK parties only) and non-domestic agreements (one or more non-UK parties). In the case of a non-domestic agreement, the court was required to stay its own proceedings providing that it was satisfied that the dispute fell within the scope of the arbitration agreement and that the agreement was otherwise valid, and providing also that the party seeking a stay had not submitted to the jurisdiction of the court by taking a step in the proceedings other than in contesting the court's jurisdiction. By contrast, in the case of a domestic arbitration agreement, the court possessed an overriding discretion to refuse a stay where sufficient reason could be shown. The July 1995 Bill re-enacted this basic structure in a simpler form, but consultation on that Bill demonstrated a possible problem in distinguishing between domestic and non-domestic agreements, as that distinction treated UK nationals differently from nationals from other parts of the EC: the Treaty of Rome prevents discrimination on the grounds of nationality. Faced with possible infringement of the Treaty of Rome, or alternatively with drawing an awkward distinction between EC agreements (where all the parties are EC nationals) and non-EC agreements, the Government chose a middle approach. The Bill, in cl 86, retains the existing distinction between domestic and non-domestic agreement and the right of the court to refuse to stay its own proceedings in the case of a

619

domestic agreement. However, cl 88 confers upon the Government the power to repeal or modify cl 86 in order to remove this distinction.

The present effect of cl 9 is, therefore, that in the case of a non-domestic agreement a court will automatically stay its own proceedings once satisfied that there is a valid and applicable arbitration clause in existence and that there has been no submission to the judicial proceedings by the party seeking to stay them. In the case of a domestic agreement, the court retains a residual discretion to refuse to stay where there are sufficient grounds for not requiring the parties to go to arbitration, but this discretion is likely to be removed in due course.

The obligation of the court to stay its own proceedings is extended, by cl 10 (re-enacting in clearer form s 5 of the 1950 Act), to interpleader cases, i.e. where party A holds property or money the ownership of which is contested by B and C: an arbitration agreement between any of the parties is to be honoured. Clause 11, again a re-enactment (of s 26 of the Civil Jurisdiction and Judgments Act 1982), applies to Admiralty proceedings in respect of which a vessel has been arrested by the claimant, the proceedings then being stayed for determination by arbitration: here, the court has the power to order the arrest to continue in force, or for equivalent security to be provided by the respondent, pending the outcome of the arbitration.

COMMENCEMENT OF ARBITRATION PROCEEDINGS

The manner in which, and the time by which, an arbitration is to be commenced is important for two reasons: the arbitration agreement itself may lay down contractual requirements for these points, upon which the jurisdiction of the arbitrators depends; and the Limitation Act 1980 (which applies to arbitration proceedings under cl 13, a re-enactment of s 34 of the Limitation Act 1980) requires proceedings to be commenced within six years of the defendant's breach of contract. In the absence of any agreement as to how and when an arbitration commences, cl 14 for the first time lays down general default provisions for both contractual and statutory limitation purposes, and these are vital in assisting the arbitrators to decide whether they may proceed with the arbitration. In the case of a named arbitrator, the arbitration commences when one party writes to the other requesting his submission to the jurisdiction of that arbitrator. If the arbitrators are to be appointed by the parties, the arbitration commences when one party serves written notice on the other requiring that other to appoint his arbitrator. Finally, if the arbitrator is to be appointed by a third party, the arbitration commences when one party serves written notice on that party asking him to make the appointment.

If the commencement of the proceedings is time-barred by the Limitation Act 1980, the arbitrators are free to hear the case provided that no objection is taken by the respondent: if he does object, he has an absolute defence and the arbitrators must deny jurisdiction. By contrast, if the arbitration has been commenced within the statutory limitation period but outside any shorter period agreed by the parties, while the arbitrators are themselves required to deny jurisdiction, the applicant may seek, under cl 12 (re-enacting s 27 of the 1950 Act), an order from the court extending the time laid down in the contract. It remains the case under the Bill that the applicant may seek a court order extending the contractual time for bringing the claim or commencing arbitration, but there are two important modifications. First, cl 12 applies to a time limit relating to the commencement of preliminary dispute resolution proceedings, which must be exhausted prior to arbitration, whereas s 27 did not. In the case of a rent review clause in a lease, for example, the landlord may be obliged to propose a new rent within a

620

given period, and there is to be arbitration in the absence of agreement: it is possible that cl 12 applies to the time limit open to the landlord for proposing the new rent and thus bringing the procedure into play. Secondly, under s 27, the court could extend time where a refusal to do so would result in "undue hardship": this was a flexible concept, and the practice of the court had become to give leave generously, e.g. because a large amount of money was at stake. The new clause tightens the requirements for an order extending time, and requires either the occurrence of circumstances outside the contemplation of the parties when the agreement was entered into, or conduct by one party which makes it unjust to hold the other to the agreement. Mere oversight which has extreme consequences will no longer be enough.

THE ARBITRAL TRIBUNAL

Appointment

The rules in the 1950 Act concerning the appointment and removal of the arbitrators are clarified by the Bill, in order to save time and cost, by, wherever possible, substituting voluntary procedures for applications to the court. The presumption in s 6 of the 1950 Act that, in the absence of agreement the tribunal shall consist of a sole arbitrator, is preserved by cl 15. The clause makes provision, for the first time, of the position which prevails where the parties have agreed that an even number of arbitrators is to be appointed (most commonly, where each party is to appoint his own arbitrator) but have failed to stipulate how any deadlock is to be broken. Under s 8 of the 1950 Act, the arbitrators were empowered to appoint an umpire to resolve the dispute in the event that they disagreed on the substance of the dispute. Clause 15, by contrast, requires the arbitrators to appoint a third arbitrator—who is to act as chairman—"forthwith" following their own appointments. The difference is, of course, that the arbitrators are then to reach their decision by majority voting, whereas an umpire is to resolve any issues alone. The Bill leaves it open to the parties to stipulate that an umpire instead of a chairman is to be appointed, or alternatively that there is to be no umpire or chairman-arbitrator: if in the latter case there is an even number of arbitrators, and there is deadlock, cl 22 rather unhelpfully states that any decisions, orders or awards are to be made by all or a majority of arbitrators. The view apparently taken is that if the parties have specifically provided for potential deadlock, they must live with the consequences if this occurs.

The provisions of cll 16 to 19 of the Bill for the appointment of arbitrators are straightforward and, unlike the Arbitration Act 1950, draw a clear distinction between the initial appointment of arbitrators and the appointment of substitutes where a vacancy arises. Turning first to initial appointment, cl 16 lays down the familiar principle that the procedure is to be agreed by the parties, failing which various default rules are laid down. Separate default rules are laid down for:

    (a) sole arbitrators (joint appointment within 28 days of a request by one party for an appointment to be made);

    (b) two arbitrators (each party to make an appointment within 14 days of a request by the other, with a third chairman-arbitrator to be appointed by the arbitrators forthwith unless the parties have agreed to the contrary—see above);

    (c) three arbitrators (each party to make an appointment within 14 days of a request by the other, with the third chairman-arbitrator to be appointed by the arbitrators forthwith); and

    (d) two arbitrators and an umpire (each party to make an appointment within 14 days of a request by the other, with the umpire to be appointed by the arbitrators at the very latest before the proceedings have commenced—under s 8 of the 1950 Act, an umpire had to be appointed only after the arbitrators had failed to agree, with the arbitrators merely being empowered, as opposed to required, to make an earlier appointment).

Clauses 17 and 18 govern the failure of the appointment procedure due to the inactivity of any person required to appoint or to agree to the appointment of an arbitrator. Clause 17 deals with the case in which the parties agree that each is to appoint an arbitrator, and one of them fails to do so: here, the party who has appointed an arbitrator is, as was the case under ss 7 and 10 of the Arbitration Act 1950, entitled to have his arbitrator treated as sole arbitrator subject to an appeal to the court by the other party. In other cases—most importantly, where the parties have agreed that a sole arbitrator should be appointed but have failed to agree as to whom that should be, or where the authority to make an appointment was vested in a third party who has failed to act—it is necessary for an application to be made to the court under cl 18. On application, the court is empowered to give directions as to how an appointment is to be made, or it may make any necessary appointments itself: in exercising its cl 18 powers, the court is required by cl 19 to take into account any agreement reached by the parties as to the qualifications of arbitrators.

Chairman and umpire

The Bill for the first time gives statutory recognition to the office of chairman. A chairman is to be appointed by the arbitrators either where the parties so require, or where the parties have agreed that there are to be two arbitrators only (in which case cl 16 steps in to require such an appointment, subject to agreement to the contrary). Under cl 20, the chairman merely has a casting vote, but does have the right to make procedural decisions and to issue the award itself in the absence of a majority in favour of a particular approach. The Bill does not indicate whether, without the agreement of the parties, the entire panel is entitled to delegate decision-making powers to the chairman: this plainly cannot be done in relation to the award itself, but it is arguable that this can be done in relation to procedural aspects of the arbitration.

Clause 21, as compared with s 8 of the 1950 Act, extends the role of the umpire. In accordance with the philosophy of the Bill, the parties are free to agree the role of the umpire, and in particular at what point he is to attend hearings and to replace the arbitrators. In the absence of express agreement, the umpire is to be appointed by the arbitrators prior to the hearing taking place, and is entitled to attend the proceedings as if he had entered on the reference. However, it is only when the arbitrators have failed to agree that the arbitrator replaces them and takes over the proceedings. Clause 21 reflects the long-standing practice of appointing the umpire at an early stage and requiring him to attend the entire proceedings, so that, if the arbitrators do disagree, there does not have to be a fresh hearing in front of the umpire. Clause 28 of the Bill also removes the doubt as to whether an umpire can recover remuneration for the period during which he has attended proceedings but has not entered on the reference: the umpire is to be treated in the same way as an arbitrator for that period.

Revocation of authority and removal

The services of arbitrators can be dispensed with in two ways: revocation of their authority by the person who appointed them; and removal by the court. Under s 1 of the 1950 Act an arbitrator's authority could, in the absence of the agreement of all of the parties, be revoked only with the leave of the court, and it remained uncertain just when the court would give its

622

leave. Clause 23 overcomes any doubts by removing the power of the court to give leave, the result being that the authority of an arbitrator can be revoked only by the joint action of the parties, agreed in writing: under cl 26, not even the death of the appointing party operates as a revocation of his arbitrator's authority unless the contrary is agreed. If the parties are not in agreement that authority should be revoked, the only method of dispensing with an arbitrator is removal, under cl 24.

There are four grounds upon which an arbitrator may be removed: these are based partly upon the 1950 Act, and partly upon judicial authority. The grounds are: justifiable doubts as to impartiality; lack of qualifications required by the arbitration agreement; physical or mental incapability to conduct the arbitration (this appears to be a new ground); and failure to conduct the proceedings properly or with reasonable despatch, giving rise to substantial injustice. To avoid delay, arbitration proceedings may continue while an application for removal is being heard.

An arbitrator who is removed will almost certainly have been in breach of contract, although insofar as his breach consists of acts done or omitted in the purported discharge of his functions, he is immune from suit under cl 29 (see below). For this reason, cl 24 gives the court, on removing the arbitrator, the power to make such order as it thinks fit with regard to his entitlement to fees and expenses, whether paid or not. A similar power to strip an arbitrator of his fees and expenses was contained in s 13 of the 1950 Act, but applied only in the situation where the arbitrator had failed to act with reasonable despatch.

Resignation

An arbitrator who resigns without the consent of the parties is, ill health or incapacity aside, likely to be in breach of contract, and is liable for damages accordingly. Such damages may be extensive, as it could prove necessary for a fresh hearing before a reconstituted panel to be held, and the arbitrator is potentially liable for the costs involved in all of this. In addition, fees and expenses may be forfeited. An arbitrator may nevertheless have good reason for resignation. It may be, for example, that the parties have, by dilatory conduct, prolonged the proceedings unduly. Alternatively, the parties may have determined a procedure for the arbitration which the arbitrator regards himself as unqualified to conduct (although this is less likely than is presently the case, given the provisions of cl 34, which allow the arbitrators to fix the procedure—see below). Accordingly, an entirely new provision, cl 25, states that where an arbitrator resigns, he may apply to the court for relief from any liability which his resignation would otherwise have attracted, and for an order in respect of his fees and expenses. If the court is of the view that the arbitrator's resignation was reasonable, it may grant the relief and order sought. It is unclear who pays the costs of such an application, particularly where it is unsuccessful.

Replacement arbitrators

Under cl 27 of the Bill, a casual vacancy for an arbitrator, due to removal, resignation or death, is to be filled in the manner agreed by the parties. In default of agreement, the vacancy is to be filled in the same way as the original appointment was made: this clarification of the law is most welcome. Clause 27 also permits the arbitration panel, when reconstituted, to decide what proportion, if any, of the earlier proceedings should stand. It will be noted that the matter is for the arbitrators and not the parties to decide.

THE IMMUNITY OF ARBITRATORS

The common law has, perhaps grudgingly, recognised the immunity of arbitrators from suit, unless they have acted in bad faith. The immunity is based primarily upon the fact that, for an action to be brought, it will be necessary to reopen the arbitration proceedings to determine whether there has been any culpable conduct on the part of the arbitrators. The common law immunity is codified by cl 29, which provides that an arbitrator is not liable for any act or omission in purported discharge of his functions as arbitrator. Liability may, however, attach where the arbitrator has totally failed to act, or where he has acted in bad faith. Immunity is, by cl 74, extended to an arbitral or other institution or person who has accepted an obligation to appoint an arbitrator for the parties: such a person is not responsible for any act or omission of his own in purported discharge of his functions (so that a negligent appointment will not attract liability) nor for any act or omission of the arbitrator. There is the usual bad faith exception, and an exception where the person has totally failed to act. The conferring of immunity settles a point which has been much debated but, until the Bill, not resolved.

JURISDICTION OF THE ARBITRATION TRIBUNAL

The Bill's provisions on jurisdiction of the arbitrators introduce major changes into existing practice. The starting point is cl 7, which provides that an arbitration clause has an existence independent of the agreement to which it relates. Confirming earlier case law, cl 7 clears the way to permitting arbitrators to act under an arbitration clause even though the main agreement to which the clause relates has come to an end, e.g. because it has been terminated for alleged breach, or where the existence of the main agreement is denied on the grounds, e.g., of want of consensus, illegality or avoidance for misrepresentation. It will be appreciated that a ruling on any of these matters requires the arbitrators to determine their own jurisdiction, for if there is no binding main agreement there can be nothing to arbitrate about. Whether arbitrators have such power is dependent upon the arbitration agreement itself. The right of the arbitrators to rule on their own jurisdiction is extended by cl 30, which provides that, subject to contrary agreement, the arbitrators can rule upon:

    (a) the validity of the arbitration clause itself;
    (b) the validity of the constitution of the arbitration tribunal, e.g. whether the arbitrators meet the parties' qualifications requirements;
    (c) what matters have been submitted to arbitration.

The 1950 Act did not deal with this question at all, and it was left to the common law to lay down the implications of a decision by the arbitrators that they possessed jurisdiction over the matters before them. In essence, a party who wished to contest such jurisdiction could press the arbitrators to make an interim award on jurisdiction, and then to appeal against the award. Alternatively, or if they refused to make an interim award, he could:

    (i) appear in the proceedings under protest, reserving his right to challenge the award on jurisdictional grounds;
    (ii) refuse to appear and risk a default award against him, but to challenge the ultimate award if it was not favourable to him; or
    (iii) at any stage before, during or after the proceedings seek a declaration from the court as to the arbitrators' jurisdiction.

The Bill, by contrast, establishes set procedures for challenging jurisdictional rulings. The relevant principles are contained in cl 31, 32, 67, 72 and 73, and may be summarised in the following way:

    (a) Where a jurisdictional point arises, the arbitrators are entitled to determine whether they have jurisdiction (cl 30), although they can presumably also refuse to do so and leave the matter to be resolved by the courts.

    (b) If the arbitrators choose to deal with the jurisdiction point, and neither party takes objection to this, a decision by them that they possess jurisdiction is binding: the right to object is lost under cl 73 unless the party seeking to object can show that he did not know and could not have discovered that there was a jurisdictional problem.

    (c) Where a party wishes to challenge the jurisdiction of the arbitrators, he has alternative approaches open to him.

        (1) He may refuse to participate in the proceedings, and may seek an injunction or declaration (cl 72).

        (2) He may refuse to participate in the proceedings, wait for the award to be made, and then challenge the award under the general provisions of cl 67, which allow an award to be challenged for want of substantive jurisdiction (cl 72).

        (3) He may participate in the arbitration proceedings, having raised an objection on jurisdictional grounds no later than the time at which he takes the first step in the proceedings, or as soon as possible after the issue arises in the course of the proceedings, although the arbitrators can extend the time in appropriate circumstances.

    (d) Where there has been an objection to jurisdiction under (c)(3) above, a number of possibilities arise. The arbitrators must do what is agreed as between the parties, but in the absence of agreement the following is the range of possibilities in cl 31.

        (1) The arbitrators may proceed to hear the entire dispute, and to make a ruling on jurisdiction in the final award, in which case the objecting party may challenge the award for want of jurisdiction under cl 67.

        (2) The arbitrators may make a ruling on their jurisdiction by award, in which case the award may be challenged under cl 67.

        (3) The arbitrators may refer the matter to the court for a preliminary ruling under cl 32. A party may not himself make an application under cl 32 unless the other party agrees or unless the arbitrators grant their permission. In the absence of the agreement of all of the parties, the court has jurisdiction to make a preliminary ruling only if it is satisfied that such a ruling would produce substantial savings in costs, that the application was made without delay and there is good reason why the matter should be dealt with by the court. The arbitrators may stay the proceedings or allow them to continue while the application is made, and in the latter case they may proceed to an award on the merits of the case.

REMUNERATION

There is little in the Arbitration Act 1950 on the remuneration of arbitrators. The effect of ss 18 and 19 of that Act was that: (i) if the remuneration or the method of its calculation has been agreed in advance between the parties and the arbitrators, the agreement is binding; (ii) in the absence of agreement, the arbitrators could fix their own remuneration in the award itself, or leave the matter to be determined by the court—in the former case, the sum fixed by the arbitrators was for all practical purposes subject to challenge only where the arbitrators insisted upon payment as a condition of the release of the award, in which case the court was entitled to tax the remuneration. The Bill sets out a number of principles governing the fixing of remuneration, in cll 28 and 56, which re-enact the old law and codify certain common law principles.

    (a) If the amount or method of calculation is fixed by contract, that contract is binding and cannot be challenged.

    (b) If the amount or method of calculation is not fixed by contract, the arbitrators are entitled to such reasonable fees and remuneration as are appropriate in the circumstances, and any sum awarded by the arbitrators to themselves may be challenged in the court by any party: if there has been overpayment, this may be ordered where reasonable. The power of review is thus available in all cases where there has been no prior agreement, and is not confined to the case in which the award is withheld as a condition of payment.

    (c) The parties are jointly and severally liable for fees and expenses, which means that the arbitrators are entitled to sue any party, as they think fit, for the full amount. It is a matter for the award itself as to which of the parties is ultimately liable, so that some adjustment between the parties may be required where payment has been made by one of them.

    (d) The arbitrators have a statutory right to retain the award (by way of lien) as security for their fees and expenses. A party may, however, apply to the court for release of the award, which the court may order on condition that the sum demanded or a lesser sum is paid into court. In all cases, the sum actually payable is to be determined in accordance with principles (1) and (2) above.

CONDUCT OF THE PROCEEDINGS

The general role of the arbitrators

The fundamental common law principle underlying the conduct of arbitrations is that they should be conducted fairly. This principle is for the first time given statutory force by cl 33, which provides that the arbitrators are to

    (a) act fairly and impartially as between the parties, giving each party a reasonable opportunity of putting his case and dealing with that of his opponent, and

    (b) adopt procedures suitable to the circumstances of the particular case, avoiding unnecessary delay or expense, so as to provide a fair means for the resolution of the matters falling to be determined.

Failure to adhere to this principle may amount to "serious irregularity", replacing the concept of "misconduct" under the 1950 Act, and may lead to the award being set aside in accordance with cl 68. The parties are entitled to legal representation under cl 36, a new provision which codifies the common law.

    There is an important hint in cl 33 to the effect that the procedure to be adopted in the arbitration is a matter for the arbitrators. This is indeed confirmed by cl 34, which allows the arbitrator to determine the procedure subject to the right of the parties to agree any matter. Clause 34 represents an important change in policy between the July 1995 Bill and the February 1996 Bill, as the former conferred autonomy on the parties whereas the latter confers autonomy on the arbitrators subject to contrary agreement on individual matters. The most important specific matters upon which the arbitrators are, subject to agreement, to decide are:

(a) the time and place of the proceedings;

(b) the language of the proceedings;

(c) whether written statements of claim and defence are to be used, and, if so, their form and time limits applicable to them;

(d) whether disclosure of documents is to be ordered, and, if so, how extensive;

(e) whether questions should be put to the parties;

(f) whether strict rules of evidence should apply as regards admissibility, relevance or weight (it should be added that the Civil Evidence Act 1995 has all but abolished the rule against the admissibility of hearsay evidence);

(g) whether the tribunal should take the initiative in ascertaining the facts and the law (i.e. whether the arbitration should be in its traditional adversarial form or whether it should take inquisitorial form);

(h) whether there should be oral evidence, or documents only.

This clause is one of the most important in the Bill, and in effect frees arbitrators from the need to lay down procedural requirements akin to those applicable to court proceedings. Whether arbitrators take advantage of these relaxations is of course another matter, and for some time it may be that arbitrators will seek comfort in established procedures. However, arbitrators should bear in mind that as long as they adhere to the overriding principles in cl 33, they can scarcely be accused of serious irregularity.

The Bill also addresses one of the major weaknesses of English arbitration law, namely the fact that parallel or chain proceedings cannot be consolidated in order to produce a single award binding between all interested parties. Clause 35 now provides that, if the parties agree, arbitrations may be consolidated into a single set of proceedings. In the absence of agreement by the parties, the arbitrators themselves have no power to order consolidation.

Procedural powers

In the absence of any agreement by the parties, cll 38 and 39 of the Bill confer upon the arbitrators a range of powers to assist them in the running of the arbitration, a number of which are new, and others of which were previously exercisable only by the court on application. The purpose is to ensure that, as far as possible, matters can be resolved in the arbitration and without recourse to the court, although if the arbitrators do not themselves have the necessary power it may still be possible in some cases to seek assistance from the court under cll 43 and 44 where the parties have not agreed that recourse to the courts is to be excluded. The list of powers, coupled with the fallback powers of the court where the arbitrators do not have the necessary power as a result of the parties' express agreement, is as follows.

(a) The power to appoint experts or legal advisers, and to charge their fees to the costs of the arbitration (cl 37). This power was generally recognised by the common law, but is given statutory force. The common law principle that decision-making must not be delegated by arbitrators to their experts is, presumably, left unaffected.

(b) The power to order security for costs from the claimant, which is to be exercised in the same manner as it would be by a court. This is a new power, previously only open to the court on application by one of the parties, and has now been transferred to

627

arbitrators from the court. The power is normally exercisable only against a claimant domiciled outside the jurisdiction, but arbitrators should be wary of making an order for security against an EC national, as it is possible that discrimination between a UK claimant and an EC claimant, by subjecting the latter to a condition which would not have been applied to the former, is an infringement of the EC Treaty, the Treaty of Rome. If the arbitrators do not have the power to order security for costs, it is not open to the court to do so.

(c) The power to give directions in relation to any property, as regards its inspection, preservation or custody. This is derived from the 1950 Act. If the arbitrators are not so empowered, the court can make an appropriate order.

(d) The power to examine a witness on oath, and to administer the oath. The court may take evidence generally or on oath if the arbitrators cannot do so, and may also use its usual procedures to secure the attendance of witnesses and the production of documents.

(e) The power to order a party to preserve evidence in his custody or control. The court may do so if the arbitrators cannot.

(f) The power to make a provisional order for the payment of money, whether referring to the sum in dispute or costs. This is a novel power as far as arbitrators are concerned, and is likely to be exercised where the issue between the parties proves to be *quantum* rather than liability. The court has a similar power in respect of judicial proceedings, but cannot intervene if the arbitrators decide not to exercise their powers in this regard. It should be stressed that this is not an interim award, but rather an interim order pending an award.

It follows from these sections that the court's assistance will be required in only two situations: where the arbitrators themselves cannot act due to a restriction on their powers; and where there is a need for a Mareva injunction freezing the respondent's assets pending the outcome of the arbitration or the enforcement of any award.

Service of documents

The Bill lays down various rules for the manner in which documents and notices may be served. These matters are for the parties themselves to determine, but in default of agreement cl 76 states that documents are to be served by post to the addressee's registered office or, in the case of a private individual, to his last known residence or business address. If such service is not reasonably practicable, cl 77 states that the matter is initially for the arbitrators, although an application to the court can be made if the arbitrators cannot deal with it.

Securing the co-operation of the parties

Section 12 of the Arbitration Act 1950 imposed an obligation on the parties to co-operate with the arbitrators in providing evidence and documents. Clause 40 derives from this provision the broader concept of doing "all things necessary for the proper and expeditious conduct of the arbitral proceedings", including, in particular, complying with the arbitrators' directions. The manner in which this obligation is to be enforced is a matter for the agreement of the parties, but in the absence of agreement the arbitrators have three implied powers under cl 41.

628

(a) To strike out the claim for inordinate and excusable delay on the part of the claimant—this is a re-enactment of s 13A of the Arbitration Act 1950, introduced in 1990.

(b) To make an *ex parte* award where a party has failed to attend an oral hearing or to provide written evidence, when requested to do so—arbitrators had this power prior to the Bill, but as it was not expressed in legislation arbitrators were understandably reluctant to take so drastic a step.

(c) Where a party has failed to comply with any order or directions, the arbitrators may make a "peremptory order", a new concept in English arbitration legislation. Failure to comply with a peremptory order empowers the arbitrators to draw the appropriate conclusions and proceed to an award on the material before them. If the order is one for the provision of security for costs, and that is disregarded, the arbitrators may give an award in favour of the respondent without more. As an alternative to action by the arbitrators themselves, the arbitrators themselves or any party may apply to the court under cl 42 for an order by it enforcing the arbitrators' peremptory order. This procedure supersedes that laid down in s 5 of the Arbitration Act 1979, whereby an application could be made to the court for an order conferring judicial enforcement powers on the arbitrators: quite what this meant was never clear.

There is some overlap between remedies (a) and (c) insofar as each procedure can result in an *ex parte* award, and clearly arbitrators will be happier to use the peremptory order procedure even without recourse to the court to enforce it, as in the event of a subsequent judicial challenge to the award there is necessarily clear evidence of non-compliance by the protesting party as well as a warning to him in the form of the peremptory order.

The role of the court

As commented earlier, the transfer from the court to the arbitrators of the powers necessary to make the arbitration work is a fundamental element in the 1996 Bill. The court's residual powers are limited to: enforcing peremptory orders made by the arbitrators (cl 42); securing the attendance of witnesses and the production of evidence (cl 43); supporting arbitration proceedings in circumstances where the arbitrators are not empowered to do so themselves, by taking evidence, preserving evidence and making orders relating to property (cl 44); protecting the proceedings by means of the grant of Mareva injunctions (cl 44); and extending any agreed time limits (cl 79). Clause 45 also preserves the procedure in s 2 of the Arbitration Act 1979, whereby under certain conditions a preliminary question of law can be referred by one of the parties to the court for its determination. The new clause is significantly more comprehensible than the original section, but the law is not changed as to its substance. As was previously the case, the Bill permits a reference provided either that all the parties agree, or that the arbitrators consent: in the latter case, the application can go ahead only if it was made without delay and the court is of the view that the determination of the point of law is likely to produce substantial savings in costs. The parties remain free to contract out of cl 45, by cl 87, but in the case of a domestic agreement contracting out is permissible only after the commencement of the arbitration: the distinction between domestic and non-domestic agreements is, however, subject to removal by the Government on the grounds that it is discriminatory and contrary to the Treaty of Rome, as discussed in the context of stays.

The only change to the law worthy of note is that the arbitrators may, subject to contrary agreement by the parties, continue the arbitration and even issue an award pending the court's decision.

629

THE AWARD

The applicable law

Clause 46 for the first time lays down the duties of arbitrators when faced with an arbitration with an international dimension. Such contracts will generally contain choice of law provisions, and under cl 46 it is the duty of the arbitrators to apply the chosen law: if the chosen law is of a foreign jurisdiction and they do not feel competent to apply that law, their course is resignation. Perhaps the greatest problems arise where there is no choice of law, as cl 46 goes on to state that if there is no choice of law the arbitrators are to apply the law determined by such choice of law rules which it considers applicable. The arbitrators must, therefore (a) decide which conflict of laws rules to apply—English arbitrators will inevitably be drawn to English conflict of laws rules; and (b) use those rules to determine the law applicable to the dispute—if English conflict of laws rules, or indeed the conflict of laws rules of any EC member state, are regarded as appropriate, the relevant rules for choice of law are contained in the notoriously and fiendishly complex Rome Convention 1980. It may be presumed that each of the procedures involved in (a) and (b) is one of law, so that errors can be corrected by appeal on point of law.

An important novel feature of cl 46 is statutory recognition of so-called "equity" clauses, whereby arbitrators are empowered by the parties to reach a result which is just and reasonable even if this means disregarding strict contract wordings and (in some cases) even rules of law. The validity of these clauses is not free from doubt, but cl 46 authorises their use by empowering the arbitrators to take account of such other considerations as are agreed between the parties. The clause indeed seems to say that arbitrators are empowered to take into account extra-legal considerations whether or not the parties have agreed that they can. The Bill does not seek to square this provision with the principle that an appeal is *prima facie* available for an error of law, as the award may be reached without reference to the law at all: the easiest method of resolving this problem is for the parties to agree that there is no right of appeal on point of law, as they are entitled to do under the Bill.

Types of award

The 1950 Act authorises the making of interim awards and full awards. The term "interim award" is misleading, but well understood as meaning a final award on a severable aspect of the dispute. Clause 47 of the Bill dispenses with the term "interim award", and replaces it with the more obvious provision that the arbitrators are entitled to make more than one award at different times and on different issues. It has already been commented that arbitrators are for the first time empowered by cl 39 of the 1996 Bill to make provisional awards, but these are not full awards and merely allow the arbitrators to anticipate their final award on issues which are not in dispute. Arbitrators are in addition, by cl 51, provided with statutory authority for the long-standing practice of making "consent awards", where the parties have reached a settlement during the course of the hearing and wish their settlement to be given formal status in the shape of an award.

Contents of an award

Form—reasons

The 1950 Act contained little on the form which an award is to take. This lacuna is remedied by cl 52 of the Bill, which also makes a significant change to English law. Under cl 52, the parties are free to agree on the form of an award, but in the absence of agreement the award is to be in writing and signed by all of the arbitrators, and it must contain reasons. The award is also to state the seat of the arbitration and the date on which it was made. The requirement for reasons is new, and is based on the principle that persons are entitled to know why their legal rights have been affected. This reversal of policy from earlier legislation means that the court no longer needs the power to order reasons—to facilitate judicial review on the basis of error of law—where none have been given. The Bill operates as follows:

(a) There is a *prima facie* obligation to give reasons, unless the parties agree to the contrary. If they have agreed that no reasons are to be given, judicial review is precluded, as is the right of either party to seek a determination on a preliminary point of law, under cl 45, and the court has no jurisdiction to require reasons. However, under cl 70, the court may apparently order reasons in the face of such an agreement, for the purpose of a challenge to the award on the grounds either of want of jurisdiction or serious misconduct: this is a change in the law.

(b) If reasons are given, but are inadequate, and there is a subsequent appeal against the award on point of law or other challenge to the award, the court is empowered under cl 70 to order reasons sufficient for the appeal to be mounted. What constitutes adequate reasons has been considered on a number of occasions by the courts, with the present view being that an award is appropriately reasoned as long as there is a clear statement of the arbitrators' decision and the considerations underlying that decision: a detailed analysis and rebuttal of the arguments put by the parties is not necessary in an award, and is to be discouraged where the parties are seeking speedy and effective dispute resolution.

(c) A failure by the arbitrators to give reasons when required to do so amounts to a serious irregularity, which may be corrected by the court by virtue of an application under cl 68.

Remedies

The remedies which may be contained in an award, as listed in cl 48, are: declaratory relief, damages (including, as a matter of common law, damages in a foreign currency), positive and negative orders as to future conduct, rectification, and specific performance (other than of a contract relating to land). This list can be extended or modified by agreement between the parties. There was no equivalent list in earlier legislation, and arbitrators will be grateful for statutory codification of this point.

Interest

Where damages are awarded, the arbitrators are empowered to award interest on more or less the same basis as was the case under ss 19A and 20 of the Arbitration Act 1950, with a number of changes. First, as regards interest on the award itself, the arbitrators are free to award simple or compound interest on the award itself, running from the date of the award until payment.

631

The rate of such interest is to be determined by the arbitrators and is no longer tied to the statutory rate under the Judgments Act 1838: it might be noted that s 20 of the Arbitration Act 1950 itself was modified in this way by the Private International Law (Miscellaneous Provisions) Act 1995, where the award of damages is in a foreign currency. Secondly, as regards interest on sums payable before the commencement of proceedings, whether or not paid by the date of the award, arbitrators are free under the Bill to award compound as well as simple interest: it remains the case under the Bill that the arbitrators cannot award interest on sums outstanding prior to the commencement of the proceedings and paid by that date.

Costs

The February 1996 Bill makes extensive provision for the award of costs by the arbitrators, and formalises well-established principles upon which costs are awardable: this is a great improvement over the 1950 Act and indeed the July 1995 Bill, as in those documents the guidance to arbitrators was at best very limited. Clauses 59 to 65 are concerned with the determination of the amount of costs, and the allocation of those costs between the parties. The arbitrators' power to award the "costs of the arbitration" extends, as previously, to the fees and costs of the arbitrators and any institution involved, and the legal and other costs of the parties.

As commented earlier, the costs which may be included in the award—the "recoverable costs"—consist of the arbitrators' fees and expenses and the parties' legal and other costs. Turning first to the arbitrators' fees and expenses, cl 64 provides that recoverable costs may not exceed reasonable fees and expenses, and if there is any dispute as to what amount this is, the dispute may be referred to the court for its determination. This does not mean, however, that any additional sum is not recoverable from the parties by the arbitrators, as cl 64 is concerned merely with what may be awarded by way of costs in the award: cl 28 allows the arbitrators to enforce a contract between themselves for a greater sum, and if in the absence of any such agreement the arbitrators demand a sum regarded by the parties as excessive, that sum must be challenged under cl 28 itself.

The recoverability of the parties' own costs is governed by cl 63. Such costs may be agreed by the parties, but in the absence of agreement it is open to the arbitrators to determine the recoverable costs on such basis as they think fit: if they do determine the recoverable costs, these are to be itemised and the basis of the calculation is to be set out. If, however, the arbitrators decide not to determine the recoverable costs, there may be an application to the court for the matter to be resolved. In the absence of judicial or arbitral determination, the amount of party costs recoverable is on a reasonable amount rather than indemnity basis.

As regards the allocation of the recoverable costs of the arbitration between the parties, it remains the case, as was the position under the 1950 Act, that any agreement between the parties allocating the costs is not enforceable unless made after the dispute in question has arisen: this removes the possibility that a party—generally the claimant—may be unable to arbitrate in the knowledge that he has to bear some costs whatever the outcome. Subject to any post-dispute agreement between the parties, the allocation of costs is a matter for the arbitrators, but now subject to the codified rule in cl 61 that costs are to follow the event unless the arbitrators decide that this is inappropriate. This is a long-standing common law principle, but now has statutory force and ought to free the arbitrators from any doubt as to how they should proceed in the vast majority of cases (at least those where there has not been a sealed offer).

632

Place and time of the award

The time by which an award is to be made may be fixed by the parties. The award itself is, under cl 54, deemed to have been made as and when it has been signed by the last of the arbitrators, although—unless the parties have agreed that this is not possible—the arbitrators may themselves fix some other date. If the arbitrators fail to meet any date specified by the parties, then, subject to contrary agreement, the court may, under cl 50, extend the time specified on application by the arbitrators or by any party. This is more or less a re-enactment of s 13 of the 1950 Act, modified to take into account the wishes of the parties (as s 13 was mandatory). Time can be enlarged by the court if failure to do so would result in "substantial injustice". This is a new test, and it remains to be seen how it will be construed by the courts.

The place where an award is made is deemed to be the place of the seat of the arbitration. This is an important change in the law, as under earlier legislation the place of the making of an award was the place where it was signed, with the result that an arbitration held in England between English parties and adjudicated upon by an English arbitrator could nevertheless result in a French award if the arbitrator happened to be in France when he signed the award. This led to complex problems concerning the judicial review powers of the court, as under the New York Convention a foreign award is to be enforced in another country, and no question can be raised as to its validity: this led the House of Lords to rule that an award which was a French award under the above circumstances nevertheless remained reviewable by the English courts despite the apparent contrary wording of the Rome Convention. Under cl 53 of the Bill, the place of signature is to be disregarded, and the earlier problems disappear.

Once the award is made, and subject to any contrary agreement between the parties, it becomes binding under cl 58, and cl 55 requires the arbitrators to notify the award to the parties, by serving copies on them "without delay" after the award is made: this is a new provision, but doubtless reflects practice. The obligation to serve copies of the award without delay is, however, without prejudice to the long-established right of the arbitrators, now re-enacted in cl 56, to retain the award as security for their fees and expenses.

Correcting the award

The 1950 Act made limited provision for the correction of an award by the arbitrators once it had been made. They were entitled to act in two situations. First, under s 17 of the 1950 Act, the "slip" rule allowed arbitrators to correct accidental clerical mistakes. Secondly, under s 18 of the Act, where the arbitrators had failed to award costs, a party could apply to them for the deficiency to be remedied. Other errors in the award could be corrected only by an application to the court for remission of the award to the arbitrators, necessarily a costly process.

Clause 57 of the Bill widens the powers of the arbitrators to correct errors without reference to the court. The additional power, subject to contrary agreement by the parties, is to "clarify or remove any ambiguity in the award". Quite what this means will have to be determined by the courts, but it seems unlikely that arbitrators will be able to use cl 57 in order to change their minds about their final decision. The operation of cl 57 is as follows. The arbitrators may make any correction themselves within 28 days of making the award, or they may respond to an application by a party and are then under an obligation to act within 28 days of receiving the application. If a new award is required, the arbitrators must make this within 56 days from the date of the first award. If the arbitrators fail to correct the award, it may be challenged on the grounds of serious irregularity, under cl 68.

633

CHALLENGING THE AWARD

The grounds contained in the 1996 Bill on which an award may be challenged are rather different from those in earlier legislation. In general terms, an award may be challenged on one of three grounds: want of jurisdiction; procedural irregularity; and error of law. Any challenge under these provisions must be made within 28 days of the award, and in all cases it is possible for the court to order better reasons from the arbitrators where inadequate reasons have been given. If the parties have agreed that no reasons should be given, the arbitrators cannot be called upon to give reasons for the purpose of an appeal on the ground of error of law, as such an agreement operates as an agreement to exclude such an appeal. However, in the case of an application to set aside an award on the basis of jurisdiction or procedural irregularity, it seems to be the case that reasons can be ordered despite the agreement: in these cases, it is nevertheless unlikely that the court would need reasons from the arbitrators in order to make its decision, but the power—new to English law—exists. Under cl 71, where the court varies the award following any challenge, the variation is to form part of the award. If the award is remitted to the arbitrators, they must produce a fresh award within three months unless the court lays down a different period. Finally, if the award is set aside, the court may in effect permit judicial proceedings on the issues to go ahead.

One important addition to English law, based upon the Model Law, is in cl 73. Under this provision, if a party becomes aware of a problem in the arbitration, whether it be jurisdictional or procedural, but does not register any objection, he is deemed to have waived the problem, and cannot later raise it before the arbitrators or the court. One clear example of this would be where a party believes that evidence has been unjustifiably excluded or ignored, but carries on regardless: his right to challenge for serious irregularity could, by such conduct, be lost.

Want of jurisdiction (cl 67)

As noted earlier, arbitrators are given by the Bill the right to determine their own jurisdiction, and there are various procedures whereby that determination can be challenged. The cl 67 procedure allows a challenge to the award itself, on the basis that it was made without jurisdiction. Such a challenge is possible where the party contesting the award has registered his objection to the proceedings, either by participating under protest or by failing to participate at all, and the court has not given a preliminary ruling on the jurisdiction point.

Serious irregularity (cl 68)

Clause 68 of the Bill replaces the "misconduct" rules in the 1950 Act. Under the earlier law, an award could be set aside or remitted to the arbitrators where the arbitrators had misconducted themselves or the proceedings. The term "misconduct" has long been criticised by arbitrators, as it inaccurately indicated some form of deliberate wrongdoing, whereas as a matter of law misconduct was nothing more or less than procedural error giving rise to injustice, often unintentional. Reform was thus called for here. Moreover, in the 1980s the court developed an apparently unwarranted interventionist jurisdiction to remit an award to the arbitrators where there had not been misconduct but merely where something had gone wrong in the proceedings, often because one of the parties had failed to put his case properly: this became known as "procedural mishap". This latter form of jurisdiction has been abolished by the Bill, and the result now is that an award can be set aside or remitted for "serious irregularity". If an award is set aside or remitted, the court retains its power to remove the arbitrators, under cl 24, but it no longer has the power conferred by the 1950 Act to put an end to the arbitration agreement: if the award is set aside, the matter must go back to arbitration. The Bill provides that there is a presumption in favour of remission, with setting aside being reserved for serious cases: this position had been reached by the courts under the 1950 Act.

Under cl 68 an award may be set aside or remitted if substantial injustice has been caused as a result of any of the following:

(a) failure by the arbitrators to act fairly and impartially or to adopt procedures suitable for a fair resolution of the case (contrary to cl 33);
(b) the arbitrators exceeding their powers;
(c) failure by the arbitrators to conduct the arbitration in accordance with the procedures agreed by the parties;
(d) failure by the arbitrators to deal with all the matters referred to them;
(e) an arbitral institution or other person with powers relating to the arbitration exceeding those powers;
(f) uncertainty or ambiguity in the award;
(g) the award being obtained by fraud or in a manner contrary to public policy;
(h) failure by the arbitrators to comply with the form of the award required by the parties or the Bill;
(i) irregularity in the proceedings admitted by the arbitrators.

Appeal on point of law (cl 69)

Clause 69 re-enacts, with clarifications and modifications, the regime applicable to appeal on point of law laid down by the Arbitration Act 1979. The new clause codifies the judicial principles applicable to appeals, developed by the House of Lords. In general terms, if the point of law is one of general public importance, the court may give leave for an appeal to be made if the arbitrators' decision is open to serious doubt. If, by contrast, the importance of the point of law is more or less restricted to the parties themselves, there is a higher threshold for leave, namely that the arbitrators must have been obviously wrong. It is possible for the parties to contract out of this jurisdiction—and they are deemed to have done so if they have agreed that no reasons are required—although in the case of a domestic agreement the contracting out is valid only if it took place after the arbitration proceedings have commenced. The distinction between non-domestic and domestic agreements is, as noted earlier, presently subject to review.

REMAINING PROVISIONS

The rest of the Bill is a re-enactment of earlier legislation. The Consumer Arbitration Agreements Act 1988 is re-enacted in cll 89 to 93. Under this Act, a consumer cannot be obliged to arbitrate unless he agrees to do so after the dispute has arisen. Finally, cll 102 to 107 re-enact the Arbitration Act 1975 on the enforceability of foreign arbitration awards. English awards are enforceable as before, under cl 66.

635

APPENDIX 5

DATE OF APPLICATION

The Bill will apply to any arbitration which is commenced after the Bill has come into force, whether or not the arbitration agreement itself was made after the Bill has come into force. It is thought likely that the new provisions will begin to apply as from the beginning of 1997.

Arbitration Bill [H.L.]

EXPLANATORY MEMORANDUM

This Bill restates existing legislation on arbitration, as set out in the Arbitration Acts of 1950, 1975 and 1979, whilst at the same time codifying principles established by recent case law. It also introduces certain changes in the law which are designed to improve arbitration as a fair, speedy and cost-effective way of resolving disputes. It reflects as far as possible the format and provisions of the UNCITRAL Model Law on International Commercial Arbitration.

The objective of the Bill is to provide for the fair, speedy and cost-effective resolution of disputes by an impartial tribunal. Apart from a limited number of clauses which are not subject to contrary agreement, the Bill gives maximum scope for the parties to an arbitration to decide for themselves how the arbitration should be handled. The provisions of the Bill come into play to support the arbitration only when the parties have not decided what should happen.

The Bill also reflects the view that the decision of the parties to choose a private tribunal rather than the courts to resolve their dispute must be respected. The Bill strengthens the powers of arbitrators and the role of the court is limited to those occasions when it is obvious that either the arbitral process needs assistance or that there has been or is likely to be a clear denial of justice. Similarly, if the parties have vested an arbitral institution with powers to act in certain situations any available process of appeal must be exhausted before the courts can be approached.

PART I   ARBITRATION PURSUANT TO AN ARBITRATION AGREEMENT

Clauses 1 to 4 are new. *Clause 1* sets out the general principles on which the Bill is founded, as indicated above. *Clause 2* defines the scope of application of Part I whilst *Clause 3* explains the concept of the "seat of the arbitration". *Clause 4* has as its purpose to distinguish between those provisions of Part I which are mandatory in the sense that they may not be displaced by contrary agreement, and those which parties can choose whether or not to apply. The mandatory provisions are set out in *Schedule 1*.

Clause 5 requires agreements to be in writing and provides a widely drawn definition of "writing". Agreements in writing include agreements evidenced in writing as well as oral agreements which refer to terms which are in writing. Writing includes anything recorded by any means.

Clause 6, which corresponds to the Model Law, defines "arbitration agreement" in essentially the same terms as section 32 of the 1950 Act. The clause also provides that agreements which incorporate by reference the terms of a written form of agreement constitute valid arbitration agreements.

Clause 7 corresponds to Article 16(1) of the Model Law and codifies the law on the separability of the arbitration clause from the main contract.

Clause 8, which deals with whether an arbitration agreement is discharged by the death of a party, reproduces the provisions of the 1950 Act with the change that subsection (1) is non-mandatory.

Clause 9, which corresponds to Article 8 of the Model Law and reproduces section 4(1) of the 1950 Act and section 1 of the 1975 Act with changes, provides for the circumstances in which an application to the court to stay legal proceedings in favour of enforcement of the arbitration agreement may be brought and how the court should treat such applications.

Clause 10 reproduces section 5 of the 1950 Act and provides for the reference of an interpleader issue to arbitration.

Clause 11 reproduces section 26 of the Civil Jurisdiction and Judgments Act 1982. It authorises the court, when it stays Admiralty proceedings in order to enforce an arbitration agreement, to order that security given to obtain release from arrest be retained pending the award.

Clause 12 reproduces with amendments section 27 of the 1950 Act which confers powers on the court, in certain circumstances, to extend a time limit imposed by an arbitration agreement for the commencement of an arbitration. The court must now be satisfied before granting an extension that circumstances have arisen which were outside the reasonable contemplation of the parties when they agreed the time limit and that it would be just to extend the time or that the conduct of one party makes it unjust to hold the other to the strict terms of their bargain.

Clause 13 re-enacts with minor modifications (but not so as to change the law) subsections (1), (5) and (7)(b) of section 34 of the Limitation Act 1980.

Clause 14 corresponds to Article 21 of the Model Law and determines when arbitral proceedings are deemed to be commenced.

Clause 15, which corresponds to Article 10 of the Model Law, provides for the composition of the arbitral tribunal and lays down default provisions in the event that the parties do not agree their own arrangements. The arrangements fill in certain gaps in the 1950 Act.

Clauses 16, 17 and 18 provide default arrangements, in the absence of party agreement, for appointing the tribunal and the procedure to be followed in the event of their failure. These clauses simplify and clarify the current law.

Clause 19 requires the court to have regard to any agreement of the parties as to the qualifications required of the arbitrators when considering whether, and if so how, to exercise its powers under *Clauses 16 and 18*.

Clauses 20 and 21 provide for the role of chairmen and umpires respectively. Current legislation does not provide for the office of chairman. *Clause 22* sets out arrangements for decision making where there is no chairman or umpire.

Clauses 23 and 24 deal with the circumstances in which the authority of an arbitrator may be revoked and an arbitrator may be removed by the court.

Clause 25 provides for the consequences of the resignation of an arbitrator.

Clause 26 provides that the authority of an arbitrator ceases on his death but that the death of a party does not revoke the authority of an arbitrator appointed by him.

Clause 27 corresponds to Article 15 of the Model Law and provides simple rules for the filling of vacancies in the tribunal and the standing of previous proceedings.

Clause 28 provides for the remuneration of the arbitrators and sets out the obligations of the parties in this regard.

Clause 29 is new and confers immunity on members of a tribunal, their employees and agents.

Clauses 30 and 31, which flow from Article 16 of the Model Law, state the existing law that an arbitral tribunal may rule on a question concerning its own jurisdiction, and provide for the timing of an objection and how the tribunal may respond.

Clause 32 is based on Article 16(3) of the Model Law and is concerned with applications to the court to consider a preliminary point of jurisdiction under *Clause 31*.

Clause 33 corresponds to Article 18 of the Model Law and sets out the duties of the tribunal in the conduct of the proceedings.

Clause 34 corresponds to Articles 19, 20, 22 to 24 and 26 of the Model law. It deals with the conduct of the proceedings. The existing statutory provision is in section 12(1) to (3) of the 1950 Act.

Clause 35 is designed to make clear that the parties are able to agree to consolidate arbitral proceedings or to hold concurrent hearings.

Clause 36 permits a party to arbitral proceedings to be represented by a lawyer or other person chosen by him.

Clause 37 gives the power to the tribunal to appoint experts, legal advisors or assessors to assist it.

Clause 38 corresponds to Article 17 of the Model Law and is concerned with the interlocutory powers exercisable by the tribunal.

Clause 39 empowers the parties to authorise the tribunal to make provisional awards. The tribunal cannot act without the agreement of the parties.

Clause 40 imposes on the parties a general duty to do all things necessary for the proper conduct of the arbitral proceedings.

Clause 41 corresponds to Article 35 of the Model Law and confers powers on the tribunal to deal with a party who refuses to co-operate. *Clause 42* provides for the enforcement of peremptory orders made under *Clause 41* which have not been complied with.

Clause 43 makes available to parties to arbitral proceedings the same processes as are available to parties to litigation to compel the attendance of witnesses. It corresponds to Article 27 of the Model Law.

Clause 44 corresponds to Articles 9 and 31 of the Model Law and confers the same powers on the court in aid of an arbitration as it has for the purposes of court proceedings. The court may only exercise these powers if the tribunal or arbitral institution has no power to act or is unable temporarily to act effectively.

Clause 45 confers a power on the court to determine a preliminary point of law arising in the arbitral proceedings. The clause is based on section 2 of the 1979 Act but does not reproduce it exactly. The court can consider only those questions of law which substantially affect the rights of one or more of the parties.

Clause 46 corresponds to Article 28 of the Model Law and determines the rules to be applied in deciding the substance of the dispute.

Clause 47 allows the tribunal to make more than one award on different aspects of the case.

Clause 48 enables the parties to agree the powers exercisable by the tribunal in relation to remedies. The clause provides a list of powers to order remedies if the parties do not otherwise agree.

Clause 49 introduces a new power to enable the tribunal, in default of agreement between the parties, to award compound interest as well as simple interest on amounts successfully claimed and to award such interest on amounts awarded at rates other than the judgment debt rate.

Clause 50 supersedes section 13(2) of the 1950 Act and provides for the court to extend any time limits for making the award set out in the arbitration agreement if satisfied that not to do so would result in substantial injustice.

Clause 51 corresponds to Article 30 of the Model Law and enables an agreed settlement of the dispute to be given the status of an arbitral award.

Clause 52 sets out a provision not included in current arbitration statute law to require the tribunal to give reasons for its award. The parties can opt out of the requirement.

Clauses 53, 54 and 55 cover various detailed aspects of the award, including where and when it is made and requirements for notifying the parties.

Clause 56 supersedes with amendments section 19 of the 1950 Act and confers on a tribunal a lien on its award to secure payment of its fees and for taxation of the fees demanded.

Clause 57 corresponds to Article 33 of the Model Law. It enlarges upon section 17 of the 1950 Act by conferring power on the tribunal to correct slips, clerical mistakes and errors in an award and to clear up any ambiguities and section 18(4) of the 1950 Act which authorises a tribunal to make an additional award in respect of any matter agreed to be referred to the tribunal but not covered by the award.

Clause 58 provides that the award is final and binding on the parties and on any persons claiming through or under them.

Clauses 59 to 65 deal with the costs of the arbitration. A new power is given in *Clause 65* to the tribunal to limit the recoverable costs of the arbitration.

Clause 66 empowers the courts to enforce an award in the same manner as a judgment, as per section 26(1) of the 1950 Act. The clause goes on to make clear expressly the circumstances in which the court may decline to enforce an award.

Clauses 67 to 69 provide for the circumstances in which applications may be made to the court to challenge the award and how the court should respond to such applications. Various changes are made to the current law. *Clause 70* restricts applications which may be made under *Clauses 67 to 69*. *Clause 71* concerns the consequences which flow from the decisions of the court.

640

Clause 72 allows a person who has taken no part in the arbitral proceedings to challenge the jurisdiction of the tribunal at any time if he finds that he is alleged to be a party to the proceedings.

Clause 73, which corresponds to Article 4 of the Model Law, sets out the circumstances in which parties forfeit their right to object to any irregularity regarding the tribunal or the proceedings.

Clause 74 introduces limited immunity for arbitral institutions. Immunity is extended to the function of the appointment or nomination of arbitrators unless it can be shown that bad faith was involved. Arbitral institutions are also not liable for the actions of the arbitrators they appoint.

Clause 75 concerns the powers of the court in relation to the payment of certain solicitors' costs.

Clause 76 allows parties to decide on the manner of service of any notice or other document. It provides a method of service in the event that the parties have not so agreed.

Clause 77 gives the court power, where service as agreed or under *Clause 76* is not reasonably practicable, to order substituted service or to dispense with service but only if any available arbitral process for resolving the matter is first exhausted.

Clause 78 makes provision for reckoning periods of time prescribed by the Bill.

Clause 79 empowers the court to extend any time limit fixed by Part I. Recourse to the tribunal or arbitral institutions (if they have been vested by the parties with the power) must first be made before the court can be approached. The court must be satisfied that not to extend the limits would result in a substantial injustice.

Clause 80 sets out the requirements as to notice in respect of legal proceedings.

Clause 81 provides that certain matters shall continue to be governed by the common law and not by Part I.

Clauses 82 and 83 define and signpost certain expressions used in Part I.

Clause 84 provides that Part I applies to all arbitral proceedings commenced on or after the coming into force of the Bill, under an arbitration agreement whenever made.

PART II   OTHER PROVISIONS RELATING TO ARBITRATION

Clauses 85 to 87 make special provision, as reflected in section 1 of the 1975 Act and section 3 of the 1979 Act, for domestic arbitrations in respect of the stay of legal proceedings and agreements to exclude the jurisdiction of the courts on points of law. *Clause 88* empowers the Secretary of State to repeal or restrict these special provisions by affirmative statutory instrument.

Clauses 89 to 93 consolidate the provisions of sections 1 to 5 of the Consumer Arbitrations Agreement Act 1988.

Clause 94 excludes the provisions of Part I in relation to small claims arbitration in the county court.

641

Clause 95 and Schedule 2 provide for the appointment of judges as arbitrators.

Clauses 96 to 100 adapt the provisions of Part I to statutory arbitrations and include a power to make further changes by statutory instrument.

Clause 101 transposes certain definitions used in Part I to Part II.

PART III RECOGNITION AND ENFORCEMENT OF CERTAIN FOREIGN AWARDS

Clauses 102 to 107 restate the current law on the enforcement of Geneva Convention awards and the recognition and enforcement of New York Convention awards.

PART IV GENERAL PROVISIONS

Clauses 108 to 112 cover certain general provisions including the binding of the Crown and arrangements for commencement. *Clause 109 and Schedules 3 and 4* deal with consequential amendments and repeals.

Effect of the Bill on public sector manpower

The Bill will have no effect on public sector manpower.

Business compliance cost assessment

There are no expected compliance costs for business.

ARRANGEMENT OF CLAUSES

PART I   ARBITRATION PURSUANT TO AN ARBITRATION AGREEMENT

Introductory

Clause
1.   General principles.
2.   Scope of application of provisions.
3.   The seat of the arbitration.
4.   Mandatory and non-mandatory provisions.
5.   Agreements to be in writing.

The arbitration agreement

6.   Definition of arbitration agreement.
7.   Separability of arbitration agreement.
8.   Whether agreement discharged by death of a party.

Stay of legal proceedings

9.   Stay of legal proceedings.
10.   Reference of interpleader issue to arbitration.

643

A BILL INTITULED

An Act to restate and improve the law relating to arbitration pursuant to an arbitration agreement; to make other provision relating to arbitration and arbitration awards; and for connected purposes.

PART I   ARBITRATION PURSUANT TO AN ARBITRATION AGREEMENT

Introductory

General principles

1. The provisions of this Part are founded on the following principles, and shall be construed accordingly—

    (a) the object of arbitration is to obtain the fair resolution of disputes by an impartial tribunal without unnecessary delay or expense;

    (b) the parties should be free to agree how their disputes are resolved, subject only to such safeguards as are necessary in the public interest;

    (c) in matters governed by this Part the court should not intervene except as provided by this Part.

Scope of application of provisions

2.—(1) The provisions of this Part apply where the law of England and Wales or Northern Ireland is applicable, or the powers of the court are exercisable, in accordance with the rules of the conflict of laws.

(2) They apply, in particular—

    (a) to matters relating to or governed by the arbitration agreement, where the applicable law is the law of England and Wales or Northern Ireland; and

    (b) to matters governed by the law applicable to the arbitral proceedings, where the seat of the arbitration is in England and Wales or Northern Ireland.

(3) The following provisions apply whatever the law applicable to the arbitration agreement or the arbitral proceedings—

    (a) sections 9 to 11 (stay of legal proceedings);

    (b) section 43 (securing the attendance of witnesses) and section 44 (court powers exercisable in support of arbitral proceedings); and

    (c) section 66 (enforcement of arbitral awards).

(4) The court may refuse to exercise any power conferred by this Part if, in the opinion of the court, the fact that the seat of the arbitration is outside England and Wales or Northern Ireland, or that when designated or determined the seat is likely to be outside England and Wales or Northern Ireland, makes it inappropriate to exercise that power.

The seat of the arbitration

3. In this Part "the seat of the arbitration" means the juridical seat of the arbitration designated—

    (a) by the parties to the arbitration agreement, or

    (b) by any arbitral or other institution or person vested by the parties with powers in that regard, or

    (c) by the arbitral tribunal if so authorised by the parties, or determined, in the absence of any such designation, having regard to the parties' agreement and all the relevant circumstances.

Mandatory and non-mandatory provisions

4.—(1) The mandatory provisions of this Part are listed in Schedule 1 and have effect notwithstanding any agreement to the contrary.

(2) The other provisions of this Part (the "non-mandatory provisions") allow the parties to make their own arrangements by agreement but provide rules which apply in the absence of such agreement.

(3) The parties may make such arrangements by agreeing to the application of institutional rules or providing any other means by which a matter may be decided.

(4) It is immaterial whether or not the law applicable to the parties' agreement is the law of England and Wales or, as the case may be, Northern Ireland.

(5) The choice of a law other than the law of England and Wales or Northern Ireland as the applicable law in respect of a matter provided for by a non-mandatory provision of this Part is equivalent to an agreement making provision about that matter.

For this purpose an applicable law determined in accordance with the parties' agreement, or which is objectively determined in the absence of any express or implied choice, shall be treated as chosen by the parties.

Agreements to be in writing

5.—(1) The provisions of this Part apply only where the arbitration agreement is in writing, and any other agreement between the parties as to any matter is effective for the purposes of this Part only if in writing.

The expressions "agreement", "agree" and "agreed" shall be construed accordingly.

(2) There is an agreement in writing—

    (a) if the agreement is made in writing (whether or not it is signed by the parties),

    (b) if the agreement is made by exchange of communications in writing, or

    (c) if the agreement is evidenced in writing.

(3) Where parties agree otherwise than in writing by reference to terms which are in writing, they make an agreement in writing.

(4) An agreement is evidenced in writing if an agreement made otherwise than in writing is recorded by one of the parties, or by a third party, with the authority of the parties to the agreement.

(5) An exchange of written submissions in arbitral or legal proceedings in which the existence of an agreement otherwise than in writing is alleged by one party against another party and not denied by the other party in his response constitutes as between those parties an agreement in writing to the effect alleged.

(6) References in this Part to anything being written or in writing include its being recorded by any means.

The arbitration agreement

Definition of arbitration agreement

6.—(1) In this Part an "arbitration agreement" means an agreement to submit to arbitration present or future disputes (whether they are contractual or not).

647

(2) The reference in an agreement to a written form of arbitration clause or to a document containing an arbitration clause constitutes an arbitration agreement if the reference is such as to make that clause part of the agreement.

Separability of arbitration agreement

7. Unless otherwise agreed by the parties, an arbitration agreement which forms or was intended to form part of another agreement shall not be regarded as invalid, non-existent or ineffective because that other agreement is invalid, or did not come into existence or has become ineffective, and it shall for that purpose be treated as a distinct agreement.

Whether agreement discharged by death of a party

8.—(1) Unless otherwise agreed by the parties, an arbitration agreement is not discharged by the death of a party and may be enforced by or against the personal representatives of that party.

(2) Subsection (1) does not affect the operation of any enactment or rule of law by virtue of which a substantive right or obligation is extinguished by death.

Stay of legal proceedings

Stay of legal proceedings

9.—(1) A party to an arbitration agreement against whom legal proceedings are brought (whether by way of claim or counterclaim) in respect of a matter which under the agreement is to be referred to arbitration may (upon notice to the other parties to the proceedings) apply to the court in which the proceedings have been brought to stay the proceedings so far as they concern that matter.

(2) An application may be made notwithstanding that the matter is to be referred to arbitration only after the exhaustion of other dispute resolution procedures.

(3) An application may not be made by a person before taking the appropriate procedural step (if any) to acknowledge the legal proceedings against him or after he has taken any step in those proceedings to answer the substantive claim.

(4) On an application under this section the court shall grant a stay unless satisfied that the arbitration agreement is null and void, inoperative, or incapable of being performed.

(5) If the court refuses to stay the legal proceedings, any provision that an award is a condition precedent to the bringing of legal proceedings in respect of any matter is of no effect in relation to those proceedings.

Reference of interpleader issue to arbitration

10.—(1) Where in legal proceedings relief by way of interpleader is granted and any issue between the claimants is one in respect of which there is an arbitration agreement between them, the court granting the relief shall direct that the issue be determined in accordance with the agreement unless the circumstances are such that proceedings brought by a claimant in respect of the matter would not be stayed.

(2) Where subsection (1) applies but the court does not direct that the issue be determined in accordance with the arbitration agreement, any provision that an award is a condition

648

precedent to the bringing of legal proceedings in respect of any matter shall not affect the determination of that issue by the court.

Retention of security where Admiralty proceedings stayed

11.—(1) Where Admiralty proceedings are stayed on the ground that the dispute in question should be submitted to arbitration, the court granting the stay may, if in those proceedings property has been arrested or bail or other security has been given to prevent or obtain release from arrest—

(a) order that the property arrested be retained as security for the satisfaction of any award given in the arbitration in respect of that dispute, or

(b) order that the stay of those proceedings be conditional on the provision of equivalent security for the satisfaction of any such award.

(2) Subject to any provision made by rules of court and to any necessary modifications, the same law and practice shall apply in relation to property retained in pursuance of an order as would apply if it were held for the purposes of proceedings in the court making the order.

Commencement of arbitral proceedings

Power of court to extend time for beginning arbitral proceedings, &c.

12.—(1) Where an arbitration agreement to refer future disputes to arbitration provides that a claim shall be barred, or the claimant's right extinguished, unless the claimant takes within a time fixed by the agreement some step—

(a) to begin arbitral proceedings, or

(b) to begin other dispute resolution procedures which must be exhausted before arbitral proceedings can be begun,

the court may by order extend the time for taking that step.

(2) Any party to the arbitration agreement may apply for such an order (upon notice to the other parties), but only after a claim has arisen and after exhausting any available arbitral process for obtaining an extension of time.

(3) The court shall make an order only if satisfied—

(a) that the circumstances are such as were outside the reasonable contemplation of the parties when they agreed the provision in question, and that it would be just to extend the time, or

(b) that the conduct of one party makes it unjust to hold the other party to the strict terms of the provision in question.

(4) The court may extend the time for such period and on such terms as it thinks fit, and may do so whether or not the time previously fixed (by agreement or by a previous order) has expired.

(5) An order under this section does not affect the operation of the Limitation Acts (see section 13).

(6) The leave of the court is required for any appeal from a decision of the court under this section.

Application of Limitation Acts

13.—(1) The Limitation Acts apply to arbitral proceedings as they apply to legal proceedings.

(2) The court may order that in computing the time prescribed by the Limitation Acts for the commencement of proceedings (including arbitral proceedings) in respect of a dispute which was the subject matter—

(a) of an award which the court orders to be set aside or declares to be of no effect, or

(b) of the affected part of an award which the court orders to be set aside in part, or declares to be in part of no effect,

the period between the commencement of the arbitration and the date of the order referred to in paragraph (a) or (b) shall be excluded.

(3) In determining for the purposes of the Limitation Acts when a cause of action accrued, any provision that an award is a condition precedent to the bringing of legal proceedings in respect of a matter to which an arbitration agreement applies shall be disregarded.

(4) In this Part "the Limitation Acts" means—

(a) in England and Wales, the Limitation Act 1980, the Foreign Limitation Periods Act 1984 and any other enactment (whenever passed) relating to the limitation of actions;

(b) in Northern Ireland, the Limitation (Northern Ireland) Order 1989, the Foreign Limitation Periods (Northern Ireland) Order 1985 and any other enactment (whenever passed) relating to the limitation of actions.

Commencement of arbitral proceedings

14.—(1) The parties are free to agree when arbitral proceedings are to be regarded as commenced for the purposes of this Part and for the purposes of the Limitation Acts.

(2) If there is no such agreement the following provisions apply.

(3) Where the arbitrator is named or designated in the arbitration agreement, arbitral proceedings are commenced in respect of a matter when one party serves on the other party or parties a notice in writing requiring him or them to submit that matter to the person so named or designated.

(4) Where the arbitrator or arbitrators are to be appointed by the parties, arbitral proceedings are commenced in respect of a matter when one party serves on the other party or parties notice in writing requiring him or them to appoint an arbitrator or to agree to the appointment of an arbitrator in respect of that matter.

(5) Where the arbitrator or arbitrators are to be appointed by a person other than a party to the proceedings, arbitral proceedings are commenced in respect of a matter when one party gives notice in writing to that person requesting him to make the appointment in respect of that matter.

The arbitral tribunal

The arbitral tribunal

15.—(1) The parties are free to agree on the number of arbitrators to form the tribunal and whether there is to be a chairman or umpire.

(2) Unless otherwise agreed by the parties, an agreement that the number of arbitrators shall be two or any other even number shall be understood as requiring the appointment of an additional arbitrator as chairman of the tribunal.

(3) If there is no agreement as to the number of arbitrators, the tribunal shall consist of a sole arbitrator.

650

Procedure for appointment of arbitrators

16.—(1) The parties are free to agree on the procedure for appointing the arbitrator or arbitrators, including the procedure for appointing any chairman or umpire.

(2) If or to the extent that there is no such agreement, the following provisions apply.

(3) If the tribunal is to consist of a sole arbitrator, the parties shall jointly appoint the arbitrator not later than 28 days after service of a request in writing by either party to do so.

(4) If the tribunal is to consist of two arbitrators, each party shall appoint one arbitrator not later than 14 days after service of a request in writing by either party to do so.

(5) If the tribunal is to consist of three arbitrators—

    (a) each party shall appoint one arbitrator not later than 14 days after service of a request in writing by either party to do so, and

    (b) the two so appointed shall forthwith appoint a third arbitrator as the chairman of the tribunal.

(6) If the tribunal is to consist of two arbitrators and an umpire—

    (a) each party shall appoint one arbitrator not later than 14 days after service of a request in writing by either party to do so, and

    (b) the two so appointed may appoint an umpire at any time after they themselves are appointed and shall do so before any substantive hearing or forthwith if they cannot agree on any matter relating to the arbitration.

(7) In any other case (in particular, if there are more than two parties) section 18 applies as in the case of a failure of the agreed appointment procedure.

Power in case of default to appoint sole arbitrator

17.—(1) Unless the parties otherwise agree, where each of two parties to an arbitration agreement is to appoint an arbitrator and one party ("the party in default") refuses to do so, or fails to do so within the time specified, the other party, having duly appointed his arbitrator, may give notice in writing to the party in default that he proposes to appoint his arbitrator to act as sole arbitrator.

(2) If the party in default does not within 7 clear days of that notice being given—

    (a) make the required appointment, and

    (b) notify the other party that he has done so,

the other party may appoint his arbitrator as sole arbitrator whose award shall be binding on both parties as if he had been so appointed by agreement.

(3) Where a sole arbitrator has been appointed under subsection (2), the party in default may (upon notice to the appointing party) apply to the court which may set aside the appointment.

(4) The leave of the court is required for any appeal from a decision of the court under this section.

Failure of appointment procedure

18.—(1) The parties are free to agree what is to happen in the event of a failure of the procedure for the appointment of the arbitral tribunal.

There is no failure if an appointment is duly made under section 17 (power in case of default to appoint sole arbitrator), unless that appointment is set aside.

(2) If or to the extent that there is no such agreement any party to the arbitration agreement may (upon notice to the other parties) apply to the court to exercise its powers under this section.

651

(3) Those powers are—
  (a) to give directions as to the making of any necessary appointments;
  (b) to direct that the tribunal shall be constituted by such appointments (or any one or more of them) as have been made;
  (c) to revoke any appointments already made;
  (d) to make any necessary appointments itself.

(4) An appointment made by the court under this section has effect as if made with the agreement of the parties.

(5) The leave of the court is required for any appeal from a decision of the court under this section.

Court to have regard to agreed qualifications

19.—In deciding whether to exercise, and in considering how to exercise, any of its powers under section 16 (procedure for appointment of arbitrators) or section 18 (failure of appointment procedure), the court shall have due regard to any agreement of the parties as to the qualifications required of the arbitrators.

Chairman

20.—(1) Where the parties have agreed that there is to be a chairman, they are free to agree what the functions of the chairman are to be in relation to the making of decisions, orders and awards.

(2) If or to the extent that there is no such agreement, the following provisions apply.

(3) Decisions, orders and awards shall be made by all or a majority of the arbitrators (including the chairman).

(4) The view of the chairman shall prevail in relation to a decision, order or award in respect of which there is neither unanimity nor a majority under subsection (3).

Umpire

21.—(1) Where the parties have agreed that there is to be an umpire, they are free to agree what the functions of the umpire are to be, and in particular—
  (a) whether he is to attend the proceedings, and
  (b) when he is to replace the other arbitrators as the tribunal with power to make decisions, orders and awards.

(2) If or to the extent that there is no such agreement, the following provisions apply.

(3) The umpire shall attend the proceedings and be supplied with the same documents and other materials as are supplied to the other arbitrators.

(4) Decisions, orders and awards shall be made by the other arbitrators unless and until they cannot agree on any matter relating to the arbitration.

In that event they shall forthwith give notice in writing to the parties and the umpire, whereupon the umpire shall replace them as the tribunal with power to make decisions, orders and awards as if he were sole arbitrator.

(5) If the arbitrators cannot agree but fail to give notice of that fact, or if any of them fails to join in the giving of notice, any party to the arbitral proceedings may (upon notice to the other parties and to the tribunal) apply to the court which may order that the umpire shall replace the other arbitrators as the tribunal with power to make decisions, orders and awards as if he were sole arbitrator.

652

(6) The leave of the court is required for any appeal from a decision of the court under this section.

Decision-making where no chairman or umpire

22.—(1) Where the parties agree that there shall be two or more arbitrators with no chairman or umpire, the parties are free to agree how the tribunal is to make decisions, orders and awards.

(2) If there is no such agreement, decisions, orders and awards shall be made by all or a majority of the arbitrators.

Revocation of arbitrator's authority

23.—(1) The parties are free to agree in what circumstances the authority of an arbitrator may be revoked.

(2) If or to the extent that there is no such agreement the following provisions apply.

(3) The authority of an arbitrator may not be revoked except—

  (a) by the parties acting jointly, or

  (b) by an arbitral or other institution or person vested by the parties with powers in that regard.

(4) Revocation of the authority of an arbitrator by the parties acting jointly must be agreed in writing unless the parties also agree (whether or not in writing) to terminate the arbitration agreement.

(5) Nothing in this section affects the power of the court—

  (a) to revoke an appointment under section 18 (powers exercisable in case of failure of appointment procedure), or

  (b) to remove an arbitrator on the grounds specified in section 24.

Power of court to remove arbitrator

24.—(1) A party to arbitral proceedings may (upon notice to the other parties, to the arbitrator concerned and to any other arbitrator) apply to the court to remove an arbitrator on any of the following grounds—

  (a) that circumstances exist that give rise to justifiable doubts as to his impartiality;

  (b) that he does not possess the qualifications required by the arbitration agreement;

  (c) that he is physically or mentally incapable of conducting the proceedings or there are justifiable doubts as to his capacity to do so;

  (d) that he has refused or failed—

    (i) properly to conduct the proceedings, or

    (ii) to use all reasonable despatch in conducting the proceedings or making an award,

  and that substantial injustice has been or will be caused to the applicant.

(2) If there is an arbitral or other institution or person vested by the parties with power to remove an arbitrator, the court shall not exercise its power of removal unless satisfied that the applicant has first exhausted any available recourse to that institution or person.

(3) The arbitral tribunal may continue the arbitral proceedings and make an award while an application to the court under this section is pending.

(4) Where the court removes an arbitrator, it may make such order as it thinks fit with

653

respect to his entitlement (if any) to fees or expenses, or the repayment of any fees or expenses already paid.

(5) The arbitrator concerned is entitled to appear and be heard by the court before it makes any order under this section.

(6) The leave of the court is required for any appeal from a decision of the court under this section.

Resignation of arbitrator

25.—(1) The parties are free to agree with an arbitrator as to the consequences of his resignation as regards—

(a) his entitlement (if any) to fees or expenses, and

(b) any liability thereby incurred by him.

(2) If or to the extent that there is no such agreement in writing the following provisions apply.

(3) An arbitrator who resigns his appointment may (upon notice to the parties) apply to the court—

(a) to grant him relief from any liability thereby incurred by him, and

(b) to make such order as it thinks fit with respect to his entitlement (if any) to fees or expenses or the repayment of any fees or expenses already paid.

(4) If the court is satisfied that in all the circumstances it was reasonable for the arbitrator to resign, it may grant such relief as is mentioned in subsection (3)(a) on such terms as it thinks fit.

(5) The leave of the court is required for any appeal from a decision of the court under this section.

Death of arbitrator or person appointing him

26.—(1) The authority of an arbitrator is personal and ceases on his death.

(2) Unless otherwise agreed by the parties, the death of the person by whom an arbitrator was appointed does not revoke the arbitrator's authority.

Filling of vacancy, &c.

27.—(1) Where an arbitrator ceases to hold office, the parties are free to agree—

(a) whether and if so how the vacancy is to be filled,

(b) whether and if so to what extent the previous proceedings should stand, and

(c) what effect (if any) his ceasing to hold office has on any appointment made by him (alone or jointly).

(2) If or to the extent that there is no such agreement, the following provisions apply.

(3) The provisions of sections 16 (procedure for appointment of arbitrators) and 18 (failure of appointment procedure) apply in relation to the filling of the vacancy as in relation to an original appointment.

(4) The tribunal (when reconstituted) shall determine whether and if so to what extent the previous proceedings should stand.

This does not affect any right of a party to challenge those proceedings on any ground which had arisen before the arbitrator ceased to hold office.

(5) His ceasing to hold office does not affect any appointment by him (alone or jointly) of another arbitrator, in particular any appointment of a chairman or umpire.

654

Joint and several liability of parties to arbitrators for fees and expenses

28.—(1) The parties are jointly and severally liable to pay to the arbitrators such reasonable fees and expenses (if any) as are appropriate in the circumstances.

(2) Any party may apply to the court (upon notice to the other parties and to the arbitrators) which may order that the amount of the arbitrators' fees and expenses shall be considered and adjusted by such means and upon such terms as it may direct.

(3) If the application is made after any amount has been paid to the arbitrators by way of fees or expenses, the court may order the repayment of such amount (if any) as is shown to be excessive, but shall not do so unless it is shown that it is reasonable in the circumstances to order repayment.

(4) The above provisions have effect subject to any order of the court under section 24(4) or 25(3)(b) (order as to entitlement to fees or expenses in case of removal or resignation of arbitrator).

(5) Nothing in this section affects any liability of a party to any other party to pay all or any of the costs of the arbitration (see sections 59 to 65) or any contractual right of an arbitrator to payment of his fees and expenses.

(6) In this section references to arbitrators include an arbitrator who has ceased to act and an umpire who has not replaced the other arbitrators.

Immunity of arbitrator

29.—(1) An arbitrator is not liable for anything done or omitted in the discharge or purported discharge of his functions as arbitrator unless the act or omission is shown to have been in bad faith.

(2) Subsection (1) applies to an employee or agent of an arbitrator as it applies to the arbitrator himself.

(3) This section does not affect any liability incurred by an arbitrator by reason of his resigning (but see section 25).

Jurisdiction of the arbitral tribunal

Competence of tribunal to rule on its own jurisdiction

30.—(1) Unless otherwise agreed by the parties, the arbitral tribunal may rule on its own substantive jurisdiction, that is, as to—
   (a) whether there is a valid arbitration agreement,
   (b) whether the tribunal is properly constituted, and
   (c) what matters have been submitted to arbitration in accordance with the arbitration agreement.

(2) Any such ruling may be challenged by any available arbitral process of appeal or review or in accordance with the provisions of this Part.

Objection to substantive jurisdiction of tribunal

31.—(1) An objection that the arbitral tribunal lacks substantive jurisdiction at the outset of the proceedings must be raised by a party not later than the time he takes the first step in the proceedings to contest the merits of any matter in relation to which he challenges the tribunal's jurisdiction.

A party is not precluded from raising such an objection by the fact that he has appointed or participated in the appointment of an arbitrator.

(2) Any objection during the course of the arbitral proceedings that the arbitral tribunal is exceeding its substantive jurisdiction must be made as soon as possible after the matter alleged to be beyond its jurisdiction is raised.

(3) The arbitral tribunal may admit an objection later than the time specified in subsection (1) or (2) if it considers the delay justified.

(4) Where an objection is duly taken to the tribunal's substantive jurisdiction and the tribunal has power to rule on its own jurisdiction, it may—

(a) rule on the matter in an award as to jurisdiction, or

(b) deal with the objection in its award on the merits.

If the parties agree which of these courses the tribunal should take, the tribunal shall proceed accordingly.

(5) The tribunal may in any case, and shall if the parties so agree, stay proceedings whilst an application is made to the court under section 32 (determination of preliminary point of jurisdiction).

Determination of preliminary point of jurisdiction

32.—(1) The court may, on the application of a party to arbitral proceedings (upon notice to the other parties), determine any question as to the substantive jurisdiction of the tribunal.

A party may lose the right to object (see section 73).

(2) An application under this section shall not be considered unless—

(a) it is made with the agreement in writing of all the other parties to the proceedings, or

(b) it is made with the permission of the tribunal and the court is satisfied—

(i) that the determination of the question is likely to produce substantial savings in costs,

(ii) that the application was made without delay, and

(iii) that there is good reason why the matter should be decided by the court.

(3) An application under this section, unless made with the agreement of all the other parties to the proceedings, shall state the grounds on which it is said that the matter should be decided by the court.

(4) Unless otherwise agreed by the parties, the arbitral tribunal may continue the arbitral proceedings and make an award while an application to the court under this section is pending.

(5) Unless the court gives leave, no appeal lies from a decision of the court whether the conditions specified in subsection (2) are met.

(6) The decision of the court on the question of jurisdiction shall be treated as a judgment of the court for the purposes of an appeal.

But no appeal lies without the leave of the court unless the court certifies that the question involves a point of law which is one of general importance or is one which for some other special reason should be considered by the Court of Appeal.

The arbitral proceedings

General duty of the tribunal

33.—(1) The tribunal shall—

(a) act fairly and impartially as between the parties, giving each party a reasonable opportunity of putting his case and dealing with that of his opponent, and

(b) adopt procedures suitable to the circumstances of the particular case, avoiding unnecessary delay or expense, so as to provide a fair means for the resolution of the matters falling to be determined.

(2) The tribunal shall comply with that general duty in conducting the arbitral proceedings, in its decisions on matters of procedure and evidence and in the exercise of all other powers conferred on it.

Procedural and evidential matters

34.—(1) It shall be for the tribunal to decide all procedural and evidential matters, subject to the right of the parties to agree any matter.

(2) Procedural and evidential matters include—

(a) when and where any part of the proceedings is to be held;

(b) the language or languages to be used in the proceedings and whether translations of any relevant documents are to be supplied;

(c) whether any and if so what form of written statements of claim and defence are to be used, when these should be supplied and the extent to which such statements can be later amended;

(d) whether any and if so which documents or classes of documents should be disclosed between and produced by the parties and at what stage;

(e) whether any and if so what questions should be put to and answered by the respective parties and when and in what form this should be done;

(f) whether to apply strict rules of evidence (or any other rules) as to the admissibility, relevance or weight of any material (oral, written or other) sought to be tendered on any matters of fact or opinion, and the time, manner and form in which such material should be exchanged and presented;

(g) whether and to what extent the tribunal should itself take the initiative in ascertaining the facts and the law;

(h) whether and to what extent there should be oral or written evidence or submissions.

(3) The tribunal may fix the time within which any directions given by it are to be complied with, and may if it thinks fit extend the time so fixed (whether or not it has expired).

Consolidation of proceedings and concurrent hearings

35.—(1) The parties are free to agree—

(a) that the arbitral proceedings shall be consolidated with other arbitral proceedings, or

(b) that concurrent hearings shall be held,

on such terms as may be agreed.

(2) Unless the parties agree to confer such power on the tribunal, the tribunal has no power to order consolidation of proceedings or concurrent hearings.

Legal or other representation

36. Unless otherwise agreed by the parties, a party to arbitral proceedings may be represented in the proceedings by a lawyer or other person chosen by him.

657

Power to appoint experts, legal advisers or assessors

37.—(1) Unless otherwise agreed by the parties—

    (a) the tribunal may—

        (i) appoint experts or legal advisers to report to it and the parties, or

        (ii) appoint assessors to assist it on technical matters,

    and may allow any such expert, legal adviser or assessor to attend the proceedings; and

    (b) the parties shall be given a reasonable opportunity to comment on any information, opinion or advice offered by any such person.

(2) The fees and expenses of an expert, legal adviser or assessor appointed by the tribunal for which the arbitrators are liable are expenses of the arbitrators for the purposes of this Part.

General powers exercisable by the tribunal

38.—(1) The parties are free to agree on the powers exercisable by the arbitral tribunal for the purposes of and in relation to the proceedings.

(2) Unless otherwise agreed by the parties the tribunal has the following powers.

(3) The tribunal may order a party to provide security for the costs of the arbitration wherever the court would have power (in proceedings before the court) to order a party to provide security for costs.

The tribunal shall exercise its power on the same principles as the court.

(4) The tribunal may give directions in relation to any property which is the subject of the proceedings or as to which any question arises in the proceedings, and which is owned by or is in the possession of a party to the proceedings—

    (a) for the inspection, photographing, preservation, custody or detention of the property by the tribunal, an expert or a party, or

    (b) ordering that samples be taken from, or any observation be made of or experiment conducted upon, the property.

(5) The tribunal may direct that a party or witness shall be examined on oath or affirmation, and may for that purpose administer any necessary oath or take any necessary affirmation.

(6) The tribunal may give directions to a party for the preservation for the purposes of the proceedings of any evidence in his custody or control.

Power to make provisional awards

39.—(1) The parties are free to agree that the tribunal shall have power to order on a provisional basis any relief which it would have power to grant in a final award.

(2) This includes, for instance, making—

    (a) a provisional order for the payment of money or the disposition of property as between the parties, or

    (b) an order to make an interim payment on account of the costs of the arbitration.

(3) Any such order shall be subject to the tribunal's final adjudication; and the tribunal's final award, on the merits or as to costs, shall take account of any such order.

(4) Unless the parties agree to confer such power on the tribunal, the tribunal has no such power.

This does not affect its powers under section 47 (awards on different issues, &c.).

General duty of parties

40.—(1) The parties shall do all things necessary for the proper and expeditious conduct of the arbitral proceedings.

(2) This includes—

    (a) complying without delay with any determination of the tribunal as to procedural or evidential matters, or with any order or directions of the tribunal, and

    (b) where appropriate, taking without delay any necessary steps to obtain a decision of the court on a preliminary question of jurisdiction or law (see sections 32 and 45).

Powers of tribunal in case of party's default

41.—(1) The parties are free to agree on the powers of the tribunal in case of a party's failure to do something necessary for the proper and expeditious conduct of the arbitration.

(2) Unless otherwise agreed by the parties, the following provisions apply.

(3) If the tribunal is satisfied that there has been inordinate and inexcusable delay on the part of the claimant in pursuing his claim and that the delay—

    (a) gives rise, or is likely to give rise, to a substantial risk that it is not possible to have a fair resolution of the issues in that claim, or

    (b) has caused, or is likely to cause, serious prejudice to the respondent,

the tribunal may make an award dismissing the claim.

(4) If without showing sufficient cause a party—

    (a) fails to attend or be represented at an oral hearing of which due notice was given, or

    (b) where matters are to be dealt with in writing, fails after due notice to submit written evidence or make written submissions,

the tribunal may continue the proceedings in the absence of that party or, as the case may be, without any written evidence or submissions on his behalf, and may make an award on the basis of the evidence before it.

(5) If without showing sufficient cause a party fails to comply with any order or directions of the tribunal, the tribunal may make a peremptory order to the same effect, prescribing such time for compliance with it as the tribunal considers appropriate.

(6) If a claimant fails to comply with a peremptory order of the tribunal to provide security for costs, the tribunal may make an award dismissing his claim.

(7) If a party fails to comply with any other kind of peremptory order, then, without prejudice to section 42 (enforcement by court of tribunal's peremptory orders), the tribunal may do any of the following—

    (a) direct that the party in default shall not be entitled to rely upon any allegation or material which was the subject matter of the order;

    (b) draw such adverse inferences from the act of non-compliance as the circumstances justify;

    (c) proceed to an award on the basis of such materials as have been properly provided to it;

    (d) make such order as it thinks fit as to the payment of costs of the arbitration incurred in consequence of the non-compliance.

Powers of court in relation to arbitral proceedings

Enforcement of peremptory orders of tribunal

42.—(1) Unless otherwise agreed by the parties, the court may make an order requiring a party to comply with a peremptory order made by the tribunal.

(2) An application for an order under this section may be made—

(a) by the tribunal (upon notice to the parties),

(b) by a party to the arbitral proceedings with the permission of the tribunal (and upon notice to the other parties), or

(c) where the parties have agreed that the powers of the court under this section shall be available.

(3) The court shall not act unless it is satisfied that the applicant has exhausted any available arbitral process in respect of failure to comply with the tribunal's order.

(4) No order shall be made under this section unless the court is satisfied that the person to whom the tribunal's order was directed has failed to comply with it within the time prescribed in the order or, if no time was prescribed, within a reasonable time.

(5) The leave of the court is required for any appeal from a decision of the court under this section.

Securing the attendance of witnesses

43.—(1) A party to arbitral proceedings may use the same court procedures as are available in relation to legal proceedings to secure the attendance before the tribunal of a witness in order to give oral testimony or to produce documents or other material evidence.

(2) This may only be done with the permission of the tribunal or the agreement of the other parties.

(3) The court procedures may only be used if—

(a) the witness is in the United Kingdom, and

(b) the arbitral proceedings are being conducted in England and Wales or, as the case may be, Northern Ireland.

(4) A person shall not be compelled by virtue of this section to produce any document or other material evidence which he could not be compelled to produce in legal proceedings.

Court powers exercisable in support of arbitral proceedings

44.—(1) Unless otherwise agreed by the parties, the court has for the purposes of and in relation to arbitral proceedings the same power of making orders about the matters listed below as it has for the purposes of and in relation to legal proceedings.

(2) Those matters are—

(a) the taking of the evidence of witnesses;

(b) the preservation of evidence;

(c) making orders relating to property which is the subject of the proceedings or as to which any question arises in the proceedings—

(i) for the inspection, photographing, preservation, custody or detention of the property, or

(ii) ordering that samples be taken from, or any observation be made of or experiment conducted upon, the property;

and for that purpose authorising any person to enter any premises in the possession or control of a party to the arbitration;

(d) the sale of any goods the subject of the proceedings;

(e) the granting of an interim injunction or the appointment of a receiver.

(3) If the case is one of urgency, the court may, on the application of a party or proposed party to the arbitral proceedings, make such orders as it thinks necessary for the purpose of preserving evidence or assets.

(4) If the case is not one of urgency, the court shall act only on the application of a party to the arbitral proceedings (upon notice to the other parties and to the tribunal) made with the permission of the tribunal or the agreement in writing of the other parties.

(5) In any case the court shall act only if or to the extent that the arbitral tribunal, and any arbitral or other institution or person vested by the parties with power in that regard, has no power or is unable for the time being to act effectively.

(6) If the court so orders, an order made by it under this section shall cease to have effect in whole or in part on the order of the tribunal or of any such arbitral or other institution or person having power to act in relation to the subject-matter of the order.

(7) The leave of the court is required for any appeal from a decision of the court under this section.

Determination of preliminary point of law

45.—(1) Unless otherwise agreed by the parties, the court may on the application of a party to arbitral proceedings (upon notice to the other parties) determine any question of law arising in the course of the proceedings which the court is satisfied substantially affects the rights of one or more of the parties.

An agreement to dispense with reasons for the tribunal's award shall be considered an agreement to exclude the court's jurisdiction under this section.

(2) An application under this section shall not be considered unless—

(a) it is made with the agreement of all the other parties to the proceedings, or

(b) it is made with the permission of the tribunal and the court is satisfied—

(i) that the determination of the question is likely to produce substantial savings in costs, and

(ii) that the application was made without delay.

(3) The application shall identify the question of law to be determined and, unless made with the agreement of all the other parties to the proceedings, shall state the grounds on which it is said that the question should be decided by the court.

(4) Unless otherwise agreed by the parties, the arbitral tribunal may continue the arbitral proceedings and make an award while an application to the court under this section is pending.

(5) Unless the court gives leave, no appeal lies from a decision of the court whether the conditions specified in subsection (2) are met.

(6) The decision of the court on the question of law shall be treated as a judgment of the court for the purposes of an appeal.

But no appeal lies without the leave of the court unless the court certifies that the question is one of general importance, or is one which for some other special reason should be considered by the Court of Appeal.

661

The award

Rules applicable to substance of dispute

46.—(1) The arbitral tribunal shall decide the dispute—

    (a) in accordance with the law chosen by the parties as applicable to the substance of the dispute, or

    (b) if the parties so agree, in accordance with such other considerations as are agreed by them or determined by the tribunal.

(2) For this purpose the choice of the laws of a country shall be understood to refer to the substantive laws of that country and not its conflict of laws rules.

(3) If or to the extent that there is no such choice or agreement, the tribunal shall apply the law determined by the conflict of laws rules which it considers applicable.

Awards on different issues, &c.

47.—(1) Unless otherwise agreed by the parties, the tribunal may make more than one award at different times on different aspects of the matters to be determined.

(2) The tribunal may, in particular, make an award relating—

    (a) to an issue affecting the whole claim, or

    (b) to a part only of the claims or cross-claims submitted to it for decision.

(3) If the tribunal does so, it shall specify in its award the issue, or the claim or part of a claim, which is the subject matter of the award.

Remedies

48.—(1) The parties are free to agree on the powers exercisable by the arbitral tribunal as regards remedies.

(2) Unless otherwise agreed by the parties, the tribunal has the following powers.

(3) The tribunal may make a declaration as to any matter to be determined in the proceedings.

(4) The tribunal may order the payment of a sum of money, in any currency.

(5) The tribunal has the same powers as the court—

    (a) to order a party to do or refrain from doing anything;

    (b) to order specific performance of a contract (other than a contract relating to land);

    (c) to order the rectification, setting aside or cancellation of a deed or other document.

Interest

49.—(1) The parties are free to agree on the powers of the tribunal as regards the award of interest.

(2) Unless otherwise agreed by the parties the following provisions apply.

(3) The tribunal may award simple or compound interest from such dates, at such rates and with such rests as it considers meets the justice of the case—

    (a) on the whole or part of any amount awarded by the tribunal, in respect of any period up to the date of the award;

    (b) on the whole or part of any amount claimed in the arbitration and outstanding at the commencement of the arbitral proceedings but paid before the award was made, in respect of any period up to the date of payment.

(4) The tribunal may award simple or compound interest from the date of the award (or any later date) until payment, at such rates and with such rests as it considers meets the justice of the case, on the outstanding amount of any award (including any award of interest under subsection (3) and any award as to costs).

(5) References in this section to an amount awarded by the tribunal include an amount payable in consequence of a declaratory award by the tribunal.

(6) The above provisions do not affect any other power of the tribunal to award interest.

Extension of time for making award

50.—(1) Where the time for making an award is limited by or in pursuance of the arbitration agreement, then, unless otherwise agreed by the parties, the court may in accordance with the following provisions by order extend that time.

(2) An application for an order under this section may be made—

    (a) by the tribunal (upon notice to the parties), or

    (b) by any party to the proceedings (upon notice to the tribunal and the other parties),

but only after exhausting any available arbitral process for obtaining an extension of time.

(3) The court shall only make an order if satisfied that a substantial injustice would otherwise be done.

(4) The court may extend the time for such period and on such terms as it thinks fit, and may do so whether or not the time previously fixed (by or under the agreement or by a previous order) has expired.

(5) The leave of the court is required for any appeal from a decision of the court under this section.

Settlement

51.—(1) If during arbitral proceedings the parties settle the dispute, the following provisions apply unless otherwise agreed by the parties.

(2) The tribunal shall terminate the substantive proceedings and, if so requested by the parties and not objected to by the tribunal, shall record the settlement in the form of an agreed award.

(3) An agreed award shall state that it is an award of the tribunal and shall have the same status and effect as any other award on the merits of the case.

(4) The following provisions of this Part relating to awards (sections 52 to 58) apply to an agreed award.

(5) Unless the parties have also settled the matter of the payment of the costs of the arbitration, the provisions of this Part relating to costs (sections 59 to 65) continue to apply.

Form of award

52.—(1) The parties are free to agree on the form of an award.

(2) If or to the extent that there is no such agreement, the following provisions apply.

(3) The award shall be in writing signed by all the arbitrators or all those assenting to the award.

(4) The award shall contain the reasons for the award unless it is an agreed award or the parties have agreed to dispense with reasons.

(5) The award shall state the seat of the arbitration and the date when the award is made.

Place where award treated as made

53. Unless otherwise agreed by the parties, where the seat of the arbitration is in England and Wales or Northern Ireland, any award in the proceedings shall be treated as made there, regardless of where it was signed, despatched or delivered to any of the parties.

Date of award

54.—(1) Unless otherwise agreed by the parties, the tribunal may decide what is to be taken to be the date on which the award was made.

(2) In the absence of any such decision, the date of the award shall be taken to be the date on which it is signed by the arbitrator or, where more than one arbitrator signs the award, by the last of them.

Notification of award

55.—(1) The parties are free to agree on the requirements as to notification of the award to the parties.

(2) If there is no such agreement, the award shall be notified to the parties by service on them of copies of the award, which shall be done without delay after the award is made.

(3) Nothing in this section affects section 56 (power to withhold award in case of non-payment).

Power to withhold award in case of non-payment

56.—(1) The tribunal may refuse to deliver an award to the parties except upon full payment of the fees and expenses of the arbitrators.

(2) If the tribunal refuses on that ground to deliver an award, a party to the arbitral proceedings may (upon notice to the other parties and the tribunal) apply to the court, which may order that—

    (a) the tribunal shall deliver the award on the payment into court by the applicant of the fees and expenses demanded, or such lesser amount as the court may specify,

    (b) the amount of the fees and expenses properly payable shall be determined by such means and upon such terms as the court may direct, and

    (c) that out of the money paid into court there shall be paid out such fees and expenses as may be found to be properly payable and the balance of the money (if any) shall be paid out to the applicant.

(3) For this purpose the amount of fees and expenses properly payable is the amount the applicant is liable to pay under section 28 or any agreement relating to the payment of the arbitrators.

(4) No application to the court may be made where there is any available arbitral process for appeal or review of the amount of the fees or expenses demanded.

(5) References in this section to arbitrators include an arbitrator who has ceased to act and an umpire who has not replaced the other arbitrators.

(6) The above provisions of this section also apply in relation to any arbitral or other institution or person vested by the parties with powers in relation to the delivery of the tribunal's award.

As they so apply, the references to the fees and expenses of the arbitrators shall be construed as including the fees and expenses of that institution or person.

(7) The leave of the court is required for any appeal from a decision of the court under this section.

(8) Nothing in this section shall be construed as excluding an application under section 28 where payment has been made to the arbitrators in order to obtain the award.

Correction of award or additional award

57.—(1) The parties are free to agree on the powers of the tribunal to correct an award or make an additional award.

(2) If or to the extent there is no such agreement, the following provisions apply.

(3) The tribunal may on its own initiative or on the application of a party—

    (a) correct an award so as to remove any clerical mistake or error arising from an accidental slip or omission or clarify or remove any ambiguity in the award, or

    (b) make an additional award in respect of any matter (including interest or costs) which was presented to the tribunal but omitted from the award.

These powers shall not be exercised without first affording the other parties a reasonable opportunity to make representations to the tribunal.

(4) Any application for the exercise of those powers must be made within 28 days of the date of the award or such longer period as the parties may agree.

(5) Any correction of an award shall be made within 28 days of the date the application was received by the tribunal or, where the correction is made by the tribunal on its own initiative, within 28 days of the date of the award or, in either case, such longer period as the parties may agree.

(6) Any additional award shall be made within 56 days of the date of the original award or such longer period as the parties may agree.

(7) Any correction of an award shall form part of the award.

Effect of award

58.—(1) Unless otherwise agreed by the parties, an award made by the tribunal pursuant to an arbitration agreement is final and binding both on the parties and on any persons claiming through or under them.

(2) This does not affect the right of a person to challenge the award by any available arbitral process of appeal or review or in accordance with the provisions of this Part.

Costs of the arbitration

Costs of the arbitration

59.—(1) References in this Part to the costs of the arbitration are to—

    (a) the arbitrators' fees and expenses,

    (b) the fees and expenses of any arbitral institution concerned, and

    (c) the legal or other costs of the parties.

(2) Any such reference includes the costs of or incidental to any proceedings to determine the amount of the recoverable costs of the arbitration (see section 63).

665

Agreement to pay costs in any event

60. An agreement which has the effect that a party is to pay the whole or part of the costs of the arbitration in any event is only valid if made after the dispute in question has arisen.

Award of costs

61.—(1) The tribunal may make an award allocating the costs of the arbitration as between the parties, subject to any agreement of the parties.

(2) Unless the parties otherwise agree, the tribunal shall award costs on the general principle that costs should follow the event except where it appears to the tribunal that in the circumstances this is not appropriate in relation to the whole or part of the costs.

Effect of agreement or award about costs

62. Unless the parties otherwise agree, any obligation under an agreement between them as to how the costs of the arbitration are to be borne, or under an award allocating the costs of the arbitration, extends only to such costs as are recoverable.

The recoverable costs of the arbitration

63.—(1) The parties are free to agree what costs of the arbitration are recoverable.

(2) If or to the extent there is no such agreement, the following provisions apply.

(3) The tribunal may determine by award the recoverable costs of the arbitration on such basis as it thinks fit.

If it does so, it shall specify—

    (a) the basis on which it has acted, and

    (b) the items of recoverable costs and the amount referable to each.

(4) If the tribunal does not determine the recoverable costs of the arbitration, any party to the arbitral proceedings may apply to the court (upon notice to the other parties) which may—

    (a) determine the recoverable costs of the arbitration on such basis as it thinks fit, or

    (b) order that they shall be determined by such means and upon such terms as it may specify.

(5) Unless the tribunal or the court determines otherwise—

    (a) the recoverable costs of the arbitration shall be determined on the basis that there shall be allowed a reasonable amount in respect of all costs reasonably incurred, and

    (b) any doubt as to whether costs were reasonably incurred or were reasonable in amount shall be resolved in favour of the paying party.

(6) The above provisions have effect subject to section 64 (recoverable fees and expenses of arbitrators).

(7) Nothing in this section affects any right of the arbitrators, any expert, legal adviser or assessor appointed by the tribunal, or any arbitral institution, to payment of their fees and expenses.

Recoverable fees and expenses of arbitrators

64.—(1) Unless otherwise agreed by the parties, the recoverable costs of the arbitration shall include in respect of the fees and expenses of the arbitrators only such reasonable fees and expenses as are appropriate in the circumstances.

(2) If there is any question as to what reasonable fees and expenses are appropriate in the circumstances, and the matter is not already before the court on an application under section 63(4), the court may on the application of any party (upon notice to the other parties)—

(a) determine the matter, or

(b) order that it be determined by such means and upon such terms as the court may specify.

(3) Subsection (1) has effect subject to any order of the court under section 24(4) or 25(3)(b) (order as to entitlement to fees or expenses in case of removal or resignation of arbitrator).

(4) Nothing in this section affects any right of the arbitrator to payment of his fees and expenses.

Power to limit recoverable costs

65.—(1) Unless otherwise agreed by the parties, the tribunal may direct that the recoverable costs of the arbitration, or of any part of the arbitral proceedings, shall be limited to a specified amount.

(2) Any direction may be made or varied at any stage, but this must be done sufficiently in advance of the incurring of costs to which it relates, or the taking of any steps in the proceedings which may be affected by it, for the limit to be taken into account.

Powers of the court in relation to award

Enforcement of the award

66.—(1) An award made by the tribunal pursuant to an arbitration agreement may, by leave of the court, be enforced in the same manner as a judgment or order of the court to the same effect.

(2) Where leave is so given, judgment may be entered in terms of the award.

(3) Leave to enforce an award shall not be given if, or to the extent that—

(a) it is so defective in form or substance that it is incapable of enforcement, or

(b) its enforcement would be contrary to public policy.

(4) Leave to enforce an award shall not be given where, or to the extent that, the person against whom it is sought to be enforced shows that the tribunal lacked substantive jurisdiction to make the award.

The right to raise such an objection may have been lost (see section 73).

(5) Nothing in this section affects the recognition or enforcement of an award under any other enactment or rule of law, in particular under Part II of the Arbitration Act 1950 (enforcement of awards under Geneva Convention) or the provisions of Part III of this Act relating to the recognition and enforcement of awards under the New York Convention.

Challenging the award: substantive jurisdiction

67.—(1) A party to arbitral proceedings may (upon notice to the other parties and to the tribunal) apply to the court—

(a) challenging any award of the arbitral tribunal as to its substantive jurisdiction; or

(b) for an order declaring an award made by the tribunal on the merits to be of no effect, in whole or in part, because the tribunal did not have substantive jurisdiction.

A party may lose the right to object (see section 73) and the right to apply is subject to the restrictions in section 70(2) and (3).

667

(2) The arbitral tribunal may continue the arbitral proceedings and make a further award while an application to the court under this section is pending in relation to an award as to jurisdiction.

(3) On an application under this section challenging an award of the arbitral tribunal as to its substantive jurisdiction, the court may by order—

    (a) confirm the award,

    (b) vary the award, or

    (c) set aside the award in whole or in part.

(4) The leave of the court is required for any appeal from a decision of the court under this section.

Challenging the award: serious irregularity

68.—(1) A party to arbitral proceedings may (upon notice to the other parties and to the tribunal) apply to the court challenging an award in the proceedings on the ground of serious irregularity affecting the tribunal, the proceedings or the award.

A party may lose the right to object (see section 73) and the right to apply is subject to the restrictions in section 70(2) and (3).

(2) Serious irregularity means an irregularity of one or more of the following kinds which the court considers has caused or will cause substantial injustice to the applicant—

    (a) failure by the tribunal to comply with section 33 (general duty of tribunal):

    (b) the tribunal exceeding its powers (otherwise than by exceeding its substantive jurisdiction: see section 67);

    (c) failure by the tribunal to conduct the proceedings in accordance with the procedure agreed by the parties;

    (d) failure by the tribunal to deal with all the issues that were put to it;

    (e) any arbitral or other institution or person vested by the parties with powers in relation to the proceedings or the award exceeding its powers;

    (f) uncertainty or ambiguity of the award;

    (g) the award being obtained by fraud or the award or the way in which it was procured being contrary to public policy;

    (h) failure to comply with the requirements as to the form of the award; or

    (i) any irregularity in the conduct of the proceedings or in the award which is admitted by the tribunal or by any arbitral or other institution or person vested by the parties with powers in relation to the proceedings or the award.

(3) If there is shown to be serious irregularity affecting the tribunal, the proceedings or the award, the court may—

    (a) remit the award to the tribunal, in whole or in part, for reconsideration,

    (b) set the award aside in whole or in part, or

    (c) declare the award to be of no effect, in whole or in part.

The court shall not exercise its power to set aside or to declare an award to be of no effect, in whole or in part, unless it is satisfied that it would be inappropriate to remit the matters in question to the tribunal for reconsideration.

(4) The leave of the court is required for any appeal from a decision of the court under this section.

Appeal on point of law

69.—(1) Unless otherwise agreed by the parties, a party to arbitral proceedings may (upon notice to the other parties and to the tribunal) appeal to the court on a question of law arising out of an award made in the proceedings.

An agreement to dispense with reasons for the tribunal's award shall be considered an agreement to exclude the court's jurisdiction under this section.

(2) An appeal shall not be brought under this section except—

    (a) with the agreement of all the other parties to the proceedings, or

    (b) with the leave of the court.

The right to appeal is also subject to the restrictions in section 70(2) and (3).

(3) Leave to appeal shall be given only if the court is satisfied—

    (a) that the determination of the question will substantially affect the rights of one or more of the parties,

    (b) that the question is one which the tribunal was asked to determine,

    (c) that, on the basis of the findings of fact in the award—

        (i) the decision of the tribunal on the question is obviously wrong, or

        (ii) the question is one of general public importance and the decision of the tribunal is at least open to serious doubt, and

    (d) that, despite the agreement of the parties to resolve the matter by arbitration, it is just and proper in all the circumstances for the court to determine the question.

(4) An application for leave to appeal under this section shall identify the question of law to be determined and state the grounds on which it is alleged that leave to appeal should be granted.

(5) The court shall determine an application for leave to appeal under this section without a hearing unless it appears to the court that a hearing is required.

(6) The leave of the court is required for any appeal from a decision of the court under this section to grant or refuse leave to appeal.

(7) On an appeal under this section the court may by order—

    (a) confirm the award,

    (b) vary the award,

    (c) remit the award to the tribunal, in whole or in part, for reconsideration in the light of the court's determination, or

    (d) set aside the award in whole or in part.

The court shall not exercise its power to set aside an award, in whole or in part, unless it is satisfied that it would be inappropriate to remit the matters in question to the tribunal for reconsideration.

(8) The decision of the court on an appeal under this section shall be treated as a judgment of the court for the purposes of a further appeal.

But no such appeal lies without the leave of the court unless the court certifies that the question is one of general importance or is one which for some other special reason should be considered by the Court of Appeal.

Challenge or appeal: supplementary provisions

70.—(1) The following provisions apply to an application or appeal under section 67, 68 or 69.

(2) An application or appeal may not be brought if the applicant has not first exhausted—

    (a) any available arbitral process of appeal or review, and

    (b) any available recourse under section 57 (correction of award or additional award).

(3) Any application or appeal must be brought within 28 days of the date of the award or, if

669

there has been any arbitral process of appeal or review, of the date when the applicant was notified of the result of that process.

(4) If on an application or appeal it appears to the court that the award—

    (a) does not contain the tribunal's reasons, or

    (b) does not set out the tribunal's reasons in sufficient detail to enable the court properly to consider the application or appeal,

the court may order the tribunal to state the reasons for its award in sufficient detail for that purpose.

(5) Where the court makes an order under subsection (4), it may make such further order as it thinks fit with respect to any additional costs of the arbitration resulting from its order.

(6) The court may on an application under section 67 or 68—

    (a) order the applicant to provide security for the costs of the application, and

    (b) order that any money payable under the award shall be brought into court or otherwise secured pending the determination of the application;

and the court may direct that the application shall be dismissed if that order is not complied with.

Challenge or appeal: effect of order of court

71.—(1) The following provisions have effect where the court makes an order under section 67, 68 or 69 with respect to an award.

(2) Where the award is varied, the variation has effect as part of the tribunal's award.

(3) Where the award is remitted to the tribunal, in whole or in part, for reconsideration, the tribunal shall make a fresh award in respect of the matters remitted within three months of the date of the order for remission or such longer or shorter period as the court may direct.

(4) Where the award is set aside or declared to be of no effect, in whole or in part, the court may also order that any provision that an award is a condition precedent to the bringing of legal proceedings in respect of a matter to which the arbitration agreement applies, is of no effect as regards the subject matter of the award or, as the case may be, the relevant part of the award.

Miscellaneous

Saving for rights of person who takes no part in proceedings

72.—(1) A person alleged to be a party to arbitral proceedings but who takes no part in the proceedings may question—

    (a) whether there is a valid arbitration agreement,

    (b) whether the tribunal is properly constituted, or

    (c) what matters have been submitted to arbitration in accordance with the arbitration agreement,

by proceedings in the court for a declaration or injunction or other appropriate relief.

(2) He also has the same right as a party to the arbitral proceedings to challenge an award—

    (a) by an application under section 67 on the ground of lack of substantive jurisdiction in relation to him, or

    (b) by an application under section 68 on the ground of serious irregularity (within the meaning of that section) affecting him;

and section 70(2) (duty to exhaust arbitral procedures) does not apply in his case.

Loss of right to object

73.—(1) If a party to arbitral proceedings takes part, or continues to take part, in the proceedings without making, either forthwith or within such time as is allowed by the arbitration agreement or the tribunal or by any provision of this Part, any objection—

(a) that the tribunal lacks substantive jurisdiction,

(b) that the proceedings have been improperly conducted,

(c) that there has been a failure to comply with the arbitration agreement or with any provision of this Part, or

(d) that there has been any other irregularity affecting the tribunal or the proceedings,

he may not raise that objection later, before the tribunal or the court, unless he shows that, at the time he took part or continued to take part in the proceedings, he did not know and could not with reasonable diligence have discovered the grounds for the objection.

(2) Where the arbitral tribunal rules that it has substantive jurisdiction and a party to arbitral proceedings who could have questioned that ruling—

(a) by any available arbitral process of appeal or review, or

(b) by challenging the award,

does not do so, or does not do so within the time allowed by the arbitration agreement or any provision of this Part, he may not object later to the tribunal's substantive jurisdiction on any ground which was the subject of that ruling.

Immunity of arbitral institutions, &c.

74.—(1) An arbitral or other institution or person designated or requested by the parties to appoint or nominate an arbitrator is not liable for anything done or omitted in the discharge or purported discharge of that function unless the act or omission is shown to have been in bad faith.

(2) An arbitral or other institution or person by whom an arbitrator is appointed or nominated is not liable for anything done or omitted by the arbitrator (or his employees or agents) in the discharge or purported discharge of his functions as arbitrator.

(3) The above provisions apply to an employee or agent of an arbitral or other institution or person as they apply to the institution or person himself.

Charge to secure payment of solicitors' costs

75. The powers of the court to make declarations and orders under section 73 of the Solicitors Act 1974 or Article 71H of the Solicitors (Northern Ireland) Order 1976 (power to charge property recovered in the proceedings with the payment of solicitors' costs) may be exercised in relation to arbitral proceedings as if those proceedings were proceedings in the court.

Supplementary

Service of notices, &c.

76.—(1) The parties are free to agree on the manner of service of any notice or other document required or authorised to be served in pursuance of the arbitration agreement or for the purposes of the arbitral proceedings.

(2) If or to the extent that there is no such agreement the following provisions apply.

671

(3) A notice or other document may be served on a person by any effective means.

(4) If a notice or other document is addressed, pre-paid and delivered by post—

    (a) to the addressee's last known principal residence or, if he is or has been carrying on a trade, profession or business, his last known principal business address, or

    (b) where the addressee is a body corporate, to the body's registered or principal office,

it shall be treated as effectively served.

(5) This section does not apply to the service of documents for the purposes of legal proceedings, for which provision is made by rules of court.

(6) References in this Part to a notice or other document include any form of communication in writing and references to service shall be construed accordingly.

Powers of court in relation to service of documents

77.—(1) This section applies where service of a document on a person in the manner agreed by the parties, or in accordance with provisions of section 76 having effect in default of agreement, is not reasonably practicable.

(2) Unless otherwise agreed by the parties, the court may make such order as it thinks fit—

    (a) for service in such manner as the court may direct, or

    (b) dispensing with service of the document.

(3) Any party to the arbitration agreement may apply for an order, but only after exhausting any available arbitral process for resolving the matter.

(4) The leave of the court is required for any appeal from a decision of the court under this section.

(5) References in this section to a document include any form of communication and references to service shall be construed accordingly.

Reckoning periods of time

78.—(1) The parties are free to agree on the method of reckoning periods of time for the purposes of any provision agreed by them or any provision of this Part having effect in default of such agreement.

(2) If or to the extent there is no such agreement, periods of time shall be reckoned in accordance with the following provisions.

(3) Where the act is required to be done within a specified period after or from a specified date, the period begins immediately after that date.

(4) Where the act is required to be done a specified number of clear days after a specified date, at least that number of days must intervene between the day on which the act is done and that date.

(5) Where the period is a period of seven days or less which would include a Saturday, Sunday or a public holiday in the place where anything which has to be done within the period falls to be done, that day shall be excluded.

In relation to England and Wales or Northern Ireland, a "public holiday" means Christmas Day, Good Friday or a day which under the Banking and Financial Dealings Act 1971 is a bank holiday.

Power of court to extend time limits relating to arbitral proceedings

79.—(1) Unless the parties otherwise agree, the court may by order extend any time limit agreed by them in relation to any matter relating to the arbitral proceedings or specified in any provision of this Part having effect in default of such agreement.

This section does not apply to a time limit to which section 12 applies (power of court to extend time for beginning arbitral proceedings, &c.).

(2) An application for an order may be made—

(a) by any party to the arbitral proceedings (upon notice to the other parties and to the tribunal), or

(b) by the arbitral tribunal (upon notice to the parties).

(3) The court shall not exercise its power to extend a time limit unless it is satisfied—

(a) that any available recourse to the tribunal, or to any arbitral or other institution or person vested by the parties with power in that regard, has first been exhausted, and

(b) that a substantial injustice would otherwise be done.

(4) The court's power under this section may be exercised whether or not the time has already expired.

(5) An order under this section may be made on such terms as the court thinks fit.

(6) The leave of the court is required for any appeal from a decision of the court under this section.

Notice and other requirements in connection with legal proceedings

80.—(1) References in this Part to an application or other step in relation to legal proceedings being taken "upon notice" to the other parties to the arbitral proceedings, or to the tribunal, are to such notice of the originating process as is required by rules of court and do not impose any separate requirement.

(2) Rules of court shall be made—

(a) requiring such notice to be given as indicated by any provision of this Part, and

(b) as to the manner, form and content of any such notice.

(3) Subject to any provision made by rules of court, a requirement to give notice to the tribunal of legal proceedings shall be construed—

(a) if there is more than one arbitrator, as a requirement to give notice to each of them; and

(b) if the tribunal is not fully constituted, as a requirement to give notice to any arbitrator who has been appointed.

(4) References in this Part to making an application to the court within a specified period are to the issue within that period of the appropriate originating process in accordance with rules of court.

(5) Where any provision of this Part requires an application to be made to the court within a specified time, the rules of court relating to the reckoning of periods, and the consequences of not taking a step within the period prescribed by the rules, apply in relation to that requirement.

(6) Provision may be made by rules of court amending the provisions of this Part—

(a) with respect to the time within which any application to the court must be made,

(b) so as to keep any provision made by this Part in relation to arbitral proceedings in step with the corresponding provision of rules of court applying in relation to proceedings in the court, or

(c) so as to keep any provision made by this Part in relation to legal proceedings in step with the corresponding provision of rules of court applying generally in relation to proceedings in the court.

673

(7) Nothing in this section affects the generality of the power to make rules of court.

Saving for certain matters governed by common law

81.—(1) Nothing in this Part shall be construed as excluding the operation of any rule of law consistent with the provisions of this Part.

(2) This applies, in particular, to any rule of law as to—

(a) the effect of an oral arbitration agreement; or

(b) the enforcement of an arbitral award by an action on the award.

(3) Nothing in this Act shall be construed as reviving any jurisdiction of the court to set aside or remit an award on the ground of errors of fact or law on the face of the award.

Minor definitions

82.—(1) In this Part—

"arbitrator", unless the context otherwise requires, includes an umpire;

"available arbitral process", in relation to any matter, includes any process of appeal to or review by an arbitral or other institution or person vested by the parties with powers in relation to that matter;

"claimant", unless the context otherwise requires, includes a counterclaimant, and related expressions shall be construed accordingly;

"the court", unless the context otherwise requires, means the High Court or a county court;

"dispute" includes any difference;

"enactment" includes an enactment contained in Northern Ireland legislation;

"legal proceedings" means civil proceedings in the High Court or a county court;

"peremptory order" means an order made under section 41(5) or made in exercise of any corresponding power conferred by the parties;

"premises" includes land, buildings, moveable structures, vehicles, vessels, aircraft and hovercraft;

"question of law" means—

(a) where the seat of the arbitration is in England and Wales, a question of the law of England and Wales, and

(b) where the seat of the arbitration is in Northern Ireland, a question of the law of Northern Ireland;

"substantive jurisdiction", in relation to an arbitral tribunal, refers to the matters specified in section 30(1)(a) to (c), and references to the tribunal exceeding its substantive jurisdiction shall be construed accordingly.

(2) References in this Part to a party to an arbitration agreement include any person claiming under or through a party to the agreement.

Index of defined expressions: Part I

83. In this Part the expressions listed below are defined or otherwise explained by the provisions indicated—

agreement, agree and agreed	section 5(1)
agreement in writing	section 5(2) to (5)
arbitration agreement	sections 6 and 5(1)

arbitrator	section 82(1)
available arbitral process	section 82(1)
claimant	section 82(1)
commencement (in relation to arbitral proceedings)	section 14
costs of the arbitration	section 59
the court	section 82(1)
dispute	section 82(1)
enactment	section 82(1)
legal proceedings	section 82(1)
Limitation Acts	section 13(4)
notice (or other document)	section 76(6)
party—	
—in relation to an arbitration agreement	section 82(2)
—where section 108(2) or (3) applies	section 108(4)
peremptory order	section 82(1) (and see section 41(5))
premises	section 82(1)
question of law	section 82(1)
recoverable costs	sections 63 and 64
seat of the arbitration	section 3
serve and service (of notice or other document)	section 76(6)
substantive jurisdiction (in relation to an arbitral tribunal)	section 82(1) (and see section 30(1)(a) to (c))
upon notice (to the parties or the tribunal)	section 80
written and in writing	section 5(6)

Transitional provisions

84.—(1) The provisions of this Part do not apply to arbitral proceedings commenced before the date on which this Part comes into force.

(2) They apply to arbitral proceedings commenced on or after that date under an arbitration agreement whenever made.

(3) The above provisions have effect subject to any transitional provision made by an order under section 111(2) (power to include transitional provisions in commencement order).

PART II   OTHER PROVISIONS RELATING TO ARBITRATION

Domestic arbitration agreements

Modification of Part I in relation to domestic arbitration agreement

85.—(1) In the case of a domestic arbitration agreement the provisions of Part I are modified in accordance with the following sections.

(2) For this purpose a "domestic arbitration agreement" means an arbitration agreement to which none of the parties is—

(a) an individual who is a national of, or habitually resident in, a state other than the United Kingdom, or

(b) a body corporate which is incorporated in, or whose central control and management is exercised in, a state other than the United Kingdom,

and under which the seat of the arbitration (if the seat has been designated or determined) is in the United Kingdom.

675

(3) In subsection (2) the "seat of the arbitration" has the same meaning as in Part I (see section 3).

Staying of legal proceedings

86.—(1) In section 9 (stay of legal proceedings), subsection (4) (stay unless the arbitration agreement is null and void, inoperative, or incapable of being performed) does not apply to a domestic arbitration agreement.

(2) On an application under that section in relation to a domestic arbitration agreement the court shall grant a stay unless satisfied—

    (a) that the arbitration agreement is null and void, inoperative, or incapable of being performed, or

    (b) that there are other sufficient grounds for not requiring the parties to abide by the arbitration agreement.

(3) The court may treat as a sufficient ground under subsection (2)(b) the fact that the applicant is or was at any material time not ready and willing to do all things necessary for the proper conduct of the arbitration or of any other dispute resolution procedures required to be exhausted before resorting to arbitration.

(4) For the purposes of this section the question whether an arbitration agreement is a domestic arbitration agreement shall be determined by reference to the facts at the time the legal proceedings are commenced.

Effectiveness of agreement to exclude court's jurisdiction

87.—(1) In the case of a domestic arbitration agreement any agreement to exclude the jurisdiction of the court under—

    (a) section 45 (determination of preliminary point of law), or

    (b) section 69 (challenging the award: appeal on point of law),

is not effective unless entered into after the commencement of the arbitral proceedings in which the question arises or the award is made.

(2) For this purpose the commencement of the arbitral proceedings has the same meaning as in Part I (see section 14).

(3) For the purposes of this section the question whether an arbitration agreement is a domestic arbitration agreement shall be determined by reference to the facts at the time the agreement is entered into.

Power to repeal or amend ss. 85 to 87

88.—(1) The Secretary of State may by order repeal or amend the provisions of sections 85 to 87.

(2) Any such order may also make any corresponding or consequential repeal or amendment of sections 89 to 93 (provisions relating to consumer arbitration agreements) which appears to the Secretary of State to be appropriate.

(3) An order under this section may contain such supplementary, incidental and transitional provisions as appear to the Secretary of State to be appropriate.

(4) An order under this section shall be made by statutory instrument and no such order shall be made unless a draft of it has been laid before and approved by a resolution of each House of Parliament.

Consumer arbitration agreements

89.—(1) A consumer arbitration agreement means an agreement that future disputes arising between parties to a contract entered into by a person as a consumer shall be referred to arbitration.

(2) For this purpose a person enters into a contract as a consumer if—

(a) he neither makes the contract in the course of a business nor holds himself out as doing so,

(b) the other party makes the contract in the course of a business, and

(c) in the case of a contract governed by the law of sale of goods or hire-purchase, or by section 7 of the Unfair Contract Terms Act 1977 (miscellaneous contracts under which goods pass), the goods passing under or in pursuance of the contract are of a type ordinarily supplied for private use or consumption.

But on a sale by auction or by competitive tender the buyer is not in any circumstances to be regarded as entering into the contract as a consumer.

(3) In subsection (2)—

"business" includes a profession and the activities of any government department, Northern Ireland department or local or public authority; and

"goods" has the same meaning as in the Sale of Goods Act 1979.

(4) It is for those claiming that a person entered into a contract otherwise than as a consumer to show that he did so.

Restriction on enforcement of certain consumer arbitration agreements

90.—(1) A consumer arbitration agreement cannot be enforced against the consumer in respect of a cause of action to which this section applies (see section 92), except—

(a) with his written consent signified after the dispute in question has arisen, or

(b) where he has taken part in arbitral proceedings in pursuance of the agreement, whether in respect of that or any other dispute, or

(c) where the court makes an order under section 93 (power to exclude restriction in certain cases where no detriment to consumer).

(2) Sections 9 to 11 in Part I (which relate to the staying of legal proceedings) do not apply to the extent that an arbitration agreement cannot be enforced by virtue of this section.

Exclusions from section 90

91.—(1) Nothing in section 90 affects—

(a) the enforcement of an arbitration agreement other than a domestic arbitration agreement within the meaning of section 85; or

(b) the resolution of a dispute arising under any contract so far as it is, by virtue of section 1(2) of, and Schedule 1 to, the Unfair Contract Terms Act 1977, excluded from the operation of section 2, 3, 4 or 7 of that Act.

(2) For the purposes of this section the question whether an arbitration agreement is a domestic arbitration agreement shall be determined by reference to the facts at the time it is sought to enforce the agreement.

677

Causes of action to which restriction applies

92.—(1) Section 90 (restriction on enforcement of certain consumer arbitration agreements) applies to a cause of action if—

    (a) proceedings in respect of it would be within the jurisdiction of a county court, or

    (b) it satisfies such other conditions as may be prescribed by order under this section.

(2) Orders under this section may make different provision for different cases and for different purposes.

(3) The power to make orders under this section for England and Wales is exercisable by statutory instrument made by the Secretary of State with the concurrence of the Lord Chancellor.

No such order shall be made unless a draft of it has been laid before and approved by resolution of each House of Parliament.

(4) The power to make orders under this section for Northern Ireland is exercisable by the Department of Economic Development for Northern Ireland with the concurrence of the Lord Chancellor.

Any such order—

    (a) shall be a statutory rule for the purposes of the Statutory Rules (Northern Ireland) Order 1979; and

    (b) shall be subject to affirmative resolution, within the meaning of section 41(4) of the Interpretation Act (Northern Ireland) 1954.

(5) An order under this section may provide that section 93 below (power to exclude restriction where no detriment to consumer) applies to a cause of action which satisfies the conditions prescribed by the order.

Power to exclude cases where no detriment to consumer

93.—(1) The court may, if it is satisfied that it is not detrimental to the interests of the consumer for the dispute in question to be referred to arbitration in pursuance of the arbitration agreement, order that the restriction in section 90 on enforcement of a consumer arbitration agreement does not apply.

(2) An application for such an order may only be made after the dispute in question has arisen.

(3) In determining whether a reference to arbitration is or is not detrimental to the interests of the consumer, the court shall have regard to all factors appearing to be relevant, including, in particular, the availability of legal aid and the relative amount of any expense which may result to him—

    (a) if the dispute in question is referred to arbitration in pursuance of the arbitration agreement, and

    (b) if it is determined by proceedings before a court.

(4) This section does not apply to a cause of action if proceedings in a county court in respect of it would fall within the small claims limit, that is, if—

    (a) in England and Wales, they would stand referred to arbitration (without any order of the court) under rules made by virtue of section 64(1)(a) of the County Courts Act 1984;

    (b) in Northern Ireland, the action would be dealt with by way of arbitration by a district judge by virtue of Article 30(3) of the County Courts (Northern Ireland) Order 1980.

678

(5) This section does not apply to a cause of action to which section 90 applies by virtue of an order under section 92(1)(b) unless the order provides that this section shall apply.

(6) The reference in section 90(1)(b) to a consumer taking part in arbitral proceedings in pursuance of the agreement does not include his taking part in arbitral proceedings in consequence of an order under this section.

Small claims arbitration in the county court

Exclusion of Part I in relation to small claims arbitration in the county court

94. Nothing in Part I of this Act applies to arbitration under section 64 of the County Courts Act 1984.

Appointment of judges as arbitrators

Appointment of judges as arbitrators

95.—(1) A judge of the Commercial Court or an official referee may, if in all the circumstances he thinks fit, accept appointment as a sole arbitrator or as umpire by or by virtue of an arbitration agreement.

(2) A judge of the Commercial Court shall not do so unless the Lord Chief Justice has informed him that, having regard to the state of business in the High Court and the Crown Court, he can be made available.

(3) An official referee shall not do so unless the Lord Chief Justice has informed him that, having regard to the state of official referees' business, he can be made available.

(4) The fees payable for the services of a judge of the Commercial Court or official referee as arbitrator or umpire shall be taken in the High Court.

(5) In this section—

"arbitration agreement" has the same meaning as in Part I; and

"official referee" means a person nominated under section 68(1)(a) of the Supreme Court Act 1981 to deal with official referees' business.

(6) The provisions of Part I of this Act apply to arbitration before a person appointed under this section with the modifications specified in Schedule 2.

Statutory arbitrations

Application of Part I to statutory arbitrations

96.—(1) The provisions of Part I apply to every arbitration under an enactment (a "statutory arbitration"), whether the enactment was passed or made before or after the commencement of this Act, subject to the adaptations and exclusions specified in sections 97 to 100.

(2) The provisions of Part I do not apply to a statutory arbitration if or to the extent that their application—

(a) is inconsistent with the provisions of the enactment concerned, with any rules or procedure authorised or recognised by it, or

(b) is excluded by any other enactment.

679

(3) In this section and the following provisions of this Part "enactment"—

    (a) in England and Wales, includes an enactment contained in subordinate legislation within the meaning of the Interpretation Act 1978;

    (b) in Northern Ireland, means a statutory provision within the meaning of section 1(f) of the Interpretation Act (Northern Ireland) 1954.

General adaptation of provisions in relation to statutory arbitrations

97.—(1) The provisions of Part I apply to a statutory arbitration—

    (a) as if the arbitration were pursuant to an arbitration agreement and as if the enactment were that agreement, and

    (b) as if the persons by and against whom a claim subject to arbitration in pursuance of the enactment may be or has been made were parties to that agreement.

(2) Every statutory arbitration shall be taken to have its seat in England and Wales or, as the case may be, in Northern Ireland.

Specific adaptations of provisions in relation to statutory arbitrations

98.—(1) The following provisions of Part I apply to a statutory arbitration with the following adaptations.

(2) In section 30(1) (competence of tribunal to rule on its own jurisdiction), the reference in paragraph (a) to whether there is a valid arbitration agreement shall be construed as a reference to whether the enactment applies to the dispute in question.

(3) Section 35 (consolidation of proceedings and concurrent hearings) applies only so as to authorise the consolidation of proceedings, or concurrent hearings in proceedings, under the same enactment.

(4) Section 46 (rules applicable to substance of dispute) applies with the omission of subsection (1)(b) (determination in accordance with considerations agreed by parties).

Provisions excluded from applying to statutory arbitrations

99. The following provisions of Part I do not apply in relation to a statutory arbitration—

    (a) section 8 (whether agreement discharged by death of a party);

    (b) section 12 (power of court to extend agreed time limits);

    (c) sections 9(5), 10(2) and 71(4) (restrictions on effect of provision that award condition precedent to right to bring legal proceedings).

Power to make further provision by regulations

100.—(1) The Secretary of State may make provision by regulations for adapting or excluding any provision of Part I in relation to statutory arbitrations in general or statutory arbitrations of any particular description.

(2) The power is exercisable whether the enactment concerned is passed or made before or after the commencement of this Act.

(3) Regulations under this section shall be made by statutory instrument which shall be subject to annulment in pursuance of a resolution of either House of Parliament.

Supplementary

Interpretation

101. In this Part, except as otherwise provided, the following expressions have the same meaning as in Part I—

"arbitration agreement",

"commenced", in relation to arbitral proceedings,

"the court",

"dispute",

"seat of the arbitration".

PART III   RECOGNITION AND ENFORCEMENT OF CERTAIN FOREIGN AWARDS

Enforcement of Geneva Convention awards

Continuation of Part II of the Arbitration Act 1950

102. Part II of the Arbitration Act 1950 (enforcement of certain foreign awards) continues to apply in relation to foreign awards within the meaning of that Part which are not also New York Convention awards.

Recognition and enforcement of New York Convention awards

New York Convention awards

103.—(1) In this Part a "New York Convention award" means an award made, in pursuance of an arbitration agreement, in the territory of a state (other than the United Kingdom) which is a party to the New York Convention.

(2) For the purposes of the provisions of this Part relating to such awards, "arbitration agreement" means an arbitration agreement in writing (including an agreement contained in an exchange of letters or telegrams).

(3) If Her Majesty by Order in Council declares that a state specified in the Order is a party to the New York Convention, or is a party in respect of any territory so specified, the Order shall, while in force, be conclusive evidence of that fact.

(4) In this section "the New York Convention" means the Convention on the Recognition and Enforcement of Foreign Arbitral Awards adopted by the United Nations Conference on International Commercial Arbitration on 10th June 1958.

Recognition and enforcement of awards

104.—(1) A New York Convention award shall be recognised as binding on the persons as between whom it was made, and may accordingly be relied on by those persons by way of defence, set-off or otherwise in any legal proceedings in England and Wales or Northern Ireland.

(2) A New York Convention award may, by leave of the High Court or a county court, be enforced in the same manner as a judgment or order of that court to the same effect.

681

(3) Where leave is so given, judgment may be entered in terms of the award.

Evidence to be produced by party seeking recognition or enforcement

105.—(1) A party seeking the recognition or enforcement of a New York Convention award must produce—
(a) the original award or a duly authenticated copy of it, and
(b) the original arbitration agreement or a duly authenticated copy of it.

For this purpose "duly authenticated" means authenticated in the manner required by the law of the country in which the award or agreement was made or in such other manner as the court may direct.

(2) If the award or agreement is in a foreign language, the party must also produce a translation of it certified by an official or sworn translator or by a diplomatic or consular agent.

Refusal of recognition or enforcement

106.—(1) Recognition or enforcement of a New York Convention award shall not be refused except in the following cases.

(2) Recognition or enforcement of the award may be refused if the person against whom it is invoked proves—
(a) that a party to the arbitration agreement was (under the law applicable to him) under some incapacity;
(b) that the arbitration agreement was not valid under the law to which the parties subjected it or, failing any indication thereon, under the law of the country where the award was made;
(c) that he was not given proper notice of the appointment of the arbitrator or of the arbitration proceedings or was otherwise unable to present his case;
(d) that the award deals with a difference not contemplated by or not falling within the terms of the submission to arbitration or contains decision on matters beyond the scope of the submission to arbitration (but see subsection (4));
(e) that the composition of the arbitral tribunal or the arbitral procedure was not in accordance with the agreement of the parties or, failing such agreement, with the law of the country in which the arbitration took place;
(f) that the award has not yet become binding on the parties, or has been set aside or suspended by a competent authority of the country in which, or under the law of which, it was made.

(3) Recognition or enforcement of the award may also be refused if the award is in respect of a matter which is not capable of settlement by arbitration, or if it would be contrary to public policy to recognise or enforce the award.

(4) An award which contains decisions on matters not submitted to arbitration may be recognised or enforced to the extent that it contains decisions on matters submitted to arbitration which can be separated from those on matters not so submitted.

(5) Where an application for the setting aside or suspension of the award has been made to such a competent authority as is mentioned in subsection (2)(f), the court before which the award is sought to be relied upon may, if it considers it proper, adjourn the decision on the recognition or enforcement of the award.

It may also on the application of the party claiming recognition or enforcement of the award order the other party to give suitable security.

Saving for other bases of recognition or enforcement

107. Nothing in the preceding provisions of this Part affects any right to rely upon or enforce a New York Convention award at common law or under section 66.

PART IV   GENERAL PROVISIONS

Crown application

108.—(1) Part I of this Act applies to any arbitration agreement to which Her Majesty, either in right of the Crown or of the Duchy of Lancaster or otherwise, or the Duke of Cornwall, is a party.

(2) Where her Majesty is party to an arbitration agreement otherwise than in right of the Crown, Her Majesty shall be represented for the purposes of any arbitral proceedings—

    (a) where the agreement was entered into by Her Majesty in right of the Duchy of Lancaster, by the Chancellor of the Duchy or such person as he may appoint, and

    (b) in any other case, by such person as Her Majesty may appoint in writing under the Royal Sign Manual.

(3) Where the Duke of Cornwall is party to an arbitration agreement, he shall be represented for the purposes of any arbitral proceedings by such person as he may appoint.

(4) References in Part I to a party or the parties to the arbitration agreement or to arbitral proceedings shall be construed, where subsection (2) or (3) applies, as references to the person representing Her Majesty or the Duke of Cornwall.

Consequential amendments and repeals

109.—(1) The enactments specified in Schedule 3 are amended in accordance with that Schedule, the amendments being consequential on the provisions of this Act.

(2) The enactments specified in Schedule 4 are repealed to the extent specified.

Extent

110.—(1) The provisions of this Act extend to England and Wales and, except as mentioned below, to Northern Ireland.

(2) The following provisions of Part II do not extend to Northern Ireland—

    section 94 (exclusion of Part I in relation to small claims arbitration in the county court), and

    section 95 and Schedule 2 (appointment of judges as arbitrators).

(3) The provisions of Schedules 3 and 4 (consequential amendments and repeals) extend to Scotland so far as they relate to enactments which so extend, subject as follows.

(4) The repeal of the Arbitration Act 1975 extends only to England and Wales and Northern Ireland.

Commencement

111.—(1) The provisions of this Act come into force on such day as the Secretary of State may appoint by order made by statutory instrument, and different days may be appointed for different purposes.

683

(2) An order under subsection (1) may contain such transitional provisions as appear to the Secretary of State to be appropriate.

Short title

112. This Act may be cited as the Arbitration Act 1996.

SCHEDULES

SCHEDULE 1   MANDATORY PROVISIONS OF PART I (SECTION 4(1))

sections 9 to 11 (stay of legal proceedings);
section 12 (power of court to extend agreed time limits);
section 13 (application of Limitation Acts);
section 24 (power of court to remove arbitrator);
section 26(1) (effect of death of arbitrator);
section 28 (liability of parties for fees and expenses of arbitrators);
section 29 (immunity of arbitrator);
section 31 (objection to substantive jurisdiction of tribunal);
section 32 (determination of preliminary point of jurisdiction);
section 33 (general duty of tribunal);
section 37(2) (items to be treated as expenses of arbitrators);
section 40 (general duty of parties);
section 43 (securing the attendance of witnesses);
section 56 (power to withhold award in case of non-payment);
section 60 (effectiveness of agreement for payment of costs in any event);
section 66 (enforcement of award);
sections 67 and 68 (challenging the award; substantive jurisdiction and serious irregularity), and sections 70 and 71 (supplementary provisions; effect of order of court) so far as relating to those sections;
section 72 (saving for rights of person who takes no part in proceedings);
section 73 (loss of right to object);
section 74 (immunity of arbitral institutions, &c.);
section 75 (charge to secure payment of solicitors' costs).

SCHEDULE 2   MODIFICATIONS OF PART I IN RELATION TO JUDGE-ARBITRATORS (SECTION 95(6))

Introductory

1. In this Schedule "judge-arbitrator" means a judge of the Commercial Court or official referee appointed as arbitrator or umpire under section 95.

684

General

2.—(1) Subject to the following provisions of this Schedule, references in Part I to the court shall be construed in relation to a judge-arbitrator, or in relation to the appointment of a judge-arbitrator, as references to the Court of Appeal.

(2) The references in sections 32(6) and 45(6) to the Court of Appeal shall in such a case be construed as references to the House of Lords.

Arbitrator's fees

3.—(1) The power of the court in section 28(2) to order consideration and adjustment of the liability of a party for the fees of an arbitrator may be exercised by a judge-arbitrator.

(2) Any such exercise of the power is subject to the powers of the Court of Appeal under sections 24(4) and 25(3)(b) (directions as to entitlement to fees or expenses in case of removal or resignation).

Exercise of court powers in support of arbitration

4.—(1) Where the arbitral tribunal consists of or includes a judge-arbitrator the powers of the court under sections 42 to 44 (enforcement of peremptory orders, summoning witnesses, and other court powers) are exercisable by the High Court and also by the judge-arbitrator himself.

(2) Anything done by a judge-arbitrator in the exercise of those powers shall be regarded as done by him in his capacity as judge of the High Court and have effect as if done by that court.

Nothing in this sub-paragraph prejudices any power vested in him as arbitrator or umpire.

Extension of time for making award

5.—(1) The power conferred by section 50 (extension of time for making award) is exercisable by the judge-arbitrator himself.

(2) Any appeal from a decision of a judge-arbitrator under that section lies to the Court of Appeal with the leave of that court.

Withholding award in case of non-payment

6.—(1) The provisions of paragraph 7 apply in place of the provisions of section 56 (power to withhold award in the case of non-payment) in relation to the withholding of an award for non-payment of the fees and expenses of a judge-arbitrator.

(2) This does not affect the application of section 56 in relation to the delivery of such an award by an arbitral or other institution or person vested by the parties with powers in relation to the delivery of the award.

7.—(1) A judge-arbitrator may refuse to deliver an award except upon payment of the fees and expenses mentioned in section 56(1).

(2) The judge-arbitrator may, on an application by a party to the arbitral proceedings, order that if he pays into the High Court the fees and expenses demanded, or such lesser amount as the judge-arbitrator may specify—

(a) the award shall be delivered,

685

(b) the amount of the fees and expenses properly payable shall be determined by such means and upon such terms as he may direct, and

(c) out of the money paid into court there shall be paid out such fees and expenses as may be found to be properly payable and the balance of the money (if any) shall be paid out to the applicant.

(3) For this purpose the amount of fees and expenses properly payable is the amount the applicant is liable to pay under section 28 or any agreement relating to the payment of the arbitrator.

(4) No application to the judge-arbitrator under this paragraph may be made where there is any available arbitral process for appeal or review of the amount of the fees or expenses demanded.

(5) Any appeal from a decision of a judge-arbitrator under this paragraph lies to the Court of Appeal with the leave of that court.

(6) Where a party to arbitral proceedings appeals under sub-paragraph (5), an arbitrator is entitled to appear and be heard.

Correction of award or additional award

8. Subsections (4) to (6) of section 57 (correction of award or additional award: time limit for application or exercise of power) do not apply to a judge-arbitrator.

Costs

9. Where the arbitral tribunal consists of or includes a judge-arbitrator the powers of the court under section 63(4) (determination of recoverable costs) shall be exercised by the High Court.

10.—(1) The power of the court under section 64 to determine an arbitrator's reasonable fees and expenses may be exercised by a judge-arbitrator.

(2) Any such exercise of the power is subject to the powers of the Court of Appeal under sections 24(4) and 25(3)(b) (directions as to entitlement to fees or expenses in case of removal or resignation).

Enforcement of award

11. The leave of the court required by section 66 (enforcement of award) may in the case of an award of a judge-arbitrator be given by the judge-arbitrator himself.

Solicitors' costs

12. The powers of the court to make declarations and orders under the provisions applied by section 75 (power to charge property recovered in arbitral proceedings with the payment of solicitors' costs) may be exercised by the judge-arbitrator.

Powers of court in relation to service of documents

13.—(1) The power of the court under section 77(2) (powers of court in relation to service of documents) is exercisable by the judge-arbitrator.

(2) Any appeal from a decision of a judge-arbitrator under that section lies to the Court of Appeal with the leave of that court.

Powers of court to extend time limits relating to arbitral proceedings

14.—(1) The power conferred by section 79 (power of court to extend time limits relating to arbitral proceedings) is exercisable by the judge-arbitrator himself.

(2) Any appeal from a decision of a judge-arbitrator under that section lies to the Court of Appeal with the leave of that court.

SCHEDULE 3 CONSEQUENTIAL AMENDMENTS
(SECTION 109(1))

Merchant Shipping Act 1894 (c.60)

1. In section 496 of the Merchant Shipping Act 1894 (provisions as to deposits by owners of goods), after subsection (4) insert—

"(5) In subsection (3) the expression "legal proceedings" includes arbitral proceedings and as respects England and Wales and Northern Ireland the provisions of section 14 of the Arbitration Act 1996 apply to determine when such proceedings are commenced.".

Stannaries Court (Abolition) Act 1896 (c.45)

2. In section 4(1) of the Stannaries Court (Abolition) Act 1896 (references of certain disputes to arbitration), for the words from "tried before" to "any such reference" substitute "referred to arbitration before himself or before an arbitrator agreed on by the parties or an officer of the court".

Tithe Act 1936 (c.43)

3. In section 39(1) of the Tithe Act 1936 (proceedings of Tithe Redemption Commission)—

(a) for "the Arbitration Acts 1889 to 1934" substitute "Part I of the Arbitration Act 1996";
(b) for paragraph (e) substitute—
"(e) the making of an application to the court to determine a preliminary point of law and the bringing of an appeal to the court on a point of law;";
(c) for "the said Acts" substitute "Part I of the Arbitration Act 1996".

Education Act 1944 (c.31)

4. In section 75(2) of the Education Act 1944 (proceedings of Independent School Tribunals) for "the Arbitration Acts 1889 to 1934" substitute "Part I of the Arbitration Act 1996".

687

APPENDIX 5

Commonwealth Telegraphs Act 1949 (c.39)

5. In section 8(2) of the Commonwealth Telegraphs Act 1949 (proceedings of referees under the Act) for "the Arbitration Acts 1889 to 1934, or the Arbitration Act (Northern Ireland) 1937," substitute "Part I of the Arbitration Act 1996".

Lands Tribunal Act 1949 (c.42)

6. In section 3 of the Lands Tribunal Act 1949 (proceedings before the Lands Tribunal)—
    (a) in subsection (6)(c) (procedural rules: power to apply Arbitration Acts), and
    (b) in subsection (8) (exclusion of Arbitration Acts except as applied by rules),
for "the Arbitration Acts 1889 to 1934" substitute "Part I of the Arbitration Act 1996".

Wireless Telegraphy Act 1949 (c.54)

7. In the Wireless Telegraphy Act 1949, Schedule 2 (procedure of appeals tribunal), in paragraph 3(1)—
    (a) for the words "the Arbitration Acts 1889 to 1934" substitute "Part I of the Arbitration Act 1996";
    (b) after the word "Wales" insert "or Northern Ireland"; and
    (c) for "the said Acts" substitute "Part I of that Act".

Patents Act 1949 (c.87)

8. In section 67 of the Patents Act 1949 (proceedings as to infringement of pre-1978 patents referred to comptroller), for "The Arbitration Acts 1889 to 1934" substitute "Part I of the Arbitration Act 1996".

National Health Service (Amendment) Act 1949 (c.93)

9. In section 7(8) of the National Health Service (Amendment) Act 1949 (arbitration in relation to hardship arising from the National Health Service Act 1946 or the Act), for "the Arbitration Acts 1889 to 1934" substitute "Part I of the Arbitration Act 1996" and for "the said Acts" substitute "Part I of that Act".

Arbitration Act 1950 (c.27)

10. In section 36(1) of the Arbitration Act 1950 (effect of foreign awards enforceable under Part II of that Act) for "section 26 of this Act" substitute "section 66 of the Arbitration Act 1996".

Interpretation Act (Northern Ireland) 1954 (c.33 (N.I.))

11. In section 46(2) of the Interpretation Act (Northern Ireland) 1954 (miscellaneous definitions), for the definition of "arbitrator" substitute—

" "arbitrator" has the same meaning as in Part I of the Arbitration Act 1996;".

Agricultural Marketing Act 1958 (c.47)

12. In section 12(1) of the Agricultural Marketing Act 1958 (application of provisions of Arbitration Act 1950)—
   (a) for the words from the beginning to "shall apply" substitute "Sections 45 and 69 of the Arbitration Act 1996 (which relate to the determination by the court of questions of law) and section 66 of that Act (enforcement of awards) apply"; and
   (b) for "an arbitration" substitute "arbitral proceedings".

Carriage by Air Act 1961 (c.27)

13.—(1) The Carriage by Air Act 1961 is amended as follows.
   (2) In section 5(3) (time for bringing proceedings)—
   (a) for "an arbitration" in the first place where it occurs substitute "arbitral proceedings"; and
   (b) for the words from "and subsections (3) and (4)" to the end substitute "and the provisions of section 14 of the Arbitration Act 1996 apply to determine when such proceedings are commenced.".
   (3) In section 11(c) (application of section 5 to Scotland)—
   (a) for "subsections (3) and (4)" substitute "the provisions of section 14 of the Arbitration Act 1996"; and
   (b) for "an arbitration" substitute "arbitral proceedings".

Factories Act 1961 (c.34)

14. In the Factories Act 1961, for section 171 (application of Arbitration Act 1950), substitute—
   "Application of the Arbitration Act 1996
   171. Part I of the Arbitration Act 1996 does not apply to proceedings under this Act except in so far as it may be applied by regulations made under this Act.".

Clergy Pensions Measure 1961 (No. 3)

15. In the Clergy Pensions Measure 1961, section 38(4) (determination of questions), for the words "The Arbitration Act 1950" substitute "Part I of the Arbitration Act 1996".

Transport Act 1962 (c.46)

16.—(1) The Transport Act 1962 is amended as follows.
   (2) In section 74(6)(f) (proceedings before referees in pension disputes), for the words "the Arbitration Act 1950" substitute "Part I of the Arbitration Act 1996".
   (3) In section 81(7) (proceedings before referees in compensation disputes), for the words "the Arbitration Act 1950" substitute "Part I of the Arbitration Act 1996".
   (4) In Schedule 7, Part IV (pensions), in paragraph 17(5) for the words "the Arbitration Act 1950" substitute "Part I of the Arbitration Act 1996".

689

APPENDIX 5

Corn Rents Act 1963 (c.14)

17. In the Corn Rents Act 1963, section 1(5) (schemes for apportioning corn rents, &c.), for the words "the Arbitration Act 1950" substitute "Part I of the Arbitration Act 1996".

Plant Varieties and Seeds Act 1964 (c.14)

18. In section 10(6) of the Plant Varieties and Seeds Act 1964 (meaning of "arbitration agreement"), for "the meaning given by section 32 of the Arbitration Act 1950" substitute "the same meaning as in Part I of the Arbitration Act 1996".

Lands Tribunal and Compensation Act (Northern Ireland) 1964 (c.29 (N.I.))

19. In section 9 of the Lands Tribunal and Compensation Act (Northern Ireland) 1964 (proceedings of Lands Tribunal), in subsection (3) (where Tribunal acts as arbitrator) for "the Arbitration Act (Northern Ireland) 1937" substitute "Part I of the Arbitration Act 1996".

Industrial and Provident Societies Act 1965 (c.12)

20.—(1) Section 60 of the Industrial and Provident Societies Act 1965 is amended as follows.

(2) In subsection (8) (procedure for hearing disputes between society and member, &c.)—
    (a) in paragraph (a) for "the Arbitration Act 1950" substitute "Part I of the Arbitration Act 1996"; and
    (b) in paragraph (b) omit "by virtue of section 12 of the said Act of 1950".

(3) For subsection (9) substitute—
    "(9) The court or registrar to whom any dispute is referred under subsections (2) to (7) may at the request of either party state a case on any question of law arising in the dispute for the opinion of the High Court or, as the case may be, the Court of Session.".

Carriage of Goods by Road Act 1965 (c.37)

21. In section 7(2) of the Carriage of Goods by Road Act 1965 (arbitrations: time at which deemed to commence), for paragraphs (a) and (b) substitute—
    "(a) as respects England and Wales and Northern Ireland, the provisions of section 14(3) to (5) of the Arbitration Act 1996 (which determine the time at which an arbitration is commenced) apply;".

Factories Act (Northern Ireland) 1965 (c.20 (N.I.))

22. In section 171 of the Factories Act (Northern Ireland) 1965 (application of Arbitration Act), for "The Arbitration Act (Northern Ireland) 1937" substitute "Part I of the Arbitration Act 1996".

Commonwealth Secretariat Act 1966 (c.10)

23. In section 1(3) of the Commonwealth Secretariat Act 1966 (contracts with

Commonwealth Secretariat to be deemed to contain provision for arbitration), for "the Arbitration Act 1950 and the Arbitration Act (Northern Ireland) 1937" substitute "Part I of the Arbitration Act 1996".

Arbitration (International Investment Disputes) Act 1966 (c. 41)

24. In the Arbitration (International Investment Disputes) Act 1966, for section 3 (application of Arbitration Act 1950 and other enactments) substitute—
   "Application of provisions of Arbitration Act 1996
   3.—(1) The Lord Chancellor may by order direct that any of the provisions contained in sections 36 and 38 to 44 of the Arbitration Act 1996 (provisions concerning the conduct of arbitral proceedings, &c.) shall apply to such proceedings pursuant to the Convention as are specified in the order with or without any modifications or exceptions specified in the order.
   (2) Subject to subsection (1), the Arbitration Act 1996 shall not apply to proceedings pursuant to the Convention, but this subsection shall not be taken as affecting section 9 of that Act (stay of legal proceedings in respect of matter subject to arbitration).
   (3) An order made under this section—
      (a) may be varied or revoked by a subsequent order so made, and
      (b) shall be contained in a statutory instrument.".

Poultry Improvement Act (Northern Ireland) 1968 (c. 12 (N.I.))

25. In paragraph 10(4) of the Schedule to the Poultry Improvement Act (Northern Ireland) 1968 (reference of disputes), for "The Arbitration Act (Northern Ireland) 1937" substitute "Part I of the Arbitration Act 1996".

Industrial and Provident Societies Act (Northern Ireland) 1969 (c. 24 (N.I.))

26.—(1) Section 69 of the Industrial and Provident Societies Act (Northern Ireland) 1969 (decision of disputes) is amended as follows.
   (2) In subsection (7) (decision of disputes)—
      (a) in the opening words, omit the words from "and without prejudice" to "1937";
      (b) at the beginning of paragraph (a) insert "without prejudice to any powers exercisable by virtue of Part I of the Arbitration Act 1996,"; and
      (c) in paragraph (b) omit "the registrar or" and "registrar or" and for the words from "as might have been granted by the High Court" to the end substitute "as might be granted by the registrar".
   (3) For subsection (8) substitute—
   "(8) The court or registrar to whom any dispute is referred under subsections (2) to (6) may at the request of either party state a case on any question of law arising in the dispute for the opinion of the High Court.".

Health and Personal Social Services (Northern Ireland) Order 1972 (N.I. 14)

27. In Article 105(6) of the Health and Personal Social Services (Northern Ireland) Order

691

1972 (arbitrations under the Order), for "the Arbitration Act (Northern Ireland) 1937" substitute "Part I of the Arbitration Act 1996".

Consumer Credit Act 1974 (c.39)

28.—(1) Section 146 of the Consumer Credit Act 1974 is amended as follows.

(2) In subsection (2) (solicitor engaged in contentious business), for "section 86(1) of the Solicitors Act 1957" substitute "section 87(1) of the Solicitors Act 1974".

(3) In subsection (4) (solicitor in Northern Ireland engaged in contentious business), for the words from "business done" to "Administration of Estates (Northern Ireland) Order 1979" substitute "contentious business (as defined in Article 3(2) of the Solicitors (Northern Ireland) Order 1976.".

Friendly Societies Act 1974 (c.46)

29.—(1) The Friendly Societies Act 1974 is amended as follows.

(2) For section 78(1) (statement of case) substitute—

"(1) Any arbitrator, arbiter or umpire to whom a dispute falling within section 76 above is referred under the rules of a registered society or branch may at the request of either party state a case on any question of law arising in the dispute for the opinion of the High Court or, as the case may be, the Court of Session.".

(3) In section 83(3) (procedure on objections to amalgamations &c. of friendly societies), for "the Arbitration Act 1950 or, in Northern Ireland, the Arbitration Act (Northern Ireland) 1937" substitute "Part I of the Arbitration Act 1996".

Industry Act 1975 (c.68)

30. In Schedule 3 to the Industry Act (arbitration of disputes relating to vesting and compensation orders), in paragraph 14 (application of certain provisions of Arbitration Acts)—

    (a) for "the Arbitration Act 1950 or, in Northern Ireland, the Arbitration Act (Northern Ireland) 1937" substitute "Part I of the Arbitration Act 1996", and

    (b) for "that Act" substitute "that Part".

Industrial Relations (Northern Ireland) Order 1976 (N.I. 16)

31. In Article 59(9) of the Industrial Relations (Northern Ireland) Order 1976 (proceedings of industrial tribunal), for "The Arbitration Act (Northern Ireland) 1937" substitute "Part I of the Arbitration Act 1996".

Aircraft and Shipbuilding Industries Act 1977 (c.3)

32. In Schedule 7 to the Aircraft and Shipbuilding Industries Act 1977 (procedure of Arbitration Tribunal), in paragraph 2—

    (a) for "the Arbitration Act 1950 or, in Northern Ireland, the Arbitration Act (Northern Ireland) 1937" substitute "Part I of the Arbitration Act 1996", and

(b) for "that Act" substitute "that Part".

Patents Act 1977 (c.37)

33. In section 130 of the Patents Act 1977 (interpretation), in subsection (8) (exclusion of Arbitration Act) for "The Arbitration Act 1950" substitute "Part I of the Arbitration Act 1996".

Employment Protection (Consolidation) Act 1978 (c.44)

34. In Schedule 9 to the Employment Protection (Consolidation) Act 1978 (industrial tribunals), for paragraph 4 (and the heading preceding it) substitute—

"Exclusion of Part I of Arbitration Act 1996

4. Part I of the Arbitration Act 1996 does not apply to any proceedings before an industrial tribunal.".

Judicature (Northern Ireland) Act 1978 (c.23)

35. In section 35(2) of the Judicature (Northern Ireland) Act 1978 (restrictions on appeals to the Court of Appeal), after paragraph (f) insert—

"(fa) except as provided by Part I of the Arbitration Act 1996, from any decision of the High Court under that Part;".

Health and Safety at Work (Northern Ireland) Order 1978 (N.I.9)

36. In Schedule 4 to the Health and Safety at Work (Northern Ireland) Order 1978 (licensing provisions), in paragraph 3, for "The Arbitration Act (Northern Ireland) 1937" substitute "Part I of the Arbitration Act 1996".

County Courts (Northern Ireland) Order 1980 (N.I.3)

37. In Article 30 of the County Courts (Northern Ireland) Order 1980 (civil jurisdiction exercisable by district judge), for paragraph (5) substitute—

"(5) County court rules may—
(a) apply any of the provisions of Part I of the Arbitration Act 1996 to arbitrations under paragraph (3) with such modifications as may be prescribed;
(b) prescribe the rules of evidence to be followed on any arbitration under paragraph (3) and, in particular, make provision with respect to the manner of taking and questioning evidence.

(5A) Except as provided by virtue of paragraph (5)(a), Part I of the Arbitration Act 1996 shall not apply to an arbitration under paragraph (3).".

Supreme Court Act 1981 (c.54)

38.—(1) The Supreme Court Act 1981 is amended as follows.

693

(2) In section 18(1) (restrictions on appeals to the Court of Appeal), for paragraph (g) substitute—

"(g) except as provided by Part I of the Arbitration Act 1996, from any decision of the High Court under that Part;".

(3) In section 151 (interpretation, &c.), in the definition of "arbitration agreement", for "the Arbitration Act 1950 by virtue of section 32 of that Act;" substitute "Part I of the Arbitration Act 1996;".

Merchant Shipping (Liner Conferences) Act 1982 (c.37)

39. In section 7(5) of the Merchant Shipping (Liner Conferences) Act 1982 (stay of legal proceedings), for the words from "section 4(1)" to the end substitute "section 9 of the Arbitration Act 1996 (which also provides for the staying of legal proceedings).".

Agricultural Marketing (Northern Ireland) Order 1982 (N.I. 12)

40. In Article 14 of the Agricultural Marketing (Northern Ireland) Order 1982 (application of provisions of Arbitration Act (Northern Ireland) 1937)—

(a) for the words from the beginning to "shall apply" substitute "Section 45 and 69 of the Arbitration Act 1996 (which relate to the determination by the court of questions of law) and section 66 of that Act (enforcement of awards) apply"; and

(b) for "an arbitration" substitute "arbitral proceedings".

Mental Health Act 1983 (c.20)

41. In section 78 of the Mental Health Act 1983 (procedure of Mental Health Review Tribunals), in subsection (9) for "The Arbitration Act 1950" substitute "Part I of the Arbitration Act 1996".

Registered Homes Act 1984 (c.23)

42. In section 43 of the Registered Homes Act 1984 (procedure of Registered Homes Tribunals), in subsection (3) for "The Arbitration Act 1950" substitute "Part I of the Arbitration Act 1996".

Housing Act 1985 (c.68)

43. In section 47(3) of the Housing Act 1985 (agreement as to determination of matters relating to service charges) for "section 32 of the Arbitration Act 1950" substitute "Part I of the Arbitration Act 1996".

Landlord and Tenant Act 1985 (c.70)

44. In section 19(3) of the Landlord and Tenant Act 1985 (agreement as to determination of matters relating to service charges), for "section 32 of the Arbitration Act 1950" substitute "Part I of the Arbitration Act 1996".

694

Credit Unions (Northern Ireland) Order 1985 (N.I. 12)

45.—(1) Article 72 of the Credit Unions (Northern Ireland) Order 1985 (decision of disputes) is amended as follows.

(2) In paragraph (7)—

(a) in the opening words, omit the words from "and without prejudice" to "1937";

(b) at the beginning of sub-paragraph (a) insert "without prejudice to any powers exercisable by virtue of Part I of the Arbitration Act 1996,"; and

(c) in sub-paragraph (b) omit "the registrar or" and "registrar or" and for the words from "as might have been granted by the High Court" to the end substitute "as might be granted by the registrar".

(3) For paragraph (8) substitute—

"(8) The court or registrar to whom any dispute is referred under paragraphs (2) to (6) may at the request of either party state a case on any question of law arising in the dispute for the opinion of the High Court.".

Agricultural Holdings Act 1986 (c.5)

46. In section 84(1) of the Agricultural Holdings Act 1986 (provisions relating to arbitration), for "the Arbitration Act 1950" substitute "Part I of the Arbitration Act 1996".

Insolvency Act 1986 (c.45)

47. In the Insolvency Act 1986, after section 349 insert—

"Arbitration agreements to which bankrupt is party

349A.—(1) This section applies where a bankrupt had become party to a contract containing an arbitration agreement before the commencement of his bankruptcy.

(2) If the trustee in bankruptcy adopts the contract, the arbitration agreement is enforceable by or against the trustee in relation to matters arising from or connected with the contract.

(3) If the trustee in bankruptcy does not adopt the contract and a matter to which the arbitration agreement applies requires to be determined in connection with or for the purposes of the bankruptcy proceedings—

(a) the trustee with the consent of the creditors' committee, or

(b) any other party to the agreement,

may apply to the court which may, if it thinks fit in all the circumstances of the case, order that the matter be referred to arbitration in accordance with the arbitration agreement.

(4) In this section—

"arbitration agreement" has the same meaning as in Part I of the Arbitration Act 1996; and

"the court" means the court which has jurisdiction in the bankruptcy proceedings.".

Building Societies Act 1986 (c.53)

48. In Part II of Schedule 14 of the Building Societies Act 1986 (settlement of disputes: arbitration), in paragraph 5(6) for "the Arbitration Act 1950 and the Arbitration Act 1979 or,

695

in Northern Ireland, the Arbitration Act (Northern Ireland) 1937" substitute "Part I of the Arbitration Act 1996".

Mental Health (Northern Ireland) Order 1986 (N.I.4)

49. In Article 83 of the Mental Health (Northern Ireland) Order 1986 (procedure of Mental Health Review Tribunal), in paragraph (8) for "The Arbitration Act (Northern Ireland) 1937" substitute "Part I of the Arbitration Act 1996".

Multilateral Investment Guarantee Agency Act 1988 (c.8)

50. For section 6 of the Multilateral Investment Guarantee Agency Act 1988 (application of Arbitration Act) substitute—

"Application of Arbitration Act

6.—(1) The Lord Chancellor may by order made by statutory instrument direct that any of the provisions of sections 36 and 38 to 44 of the Arbitration Act 1996 (provisions in relation to the conduct of the arbitral proceedings, &c.) apply, with such modifications or exceptions as are specified in the order, to such arbitration proceedings pursuant to Annex II to the Convention as are specified in the order.

(2) Except as provided by an order under subsection (1) above, no provision of Part I of the Arbitration Act 1996 other than section 9 (stay of legal proceedings) applies to any such proceedings.".

Copyright, Designs and Patents Act 1988 (c.48)

51. In section 150 of the Copyright, Designs and Patents Act 1988 (Lord Chancellor's power to make rules for Copyright Tribunal), for subsection (2) substitute—

"(2) The rules may apply in relation to the Tribunal, as respects proceedings in England and Wales or Northern Ireland, any of the provisions of Part I of the Arbitration Act 1996.".

Fair Employment (Northern Ireland) Act 1989 (c.32)

52. In the Fair Employment (Northern Ireland) Act 1989, section 5(7) (procedure of Fair Employment Tribunal), for "The Arbitration Act (Northern Ireland) 1937" substitute "Part I of the Arbitration Act 1996".

Limitation (Northern Ireland) Order 1989 (N.I.11)

53. In Article 2(2) of the Limitation (Northern Ireland) Order 1989 (interpretation), in the definition of "arbitration agreement", for "the Arbitration Act (Northern Ireland) 1937" substitute "Part I of the Arbitration Act 1996".

Insolvency (Northern Ireland) Order 1989 (N.I. 19)

696

54. In the Insolvency (Northern Ireland) Order 1989, after Article 320 insert—

"Arbitration agreements to which bankrupt is party

320A.—(1) This Article applies where a bankrupt had become party to a contract containing an arbitration agreement before the commencement of his bankruptcy.

(2) If the trustee in bankruptcy adopts the contract, the arbitration agreement is enforceable by or against the trustee in relation to matters arising from or connected with the contract.

(3) If the trustee in bankruptcy does not adopt the contract and a matter to which the arbitration agreement applies requires to be determined in connection with or for the purposes of the bankruptcy proceedings—

    (a) the trustee with the consent of the creditors' committee, or

    (b) any other party to the agreement,

may apply to the court which may, if it thinks fit in all the circumstances of the case, order that the matter be referred to arbitration in accordance with the arbitration agreement.

(4) In this Article—

"arbitration agreement" has the same meaning as in Part I of the Arbitration Act 1996; and

"the court" means the court which has jurisdiction in the bankruptcy proceedings.".

Social Security Administration Act 1992 (c.5)

55. In section 59 of the Social Security Administration Act 1992 (procedure for inquiries, &c.), in subsection (7), for "The Arbitration Act 1950" substitute "Part I of the Arbitration Act 1996".

Social Security Administration (Northern Ireland) Act 1992 (c.8)

56. In section 57 of the Social Security Administration (Northern Ireland) Act 1992 (procedure for inquiries, &c.), in subsection (6) for "the Arbitration Act (Northern Ireland) 1937" substitute "Part I of the Arbitration Act 1996".

Trade Union and Labour Relations (Consolidation) Act 1992 (c.52)

57. In sections 212(5) and 263(6) of the Trade Union and Labour Relations (Consolidation) Act 1992 (application of Arbitration Act) for "the Arbitration Act 1950" substitute "Part I of the Arbitration Act 1996".

Industrial Relations (Northern Ireland) Order 1992 (N.I. 5)

58. In Articles 84(9) and 92(5) of the Industrial Relations (Northern Ireland) Order 1992 (application of Arbitration Act) for "The Arbitration Act (Northern Ireland) 1937" substitute "Part I of the Arbitration Act 1996".

Registered Homes (Northern Ireland) Order 1992 (N.I.20)

59. In Article 33(3) of the Registered Homes (Northern Ireland) Order 1992 (procedure of

Registered Homes Tribunal) for "The Arbitration Act (Northern Ireland) 1937" substitute "Part I of the Arbitration Act 1996".

Education Act 1993 (c.35)

60. In section 180(4) of the Education Act 1993 (procedure of Special Educational Needs Tribunal), for "The Arbitration Act 1950" substitute "Part I of the Arbitration Act 1996".

Roads (Northern Ireland) Order 1993 (N.I.15)

61.—(1) The Roads (Northern Ireland) Order 1993 is amended as follows.

(2) In Article 131 (application of Arbitration Act) for "the Arbitration Act (Northern Ireland) 1937" substitute "Part I of the Arbitration Act 1996".

(3) In Schedule 4 (disputes), in paragraph 3(2) for "the Arbitration Act (Northern Ireland) 1937" substitute "Part I of the Arbitration Act 1996".

Merchant Shipping Act 1995 (c.21)

62. In Part II of Schedule 6 to the Merchant Shipping Act 1995 (provisions having effect in connection with Convention Relating to the Carriage of Passengers and Their Luggage by Sea), for paragraph 7 substitute—

"7. Article 16 shall apply to arbitral proceedings as it applies to an action; and, as respects England and Wales and Northern Ireland, the provisions of section 14 of the Arbitration Act 1996 apply to determine for the purposes of that Article when an arbitration is commenced.".

SCHEDULE 4 REPEALS (SECTION 109(2))

Chapter	Short title	Extent of repeal
1892 c. 43.	Military Lands Act 1892.	In section 21(b), the words "under the Arbitration Act 1889".
1922 c. 51.	Allotments Act 1922.	In section 21(3), the words "under the Arbitration Act 1889".
1937 c. 8 (N.I.).	Arbitration Act (Northern Ireland) 1937.	The whole Act.
1949 c. 54.	Wireless Telegraphy Act 1949.	In Schedule 2, paragraph 3(3).
1949 c. 97.	National Parks and Access to the Countryside Act 1949.	In section 18(4), the words from "Without prejudice" to "England or Wales".

Chapter	Short title	Extent of repeal
1950 c. 27.	Arbitration Act 1950.	Part I.
		Section 42(3).
1958 c. 47.	Agricultural Marketing Act 1958.	Section 53(8).
1962 c. 46.	Transport Act 1962.	In Schedule 11, Part II, paragraph 7.
1964 c. 14.	Plant Varieties and Seeds Act 1964.	In section 10(4) the words from "or in section 9" to "three arbitrators)".
		Section 39(3)(b)(i).
1964 c. 29.	Lands Tribunal and Compensation Act (Northern Ireland) 1964.	In section 9(3) the words from "so, however, that" to the end.
1965 c. 12.	Industrial and Provident Societies Act 1965.	In section 60(8)(b), the words "by virtue of section 12 of the said Act of 1950".
1965 c. 37.	Carriage of Goods by Road Act 1965.	Section 7(2)(b).
1965 c. 13 (N.I.).	New Towns Act (Northern Ireland) 1965.	In section 27(2), the words from "under and in accordance with" to the end.
1969 c. 24 (N.I.).	Industrial and Provident Societies Act (Northern Ireland) 1969.	In section 69(7)— (a) in the opening words, the words from "and without prejudice" to "1937"; (b) in paragraph (b), the words "the registrar or" and "registrar or".
1970 c. 31.	Administration of Justice Act 1970.	Section 4.
		Schedule 3.
1973 c. 41.	Fair Trading Act 1973.	Section 32(2)(d).
1973 N.I. 1.	Drainage (Northern Ireland) Order 1973.	In Article 15(4), the words from "under and in accordance" to the end.
		Article 40(4).
		In Schedule 7, in paragraph 9(2), the words from "under and in accordance" to the end.
1974 c. 47.	Solicitors Act 1974.	In section 87(1), in the definition of "contentious business", the words "appointed under the Arbitration Act 1950".
1975 c. 3.	Arbitration Act 1975.	The whole Act.

699

Chapter	Short title	Extent of repeal
1975 c. 74.	Petroleum and Submarine Pipe-Lines Act 1975.	In Part II of Schedule 2— (a) in model clause 40(2), the words "in accordance with the Arbitration Act 1950"; (b) in model clause 40(2B), the words "in accordance with the Arbitration Act (Northern Ireland) 1937". In Part II of Schedule 3, in model clause 38(2), the words "in accordance with the Arbitration Act 1950".
1976 N.I. 12.	Solicitors (Northern Ireland) Order 1976.	In Article 3(2), in the entry "contentious business", the words "appointed under the Arbitration Act (Northern Ireland) 1937". Article 71H(3).
1977 c. 37.	Patents Act 1977.	In section 52(4) the words "section 21 of the Arbitration Act 1950 or, as the case may be, section 22 of the Arbitration Act (Northern Ireland) 1937 (statement of cases by arbitrators); but". Section 131(e).
1977 c. 38.	Administration of Justice Act 1977.	Section 17(2).
1978 c. 23.	Judicature (Northern Ireland) Act 1978.	In section 35(2), paragraph (g)(v). In Schedule 5, the amendment to the Arbitration Act 1950.
1979 c. 42.	Arbitration Act 1979.	The whole Act.
1980 c. 58.	Limitation Act 1980.	Section 34.
1980 N.I. 3.	County Courts (Northern Ireland) Order 1980.	Article 31(3).
1981 c. 54.	Supreme Court Act 1981.	Section 148.
1982 c. 27.	Civil Jurisdiction and Judgments Act 1982.	Section 25(3)(c) and (5). In section 26— (a) in subsection (1), the words "to arbitration or"; (b) in subsection (1)(a)(i), the words "arbitration or"; (c) in subsection (2), the words "arbitration or".

Chapter	Short title	Extent of repeal
1982 c. 53.	Administration of Justice Act 1982.	Section 15(6). In Schedule 1, Part IV.
1984 c. 5.	Merchant Shipping Act 1984.	Section 4(8).
1984 c. 12.	Telecommunications Act 1984.	Schedule 2, paragraph 13(8).
1984 c. 16.	Foreign Limitation Periods Act 1984.	Section 5.
1984 c. 28.	County Courts Act 1984.	In Schedule 2, paragraph 70.
1985 c. 61.	Administration of Justice Act 1985.	Section 58 In Schedule 9, paragraph 15.
1985 c. 68.	Housing Act 1985.	In Schedule 18, in paragraph 6(2) the words from "and the Arbitration Act 1950" to the end.
1985 N.I.12.	Credit Unions (Northern Ireland) Order 1985.	In Article 72(7)— (a) in the opening words, the words from "and without prejudice" to "1937"; (b) in sub-paragraph (b), the words "the registrar or" and "registrar or".
1986 c. 61.	Insolvency Act 1986.	In Schedule 14, the entry relating to the Arbitration Act 1950.
1988 c. 8.	Multilateral Investment Guarantee Agency Act 1988.	Section 8(3).
1988 c. 21.	Consumer Arbitration Agreements Act 1988.	Sections 1 to 5. In section 9(4) the words from the beginning to "Scotland" and from "and" to the end.
1989 N.I. 11.	Limitation (Northern Ireland) Order 1989.	Article 72. In Schedule 3, paragraph 1.
1989 N.I. 19.	Insolvency (Northern Ireland) Order 1989.	In Part II of Schedule 9, paragraph 66.
1990 c. 41.	Courts and Legal Services Act 1990.	Sections 99 and 101 to 103.
1991 N.I.7.	Food Safety (Northern Ireland) Order 1991.	In Articles 8(8) and 11(10), the words from "and the provisions" to the end.
1992 c. 40.	Friendly Societies Act 1992.	In Schedule 16, paragraph 30(1).
1995 c. 8.	Agricultural Tenancies Act 1995.	Section 28(4).
1995 c. 21.	Merchant Shipping Act 1995.	Section 96(10) Section 264(9).

701

Table of Destinations and Derivations

AA 1950	**1996 Bill**
1	Cl. 23(3)
2(1)	Cl. 8(1)
(2)	Cl. 26(2)
(3)	Cl. 8(2)

1(2) .... Cll. 69(1), (7), 71(2)
  (3) .... Cl. 69(1), (2)
  (4) .... Cl. 69(3)
  (5) .... Cl. 70(4)
  (6) .... REPEALED
  (6A) .... Cl. 69(8)
  (7) .... Cl. 69(6)
  (8) .... Cl. 71(8)
2(1) .... Cl. 45(1)
  (2) .... Cl. 45(2)
  (2A) .... Cl. 45(5)
  (3) .... Cl. 45(6)
3(1) .... Cl. 69(1)
  (2) .... REPEALED
  (3) .... REPEALED
  (4) .... REPEALED
  (5) .... REPEALED
  (6) .... Cl. 87(1)
  (7) .... Cl. 85(2)
4(1) .... REPEALED
  (2) .... REPEALED
  (3) .... REPEALED
  (4) .... REPEALED
  (5) .... REPEALED
5(1) .... Cll. 41(4), 42(1), (4)
  (2) .... Cl. 41(4)
  (3) .... REPEALED
  (4) .... REPEALED
  (5) .... REPEALED
  (6) .... REPEALED
6(1) .... REPEALED
  (2) .... REPEALED
  (3) .... REPEALED
  (4) .... REPEALED
7(1) .... REPEALED
  (2) .... REPEALED
  (3) .... REPEALED
8(1) .... REPEALED
  (2) .... REPEALED
  (3) .... REPEALED
  (4) .... REPEALED

LA 1980   **1996 Bill**

34(1) .... Cl. 13(1)
  (2) .... Cl. 13(3)
  (3) .... Cl. 14(3)–(5)
  (4) .... Cl. 76(1), (4)
  (5) .... Cl. 13(2)
  (6) .... REPEALED
  (7) .... Cl. 13(4)

CJJA 1982   **1996 Bill**

26(1) .... Cl. 11(1)
  (2) .... N/A
  (3) .... Cl. 11(3)

CAAA 1988   **1996 Bill**

1(1) .... Cll. 89(1), 90(1)
  (2) .... Cl. 92(1)
  (3) .... Cl. 90(2)
2(1) .... Cl. 91(1)
  (2) .... Cl. 91(1)
3(1) .... Cl. 89(2)
  (2) .... Cl. 89(3)
  (3) .... Cl. 89(4)
4(1) .... Cl. 93(1)
  (2) .... Cl. 93(2)
  (3) .... Cl. 93(3)
  (4) .... Cl. 93(4)
  (5) .... Cl. 93(4)

TABLE OF DESTINATIONS AND DERIVATIONS

Index

[The prefixes "I/..." and "II/..." indicate page numbers in Volume 1 and Volume 2 respectively]

716

733